CHINA AND ISL

CW00967787

China and Islam examines the intersection of two critical issues of the contemporary world: Islamic revival and an assertive China, questioning the assumption that Islamic law is incompatible with state law. It finds that both Hui and the Party-State invoke, interpret, and make arguments based on Islamic law, a *minjian* (unofficial) law in China, to pursue their respective visions of "the good." Based on fieldwork in Linxia, "China's Little Mecca," this study follows Hui clerics, youthful translators on the "New Silk Road," female educators who reform traditional madrasas, and Party cadres as they reconcile Islamic and socialist laws in the course of the everyday. The first study of Islamic law in China and one of the first ethnographic accounts of law in postsocialist China, *China and Islam* unsettles unidimensional perceptions of extremist Islam and authoritarian China through Hui *minjian* practices of law.

MATTHEW S. ERIE, an anthropologist and a lawyer, is an associate professor of Modern Chinese Studies at the University of Oxford. His earlier works on law and society have appeared in publications such as *American Ethnologist, Law and Social Inquiry,* the *Hong Kong Law Journal,* and the *Oxford Encyclopedia of Islam and Law.* He has lived and studied in China and the Middle East, and has practiced law in New York City and Beijing.

CAMBRIDGE STUDIES IN LAW AND SOCIETY

Cambridge Studies in Law and Society aims to publish the best scholarly work on legal discourse and practice in its social and institutional contexts, combining theoretical insights and empirical research.

The fields that it covers are: studies of law in action; the sociology of law; the anthropology of law; cultural studies of law, including the role of legal discourses in social formations; law and economics; law and politics; and studies of governance. The books consider all forms of legal discourse across societies, rather than being limited to lawyers' discourses alone.

The series editors come from a range of disciplines: academic law; socio-legal studies; sociology; and anthropology. All have been actively involved in teaching and writing about law in context.

Series editors

Chris Arup
Monash University, Victoria

Sally Engle Merry
New York University

Susan Silbey
Massachusetts Institute of Technology

A list of books in the series can be found at the back of this book.

CHINA AND ISLAM

The Prophet, the Party, and Law

MATTHEW S. ERIE
University of Oxford

CAMBRIDGE
UNIVERSITY PRESS

University Printing House, Cambridge CB2 8BS, United Kingdom

One Liberty Plaza, 20th Floor, New York, NY 10006, USA

477 Williamstown Road, Port Melbourne, VIC 3207, Australia

4843/24, 2nd Floor, Ansari Road, Daryaganj, Delhi - 110002, India

79 Anson Road, #06-04/06, Singapore 079906

Cambridge University Press is part of the University of Cambridge.

It furthers the University's mission by disseminating knowledge in the pursuit of education, learning and research at the highest international levels of excellence.

www.cambridge.org
Information on this title: www.cambridge.org/9781107670112

© Matthew S. Erie 2016

First published 2016
First paperback edition 2017

A catalogue record for this publication is available from the British Library

Library of Congress Cataloging in Publication data
Names: Erie, Matthew S., author
Title: China and Islam: the prophet, the party, and law / Matthew S. Erie.
Description: Cambridge: Cambridge University Press, 2016. |
Series: Cambridge studies in law and society |
Includes bibliographical references and index.
Identifiers: LCCN 2016003010 | ISBN 9781107053373 (hardback)
Subjects: LCSH: Islamic law – China. | Law – China.
Classification: LCC KBP69.C5 E75 2016 | DDC 342.5108/5297–dc23
LC record available at http://lccn.loc.gov/2016003010

ISBN 978-1-107-05337-3 Hardback
ISBN 978-1-107-67011-2 Paperback

To my mother and father, and
In memory of Loren V. Erie

Zhengjiao bu zhengquan.
(Contend for the teaching, do not contend for power.)
A Hui saying

CONTENTS

FIGURES

TABLES

ACKNOWLEDGMENTS

In its entirety, my pilgrimage to China's Little Mecca has taken place over a period of approximately thirteen years. Like any journey, this one would have been meaningless and indeed impossible without those who prepared and guided me. In reflecting on those who have kindly provided support to the writing of this book, my concerns are twofold. The first is that I may unintentionally omit someone who has been a resource in some way during this time. In the event that I do so, I can only express my sincerest apologies. The second concern is more specific to China: I cannot name the majority of the people based in China who were the most helpful to me. To those individuals, I can only say that the fact that you cared to assume the risk of helping a non-Muslim foreigner speaks volumes of your inclusiveness and gives hope for surmounting the various cultural, national, and political divides that are too often reified rather than overcome.

I express my gratitude first and foremost to my mentors, especially Steven Sangren and Jacques deLisle, who, respectively, taught me how to think like an anthropologist and how to think like a lawyer, and then how to think against the grain in both disciplines. China, as I have learned from them, requires one to do so. They have taught me that producing scholarship is a commitment to principles, moral ones as much as intellectual ones. Much of this project has been animated by their lessons.

In my ungraceful attempts to straddle the two worlds of anthropology and law, I have benefited from numerous teachers. At Cornell, Andrew Willford, Viranjini Munasinghe, and Magnus Fiskesjö spent countless hours in their homes, in Ithaca diners, or in Shanghai coffee houses taking me through the anthropological traditions from taboo to ethnicity. Also at Cornell, I thank the late Terry Turner, Allen Carlson, Chris Garces, Eric Tagliacozzo, David Powers, Shawkat Toorawa, Vilma Santiago-Irizarry, Annelise Riles, Nimat Barazangi, and Mark Selden for enriching my graduate training. Among Cornell anthropology students, I thank especially Sara Shneiderman, Zhang Yinong, Eric Henry, Jen

Shannon, and Amy Levine for their astute criticisms and reflections both in class and in writing during graduate school and after.

I owe a tremendous debt to the incredible community of scholars who pursue "law and society" studies and have been particularly formative in my thinking. These scholars have taught me how to identify and analyze a problem and to assess its importance beyond the immediate context. It has been one of the great privileges of my professional career to work with Sally Engle Merry on the writing of this book. She has given her time and experience toward improving the lucidity of my writing. In addition, such scholars as Frank Upham, Tom Ginsburg, Kim Lane Scheppele, and Justin Richland have not only provided intellectual inspiration but have also been guides in the broadest sense of the word.

On the law side, I am indebted to William Burke-White, Sally Gordon, Eric Feldman, and Gideon Parchomovsky, all of whom taught me that the study of law can be much more than doctrine. I also thank Wang Chenguang, Gao Qicai, and the late He Meihuan at Tsinghua University Law School for first exposing me to the human side of Chinese law. Jerome Cohen, William Alford, Zhu Suli, Eva Pils, Zhang Xisheng, Teemu Ruskola, Rachel Stern, Liu Sida, John Ohnesorge, Benjamin Liebman, Zhao Xudong, Carl Minzner, Ethan Michelson, Timothy Webster, Benjamin van Rooij, Stéphanie Balme, Michael Dowdle, Mo Zhang, Jedidiah Kroncke, Neysun Mahboubi, and others who have shared their knowledge of law and society in China have been invaluable to my writing. I am particularly thankful to David Livdahl for bringing Norwegian humor to the practice of law in China.

Numerous scholars have patiently exposed me to the breadth and minutiae of Islamic legal studies, including, at Princeton, Michael Cook, Hossein Modarressi, Bernard Haykel, and Max Weiss. In addition, scholars across the academy, including Tamir Moustafa, Brinkley Messick, Timothy Daniels, Saba Mahmood, Asifa Quraishi-Landes, Anver Emon, Jonathan Brown, Sherif Omar Hassan, Mitra Sharafi, Mark Massoud, Darryl Li, Nurfadzilah Yahaya, Guy Burak, Mariam Amin Shehata, Ambassador Sallama Shaker, Hussein Rashid, and Frank Stewart, have encouraged me to realize where the Hui experience approximates that of Muslims elsewhere and where it diverges.

I have benefited in countless ways from the two founders of the modern study of Islam in China, Dru Gladney and Jonathan Lipman. From how to take notes during an interview to how to correctly pronounce the name of Xunhua's "Jiezi" Mosque (it's "Gazi"), the founders have shared their encyclopedic knowledge of this topic. This book is indebted to them beyond the mere number of citations to their works. Liu Wei, Zvi Ben-Dor Benite, Ding Hong, Rahile Dawut, Gao Zhanfu, Wang Jianping, Yang Wenjiong, Zhou Chuanbin, Xu Lili, Chang Chung-fu, Rian Thum, James Frankel, Ma Haiyun, and Roberta Tontini, among others, have also enhanced my understanding of the historical, textual, and intellectual dimensions of Muslims in China.

In preparing my book, I have benefited from the feedback I received during presentations at various institutions (in reverse chronological order): Louisa Schein organized a group reading of a portion of my book by China specialists at Rutgers University, which provided well-rounded feedback, particularly on my characterization of the *minjian*. William Nelson hosted my talk at the New York University Law School's Golieb Legal History Colloquium, whose participants pushed me to improve the precision of the book—namely, my discussion of custom. William Alford and Intisar Rabb created a lively environment in their International and Comparative Law Workshop at Harvard Law School, and their students provided piercing comments regarding the viability of shariʿa in secular systems. Michael Gilsenan graciously twice invited me to speak at the Kevorkian Center for Near Eastern Studies, including at his Islamic Law in Society Symposium, during which scholars from NYU and elsewhere provided critical responses to the question of Islamic law's localization in Chinese society. In addition, Mark Turin and Sienna Craig spearheaded the Himalayan Studies Conference at Yale University, during which I presented on a panel organized by Tenzin Jinba that helped me contextualize the role of ethnicity in my study in the Sino-Tibetan borderlands. Lastly, I thank the organizers of various panels at the Law and Society Association, American Anthropological Association, and Association of Asian Studies for allowing me to present portions of the book in progress. I am thankful to all participants during these various presentations, and especially John Osburg, Hans Steinmüller, Luo Yu, Megan Steffen, and Marissa Smith.

A number of people have read various drafts or parts of drafts. Max Oidtmann's firsthand insights on Northwest China were invaluable in transforming the dissertation into the book manuscript. Tim Haupt lent his ethnographic eye to the draft manuscript and was a true writing companion. Michael Gilsenan, Adnan Zulfiqar, and Michael Meyer not only read the manuscript in full but have also been co-travelers in different trajectories across disciplines, area studies, and professions. I owe them much.

This study has required that I gain familiarity with a number of languages, and I want to thank my language teachers—in particular, Amy Shen, Li Bing, Sharif Rosen, Albert Johns, Frances Yufen Lee Mehta, Qiuyun Teng, Namgyal Tsepak, Nizar Hermes, Wasim Shiliwala, Brenton Sullivan, and Hamza Zafer—for their patient guidance.

At Princeton, Jeremy Adelman and Mark Beissinger created an ideal environment in which to write this book. I also thank the late Paul Sigmund III, my gracious housemate, for the many conversations over early-night dinners of roast chicken and creamed spinach to discuss Christian and Islamic theologies.

I would like to thank the various libraries and archives where I conducted research for this book—namely, the Linxia City Library, Linxia Prefectural Archives, the Beijing Center's Donald Daniel Leslie Collection, the Chinese University of Hong Kong's University Services Center, the Gansu Provincial Archives, the Xinjiang Uyghur Autonomous Region Archives, the Christian and Missionary Alliance Archives at the Billy Graham Center, the Harvard-Yenching Library's Carter D. Holton Collection, Cornell University's Wason Collection, and Princeton University's East Asian Library.

Certainly, administrative staff at universities, my former law firm, and various libraries made my life easier during the various stages of the book's production. I owe a sincere thank-you to Camellia Liu, Donna Duncan, Elizabeth Edmondson, Liren Zheng, the late Raymond Lum, Diane Natanson, Jayne Bialkowski, and Carole Frantzen.

Some portions of Chapters 1 and 7 of this book draw from two previously published works: "Muslim Mandarins in Chinese Courts: Dispute Resolution, Islamic Law, and the Secular State in Northwest China" in *Law & Social Inquiry*, (40(4): 1001–30, 2015), and "Defining Shari'a in China: State, Ahong, and the Post-secular Turn" in a special issue of *Cross-Currents: East Asian History & Culture Review* (no. 12, September 2013). I am grateful to *Law & Social Inquiry*, *Cross-Currents*, and Cambridge University Press for allowing me to do so. The *Cross-Currents* special issue was the result of an international conference I organized at Cornell in 2012, and I thank the participants from China, Taiwan, and the United States as well as the Jeffrey Lehman Fund for Scholarly Exchange with China for funding the conference.

This book is based on my dissertation, fieldwork for which was funded by the National Science Foundation Doctoral Dissertation Research Improvement Grant, the Fulbright-Hays Doctoral Dissertation Research Abroad Grant, and various Cornell grants. The book was written with funding from the Princeton Institute for International and Regional Studies, the Luce/ACLS Program in China Studies Postdoctoral Fellowship, and the Smith Richardson Foundation Strategy and Policy Fellows Program.

I owe a special thanks to John Berger and his production team at Cambridge University Press for their support. The manuscript was copyedited by Allison Brown and Allan Edmands. I am indebted to Tsering Wangyal Shawa and Sorat Tungkasiri for their help with generating the maps.

Most of all, I thank the people of Linxia and elsewhere in China, who took the time to speak to me when they had very little to gain from doing so. I am grateful to them for sharing with me their stories, their complaints, their victories, and their aspirations.

My journey would not have been possible without the support of my wife, Yaeji Regina Park, who has been with me every step of the way – from late-night Skype calls in smoke-filled *wangba* during fieldwork to early-morning conversations years later at the kitchen table honing "The Argument" with all her precision as a lawyer. She is a fellow pilgrim and makes the journey worthwhile.

ABBREVIATIONS

Ar.	Arabic
AR	autonomous region
BCA	Bureau of Civil Affairs
BEA	Bureau of Ethnic Affairs
BON	Bank of Ningxia
BRA	Bureau of Religious Affairs
CBRC	China Banking Regulatory Commission
CCP	Chinese Communist Party
Ch.	Chinese
CPPCC	Chinese People's Political Consultative Conference
EAGC	Education Administration Guidance Committee
GWDP	Great Western Development Policy
ICBC	Industrial and Commercial Bank of China
IRC	Islamic resource center
KTV	karaoke bar
MCA	Ministry of Civil Affairs
NGO	nongovernmental organization
NPC	National People's Congress
PLA	People's Liberation Army
PMC	people's mediation committee
PRC	People's Republic of China
PSB	Public Security Bureau
Q.	Qur'an
RMB	renminbi, the official currency of China
SAEA	State Administration of Ethnic Affairs
SARA	State Administration of Religious Affairs
SARS	severe acute respiratory syndrome
SCO	Shanghai Cooperation Organization
SEAC	State Ethnic Affairs Commission
SEZ	special economic zone
U.	Uyghur
UFWD	United Front Work Department
Yi-Xie	China Islamic Association (Zhongguo Yisilanjiao Xiehui)

A NOTE ON LANGUAGE

I have endeavored to minimize foreign terms. However, because much of the work of making sense of Islamic law in Chinese society among Hui requires translation, this book necessarily tracks several concepts across languages (Arabic or Persian, Chinese, and English). Where foreign language terms or phrases are of particular salience to the text, I gloss them in English, although I do not gloss a few key terms, such as *minjian*, in order to retain some of the term's texture. Chinese terms are rendered in pinyin with the exception of a handful of Taiwanese names and such pre-PRC figures as Chiang Kai-shek and Sun Yat-sen, which I render in Wade-Giles. Where two different Chinese words have the same pinyin, I provide the Chinese characters to distinguish. I have provided the names of laws and regulations in pinyin after the English translation. For Arabic terms, I have followed the transliteration system of the *International Journal of Middle East Studies* ("IJMES style"). Pursuant to the IJMES style, I use half-rings for *ʿayn* (e.g., shariʿa) and hamza (e.g., Qurʾan) and *–ay* and *–aw* endings for diphthongs. For Chinese names within the text and in the Chinese language reference list, following standard Chinese usage, I begin with the family name and then provide the given name (e.g., "Ma Laichi" in text or "Ma, Laichi" in the reference list). For Arabic names in the reference list that begin with "al-" I alphabetize them according to the first letter after "al-." When citing works in foreign languages, I have retained the original spelling of and capitalization in foreign language titles pursuant to the preference of the author. For interview material, I have attempted to minimize transliterations, but I have included the pinyin for Chinese and used IJMES style for Modern Standard Arabic where applicable. In transliterating terms from the local dialect of Bafanghua, which includes Chinese and Arabic as well as other languages, in accordance with Hui phonetics, I have modified pinyin for terms that diverge from the Chinese or Arabic original languages (e.g., *bei homo* for the Chinese *bai maozi* ["white cap"] and *nietie* for the Arabic *niyya* ["intent"]). Following the main text is a multilanguage glossary, which includes both the Chinese and Arabic scripts for relevant words.

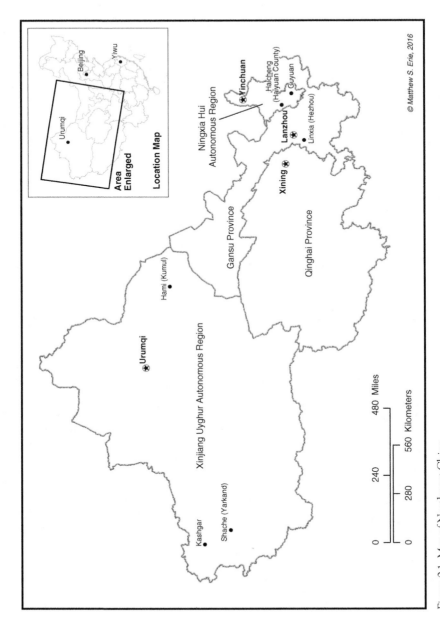

Figure 0.1 Map of Northwest China
Source: the author

INTRODUCTION

THE PARTY-STATE ENTERS THE MOSQUE

> *There is a conflict. Communism is a belief. One cannot have two beliefs. Even if we don't think of Communism as a belief and rather as political thought, then it says no one can have a religious belief. The two are mutually exclusive.*
> A Muslim cleric in Linxia

THE LETTERS ON THE WALL

The quiet courtyard of the mosque where Nasim[1] is a cleric will soon be filled with the faithful arriving for the noon prayer. As a member of the Yihewani "teaching school," which sees itself as tied to the Hijaz (the western portion of Saudi Arabia containing Mecca and Medina), he prefers his Arabic name over his Chinese one. I sit in Nasim's office in the mosque where he is a cleric (*ahong*[2]) in Linxia (formerly Hezhou), a city in Gansu Province in Northwest China.[3] Hui, the largest of China's Muslim minority groups, call Linxia, a trading city on the historic Silk Road, "China's Little Mecca," as it has served as the center for all the revivalist strains of Islam that have entered China since the seventeenth century.

When Nasim returns from a late morning meeting with the Bureau of Religious Affairs (BRA) to prepare for prayer, he finds three people waiting for him. One is a student loitering in the mosque library. The second person is a plainclothes policeman, sitting and waiting for Nasim while sipping a thermos full of green tea and looking at the posters of the Sacred Mosque in Mecca that hang on the wall of the reception room.

---

[1] All names of the living are pseudonyms, unless they are of public record.

[2] *Ahong* is the Chinese transliteration for the Persian word *ākhūnd* (the learned).

[3] By Northwest China, I refer to Gansu Province, the Ningxia Hui Autonomous Region ("Ningxia"), Qinghai Province, and the Xinjiang Uyghur Autonomous Region ("Xinjiang").

Also sitting in the reception room is the third person, who, unexpectedly, is a stranger—a white, non-Muslim American anthropologist, no less.

Nasim goes to the policeman first, and the two enter the cleric's inner chamber, where they talk and then reemerge to the outer reception room. The policeman nods to Nasim and then leaves the mosque courtyard in his unmarked, black Santana. Meanwhile, the student, realizing this is not the time to ask which sura (Qur'anic chapter) is the subject for tomorrow's lesson, returns to his dorm room just across the courtyard, where he lives with eighty other young Chinese Muslim men studying Islam.

Nasim glides into the room where I sit, takes my hand warmly, and sits next to me. He wears the white skullcap commonly worn by Muslim men, called *bai maozi* in standard Chinese and pronounced *bei homo* in the local dialect. Like most of Linxia's clerics, he is not yet forty. The walls of the reception room prominently display the laws and regulations governing areas of religious activity. The national, provincial, and prefectural laws hang from top to bottom, a kind of visual hierarchy of the legislative sources. On an adjacent wall hang passages from the Qur'an, written in elegant black Arabic calligraphy. Nasim sits in a hard-backed armchair, the People's Republic of China (PRC) regulations above his right shoulder and the prescriptions from the revealed sources of Islam to his left—the word of the Party-State and the word of God.

With no small amount of caution, I turn to Nasim sitting next to me. It is the summer of 2009, and the worst interethnic riots in modern Chinese history have just rocked the country. On July 5, 2009, over a thousand Uyghurs (Turkic Muslims) and Han Chinese in Urumqi, the capital of Xinjiang, had cut each other down in the streets, resulting in 197 people, including Han and Uyghur, being killed and approximately 1,700 more injured. In the aftermath of the riots, Uyghurs had fled Xinjiang for nearby provinces, and the security forces had instructed Hui clerics and mosque leaders to expel any Uyghurs for fear that they were terrorists. Several times during the early part of my fieldwork that consisted of visiting mosques, Hui had turned me away after misidentifying me as a Uyghur. The multiple levels of surveillance were so pervasive as to ensnare even me, someone who looks very little like a Uyghur.

Nasim smiles at my nervousness. After introducing myself, I ask him why the policeman came to see him and if there was any danger in my being there. Nasim smiles his small, compact smile: "No, there is no danger. He is a member of the Linxia City Public Security Bureau who came to consult me. I will go soon to the police headquarters to give further assistance." He continues, "This happens frequently. They often come to consult me on cases that touch on a matter of religious law [jiaofa]. The municipal police, the traffic police, the judicial organs at the city and prefecture level—they all come. In this matter, a Chinese Muslim man has been run over by a Han Chinese taxi driver, just two days earlier. The bereaved family sought 30,000 yuan[4] in compensation, which the taxi driver was unable to pay. The policeman sought my help in resolving the dispute."

When I ask why the need for a cleric, Nasim explains, "Linxia is a Muslim city. It is majority Muslim. As Muslims, we abide by religious law [jiaofa] and state law [guofa]. Most people, in the event of an accident, will want to resolve the problem by invoking religious law, the rule here being that compensation is owed to the family. When the amount of compensation is at issue, a compromise is made. So, I told the policeman to suggest to the family that they lower the amount to something the Han can afford. Islamic law [Yisilanfa] requires justice, not revenge."

This scene is repeated throughout Linxia: public security officers, officials of ethnic and religious affairs, and other cadres of the Chinese Communist Party (CCP, or "the Party") regularly solicit the aid of clerics who are the leaders of mosque communities. The acquiescence of a non-Muslim Han wrongdoer to the extralegal jurisdiction of a Muslim cleric is likewise frequent in Linxia. Also common: clerics such as Nasim would leave no record of the dispute and thus provide no written basis for an indigenous jurisprudence. Cases like these comprise everyday life in Linxia.

Yet, as the PRC is a socialist legal system, it provides no legal basis for religious law. At periods in the PRC's history, the Party-State has been outright hostile toward any institution or person that would endorse religious authority. In Nasim's office, however, the seemingly inimical letters of two legal orders, Islamic law and state law, are showcased side by side. On the surface, there is no conflict. Nonetheless, the actions of Nasim and the policeman suggest their agreement may not accord with the letter of state law. Personalistic relationships between representatives of Muslim communities and the Party-State fill the gaps between their respective legal orders. Such collaborations, however, are fragile. Visits by police officers could just as well result in the cleric being detained, rather than

---

[4] At the time of my fieldwork, 6.83 yuan was equal to 1 US dollar.

consulted, as happened several times during my fieldwork. The line that divided permissible from prohibited behavior seemed to shift; as a result, violence, while not visible in such encounters, was nevertheless latent and unpredictable. Nasim's confidence that there was "no danger" struck me as misplaced, or perhaps it was my own ability to fathom where lines were drawn (and by whom) that was inadequately attuned.[5]

As someone who is trained as a lawyer, in addition to being an anthropologist, I found that the scene in Nasim's office certainly did not conform to my expectations of law. In the United States, Americans learn that police officers are the face of the law. In Linxia, however, not only did state law and therefore the police appear to have limits, the cleric also seemed to have considerable influence, because there was an entirely different type of law that operated in the mosque office. While working for an international law firm in Beijing in the mid-2000s, I came to appreciate the Chinese lawyers who had previously worked in such governmental bureaus as the Ministry of Commerce, upon whom the firm relied to glean information from their former governmental colleagues concerning the implementation and enforcement of a regulation that would impact a deal. I learned in China, to a greater degree than in US legal practice, that it was relationships that gave meaning to law, and while actors operate within asymmetries of power, there are asymmetries within asymmetries. Depending on the context, the application of local rules could result in power relations being inverted even if they are not overturned.

It was my earliest exposure to the practice of law in China that propelled my interest in understanding the operation of law in Chinese society, and what such a study could teach about law more generally. Further, I wanted to study law beyond the glassed-in cubicles and recycled air of a corporate law firm to where Chinese outside the urban cores of the east coast encountered the law in their everyday. This impulse led me to Linxia. Yet in Linxia the nature of the controlling law itself was at question. What was this "law" that Nasim called *jiaofa*? How did Hui practice this form of Islamic law? Under what conditions did the state tolerate it? What could be learned from Linxia to understand Islam? China? And how could someone such as Nasim live with such uncertainty, of not knowing where collaboration ends and conflict begins?

---

[5] Another possibility is that Nasim and others intentionally misrepresented themselves to me. As I conducted my fieldwork during a period of anti-American sentiment in many Muslim communities across the globe, including Hui regions, the degree to which my interlocutors were forthcoming was a constant concern.

This book considers how a historically marginalized minority group that has a vision of "the good" that differs from that of the majority pursues that vision under a condition of arbitrary rule, in reform-era China.[6] This problem occurs at the overlap of two critical global trends: the revival of Islam and the ascendance of China. Whereas an expanding literature studies Muslim minorities and their law in Western liberal states,[7] I address this question through the case of Hui in China. In China, state law severs religion from religious law, yet following Islamic law is central to Muslim minorities' ideas of the good life, defined by such values as authenticity, piety, orthodoxy, and purity. This book is a study about how Hui exercise this capacity when the Party-State, backed by its monopoly on force, mobilizes considerable institutional and discursive resources to make Islam conform to Chinese socialism and nationalism.

Much of the public perception of Islam following the attacks of September 11, 2001 has been informed by the "clash of civilizations" thesis,[8] a thesis that has been rigorously criticized.[9] In recent years, the problem has been reframed by the radicalization of Muslims and the conversion of non-Muslims to neofundamentalist strains of Islam in continental Europe, the United Kingdom, and the United States who may or may not have affiliations with overseas groups such as al-Qaʻida and the so-called Islamic State in Iraq and Syria. "Homegrown terror" has led to attacks in a number of countries in North America, Europe, and Asia. The danger, as understood, is no longer "us versus them" but rather "we are becoming them."[10] Instead of national interests and citizens being

---

[6] The term *reform-era* refers to the "opening and reform" inaugurated by Deng Xiaoping in 1978, which has modernized the state economy and sought to integrate China into the global economic order. This era continues to the present day.

[7] For a partial selection, see Shah (1994), Moore (2002), Mamdani (2002), Abdo (2006), Rohe (2007), Emon (2006, 2007), An-Naʻim (2008a, 2008b), Fadel (2009), Shryock (2010), Christoffersen (2010), Nielsen (2010), Esposito and Kalin (2011), Giunchi (2014), and Grillo (2015).

[8] Samuel Huntington (1993) argued that following the end of the Cold War, warfare would increase along civilizational lines, which he defined as Western, Confucian, Japanese, Islamic, Hindu, Slavic-Orthodox, Latin American, and "possibly" African. Later, Huntington (1996) changed the civilizations to Western, Sinic, Orthodox, Islamic, Hindu, Japanese, and African.

[9] Important criticisms of the "clash" thesis include Mottahedeh (1996), Rashid (1998), and Abrahamian (2003). For an illuminating critique based on evidence from China, see Gladney (1998).

[10] The shift from Islamic radicalism as a purely foreign policy matter to one that is also domestic is reflected in the approach of the US government. A 2008 report by the United States Senate Committee on Homeland Security and Governmental Affairs concludes, "Violent Islamist ideology and the terrorism it inspires pose a substantial threat to America's homeland security. The core tenets of this violent ideology are straightforward, uncompromising, and absolute. The ideology calls for the pursuit and creation of a global Islamist state—a Caliphate—that unites all

harmed "over there," the fear is that the enemy is the next-door neighbor, a politician, or a sister.[11] Perceptions of Islamic law and its impact in state legal systems are central to such global currents of fear. Public concern stems from some groups' neofundamentalist views of Islamic law, including corporal punishment such as public flogging, stoning, and beheading, and the influence of such practices on domestic legal orders. Anxieties have caused pundits to reduce the complexity and diversity of Islamic law to the law-of-terror that is infiltrating state law, and have deemed Muslims and Islamic law to be incompatible with the law of the modern state.[12]

This book questions whether the relationship between Muslim minorities and the modern state is one of irreducible antagonism because of conflicts between Islamic law and state law. Muslims and the state can work toward a common ground—however precarious—where they *both* pursue their vision of "the good," partly by accessing Islamic law. I use China as an unlikely testing ground for this assertion. China is distinct, because it is a socialist legal system that formally excludes religious law, and yet, for purposes different from those of Muslim minorities in China, the Party-State mobilizes Islamic law for its own ends.

Hui of various "teaching schools" (*jiaopai*), communities of believers, and representatives of the Party-State have created an environment for the flourishing of nonradical forms of Islam. Muslims in Northwest China are unique among Muslims elsewhere in China and in other places in the world in that all Muslims, down to the last child, identify with a teaching school. At the same time almost all Hanafi,[13] the teaching schools that have formed in China, are distinguished by their particular views of doctrine and law. Teaching schools are not physical places of instruction, although they do operate schools in this sense. Rather, they are ideologically driven groups of Muslims who establish mosques or Sufi tomb complexes[14] to cultivate specific understandings of Islam.

Muslims—the *Ummah*—and is governed by Islamic law—*Sharia*" (Lieberman 2008: 2). Following several post-9/11 actual or attempted terrorist attacks in the United States, in February 2015 the Department of Homeland Security convened a "Countering Violent Extremism" summit in three US cities to address the problem of homegrown terrorists, including those who have received training from groups abroad.

[11] On the problem of radicalization of Muslims in Europe and North America and the conversion of non-Muslims to extremist Islam, see Roy (2004), Abbas (2011), and Goerzig and al-Hashimi (2015).

[12] A number of writers, academic and popular, with a variety of agendas, have assumed this position. See, e.g., Lewis (1990), Horowitz (2004), Spencer (2008), McCarthy (2012), and Bostom (2012).

[13] Hanafi is one of the four traditional schools of jurisprudence in Islamic law, named after its founder, Imam Abu Hanifa (699–767 CE).

[14] Sufi tomb complexes (*gongbei*) are sites where a founder or an important member of the Sufi order is buried. The complexes, which may include grand courtyards, prayer halls, dining halls, and

Thus, the picture from the Northwest is not a binary of "Hui-state relations" but rather a number of relationships between and among teaching schools and the Party-State, who are all jostling to realize their view of the good life.

Led by the orientation of their teaching school, Hui work toward a middle ground through negotiation and collaboration with officials and cadres, translation, vernacularization, localization, and gendering of Islamic law as well as mediation of conflicts between state law and Islamic law. Yet to call the result a "depoliticized" Islam may be going too far. Although Hui and the Party-State's views of the good life may overlap, they are not seamless; as a result, the process by which actors on the ground use Islamic law is riddled with micro-conflicts. Thus, the boundaries that the state constructs between the private realm of belief and the public sphere of secular nationalism are unclear. Ongoing interpretive contests over what Islamic law means and what role it should play in China's reengagement with the global *umma* (Ar. lit. "people, community," meaning "the Muslim community"), among Hui as well as with the Party-State, constantly redefine the parameters of Islam in public life in contemporary China.

The study of Hui contributes to deepening contemporary understandings of Muslim minorities in secular societies. More specifically, it does so through their practice of law. At the outset, I underscore that my use of "law" is deliberately broad. This book extends understandings of law that are based on religious rather than state authority, as I explain in more detail below. My approach thus weighs the subjective along with the objective, the "emic" beside the "etic," and the users' view of the law in addition to familiar conceptions. In the remainder of this introduction, I provide the context of China's Islamic revival, of which Islamic legal practice is a constitutive part. I then provide a framework, broadly anthropological, through which to understand problems, attendant to the study of law, of terms, translation, and analytics that balances Hui views of law with received accounts of law. The China case resonates with concerns in both the study of Islam and of ethics; and I situate the Hui within converging theoretical views. Following this, I assess the political aspects of the question of Hui law via the Party-State's approach to governing ethnic minority regions. Lastly, I discuss my methodology, and I conclude with an overview of the subsequent chapters.

residential quarters for students, are vital not just for ceremonial observances but also for the broader social life of Sufi orders.

CHINA'S ISLAMIC REVIVAL

Following postcolonialism and the popular revolutions known as the "Arab Spring" in the Middle East, Islamic law is gaining traction in political reform across the region. China's Islamic law revival differs from those in such Muslim-majority contexts as the Middle East, where Muslims have a thick repertoire of public symbols with which to make arguments about ways to achieve a good life in accordance with Islam. Whether by Islamic political parties, public intellectuals, Islamic courts and qadis (judges), or academic and popular media, Muslims in such states can pursue their ethical projects in accordance with Islamic law, because Islam saturates institutional life. Islam is present in formal law as well. Constitutions, for instance, may formally recognize Islamic law as a source of law in general.[15]

What is remarkable about the Hui Islamic revival is that they are reintegrating China into the global *umma* largely without formal political representation, participation in policy formation, or religious associations independent of the state. Before analyzing how Hui do so, I first address the question of Hui themselves. As of 2010, the date of the most recent census, China has more than twenty-three million Muslims, more than Libya, Malaysia, or Russia, a population that falls between the number of Muslims in Syria and that in Saudi Arabia. The Party-State identified ten distinct Muslim ethnic groups as part of its nation-building efforts in the 1950s. In contemporary China, the largest group is Hui, of whom there are over ten million, followed by Uyghurs, of whom there are slightly fewer (see Table 1.1). When English-speaking audiences hear "Muslims in China," they tend to think of Uyghurs. This book is not about Uyghurs. However, as events in the recent history of Xinjiang have cast a pall over non-Uyghur Muslim minorities, some familiarity with the situation of Uyghurs is essential to understand China's Islamic revival and the place of Islamic law in it.

Uyghurs and Hui have had different historical relationships to the Han majority and the Chinese state. Uyghurs are geographically concentrated in Xinjiang, especially in such oasis cities in southern Xinjiang as Kashgar and Shache (Yarkand). They speak their own language, which is a Turkic language, and physically they look more like Central Asians than like Han Chinese. As a result, Uyghurs identify strongly with Turkic-speaking

---

[15] Regarding constitutional reform from the Middle East before and after the "Arab Spring" to Southeast Asia, where Brunei adopted Islamic law in 2014, shari'a is gaining salience in state legal systems (Lombardi 2006, 2013; Feener and Cammack 2007; Rabb 2008; Hefner 2011; Crouch forthcoming).

TABLE 1.1 Population size of officially recognized Muslim minority ethnic groups over time

Muslim minority	1982 population	2010 population	Percent change
Hui	7,228,398	10,586,087	+46
Uyghur	5,963,491	10,069,346	+69
Kazakh	907,546	1,462,588	+61
Dongxiang	279,523	621,500	+122
Kyrgyz	113,386	186,708	+65
Salar	69,135	130,607	+89
Tajik	26,600	51,069	+92
Bonan	9,017	20,074	+123
Uzbek	12,213	10,569	−13
Tatar	4,122	3,556	−14
Total	14,613,431	23,142,104	+58

Sources: 1982 and 2010 Censuses (Population Census Office 1985: 18–19; 2012: 74). One possible factor in explaining the decrease in Uzbek and Tatar populations is immigration to Kazakhstan and the other newly independent states following the dissolution of the Soviet Union in 1991. As a whole, these statistics most likely under-report the actual number of Muslims in China

Muslims of Central Asia. Their practice of Islam is one element of their Central Asian heritage. Uyghurs were not always Muslim, and pre-Islamic faiths continue to influence the Uyghur practice of Islam, particularly among Sufis in southern Xinjiang. Many urban Uyghurs today identify as "Sunnis" (by which they mean "other than Sufis"). In terms of political organization, from the ninth to the thirteenth centuries CE, Uyghur kings ruled over much of the northern Turpan basin, and in the seventeenth century Naqshbandi Sufis consolidated power over the southern Tarim basin until Qing soldiers overthrew them in the mid-eighteenth century. Xinjiang was thus incorporated rather late into the Chinese Empire. The result of these linguistic, racial, religious, and political traits is that Uyghurs have a strong sense of identity, one that is largely defined against that of the Han (and Hui) migrants in Xinjiang.[16]

[16] For readings on Uyghur history, including Islam and contacts with Central Asia, see Rudelson (1997), Millward (1998, 2007), Bellér-Hann et al. (2007), and Thum (2014). For literature on Uyghur politics in the socialist period, see Becquelin (2000), Starr (2004), Gladney (2004b), and Bovingdon (2010).

Unlike Uyghurs, Hui[17] are geographically dispersed throughout China. Hui identify as the descendants of the Persian and Arab merchants, migrants, and envoys who entered China beginning in the Tang Dynasty (618–907 CE).[18] Following a long history of movement throughout present-day China and along the historic Silk Road, both the overland route that connected western China to Central Asia and the maritime version that enabled trade with merchants from origins as diverse as Southeast Asia to the Arabian peninsula, today's Hui are found in almost all major cities in China. However, there are larger concentrations of Hui in Gansu, Ningxia, Qinghai, and eastern Xinjiang. As a result of their dispersion, Hui have had a much longer history of interaction and intermarriage with Han as well as with other ethnic groups, including Mongolians and Tibetans. Consequently, Hui outwardly look like Han; furthermore, they speak Mandarin (although their language is often inflected with Arabic, Persian, and other languages).

Hui are often perceived as the model minority, who are complicit with state power—the "good Muslims" in contrast with the Uyghurs as "bad Muslims." Such analogies suffer from historical amnesia, however, since the relationship between Hui in the Northwest and the historic state has hardly been one of quiescence. There were movements by Hui leaders to establish sultanates in southwestern China during the Qing Dynasty, and Hui originally from Linxia founded their own governments in the 1930s throughout Northwest China, governments that were anti-Communist. Generally, however, Hui today do not wish to establish their own political state. Hui have enjoyed a higher degree of integration into the Chinese state than have Uyghurs. In the Ming Dynasty (1368–1644), for instance, Hui attained positions of prominence in the official bureaucracy, particularly as astronomers.[19]

---

[17] As with most ethnonyms in China, the designation Hui is partly a product of nation building, although the term predates the founding of the PRC. Hui today may refer to themselves as "Musilin" (Muslim) and thus privilege their religious identity in association with Muslims elsewhere. From the view of the state, Hui are an aberration, because they are the only ethnic group in China defined by religion (Nationality Problem Research Committee [1941] 1980). I retain the use of "Hui" not to reinforce official ethnic categories but to observe that Hui, who also use the term in self-descriptions, consider the name to refer to their particularly Chinese form of Islam.

[18] All dates are Gregorian calendar and Common Era unless otherwise stated.

[19] For background reading on Hui, see Bai (1944), Lipman (1996), Dillon (1999), Gillette (2000), Chang (2001), Israeli (2002c), Benite (2005), and Gladney (2008, 2009).

Hui have had an ambiguous relationship with the Han majority, a relationship summarized in historian Jonathan Lipman's (1997) phrase "familiar strangers"; and their familiar strangeness has intensified in recent years, pursuant to global discourses that equate "Muslim" with "terrorist." Despite their phenotypical similarity to the ethnic majority, as Muslims they are different from Han Chinese. As a result, Hui have generally been confined to a second-class citizenship in China. During certain periods, such as during the Qing Dynasty (1644–1912), Hui have suffered considerable discrimination. These conditions have caused Hui to feel alienated from Muslims outside of China, an estrangement that, in part, fuels their interest in Islamic law. Their co-participation with the Party-State in the Islamic revival is not generally an experience shared by Uyghurs, however, whose attitudes toward Han and the state are less amenable to collaboration.[20] While this book is concerned with the experience of Hui, I make comparisons, where applicable, with other Muslim minority groups in the Northwest.

China's Islamic law revival is part of an Islamic renaissance in the country, one that is particularly visible among Hui communities. This resurgence is a result of both governmental policies over the past thirty-plus years and larger global renewals of Muslim identities and political action—these different sources not always working toward the same ends or even sharing similar assumptions about religion and politics. As a consequence of the revival, the number of mosques in China has grown from approximately 20,000 in 1994 to 35,535 in 2010, a 78 percent increase.[21] Islam is one of the fastest growing religions in the country, particularly among youth, mostly as a result of Muslim minorities' fertility rates following exceptions to the one-child policy and less due to conversion, although this happens on the fringes of Han and Tibetan societies.[22] The number of clerics and students in madrasas has likewise increased from

---

[20] Whereas research has been done on the historical presence of Islamic law in Uyghur communities (see, e.g., Bellér-Hann 2004, 2008) and several scholars in the United States, Japan, and China are conducting important research on Uyghur practice of law during the Qing Dynasty, research still needs to be done on contemporary Uyghur practices of law.

[21] The book *A General Survey of China's Mosques* (*Zhongguo qingzhensi zonglan*) gives the number as more than 1,000 registered mosques (Wu 1995: 13). In 2010 most Hui I spoke with put the number at well more than 30,000 mosques (registered and unregistered), of which there are roughly 8,000 in Gansu and Ningxia alone (with the two areas having approximately the same amount). The number provided for 2010 is the official mosque count (Yang 2010: 1).

[22] See, e.g., the *Report on Chinese Religions Survey* (*Zhongguo zongjiao diaocha baogao*) (2015) completed by the China Renmin University Philosophy Department (Zhongguo renmin daxue zhexueyuan) and the China Renmin University China Survey and Statistics Center (Zhongguo renmin daxue Zhongguo diaocha yu shuju zhongxin).

45,000 in 1998 to 53,383 in 2010.[23] To put the growing contacts between China and the Middle East in perspective, the number of hajjis (those who have performed the annual pilgrimage to Mecca) in 1952, the year of the first official PRC delegation, was 16, whereas in 2015, 14,500 Chinese Muslims completed the hajj.[24] The revival is further seen in the proliferation of halal food restaurants and factories, the growing communities of foreign Muslims who reside permanently in southeastern China, and the ubiquitous signs of Islam in public life in most cities, from mosques to stores that sell "Muslim use products" such as perfumes and soaps that are "free of any porcine products."

The Islamic revival has taken an "official" form, as a response to state law and policy. The PRC Constitution, statutes, and regulations guarantee freedom of religion.[25] However, policy that originates from the Party, which trumps state law, specifies that only "normal" religious activities receive state protection.[26] This qualification allows the officials in the BRA to determine which practices qualify as orthodox religions and which are heterodox and illegal. Such denigrations were often politically motivated. In the early decades of Communist rule, for example, practices such as Sufism were labeled "evil cults" (xiejiao).

At the same time, China's Islamic revival has also been elaborated through a number of practices[27] collectively known as minjian, which inform Hui religious belief and which are diversifying and deepening partly in response to state-led reform. Minjian literally means "between people" and is variously translated as "among the people," "popular," "unofficial," "folk," "nongovernmental," "nonstate," and "grassroots."

[23] The source of these statistics is the Ningxia Hui Autonomous Region Civil Servant Exam Employment and Professional Management Office (Yang 1998: 20; 2010: 1), which produces reports on clerical training. There is some discrepancy in the numbers, as to whether the figure applies to just clerics or to both clerics and students.

[24] These figures are the official statistics of the China Islamic Association (Zhongguo Yisilanjiao Xiehui) that organizes the hajj.

[25] See Chapter 1.

[26] The policy document *The Basic Viewpoint and Policy on the Religious Question during Our Country's Socialist Period* (Document No. 19) provides a definition of freedom of religion that guides Party work to this day. Document 19 clarifies that freedom of religion means freedom to believe but also freedom not to believe. Document No. 6, issued by the CCP Central Committee in 1991, clarifies that only "normal" religious activities are protected from noninterference (Potter 2003: 320).

[27] The sociologist Pierre Bourdieu provided one understanding of "practice" as a product of the dialectical relationship between what he called "habitus," or habitual ways of acting, and the "social field," which he understood as an "area of structured, socially patterned activity" (1987: 805; [1991] 2002: 14). Bourdieu's approach is generally helpful, although, as I emphasize in the rest of this book, Hui practice is heterogeneous and subject to debate.

12

Minjian refers to those institutions and norms that have not (necessarily) received the state's imprimatur. Hui use *minjian* to describe those people, places, and things that are not registered or sanctioned by state law (e.g., clerics, students, mosques, tombs, prayer halls, publications, property transactions, and so forth). The *minjian*, however, cannot be reduced to such social scientific concepts as "public sphere" or "civil society," which, although they also define a realm that is not dominated by the state, unfairly suggest coordinated action, autonomy, or transparency. Although the *minjian* can assume institutional form, it is broader than institutions and is practiced by means of rules that may be neither established nor systemic. Likewise, *minjian* should not necessarily be equated with "illegal." Rather, it may not (yet) have a basis in state law or be expressly prohibited by state law; it is potentially illegal or legal or, as a third possibility, inheres in those activities, domains, places, or roles on which the law is silent. The relationships between the official and *minjian* are far from static and are constantly on the move.

The *minjian* encompasses "person-to-person" or social activities outside the reach of the state but that maintain boundaries with the state. State power, however, partially subsists on the *minjian* and its relationships. Whereas the *minjian* is constrained by the official, the official—including legislation, litigation, governmental propaganda, and policy making and enforcement (i.e., the official world of Chinese law)—is even more constrained by the socialist ideology of the Party-State. The two domains of the *minjian* and the official coexist easily only on the surface, as demonstrated by the texts of PRC and Islamic laws hanging side by side in Nasim's office. Meanwhile, in the backrooms of mosque offices and other private spaces, the *minjian* and official intermingle but not without an element of danger, despite Nasim's claim to the contrary. It is at the points of contact between the *minjian* and the official where the former could potentially eclipse the latter, upsetting the public secret of the *minjian* and endangering the legitimacy of the official. Hui cadres who are enmeshed in multiple overlapping networks—those of their religious and work communities—particularly embody such tensions.

The *minjian* and the state may just as likely tolerate each other. The state may employ the category *minjian* or the state may try to transform the *minjian* into the realm of the official. In the context of maintaining social order, their relationship is akin to what scholar of religion Louis Dumont (1980: 245) called "the encompassing of the contrary," although the result is less hierarchy (his term) than what a young Mao Zedong ([1937] 1970) called "contradiction," a "unity of opposites." More broadly, the story of reform-era China—whether state-society relations, knowledge production, relations between the private and public sectors, or transnational links—is the story of *minjian* and its contingent relation to power.

Much of the dynamism of the Islamic revival or religious awakenings more generally in China can be attributed to the continual pull-and-tug of the *minjian* and the state, as highlighted by law. Secular policies[28] mold Daoism, Buddhism, Catholicism, Protestantism, and Islam (the five officially recognized faiths) into belief systems that are culturally expressive and emphatically Chinese.[29] Following such transformations, China is witnessing the prolific construction of places of worship, the performance of rites, and elaborate costumes, while certain types of religious texts that subordinate temporal to transcendent authority are banned. The sanctification of religion by the state further deprives it of its law. Thus, when Chinese refer to "popular law" (*minjianfa*), such a category includes "religious law."[30] Like "popular faith" (*minjian xinyang*), "popular law" has no basis in formal law. So while no type of popular law, including religious law, is regulated, it is the religious law of those ethnic groups—i.e., Uyghurs and Tibetans, and to some extent Mongolians and Hui, groups that have transnational connections and that do not necessarily adhere to national jurisdiction—that has proven nettlesome to socialist rule.

As applied to the question of secularizing Islam, the Party-State encourages certain forms of international connections between those Muslims in China and their coreligionists abroad, as I saw in such eastern cities as Yiwu, Shenzhen, and Shanghai. These exchanges are mainly economic, but they are also intellectual, such as study abroad, and spiritual, such as the hajj. Yet Hui additionally create their own links abroad, such as the *minjian* hajj, by which they attend the pilgrimage on the quota of such other countries as Thailand, and Sufi pilgrimages to Central Asia and India. Evidence for such revived connections is provided by the increased

---

[28] My use of the term "secular" is influenced by recent writings in anthropology (Asad 2003; Scott and Hirschkind 2006; Bubandt and van Beek 2012; van der Veer 2014) and law and religion (An-Na'im 2005; Kuru 2009, 2012; Stepan 2011; Fox 2012) that have argued that secularism is not neutrality toward religion (as in "separation of church and state"); rather it is the active management of religious institutions and ideas by temporal authorities. What distinguishes the China case is the extreme nature of its secularism in formally espousing freedom of religion by law but actively intervening in nearly all aspects of religion, from scripture and places of worship to dress and speech.

[29] See, for instance, Yang (2008), Goossaert and Palmer (2011), Yang Fenggang (2011), and Katz (2014).

[30] Chinese scholars use *minjianfa* to signify all nonstate legal orders, whether based on religion, custom, locality, clan, or group (see, e.g., Chen and Xie 2002; Tian 2005; Xie 2012).

circulation of Arabic and Persian texts, some of which escape the governmental censor. Collectively, these media and points of contact are expanding and deepening Hui knowledge of Islamic law.

Islamic revival has reached a tipping point, however. In the past decade, in a kind of vicious spiral, the state has increasingly curtailed Uyghurs' religious practice, which in turn has radicalized a small segment of the population, incurring greater state restriction and surveillance. It was primarily Uyghur discontent with this state of affairs that led to the July 5, 2009 riots in Urumqi. A number of terrorist attacks have followed that have spilled out of Xinjiang, including in Beijing in 2013 and in Kunming in 2014. Despite their difference from Uyghurs, Hui, because they are Muslims, have a relationship with the Party-State that is colored by both Chinese and international discourses on Islam. Not infrequently, in terms of the actual implementation of ethnic and religious policy, they are "lumped together" with Uyghurs. A Hui cleric in Linxia summarizes this problem: "The government is concerned about Islamic extremism through contacts between Muslims in China and those in Central Asia. As Xinjiang is close to Central Asia, so too is Linxia dangerous. It doesn't make any sense, but that's how they think." To some extent, to be Muslim in post-2009 China is to be a suspect class.

ANTHROPOLOGIES OF LAW

Whereas normative indeterminacy—that is, diverse norms that are not of themselves easily understood but require interpretation—is found everywhere, China provides a particularly rich reservoir of plural and potentially conflicting norms.[31] China's extreme pluralism is a result of the diversity of communities, distinguished by faith, ethnicity, lineage, profession, and geography, that are subsumed within the modern nation-state. Over the past three and a half decades, the state has built a modern legal system to bring order to this diversity. Modern law differs from imperial law in that, chiefly, the state has defined law as state law, and it is this state law that applies to all, universally throughout the nation. Modern law consists of courts, lawyers, police, procuratorates, codes and statutes, law schools, and an array of administrative bodies. Yet this construction of modern law has not necessarily led to the decline of nonstate norms, and in some cases it has revitalized them.

---

[31] For a sample of the literature, see Zhang and Wang (2003), Zhao (2003), Wang (2009), and Hillman (2014).

Thus far I have called the local rules of the Hui "Islamic law," yet the assumption begs the question, is it really "law"? On the muddy banks of the Yellow River in Lanzhou, the provincial capital of Gansu, I asked a senior member of a Yihewani mosque this question. Can Islamic law really be called "law" in the absence of an Islamic state or jurists and Islamic courts to make and enforce that law? His jaw dropped. "We consider it law," he sputtered. "If we fail to abide by what the Qur'an says in this life, then we will be punished in the afterlife. Activities such as daily prayer, fasting, and giving alms [ṣadaqa]—these we must do! If you do not think these are law, then you do not understand Islam."

By using the preferred Hui term *jiaofa* (religious law), the Yihewani elder made a couple of associations that were unequivocal: their practice is "law" (*fa*), not its traditional complement *li*, meaning social etiquette or, more formally, rites, that are standards of behavior and order social relationships, and it derives from the religion of Islam. Most Hui would agree with this usage. By linking their conception of Islamic law to the "teaching," they invoke the divine authority of the Qur'an, as revealed to the Prophet Muhammad.

Jiaofa suggests a broadening of conventional understandings of law. To take a baseline, generally Weberian, definition of law as a system of rules that is applied to a distinct population and that is enforced through institutions designed specifically for such purposes,[32] this definition encompasses a number of different types of law. The most typical is state law, including constitutions, legislation, and court decisions that both balance the interests of citizens with those of the state and allocate rights and duties between individuals. This understanding of law has attained prominence with the rise of the modern nation-state, yet the scope of law can be broadened to include nonstate law, such as religious law. The defining characteristic of state law is its enforcement by the coercive apparatus of the state. The distinguishing feature of religious law is the divine nature of the lawmaker. Human intermediaries interpret revealed law through a corpus of texts and methods of reasoning that may be backed by formal institutions such as courts. Islamic law, for instance, is sometimes understood to qualify as "law" only when it is incorporated into state law. However, religious law is also a matter of individual conscience; enforcement can operate in the absence of state-backed institutions, such as in the case of Muslim minorities in secular states, and informally through

---

[32] Weber defined law as that which is externally guaranteed by the probability of coercion applied by a staff of people whose position is specific to that function ([1922] 1967: 5).

a critical mass of believers, the teaching schools in the Hui case, and the basis of the "must" in the Yihewani elder's statement. More fundamentally, as with state (i.e., secular) law, religious law is rooted in the intersections between justice and violence.[33]

The question "is it really law?" has implications beyond terminology to the core analytics of anthropology.[34] In its task to open up novel ways to think about foundational aspects of social life, anthropology can work to expand formalist conceptions of positive law that equate law with the state,[35] but it can do so only by taking adequate analytical precautions. On the one hand, the anthropologist errs in shoehorning culture into Western categories, for example, "law." On the other hand, a core feature of the discipline is privileging the concepts and language of interlocutors in the field; and so, cultural intimacy and translation are required to make such knowledge "knowable" to wider audiences. In understanding the key term *jiaofa*, the generic term for Hui normativity,[36] local language and perspectives may go only so far. For one thing, the Yihewani elder's statement showed that *jiaofa* also entails ethical obligations, personal conduct that brings one closer to God. So already the category "law" is elusive, because it includes the subcategory of ethics.

To be more precise, *jiaofa* is really closer to something like an amalgamation of legalistic rules, ethical evaluations, moral commandments, and localized customs. Hui may distinguish among these sources, for example, calling Qur'anic inheritance shares, the husband's duties to his wife, or the requirements for establishing a *waqf* (pious endowment) *fa* (law), whereas obligations like wearing head coverings, dietary restrictions, or post-copulation ablutions are *daode* (ethics or morality) or *meide*

---

[33] A critical line of thought, initiated by Karl Marx, has investigated this parallel and has been most robustly developed by Walter Benjamin ([1921] 2000), Jacques Derrida (1990), and Giorgio Agamben (1999).

[34] See, e.g., the classic debate between Max Gluckman (1955) who preferred "universal" (i.e., Western) terms and Paul Bohannan (1957) who distinguished between analytical and "folk" categories. The implications of this debate are still felt today in anthropology. It has echoes in concerns about projects that underscore "difference" versus "commonality" (Sahlins 1995; Obeyesekere [1992] 1997) and the possibilities of universals in the face of "ethnographic theory" (e.g., Strathern 1990; Sangren 2009; de Col and Graeber 2011). The view that animates this book is that anthropology has dual commitments: to illuminate social worlds that differ from familiar ones while providing grounds for cross-cultural comparison.

[35] See, e.g., Malinowski (1926), Geertz (1983), Greenhouse (1986), Bourdieu (1987), Rosen (1989), Merry (1990), Mundy (2004), Riles (2004), Dresch (2012a, 2012b), and Pirie (2013a).

[36] Hui also refer to Islamic law as a number of phonetic transliterations, including Yisilanjiaofa ("Islamic (religious) law") and Yisilanfa ("Islamic law") or one of the transliterations of shari'a, such as *sheruo'ati*.

(virtue). The grounds upon which they distinguish them are based on Hui conceptions of law versus ethics (which instruct people on how to live), morality (as obligations that constrain behavior), or virtue (ethical and moral embodiment). For Hui, law is the language of prescription and prohibition (again, the "must"), whereas the latter are behavioral standards. Moreover, adherence to law is rewarded or punished in the afterlife, while unethical behavior may not carry such consequences. Some learned clerics link such sources, saying, for example, that ethics and morality are based in the juridical rules of the revealed law. Yet, more often than not, "lay" Hui refer to these sources collectively as *jiaofa*.

For purposes of this book, my use of "law" is shorthand for what would otherwise be an enumeration (i.e., "law" plus "ethics" plus "morals" plus "customs"). My use is a compromise between the anthropological ethics of taking interlocutors' concepts seriously while also maintaining distance for critique. Where relevant, I distinguish Hui usage of *jiaofa* from non-legal rules (e.g., ethics, customs, etc.). However, it is not always easy to draw clear lines. For instance, whereas Nasim's rule on compensation for accidental death has a basis in Islamic law, specifically, the law on retaliation (Ar. *qiṣāṣ*) which is often mitigated to compensation (Ar. *diya*) and Nasim broadly cites *jiaofa*, his reasoning is more moral than legal. As the example shows, Hui moralize law and, elsewhere, render ethics "law-like." Indeed, conceptual blurring at the margins of law/ethics is part of Hui representations of their norms. My strategy is explicitly cross-cultural, and thus differs from my approach to *minjian* that, while it may also have analogues in non-Chinese cultures, I prefer to leave it untranslated to demonstrate some of the nuance of the Hui experience. To call the rules that order Hui social life "law" is not to conflate such order with state law. Hui make clear distinctions, as did Nasim, in differentiating the two. Hui often began explaining to me how Islamic law works in China by stating that China is not a theocracy and their law inheres in the *minjian* rather than the political, although this separation, as I found, was far from absolute.

The problems of translating *jiaofa* echo the difficulties of understanding shari'a, ultimately the referent for *jiaofa*. Technically, shari'a refers to the divine path, or God's will. It includes the sacred sources: the revealed text of the Qur'an and the sunna, the practice established by the Prophet Muhammad as well as that of the earliest generations of pious Muslims and which includes the hadith tradition, the sayings and deeds of the Prophet Muhammad. In popular understandings outside of China, shari'a also includes the secondary sources: *qiyās* (analogies) and *ijmā'* (consensus), which Hui may also reference, although they rarely develop in written form their own rules based on these sources. *Fiqh* (lit. "understanding") refers to the human effort to know and apply shari'a, and it takes the form of a body of derived rules. As Hui are almost uniformly Sunni and mainly follow the Hanafi *fiqh*, they reference and translate Hanafi works. In this book, following Hui usage, I distinguish between shari'a and *fiqh*, and for descriptive purposes call them "Islamic law."[37] There are important differences between Islamic law among Muslim populations who live in states that apply such sources as state law (e.g., Pakistan, Egypt, Saudi Arabia, Malaysia, etc.) and Islamic law for Muslim minorities who abide in states that do not apply Islamic law, as Hui do. As with American Muslims, for example, Hui like Nasim discuss Islamic law (i.e., Yisilanfa) as law that derives from the authority of religion and not that of the state, yet this authority is no less palpable.

As I discovered in mosques, shari'a is more prominent in Hui practice than *fiqh*. *Fiqh* remains largely fragmented and oral; clerics for the most part do not write opinions of matters they hear as such records could be used against them by state authorities. At one level, Hui, like Muslims elsewhere, view shari'a as a "'total' discourse" (Messick 1993: 2), which they call their "life rule" (*shenghuo guilü*). Much more than a set of commandments, it provides both a normative framework through which Hui organize their personal, familial, communal, and religious lives as well as a set of ethics by which they measure their and others' deeds and thoughts according to a standard most conventionally embodied in the words and acts of the Prophet Muhammad, but which may be realized more immediately by a Hui Sufi shaykh, cleric, or teacher, the models of and for Hui. Hui acquire knowledge of Islamic law primarily through mosque-based clerics such as Nasim, who have a monopoly on applying rules from shari'a to everyday matters, producing a rudimentary *fiqh*.

Practice takes the form of 'ibādāt (rituals), or aspects of worship that include ṭahāra (concerns of purity), and mu'āmalāt (the laws of social

[37] The issues attending to translating shari'a or *fiqh* as "law" differ slightly from those of *jiaofa*. I translate *jiaofa* as "religious law" because Hui consider it as such; nonetheless, this translation is the starting point (not conclusion) of my analysis. Shari'a or *fiqh* as "Islamic law" has its own history, and scholars acknowledge that the term "Islamic law" is mostly a European invention. This history would seem to warrant the anthropologist's aversion to imposing colonial categories. Yet many of these same scholars retain the term, for a number of reasons. One of these is that "law" draws attention away from a mystified notion of shari'a as exclusively revelation and to one that emphasizes the work of those who derive and apply its rules (*fiqh*), work that is as "legal" as that of a US court clerk or judge. See, e.g., Kamali ([1991] 2003: 1), Weiss (1998: 8, 120), Johansen (1999: 2), Hallaq (2009a: 2–5; 2009b), and Rabb (2014: 9, 12–13).

relations). At a general level, *'ibādāt* is more "ethical" whereas *mu'āmalāt* is more "transactional," although such distinctions frequently break down. Islamic law is expansive, regulating not just ritual matters, but also economic ones that obtain political significance by influencing the relative power between parties, whether between husband and wife or even between China and Middle Eastern states through the hajj. Nonetheless, Hui understand the spectrum of Islamic law as a matter of "religious belief" (*zongjiao xinyang*, Ar. *īmān*). The framing work they do that underscores the religious rather than the economic or political nature of Islamic law is partly a result of the nature of shari'a (its primary sources are concerned chiefly with matters of worship, and legal rules only secondarily) and also their socialization in a Han-majority nation under a socialist state. At the same time, for some Hui, belief may entail the provision of welfare and public goods, the reallocation of power between parties, and the determination of justice—functions usually associated with the state, particularly when it is "authoritarian."[38]

In spite of Hui's aspiration for a total law, however, even if they emphasize its religious nature, Islamic law in their communities is piecemeal and internally disunited, as I learned very quickly upon visiting different mosques. Just as Hui use the term *jiaofa* to refer to non-legalistic bases of personal and communal behavior such as ethics and morality, so too does the Hui longing to live in accordance with shari'a exceed their practice, although this is changing with increased contact with coreligionists from abroad. Their practice responds to pressures from the Han majority, the Party-State's varied and sometimes contradictory attempts to restrict or mobilize Islamic law, and evolving trends in the global *umma*. To put it another way, Hui practice is molded by both Chinese custom and state law.

The relationship between Islamic law and local custom is a result of a long process of localization of Islamic law in Chinese society. As a doctrinal matter, Islamic law permits a limited application of *'urf* (lit. "what is known," or custom) as a subsidiary source of law (Coulson 1959: 15). Such sources were permissible, provided *'urf* did not contravene the revealed sources. Actual practice, however, has shown that custom has had a much more expansive role than classical theory admitted.[39] While Hui do not

---

[38] In Hui communities such as Linxia, the authoritarian state is not only "fragmented" (Lieberthal 1992) but looks quite Muslim. For literature on power sharing between state and nonstate providers of public goods in China, see Tsai (2007), Mertha (2008), Saich (2008), Cao (2010), and Lee and Zhang (2013).

[39] Case studies come from West Africa (Oba 2002) and Ottoman Syria (Mundy and Smith 2007: 234), as well as from the Bedouin (Stewart 2006) and the South Asian Muslim diaspora (Ballard 2006).

use the term *'urf*, custom is an integral part of how they practice Islam, influencing, for example, practices of worship and the regulation of property, marriage, and inheritance.

Chinese customs may either enhance certain rules of Islamic law or transform them. Muslim minorities in China are subject to formidable pressures to assimilate. In a famous debate, one Chinese scholar viewed Sinicization (or Sinification), knowledge of the Chinese classics and acceptance of Confucian values, as an inevitable and benign process (Ho 1998: 129, 136).[40] Hui practices of Islamic law are thus paramount for maintaining boundaries with Han. The kernel of *ṭahāra*, for example, is the prohibition against eating pork.[41] The pork taboo is an effect of the Hui cohabitation with Han, for whom pork is a staple. Just as the pork taboo is central to Hui *'ibādāt*, so the taboo "against marrying women out"[42] is the nucleus of the *mu'āmalāt*. That taboo is both a localization of Islamic marriage law and a specifically ethnic prohibition against Hui women marrying Han men. The importance of the pork taboo and the taboo "against marrying women out" goes well beyond dietary restrictions and marriage law, respectively, as such rules have become organizing principles of Hui sociality. Hui have adapted to living in a non-Muslim-majority society by enhancing such fundamental rules of their social organization. As Dru Gladney (1987b, [1991] 1996) and others (see, e.g., Pillsbury 1974; Ma 1998) have pointed out, such embodied practices are productive of Hui as a distinct group that is continually maintaining its identity vis-à-vis the Han majority. I would underscore that it is their localizing of Islamic law that does much of this work.

At the same time, and contravening conventional views of law in anthropology,[43] certain practices of Hui localized law may actually erase interethnic boundaries. In the long process of Islamic law's localization in China, some Chinese customs have shaped Hui behavior and interpersonal norms. It is unclear where to draw the line between those of Han

[40] For a view critical of such assertions, see Crossley (1990b).

[41] Q. 5:3.

[42] Q. 60:10.

[43] Influenced by A. R. Radcliffe-Brown's (1950) structural-functionalism, early anthropologists sought to explicate how rules functioned to cohere social groups (see, e.g., Fortes 1949; Evans–Pritchard 1951; Beidelman 1961). The structuralist approach advocated by Claude Lévi–Strauss ([1967] 1969, 1976) focused on taboo as a kind of universal norm resulting from binaries in the human mind that are linguistically expressed. Fredrik Barth's (1969) "transactional" approach, a reaction to structuralism, emphasizes such prohibitions as taboo as continually redefining ethnic identities. For key readings in the anthropology of law, see Mundy (2002) and Moore (2005).

provenance (in which case, "Hanification" may be more appropriate than Sinicization) and those that are "Hui customs." From such ritual matters as the use of incense to such economic concerns as the giving of charity to familial relationships as in polygamous marriages, Chinese customs have influenced how Hui understand the rules that underlie their social production.

The question of the purity of their law is a chief concern for Hui and has become "politicized"—that is, made an object of interpretive rivalry and power struggle—by teaching schools, which have formed and divided over such matters. For Hui, making sense of Islamic law for their constituencies, as minorities, is pivotal to their significance. The teaching schools do so with reference to their respective "centers," which may be inside or outside China. In terms of the consequences of Chinese custom for Islamic law, Hui use law as a means of boundary maintenance vis-à-vis the Han majority, but in certain fields of law, this use may efface those very boundaries. At the same time, Hui interpretations of law internally differentiate teaching schools. In terms of interethnic boundary maintenance, Hui adopt such bodily markers and practices as the wearing of a white skullcap or hijab as well as daily prayer and the consumption of only halal foods. These markings gain a finer level of distinctiveness between teaching schools, since membership is designated by wearing certain types or colors of head covering and praying only at the mosque of one's teaching school or fellow members' restaurants.

Just as the Hui practice of Islamic law reacts to the presence of Chinese customs, pursuant to inter-teaching-school contests, it also responds to state law. As mentioned, state law provides no basis for religious law. Unlike such states as Indonesia, China has no Islamic law courts.[44] And unlike in the United States, where courts may, under certain conditions, regard Islamic law as a foreign law, or in the United Kingdom, where state law provides for shari'a councils that work with civil courts,[45] PRC courts expunge any reference to Islamic law mentioned during legal proceedings by parties to a dispute.

Despite its lack of formal recognition of Islamic law, the state uses law based on such faiths as Islam as a resource for its own rule. More precisely, the Party-State has structurally blocked the practice of Islamic law; law and policy interact with *'ibādāt* and *mu'āmalāt* differently, permitting more freedom for the former than for the latter. Hui can pray, fast, and

---

[44] On Islamic courts in Indonesia, see Lev (1972), Lindsey and Steiner (2012), and Feener (2013).

[45] On the status of Islamic law under US law, see Volokh (2014). For the debates concerning shari'a councils under English law, see Bowen (2011) and Griffith-Jones (2013).

give zakat (obligatory alms), but marrying and dividing property in accordance with the Hanafi *fiqh* on *muʿāmalāt* must be done in the realm of the *minjian*. Control over the family and over property is foundational to state power, as is the use of organized force to implement law. Consequently, the Party-State has monopolized certain fields of law—for instance, criminal law—while delegating powers of law making and law enforcement to Hui (as well as to other minorities) in fields that touch on public safety, such as the areas of traffic control and food quality. Between these two fields of law is a wide gray area that includes market transactions, small-scale dispute resolution, and public welfare, where the state has not provided an express grant of authority but where Hui have nonetheless carved out domains where they bring Islamic law to bear on legal questions.

The result is that for such matters, including marriage and divorce as well as property and inheritance, there may be a "dual track" of state law and Islamic law that leads either to choices or to conflicts of law in terms of both substantive and procedural rights. One aim of this book is not just to describe how legal arguments, disputes, and claims of Hui cut across the official and *minjian*, but also to explain those factors that lead the Party-State to decide which areas to permit and which to prohibit—or to decide in which areas to tolerate Islamic law, as the Hui say by "opening one eye while closing the other" (*zheng yi zhi yan, bi yi zhi yan*).

To summarize, then, among Hui Islamic law is both a regulating pattern of rules that organize their everyday life and a body of ethics by which they assess aspects of "the good," namely authenticity and piety, as well as purity and orthodoxy. To the Party-State, however, Islamic law is a resource through which it can leverage its rule in Hui areas. It does so by delegating certain types of authority to clerics such as Nasim for purposes not just of social stability, but, as I show in the following chapters, also of economic development and the Party's own legitimacy.

LAW AND ETHICS

The cultural translation of concepts is closely linked to their analysis, as *jiaofa*, shariʿa, and Islamic law show. While Hui explanations provide a basis for making sense of Islamic law in China, given that their terms are sometimes more aspirational than fact-based, I supplement their own analytics with those that are removed from local epistemologies. In her study that drew on ethnographic data from diverse sites, including the Chagga of Tanzania and workers in the dress industry in New York, anthropologist Sally Falk Moore (1973, 1978) developed the idea of the "semi-autonomous social field." Her underlying concept is that contrary to legal positivism, the state is not the only lawmaker, and sub-state communities may have their own systems of justice. Moore (1973: 720) defined the semi-autonomous social field as one that can "generate rules and customs and symbols internally, but that is also vulnerable to rules and decisions and other forces emanating from the larger world by which it is surrounded." Although Moore's semi-autonomous social field derived from a particular provenance, alongside Hui conceptions it is helpful to think through the relationship between Islamic law, state law, and Chinese customs that generate the Hui social field.[46] By "Hui social field," I mean mosque-based Hui communities and the transnational links, both material and imaginary, fostered by the teaching schools. The Hui social field generates its own set of norms in accordance with Islamic law, and yet Hui practice is thoroughly localized according to the various pressures of Chinese society. Specifically, it is through the social field that Hui make sense of the interrelationships between their law, that of the state, and pre- or non-Islamic customs.[47]

The Hui social field, however, differs from Moore's definition in several regards. For one, Moore (1973: 723), consistent with her processual approach to law, which incorporates temporality and change into the study of rules, acknowledges that the social field is shaped by the state order external to it as actors make recourse to state law. However, one of the contradictions of the Hui social field is that the state has already defined the very jurisdictional fields of *minjian* Islamic law, as I show in more detail in Chapter 1. Nonetheless, and in tension with the foregoing, the fact remains that Hui have developed transnational ties primarily through teaching-school networks that challenge limits imposed by the Party-State. So while the regime, as explained below, tries to "domesticate" Islamic

---

[46] Moore's definition of "social field" is more helpful in understanding the Hui case than that of Bourdieu (1987: 805; [1991] 2002: 14—discussed in an earlier footnote), because she underscores the distinction between state and nonstate norms.

[47] The Hui social field is not unique in this regard. Muslim communities outside China are also regulated by the state, Islam, and customary authority. Among case studies, see Dupret, Berger, and al-Zwaini (1999), Bowen (2005), Yilmaz (2005), Dahlgren (2012), and Benda–Beckmann and Benda–Beckmann (2013). Nonetheless, China diverges from situations in Indonesia, Turkey, and the Middle East, particularly in regard to the relationship between state and religion. Whereas "legal pluralism" in many areas of the world was a result of colonialism, China, officially "semi-colonial" after the Opium War of 1839–1842, was impacted by colonialism predominantly in the coastal southeast. Western imperialism did not shape Islamic law among Muslim communities in the Northwest to the same degree that Chinese imperial law did, although the Chinese Empire adapted methods of governance from Western and Japanese empires that transformed Islamic law in China.

law, the teaching schools, though conscious of Hui belonging in China, link their communities with centers that may be based outside China. Furthermore, different interpretations by teaching schools demonstrate that the Hui social field is hardly homogenous; it constantly changes as Hui interact with Muslims and non-Muslims domestically and abroad. Interpreting Islamic law in the social field takes the forms of ritual behavior, textual production, sermons, and, sometimes, back-alley brawls. The interface between Islamic law and state law is similarly dynamic, although for different reasons. Due to its own ideological constraints, the state may publicly recognize only certain interactions with Hui while others remain shaded over. Similarly, Hui leaders need to be wary of too intimate a contact with state representatives and their law, which may otherwise endanger their legitimacy.

Further complicating Moore's model involving externally imposed constraints, the Party-State, in its efforts to produce its own version of Islam, governs through Muslim authorities and Islamic law itself.[48] Michel Foucault, in his later writings, called the use of resources and authorities in addition to state law and policy for purposes of rule "governmentality." Foucault (1991, 2008) analogized governmentality to the ordering of a household by which a family attains order through the "disposition of things." Governmentality operates not only through law but also through discipline and security; moreover, governmentality does not work through forceful imposition from the outside in but through shaping ethics internally. This approach is apparent in state-run Islamic schools and Arabic vocational schools, quasi-governmental organizations' guidelines for the contents of clerics' sermons, and regulations on Islamic finance, among other examples that will be further discussed throughout the book.

By trying to shape the Hui social field through its elite, its institutions, and even Islamic law, the Party-State, to some extent, subjects itself to the rules of Hui. The Party-State attains legitimacy among Hui by presenting itself as the sovereign that provides justice, fairness, and prosperity, consonant with Islamic principles. As a consequence, the Hui social field can also constrain the state or, at least, the state's legitimate rule in the eyes of Hui. The impact of non-Muslim custom and state law does not invalidate the "purity" of Islamic law, for it is precisely the working out of "correct"

---

[48] China is distinct from comparative cases, such as Malaysia, where the state officially recognizes Islamic law and claims exclusive powers over its interpretation (Peletz 2002, 2015; Moustafa 2014).

practice and the ethical reflection it entails that comprises the Hui effort for authenticity and piety in their interpreting of the law.

The Hui social field is not just a matter of external relations—observable social or legal interactions among Hui or between Hui and Han or Tibetans—but also of internal dimensions of the law. Teaching schools consciously try to craft what they view as "legitimate Muslims" (*hege de Musilin*) through their distinct interpretations of Islamic law. Such a task is at the core of their attempt to realize a particular vision of Islam in China. One of the major contributions of the recent anthropology of Islam has been to explain the ethical dimensions of shari'a (Mahmood 2005; Hirschkind 2006; Agrama 2010)[49] rather than reducing shari'a to law (where it often becomes mistranslated as "code").

The anthropology of Islam intersects with the ascendance of the study of ethics in anthropology.[50] Drawing on social theory from Émile Durkheim and Foucault as well as moral philosophy from Alasdair MacIntyre, such inquiries examine the ways in which societies evaluate the good life. Anthropologist James Laidlaw (2014: 4), in particular, has promoted ethics as an ethnographic counterpunch to the mechanistic application of "structure," "neoliberalism," or "globalization" to the study of self and culture. Laidlaw takes issue with Talal Asad's anthropology of Islam ([1986] 2009b) for perpetuating such a mechanistic outlook. To Laidlaw (2014: 167), recent works on Islam conceive of piety as a mechanical process, a kind of input-output approach to human action. Muslims in such accounts seek "a coherent, consistent, and self-reinforcing programme ... which they experience increasingly at an unreflective, taken-for-granted, and affective level." Laidlaw (2014: 169–73) suggests that the depiction of Islamism as the assertion of Islamic doctrine in the public sphere should not override a description of the experience of piety.

Hui practice of shari'a raises questions for both the anthropology of Islam and the anthropology of ethics. Contrary to Asad's line of inquiry, Morgan Clarke (2012) has argued that underscoring the ethical aspects of shari'a does not necessarily mean excluding its legal aspects. Clarke's assertion that an anthropology of rules should accompany the anthropology of ethics finds traction in Hui attitudes toward what the cleric Nasim called "Yisilanfa" (Islamic law).[51] Unlike in the Middle East, however, as shari'a in China is

---

[49] For an earlier analysis of Islamic law as ethics, see Reinhart (1983).

[50] The major readings include Laidlaw (2002), Lambek (2010b), Faubion (2011), Fassin (2012), and Stafford (2013). David Graeber (2001) has also engaged the question of ethics through a different intellectual trajectory, that of Marx and Marcel Mauss on value.

[51] Morgan's intervention finds support in the anthropology of law that has focused on rules (see, e.g., Comaroff and Roberts 1981; Conley and O'Barr 1990). Indeed, the "ethical turn" is in part

neither backed by courts nor produced by jurists, its status as law from either an Islamic or secular view is open to question. Nonetheless, as I show in this book, Hui follow rules such as giving the bride a *mahr* (bridal gift) or burial protocols as religious obligations. Duty-based rules, like ethics, can be a source of normative action and, pursuant to Laidlaw's intervention, reflection can inform ideas of authenticity, as seen in the case of teaching schools.

An analysis that includes both the legal and the ethical aspects of shariʻa and how they inform the socialization of Muslims finds particular resonance in the study of China. The category of law has suffered an impoverished reputation in China.[52] One reason is that much of the English literature on Chinese law has historically privileged Western notions of law and denigrated those of China (Alford 2000; Ruskola 2013). As a result, one frequently hears that "China has no law" or that the Party has established "rule by man" instead of "rule of law."

Sulayman al-Tajir, a ninth-century Iranian merchant, provides a different lens with which to examine Chinese law. In his *Accounts of India and China* (*Akhbar al-Sin wa-l-Hind*), al-Tajir depicts the access to justice in rural imperial China, based upon his observations of life in Guangdong: "Every town has a thing called *al-dara*. This is a bell placed near [lit. 'at the head of'] the ruler of the town and is tied to a cord stretching as far as the road for the [benefit] of the common people." If a person is wronged by another person, he or she shakes the cord that is linked to *al-dara*. Then, al-Tajir observes, "the bell near the ruler starts ringing. So he [the wronged] is allowed to enter [the palace] to relate personally what the matter is and to explain the wrong done to him" (Hermes 2013: 214). However embellished al-Tajir's account of the justice bell, or *al-dara* (Ch. *duo*), may be, his description of law in China is very different from the earliest European and American assessments. By moving away from the China-West axis, this book brings fresh insights to bear on how the study of Chinese law can contribute to thinking through the ways in which nonstate orders mediate relationships between minorities, religion, and the state.

In contrast to law, ethics has been deemed an enduring feature of Chinese society. In imperial China, government was tied to metaphysics, and rule to human nature. In Confucian methods of self-cultivation, the ruler was meant to perform rites, or *li*, that ensured harmony among

---

a reaction to such an approach. The China material suggests an accommodation between rules and ethics.

[52] For classical treatments of the question, see Granet (1934: 341), Fei ([1947] 1992: 43), and Weber (1951: 147).

social relationships. The sovereign traditionally stood in a (superior) relationship to law, and sovereignty was performed through ritualized ethics; the two were inseparable. In addition to being political, Neo-Confucian ethics were also interpersonal, and were based on duty just as much as on will. The religious revival in the reform period has reawakened such ethical practices (Yan 2009).

Due to their long history in China, Hui have developed their own ethical and moral practices that are reviving. These stem from a variety of inspirations, including Sufism, Qing-era textual explanations of Islam through Neo-Confucian cognates,[53] and modernist interpretations of Islam. At the same time, Hui regard interpersonal ethics (as well as bodily and dietary ones) as imperatives and emphasize the lawlike nature of shari'a vis-à-vis the Han majority. Thus, the Hui experience demonstrates how ethicized law (or legalistic ethics), as an alternative to that of the state and which it may have historically repressed, are once again thriving in China.[54]

In listening to their reflections about their law, Hui were uniform in their conviction that following Islamic law is a requirement of being a Muslim, as understood and reinforced within the teaching schools, although they would condition such statements in various ways, acknowledging that they are citizens of a socialist state. Technically, if Muslims follow the Hanafi school of jurisprudence and reside outside the "Abode of Islam" (dār al-Islām), such as Hui, then Islamic courts have no jurisdiction over them and they must follow most of the prohibitions of Islamic law (e.g., adultery, theft, murder, alcohol, and so on) as moral imperatives. The Hanafi school is exceptional in that it exempts such Muslims from certain prohibitions in Islamic law when conducting business with non-Muslims to the extent that such transactions are permitted under the law of the land—namely, usury, selling alcohol or pork, or engaging in such forms of risk as insurance and gambling (Abou el-Fadl 1994: 173–74). Hanafi jurists thus permit a high degree of flexibility for such Muslims when dealing with the property of non-Muslims. However, for reasons ranging from the pragmatic to the ideological, many Hui believe they are beholden to all the obligations of shari'a.[55]

---

[53] One such touchstone is the work of Liu Zhi, an eighteenth-century Chinese Muslim scholar whose *Tianfang dianli* (*Laws and Rites of Islam*) (1710) explained shari'a through multiple interrelated referents, including rites (*li*) and law (*fa*) (Frankel 2011: 72–75; Tontini 2011: 518–19).

[54] For work on religious law in China, see Peerenboom (1993, 2002) and Katz (2009).

[55] It is little known among Hui that in 1930 the Yunnanese Muslim Ma Ruitu, writing in Arabic, asked the Egyptian journal *al-Manar* if China was the "Abode of Islam" or the "Abode of War" (*dār al-ḥarb*). Muhammad Rashid Rida, the editor, responded in a fatwa that China was indeed

Complicating matters is that different official rules are applied to three inclusive sets of populations among Hui and other Muslim minorities. The first and most inclusive population is Hui at large. Hui are subject to both state law and religious and ethnic policy. One aspect of *'ibādāt*, the annual hajj, illustrates the tension between religious obligation and the demands of citizenship in a socialist state. The Party-State has limited the number of pilgrims who may undertake the hajj each year, since the pilgrimage to Mecca has been the most powerful conduit for destabilizing and revivalist strains of Islam to enter China. The second population, a subset of the first, comprises those Hui who work for the government, either in the public sector or for a state-owned enterprise. In Muslim cities such as Linxia, where the government is the largest employer, most upwardly mobile Hui are civil servants, a broad category in China. These Hui, including not just officials but also other public servants, such as teachers, cannot wear religious signs (e.g., headscarves and white caps) in public places. They also cannot pray at work.

Some civil servants may join the Party; Hui cadres are the third and smallest population. They are subject to the internal rules of the Party that prohibit religious belief. For Hui cadres, any outward sign of their adherence to Sunni Islam's Five Pillars, including pronouncing the *shahāda* (testimony of the faith), prayer, zakat, fasting, and the hajj, is impermissible. Fasting during the month of Ramadan is particularly problematic, since it is believed to slow productivity in the workplace. Hui, as subject to both secular and religious mandates, experience different degrees of "value conflict" (Laidlaw 2014: 173), not unlike Muslims elsewhere. The Hui experience of normative indeterminacy is fraught with such micro-conflicts, the intensity of which is inversely proportional to the size of the affected population (i.e., Hui cadres experience the most acute conflict).

To review, though the Hui social field is a spatial metaphor, it is used not to describe the physical community but rather the Hui capacity to generate their own norms in accordance with how they interpret the injunctions of Islam. Their versions of Islamic law are *minjian*, because Hui generate them largely outside the view of the state. One of the contradictions of Islamic law as *minjian* is that its jurisdiction, if that term can be used, is mostly a carve-out from state law. The state is complicit in the *minjian*, and yet Hui are Islamic law's main proponents. Because the Hui

the latter but that this designation was advantageous to Hui, because they could engage in wider commercial activities (Halevi 2013).

social field generates its own rules based on a localized form of Islamic law that is nonetheless shaped by state law, its boundaries are formed by those points of contact or conflict with the state. At these points, Hui reconcile through the paths of teaching schools their self-directed action with the structural dismantling of Islamic law by the Party-State. Through the social field, Hui navigate contradictions between the secular and ecclesiastical, localized and transnationalized, and *minjian* and official. Hui are every day transgressing such boundaries in using such state institutions as the police or courts, attending school, trading in the markets, or even just showing up at work. Through their social field, Hui make sense of being postsocialist[56] citizens, slaves of God, and cultural subjects of China.

AUTONOMY IS NOT SOVEREIGNTY

Thus far, I have described PRC state law and policy in the abstract; in this section, I introduce the framework through which the state manages ethnic minorities and their own legal and political institutions. PRC state law provides for a system whereby ethnic minorities in certain areas may, in theory, enjoy a limited right to govern themselves according to their own prerogatives. Linxia, for example, is the capital of Linxia Hui Autonomous Prefecture, one of thirty such autonomous prefectures in the country. By law, the people's government at the prefectural level is empowered to issue regulations that respond to the specific needs of the minority who reside there. This system of *zizhi*, usually translated as "autonomy" but which literally means "self-rule" or "self-government," is a core feature of China's political system, a system formally known as "regional ethnic autonomy" (*minzu quyu zizhi*), hereinafter "ethnic autonomy."[57] Ethnic autonomy, which has resulted in a number of "autonomous areas," is a response to a very old question in China: how to rule those non-Han populations concentrated on the sensitive borders of the state.

Whereas the liberal approach to multiculturalism is predicated on negative rights (i.e., freedom of religion, assembly, and speech) that are held by the individual against the state, the Chinese socialist approach

---

[56] The term "postsocialist" here refers to China's transition from a planned to a market economy. Although marketization has altered the relationship of citizens to the state, the state maintains a strong hand in the economy through state-owned enterprises and ownership of property. I retain the term "socialist" to describe administrative or legal rules.

[57] For a bibliography of works written on ethnic autonomy, see Que (2013), who identifies 15,054 periodical publications, from 1915 to 2012, that include "ethnic autonomy" or its corollaries in their title or as their subject.

to cultural difference has been for the state to grant all individuals a baseline measure of positive rights. This approach places a premium on social and economic rights over civil and political ones but, as mentioned, does include a limited freedom of religion. Ethnic autonomy is applied to certain areas within the territorial PRC with high concentrations of ethnic minorities. According to the relevant law, local governments in such areas ensure additional rights, such as the protection of local language, customs, and traditions. Nevertheless, the central government is the source of all rights, as applied to all Chinese citizens, including ethnic minorities, and the purpose of rights, whether based on citizenship or on ethnic minority status, is not to provide a legal basis to challenge state action but to unify and manage diverse populations within the multiethnic state.[58]

In what could be called the "first generation of ethnic policy" in the 1950s, the CCP adapted Soviet policies for categorizing and governing minorities. PRC policy toward minorities began with the "ethnic identification project," which incorporated Stalin's definition of "nationality" in addition to such other imperial categories as those of Great Britain (Mullaney 2011). As the Party-State consolidated its rule over the multiethnic populations of China's peripheries, it elicited applications for "minority nationality" status.[59] Some four hundred groups applied, but only fifty-five *minzu* (ethnic minorities)[60] were eventually officially recognized (Fei 1980: 147). The state incorporated minority citizens by implementing ethnic autonomy and conferring preferential policies (*youhui zhengce*), which give benefits to minorities by virtue of their ethnic minority identity, particularly in the fields of education and employment. These benefits are tied to the person and apply to ethnic minorities regardless of where they live.[61]

As part of constructing the multiethnic nation, the Party-State gave each ethnic minority its own "customary law" (*xiguanfa*)—for instance, "Hui customary law" (*Huizu xiguanfa*). "Hui customary law," however, is

---

[58] For studies of citizens' use (or nonuse) of rights and the limits of legal mobilization, see Michelson (2006, 2007a, 2008b), O'Brien and Li (2006), and Lee (2007).

[59] The English translation "ethnic minority" has gradually replaced "minority nationality" in recent years, as the latter has a closer nexus to international law and rights of self-determination (China and the Principle 2010: 85).

[60] "Ethnic minorities" is an imprecise but passable translation of *minzu*, a key term in ethnic policies in the PRC and one that has changed over time. For a fuller discussion of *minzu*, see Chapter 1.

[61] For analyses of preferential policies, see Zhou and Hill (2009), Sautman (2010, 2012, 2014), and Yamada (2012).

not the same as Islamic law; as used in Chinese academic literature, it normally refers to devotional or ritual aspects of Islamic law, including dress, prayer, dietary restrictions, and so on, but it largely excludes personal status law pertaining to marriage, divorce, inheritance, and property relations. The Party-State's construction of Hui customary law demonstrates that norms in Hui communities, rather than forming rigid binaries (i.e., Islamic law/state law and Islamic law/custom), interact, transform, and subsume one another. One consequence of the Party-State's tight control over Muslim autonomous areas is that Hui have been unable to enact legislation in accordance with their customary law, let alone with Islamic law. Local people's courts in autonomous areas also cannot enforce Hui customary law.

Following the interethnic violence in Tibet in 2008 and the riots in Urumqi in 2009, ethnic autonomy has become the centerpiece of an international debate known as the "second generation of ethnic policy."[62] Critics have focused in particular on the problem of "popular law" (*minjianfa*) under the current constitutional order of ethnic autonomy (Xie 2014; Xu 2014).[63] Debates, however, often elide the actual experience of minorities who reside within "autonomous areas."

---

[62] Chinese readers have grouped opinions into two camps: libertarians and conservatives. On the one side, libertarians suggest a dismantling of ethnic autonomy and preferential policies to increase integration of minorities (Liu 2014). Ma Rong (2004, 2009a, 2009b, 2009c, 2010), an American-trained Hui sociologist at Peking University, has argued for dismantling ethnic minority policy on the grounds that it reifies ethnic consciousness and encourages separatism. Ma Rong favors governmental assistance and subsidies based on economic need rather than on ethnic identity, in order to weaken ethnic cohesiveness and cultivate a consciousness of the "Chinese nation" (*Zhonghua minzu*) (2004: 125). See also Hu and Hu (2011). On the other side, conservatives such as Hao Shiyuan (2011a, 2011b, 2012a, 2012b), deputy secretary general of the Chinese Academy of Social Sciences, acknowledge faults with ethnic policy and seek a more comprehensive implementation, also for the benefit of the "Chinese nation." For an excellent discussion that maps out some of the key positions, including those of Hao Shiyuan, Ma Rong, and Zhang Haiyang, Minzu University professor and assistant dean of the Institute for Ethnic Studies and Sociology, see Hao, Zhang, and Ma (2013). For foreign assessments of the "second generation of ethnic policy" debate, see Bovingdon (2013), Leibold (2013), and Elliott (2015).

[63] Zhu Suli, China's preeminent sociolegal scholar, wrote in a programmatic article, "In my opinion, the most basic problem [for Chinese law] is conflicts between so-called Chinese society's traditional law—as expressed in popular law [*minjianfa*]—and modern state law" (1993: 18). Zhu authored a book entitled *Rule of Law and Native Resources* (*Fazhi jiqi bentu ziyuan*) ([1996] 2004), which advocates building on indigenous Chinese forms of law, as an alternative to building on Western models, for China's legal development. Zhu's program has spurred a line of inquiry that has opened up a new field of sociolegal studies in China. For a partial list, see Wang and Wang (1997), Liang (1999), Zhu and Hou (2008), and Wang Qiliang (2009).

Taking a step back from the current policy debates,[64] this book considers the broader role of the *minjian* in Chinese law and governance, what it means for those marginalized by the law and for the Party-State as lawmaker. In reform-era China, there is an increasing gap between official claims of political representation, which may be absolutist in rhetoric but attain a level of performativity, and the day-to-day conduits of power (Erie 2012). A view that considers the *minjian* shows that decision making does not always occur in the legislative halls of people's congresses or in the basic-level people's courts, but rather in mosque offices and even such "neutral" spaces as halal restaurants. For itself, the moral demise of Maoism has led the Party into an uncomfortable embrace of faith. In ethnic and religious minority areas, the Party must maintain its own boundaries between itself and the faithful.[65] Whereas critical approaches to sovereignty, most notably that of Italian philosopher Giorgio Agamben (1998, 2005), have defined the sovereign as that which excepts itself from the law, the recent history of Greater China suggests that for the sovereign, law has meaning not only in its suspension: the choice and interpretation of law is at the core of these evolving relationships.[66] Moreover, it is not just the law of the state that is the basis for articulating one's relationship with the state; instead, *minjian* law, such as Islamic law, provides interlocutors (Hui clerics, "lay" Hui, Hui cadres, and even Han) with a way to mediate their relationship with nodes of power, whether in Linxia, Mecca, Cairo, Kuala Lumpur, Beijing, or elsewhere.

---

[64] Elite debates have not been without effect on official policy. Recent years have seen a break from the "first generation" model of ethnic distinctiveness to one that encourages "melting pot" assimilation. Beginning in 2010, the Tibet and Xinjiang Work Forums, convened by the Central Committee of the CCP, advocated "ethnic association, exchange, and blending" (*minzu jiaowang, jiaoliu, jiaorong*). On September 30, 2014, the decennial Central Ethnic Work Committee, a forum of top leaders and "model ethnic" officials, reiterated the mixture model and called attention not only to the "material aspects" (*wuzhi fangmian*) of development but also to its "spiritual aspects" (*jingshen fangmian*) (Central Ethnic Work Committee 2014). (For bibliographic purposes, I cite anonymous documents (Chinese or English) with a shortened version of the title in English.)

[65] For anthropological accounts of the local state and its construction of ethnicity, see Gladney ([1991] 1996), Litzinger (2000), Harrell (2001), Mueggler (2001), Fiskesjö (2006), McCarthy (2009), Wellens (2010), and Tenzin (2014).

[66] In 2014 both Taiwan and Hong Kong experienced mass protests over the definition of their formal legal relationship with the PRC. In the "Sunflower Student Movement," Taiwanese students occupied the Legislative Yuan to call for a review of cross-Strait economic agreements. In the "Umbrella Movement," Hong Kong protesters sought enforcement of the 1997 Basic Law to ensure free elections.

BECOMING *MINJIAN* IN CHINA

To understand how Hui abide by a *minjian* law, it is necessary to peek behind the curtain of the state law's performance. In recent years, a number of studies have deepened the contemporary understanding of how law works in Chinese society.[67] For the most part, anthropologists have had a more difficult time contributing to Chinese legal studies. One reason for anthropology's marginal contribution has been methodological. To conduct long-term ethnographic fieldwork on law in any setting—formal or informal—requires the researcher to confront a laundry list of difficulties, some of which are more onerous than others.

The impetus behind this book has been to collect empirical data regarding the contemporary practice of Islamic law by Hui, including elites and commoners, men and women, to illustrate how Islamic law works in an East Asian "authoritarian" context. With few exceptions, social scientists have been largely unable to study nonstate normative orders as practiced by non-Han peoples in China.[68] One reason why the category of "law" has been denied to minorities (Muslim or otherwise) in China is because the state has monopolized not only the law itself but also the production of knowledge about its forms.

To understand the dynamics of the localization and revitalization of Islamic law, in 2004 I began examining potential field sites during preliminary fieldwork. From 2009 to 2011 I conducted eighteen months of fieldwork in Northwest China, with follow-up fieldtrips in 2012 and 2015, for a total of twenty months in the field. Against the backdrop of heightened disquiet in the region after the July 2009 riots in Urumqi, a foreign researcher was a liability to any potential local sponsor. The competitive advantage of anthropology is "being there" (Borneman and Hammoudi 2009). Yet being there can also be the worst of things—for one's interlocutors and for oneself. As a matter of pragmatics, one learns in China that there is the official way and the unofficial way to do things. I spent a great amount of time, effort, and funds trying the former. Eventually, I realized that not only was the latter preferred by most Chinese (Han or minority), but it would also allow me a window into those practices that occur beyond the pale of formal law.

---

[67] See, for instance, Diamant, Lubman, and O'Brien (2005), Liebman (2005), Gallagher (2007), Ginsburg (2008), Michelson (2008a), van Rooij (2010), Liu and Halliday (2011), Woo and Gallagher (2011), He (2014), Stern (2013), and Pils (2014).

[68] One such noteworthy exception is Fernanda Pirie's research on Amdo Tibetans (2005, 2006, 2013b).

Given the extreme difficulty of conducting field research in the shadow of the Urumqi riots, my fate was determined by a gathering of three individuals—a police officer, a local legislator, and a scholar (all Hui)—during a meeting in Linxia to which I was not invited. Because two of the three people in the room were my allies, I was allowed to stay. I developed a complex relationship of mutual irritation/tolerance with the third participant at the meeting, a police officer I will name Officer Zeng. After the meeting, we became beeping red dots on each other's radars. When passing me on the street, Officer Zeng would pretend to ignore me as he wrestled control over the involuntary snarl that would appear on his face. When ignoring each other became untenable and we engaged in conversation, for instance in a public park, we would inevitably start arguing through forced smiles as we found ourselves defending our respective countries' views on social justice. He would stop by unannounced at my place of residence to "check in" with me as he casually fingered through the books on my desk. We eventually settled into a kind of uneasy equilibrium. I became both his daughter's English tutor and convenient dinner table scapegoat for US foreign policy gaffes, as we participated in the exchange of favors and verbal barbs. He advised me that "Linxia is not like other places" and "I should be careful." I initially dismissed such warnings as Chinese paternalism, but after experiencing subtle shades of hostility that once flared up into face-to-face confrontation, I can reflect that Officer Zeng was correct.

In short, our relationship was confounding and yet, over time, became familiar. Although my status was never clearly defined in legal terms, it was only because of our relationship (however ambivalent it was) that I was allowed to conduct my research. Thus, my fieldwork was directed by some of the same forces that shape the *minjian* in China as experienced by Hui: on the one hand, constraints, if not blockages, imposed by state law and policy and, on the other hand, the obligations of personal and communal (in my case, anthropologists') ethical and professional commitments. The friction between these impositions and drives forced me to reflect empathetically on being Muslim in postsocialist China.

I established myself in the old Muslim quarter of the city known as Bafang. I realized that given the importance of the teaching schools to the localization of Islamic law in China, I would have to conduct visits to other field sites in the Northwest. I visited additional areas in Gansu, including Dongxiang Autonomous County, home of the Dongxiang, and the Hui-Han-Tibetan town of Lintan (formerly Taozhou), the base of the Xidaotang. In Qinghai I traveled to Xunhua Salar Autonomous County, the seat of the Salars, and also to the great Hui center of Xining.

I took overnight trains with Hui students to Ningxia, visiting Guyuan and Haiyuan, places of extremely low socioeconomic levels but centers of Hui, particularly Khufiyya Sufi, communities. I also took several trips to Yinchuan, the capital of the autonomous region and the city that is perhaps the most flourishing in the contemporary Islamic revival. Since 2004 I have taken half a dozen trips to Xinjiang, ranging from two to four weeks in length. These research trips entailed data collection in Hami (Kumul), Urumqi, and oasis cities around the Taklamakan Desert, including Kashgar and Shache (Yarkand). My approach was thus a modified multi-sited ethnographic study (Marcus 1995, Hannerz 2003).

Though my study was heavily focused on Linxia, my collection of data gathering radiated outward, following missionaries, circulating texts, and Sufi pilgrimage routes. Such an approach enabled me to obtain a depth of knowledge in the "intensively-focused-upon single site of ethnographic observation and participation" (Marcus 1995: 96) while recognizing that China's Little Mecca is located in larger "wholes" (Cook, Laidlaw, and Mair 2012: 57). Plural sites enabled me to compare a number of variables across the Northwest, including the effects of the Islamic law revival and the impacts of Communist policy on Hui communities.

The bulk of the data analyzed in this book comes from more than two hundred interviews. Over half of these were with Muslim authorities, including clerics, Sufi shaykhs, madrasa teachers, and other administrative personnel in mosques and Sufi tomb complexes. A smaller proportion were conducted with officials and Party cadres in legal, judicial, and public safety bureaus as well as with entrepreneurs, teachers in state-run schools, students, and merchants. I collected interviews by use of "snowball sampling" (Atkinson and Flint 2003; Bernard 2006), which enabled me to extend my network of interlocutors through the social connections of individuals I had previously interviewed.

The core data set of my study comes from time spent at thirty-four mosques and the twenty-three main Sufi tomb complexes in Linxia. Mosques (and also schools, Islamic banks, and sheep hide markets) are arenas in which Hui make sense of their adherence to state law and Islamic law, the site where the Hui social field is most visible. Interviews were conducted principally in Mandarin. The local dialect is called Bafanghua, "the language of Bafang." Bafanghua incorporates Arabic, Persian, Urdu, Tibetan, Mongolian, and various other local dialects of Muslim ethnicities, including Dongxiangyu and Salarhua. I studied Arabic, one of the main foreign languages in Bafanghua, in Linxia and, in between field trips, in Amman, Jordan, so as my ability in the dialect increased, I was able to introduce more Bafanghua into my conversations. Interviews were semistructured, and wherever possible, more informal interviews were conducted as follow-up. To develop extended case studies, I selected several influential clerics, as defined by their leadership at "administrative mosques" (*hanyi dasi*, or *hanyisi*[69]) or at Sufi tombs where founders of orders are buried. Given the sensitivity of the topic of Islamic law in China, I did not record conversations but took copious notes during interviews, which I immediately afterward transcribed in full. I kept these transcripts in a double-password-protected laptop that I carried with me wherever I went. (Several times, Hui prevented me from entering their mosque suspecting I carried a bomb in my backpack.) Contrary to ethnographic approaches to Islamic law in the Middle East and North Africa,[70] without recourse to courts and case filings, written petitions, collections of fatwas (legal opinions), or law-related archives, my fieldwork was shaped by the Hui experience, which is off-the-official-record. Consequently, I have elected not to disclose identifying information about my interlocutors.

In addition to interviews, I observed and, where permitted by Hui, participated in all aspects of devotional and social life. These included prayer, ritual feasting and holidays, charitable giving, and attendance at weddings and funerals. I also collected case studies of dispute resolution in a variety of forums, such as informal mediation by clerics in mosque offices and more formalized mediation jointly conducted by clerics and police. On-site data collection was supplemented by participation in Chinese Muslim online networks, blogs, and virtual communities that produce and consume matters of Islamic law.

In compliance with professional ethics, I safeguarded information entrusted to me. Furthermore, even if I was not entering into lawyer-client relationships with related privileges, my training as a lawyer instructed me to protect information. This was not always easy, given that Hui learned of my research through their networks (and on social media platforms where Hui discussed me and my intentions often quite erroneously) and sometimes knew to whom I had been speaking. In addition, I collected local histories of teaching schools, and I sometimes participated in their writing when asked to do so.

In addition to fieldwork, I conducted research in governmental archives in Linxia and Urumqi as well as the Gansu Provincial Archives

---

[69] This is a local Hui term, not a governmental designation. Administrative mosques are where members of smaller mosques go to attend the Friday prayer. Additionally, administrative mosques may have certain powers over smaller mosques, such as appointing the cleric.

[70] See, e.g., Hirsch (1998), Messick (2008), Stiles (2009), and Dahlgren (2012).

in Lanzhou, which also contain material for Ningxia and Qinghai. I also conducted archival research at the Northwest Minority Research Center Materials Room at Lanzhou University, the National Library in Beijing, and the University Services Center at the City University of Hong Kong—as well as the Harvard-Yenching Library at Harvard University, which has the finest collection of Christian missionary material from those families who visited Linxia in the tumultuous 1920s and 1930s.

While my analysis is informed by the discipline of anthropology, it is eclectic in taking insights from law and society, history, political science, and moral philosophy. For generalist readers, this book presents a case study of the practice of Islamic law outside the setting of Western democracies. It is a context where what Agamben (2011), drawing on Foucault's governmentality and Carl Schmitt's political theology, calls "glorification"[71] has greater traction than violent conflict and thus challenges entrenched ideas about extremist Islam, a uni-dimensionally illiberal China, and more broadly, the incompatibility of Islamic law for plural societies in modern states. For audiences interested in the global renaissance of Islam, the book offers an in-depth case study of Chinese Muslims in a postsocialist regime during a period of simultaneous opening and control. Scholars of law and society as well as anthropologists of law will be interested in one of the first ethnographies in English of China's normative diversity. Lastly, China scholars who track developments in ethnic and religious minority policy will find a *minjian* view of policy effects from the perspective of Hui.

ORGANIZATION OF CHAPTERS

To explain the ways in which Hui pursue their law between the *umma* and a globalizing China, this book is organized around tensions (either apparent or implicit) between Hui practices of their localized Islamic law, on the one hand, and the Party-State and its secular law and policies, on the other hand. The Party-State impinges on the Hui social field across several legal and ethical domains—including ritual, education, procedure, finance, charity,

[71] Through a series of monographs, Agamben has been elaborating Carl Schmitt's ([1922] 2005) political theology, partly through Foucault's line of analysis. Agamben's *State of Exception* (2005) is an elaboration of Schmitt's first thesis that the sovereign is he who decides on the state of exception. His *The Kingdom and the Glory* (2011) is an exposition of Schmitt's second thesis: all concepts of major state theory are secularized theological concepts. Agamben draws his idea of "glorification" from this second thesis. In addition to force and consent, glory represents another dimension of power, one in which those who are ruled praise the ruler through ceremony, acclamation, protocol, and scripture.

property, and family law. But just as secular authority constrains the activities and speech of clerics, so too have cadres and officials come to rely on Hui leaders. Uneasy collaborations have enabled a "back door" to appear for the practice of Islamic law within the Hui social field. In the reform period, back doors connect to other back doors, and networks of texts, migrants, pilgrims, and new media have revived certain aspects of Islamic legal practice. The Party-State has taken notice of such revivals and tried to use Islamic law for its rule, too. The relationship between the Party and the local representatives of Muslim authority is thus not necessarily antagonistic but rather one of mutual access, information gathering, and suspicion.

Chapter 1, "History, the Chinese state, and Islamic law," provides a history of the localization of Islamic law in China, showing how this history has been effaced in the course of China's legal development. Unlike the chapters that follow it, Chapter 1 is written from the perspective of the state; that is, it is concerned with the extent to which state law has recognized Islamic law. Islamic law has undergone a long process of adaptation. The Party-State has borrowed from predecessor states the category "customary law" (*xiguanfa*) to define Islamic law, and it has tied customary law to ethnicity. In the mid-twentieth century, ethnic autonomy was built on the idea of customary law. The resilience of this category has excluded Islamic law from institutional recognition and presents one reason for the inflexibility of ethnic autonomy.

Chapter 2, "Linxia at the crossroads," moves from the status of Islamic law in the historical Chinese states to the construction of the Hui social field, as seen in one of China's holiest cities to Hui. Linxia has been central to the proliferation of a number of strains of revivalist Islam in China. These interpretations of Islamic doctrine have assumed the form of the teaching schools. The Communists imposed an administration of law over Linxia's doctrinally divisive communities, yet the imposition has been incomplete. Secular authority has become partly dependent on clerics and mosque leaders to communicate Party policy.

Chapter 3, "Ritual lawfare," shows that it is in the domain of ritual where the teaching schools enjoy the broadest capacities for self-definition. Whereas Muslims' observation of and debates over ritual aspects of shariʻa are resurgent throughout the globe, in China, Hui have adopted a particular Chinese view, which connects ritual action to "the good." Partly as a result of the Party-State's blocking of other domains of Islamic law, the teaching schools have politicized ritual as members fight over the role of incense in prayer, the practice of "turning of the *fidya*" (compensation for failure to perform an expiatory act), and who should read the Qur'an at burials. I argue that as an example of *minjian* excess, teaching schools interpret ritual matters not only as a means of establishing hermeneutical domination over school rivals but also as symbolic measures for gaining control over normative indeterminacy, particularly in areas of justice and equity that they find lacking in the official order.

Chapter 4, "Learning the law," examines the educational institutions through which Hui acquire their knowledge of Islam, Arabic, and Islamic law, in particular. The view from Linxia is that the teaching schools and the Party-State have initiated projects to cultivate ethical subjects among Hui. The way in which Hui have taught shari'a in private madrasas is as an ethical program, while legal problem solving remains a conversation topic held informally in hallways. With greater numbers of clerics studying Islamic law abroad, the Party-State has adopted a number of strategies to delink Islamic law from clerical instruction. State-run Islamic Scriptural Institutes train students to become functionaries in the government. Also, "ethnic schools" teach commercial Arabic devoid of religious content to encourage young Hui to become translators for foreign Muslim businessmen in eastern cities that are part of China's "New Silk Road."

Chapter 5, "Wedding laws," asks whether Hui women can gender Islamic law. Whereas postcolonial states have reserved in Islamic family law a privileged domain for Muslim self-regulation, the PRC has sought to aggressively reform the areas of marriage, divorce, and inheritance, with reference to the principle of gender equality. Ironically, state legal reform in family law has further marginalized women and their ability to protect their property and custodial interests. Nonetheless, Hui women creatively mobilize state law to protect their rights under both PRC and Islamic law. Patriarchal interpretations of Islamic law are a problem that Muslim women face throughout the world. The study of Hui women and their use of multiple sources of law diverges from studies that privilege women's agency through ethical piety and self-expression. Rather, Hui women operate within two incompletely functioning bodies of law, religious and secular, which are deeply patriarchal; at the same time, women work across legal orders to protect their spiritual, mental, and bodily integrity.

Chapter 6, "Moral economies," examines the financing of Islamic revival as one dimension of the *minjian*, specifically through Hui exchange, allocation of material assets, and investment of resources. Whereas Hui practice local forms of barter in the sheep hide markets of Linxia as well as engage in charitable giving mostly beyond state regulation, the state has sought to tightly control (i.e., make "official") emergent Islamic banking services in Ningxia, with their potential to create channels for funds from the Middle East into China. Hui moral economies consist of uses of money and property that are shaped by, but not wholly reducible to, "Islamic," "socialist," or "capitalist" models of economic behavior. Sources of money and the purposes to which they are put fund China's Islamic revival and the forms it is taking, whether "official," neoconservative, mystical, or so on. The flow of such resources within the Northwest and across borders further tests the boundary between the Hui social field and the security state.

Chapter 7, "Procedural justice," moves from the substantive areas of the law to examine processes of dispute resolution in Hui communities. Clerics play a pivotal role in negotiating Islamic law and state law for dispute resolution. The Party-State's approach in dealing with the authority of clerics varies. In some parts of the Northwest, such as Linxia, clerics are loosely enveloped in the legal and judicial bureaucracy. They may assist judges in solving disputes, in which case they may apply shari'a to the case at hand, but state judges' dependence on clerics is *minjian*. Elsewhere, such as in Ningxia, there are highly publicized forms of dispute resolution—for example, "Islamic people's mediation committees"—through which mosque leaders mediate in accordance with state rules and regulations. Officials' and cadres' use of clerics illustrates the Party-State's pragmatic treatment of Muslim authorities and, more broadly, the ideological role of law in securing order over freedom in the post-9/11 period.

The conclusion, "Law, *minjian*, and the ends of anthropology," reasserts that Hui, in the form of teaching schools, and the Party-State work toward a common ground in pursuing their projects—in part, through Islamic law. The Hui case shows that Islamic law and modern state law are not inherently antagonistic. Whether in Muslim countries or secular states, Muslims all over the world are engaged in a number of jurisprudential, legislative, and intellectual projects to find points of convergence between Islamic and state law. Diverging from models of Western liberal democracies or transitional states in the Middle East, Hui and the Party-State do such work through the *minjian*. As opposed to the official sphere, which can be performative, the *minjian* allows for flexible, pragmatic, and adaptive action. Through it, Hui elite and state officials and cadres solve problems and share power while pursuing their respective versions of the public good. At the same time, an excess of the *minjian* can lead to an abuse of Islamic law. The conclusion draws together the foregoing to assess which domains of law in the Hui social field are amenable to the *minjian* versus those where the Party-State has asserted its ownership over law.

1

HISTORY, THE CHINESE STATE, AND ISLAMIC LAW

What the State fears (the State being law in its greatest force) is not so much crime ... [but] fundamental, founding violence, that is, violence able to justify, to legitimate ... or to transform the relations of law (Rechtsverhältnisse, 'legal conditions'), and so to present itself as having a right to law.

Jacques Derrida (1990)

THE FOUNDATIONS OF CHINA'S ISLAMIC LAW

Islamic law has a history in China for as long as Muslims have been in China—that is, since the eighth century, a mere century after the death of the Prophet Muhammad. In the ensuring centuries, following Muslims' accommodation to Chinese society, Islamic law underwent transformations in the imperial period in its jurisdiction, substance and procedures, sources, and institutions. In addition, at various points the Chinese state integrated Muslim elite into the Confucian bureaucracy. In the modern era new ideologies, including secularism, nationalism, and socialism, reinterpreted law. The state designed a legal system that emphasized horizontal institutions under which citizens officially enjoyed equal rights. At the same time, law based on citizenship normalized a new kind of hierarchy of difference based on ethnicity. Crucially, the transition from empire to nation-state saw the state's monopoly on law as the defining element of "modern" law, by marginalizing any alternative lawmaker.

In this chapter, I examine the ways by which sovereign China has managed Islamic law as an example of how, by distinguishing state law from nonstate law, it has, perhaps in the face of its own state-building projects, given life to the *minjian*. Arguing that secular projects are historical just as they are modernist, this chapter provides evidence from successive Chinese regimes' treatment of Islamic law to show that the PRC's approach is both an inheritance from previous states and a reinterpretation of received categories. During the transition from empire to nation, state institutions and discourses transformed Islamic law, gradually narrowing it. Official discourse concerning Islamic law shaped its substance and procedures so that it became "custom"-like, religious without being political, and emphatically Chinese. In the case of the history of Islamic law in China, the form that Islamic law assumed was something the state calls "Hui customary law" (*Huizu xiguanfa*), its descriptor for the *minjian*. I thus use "Hui customary law" to explore the *minjian* as both a product of the state and that which lies beyond its reach, and perhaps beyond its control.

The narrowing of Islamic law in the late imperial period and its reformulation as sub-legal custom is symptomatic of the emergence of the modern notion of sovereignty in China. Imperial China did not develop the Western notion of sovereignty, as in the recognition of equality between states that have complete and exclusive control over their own territory and peoples. Traditional accounts describe a "Chinese world order," in which the emperor was the ruler of "all under heaven" (*tianxia*). The emperor was the ethico-political center who held dominion over lesser rulers, who in turn had to pay tribute.[1] Subsequent historiography has nuanced (but not decentered) this view by arguing, on the one hand, that the modern Eurocentric notion of sovereignty is itself a recent invention[2] and, on the other hand, that the Chinese Empire was articulated through sophisticated rituals of ceremony, hosting, and ideographic distinctions.[3] These practices and the worldview they supported were radically altered in the early twentieth century by Chinese intellectuals' and foreign missionaries' translation of international law. By the end of the Qing Dynasty in 1912, law had become the basis for modern sovereignty in China,[4] and yet law did not displace ethics, ceremony, and the religiosity that was constitutive of the relationship between ruler and ruled.

---

[1] John K. Fairbank first described this system in his *The Chinese World Order: Traditional China's Foreign Relations* (1968).

[2] See, e.g., Hinsley (1986) and Biersteker and Weber (1996).

[3] For writings representative of this shift, see Hevia (1995), Liu (2009), and Mosca (2013).

[4] In many respects, late Qing jurists' attempts to develop a modern constitution were driven by their earliest experiences with international law, namely, the Unequal Treaties of the Opium War (1839–1842). On the formation of sovereignty between the Qing's subjugation to a Eurocentric international legal order and domestic legal modernization, see Cohen (1970), Ogden (1974b), Svarverud (2007), Duara (2009), Ocko and Gilmartin (2009), and Ruskola (2013).

As law became the exclusive purview of the modern sovereign and essential to its authority (as the state and not a person), then the sovereign became ambivalent toward nonstate law. The relationship between state law and Islamic law, which exemplifies this ambivalence, has assumed a variety of forms, including recognition, nonrecognition, misrecognition, co-optation, competition, eradication, manipulation, codependence, and valorization. This relationship varies according to the historical Chinese state (i.e., late imperial, Republican, or Communist) as well as the Muslim community in question. The troubled history of Islamic law in China suggests that current theories of secularism do not account for the diverse effects of secular states on religion and religious law.

Further, theories of secularism inadequately conceptualize the agent of secularization itself. Such theories cast the "state" as the default agent, influencing religion through such institutions as courts, legal rights, and education, as well as policy implementation (e.g., "religious" and "ethnic affairs"). In the PRC, however, the CCP is the ideological corps that operates through the state's rule-making apparatus to form a patriotic Islam in China. In recent years, the Party-State's approach to Islam is as much about its own ideological decay and estranged relationship to the law as it is about the perceived threat of Islamic extremism.

In addition to state categories, the Communists, who assumed power in 1949, adapted a number of Soviet-inspired institutions and policies that survive to the present day. These institutions further marginalize Islamic law in the public sphere through legislation, so-called representative bodies, and policy making. But the history of Islamic law in China is not one of the "structural death" of shari'a (Hallaq 2009a: 15–16). Rather, it has survived and returned in the reform era through the *minjian*. Historically, the adaptation of Islamic law that preceded the modern state resulted more in atrophy than amputation. The nation-state, particularly under socialist law and Communist policy, has nevertheless altered the viability of Islamic law in the everyday lives of Muslim minorities in China. The Islamic revival in the reform period, however, has renewed interest in Islamic law, complicating the Party-State's definition of Islam and its monopoly on the law.

This chapter is organized chronologically, following the historical arc of Islamic law in China: (1) the imperial period, which was a long period of localization; (2) the end of the Qing Dynasty in the late nineteenth and early twentieth centuries, during which Hui practices of localized shari'a continued, while what is called shari'a elsewhere became labeled with the state category "Hui customary law," (3) the Nationalist and Communist republics, which reinterpreted customary law for their own state-building projects; and (4) the reform period, which saw greater integration of China into the *umma* and increased awareness of Islamic law among Hui and other Muslim minorities. In recent years, the Party-State has tried to secularize Islamic authority and Islamic law—to mold Islam in its own socialist and nationalist image. Contrarily, secularization has led to an expansion of the *minjian* and the Islamization of CCP sovereignty in the Muslim Northwest.

THE TRANSFORMATION OF ISLAMIC LAW IN THE CHINESE EMPIRE

Recent insights from the study of imperial legacies and postcolonialism have shown that the formation of nation-states marks not a rupture from the imperial past but rather (sometimes uncomfortable) modifications of governance over multiethnic populations.[5] To understand the place of Islamic law in contemporary China, it is essential to understand its broader historical trajectories. In the imperial period, as Chinese Muslims adapted to Chinese society, Islamic legal practice was increasingly relegated to private and familial matters. At times, namely during the Yuan Dynasty (1271–1368) and the Qing Dynasty (1644–1912), the state used Islam and its law to govern Muslim populations. In different moments, imperial governance variously operated to marginalize, bureaucratize, and customize Islamic law. At a broad level, the history of Islamic law in the imperial period parallels trajectories of Islamic and state law in the Russian and Ottoman Empires as well as during the British colonization of India and Malaysia. In these imperial formations, through a variety of institutional and jurisprudential forms, officials used Islamic law to buttress their rule.

By the Tang Dynasty (618–907) there were growing communities of Arab and Persian traders, merchants, and envoys on the southeastern coast of China. In what has become known as the "maritime Silk Road," Muslim businessmen who traded in Chinese porcelain and silk took up residence in coastal cities. There were legal restrictions on the ability of foreign Muslims to enter into marriages with Han Chinese women, own real

---

[5] See Stoler (2006), Hirschhausen (2008), and Burbank and Cooper (2010: 413–43).

property,[6] and inherit.[7] Beyond formal law, and in the context of increasing conflicts between the growing foreign Muslim population and the Chinese, informal sanctions in the form of racism and distrust led Arabs and Persians to live in their own communities.[8] Within these enclaves,[9] the Muslims practiced Islamic law. For example, in the Guangzhou Muslim quarters, called "foreigner districts" (*fanfang*), Muslim residents chose their own leader, who was considered a local magistrate. This leader, almost always male, was integrated into the Chinese bureaucracy at the lowest level and collected taxes for the imperial government, but he exercised discretion and could enact special policies, including mosque building and religious activities. Further, foreigner districts had their own courts. In one of the earliest accounts of Islamic law in China, Sulayman al-Tajir described Islamic courts in Canton (Guangzhou):

> At *Canfu*, which is the principal Scale for Merchants, there is a *Mohammadan* appointed Judge over those of his Religion, by the Authority of the Emperor of *China*; and that he is Judge of all the *Mohammedans* who report to these Parts. Upon Festival Days he performs the public Service

[6] See *General Mirror for the Aid of Government* (*Zizhi tongjian*), compiled by the Northern Song official Sima Guang (d. 1086), stating, "Li Mi [Tang cabinet minister, d. 789] knows that the bearded visitors [*huke*] that have lived in Chang'an for a long time, or forty years or more, all have wives, buy real property, profit from holding property rights, and live a peaceful life with no desire to return home" (Lu 2001: 51). But see the *Ancient Record of the Tang Dynasty*, indicating that miscegenation was banned: "Your Excellency promulgates the law, in order to distinguish Chinese from barbarian, to outlaw intermarriage, and prohibit barbarians [*manren*] from taking real property" (Qiu 2001b: 34). Both the Tang and Song Codes prohibited foreign Muslims' ability to return to their countries with their Chinese wives (Dou 1984; Liu 1999a: 193–94). Further, the Song encyclopedia *The Prime Tortoise of the Record Bureau* (*Cefu yuangui*) records that the Tang Dynasty imposed restrictions on relations between male Muslims and female Chinese by outlawing the traffic of women (Zheng 2003: 27). The work also records that in Jingzhao (Xi'an), the government proclaimed: "Chinese people shall not in private travel with, conduct business with, marry, have dealings with or receive money from foreigners [*fanke*]; as for property and slaves and maid-servants, possession [by foreigners] is strictly prohibited" (Qiu 2001b: 34).

[7] In the Song Dynasty, efforts were made to ban foreign Muslims from cities by law. In Wenzhou, for example, an assistant prefectural magistrate issued a legal regulation (*falü guiding*) outlawing urban residence for Muslims. The law, however, was largely ignored by foreign merchants and government officials alike (Zhang 2002).

[8] As opposed to the more common appellation for foreigners—"foreign ghost" (*fangui* 番鬼), which denoted Westerners—many of the official histories use the denigration "foreign animals" (*fanliao*), which was conventionally used to describe Persians (see, e.g., Bai 1995).

[9] As hermetic spheres of bounded foreign law, these Muslim quarters were imperial China's first sites of extraterritoriality and are a precedent of sorts for the extraterritorial zones established in coastal cities by Western powers from the seventeenth to late nineteenth centuries. At least one authoritative commentator has made the comparison, forming the questionable conclusion that the first of the extraterritorial treaties, the Treaty of Nerchinsk (1689), was not met with objection

with the *Mohammedans*, and pronounces the Sermon or *Kotbat*, which he concludes, in the usual form, with Prayers for the Soltan of the *Moslems* (or *Muslemen*). The Merchants of *Irak* who trade hither, are no way dissatisfied with his Conduct, or his Administration in the Post he is invested with; because his Actions, and the Judgments he gives, are just and equitable, and conformable to the *Koran* (or *Alcoran*) and according to the *Mohammedan* Jurisprudence.

Renaudot (1733: 8), original emphasis[10]

This Central Asian traveler observed the operation of Islamic courts as one of autonomy from the Chinese government and authenticity vis-à-vis the dominant culture of the Han Chinese. In the course of imperial history, such autonomy gradually fell away in the face of both Chinese administration and the Han majority.

The Tang Code established the precedent of acknowledging the existence of foreign law among foreigners domiciled within the territorial empire. In the earliest legal article dealing with foreign affairs in Chinese legal history, the Tang Code recognized foreign law by permitting foreigners to settle disputes according to their own law:

> For all those outside the pale of Chinese civilization, when those of the same group commit a crime against each other, their dispute is to be settled in accordance with their own custom and law [*sufa*]. When a member of one group commits a crime against a member of a different group, then their dispute will be settled in accordance with the legal theory [i.e., Tang Code].

(Liu 1999b: 144)

The imperial bureaucracy incorporated qadis (judges) into its lowest rung. Such jurisdictional accommodations continued throughout the Song period.

Events preceding the Yuan Dynasty marked a change in the history of Muslims, and with it Islamic law, in China. The Mongolian army's campaigns, namely their destruction of the Kara-Khitai Khanate and the Khwarezmian Empire in western Central Asia in 1219–1220, displaced large populations of Persians and Turks. As a wave of Muslims moved

---

by the Chinese side, "since when the Arabs had traded at Canton, Amoy, Foochow, and Ningpo in the eighth and ninth centuries they had been permitted to retain their own laws" (Keeton 1969: 90).

[10] L'Abbé Eusèbe Renaudot in 1718 was the first to translate into a Western language the travelogue *Accounts of India and China* (*Akhbar al-Sin wa-l-Hind*), attributed to al-Tajir, who allegedly traveled to China in the ninth century. Jean Sauvaget (1948) published a French translation of al-Tajir that generally accords with this excerpt of the English version of Renaudot with some

eastward, the pattern of Muslims living in large cities shifted to one of small settlements dispersed over large areas in Northwest China, a pattern that has come to characterize Chinese Muslim communities to the present.

The emergence of what is today called Hui (also Huihui, *huimin*, or Huizu) through intermarriage, migration, conversion, and cultural mixture between Han and foreign Muslims followed divergent trajectories in different parts of China.[11] Reflecting the Mongols' valorization of Muslim talent, the Yuan government implemented the Bureau of the Qadis (Huihui Hade Si) to govern Hui populations.[12] Like the Muslim officials during the Tang-Song period, the Bureau of the Qadis was integrated into the lowest level of the administration. The qadis assisted the local officials in handling administrative affairs, and they adjudicated marriage, property, and inheritance disputes among Muslims in accordance with Islamic law.[13]

By the thirteenth century there was already a narrowing of the scope of Islamic law to matters of family law, as occurred in the Russian Empire in the eighteenth century and in portions of the former Ottoman Empire in the nineteenth century when the British took over Egypt (Asad 2003: 210; Spannaus 2013). The Bureau of the Qadis was a kind of predecessor to the Ecclesiastical Assembly of the Muhammadan Creed, established by Catherine the Great in 1788 in Ufa, through which the tsarist state backed mullas, who heard cases on matters of marriage, divorce, and other family matters (Crews 2006: 52). The Bureau of the Qadis demonstrates the Yuan Empire's recognition of plural sources of law, even if state law had already limited the content of Islamic law. Extant historical documents pertaining to the Bureau of the Qadis refer to its activity in the coastal cities, such as Wenzhou and Guangzhou, as well as Inner Mongolia.[14]

---

minor differences; for example, Sauvaget wrote "*droit de Islam*" (law of Islam) where Renaudot wrote "*Mohammedan* Jurisprudence." The Arabic original is "*aḥkām al-Islām*" or "rules of Islam."

[11] Scholarly opinion varies, in some cases significantly, as to when the Hui first formed as a cognizable group—that is, when Hui began to think of themselves as belonging to a distinct identity. The view among PRC scholars is that the Hui emerged during the Yuan period, although many of the defining features such as "scriptural hall education" did not appear until the Ming period (Yang 2006; Ding 2008). Western scholars, such as Gladney (1987b) and Lipman (1997), adopting constructivist analyses, emphasize the recent construction of the Hui as part of the building of the modern nation.

[12] In southwestern China, the Yuan used foreign Muslims to govern not only Chinese Muslims but also non-Muslims. When the Mongols arrived in Yunnan in 1253, they appointed a Central Asian administrator named Sayyid 'Ajjal Shams al-Din to rule over the polyethnic population (Armijo-Hussein 1997).

[13] See Wang (2002), Ma (2005), and Liu and Wang (2011).

[14] In 1984 Chinese archaeologists discovered documents in the ancient Tangut city of Eji Nai, or Khara-Khoto in Mongolia (Ch. Heicheng, "Black City"), the capital of the Yijinai Prefecture in

The Ming government (1368–1644), which overthrew the Yuan Dynasty, dismantled the Bureau of the Qadis and pursued generally more restrictive policies toward Muslims and their law. At the same time, the Ming and Qing Dynasties saw the elaboration of institutions that gave limited recognition to Islamic law. The revisionist historiographical school "New Qing History" has demonstrated that while the Great Qing Law Code was applied to the borderlands, the Qing did not force assimilation on non-Chinese populations (Crossley 1990a, Elliott 2001). The Qing established legal institutions such as the Court of Colonial Affairs (Lifanyuan) to deal with Mongols, Tibetans, Chinese Muslims, and Turkic Muslims (Dreyer 1976: 9–10; Yuan and Gao 2001: 38). These courts implemented Qing law while allowing non-Han legal specialists—for instance, qadis in the area the Qing conquered in 1759 (known today as Xinjiang)—to handle most familial matters in accordance with Islamic law (Bellér-Hann 2008; Tian 2012).

Among Turkic Muslims, Islamic legal institutions enjoyed a long history, one that survived up until the socialist period. The Qing adopted forms of indirect rule that permitted such institutions a degree of political autonomy. In the oases cities around the Taklamakan Desert in Xinjiang, qadis implemented a combination of shariʻa and Uyghur customary law in courts called *qadihana* ("house of the qadi") in Uyghur language. In 1874, the Qing court abolished the use of Islamic law in handling penal cases but continued to allow for Islamic law and local custom to address noncriminal matters through qadis (Yuan and Gao 2001). The Japanese scholar Jun Sugawara (2009, 2010) has shown, based upon qadi court documents discovered in Kashgar, that from this period until the early 1950s qadis often authenticated legal documents, although Chinese administrators sought increasingly to standardize such legal forms. Uyghur fables often feature qadis, sometimes in the form of the populist wise man Afanti,[15] demonstrating the strong position of the institution in Uyghur collective consciousness.

the Yuan Dynasty. Called the *Case Documents of Shi Lin's Marriage Contract* (*Shilin hunshu an wenjuan*), the trove contains some one hundred documents pertaining to lawsuits dated to ca. 1311. Three documents refer to the role of the Bureau of the Qadis in adjudicating suits between Hui in the qadi's jurisdiction. In one case, a Hui man named Awu sued a Han not in the court of the Bureau of the Qadis but in the (Han) main administrative center. Scholars have interpreted this forum shopping as Hui considering the Bureau of the Qadis not to be a particularly favorable venue (Qiu 2001a: 158; Hou 2007), although it is equally possible that the Bureau of the Qadis did not have jurisdiction over non-Muslims.

[15] In 2009, in Hotan, I found a VCD series called *Uyghur Popular Stories: Afanti* (*Weiwu'erzu minjian gushi: Afanti*), which features several films centered on the legendary figure of Afanti, a half wise man and half fool who dispenses advice and local justice.

A less well-known case of Islamic legal institutions among Turkic Muslims is that of the Salars, based in Xunhua County, one hundred kilometers west of Linxia. The Salars had their own tradition of qadis. Salar history centers on Jiezi Mosque,[16] built near the site of a holy spring. Salars say the camel of the two brothers Kharaman and Akhman, who led the Salars to China from Samarkand in the eighth century, turned to stone at the spring, indicating the land God had chosen for them. Down the hill from the mosque, covered in overgrowth, is a modest mausoleum, dated to 1851, for several Salar qadis (see Figure 1.1).[17] According to the current head of Jiezi Mosque, qadis served until the latter years of the Republican period, when the warlord Ma Bufang replaced them with appointees whom he empowered to enforce Islamic law, mainly on civil matters. Views differ on whether the institution of the qadi was an inherited one, passed from father to son.[18] A nonagenarian fifth-generation descendant of the last qadi told me that the institution was hereditary. According to the elder Salar, there were seven generations of qadis, and they were the custodians of the handwritten Qur'an, following the examples of Kharaman, an expert on Qur'anic exegesis, and Akhman, an imam.

As seen in the case of Uyghurs and Salars, Turkic Muslim communities maintained Islamic legal institutions much longer than did Chinese Muslims in Gansu Province.[19] The erosion of qadi courts and legal textual production occurred relatively early in the history of Chinese Muslims. Reasons for this include cultural, linguistic, and geographic factors. The geographical distribution of Hui and the lower population density of their communities, for example, have made them more susceptible to the pressures of Hanification.

In addition to the Chinese language and customs, imperial law has also retarded the development of Hui legal institutions. In Hui-dominated areas of the Northwest there were no such institutions as the Court of Colonial Affairs that permitted indirect rule through

---

[16] The mosque name means "street." It is also known colloquially as Gazi Dasi, meaning "Small Lane Grand Mosque."

[17] The inscription on the mausoleum reads "eighth lunar month of the first year of the Xianfeng period [1851–1861]" (*Xianfeng yuannian guiyue*).

[18] The Muslim scholar Mian Weilin (1988: 54) attributes the hereditary nature of such titles, which he argues was established as early as the late Ming, to the influence of "the Han feudal clan system".

[19] Gansu in the late Qing period was significantly larger than Gansu Province in the PRC. It included parts of southwestern Inner Mongolia, eastern Qinghai, northeastern Xinjiang, and all of Ningxia.

Figure 1.1 Mausoleum containing the graves of two qadis, near Jiezi Mosque in Xunhua County, Qinghai Province. One of the qadis is identified by his descendants as Wu Shidan

Source: the author

Islamic law. Unlike for Turkic Muslims, where formal legal institutions could reproduce Islamic legal consciousness, for Hui during the Qing period both Islamic law and legal institutions lost importance in everyday life. Following Sufi rebellions, such as the 1781 Jahriyya revolt, the Qing restricted Hui movement, banned proselytizing, and reformed mosque administration in Muslim cities in Gansu (Ma 2006: 170–71). During this time, the use of qadis in mosques fell out of favor, although it seems this shift had begun as early as the Yuan period, centuries before.[20]

Thus, unlike in Xinjiang, there was a consolidation of judicial power by the Qing court over Chinese Muslims in Gansu. Regular civil officials held jurisdiction over legal matters pertaining to Muslims (Lipman 2005: 88), and the Great Qing Law Code contained many provisions

[20] By 1328 it had been ordered that the qadis were to be abolished, although Ibn Battuta observed them during his visit in 1345 (Chaffee 2006: 416).

specific to Hui, some of which—for example, in the area of penal law—set a higher penalty for Hui defendants (Lipman 1999: 573; Ma 2006: 165). In addition, provisions on civil affairs prohibited intermarriage between Hui and other Muslims (Ma 2006: 167). The Hui historian Bai Shouyi (1992b: 450) relates that Qing governance over Chinese Muslims was permeated by the spirit of the saying "Hui have the character of dog or sheep. They know how to threaten but lack morals." Hui were thus not only subject to Qing law but assigned an inferior status.

In addition to discrimination in Qing law, scholars have argued that court cases between Han and Hui touching on matters of family, marriage, and land contributed to tensions that caused the Hui uprising of 1862 in Shaanxi. Over the next decade, Zuo Zongtang, the Han Chinese general who put down the Taiping rebellion, killed some 700,000 Hui (Dillon 1999: 58–59). In Yunnan and Kashgar, Du Wenxiu and Yaqub Beg, respectively, chafed at Qing attempts to consolidate rule over frontier Muslim populations, and sought to establish sultanates based on Islamic law (Kim 2004: 91; Atwill 2005a: 147). Their attempts to found Islamic states directly challenged the legitimacy of Qing rule. In the Hui experience, shari'a was anti-empire, and its institutions were dismantled along with the governments of the short-lived sultanates.

Qing law's monopolization of the adjudication of Muslim disputes should not, however, be seen as a fait accompli. While Chinese Muslims solicited the state to intervene in disputes between Muslims, there were Muslim authorities not backed by the state—namely, the clerics (ahong), who mediated disputes touching on everyday concerns. Here, the experience of Muslims in the Russian Empire is illustrative. Whereas mullas collaborated with the tsarist state (Crews 2006), scholars have argued that in the study of such relationships, reliance on official petitions leads to overstating the degree to which Muslims viewed the state as the arbiter of orthodoxy (see, e.g., Morrison 2008). Similarly, despite the scarcity of textual evidence for imams[21] handling disputes in the late imperial period in Northwest China, given the paramount role of imams in mosque governance in the contemporary Northwest, it is unlikely that such a role is a recent invention. The history of Chinese Muslims' practices of Islamic law in the imperial period shows a gradual falling away of institutions. The decline of Islamic law was an effect just as much of cultural assimilation as of state design.

---

[21] Generally, the Hui use ahong and yimamu ("imam") interchangeably and use "mulla" less to designate the person in charge of the mosque community.

THE CUSTOMIZATION OF ISLAMIC LAW

The legal modernization of the Qing court through the New Policies (1898–1912) marks a turning point in the history of Islamic law in China. Through such reforms, Islamic law became cognizable under state law as "customary law." Together, law and its obverse, customary law, constituted modern Chinese sovereignty. In the first decade of the twentieth century the court conducted an empire-wide survey of the customs of the people as part of its attempt to modernize the Great Qing Law Code. The Qing surveys became a precedent, as both glossary and methodology, for categorizing nonstate law under a modern legal system. The late Qing legal reform occurred against a backdrop of epochal crisis: war with Japan and aggression by the Eight-Nation Alliance as well as domestic turmoil in the form of the anti-Manchu, anti-imperialist Boxer Rebellion. Chinese law was excoriated as the source of Chinese weakness against foreign and internal forces. The Great Qing Law Code was faulted for its lack of sophistication, for not developing substantive and procedural law as separate branches, and for not distinguishing civil law from criminal law.

In response, Chinese reformers looked to the Japanese experience for lessons in legal modernization. Meiji Japan had undergone legal modernization prior to China, and the Qing government regarded its use of legal concepts borrowed from Germany and France, among other foreign nations, as a model for adapting Western law to Asian sociopolitical realities. It was during the New Policies that Chinese intellectuals began translating concepts of constitutionalism, state theory, and international law, which transformed the way they thought about sovereignty.[22] Following foreign models of reform, the Qing modernizers began by taking stock of native legal sources for localized customs, for the specific purpose of devising new civil and commercial legal codes. At this time, Islamic law was labeled "custom" (*xiguan*) or "customary law" (*xiguanfa*), lexical adaptations from Japan's legal modernization.

The parameters of the customs survey were outlined in 1904. In that year, cabinet ministers of the Qing government established the Bureau for the Revision of the Laws (Xiuding Falüguan, hereinafter "the Bureau"). The Bureau had two main responsibilities: one, collect, compile, and systemize Qing law for the purpose of deletion or revision, and two, translate foreign laws.[23] The customs survey was a component of the first responsibility. The

---

[22] See Ogden (1974a), Reynolds (1993), and Zarrow (2006).
[23] The Guiding Measures for the Revision of the Laws by the High Officials for Legal Revision (*Xiuding falü dachen zouni xiuding falü dagai banfa zhe*), 1907, state that before the laws can be

mandate of the Bureau was broad, encompassing civil, commercial, and criminal law.

The customs survey aimed to collect and document the body of customs in traditional Chinese culture. The survey planning began in 1907, and fieldwork began a year later.[24] Each province established a "survey bureau" (*diaochaju*) at the prefectural and county levels, under which a "legal system department" (*fazhike*) carried out the actual fieldwork. Even Xinjiang, the last province to be created under the Qing Empire in 1884, established a survey bureau in 1909 (Sui 2004: 39). The first survey was focused on commercial affairs and the second on civil affairs. The first survey[25] was directed at collecting data on the social strata of businessmen, the size and operation of markets, systems of registration for businessmen, and mortgaging (Li 2005: 163).

The first survey's dependence on the coordination of local officials resulted in inconsistencies. The second survey, which dealt with civil-affairs customs, saw a greater degree of standardization. In preparation for the survey, the Bureau issued *The Regulations on the Civil Customs Survey in Ten Articles* (hereinafter "the Regulations").[26] The Regulations gave general guidelines on both the administration and content of the civil-customs survey. They specified that local businessmen and gentry, in consultation with surveyors from the relevant level of the survey bureau, would conduct fieldwork and that officials dispatched from the Bureau would oversee the surveys (articles 3 and 4). The Bureau regulated even the minutiae of methodology. Survey teams had a standardized set of observation protocol specifying methods of data collection, time duration of surveys, type of ink and paper to be used on forms, and so on (Hu 2000: 3).

revised, there must be a survey covering foreign laws, the Qing code of etiquette (*lizhi*), and civil and commercial customs. Note that traditional Chinese sources of criminal law were excluded, and thus foreign models predominated in the field of criminal law. Specifically, the foreign penal codes translated were those of France, Germany, Holland, Russia, Japan, Belgium, the United States, Sweden, and Finland (Li 2005: 115–16).

[24] The traditional date is 1907 or 1908. Hu Xusheng, citing the *Hubei Survey Bureau Legal System Department First Survey Subject List* (*Hubei diaochaju fazhike diyici diaocha kemu*), dates the beginning of the survey to 1904 (Hu 2000: 2).

[25] The guiding rules for the first survey, directing its contents and methods, were the *Law Bureau Regulations on the Survey of Provincial Commercial Customs* (*Falüguan diaocha gesheng shangxiguan tiaoli*), issued in 1909.

[26] As to the date of the Regulations, article 3 specifies that they were announced in 1909 (Bureau for the Revision of the Laws 1909).

The production of knowledge about customs through the surveys approximates other colonial projects, in the making of sovereign law at the beginning of the modern period. The Regulations specifically cite the drafting of the civil law—that is, the Great Qing Civil Law Draft—as the reason for the surveys. Along these lines, the compilers instructed the surveyors to "rectify" customs. Article 7 specifies, "The legal terms should not be lightly used. If [one were] to follow each locality's expression, it is certain that one could not attain their unification. The surveyor has to state them clearly, and prevent any answers from taking the form of local expressions and thereby eliciting confusion" (see also Bourgon 1999: 1086). Not unlike British anthropologists in colonial Africa and India, Chinese legal reformers faced the difficulty of translating so-called premodern laws into terms cognizable under Western law. The Qing officials required surveyors to translate local norms embodied in popular expressions into legal precepts that accorded with European and Japanese civil law categories. Working under considerable time pressure, the Bureau collected in total 828 volumes (Sui 2004: 45). Surveying was stopped in 1911 with the fall of the empire.

The customs survey was most immediately shaped by Japanese colonial practices[27] but shares commonalities with early-twentieth-century colonialism in the global South. The customs survey is an instantiation of what Nicholas Dirks (2011), writing about British India, calls the "ethnographic state." Through census, map, and archive, the ethnographic state in British India created caste as the explanatory paradigm of Indian society (Cohn 1987). The customs survey parallels British colonial administrators' construction of so-called Anglo-Muhammadan law in India. To govern India's Muslim population, British administrators consulted scholars ('ulama'), who submitted fatwas to colonial judges. Eventually, Anglo-Muhammadan law was consolidated in textbooks, digests, and precedents (Anderson 1990), ossifying rules that were otherwise negotiated, debated, elastic, and context-dependent (Hooker 1975: 94–95).

Taking a different approach, colonial administrators in the Punjab privileged customary law over shari'a and conducted surveys to codify customs (riwaj, in Persian and Urdu) (Bhattacharya 1996: 21–22). The division between customary law and shari'a and the preference for the former over the latter was carried out elsewhere. Dutch colonial law, for

---

[27] In 1908 Japanese colonists completed and published a volume on customary law in Taiwan, *Private Law in Taiwan*, which became a reference for Chinese reformers (Bourgon 2005: 96), and the Meiji jurist Ume Kenjirō conducted a customary law survey in Korea from 1908 to 1910 (Kim 2008).

instance, preferred *adat* (custom) over sharī'a in Southeast Asia (Bowen 1988; Gilmartin 1988: 45–47). Islam's accommodation to Malaysian and Indonesian society meant Islamic rules were incorporated into adat, particularly in the areas of marriage, divorce, and polygamy. Dutch administrators wrote codes of customary law (*adatrecht*) instead of sharī'a to minimize the influence of Islam.[28] Russian colonialists in Turkestan likewise privileged adat over Islamic law in the administration of pluralistic colonial law in the second half of the nineteenth century.[29] Adat-oriented colonial law effectively marginalized sharī'a in its preference for codified custom.

The Qing customs survey thus shared attributes with British, Dutch, and Russian colonial projects, but did so by objectifying the interpersonal customary law of its own subjects rather than those of a distant colony. Customs were used to describe all Chinese, whether Han or non-Han, including Muslims. It is tempting to call the customs survey proto-nationalistic in its homogenizing aspirations. Yet at the same time, like Anglo-Muhammadan law and adat, it created a limited set of rigid and decontextualized customs based on sharī'a.

The Qing Empire utilized a wide array of nonstate legal institutions and sources of law in service of the empire. In her study of legal pluralism in empires, Lauren Benton notes the high degree of tolerance for unofficial legal systems within imperial administration, without claims of legal hegemony by the empire-state (Benton 2002, 2012; Benton and Ross 2013). To some extent, nonstate law or custom coexisted with state law. Legal historian Liang Zhiping (1996: 36–37) has argued that a number of unofficial sources of law, including *minjian* law, oral, or written rules stemming from one's clan or ethnic group, supplemented state law during the Qing period. Moreover, Qing courts could deviate from the Great Qing Law Code in order to more accurately reflect local custom (Huang 2001).

Historian Jérôme Bourgon has taken issue with the thesis that the Qing looked to custom as a source of civil law. Bourgon argues that customary law is a Western invention, which entered China only during the late Qing period and was exploited by Republican reformers (1999, 2002, 2005). Bourgon's analysis is predicated on a highly formalistic definition of customary law, as understood in continental civil law. Bourgon's civil-law-defined customary law and Liang's unofficial sources of law may not be mutually exclusive. That is, during the late Qing period civil law definitions came to characterize the

---

[28] For readings, see Hooker (1978), Bowen (1988: 280), and Rahman (2006).
[29] See, for instance, Bobrovnikov (2001), Bellér-Hann (2004), and Brusina (2006).

relationship between *minjian* law and state law. The Qing began the process the Republicans would try to carry through: using customs for the purpose of writing legal codes pursuant to continental law theory. The difference was that the Qing operated under a different set of assumptions, including the integrity and viability of the empire, and an imperial worldview that, albeit challenged, still held at the center.

CUSTOM AND THE NATION

Customs of the colonized, which were often reified by colonialists through codification, textualization, and judicial work, frequently became the basis for legislation in young nations. For instance, when India gained independence from Britain, the Constitutional Assembly incorporated British Anglo-Muhammadan law as "religious personal law," and it remains an object of debate to this day (Parashar 2013). Modern China also inherited imperial strategies of rule over multiethnic populations. Realizing the nationalistic potential of the customs survey, the Nationalist Beiyang government (1912–1927) continued the project started by the Qing, although the discourse on customary law was transformed to serve the purposes of the new nation.[30] In the modern period, the Republicans adopted a secularist approach to nation building, which drew upon the customs surveys of the Qing and tolerated the religious basis of customs to the extent they were rational (as opposed to superstitious). The Republican customs survey illustrates one procedure of rationalization, the result of which would form a pillar of the sovereign nation: the deepening distinction between law and custom.

After an initial, failed attempt at a nationwide survey led by the Ministry of Justice in 1918, the survey was conducted by the reconstituted Bureau in 1919. It covered sixteen provinces and three special administrative areas, excluding Guangdong, Guangxi, Yunnan, Guizhou, Sichuan, and Xinjiang, which at the time had either declared independence from the Republican government or were too war-torn for administrative coordination. The survey work continued until 1921. In 1926 the Beiyang government's Ministry of Justice edited *The Complete Collection of Chinese Civil Customs* (*Zhongguo minshi xiguan daquan*). It subsequently reorganized

---

[30] The years 1912 to 1927 saw a series of competing cliques and warlords, whose reign in Beijing is collectively known as the Beiyang government. The Beiyang government was opposed by Sun Yat-sen's Nationalist (Guomin), or Nanjing, government, established in 1917, and was defeated by them in 1928, which led to the Nationalist-led Republic. Anthony Dicks (1990: 366–67) discusses Islamic law's customization in this period.

the compilation, organized by province, and published it as *The Record of the Civil and Commercial Affairs Customs Survey* (*Minshang shi xiguan diaocha lu*, hereinafter the *Record*), although this document has since been lost.[31] Meanwhile, in 1930 the rival Nanjing government's Ministry of Justice published the abridged form of the *Record*, named the *Abstracts of the Record of the Civil and Commercial Affairs Customs Survey* (*Minshang shi xiguan diaocha baogao lu*, hereinafter the *Abstracts*). In addition to the 828 volumes collected under the Qing survey, 72 volumes were gathered under the Republican survey. The *Abstracts* catalog some 3,432 customs, dividing them into the following parts: 12 general customs, 985 debt customs, 1,389 property customs, and 1,046 family inheritance customs (Hu 2000).

Following the Japanese, who looked to the German historical school, which advocated a study of customary law as an expression of the *Volksgeist*, the Chinese Nationalists—who ruled from the fall of the Qing in 1912 until 1949, when they lost the civil war to the Communists—compiled customary law as the raw ingredients for the laws of the new nation. Principles would be derived from local customs and would then serve as the basis for writing law codes (Bourgon 2005: 95). While the Republican surveys use *xiguan* (custom), as did their Qing forebears, the concept of *xiguanfa* (customary law) also entered nationalist discourse at this time.[32] "Custom" became linked to rights that could be upheld in a civil law system. Thus, the Republicans adopted a much more robust continental notion of customary law than that of the Qing, but such legal translation occurred through the specific needs of the Republicans' nationalist project. In short, the customs survey became an instrument of nation building. Consequently, customary law, as I show below, was tied to *minzu*, the "nation."[33] Customary law was crucial to the transformation of the Chinese people from imperial subjects into citizens of the Republic.

Throughout the Republican period customary law referred to the customs of the Chinese people, meaning Han Chinese. In the *Record* and the *Abstracts*, geography, in the form of provinces and counties, rather than ethnic difference is the primary criterion for distinguishing different

---

[31] Parts of the *Record* have been retained in various publications, such as its preface, which can be found in the periodical *Communiqué of the Judiciary* (*Sifa gongbao*) (1927) (Hu 2000: 7).

[32] *Xiguanfa* was derived from the Japanese *kanshūhou*. *Kanshū* was a Meiji neologism that reinterpreted "custom" as an enforceable right. *Kanshūhou* emphasizes the legal nature of customs. One of the first uses of the neologism *xiguanfa* was by the philologist Hu Yunyu (1914).

[33] *Minzu* (lit. "people" plus "descent") is another loanword from Japanese. First used by Liang Qichao in 1898, the term was invoked by Sun Yat-sen to mean "nation" as a lineage that shared

customs.[34] The contemporary notion of ethnicity had not yet permeated Chinese ideas of cultural difference, yet the *Abstracts* reflect some native categories of cultural difference. In the reports for Gansu Province, the *Abstracts* include three non-Han ethnonyms: *fanmin*, *huimin*, and *samin*. *Fanmin* (lit. "foreign peoples") refers to Tibetans (Fiskesjö 1999: 140; Wang 2008: 162). *Huimin* means, loosely, "those who follow Islam," including those called Hui and Uyghur in contemporary China. *Samin* denotes the Salars, who are also Muslim but are given their own ethnonym. The reports do not particularly emphasize cultural difference in categorizing customs.

For each of the three types of customs included in the *Abstracts*—property, debt, and kinship inheritance—there is a chapter on Gansu. However, one conspicuous absence in the Gansu chapter on property is the institution of Islamic pious endowments (Ar. *awqāf*, sing. *waqf*). It includes customs pertaining to temple-owned land (*miaochan*) and land belonging to an ancestral temple (*jiamiao*) (Hu, Xia, and Li 2000: 388) but not that of mosques or Sufi tomb complexes (*gongbei*), which collectively had vast land holdings in areas of contemporary Ningxia and central and southern Gansu up until Communist land reforms in 1949.

CCP historical documents from the 1950s, by contrast, obsessively catalog the land holdings of Muslim mosques and shrines. In fact, the CCP largely legitimated its land policies in the Northwest based on the widespread existence of such Islamic institutions and their alleged exploitation of the masses. Yet there is no mention of such practices in the *Abstracts*, even in such counties as Guyuan and Tianshui, which historically have been primarily Muslim. In the chapter on debt, the section on Xunhua County mentions the buying and selling of land by Tibetans according to "Tibetan regulations" (*fangui* 番规) and not contracts (Hu, Xia, and Li 2000: 737). Curiously, it does not mention the majority Salars, who have lived in Xunhua since at least the Yuan Dynasty. Likewise, it mentions the many Tibetan Buddhist monasteries (*fansi*) in Xunhua (Hu, Xia, and Li

a territory and an ancestor (Dikötter 1992: 91). The term has undergone semantic revision in the reform period. Whereas English translations of official PRC documents in the early socialist period favored "nationality" as the equivalent for *minzu*, beginning in the 1990s the English translation has increasingly used "ethnicity," perhaps demonstrating both sensitivity to the failed Soviet policy and also concerns about PRC obligations under international law. In this book I use "ethnicity" for analytical purposes, but retain "nationality" when the official translation (of a governmental body, for example) uses the older translation.

[34] This approach of not using ethnicity as a criterion for organizing data is broadly consonant with the Republican government's approach to census taking. The 1912 census does not include information pertaining to ethnic or cultural identity (Liu 1931).

2000: 738) but not the mosques, which most likely outnumbered lamaseries in the late Qing period.[35]

Only in the 1930 *Abstracts'* Gansu chapter on kinship inheritance do we see explicit reference to "Islamic customs" (*Huijiao xiguan*). The twenty-fourth section begins with "Islamic polygamy:"

> Under Islam, a husband may marry four wives. They are all bound by ceremony. The system is based on equality. If the husband takes a fifth woman, then the fifth is called a "concubine" [*qie*]. The concubine and the wives are not necessarily equal. If among the four wives, something happens to one, then the fifth woman is called a wife.
>
> As reported by the committee's Xu
> members in Hu, Xia, and Li 2000

Another entry is called "a widow remarries [and] the late husband's family cannot take back the bride price [*caili*]:"

> Islamic family rules state that in the event a widow remarries and if her deceased husband has no debts, then she cannot receive a bride price from her second husband. Even if he has debts, and his inheritance is used to pay back his creditors, then she also cannot receive a bride price. Once someone has violated the religious rules and without authorization received wealth, then the imam of that place must inform the local government office. The official takes the bride price from the offending party and uses it for the expenses of the religion's public welfare.
>
> As reported by Longde County Deng Committee
> members in Hu, Xia, and Li 2000: 1047–48

The twenty-sixth section on customs in Lintan County (formerly Taozhou), the home of the Xidaotang Muslim collectivity, includes as its second entry "using the scripture to replace the witness to a wedding:"

> When Hui marry, they do not draw up a marriage contract. Rather, the matchmaker and the male or female heads of the two families swear upon the Qur'an and shake hands. When this is done, the marriage is established. This is called using the scripture to replace the witness to a wedding.
>
> As reported by the Lintan County Yao Committee
> in Hu, Xia, and Li 2000: 1049

---

[35] Likewise, in the chapter on debt customs, the section on Daohe County, later known as Hezhou and, after 1949, Linxia, has no record of such debt instruments as the contract. While it is highly possible that Muslim minorities did not use contracts under Islamic law, the absence of a record for pious endowments under the property part of the Gansu chapter is striking.

To pause in the chronology of Chinese customization of Islamic law, it is important to consider the matter of whether these customs can really be called "Islamic." The first and second of the three customs make a distinction between what Islamic law allows and the local custom, which is a modification of those rules. The customs are thus purported observations of actual practice that either Chinese Muslims or the compilers of the *Abstracts* (or both) considered "Islamic." However, most Hanafi jurists would question whether the custom qualifies as "Islamic," as they do not cite Islamic sources. As to the first custom that acknowledges the limit of four wives, medieval Hanafi law allowed men to take concubines with restrictions,[36] although slavery and thus concubinage has been deemed unlawful by consensus.

The second custom includes two different prohibitions: one, the family of the deceased husband cannot take back the "bride price" (*caili*) that he gave the wife, and two, she cannot receive a new bride price from her second husband. As an initial matter, both prohibitions draw attention to slippage between the Chinese bride price and the Islamic *mahr*, a problem that I take up in detail in Chapter 5. In terms of the first prohibition, there is a consensus among all schools of Islamic jurisprudence that the family of the deceased husband cannot take back the *mahr*, and thus that prohibition conforms to Hanafi law. The second prohibition, however, violates Hanafi law in refusing a widow a bride price upon her remarriage.

The third custom raises several issues. First, an oral contract was permissible but was not the preferred method of marriage.[37] Second, a woman's consent to the marriage is generally required under Islamic law; consent, however, took the form of that of an adult male guardian who spoke on behalf of a previously unwed woman (i.e., a virgin). Hanafi law made a distinction in this regard, stating that consent (which could be conferred implicitly through silence) was required of any woman of majority age.[38] However, and third, Hanafi law requires two witnesses to publicize the union, and the use of the Qur'an as a substitute would not fulfill that same function.

The customs illustrate how non-Muslim Chinese customs came to shape actual practice. The customs (as recorded) make explicit reference

---

[36] In the medieval period a man could not have sexual intercourse with his wife's slaves or with a married female slave, and in the Ottoman Empire, where Hanafi law predominated, a man who sired a child from a slave had to recognize that child as his own (Fay 2012: 80–81).

[37] Q. 2:282.

[38] See Esposito (2001: 15), Ali (2010: 41), and Spectorsky (2010: 65, 70, 97, 148–49).

to Islamic rules, but the customs' characterizations of those rules are nonetheless muted or contradicted by Chinese preferences. Although Islamic law allows for local custom, or ʿurf, custom cannot contravene doctrine. In these recordings of "Islamic customs," long-term socialization in Chinese society has transformed family law rules. Most of these customs are no longer practiced by Hui, with a few possible exceptions. For instance, the first custom appears to have been shaped primarily by traditional Chinese practices of polygamy that have revived in the reform era; it may also have possible roots in the Shiʿi practice of "temporary marriage" (mutʿa). Although "temporary marriage" is unlawful in Sunni Islam,[39] a small minority of Hui have "tryout marriages," which last only a brief time and often survive only upon the husband's confirmation that his wife is a virgin. However, no Hui I spoke to used the Arabic term mutʿa, and the temporary marriage appears much more shaped by Chinese than by Shiʿi traditions. Neither of the other two customs appears to be practiced today, although traditionalist Hui continue to place a premium on the Qurʾan and its substitutive function, as seen in the ritual of the fidya.[40]

As a means of knowledge production, the Abstracts select which rules to represent and record (and which to discard). The view that emerges from these few references to Muslim customs is that Muslim minorities in China historically practiced a highly localized form of what are known elsewhere as the laws of social relations (muʿāmalāt). This area of the law provided guidance on topics such as polygamy, marriage and remarriage, guardianship, inheritance, and such life-cycle events as the wedding ceremony. Yet the Abstracts, as noted, are selective and omit more than they include. They were thus one edge of the secularist project of building the nation. As Rebecca Nedostup (2009: 4) has chronicled, the Republican government's policy toward religion in the first decades of the twentieth century—"iconoclasm, categorization, and national mobilization"—was instrumental to the process of

---

[39] For analyses of "temporary marriage," see Murata (1987) and Vikør (2005: 137).

[40] The fidya (lit. "ransom") is an expiatory act for the recently deceased through which family members and friends atone for the sins committed by the dead or to accrue merit for obligations left unfulfilled. Hui cite the Qurʾan (2:184, 196) as the basis for this practice. In almost all teaching-school practices, members gather in the mosque or home (sometimes forming a circle) to perform the ritual. Reformist Hui (who in this book I call, following Hui terms, Yihewani and Salafiyya) pass or "turn" money that is then either given to surviving family members or donated to the poor. Traditionalist Hui (e.g., Gedimu and Sufi) may use the Qurʾan as a symbolic substitute for money, in order to accrue merit for the deceased. Reformist Hui strongly disagree with this use of the Qurʾan, considering it a violation of sacred law.

transforming notions of authority from one based on cosmology (i.e., emperor/heaven) to popular sovereignty. Part of this project meant channeling spirituality from old superstitions toward a new "faith" in the state.

Two conclusions can be drawn from the extent of minority customs recorded in the customary law surveys in the late Qing and early Republican periods. First, during this time customary law referred not just to minorities, but to Han Chinese, too. With the exception of the customs excerpted above, the vast majority of the over three thousand customs recorded in the *Abstracts* were those of the Han. In accord with Chiang Kai-shek's theory of the "Chinese nation" (*Zhonghua minzu*), collective national identity was embedded in customary law of and for the nation. The Republican version of the customs survey was similar to the reconstruction of adat in 1950s Indonesia, where the Supreme Court reconstructed codes of adat, initially written by Dutch colonialists, as blueprints for the post-revolutionary nation. By "nationalizing" adat, the state sought to extend rules specific to local communities to the nation as a whole (Bowen 1988: 280).

Second, although Islamic law was not a major field of investigation in the survey, it was named "Islamic custom" (*Huijiao xiguan*)—perhaps the first time official writings had named it as such. Whereas scholars have focused on the entry of notions of race and ethnicity (as well as class) into China during this period,[41] the importance of the survey's interpellation of Islamic law as custom shows that the dichotomy of law and custom was another descriptive theory that formed the nation. Islamic law is not conceived of as a foreign legal system or even the local substantiation of a global religion with roots outside of China, but rather it is a primordial artifact of an indigenous Chinese group: *huimin*, those who believe in Islam. The *Record* created an archive of customary law, despite the fact that, in terms of creating legislation, the survey was "a spectacular failure after two decades of patient efforts" (Bourgon 2005: 101).

THE ETHNICIZATION OF CUSTOM

The Communists also invoked the concept of customary law as they undertook their nationwide survey of ethnic groups in 1954. Consistent with studies that have identified the bureaucratic classification of the ethnic other as a continuity between Communist and Republican forms of rule (Mullaney 2004; Fiskesjö 2012), the Communists inherited the

---

[41] See, for instance, Dikötter (1992), Fitzgerald (1995), and Harrison (2001).

discourse of customary law from the Republicans (and the Qing before them). However, the meaning of the term was again transformed, as the Communists reinterpreted it in accordance with Marxism-Leninism and the evolutionary thought of the lawyer and anthropologist Lewis Henry Morgan. Their "ethnic identification" (*minzu shibie*) project identified language as a chief marker of ethnic difference (Mullaney 2011). The collection of customary law was an important goal of the project as well, though customary law was considered both "ethnic" and "feudal," and inferior to modern state law. As I explain below, under the CCP the state became the sole legislator, and the Party positioned itself as transcending competing belief systems, which were labeled "superstition."

In the earliest CCP regulations on social life in Gansu and other border areas during the civil war period (1927–1950), customary law was recognized and enforceable to the extent that it did not contravene state law.[42] While this nominal recognition was later enshrined in statutory law, customary law became a signifier of feudalism and ethnic backwardness that demanded liberation in the form of state law. In the ethnic identification project, which generally addressed customary law,[43] reports on Hui in the Northwest, such as *The Compilation of Gansu Hui Survey Materials* and *The Compilation of Qinghai Hui Survey Materials*, categorize Islamic law as "social habits and customs" (*fengsu xiguan*), the Chinese socialist term for customary law.[44]

---

[42] Article 3 of the Revised Provisional Marriage Regulations of the Shaanxi-Gansu-Ningxia Border Region (*Xiuzheng Shaan-Gan-Ning bianqu hunyin zanxing tiaoli*), promulgated March 20, 1944, states, "In the case of marriage contracted by members of national minorities, while the principles of these Regulations shall be observed, their customary laws shall [also] be respected" (cited in Meijer 1971: 289).

[43] Many of these reports have been collected in the series *A Collection of the Social and Historical Survey Materials of Chinese Ethnic Minorities* (*Zhongguo shaoshu minzu shehui lishi diaocha ziliao congkan*), printed originally in the mid-1980s by provincial social science academies. In the 2000s the Nationalities Affairs Commission published a series of this same material as part of its *Nationality Problem Five Collections* (*Minzu wenti wuzhong congshu*). However, the recent edition features contemporary scholars writing brief articles on ethnic minorities based on the survey materials and is not a reprinting of the survey materials themselves. See also the volume *Sixty Years of China's Ethnic Laws* (*Zhongguo minzu fazhi 60nian*) (Xiong 2010), which commemorates the sixtieth anniversary of Communist rule in minority regions and includes excerpted reports.

[44] See, e.g., *The Compilation of the Gansu Hui Survey Materials* (Chinese Academy of Social Sciences Nationalities Research Institute 1964a). In addition to the provincial reports on Hui in the Northwest, there are also reports on Hui autonomous prefectures, such as *The General Condition of the Changji Hui Autonomous Prefecture* (Editorial Group for the General Situation of the Changji Huizu Autonomous Prefecture 1985) in Xinjiang. Other reports specifically on Hui include *The Heilongjiang Hui Social-Historical Survey Report* (Chinese Academy of Social Sciences

Materials from the survey covering Hui include summaries describing "Hui family law," namely, early marriage (*zaohun*), marriage form, the scope of intermarriage, and the processes of engagement, divorce, remarriage, and property inheritance (Huang 2009; Xiong 2010: 95). Additionally, there are site-specific descriptions for marriage, burial, and "religious belief customary law" as well as for systems of land ownership, leasing, borrowing and lending money, and employment (Xiong 2010). There are similar summaries for the Salar, Bonan, Kyrgyz, Dongxiang, Tajik, Uzbek, Kazakh, Tatar, and Uyghur ethnicities. In short, in the first decade of Communist rule, customary law became wedded to the concept of *minzu*, which along with denoting the "Chinese nation," came to mean ethnic minorities and not Han. Through such discursive connections, Islamic law was labeled customary law, or "ethnic law" (*minzufa*). Whereas the term *xiguanfa* was an elastic term as used in the Republican period, even applying to US common law (Huang 1936), the Communists used the term to refer to nonstate law, primarily that of ethnic minorities.[45]

In the transition from empire to nation-state, Islamic law in China has thus undergone "lawfare," or the creation of customary law (Comaroff 2001: 306; Comaroff and Comaroff 2009: 56). Like adat and Anglo-Muhammadan law, "Hui customary law" in China is a vestige of empire. While adat and custom predated colonial administration, through digests, precedents, codes, and cases, colonial courts objectified these sources of authority. Whereas custom was deeply contextual, rules were made rigid (Anderson 1990; Bhattacharya 1996). Moreover, in the Communist period custom has been ethnicized—that is, discursively linked to the notion of *minzu*. As a result, it becomes inconceivable semiotically to disarticulate customary law from *minzu*. Official discourse in the PRC reproduces Islamic law as Hui customary law, a localized, detextualized, and depoliticized foil to modern state law. As Talal Asad (2003: 23) has remarked, the "binaries that pervade modern secular discourse"—in this case, custom/law—are constitutive of secularism itself.

Nationalities Research Institute 1958), *The Guangdong Hui Social-Historical Situation* (Team of the Guangdong Social-Historical Survey 1963), and *The Yunnan Hui Social-Historical Survey* (Yunnan Provincial Editors Group 1985).

[45] Gao Qicai, professor at Tsinghua Law School and leading expert on customary law, has defined customary law in the following terms: "Customary law is the opposing counterpart to law formulated by the state. It is born of all kinds of social organizations, social authorities, norms of certain social organizations, and the behaviors of all members of certain societal regions for the purpose of their general compliance" (Gao 2003: 8).

In addition to the ethnicization and localization of Islamic law in the Communist period, there is also a bifurcation between what the Hanafi school of jurisprudence terms devotional law (*'ibādāt*) and the law of social relations (*muʿāmalāt*). As in the European setting (Rohe 2006; Shah 2010), Chinese state law resists integrating the full panoply of Islamic rules concerning social relations. Official and academic representations of Hui customary law are limited primarily to ritualistic matters, including dietary law and prayer. Where they touch upon the law of social relations, it is those rules that are most aberrational to state law—for instance, polygamy—that attract attention. Highlighted behaviors are framed as customs that are immutable.[46] There is no sense of the continuous negotiation and debate by members of Hui communities, including women, about such practices.

In sum, the discourse of customary law traveled across linguistic-cultural-jurisprudential distinctions (continental, Japanese, and Chinese) as well as through political regimes within China. Customary law is a trans-regime discourse that has served different purposes in the imperial, Republican, and Communist periods. At the same time, the trajectory of customary law challenges what are often entrenched periodizations in the historiography of Chinese law. The Communists' inheritance of the Qing discourse on customary law will not surprise students of nationalism (Anderson 1983: ch. 10). Across the history of the customary law discourse, however, there is a gradual narrowing, if not hardening, of the state's view of nonstate law. Whereas the empire was generally tolerant of nonstate law, the PRC has excluded such sources of law. The *minjian* is born of this exclusion. This narrowing process is a result of socialist ideology just as much as of state-led nation building. Indeed, Islamic law presented an ideological challenge to the Party's monopoly on defining law. The nonrecognition of religious law is congruent with the broader "imagined linking of the law to foundations of sovereignty" (Ocko and Gilmartin 2009: 56) in modern China. Any threat Islamic law presented was objectified and made manageable as customary law, which always required the recognition of the Party-State's legal institutions.

---

[46] For example, Gao Qicai (2003: 9) states, "The stability of customary law and other basic entrenched aspects are related to human nature. That is, due to the intimate relationship between customary law and human nature, and because human nature is fixed since time immemorial, human nature does not change and customary law also does not change."

GRANTING AUTONOMY

State discourse of customary law has been a building block of the PRC's governance over ethnic minorities and a source of legitimation for the Party-State's institutions of ethnic autonomy and preferential policies, mainly in the fields of education and employment.[47] Such institutions omit or exclude the capacity of Muslims to practice Islamic law, including building institutions, whether juridical, administrative, or educational, that would cultivate Islamic legal consciousness. My focus here is on ethnic autonomy as the foundation for governance over large numbers of Muslim minorities in the Northwest. Ethnic autonomy exists, according to law, to protect the customs of such ethnic minorities as Muslims, and yet practice shows the opposite result.

Scholars have called the legislative structure of the PRC "a monistic system with several levels" (Wang 1997: 14), and as such the legal system is an indelible part of the PRC's national, territorial, and political unity. The National People's Congress (NPC) is the main legislative body that promulgates laws for the entire nation. Within the nation, the PRC has five "autonomous regions" (ARs): the Inner Mongolia Autonomous Region, the Guangxi Zhuang Autonomous Region, the Tibet Autonomous Region, the Ningxia Hui Autonomous Region ("Ningxia"), and the Xinjiang Uyghur Autonomous Region ("Xinjiang"). Beneath ARs are lower administrative units, including autonomous prefectures, autonomous counties, autonomous municipalities, and autonomous towns; collectively these units are considered "autonomous areas."[48] There are 40 autonomous prefectures and 120 autonomous counties.[49] Autonomous prefectures or counties do not have to be located within an AR. For example, Linxia is located in the Linxia Hui Autonomous Prefecture in southwestern Gansu Province. Together, the autonomous areas comprise nearly two-thirds, or 64 percent, of the landmass of the PRC, and Xinjiang in particular contains many of China's natural resources in oil

---

[47] A growing literature cutting across the social sciences and policy examines problems attendant to the regional autonomy system and preferential policies and calls for reform (Ghai 2000; Ma Rong 2004; Ghai and Woodman 2009; Wang Jian 2010; Zhang Rui 2010; Leibold 2013; and Ma Wen 2014).

[48] Such areas operate within a centralized system: pursuant to the Preamble of the Common Program of the Chinese People's Political Consultative Conference (*Zhongguo renmin zhengzhi xieshang huiyi gongtong gangling*), adopted September 29, 1949, the PRC is a unitary state, meaning that "all local people's governments throughout the country shall obey the Central People's Government."

[49] Three of these are autonomous banners (*qi*), county-level administrative divisions located in the Inner Mongolia Autonomous Region.

and natural gas. Over 80 percent of ethnic minorities reside in autonomous areas. From the perspectives of national security and border control, energy, and internal stability, the question of autonomy looms large as China embarks on possible reforms of the system.

Ethnic autonomy highlights the PRC's adoption of Soviet institutions. In the first generation of ethnic policy formulation, ethnic autonomy was a result of Soviet nationality policy.[50] Mao Zedong retreated from the CCP's earliest statements of policies toward non-Han that promised self-determination and the right to secede from the Chinese state.[51] The prioritization of the Han Chinese and the call for unity over diversity and federalism prevailed. While China's policies toward ethnic minorities have varied according to the ethnic minority population and have further changed over time, the basics of ethnic autonomy have remained remarkably resilient to reform.

The people's congresses of autonomous areas may—according to the Constitution, the 1984 Law of the PRC on Regional Ethnic Autonomy, and the 2000 Legislation Law of the PRC—promulgate laws to protect minority customs, traditions, and languages.[52] Specifically, these legislative bodies may issue three types of regulations: (1) autonomous regulations

---

[50] Regarding the early legislative history of ethnic autonomy, the CCP began deliberating ethnic autonomy during the Seventh Central Committee of the CCP in 1945. Party leaders advocated autonomy for minority-concentrated regions partly as a response to the war with Japan. The rationale for ethnic autonomy was that it would unite the minorities against the Japanese. In May 1947—before the founding of the PRC—the first autonomous region was established in Inner Mongolia. In September 1959 the Common Program (Gongtong Gangling) gave ethnic autonomy legal status: "Where ethnic minorities inhabit a region in a compact community, ethnic regional autonomy shall be implemented, in accordance with the number of the ethnic inhabitant population and the size of the area, and ethnic regional autonomy organs shall be individually established." In August 1952 the Implementing Program for PRC Ethnic Regional Autonomy (Zhonghua renmin gongheguo minzu quyu zizhi shishi gangyao) further elaborated the principles of ethnic autonomy. The PRC's first constitution, in 1954, enshrined the system of ethnic autonomy and recognized three levels: autonomous regions, autonomous prefectures, and autonomous counties. For the legislative history of ethnic autonomy, see Sun (2009).

[51] The Manifesto of the Second National Congress of the CCP (Zhongguo gongchandang di er ci quanguo dahui xuanyan), July 16–23, 1922, declared Tibet, Mongolia, and Xinjiang (Huijiang) to be "autonomous states" (zizhi bang) as part of the Federal Republic of China. The Manifesto further used the term "self-determination" (zijue), which appeared in CCP policy documents throughout the mid-1940s to unite the minorities against the Nationalists but which was dropped in favor of "autonomy" (zizhi) in 1949.

[52] See the Constitution of the PRC (Zhonghua renmin gongheguo xianfa), passed by the First Meeting of the First Session of the NPC, September 20, 1954, art. 3; Law of the PRC on Regional Ethnic Autonomy (Zhonghua renmin gongheguo minzu quyu zizhifa), promulgated May 31, 1984, amended February 28, 2001, art. 19; and the Legislation Law of the PRC (Zhonghua renmin gongheguo lifafa), passed by the Third Session of the Ninth NPC, March 15, 2000, art. 66.

(*zizhi tiaoli*), (2) individual regulations (*danxing tiaoli*), and (3) flexible or supplementary regulations (*biantong huo buchong guiding*). Autonomous regulations are comprehensive in scope and lay out the general powers of the people's government and local people's congress, as well as some of the overall policy aims. Individual regulations address such narrowly defined matters as financial management, technology, hygiene, natural resource acquisition, and environmental protection. Flexible or supplementary regulations specifically modify legislation from higher levels of government for the autonomous area in question.

As of 2015, however, no AR has issued an autonomous regulation.[53] Since 2009, the State Ethnic Affairs Commission and the NPC's Nationalities Affairs Commission have held a number of symposia, along with experts on "ethnic law," to discuss the problem without any concrete results. The reasons for the absence of autonomous regulation at the AR level are several. Autonomous regulations and individual regulations require approval from the legislative body at the next higher level.[54] Procedurally, the Standing Committee of the NPC must review and approve draft autonomous regulations issued at the AR level.[55] The CCP also plays a role in reviewing proposed autonomous regulations. Thus, lawmaking in autonomous areas is a political process that entails "bargaining and compromise between the autonomous areas and higher organs" (Xia Chunli 2009: 558). Ultimately, the political authority of the CCP backs the legislative power of the NPC. The administrative and legal structure of the state makes lawmaking difficult for autonomous areas, and the Party's right to veto any politically sensitive regulations constrains ethnic autonomy. As scholar of ethnic relations Zhang Haiyang (2014) has written, "Some people believe that autonomy will have the risk of division. They say 'today autonomy, tomorrow federalism, and the day after they want independence'." Hence, the possibility of autonomous regulations, the ostensible mainstay of ethnic autonomy, is foreclosed by Party fiat.

---

[53] The Inner Mongolia Autonomous Region Regulations on People's Prairie Management (*Neimenggu zizhiqu caoyuan guanli tiaoli*), issued by the Inner Mongolia Autonomous Region People's Congress, effective January 1, 2005, were passed not as an autonomous regulation, but as a "local statute" (*difang fagui*). Local statutes have a more limited scope of authority than autonomous regulations but do not need to be approved by the NPC.

[54] See the Law of the PRC on Regional Ethnic Autonomy, art. 19.

[55] Pursuant to the Law of the PRC on Regional Ethnic Autonomy, art. 15, the people's governments of all ethnic autonomous areas are subordinate to the State Council, and pursuant to the PRC Constitution, art. 67(8), the Standing Committee of the NPC has the power to annul the local regulations of autonomous areas.

Where local people's congresses of some autonomous areas have been successful is in implementing regulations regarding custom. Despite the relative inactivity of the people's congresses of ARs, at the level of autonomous prefectures and autonomous counties the people's congresses have, over the last sixty years, issued numerous autonomous regulations and individual regulations, some of which are based on custom. There are no comprehensive official statistics of sub-AR autonomous regulations and individual regulations publicly available, but Chinese scholars estimate that as of 2015 there are approximately 139 autonomous regulations, 658 individual regulations, and 74 flexible or supplementary regulations issued at the sub-AR level.[56] Many of these protect minority rights in the areas of language and rules governing social relationships, especially marriage.

In assessing PRC law's treatment of ethnic-minority customary law, a distinction must be made between those groups who have resisted assimilation and those who have undergone a greater degree of Hanification. Certain ethnic minority groups who have lived in greater proximity to Han, such as the Yao, Miao, and Tai, primarily in southeastern China, have had greater success in implementing custom-compliant regulations.[57] These groups have codified their legal orders at the lowest level as "popular agreements of village rules" (*cungui minyue*) that may be enforced by basic people's courts (Gao 2003: 307–8; Ou 2006). Those ethnic minorities who practice religions with textual and institutional traditions transcending the boundaries of modern nation-states and belonging to communities that similarly cross national boundaries, such as Tibetans, Muslims, and Mongolians, have been more resistant to both Han pressures and state policy.[58] Political control is much tighter in these areas than in southeastern China. There are exceptions to the rule that religious law is not recognized under PRC law. In parts of Amdo, Tibet, for example, basic people's courts have also been known to look to "Tibetan customary law" in judicial decision making.[59] PRC governance over Muslim customary

---

[56] These figures are from Chinese scholars who work on ethnic policy but who wish to remain anonymous. The figures are generally on track with statistics from prior years. For instance, Sautman (2012: 151) has 135 autonomous regulations, 474 individual regulations, and 70 flexible or supplementary regulations. An official count has 133 autonomous regulations, 384 individual regulations, and 68 flexible or supplementary regulations. For an incomplete database of such regulations, see State Ethnic Affairs Commission (2011).

[57] On the study of the Zhuang under "ethnic autonomy," see Kaup (2000, 2003).

[58] For studies on specific minority groups, see Bovingdon (2002), Bulag (2002), Gladney (2004b), and Yu (2011). For broader overviews, see Mackerras (2003) and Han (2013).

[59] Judges in people's courts may consider "Tibetan customary law" in fact finding. However, the court cites "normative facts" (*guifan shishi*) as the legal basis for customary law.

law is the outlier in this regard. Muslim minorities in the Northwest have had little success in codifying shariʿa through lawmaking in autonomous areas or in having shariʿa enforced in people's courts. As a result, the people's congresses of many ARs are in legislative doldrums. Although two of the five autonomous regions, Xinjiang (est. 1955) and Ningxia (est. 1958), are home to significant Muslim populations, they have limited capacity to enact laws in accordance with Islamic law.

Similarly, sub-AR autonomous areas that have been established for Muslim minority communities and that have been particularly difficult to rule, such as Linxia Hui Autonomous Prefecture (see Chapter 2), also have restricted lawmaking capacity. Generally, people's courts in nominally Hui autonomous areas in Gansu and Qinghai are not empowered to enforce the customary law of Hui. Ethnic autonomy's particular "cunning of recognition" (Povinelli 2002) is to recognize customs in legal text but not in legislative practice.[60] That is, the Party-State accords recognition to Hui customary law within the institutional framework of ethnic autonomy, but building institutions to accord recognition is not the same as building institutions that represent communities *"claiming, demanding, or asking"* (Twining 2012: 119, original emphasis) for recognition of their own interests by the state. As happened elsewhere in the encounter between the nation-state and Islamic law, in China the imposition of administrative and legal structures over the nation-state has served to dissociate Islamic law, as customary law, from the global *umma* of Muslims.

The incorporation of the Northwest into the modern Chinese nation-state did not cause the disintegration of Islamic law, however. The Communists used Islamic legal traditions to validate their own assumption of power and monopoly on lawmaking. Consistent with its own "internal Orientalism" (Schein 1997), the state's degradation of Islamic law institutions justified liberation and the establishment of socialism as a new theology. This process was clear to me when I visited a *qadihana* ("house of the qadi"), one of the few that survive in Xinjiang, located in the Kuqa Qingzhen Grand Mosque. Built in 1559 in the oasis city Kuqa, the mosque was a major center of pilgrimage, prayer, and learning. Its

---

[60] According to a study conducted by Gao Qicai (2013), of the 239 laws passed as of 2012, at least 24 contain articles that touch upon customary law.

reputation further stemmed from the court that handled cases from throughout Xinjiang.

I visited the mosque in the winter of 2010. It contains a large cupola for a muezzin (the person who calls Muslims to prayer), a sprawling prayer hall, a courtyard with surveillance cameras, and, in the southeast corner of the complex, the *qadihana*. Marking what is currently a cultural heritage protection site, outside the *qadihana* hangs a small sign that says "old location of a religious court" in Uyghur and Chinese. Inside is another small courtyard with a door that leads into a souvenir shop and, off to the right, the actual courtroom. There is a raised platform that is most likely where the qadi sat. On the south wall, the one I face as I walk in, is a large window, the main source of light in the room, and two photos. The one to the right is of Ahmad Grand Mulla Hajji. He was a great imam, the local Uyghurs say, and a qadi. The last qadi to hold power before the Communists took control in 1949, he died in 1991. The photo to the left is of his predecessor, named Yimid Qazi (qadi) Hajji, who died before 1949. The light from the window illuminates a short table on the raised platform displaying four whips (U. *dahray*), each made of blackened leather. As one worshipper told me, the qadis used the two thinner ones to punish minor offenses and the heavier ones for major offenses. Outside the courtroom, the room that sells souvenirs is laden with colorful Xinjiang tourism books, postcards, and jewelry—and whips.

The conspicuous display of the whips (see Figure 1.2) evidences the Party-State's reinterpretation of Islamic law and Xinjiang history. Islamic law is reduced to harsh, corporal punishment and, by implication, the qadi as well as the *khwāja* (religious leaders) above him were the dispensers of a brutish and physical justice. Indeed, Kuqa residents admit that the whips were used to punish transgressors, that thieves had their hands cut off and adulterers their penises, and in fact the death penalty was also enforced by the qadi.[61] However, the qadi also addressed civil law matters, including issues of family law, inheritance, and property, but there is no evidence remaining of these aspects of justice.

Like state displays of "ethnic tourism" in southern China, including orchestrated performances of song and dance whereby the Han majority consumes ethnicity as something exotic, a foil to the modernity-bearing Han, the display of the whips and the signage at Kuqa Qingzhen Grand Mosque

---

[61] The *Authentic Records of the Muslim Religion in the Qing Dynasty* (*Qing Muzong shilu*) states that between the Xianfeng and Tongzhi periods (i.e., 1850 to 1874), the Qing prohibited Uyghur qadis from adjudicating crimes (Yuan and Gao 2001: 38).

Figure 1.2 One of the few remaining *qadihanas* in China, located in Kuqa, Xinjiang. Note the whips prominently displayed in the middle

Source: the author

demonstrates a set of oppositional symbols. As one of the few vestiges of an Islamic legal institution in the PRC, the *qadihana* symbolizes a harsh legal other to the enlightened order of secular state law. The contrast between Islamic law as physical brutality and patriarchal oppression, on the one hand, and proportionate force in punishment and gender equality under state law, on the other hand, is metonymized in social life in Xinjiang, where women are discouraged from wearing veils in public buildings. The internal legal other of Islamic law belies Chinese law's own past, however. Imperial Chinese law also featured instruments of torture as corporal punishment. The two whips, one thin, one thick, are reminiscent of the light and heavy bamboo sticks (*chi* and *chang*, respectively) used in corporal punishment by the Qing (Bodde and Morris 1967: 77, 80)[62] and that were reinstated by Yuan Shikai in 1914 (Dikötter 2002: 86–87). While the early Communist period witnessed a great deal of discourse that labeled Qing law anti-modern, contemporary visitors to Kuqa can see similar public displays describing Uyghur practices as such.

---

[62] Margery Wolf (1972) observed that corporal punishment was used by mothers in the home in rural Taiwan.

In addition to the Uyghur *qadihana*, Communists have also appropriated property law to reinterpret the legacy of Islamic law in China. CCP archives in Lanzhou, for example, are filled with records of landholdings by Hui mosques and Sufi tomb complexes, the latter held in the name of a shaykh (master).[63] Property relations, especially between the Sufi shaykh and his followers, were interpreted through Marxist property theory to demonstrate the exploitative nature of Sufism. The Party presents itself as liberating subjugated ethnics from their own oppressive law.

REFORM, RELIGION, AND THE RETURN OF THE REPRESSED

Religious belief versus faith in the Party has been one of the defining oppositions of modern Chinese history. The nadir of religious policy over the last sixty years was the Cultural Revolution (1966–1976), a tragedy for Muslim minorities. During the Tenth Plenary Session of the Eighth Central Committee of the Party, Mao Zedong ushered in a "new stage in the socialist revolution" by declaring: "To overthrow a political power [i.e., the bourgeoisie], it is always necessary first of all to create public opinion, to do work in the ideological sphere" (Chai 1972: 405). According to one report, in 1966 "some 30 million youthful Red Guards marched and counter-marched across the face of Communist China, repeating with religious fervor quotations from Mao Zedong" (Chai 1972: 405). As part of the attack on the "four olds"—old ideas, old culture, old customs, and old habits—impassioned Red Guards, some of whom were Muslim, attacked Islamic institutions. The Red Guards denounced imams and Sufi shaykhs and prosecuted them in sham trials. Many were forced to perform hard labor. Some were killed. Sufi tombs were desecrated, and wood from mosques was torn down and consumed in bonfires. Qur'ans and scripture were likewise burned. Officials confiscated land designated as pious endowments by Muslim communities. Frenzied conviction in the Party and its utopian vision marked the point of greatest violence against alternative belief systems, including Islam.

---

[63] The primary sources from the Gansu Provincial Archives include the Report on Solving Linxia City's Mosque and Sufi Complex Land Problem (Linxia Prefecture Committee United Front Work Department 1952) and the Report Communicated in the Spirit of the Meeting by the Provincial Party Committee United Front Work Department on the Mosque and Tomb-Complex Land Problem and Ethnic-Religious Personnel Placement Problem (United Front Work Department of the Wudou Prefectural CCP 1956).

The reform period beginning in 1978 marks a new stage in the relationship between socialism as a belief and Islam. Instead of overtly opposing Islam, the Party-State has tried to craft it in accordance with Chinese socialism and nationalism. Liberalization of religious policy has allowed for an unprecedented resurgence in popular and official religions.[64] In trying to discursively and institutionally manage Islam and its law, the Party-State's policies have alternated relaxation and tightening and have also varied according to Muslims' location, ethnicity, and doctrinal affiliation. More recently and cutting across policy differentiation at the local level, events in Xinjiang since the 2009 riots have set the tone for policy toward Muslims generally.

Liberalization of religious policy has enabled an Islamic revival. Following the destructive decade of the Cultural Revolution, mosques and Sufi tombs have been rebuilt and registered, madrasas have been filled with students learning Arabic and Persian, economic networks again flourish both within the Northwest and between Muslim minorities in China and coreligionists abroad, and more Muslims perform the annual hajj. In spite of these aspects of revival, however, the Party-State has, for the most part, not altered course on refusing to recognize Islamic law. At the discursive level, despite the State Council's adoption of *Yisilanjiao* as the Chinese translation of Islam to replace *Huijiao* as early as 1956 (Goossaert and Palmer 2011: 157), only recently have PRC scholars begun writing about Islamic law (Yisilanjiaofa) (Ha 2007)—and even then, such treatments mostly concern Islamic law outside of China (Gao 2004; Ma Mingxian 2011).[65] Similarly, whereas scholars have drawn attention to China's "legislative explosion" (Lubman 1999: 173), people's congresses in autonomous regions remain mostly underused, if not inactive.

Despite the Party-State's maintenance of its monopoly on defining law, there has been a quiet new awareness among Muslim minorities of Islamic law in everyday life, which is a result not just of state policy but also of the rebirth of the *minjian*. One cause of this consciousness is renewed engagement with foreign Muslims. While Uyghur militants' training in Afghanistan has dominated state-controlled media, Muslim minorities are involved in a number of economic, spiritual, and intellectual exchanges

---

[64] For a nonexclusive selection of the literature on China's religious revival, see Xie (2006), Palmer (2007), Lagerwey (2010), Chau (2011), Madsen (2011), Yang Fenggang (2011), Jansen, Klein, and Meyer (2014), and Katz (2014).

[65] Recently, Ding Shiren (2014) of Lanzhou University has begun writing about Islamic law in China.

with Muslims abroad. Evidence of such transnational networks are everywhere, with Muslims performing the hajj, studying abroad in Cairo and Amman, conducting Islamic finance delegations to Kuala Lumpur, and participating in Sufi pilgrimages to Sirhind.

One of the great examples of exchange is the city of Yiwu in Zhejiang Province. In Yiwu, a gem in China's export-driven economy, businessmen from Pakistan, Sudan, Egypt, Indonesia, and elsewhere purchase clocks, stationery, sandals, religious paraphernalia, stuffed animals, cell phones, picture frames, and sex toys for resale in their home countries. These foreign Muslims are one segment of a network of vendors, business trade companies, translators, middlemen, transporters, and distributors that link Yiwu, "the world's largest small commodities market" (Wu 2010), to consumers from Marrakech to Jayapura in what some commentators have called the "New Silk Road" (Ho Wai-Yip 2013; Simpfendorfer 2009).

The people's government of Ningxia, a small diamond-shaped region in central China, built a halal food industrial zone in 2003 and three years later established trade relations with Saudi Arabia, Kuwait, the United Arab Emirates, Egypt, and Malaysia, among other Muslim countries. Since 2008, Ningxia halal food production has benefited from US$6.28 million in foreign investment. In 2009 halal food production enterprises had realized a total value in output of RMB 20 billion. Since 2010, thirty-seven halal food production enterprises have received approval and special loans from the finance administration.[66] As a result of these transnational networks, Muslim minorities in China are relearning the fundamentals of Islamic law in their transactional and intimate lives.

The Party-State's role in China's Islamic reawakening, of which Islamic legal consciousness is a part, proceeds from two tensions. First, the Party-State supports those ties abroad and growing foreign Muslim communities within China that facilitate China's economic development and national interests, but it rejects domestic or transnational Muslim networks that do not. Following China's reform and opening, domestic affairs have increasingly affected international relations, and vice versa. Positive relations with its own Muslim minorities are seen as part and parcel of its ties to oil-rich states, including Saudi Arabia, Iran, and Sudan (Kemp 2012; Olimat 2012). While human rights (often understood in their Western guises) may not be a product of increasing exchange between China and the Middle East, Islamic legal consciousness, which

---

[66] Data obtained from the Ningxia Academy of Social Sciences, on file with the author.

carries its own notions of rights, has grown along with such ties. Yet the Party-State impedes those nascent networks that it perceives as not supporting its interests. Education, travel abroad, and pilgrimage have been points of contention between Muslims and the government, and Muslim minorities have adopted a number of strategies to circumvent blockades on their cross-border mobility, including obtaining counterfeit passports and making the hajj through other countries' quotas.

A second tension characterizing the Party-State's intervention in Islamic law revival is the bifurcation between the Party-State's nonrecognition of Islamic law and its reliance upon clerics, Sufi shaykhs, and madrasa teachers. These religious leaders, almost all male in the patriarchal Northwest, are incorporated by the state into the lowest rungs of its bureaucracy for purposes of social control in Muslim communities. The Party-State law's approach to Islamic law diverges from its integration of such elite. For instance, whereas the state may nullify any legal basis for Islamic law, it depends for pragmatic purposes on Hui elite. Furthermore, relationships between officials and Hui elite at the local level may not reflect central policy making. The modern history of Islamic law in China hence complicates anthropological theories of secularism (Asad 2003; Mahmood 2006; Agrama 2012). The Chinese state's relationship with Islam draws attention to the different—and potentially contradictory—ways the state mobilizes the authority of law as opposed to that of social and political relationships.

While state law's relationship with Islamic law turns on recognition/nonrecognition, the modern state's relationship with Hui elite hinges on anxious collaborations. Such collaborations shift between co-optation and competition. From the vantage of the state, the leadership of Hui elite must be routinized and contained. The ideological imperatives of the Party have not fully gone away, however. Scholars have noted that the Party has appropriated many of the symbols of religion, including sacred texts, charismatic authority, pilgrimage sites, ritual transformation, and utopianism (formerly based on Marxism-Leninism, but in postsocialist China, defined as urbanism-consumerism). Similar to the Nationalist Party, the Communist Party is an "affective regime," engaged in "ritual competition" with religious faiths (Nedostup 2009: 227–29). In this approach, the Party-State admits that it cannot fully co-opt a religion and so competes with it at the local and national level.

Goossaert and Palmer (2011: 168) call this process that leads to political religiosity the "sacralization of the state." Their analysis shares affinities with Carl Schmitt's ([1922] 2005) "political theology." Talal Asad (2003: 189), on the other hand, cautions that such analogizing assumes essential aspects of religion. My approach differs from approaches to religion in China, political theology, and the anthropology of secularism by emphasizing that sacralization occurs not on the "State" side of the hyphenated Party-State but rather in service to the Party. The Party is a community of believers, yet one that has largely lost its faith, a community that operationalizes state law and policy to maintain order. In the reform era, the tenets of Marxism-Leninism have fallen away in favor of rampant marketization and material acquisition. Hui in most parts of the Northwest have been mainly excluded from this process. In these areas, the Party looks to Islam for its own legitimization. Power and consent are vectors of the "strange bedfellows" relationship between Islam and Chinese socialism in the Northwest.

ISLAM IN THE IMAGE OF THE PARTY

As part of its entry into the global community of nation-states and commitments to domestic and international law, the PRC in the reform period has accorded a limited "freedom of religion" to Muslims. While there is no specific legislation on religion, article 36 of the 1982 Constitution and article 11 of the 1984 Law of the PRC on Regional Ethnic Autonomy guarantee "freedom of religion."[67] The meaning of freedom of religion, however, is not articulated in state law but in a CCP policy document. *The Basic Viewpoint and Policy on the Religious Question during Our Country's Socialist Period* (commonly called "Document No. 19") provides a definition of freedom of religion that guides Party work to this day. Document No. 19 clarifies that freedom of religion means not only freedom to believe but also freedom not to believe. Furthermore, as Donald E. MacInnis (1989: 15) writes in his study of religious policy, "The crux of the policy of freedom of religious belief is to make the question of religious belief a private matter, one of individual free choice for citizens." PRC state law draws a line between private and public, and between

---

[67] See also arts. 1 and 2 of the Religious Affairs Regulations (*Zongjiao shiwu tiaoli*), passed by the State Council on June 7, 2004, amended March 1, 2005. Moreover, PRC Criminal Law makes it illegal for cadres to "deprive citizens of the freedom of religious belief and violate the beliefs and customs of ethnic minorities." See the PRC Criminal Law (*Zhonghua renmin gongheguo xingfa*), passed by the Second Session of the Fifth NPC on July 1, 1979, revised July 1, 2011, art. 251.

79

behavior that can be pursued since birth and that which can be pursued only in adulthood. As with French *laïcité* or Turkish secularism, Chinese freedom of religion holds that Islam, to be acceptable, can only be a private adult matter.

While state law provides a veneer of limited religious freedom, it is really Party policy that gives shape to state-sanctioned Islam on the ground. Party policy often takes the form of what is colloquially referred to as "red-headed documents" (*hongtou wenjian*), policy statements and directives from governmental or Party units so named because of the red lettering used at the top of the document. Ethnic and religious affairs bureaus as well as public security organs produce such documents, which are distributed to mosques, madrasas, or other Islamic institutions for compliance. "Red-headed documents" are a supplementary source of authority that can be more responsive to social change or conflict than can state law.

One of the chief mechanisms of crafting an Islam consonant with Chinese socialism has been the Party-State's monopoly on the public sphere. By dominating the public sphere in which religious values may be discussed, proselytized, acquired, or assessed, the Party-State has crafted its own version of Islam. Specifically, it has done so by appropriating the very terms through which religious discourse is communicated. Law has been a central site for the Party-State's redefinition of Islam. As described above, the production of Islamic law as customary law was bound up in the construction of Chinese Muslims as Hui. Moreover, by classifying Islamic law as custom, state law maintained its monopoly on the power of calling groups, believers, citizens, or subjects into being. Thus, by fiat of statutory law and religious regulations, clerics are not 'ulama', or scholars, but, rather, "religious personnel" (*zongjiao renshi*). Formally, mosques are "religious activity areas" (*zongjiao hudong changsuo*), and communities of believers are known as "religious social organizations" (*zongjiao shehui tuanti*). Part of the history of Islamic law in China is the erasure of the terms through which such a history can be written. State law and religious regulations act on and through "religious personnel," "religious activity areas," and "religious social organizations" to define state-approved Islamic orthodoxy. A number of ethnic and religious bureaus as well as Party organs license individuals and register all mosques, Sufi tombs, and Muslim organizations. The creation of registers and archives assists the state in monitoring Muslim populations.

SECULARIZING SHARI'A

There are limits, however, to efforts of selectively transforming the *minjian* into the official, as illustrated by the short history of "official" Islamic law in reform-era China. A centerpiece of the Party-State's definition of Islam and of its experiments to interpret Islamic law in accordance with Party principles is the China Islamic Association (Zhongguo Yisilanjiao Xiehui, or Yi-Xie). The Yi-Xie is introduced in its literature as the "patriotic religious group of all China's Muslim ethnicities." The National Representative Assembly of the Yi-Xie, the highest organ within the Yi-Xie, first met in Beijing on May 9, 1953, and passed the General Regulations of the Yi-Xie,[68] which laid out the aims of the association, including, inter alia, implementing Party-State religious policies, developing the fundamental spirit and great traditions of Islam, representing the lawful rights of all Muslims, training Islamic talent, producing scholarship, providing consultation in developing new laws and regulations, and developing Islamic curricula for the ten Islamic Scriptural Institutes (state-approved madrasas). The Yi-Xie is headquartered in Beijing's Muslim quarter, known as Oxen Street.

The Yi-Xie coordinates relations between the Party, the Muslim masses, and overseas Muslims. To facilitate its domestic mission, the association operates at all administrative levels. Its branch offices in the Northwest—such as the Ningxia Islamic Association (or "Ningxia Yi-Xie"), the Linxia Prefectural Yi-Xie, and the Linxia City Yi-Xie—are housed in offices attached to influential mosques. Yi-Xies at the autonomous region, prefectural, county, or city levels are usually administered under religious affairs bureaus (and the Party organs behind them) at the same administrative level. Thus, their funding and resources come from governments at the relevant administrative level rather than through the Yi-Xie in Beijing.

In terms of channeling funds from the oil-rich Gulf, the Yi-Xie has been prominent in shaping the PRC's international relations with Saudi organizations. For instance, the Yi-Xie established ties with the Muslim World League, a consortium of Islamic NGOs, funded by the Saudi government in the early 1980s (Allès, Chérif-Chebbi, and Halfon 2003: 17). Funding

---

[68] General Regulations of the Yi-Xie (*Zhongguo Yisilanjiao xiehui jianzhang*) passed May 11, 1953. In accordance with broader shifts in Party-State reform from the 1950s to the 1980s, the name of the governing rules was changed in the 1980s from the Soviet-sounding "general regulations" (*jianzhang*) to the more globally fashionable "constitution" (*zhangcheng*).

provided by the Islamic Development Bank, an affiliate of the Muslim World League, has been instrumental to the development of a number of state-backed Islamic institutions.

Although the Yi-Xie has been seen in the past as a mouthpiece of the Party-State and evidence of the state's mobilization of Islam as a tool of governance, its role in balancing the needs of the government and those of Muslim minorities is situation-dependent. The Party-State's approach to governing Islam, and the key role of the Yi-Xie, changed in 2000 and 2001, as a response primarily to domestic affairs but also to international events regarding the "War on Terror." By the late 1990s violence between Uyghurs and Han Chinese in Xinjiang had increased. In 1999 there were a reported sixteen incidents of interethnic violence (Bovingdon 2002: 186–88). Battling the so-called three evil forces—religious extremism, splittism, and terrorism—has formed the basis of the government's policies toward the westernmost provinces. Following the 9/11 attacks in the United States, the state's depiction of violence in Xinjiang as terrorism enjoyed greater support, partly because the Bush administration in 2002 added the East Turkestan Islamic Movement to its list of outlawed terrorist organizations. Although turmoil in Xinjiang had long predated the People's Republic of China, after 9/11 any violence or anti-state behavior by Uyghurs in Xinjiang has been couched as "terrorism."

Beginning in 2001, policies toward Islam in China have thus focused on the Xinjiang problem.[69] But the policies also have an impact on Muslims outside that region, including Hui. Riots or anti-state attacks in Xinjiang have the effect of tightening public security controls over movement throughout the Northwest. Roadblocks are established, armed police patrol Muslim-heavy cities, and international travel, which depends on securing a passport in the PRC, becomes onerous.

Against the backdrop of political and academic discourses that continue to cast Islamic law as customary law, the Yi-Xie has stepped up its efforts to instill "patriotic education" in clerics through both formal instruction and state-sanctioned weekly prayer sermons. Furthermore, the Yi-Xie established a committee tasked with interpreting shariʿa in accordance with Party policy and state law. The Education Administration

---

[69] Scholarship on state policy in Xinjiang following 9/11 makes particular reference to the Shanghai Cooperation Organization (SCO). The SCO was founded in 2001 in Shanghai by its members, including China, Kazakhstan, Kyrgyzstan, Russia, Tajikistan, and Uzbekistan. The multilateral organization coordinates security, military, and economic affairs in the region and has consistently identified anti-terrorism as a unifying objective (Bovingdon 2002; Gladney 2004a; Rudelson and Jankowiak 2004).

Guidance Committee (EAGC), formed in 2001,[70] was conceived to be China's 'ulama', the most learned of China's clerics, who would advise the state. According to internal Yi-Xie memoranda, the EAGC was created to "actively guide innovative measures for the adaptation of Islam to socialist society." Significantly, the EAGC was to accomplish such harmonization through "correctly expounding the classical religious doctrine."[71]

The EAGC's project centers on the concept of "expounding the classics" (*jiejing*), or explaining shari'a. *Jiejing* appears to be a cognate for the Arabic term for methods of deriving law in the Islamic tradition. The EAGC can be seen as a postsocialist Chinese instantiation of a long line of attempts by political authorities, from the Ottoman Empire to post-independence Indonesia, to commandeer Islamic jurisprudence for purposes of rule (Feener 2007; Burak 2013, 2015). Indeed, in the contemporary post-9/11 period secular governments' construction of "official" Islam to counter radicalization of Muslim citizens and immigrants is not unique to China (see, e.g., Rascoff 2012).

An examination of the materials produced by the EAGC demonstrates that they are more propaganda than Chinese Islamic jurisprudence. The EAGC performs the work of exegesis mainly through two forms of media. The first one is familiar: the sermon. The EAGC has published some forty-six sermons in several edited volumes called *Collections of Newly Edited Wo'erzi Speeches* (Chen 2011: 13). These collections, of which some eight hundred thousand copies have been distributed to mosques throughout China, explain state interests through the Qur'an and the hadith (Chen 2011: 13–14). In particular, the sermons communicate such principles as "love state, love religion" (*aiguo aijiao*), "maintain ethnic unity" (*weihu minzu tuanti*), "social stability" (*shehui wending*), and "[state] law dignity and national unity" (*falü zunyan he guojia tongyi*). Applying Weber's ([1922] 1967) analysis of legal thought, members of the EAGC and clerics who use their sermons can be seen as exercising a substitutive substantive rational thinking. They explain Islam not necessarily through a set of principles expounded by the Prophet Muhammad but through Party propaganda.

For instance, one sermon, entitled "Islam Advocates Unity and Harmony" (*Yisilanjiao tichang tuanjie hemu*), begins with the favored

---

[70] The establishment of the EAGC, on April 23, 2001, predated the 9/11 attacks; however, the committee appears to have taken on greater significance following the Chinese government's response to perceived terrorist activity in Xinjiang.

[71] The source is internal Yi-Xie memoranda, on file with the author.

Qur'anic verse of the Yi-Xie that commands, "And hold fast, all together, by the Rope which Allah (stretches out for you), and be not divided among yourselves"[72] ("*Nimen dangquanti zhichi Zhenzhu de sheng-shuo, bu yao fenlie*"). The remainder of the sermon discursively echoes the theory of "harmonious society" (*hexie shehui*) by Hu Jintao, who was General Secretary of the CCP at the time of the EAGC project:

> From the above teachings derived from the classics, we can grasp that Islam advocates unity and opposes division. Unity is the virtue of us Muslims, it is the core of one family, one collective, one society, and the source of Muslims' strength. The early Muslims obeyed the commands of Allah and the teachings of the Prophet. They were of universal agreement in creating, in the history of humanity, the great Islamic civilization. With the lapse of time, we cannot fail to see that there are a few among us for whom the scriptures' call for unity and opposition to division has faded from memory.
>
> (Chen Guangyuan 2003: 90)

The sermon also recalls earlier Leninist techniques of the "mass line," which used persuasion, exhortation, and propaganda to create solidarity vis-à-vis class enemies (Lubman 1999: 42). Rather than use Maoist slogans to raise class consciousness or glorify the proletariat, the Yi-Xie sermons employ the language of Islam, as interpreted through the lens of social-ism, to elevate Islamic legal consciousness among Chinese Muslims and unite followers under the authority of the Party, which itself has under-gone significant transformation over the past sixty years (Li 2008). The Party's response to Islamic resurgence thus has not been to exclude Islam ideologically but to assimilate it.

In addition to sermons, the EAGC's "expounding of scriptures" also produces a body of what it deems "Islamic law," broadly defined. From 2001 to 2011, the EAGC produced some six collections of what it termed "fatwas," or legal opinions on specific matters. These so-called fatwas are published in the *Jiaowu zhidao tongxun* (EAGC communica-tions, hereinafter, *tongxun*). The *tongxun* address a range of issues, from defining jihad to proper dress for Muslims. Furthermore, the *tongxun* claim that the members of the EAGC consulted foreign sources in compiling the *tongxun*. For example, in 2003, when the severe acute res-piratory syndrome (SARS) epidemic spread through China, the EAGC consulted bodies of legal authorities in Muslim countries to gain insight on minimizing the spread of SARS, particularly with reference to legal

---

[72] Q. 3:103. In this book, I use the English translation of the Qur'an by Abdullah Yusuf Ali in *An English Interpretation of the Holy Qur-ān: Arabic Text and Translation* (1938).

regulations derived from *fiqh* regarding disposal of the remains of SARS victims (Chen 2011).

While the EAGC's sermon collections can be found in mosques throughout the Northwest, the *tongxun* have been "harmonized," to use the Chinese netizens' term for censorship. While the reason for the EAGC project's fate is unclear, it seems that the Bureau of Religious Affairs deemed the EAGC to have exceeded its mandate and terminated the project. Although the *tongxun* interpreted shariʿa in accordance with socialism, it is likely that the state deemed any circulation of *fiqh*-like texts as a potential challenge to its sovereignty. The jurisdictional conflicts between the Yi-Xie, a religious organization constituted under the Party, and the state reveal that the Party-State does not think with one mind. As a result, the Party-State's monopoly on the public sphere is incomplete, just as its imposition of state law over nonstate law or secular bureaucracy over religious hierarchies is also an unfinished process.

In summary, the meanings of "customary law" have shifted since the early twentieth century. Originally designated by Qing jurists and later Republican reformers as a basis for writing state law, customary law has been designated by the CCP as a non-law. What was once of the nation has become distinctively for the ethnic. At the same time, in accordance with the Party-State's attempt to conform Islam to its own image, attempts have been made to use Islamic law as a form of governmentality. "Hui customary law" and its derivative relationship with Islamic law provide a window, then, into the contradictions of the *minjian*. Hui customary law shows that the *minjian* and its relation to the state have been contingent on an array of factors, from international pressures to domestic strife. The *minjian* is defined by its exclusion from the universe of norms sanctioned by the state; yet it is artfully included into state governmentality as a kind of untapped resource in the guise of Islamic law. The *minjian*, that which could potentially undermine the official, can be made official, an object and tool of rule. This ambiguity is a defining feature of the *minjian*: who can use it and for what purposes. In the reform era, *minjian* Islamic practices, including legal ones, are reviving, not necessarily as opposed to the Party-State but in uncertain tandem with it.

2

LINXIA AT THE CROSSROADS

Linxia ... hao fuza le (Linxia ... is very complicated).

Hui elder from Lanzhou

BAFANG

The *adhān* blares out over the mosque's speaker systems, calling the faithful to the Friday prayer. The sound unfolds like a blanket over the Muslim quarter of Bafang (lit. "eight precincts"), in the southwest of Linxia. The voice stretches out to the Han Chinese section of the city, where it contends with the static of pop music, honking cars, and the errant firecracker. The calls radiate from the mosques' minarets one after another. The messages glorifying God are the same, but as their timing and direction are all different, the message loses its coherence. In Bafang, each mosque is the center of a community (Ar. *jamā'a*, Ch. *zhemate*, or *jiaofang*), and each community belongs to a teaching school or Sufi order. With each teaching school adhering to its own astronomical calculation for the call, concert becomes cacophony in China's Little Mecca.[1]

---

[1] Many Muslims in Linxia attribute the epithet to the journalist Fan Changjiang. Fan, however, never actually used the expression. The attribution comes from his *China's Northwest Corner* (*Zhongguo de xibei jiao*), in which he wrote:

> Hezhou is the holy land of China's Northwest. Of the famous personages of the Islam of China's Northwest, whether based on religion, military, or politics, most come from Hezhou. The city wall and moat are not large, and lie on the plains, not a strategic point. Hezhou's fame, however, reverberates through the eardrums of all ethnicities in the Northwest. When Hui hear Hezhou, they are very happy. This is their home. It is the center of their financial affairs, the concentration of their population, and the base of all movements (Fan [1937] 1991: 89).

Others, such as the editors of *Gansu Religion* (*Gansu zongjiao*) (1989), attribute the expression to the Tongzhi period (1862–1874) (Li 2006: 109). The earliest reference I have found is by David P. Ekvall, Christian missionary father to the famous Robert Ekvall (1898–1978), who was born in Minchow, Gansu, himself becoming a missionary and later a Chicago-trained

As I stand in the intersection of two lanes in the center of Bafang, the residents come out of their courtyard homes, ambling toward their mosque. The attendees are mostly male, although a few women congregate in the women's prayer halls that are found in some of Bafang's mosques. Most of the men are elders who have retired or who work part time in one of the shops along the periphery of the quarter.

The lanes resemble Beijing's *hutong* or Kashgar's *holta kucha*. They have developed organically without reference to an orthogonal urban plan. The walls, which muffle the sounds of the city beyond, extend several meters overhead, ensuring privacy for those who live in courtyard homes within. Behind the walls of the lanes, I hear Bafanghua, the local dialect of Bafang Hui,[2] a linguistic palimpsest of those traders, soldiers, and envoys who centuries before traveled to China over the Silk Road.

I walk north from the intersection through Bafang and find a walled courtyard tucked behind a series of tight turns. The courtyard is larger than most, at thirty-seven square meters. It has two-story buildings on all sides and smaller haphazard shacks in the center. A mastiff barks protectively over his bowl of sheep bones and grease. A thin layer of loess dust covers all surfaces. Bafang Hui call this residential compound Eighteen Courtyards, a reference to its large size. Despite its dilapidated appearance, it is, arguably, one of the most important historical sites in Linxia.

Eighteen Courtyards was the residence of Ma Tingxiang (1889–1930), grandson of Ma Zhan'ao (1830–1886), one of the "Hezhou Three Mas," warlords who ruled most of Northwest China during the decline of the Qing Dynasty and the transition from empire to nation. Beyond the size of Eighteen Courtyards, there is no sign of the opulence of Ma Tingxiang's family. Whereas most homes in Bafang have a plaque over the door proclaiming, in golden Arabic letters, *Allahu akbar* (God is great) alongside a government-administered *hexie jiating* (peaceful family) sign, here the doors are plain. Painted on the columns flanking the entrance of the main southern room are fading blue Chinese characters, a remnant of the People's Liberation Army (PLA). The ones still visible on the former residence of Ma Tingxiang, whose family fought for the Nationalist Army, read, "Dispute the

---

anthropologist. In an entry for the Christian and Missionary Alliance newsletter, dated December 21, 1908, the elder Ekvall writes with undisguised glee: "Hochow, the Mecca of Kansuh Moslems, is finally open to the Gospel!" (Ekvall 1908: 1).

[2] I reserve the term "Bafang Hui" for those Hui living within Bafang, and I use "Linxia Hui" for those who inhabit the larger city and surrounding countryside. Thus, Linxia Hui includes Bafang Hui.

lesson ... smash the stone-leaning conservatism." Positioned in the center of Bafang, Eighteen Courtyards is insulated by Bafang's mud-brick walls from the Han city beyond, whose noise pollution, high-rise construction, night-clubs, and bars nonetheless encroach upon the quarter.

Bafang is a physical representation of the Hui social field of Islamic law and ethics in Northwest China. Sally Falk Moore (1978: 57) defined the "semi-autonomous social field" not as an organization or commu-nity but as a domain with the capacity to generate its own rules and induce compliance to them. Bafang demonstrates that the Hui social field may also have communal and even material aspects. I understand the Hui social field broadly as Muslim communities and networks that are informed by the traditions of the teaching schools, and many of China's teaching schools have their base in Bafang, in its mosques and tightly packed neighborhoods. PRC state law and policy have, since the 1950s, tried to influence or eradicate the social fields of teaching schools centered here.

In this chapter, I provide a history of Linxia to illustrate the formation of the Hui social field and the working of plural law, including Islamic law, in Northwest China. Eighteen Courtyards, with its brick, stone, alu-minum, and graffiti, encapsulates the many layers of Linxia's history. Specifically, Eighteen Courtyards illustrates the making of China's Little Mecca as a market town on the historic Silk Road that functioned as the base for revivalist strains of Islam. It was the birthplace of the Ma family warlords and the anti-Qing rebellions. Bafang has also been a test case for Communist rule, and finally, it has challenged the Party-State's economic reform. The influences that have shaped Linxia have similarly formed its cultures of law.

The teaching schools, the source of Bafang's *adhān* (call to prayer) med-ley, have sought to popularize their interpretation of Islamic law and ethics as orthodoxy in the Northwest. Views among teaching schools nat-urally differ as to which practices constitute correct law. Teaching schools' efforts to define their piety and authenticity have not necessarily led to their recognition of that right among others. In other words, their drive to "enforce" their law in the field of intra-Muslim relations often leads to intolerance.[3]

---

[3] Against assumptions in certain strains of normative political theory, it is not apparent to me that most Hui "greatly value autonomy in others," to quote one philosopher (Pendlebury 2004: 45). At the same time, Hui may espouse pan-Hui (albeit rarely Hui-Uyghur) commonality and solidarity.

With the arrival of the Communists, what was imposed on Linxia's internally contested and heterogeneous Islam was not only secular law but also the very distinction between state and nonstate law itself. Thereafter, Islamic law was "Hui customary law," and yet the history of Linxia demonstrates how the local Party-State and Muslim authorities came to rely on each other as the Party-State had to grapple with the meaning of Islamic law. One consequence of this is that the Party-State, as secularizing agent, itself attained a sectarian presence, as one doctrinal group among others trying to define Islam in China. The imposition of law, however, is never a fait accompli (Burman and Harrell-Bond 1979). Rather, the Communists' construction of a legal system and administrative bureaucracy over the internal system of management and control among Linxia's mosques has resulted in a set of triangular relationships between teaching schools and the Party-State. Hui teaching schools make claims for their authenticity not only through and against other teaching schools but also through and against the Party-State. The experience of Hui shows that it is at the points of negotiation, subterfuge, evasion, collaboration, and disagreement—*minjian* practices—that the parameters of the Hui social field are continually redefined.

In what follows, I move out from Bafang, the Muslim quarter, to describe the multiethnic city of Linxia in which it is located. Space in Linxia is divided primarily by ethnicity and secondarily by teaching school. The selection of Linxia[4] as a prefectural capital in the socialist era has created an urban landscape of seemingly contradictory Muslim and Communist authorities that define the contours of the Hui social field. Next, I explain the historical development of this social field, with particular reference to the question of how Hui have managed a set of relationships vis-à-vis temporal rule. This section includes an overview of the teaching schools and their establishment in Linxia. Whereas previous studies have described the teaching schools (Gladney [1991] 1996; Lipman 1997), I emphasize their formation as jural communities in Linxia, which by the early twentieth century had emerged as one of the great centers of Islamic learning in China. In the subsequent two sections, I assess first the Communists' attempts to impose rule over the Muslim social field and then the impacts of reform and opening on Bafang Hui. The net effect of these historical

---

[4] Linxia is the name of the city, the prefecture of which the city is the capital, and a county that is southwest of the city and within the prefecture. As used in this book, Linxia refers to the city unless otherwise stated.

shifts has been both to suppress the emergence of the types of civil society institutions, familiar to Western audiences, that support autonomous action and to build on Hui modes of sociality, bargain, and compromise—the hallmarks of their practice of *minjian*.

LINXIA

Contradictions inhere in Linxia. In a country that is overwhelmingly Han Chinese, Linxia is a Muslim city—architecturally, aurally, and spiritually. It is both isolated from and peripheral to China's drive to urbanized modernity and yet central to the history of the Northwest region, and it remains connected to Muslim centers inside and outside China. In terms of material wealth and conspicuous consumption, Linxia pales in comparison with other Chinese cities, but for spiritual life, whether considered in terms of the number of Sufi pilgrimage sites or the level of daily mosque attendance, there are few places in China that rival Linxia. It is the capital of a prefectural autonomous region under the laws and regulations of the PRC and the leadership of the CCP, and yet everywhere Hui read the Qur'an for a host of reasons, including for its ethical and legal precepts. Linxia Muslims demonstrate a degree of unanimity in their idea of the ethical life (e.g., piety, industriousness, humility) vis-à-vis the majority and generally more urbanized Han Chinese. At the same time, Hui unanimity is internally marked by radical alterity in interpretations of doctrine and law.

To put Linxia in context, Gansu Province has a total population of 25.5 million people, with some 1.7 million Muslims, of whom 1.2 million are Hui (Ma Wenlong 2011: 34; Feng and Shi 2012: 69). Linxia Hui Autonomous Prefecture, of which Linxia is the capital city, is one of the densest Muslim prefectures in China in terms of Muslim population. It has 1.95 million people, of whom over half, or 1.1 million, are Muslims (Ding 2011: 25). Linxia's population is roughly half Muslim and half non-Muslim, although Linxia Han believe it is slightly majority Han, and Hui argue the opposite. Officially, as of 2010, the city's total population was 274,466, composed of 129,628 Han (47.23 percent), 119,648 Hui (43.59 percent), and a smaller number of non-Hui Muslim minorities, including Dongxiang, Salar, Bonan, and Uyghur, making Muslims a slight majority in Linxia (see Table 2.1).

The city is organized by ethnicity roughly into two spheres of activity, a legacy of Linxia's imperial past. The old imperial walls enclosed what residents call the "inner city." Today, this area is occupied mainly by Han. Although the city wall was razed in the 1950s, removing the physical boundary, Linxia

TABLE 2.1 Linxia City population by ethnic group

	Han	Hui	Dongxiang	Tuzu/Monguor	Tibetan	Bonan	Salar	Uyghur	Misc.	Total
Number	129,628	119,648	20,704	1,467	1,020	858	837	11	293	274,466
%	47.23	43.59	7.54	0.53	0.37	0.31	0.30	–	0.11	~100

Source: Feng and Shi (2012: 68-107).

residents have retained a division between inner city, or Han space, and "outer city," or Hui space. In contemporary Linxia, the inner city is where the supermarkets and shopping malls selling the latest in Euro-American fashion imitations are located. Bars, clubs, KTVs (karaoke bars), massage parlors, and Internet cafés also predominate in the inner city. This has also been the location for the government buildings for both the city and the prefectural governments (although the former was relocated to the east-ern suburbs in 2007). Streets are wide and paved, there are trash bins on every corner, and police officers at every intersection. Signs on restaurants read *dazhong*, meaning literally "the masses" but understood in Linxia to mean "of and for Han," the lexical antonym to *qingzhen* (lit. "clear and true," meaning halal), found on Hui restaurants in Bafang.

Hui dominate the outer city, or Bafang. Occupying a total area of 1.24 square kilometers to the immediate southwest of what used to be the south gate of the imperial wall, Bafang contains Hui mosques, homes, and madrasas. Many Hui decline to move to the inner city, citing the traffic, noise, scarcity of halal restaurants, and distance from mosques. Frequently, Hui denounce the moral quality of inhabitants in the inner city for drinking, dancing, gambling, online surfing, smoking, using her-oin, and other haram activities, such as soliciting prostitutes. Yet the boundaries between Han inner city and Hui Bafang are simultaneously affirmed and transgressed in the course of the everyday. The inner city's Internet cafés are filled at night with Hui youths (boys and girls), and middle-aged Hui men surreptitiously patronize its bars and brothels (minus white skullcap and thereby passing as Han). Likewise, many halal restaurants in Bafang are frequented by Han and Tibetans, who are major non-Muslim consumers of *qingzhen* food.

Hui residential patterns have widened around the city follow-ing the construction of more mosques and the general urban sprawl. Nevertheless, Bafang remains the core of the Muslim quarter. As of 2010, Bafang had a total of 4,507 households, or 14,384 people according to the statistics of the General Survey of Bafang Neighborhood.[5] Official population statistics are based on three people per household, which is most likely an underestimate. Most households I visited had at least four if not five or more individuals. Ninety-eight percent of the households are Hui. There are twenty-seven mosques in Bafang: eleven Gedimu, eleven

---

[5] Official statistics also distinguish between permanent residents and the "floating population." The statistics as of 2010 are 2,216 permanent homes, or 8,936 people, and 1,060 people for the floating population. These figures, however, do not add up to the total of 14,384.

Yihewani, four Salafi, and one Xidaotang. Outside Bafang, but within the environs of the city, there are another seven mosques. Additionally, a number of Khufiyya tomb complexes (*gongbei*) are located on the western outskirts of Bafang. Farther north is the Qadiriyya cluster of tombs centered on the Grand Tomb complex. Although the tombs were initially outside the city limits, the modern city has spread to include them.[6] Linxia, in short, presents one of the densest and most doctrinally diverse Muslim communities in East Asia (see Figure 2.1).

To describe the historical formation of Linxia Muslims' social field, I draw upon the official local gazetteers (*difangzhi*);[7] "literature and historical materials" (*wenshi ziliao*);[8] local histories composed by mosques and Sufi orders;[9] a growing body of secondary literature, much of it produced by Muslim scholars from Linxia; accounts from early twentieth-century Christian missionaries; and interviews with Linxia Muslims and non-Muslims. I do not use these sources uncritically and, at the outset, foreground the multiple layers of biases, political and doctrinal, that infuse historical accounts in Linxia to this day. Disputes over history are part of the production of Linxia historiography.

THE MAKING OF "CHINA'S LITTLE MECCA"

Tea and horses

For most of its history, Linxia has been a commercial hub known as a civilizational crossroads vital to trade throughout the Northwest rather

---

[6] According to official statistics, for the administrative unit of Linxia City, which is 88 square kilometers, there are 122 "Islamic areas," including 98 mosques and 24 Sufi tombs and cloisters (Linxia City Chronicles Committee 2011: 729).

[7] The primary historical sources for Linxia in imperial and Republican times are five gazetteers that were written before the Communist period. These are the *Hezhou Annals in the Period of the Jiajing Emperor* (Jiajing Hezhou zhi) (1546, four volumes), *Hezhou Annals in the Period of the Kangxi Emperor* (Kangxi Hezhou zhi) (1687, two volumes), *Hezhou Annals in the Period of the Kangxi Emperor* (Kangxi Hezhou zhi) (1707, six volumes), *The Continuous Manuscript of the Hezhou Annals* (Hezhou xuzhigao) (1909, six volumes), and the *Continuously Revised Leading River County Annals* (Xuxiu daohe xianzhi) (1931, eight volumes). Additionally, upon the founding of the PRC, the local government produced the "modern" equivalent in the *Linxia Hui Autonomous Prefecture Gazetteers* (Linxia Huizu zizhizhou zhi), of which there are multiple versions organized by topic.

[8] The "literature and historical materials," also an official source, consists of short monographs compiled by CCP committees under relevant administrative levels of government. For Linxia, the series was produced at the level of the Linxia Hui Autonomous Prefecture. The series, consisting of approximately a dozen books, was begun in the mid-1980s.

[9] During my fieldwork from 2009 to 2012, many of the mosques and Sufi tomb complexes were in the process of either writing their local history or had already finished doing so. Such unofficial sources that have not undergone the publication censorship present nonstate versions of local history.

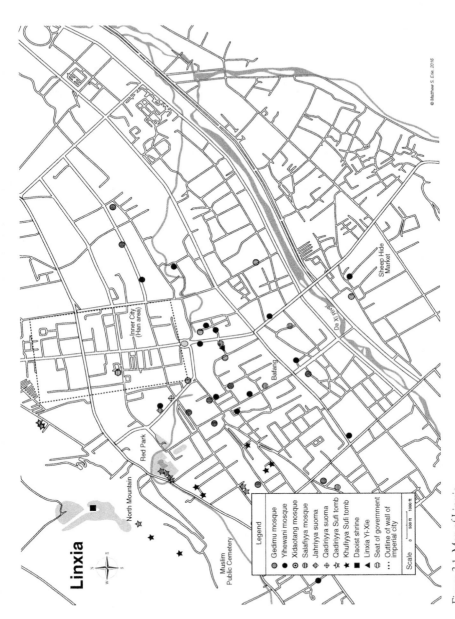

Figure 2.1 Map of Linxia

Source: the author

than as a seat of administration. Linxia lies at the intersection of the great culture zones of China: the Han Chinese of the Sichuan Basin to the southeast, the Mongolians of the Gobi Desert to the northeast, the Turkic Muslims in the Tarim Basin beyond the Altun Mountains to the north-west, and the Tibetans of the Tibetan Plateau to the southwest. Each of these groups has left its trace in Linxia's history, religion, ethnic compos-ition, language, and law. The earliest inhabitants of the area and their ancestors, proto-Tibetans, referred to in the Chinese dynastic histories as Tufan, came to the fertile valley as a resting station between large monas-tic centers in Labrang and Tsod (Ch. Hezuo) and Lanzhou, 140 kilom-eters to the north. While Muslim minorities dominate the area around Linxia today, historically it was mainly Tibetans who inhabited the region.

Linxia rests in an oblong valley that follows the Da Xia River east to west. This location gives Linxia its traditional name, Hezhou, which means "sand-bar."[10] The city has grown along the east-west axis and is bordered to its north by North Mountain, a loess plateau that rises high above the city, and to its south by a series of hills. The valley marks the southern rim of a maze of deeply eroded loess escarpments that stretch to Lanzhou (see Figure 2.2).

Due to its location between the Qinghai-Tibet plateau and the loess pla-teau formed by the Yellow River, which stretches eastward through central Gansu, for over a millennium Linxia has been a natural thoroughfare for commerce. It served as a commercial center for goods exchanged from Chengdu, Xining, and Lhasa. In particular, trade with Tibet was conducted through Linxia and Lintan (previously Taozhou), 175 kilometers south of Linxia. The Tang sought to monopolize the trade routes through the Gansu corridor and capitalize on Silk Road profits by taxing goods (Yu 1967: 128). However, for most of the imperial period before the Ming, control over the area was tenuous. The local gazetteers are replete with accounts of rebel-lions, uprisings, brigands, and internecine attacks on the garrison, which was more a military outpost than an administered settlement.

Beginning in the Northern Song period (960–1127), and subject to greater state regularization in the Ming period (1368–1644), the tea-horse trade (*chama hushi*) also operated through Linxia and Lintan. Nomadic Tibetans coveted lowland teas from Sichuan and Shaanxi, while Han and Hui required horses for transportation and military campaigns that could withstand the high altitudes and harsh conditions of the Qinghai-Tibet

[10] Linxia has had several names in Chinese. The earliest was Baohan, then Hezhou beginning in the Sui Dynasty (589–618) and popularized during the Tang Dynasty, then Daohe ("headwater") County from 1913 to 1928, and finally Linxia ("next to the Xia River") County in 1928.

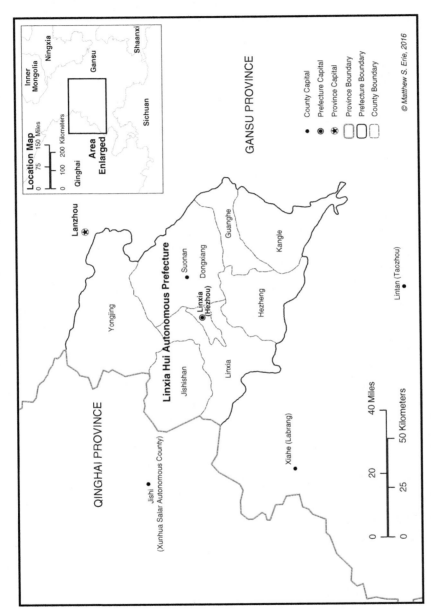

Figure 2.2 Map of southwestern Gansu Province

Source: the author

plateau. As recorded in a document from the Southern Song Dynasty (1127–1279), "Silkworm tea always enters the markets of the Tibetans, and Hu horses come from a great distance" ("*Shucha zong ru zhu fanshi, huma chang cong wanli lai*")[11] (Ma 1994: 108). Linxia was also a base for privately owned trade-mule caravans, usually operated by Muslims, called "households-on-foot" (*jiaohu*); these caravans transported tea, wool, salt, sugar, grains, silks, handwoven cloth, medicines, and sheep hide and leather throughout Tibet, Yunnan, Sichuan, and the Northwest (Yan 2007: 15, 40, 55). Beginning in the seventeenth century, Linxia functioned as a clearinghouse for opium via routes originating from the south.

The historian Valerie Hansen has shown that the Silk Road was hardly a unitary highway from Beijing to Rome, but rather was composed of such regional markets. Communities exchanged goods locally along "a patchwork of drifting trails and unmarked footpaths" (Hansen 2012: 8). Nonetheless, it was through those trails and footpaths that, beginning with the Tang Dynasty, regional trade networks linked Linxia to the Northern Silk Road via the Hexi corridor to Central Asia. Linxia gained prominence along the Southern Silk Road, which led from Lanzhou through Linxia southward into Tibetan territory and farther into modern-day Yunnan Province, following the great river systems of Southeast Asia to India.

Given its position along the Southern Silk Road and its role in the tea-horse trade, Linxia, for most of its imperial history, was a central place embedded in an economic hierarchy (Skinner 1980: 3–4), above Tibetan towns like Tsod and Labrang and below the provincial capital and Silk Road gateway of Lanzhou. Linxia existed because of its prominence in the regional economy, establishing a benchmark for relative economic and political autonomy.

The Islamization of Linxia

During the Yuan and Ming periods, the imperial government used a variety of tactics to govern Linxia, although the Muslim communities that developed in Bafang during this period were for the most part self-regulating. After the Mongolian Khanate attacked Linxia in 1227, the Mongols adopted a pragmatic approach to rule over Gansu. It was under the Yuan that many Muslims from the Ilkhanate and Chagatai Khanate were forced to migrate east into China. In particular, two Muslim groups prominent along the eastern rim of the Qinghai-Tibet plateau, the

---

[11] The reference is from the text *Casual Notes on the Ability to Change One's Vegetarian Diet* (*Nenggai zhai manlu*). The character *Hu* means "non-Han peoples in the Northwest."

Dongxiang and the Bonan, trace their ethnogenesis to these movements. Much has been made of the Mongols' use of Muslim officials to rule over the Chinese.[12] However, in the borderland outpost of Linxia, the Mongols turned not to Muslims but to the Tibetans to continue their tradition of local rule (Franke 1994: 298–99; Ma 1994: 104). The Ming appear to have employed a variety of means of rule, including the "local chieftain" (tusi) system of indirect rule (Ma 1994: 104–5). These methods included sending troops to the outpost with forced labor, mainly consisting of convicted criminals from the east.

Most oral histories of Linxia residents confirm that their ancestors migrated to Linxia as forced labor. In the words of a Han man born in 1943:

> My ancestors came with the first Hanmin to Linxia during the Hongwu period of the Ming Dynasty. They came from Nanjing city ... During the Yuan Dynasty there was an effort to cultivate the area by settlement and use it as an outpost along the borderlands of the empire, facing Tibet, Xinjiang, and beyond. The earliest settlers were sent to cultivate the land ... The families that emigrated were all forced to do so. The first emperor of the Ming Dynasty, Zhu Yuanzhang, forced out the families of criminals. If one member of the family was a criminal, then the whole family was forced to move, in a policy called implicate nine generations of a family [zhulian jiuzu], and their lands were given to members of the family or officials.

A Hui farmer living in a Sufi village on the eastern outskirts of Linxia gives a similar account of the origin of his ancestors. He says, "My lineage 'Mu' arrived during the early eighteenth century. My ancestors were sent here from Beijing as punishment for their crimes." In fact, Muslims arrived in Linxia from many different locations over an expanse of time. They migrated from Xi'an, Shaanxi, and Nanjing, congregating in the area southwest of the city wall, since they were not allowed to live inside the gated city (see Figure 2.3).[13]

---

[12] For examples, see Rossabi (1981), Morgan (2007: 97–98), and Papas (2011: 267). As previously mentioned, the dominant view in Chinese historiography is that the Chinese Muslims known as Hui today or Huihui in the imperial period formed during the Yuan period from the in-migration of foreign Muslims (see, e.g., Bai [1957] 1992a).

[13] Linxia was not unique in its Hancheng Huiguan (Han in the city, Hui outside the gate) pattern. Xining, Yinchuan, Lanzhou, and other major cities in the Northwest all featured this pattern. Some Hui scholars I talked to in Beijing argue that Muslims chose to live outside the city gate, as it was more conducive to commerce and easy transport. Most eyewitness historical sources before the destruction of the walls in the 1950s state that the city excluded Hui. David Ekvall (1908: 2), for instance, wrote: "Some of the wealthy Moslems have palatial residences to the south suburb of the city, for none are allowed to live inside the wall of the city proper."

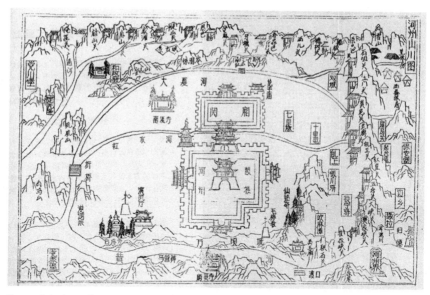

Figure 2.3 A rendering of a heavily fortified Linxia during the Kangxi period (1662–1723)

Source: Hezhou Annals in the Period of the Kangxi Emperor (1707) (reproduced as Wang Quanchen 2009)

Note the map is both inverted and reversed. Also, Bafang is not represented. It would be located in the upper-right-hand corner of the city wall on this map.

Bafang was historically organized around twelve mosques. The oldest, South Gate Grand Mosque, was built in 1273. With the construction of mosques, a conglomeration of small communities in Bafang grew into a distinctly Hui community. These homes, based on a courtyard design much like that of Eighteen Courtyards, were all within walking distance to a mosque. These courtyards interlocked to form neighborhoods around the mosques, which became the building blocks of the Hui social field.

While there was some concentration of Muslims in Linxia before the Yuan, it was not until Muslim soldiers in the Yuan and Ming armies were deployed by their commanders to open the land that Hui collected in larger numbers (Ma 1994: 111–12). According to the *Hezhou Annals in the Period of the Jiajing Emperor*, fifty thousand Muslims occupied Bafang by the sixteenth century (Ma Dongping 2010: 12). In addition to military deployment and forced migration, Muslim migrants came to Linxia because of its centrality as a market town.

For most of the imperial period, mosques were administered by the "three clerics" system consisting of the cleric (*ahong*) or imam, who led the prayer;

the *haituibu* (Ar. *khaṭīb*), who gave the Friday sermon; and the *mu'anjin* (muezzin), who called the faithful to prayer (Ma [1979] 2000: 90). Unlike the Salars, Mongols, or Uyghurs, for whom there is historical evidence for the institution of the qadi (judge), such an institution does not seem to have operated in the mosques of Bafang. Rather, the clerics were the Islamic law experts and mediated most interpersonal and family disputes, while the majority of criminal matters were handled by the local magistrate.

In the eighteenth century an alternative to the three-clerics system called "local rules and regulations" (*xiangyue*) emerged in Linxia's mosques (Wu and Chen 2006). This system consisted of elders in the mosque community who managed the mosque as a form of popular self-rule. There were struggles for power between the clerics and the elders (Lu 2010). The Qing government, as part of its attempt to gain tighter control over mosques, supported the elders in a way that was similar to local government's cultivation of gentry as subofficials. In this new system, the clerics were hired by the elders, who themselves were elected by members of the mosque community and who took care of all nonreligious matters in the mosque, including property management (Ma [1979] 2000: 90).

Throughout the Qing period, Muslim communities were thus largely self-regulating in a process by which leaders generated rules, only loosely in accordance with Islamic law, to organize the personal and social lives of their followers. Most disputes, except criminal matters, fell under the authority of clerics as proxy qadis. Although imperial walls physically separated inhabitants within Linxia from the magistrate, it appears that Muslims could seek him out for the resolution of conflicts, even those that turned on a question of Islamic law (Lipman 1999: 561). Such decisions would, however, apply Qing law. Thus, while the mosque communities that formed the Hui social field were self-governing, the late imperial period saw justice practiced across the dual tracks of an informal Muslim system and an official imperial one.

Islam, patronage, and warlords

Beginning in the late nineteenth century, as Western states colonized portions of the Middle East and East Asia, Linxia became more integrated into global currents of both imperial commerce and political Islam. These changes led to a collapse of the government in the Northwest, ending self-rule in the region. By the end of the nineteenth century, the wool trade had become so profitable that Tianjin-based firms from Russia, America, Britain, Japan, and Germany established trading networks throughout the Northwest, including Linxia, to export wool for foreign markets (Ma 1994: 171–72; Millward 1989). Many of the lineages of the Ma family warlords came to prominence by profiting from trade through Linxia. During China's civil war, the Ma warlords mobilized a number of shifting alliances and power centers, from Uyghur *begs* to Japanese imperialists, in order to consolidate their rule, resulting in conflict that caused the death of an untold number.

One of the sources of authority the Ma warlords invoked was Islam. Throughout the seventeenth century the practice of Islam was generally uniform, with Hui living in communities such as Bafang, concentrated around mosques. These Hui have come to be called the Gedimu (Ar. *qadīm*, "the ancient"), although the origins of this designation are unclear and its genesis may be more recent than its adherents profess. In their mythology, the Gedimu view themselves as the descendants of the original Arab and Persian merchants, missionaries, envoys, and soldiers who traveled to China via the Silk Road. The Gedimu pray five times a day, abstain from pork, fast during Ramadan, and study the Qur'an in madrasas attached to mosques, known as "scriptural hall education" (*jing-tang jiaoyu*). Prayer is led by a cleric who also reads the Friday sermon and mediates disputes in accordance with Islamic law.

The pattern of Hui communities growing around mosques changed in the early eighteenth century, when returning hajjis brought Sufi practices to Linxia. Ma Laichi (1681–1766) established the first great Sufi order, the Khufiyya Glory Mosque,[14] in 1734 in western Bafang after traveling to Mecca, where he studied the four Sunni schools of jurisprudence and several Sufi paths (Ar. *turuq*, sing. *tarīqa*). The official history of his tomb relates that Ma Laichi received "the light of teaching" (*zhuan guangzi*) from a twenty-fifth-generation descendant of the Prophet Muhammad, Khwaja Afaq (Ch. Haidaye Tonglahai).[15]

Another Linxia native, Ma Mingxin (1719–1781), is known for his opposition to Ma Laichi (Fletcher 1975; Bakhtyar 2000: 41–42). After studying in the Arabian peninsula and Central Asia for several years, Ma Mingxin returned to China and founded a Sufi order based on the Jahriyya. The order disagreed with Ma Laichi's order on the issues of hereditary

---

[14] While Sufi orders usually took the tomb of the founding saint as the base of their operations, their name could incorporate the title of a mosque.

[15] The title khwāja is Persian for "religious leader." Khwaja Afaq (d. 1693) was an ethnically Uyghur Sufi master and khan of Kashgaria in southern Xinjiang (where his tomb is located). He founded the Agtaghliq (Aq Tahgliq, or Afaqi), in English "White Mountain," sect of Naqshbandi Sufism (Fletcher 1977: 113; 1995: 9–16; Gladney [1991] 1996: 46–47; Millward 2007: 86–88).

succession, donations to the *murshid* (spiritual guide, pl. *murshidūn*), and silent *dhikr* (remembrance of God) (Lipman 1999; Atwill 2005b). The multigenerational dispute between the followers of Ma Laichi and Ma Mingxin—which spilled over into Xunhua and implicated the Salars as well, resulting in revenge killings—would have grave import for the formation of Sufism in China and its oppression by the Chinese state (Lipman 1984; Gladney 1987a; Israeli 2002d). The Khufiyya, known as the Old Teaching (Laojiao), were more successful in gaining support from the local government than the Jahriyya, or the New Teaching (Xinjiao). The latter were heavily persecuted for the first eight generations of their leadership and largely pushed out of Linxia, although a *suoma* (Ar. *ṣawmaʿa*), a cloister or monastery, survives in the place where Ma Mingxin lived in 1744.

A third Sufi order and one that has received far less scholarly attention is the Grand Tomb Complex order, established by Qi Jingyi (1656–1719). Like Ma Laichi, Qi Jingyi received the blessing of Khwaja Afaq but would become the *murīd* (pupil; pl. *murīdūn*) of Khwaja ʿAbd Allah (Ch. Huazhe Erbudonglaxi), a twenty-ninth-generation descendant of the Prophet who was born in Jeddah and traveled to Guangzhou in 1674. One version of the order's official history adapted from their foundational text, *The Roots of the Pure and True* (*Qingzhen genyuan*),[16] describes the first encounter between the teacher and students:

> [Khwaja ʿAbd Allah] arrived to Linxia, and after staying at the home of Muyoulin at Little South Gate [City Corner Mosque], and inquiring after Heiliali [the scriptural name of Qi Jingyi], he exhorted Muyoulin to make inquiries. Muyoulin attended hurriedly to notify City Corner Mosque, where Qi Jingyi heard from others and was delighted and went to pay homage, and as soon as the two met they were as old friends. Khwaja ʿAbd Allah on this happy day, proclaimed: "This person, in my mind's eye, is also me [*ci wu xinmuzhong zhi ren ye*]!"

Stories like this one combine an attachment to natal place with the drive to claim legitimacy from the perceived source of Islam—in this case, Central Asian Sufism.

Another group that formed in Gansu is the Xidaotang ("Hall of the Western Way," or "Western Daotang" [place of Sufi instruction]). Ma Qixi (1857–1914), born into a Sufi family, was en route to Mecca when he encountered war in Samarkand. Unable to proceed for a year, he occupied

---

[16] This text is similar to the genre of *manāqib* (hagiography), familiar to Sufis. The stories were last edited in 1981, although the date of their original composition is unknown.

himself with prayer and meditation. Upon his return to Lintan, he founded a new order based upon a concept he called the *wuma* (Ar. *umma*), a unique spiritual and economic community. The Xidaotang attracted some twenty Khufiyya Sufis, who left the Old Glory Mosque order in Linxia and founded a Xidaotang mosque in northwest Bafang in 1905.

The entry of Sufism, via the Khufiyya, Jahriyya, and Qadiriyya, and the Xidaotang changed the practice of Islam in the Northwest. The figure of the *murshid* (Ch. *laorenjia*), believed to be the intercessor between God and practitioner, dominated the moral and ethical lives of members of the order. Followers sought assistance from the shaykh on personal and familial problems. Leadership of the Sufi order became hereditary in most cases and was passed down the patriline. Through the zakat and voluntary donations (Ch. *nietie*, Ar. *niyya*), the Sufi orders accrued significant land holdings, including pious endowments (Ar. *awqāf*, sing. *waqf*), throughout Linxia and beyond.

The followers of Ma Laichi built a tomb complex in western Bafang, and those of Qi Jingyi built, in northwest Linxia outside the city wall, a sprawling tomb. Tens of thousands of Sufis from throughout the region, including Salar, Bonan, Dongxiang, Uyghur, and converted Tibetans and Han, in addition to Hui, pilgrimage to these tombs every year for the anniversary of the saint's death. Although the Xidaotang do not have a *silsila* (initiatic chain) and do not self-identify as Sufis, the decennial remembrance of Ma Qixi in Lintan likewise draws thousands of Xidaotang. A few of the Ma family warlords, such as Ma Hongbin (1884–1960) and Ma Hongkui (1892–1970), both commanders in Republican president Chiang Kai-shek's army and governors of Ningxia, patronized Hui Sufi masters in Linxia and Ningxia as well as Uyghur Khwajas in Xinjiang.

The next revivalist movement to enter Linxia was that of the Yihewani, which cannot be understood without reference to the Ma family warlords, deteriorating relations between the Qing government and Muslims, and pervasive Han-Hui and intra-Muslim violence. There were three main lineages—all Mas[17]—that dominated Gansu, Ningxia, and Qinghai from the 1860s to the 1940s. The lineages from Linxia are known as the "Hezhou Three Mas" and include Ma Zhan'ao, Ma Haiyan, and Ma Qianling (see Figure 2.4). Ma Zhan'ao (1830–1886) was a Khufiyya Sufi cleric of the Glory Mosque order. In opposition to discriminatory Qing laws and the massacre of Muslims in the Shaanxi Muslim rebellion of 1862–1872, Ma Zhan'ao led

---

[17] Northwest Hui usually explain the preponderance of the surname Ma among Hui by the fact that the pronunciation of the Chinese Ma most approximates the first syllable of Muhammad.

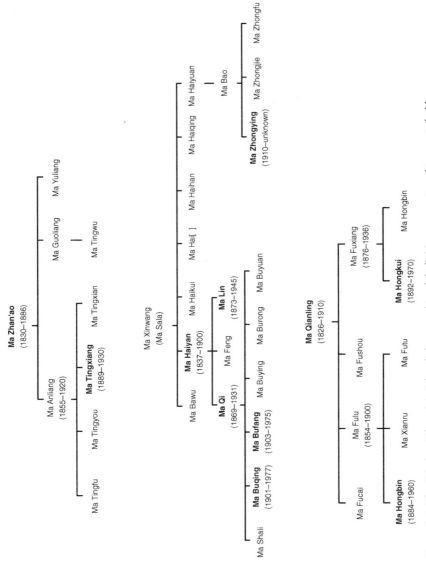

Figure 2.4 The "Hezhou Three Mas" family lineages (simplified). Names mentioned in text in bold

Source: the author

a united Khufiyya-Jahriyya attack against Linxia in 1862 (Chen 2002: 169). After a siege that allegedly lasted one thousand nights, Ma Zhan'ao broke through the city wall (Hai 1993: 26–29). The Qing thereupon dispatched Zuo Zongtang, the general who put down the Taiping rebellion, to retake Linxia. After uniting the Hui and Han, Ma Zhan'ao defeated Zuo in 1872, but then surrendered to the Qing forces to mitigate bloodshed (Ma Junhua 2004: 32–35). Ma Zhan'ao's turnabout exemplified the empress Cixi's policy of "using the Hui to control the Hui" (yi Hui zhi Hui).

A second Linxia Ma lineage began with Ma Haiyan (1837–1900), who made a living as a "household-on-foot," transporting goods throughout southern Gansu before joining Ma Zhan'ao in the long conflict with the Qing army and gaining fame for his valor. His son Ma Qi (1869–1931) formed a powerful army that gained the support of the Republican government. Ma Qi and his sons, Ma Bufang (1903–1975) and Ma Buqing (1901–1977), who inherited their father's posts, would provide the military force backing the spread of the Yihewani movement.

The Yihewani was founded and popularized by Ma Wanfu (1849–1934). Also known as Guoyuan Hajji, Ma Wanfu was a Dongxiang born in present-day Dongxiang Autonomous County. Like Ma Laichi and Ma Mingxin, Ma Wanfu traveled abroad and performed the hajj. The hajj experience, which Ma Wanfu completed in 1886, transformed his views on Islam. He returned in 1892, bringing several Wahhabi texts, including the *Kashf al-Shubuhat*, or *Clarification of the Doubts*, written by Muhammad ibn 'Abd al-Wahhab (Mingde Mosque of Linxia City 2004: 4). He advocated a scripturalist interpretation of Islam, based only on the authority of the Qur'an and the hadith. Under the slogans "base the teaching on the scripture" and "respect the scripture, reform customs," he put forth a ten-point program that attacked many of the practices of the Gedimu and Sufis and required women to wear the hijab. However, much like Muhammad ibn 'Abd al-Wahhab (1703–1766)—the eponymous founder of Wahhabism[18] whose message would have gone unheard if not for his

---

[18] The terms Yihewani, Wahhabi, and Ikhwan are problematic terms, particularly in translation, and deserve careful attention when tracing the origins of the Yihewani in China. Yihewani is understood by Hui to refer to al-Ikhwan al-Muslimun (Society of Muslim Brothers), or Ikhwan. The Ikhwan originated with Hasan al-Banna (1906–1949), who founded the Ikhwan in Egypt in the late 1920s. The Ikhwan should not be confused with the Wahhabi (who were also dubbed the Ikhwan, or "brothers"), the ultrapuritanical version of Islam, founded by 'Abd al-Wahhab (1703–1766) in what would be called the Kingdom of Saudi Arabia. The two overlapped and to some degree merged under the patronage of the Saudis, after the Ikhwan were exiled from Egypt by Nasser in the 1960s (Wickham 2013: 144; al-Arian 2014: 79). The Yihewani have undergone a process of localization in Chinese society and politics such that they fuse elements of the

alliance with a powerful backer in the person of Muhammad ibn Sa'ud (d. 1765), the founder of the first Saudi state—Ma Wanfu would most likely not have gained followers if it were not for his alliance with Ma Qi (Lipman 1997: 207). Ma Qi had consolidated his power in Xining, where Ma Wanfu accepted a leadership position at East Gate Grand Mosque. In 1918 Ma Qi installed Ma Wanfu as a leader in the mosque, and it was converted to Yihewani. As chronicled in the mosque's official record, Ma Wanfu gained support among the "ten great clerics of the new teaching"[19] in Linxia. Through implementing a new curriculum in madrasas and advocating scripturalist interpretations in sermons, the clerics proselytized Yihewani doctrine (Compilation Committee 2004: 210–12).

The ten clerics were not immediately successful, as Linxia was still in the throes of the ongoing war between the National People's Army and Muslim militias. Ma Zhongying (1910–unknown), cousin to Ma Bufang and Ma Buqing, laid siege to Linxia three times. In the final attempt in 1928, he stormed the wall and seized Linxia (Ma 1994: 194–96). In retaliation, the infamous commander of the seventeenth division of the National People's Army, Zhao Xiping, burned Bafang, including its twelve mosques and most of its Sufi tombs.[20] Elder Bafang Hui still talk about Bafang burning for eight nights, dispersing Bafang's 40,000 Hui.[21]

In the aftermath, Ma Bufang and Ma Buqing established their authority in Linxia. In the 1930s Republican president Chiang Kai-shek supported Ma Bufang's bid for power over Qinghai, regarding him as both anti-Communist and anti-Japanese. Ma Bufang ruled Linxia as his own fiefdom. During this period, he mobilized the new teaching to replace Gedimu and Sufi leaders with Yihewani clerics loyal to him (Mingde Mosque of Linxia City 2004: 26–27).

Consequently, all mosques in Bafang except for Old Wang Mosque and City Corner Mosque converted to Yihewani. Meanwhile, Ma Buqing, who also sided with the National People's Army and served as the deputy commander of the fourteenth division, conducted a series of successful

Ikhwan's program of the Islamization of society with the Wahhabis' ultraconservative call for a return to an unadulterated community founded on Islamic law.

[19] The designation "new teaching" (*xinjiao*) is particularly nettlesome in the study of Islam in China, because successive reformist movements have assumed the title.

[20] For a description, see the report written by Robert Ekvall (1938), who lived in southern Gansu during the "Mohammadan Rebellion" of 1928–1929.

[21] Bafang's Muslim population saw a significant drop from pre-Republican times during this period, most likely due to the continuous wars, famine, natural disasters, and displacements of the early twentieth century. The *Linxia City Gazetteer* (1995) gives the number 11,481 people for the year 1940 (Ma Dongping 2010: 12).

military engagements against the Red Army in Ningxia. He returned to his native Linxia, where he built primary schools, including a girls' school, and funded the construction or expansion of several Yihewani mosques, including Lower Second Society Mosque. Thus, the Yihewani movement grew in Linxia and elsewhere in the Northwest primarily due to the patronage and temporal power of the Ma warlords.

Such was not the case for the Salafiyya, a movement that also calls Linxia its base. The Salafiyya promotes a neoconservative ideology and has affinity with the Yihewani in opposing the Gedimu and the Sufis. However, it rejects what it views as the accommodation of the Yihewani to both the state and Chinese culture. Chinese Salafis, however, do not promote violence against the state and are thus more akin to Salafis in Saudi Arabia than to militant strains of Salafism, such as al-Qa'ida. Fundamentally, Salafism is a purist movement that tries to return Islam to the situation during the "first three generations" of Islam (Meijer 2009: 3–5; Lauzière 2010: 370). Thus, among Chinese Muslims Salafis are known as the "preceding three generations," or as the *santai*, for their practice of raising their hands three times to initiate prayer with the *takbīr*.

Chief among Salafism's features is their rejection of the *taqlīd* (imitation) of one of the established Sunni schools of jurisprudence, as well as some of their legal methodologies. Although non-Salafis label them followers of the Hanbali school, which is known for its strictness, Salafis in China, like their counterparts elsewhere, reject this characterization, privileging direct interface with the sources of revelation (Haykel 2009: 42). The history of the relationship between the Ikhwan and Salafiyya is convoluted, as the Ikhwan movement used Salafism as an ideology to promote its own purposes, resulting in much cross-fertilization between the two (Skovgaard-Petersen 1997: 155–56). Crucially, both the Ikhwan and Salafis employ a similar legal methodology of returning to the revealed sources. Muslims in Linxia distinguish the two groups. They do so with reference to the Salafiyya's historical entry to China, which I briefly describe here, following Gladney's (1999b) pioneering work.

There are different theories as to the genesis of Salafism in China, which, like Sufism and the Yihewani movement, is understood as stemming from the practice of the hajj and missionary activity. The most common version traces the first Chinese Salafis to a group of Muslims who participated in the hajj in 1936 and returned in that year. This group was composed of Ma Debao, Ma Yinusi from Bafang, Ma Zhengqing, and Ma Lin, who was Ma Bufang's uncle. Ma Debao met a Salafi missionary named Muhammad Habib Allah, or Habibullah (Ch. Huzhandi), in

Mecca, who, like the Egyptian reformer Muhammad 'Abdu (1840–1905), had studied the works of the fourteenth-century scholar Taqi al-Din Ahmad ibn Taymiyya, a jurist of the Hanbali school. Upon returning, the hajjis sought to proselytize Salafism in the Yihewani mosques of Bafang but were met with resistance by the established ten clerics of Ma Bufang. On February 30, 1949, six months before the arrival of the PLA, the Salafiyya held a public debate with Yihewani leaders over "*hukm* [rule], doctrine, and etiquette" (*hukun, jiaoyi, liyi*) in the hadith, and as their views were irreconcilable, the two formally split (Hanunai 1986: 128).

I discovered another dimension of the Salafiyya origin story: that a missionary named Said Buharla ("Mister Bukhara," after his native place) traveled to Xining in 1938 and established the first Salafi schools in China. I traveled the 240 kilometers from Linxia to Xining, where I learned about the two madrasas he founded at East Gate Grand Mosque and South Gate Grand Mosque. I also encountered an octogenarian Hui elder who, when he was nine years old, had met Said Buharla. He related that Said Buharla was none other than Habibullah (i.e., Muhammad Habib Allah). According to the elder, Said Buharla taught the *Sahih al-Bukhari* (a collection of hadith) at South Gate Grand Mosque.[22] Ma Yudao, the second-eldest son of Ma Wanfu, the founder of the Yihewani teaching school in China, taught the *uṣūl al-fiqh* (*faxue dagang*) or legal theory.[23] Students had to memorize these materials and apply the rules to legal problems. After two years, Muhammad Habib Allah was driven out of Xining by the Yihewani and fled to Saudi Arabia. Nonetheless, several of his students from Bafang who studied at the school returned to Linxia as the "new style ten great imams" (*xinshi shi da yimamu*), some of whom joined the Salafiyya, in contrast to Ma Bufang's "old style ten great imams" (*laoshi shi da yimamu*), who spread the Yihewani creed. An advertisement for the Xining school dated 1936 and posted on the Gedimu City Corner Mosque lists many of the Bafang clerics (see Figure 2.5).

The history of the first Salafiyya mosques in Linxia contrasts sharply with that of the earliest Yihewani enclaves backed by the warlords. Opinions differ among Linxia Salafis as to where and by whom the first

---

[22] Many Hui I spoke to made the point that Said Buharla carried this collection of the Prophet's sayings into China. Most likely he was not the first. Hui hold the collection, compiled by the Central Asian scholar Muhammad ibn Isma'il ibn Ibrahim ibn al-Mughira ibn Bardizbah al-Bukhari (810–870), in the highest regard as one of the most complete compilations of the Prophet's words.

[23] The official history of East Gate Grand Mosque confirms that Ma Yudao taught at several mosques, including South Gate Grand Mosque, from 1931 to 1945 (Compilation Committee 2004: 213).

Figure 2.5 A newspaper advertisement for one of the first Salafi schools in China

Source: Qi family archives

The advertisement reads in part: "And the Director of the College appointed two deputies, Muhammad Husayn al-Qukiyajani al-Khahawi [and] Muhammad Habib Allah al-Tujawi." Little is known about the former. The latter is the missionary from Bukhara.

congregation was formed. This difference in opinion reflects a historic split within the earliest generation of the Salafiyya. The disagreement occurred between two of the pilgrims who had returned from the hajj in 1936: Ma Debao and Ma Zhengqing. The Dongxiang Ma Debao (1867–1977) exercised a more hardline view of Salafi thought; thus, his "radical faction" encountered a greater degree of resistance from the Yihewani. Ma Zhengqing (1878–1958) held a more centrist view, known as the "moderate faction."

Just as the Salafiyya have learned to not challenge the political authority of the Party-State directly, more recent groups to enter the Northwest have also sought Islamic revival without political reform. In the 1980s a group of missionaries from the Tablighi Jama'at, which is based in India, traveled to China to proselytize among Muslims. The Tablighi Jama'at seeks to remind Muslims of what they consider to be a pure form of Islamic practice and a return to the piety exemplified by the Prophet Muhammad. As one of the missionaries reported in a 1997 account, the Tablighis were appalled by the lack of ritual cleanliness among Chinese Muslims (Metcalf 2003: 144).

The group is perhaps most well known for its advocacy of the purdah for women (Metcalf 1998, 2000). When I returned to Bafang in 2012, I discovered many more women than the year before wearing the full facial veil. Hui in and around Linxia had different explanations for this change, but some pointed to the fact that the Tablighi Jama'at had recently become more active in Lanzhou, as well as in Xining. Members regularly conducted study sessions in these cities and participated in excursions into the surrounding countryside, where they preached to other Muslims and sometimes to Han and Tibetans. During a visit in 2015, the number of full facial veils was far fewer in Bafang. Residents told me that the government had closed Tablighi Jama'at centers in Lanzhou and elsewhere. While the causal relationship between the Tablighi Jama'at and wearing of veils is not definite, it may be one reason for the increase, however temporary, in face coverings. While it is uncertain whether the Tablighi Jama'at will become a teaching school, as did the Salafiyya, its activity speaks to the dynamism of doctrinal interpretation in the region.

A brief summary of the main features of Linxia's overlapping social fields of "community justice"[24] illuminates their internal heterogeneity. The history of Linxia is the history of the entry of a succession of "tides" (Fletcher 1995) or "modes" (Gladney 1999b) of Islam into China. These successive revivalist strains of Islam have assumed a collective form as teaching schools. The crux of the debate over teaching schools is what it means to be a Chinese Muslim, the measure of which is one's

---

[24] Law and society scholars have also called such private ordering "informal justice" or "popular justice." See, e.g., Abel (1982), Harrington (1985), Hofrichter (1987), and Merry and Milner (1993).

approach to the sacred law and capacity to abide by it. Whether in the Khufiyya-Jahriyya debates about succession, the Yihewani critique of intercession and "saint worship," or the Salafiyya rejection of any authority (textual or charismatic) except for the revealed sources of Islam, disagreements between teaching schools point to different understandings of what constitutes Islamic law.

The teaching schools' elite members, namely clerics and Sufi shaykhs, attempt solutions to these questions through sermons, exhortations, admonitions, and consultation. Likewise, elites' mediation of disputes within mosque communities reinforces rules that bind the community. Teaching schools have appropriated symbols such as hajjis, missionaries, and texts to serve as evidence for their different interpretations of Islam. This social field existed largely outside and independent of the official court system during the Qing Dynasty, although community justice was upheld quite literally in the shadow of the magistrate's wall. When the Communists arrived in Linxia with their socialist legal system, they would drastically change the relationship between the social field and the juridical authority of the state.

"DISPUTE THE LESSON": COMMUNISTS IN THE HOLY LAND

On August 22, 1949 troops from the First Corps of the First Field Army of the PLA entered Linxia and seized the city from the Ma family warlords. PLA officers propagated a new teaching in Linxia's mosques. According to official sources, military units approached those at prayer armed not with guns but with ideological texts, the *Hui Work Manual* (*Huimin gongzuo shouce*), and a report called *Respecting Hui Social Habits and Customs* (*Zunshou Huimin fengsu xiguan*). Guided by the general principle of "religious freedom," they consulted clerics on matters of Hui custom (Zhao 1990: 29).

Like the Sufis, Yihewani, and Salafiyya who came before them, the Communists sought to convert Linxia Muslims to their particular doctrine. Marxism, a novelty in China's Little Mecca, was then being spread throughout the country.[25] Members of the PLA and the United Front Work Department (UFWD), a Party organ established in 1923 that

---

[25] As early as 1939, with the establishment of the Shaanxi, Gansu, Ningxia Border Region Government, the Communists took advantage of anti-Japanese sentiment to mobilize popular support for the direct election of representative assemblies and to propagate Communism. Elections at the village, county, and Border Region Government levels had begun two years

manages relations with non-Communists, altered their message according to their audience. "Liberation" for Linxia was that from oppression by warlords and the chaos of the sectarian strife that had dominated the city and much of the Northwest for the preceding half century. The Communists enjoyed a degree of mystique, following the epic Long March (1934–1935), during which the PLA fought the armies of Ma Bufang and Ma Buqing. Like other reformers, the Communists foregrounded their message as one of emancipation, and they were also able to mobilize coercive violence in support of their cause.

From the perspective of Linxia Hui, Communists seeking to incorporate Linxia into New China had to learn to follow local rules rather than simply overlay another government de novo. Since the inter-Sufi wars of the seventeenth century, and throughout the clashes between the Yihewani and traditionalist Gedimu and Sufis, the anti-Qing Hui rebellions, and the oppressive measures of the Ma warlords, Linxia had been a place of cumulative scarring. Communist rule would add additional layers.

The Communists' approach to administering Linxia—imposing secular law, policy, and bureaucracy—ultimately became dependent on the local systems it was designed to supersede. The Communists' administration continually interacts with the Hui social field. Methods of administration have varied over the past sixty years. At times, the Party-State's approach has approximated legal engineering akin to that of the Bolsheviks in the 1920s in Central Asia, where they sought to uproot nonstate law (Massell 1968). At other times, policy has been akin to that of the British in India, whose aim was the transformation of customs to aid in colonial administration (Galanter 1989). In the first decade of Communist rule, local cadres sought to establish new legal and juridical organs through Linxia Muslims' participation. But from 1958 until the end of the Cultural Revolution, clerics and shaykhs were discredited if not outright attacked. Following the reforms of the 1980s, administration has taken the form of socialist "rule of law."

The consequences of these different approaches are contradictory. On the one hand, the Communists at mid-century demolished local centers

earlier. The *Collection of Policies and Regulations of the Shaanxi, Gansu, Ningxia Border Region* (*Shaan-Gan-Ning bianqu zhengce tiaoli huiji*) (Government of the Shaanxi, Gansu, Ningxia Border Areas 1944), which is actually a supplement to the collection, provides the governing body of rules over the government, specifically, fifty-two statutes referring to administration, government organization, civil affairs, and other topics. The government's control was shaky, however. Military pressure from the Nationalists weakened its control, and the strength of Ma Bufang and Ma Buqing's militias further delayed Communist control of Linxia.

of power to force Linxia Muslims into revolutionary modernity, thereby minimizing the ability of elites to develop practices of informal justice. On the other hand, reform-era leadership has sought to transform local rules by co-opting Hui elite, drawing upon their authority to enhance state initiatives in Muslim communities. Thus, while the Party-State has imposed a secular "rule of law" system over the community-based forms of informal justice, it is a system predicated, in part, on local understandings of Islamic law. This imposition shows law to be a two-way process, which transforms the local state just as much as it does the community (Kidder 1979).

A major objective of the Communists' administration in Linxia has been to isolate the city and its inhabitants. Whereas Muslim minorities in Yinchuan (Ningxia), Shadian (Yunnan Province), and cities on the east coast have been able to take advantage of state-supported resources to reestablish networks with coreligionists abroad, Linxia Muslims have had more difficulty integrating themselves into the so-called "New Silk Road." The Party-State has isolated them from foreign Muslim influence via the hajj, trade, education and intellectual exchange, and civil society. Additionally, the Party-State has used the market to promote nation building at the local level and to depoliticize Islam. Administration helps patrol the boundaries between state law and Islamic law across the overlapping social fields of Muslim minority communities.

Administering Bafang

Immediately upon entering Bafang, the Party began consolidating its rule by replacing local systems of control with those of the state. Historically, Bafang was divided into eight precincts, which were under the administration of twelve mosques. The mosques provided education for youths, a social security net for impoverished families through collective donations, and a local authority to solve disputes within and between families. The Communists began working with the mosque communities to involve them in decision making and state institution building.

In August and September 1949 the Party-State established the Linxia County People's Government and the Linxia City People's Government. In October 1949 the First Representative Meeting of All Nationalities of All Walks of Life was convened as a venue to communicate the nascent government's policy objectives to residents (Linxia City Annals Compilation Committee 1995: 535). The meeting was attended by 150 representatives. Although Hui first refused to sit with Han, they did so during the second meeting (Hai 1993: 40). Between 1949 and 1953 there were a total of nine such representative meetings, during which representatives would review municipal work reports and address pressing issues. For instance, in 1950, during the second of such meetings, the delegates evaluated two proposals to stop opium trafficking through Linxia (Linxia City Annals Compilation Committee 1995: 535).

In 1951 the Communists established the Bafang Hui Autonomous District People's Government and the West Plain Hui Autonomous Village. These were sub-municipal administrative units and the first autonomous governments in Linxia. Their primary purpose was to establish institutions to train Muslim cadres who would be the grassroots liaisons between the mosque communities and the local government. According to Party statistics, in 1958, of 781 cadres, 217, or 28 percent, were Hui (Chinese Academy of Social Sciences Nationalities Research Institute 1964b: 5). The impetus behind the creation of such autonomous governments appears to have been an effort to win over Hui masses and to grant ethnic autonomy for minority communities, such as those in and around Linxia that had historically exercised discretion in their own affairs.[26] At the same time, the Communists sought to sever ties between Hui communities and the Ma family warlords, who were, to varying degrees, affiliated with the Nationalists. Descendants of Ma Bufang claim that as early as 1951 there were "criticism" sessions, during which any relative of Ma Bufang was persecuted.

In addition to involving Hui in local government, urban planners divided the city into six neighborhoods (*banshichu*), most of which have retained their pre-Communist place-names: South City, North City, West Gate, East Gate, Bafang, and—the exception—Red Park. The Bafang neighborhood was subdivided into four communities (*shequ*): River's Edge Front, Butterfly Villa, Dam Mouth, and Wang Mosque. For the most part, the current communities do not adhere to the pre-Communist mosque communities. Instead, the Communist administration broke up the mosque communities, overrode their jurisdictional lines, and organized households under a local neighborhood office.

In 1956 the government established the Linxia Hui Autonomous Prefecture, composed of seven counties including Linxia City (Editorial Group 2008: 78). Linxia Hui Autonomous Prefecture, in accordance with the 1954 PRC Constitution, was empowered to enact legislation in light

---

[26] For a detailed study of the establishment of the Zeku Tibetan Autonomous County in southeastern Qinghai from 1953 to 1958, and particularly the motives of the Communists, see Weiner (2012: see especially 221).

of local circumstances.[27] Theoretically, the autonomous prefecture has the power to modify national law to accord with the cultural norms of the ethnic minorities, which in the case of Hui would seem to include Islamic law. However, in the nearly sixty years of Party-State rule, the people's congress of Linxia Hui Autonomous Prefecture has passed only seven local regulations pursuant to the power of ethnic autonomy.[28] Of these, only one pertains to a subject addressed in Islam—halal food production.[29] Likewise, the Linxia Hui Autonomous Prefecture Religious Affairs Administrative Measures regulate mosques, mosque property, and mosque communities without reference to their correlates in Islamic law (e.g., mosque property as *awqāf*). State law's discursive omission of Islamic law and its concepts in an autonomous area named after a Muslim minority group is one way that secularism operates in the Northwest to produce a state-sanctioned Islam, bereft of Islamic law. Autonomous regulations are hollowed out of substance that would most approximate the religious law of those inhabiting the autonomous area.

---

[27] See Constitution of the PRC (*Zhonghua renmin gongheguo xianfa*), passed by the First Meeting of the First Session of the National People's Congress, September 20, 1954, art. 3. Autonomous administrative units (regions, prefectures, counties, and villages) would receive their own legislative basis in the Law of the PRC on Regional National Autonomy, promulgated May 31, 1984, revised February 28, 2001.

[28] The autonomous regulations were issued first as the Linxia Hui Autonomous Prefecture Autonomy Regulations (*Linxia Huizu zizhizhou zizhi tiaoli*), passed by the First Meeting of the Ninth Session of the Linxia Hui Autonomous Prefecture Congress, June 30, 1987, amended January 8, 2011. Subsequently, six individual regulations have been passed: (1) Linxia Hui Autonomous Prefecture Education Regulations (*Linxia Huizu zizhizhou jiaoyu tiaoli*), passed by the First Meeting of the Eleventh Session of the Linxia Hui Autonomous Prefecture People's Congress, March 15, 1997, amended October 25, 2003; (2) Linxia Hui Autonomous Prefecture Halal Food Administrative Measures (*Linxia Huizu zizhizhou qingzhen shipin guanli banfa*), passed by the Fourth Meeting of the Eleventh Session of the Linxia Hui Autonomous Prefecture People's Congress, April 11, 1999; (3) Temporary Administrative Measures of the Linxia Hui Autonomous Prefecture Religious Affairs (*Linxia Huizu zizhizhou zongjiao shiwu guanli zanxing banfa*), hereinafter "Linxia Religious Measures," passed by the Linxia Hui Prefectural People's Government, December 31, 2001, implemented January 7, 2006; (4) Linxia Hui Autonomous Prefecture Liujia Gorge Reservoir Ecology Environmental Protection Construction Regulations (*Linxia Huizu zizhizhou Liujia xia kuqu shengtai huanjing baohu jianshe tiaoli*), passed by the Fifth Meeting of the Twelfth Linxia Hui Autonomous Prefecture People's Congress, February 27, 2005; (5) Linxia Hui Autonomous Prefecture Fossil Protection Regulations (*Linxia Huizu zizhizhou gushengwu huashi baohu tiaoli*), passed by the Seventh Meeting of the Twelfth Session of the Linxia Hui Autonomous Prefecture People's Congress, June 7, 2006; and (6) Linxia Hui Autonomous Prefecture Administrative Measures on the Dangers of Table Salt Having Excessive or Insufficient Iodine (*Linxia Hui zizhizhou shiyan jia dian xiaochu dian quefa weihai guanli tiaoli*), passed by the Fifth Meeting of the Thirteenth Session of the Linxia Hui Autonomous Prefecture People's Congress, January 15, 2010.

[29] See the Linxia Hui Autonomous Prefecture Halal Food Administrative Measures.

In their place and violating Islamic law, the city government has implemented birth control and family planning policies in Bafang. In the 1980s such policies included forced sterilization for Hui women who had given birth to more than two children. In the early 1990s, as part of the government's preferential policies (*youhui zhengce*), Hui families could have two children as opposed to Han, who were subject to the "one-child policy." Since 1995, however, Hui and Han households can have only one child. This rule is enforced through different techniques. I heard of both a monthly reward to households (e.g., 120 yuan per month) that had only one child and also a penalty called a "social expense cost," adjusted to the father's income, for those who exceeded their one-child maximum.[30] Residents of Bafang admitted that the system is open to myriad forms of subterfuge. Hui officials from one neighborhood-level people's congress said that not only do most families have more than one child, but since the early 2000s many Hui have also moved from rural areas to Bafang, increasing the population beyond officially recognized levels.

Bafang has eight Party branches that function through the neighborhood office, which implements Party policies at the granular level. The official position is that Bafang has "widespread and severe poverty, classical vernacular architecture, joblessness, and a floating population."[31] Most households in Bafang have an income of 1,000 to 2,000 yuan per month, which is below the standard of 30,000 yuan of annual income for low-income families. According to the Linxia City Bureau of Civil Affairs, 42 percent of the households receive welfare.[32] Additionally, some families receive government subsidies for housing. Beginning in the 1980s, the government has provided water for all households, but there is no central sewer system, and most households still burn black coal in central stoves. Through replacing social services and financial support provided by mosques through their donation contributions, the Party-State has sought to reorient households away from the mosque as the center of the community and toward the various organs of the neighborhood office.

In consolidating its control of Linxia, the Party-State has reformed a number of institutions crucial to the Hui, including (1) the role of their clerics and shaykhs, (2) the system of mosque administration that was

---

[30] Salar and Dongxiang families residing within Bafang can have two children.

[31] The quotation comes from a poster outside the Bakou Residential Office in 2012.

[32] The public statistics from the Bafang Neighborhood Office gave a much lower figure for 2010: 1,550 total households, or 4,692 people. In all, 520,812 yuan per month was given in 2010, or 336 yuan per household. The amount of welfare, on average, is 170 yuan per month per household.

internal to Linxia and that predated the arrival of the Communists, (3) the operation of succession among Sufi orders, (4) communal property and sacred space, and (5) Muslim civil society institutions. Collectively, these reforms comprise what could be called the "structural interpenetration" (Santos 1980: 383) of Muslim institutions by the Party-State. The relationship between the law of the Party-State and the local Islamic law of Linxia brings the Hui social field into high relief. State law is hostile toward religious law and has "cannibalized the institutions which it presumably reinforces or with which it interacts" (Diamond 1974: 252), while preserving (if not molding) the repositories of knowledge about Islam and its law. I address these reforms in turn.

First, the position of Hui elite as the leaders of their respective communities has been a centerpiece of the Party-State's administration. As Hui elite are the mediators of all disputes in the community, the Party-State has enlisted clerics and shaykhs as key nodes in its informal administration. As seen in the precedents of Ma Laichi, Ma Mingxin, Ma Wanfu, Ma Qixi, and others, Hui leaders can combine reformist knowledge of Islam and doctrine from centers of Islamic learning abroad with "charismatic revelation of law" (Weber [1922] 1967: 80, 303) to massive effect. As a result, the Party-State has endeavored to circumscribe and transform their authority so that they act as agents of the local state. Given the centrality of Hui elite to the Party-State's administration and the efforts of that administration to neutralize the Hui elite authority through bureaucratization, I devote Chapter 7 to this issue through an analysis of the procedural aspects of Islamic law in China.

Second, in addition to targeting clerics and shaykhs, the Party-State has sought to dismantle the internal system of mosque administration. Linxia Hui call this regulatory system *hanyi dasi*, or *hanyisi*, a transliteration derived from the Arabic for "administrative mosque." The concept applies to large mosques to which Muslims of different (smaller) mosques go to attend Friday prayer. Additionally, the *hanyisi* may have administrative powers over the smaller mosques. For instance, when Ma Qi endorsed Ma Wanfu as one of the leaders of Xining's East Gate Grand Mosque in the 1920s, the mosque became the *hanyisi* of the Yihewani. As a consequence, Ma Wanfu was empowered to place clerics in smaller mosques, such as those in Linxia. The *hanyisi* also had discretion in terms of selecting the curriculum and texts in the madrasas of mosques under it. The *hanyisi* could also enjoy power over the management of subordinate mosques' property, including their donations from followers and *awqāf*.

The Communists labeled the *hanyisi* system an expression of feudal privilege and prohibited it by law.[33] As explained to me by Officer Zeng, a Hui policeman of mixed Tibetan descent and a member of the Gedimu, "Up until the Republican period, the *hanyisi* was the dominant system, but now through law and policy the system has changed to the *shudi* ['belongs to locality'] system." Under the *shudi* system each mosque is, by law, equal and independent of all others. In Linxia, however, Gedimu still consider Old Wang Mosque and Old Glory Mosque as their *hanyisi*, Yihewani consider South Gate Grand Mosque as theirs, and most Salafis consider River's Edge Front Mosque to be their *hanyisi*. Members of the respective teaching schools attend these mosques for Friday service. The other functions of the *hanyisi* survive in muted form. For example, upon graduation, a student of a *hanyisi*'s madrasa may teach at a mosque of the same teaching school, and he is often hired through the personal connections of the lead teaching cleric of the madrasa from which he graduated. That lead teaching cleric or the mosque administration of the school he graduates from may have influence over his decisions upon his assumption of his new post.

Third, if the CCP can be thought of as one the most recent teaching schools to spread an interpretation of Islam among Linxia Hui, then, like other teaching schools, it attempts to impose new rules over and against those of rival schools. Not unlike the Yihewani, who were backed by the Ma warlords, the Communists are supported by the coercive apparatus of the state. The Party-State's imposition of meta-rules over Sufi order succession clearly illustrates the third aspect of its administration of Linxia, the center of Sufism for most Muslim minority groups in Northwest China.

Chinese Sufi orders differ from mosque communities in that they are not based on domicile. Although Sufis living in close proximity to a tomb will visit it regularly, the order is a dispersed network with members throughout China. Because Sufi orders are diffuse, they are harder to control. The state has not sought to control Sufi orders by banning saints' days (although they were stopped from the 1950s to the 1970s). Rather, the state has tried to prevent the spread of Sufi orders

---

[33] See Measures on Gansu Province Mosque Administration (*Gansu sheng Yisilanjiao qingzhensi guanli banfa*), passed by the Sixth Representative Gansu Province Islamic Meeting, November 17, 1999, art. 2, stating, "Mosques must implement the single *fang* system; there cannot be any subordinate relations between mosques. Important issues with a mosque should be decided by the masses of that mosque and in accordance with relevant regulations; outside mosques and people cannot interfere with their decision making." See also the Linxia Religious Measures, art. 11, stating in part, "Religious activity areas are all equal."

by regulating the process of succession. The orders grow as a result of a *murshid* acquiring *murīdūn*, who in turn become *murshidūn* to *murīdūn* and so on, like a branching tree. In fact, the *silsila* is often graphically represented as a treelike growth. As each *murshid* dies, his tomb acquires a vaulted position in the order's cosmological map, attracting *murīdūn* and pilgrims, and becoming a site of devotion. The entire process of the order's growth depends on and begins with the ability of the master to proselytize.

The passing of what Hui call the *kouhuan* is one of the most important links in the process of spreading a *ṭarīqa*. The *kouhuan* (Ar. *ijāza*, "permission") is what a *murshid* gives a *murīd*, authorizing the *murīd* to transmit the accumulated and secret knowledge of the order. The *kouhuan* is occasionally accompanied by sacred relics, scriptures, or the text of the *silsila*. Religious policy in the Communist era has short-circuited the process of the order's growth by arresting the spread of the *ṭarīqa* at its source. PRC religious policy greatly curbs the proselytizing of religion, that is, the passing of the *kouhuan*.[34] The constraints placed on proselytizing make it difficult for a master to attract students. While the regulation of proselytization affects all teaching schools equally, it has been particularly deleterious to Sufi groups.

Nonetheless, almost all Sufi masters I met proselytize. Some younger teachers do so actively, by traveling nonstop through Northwest China. The shaykh of an order based in Lanzhou, for example, travels by an SUV, driven by his son, on a weekly basis. Others have acquired an age and status such that interested parties travel to them. Qi Jiequan (d. 2012) of the Bright Heart order hosted guests on a daily basis, some of whom were young would-be *murīdūn*, from as far away as Yining (Gulja), Xinjiang, 2,740 kilometers from Linxia.

Fourth, part of dismantling the *hanyisi* system and interrupting the spread of Sufi orders has been the expropriation of their assets, mainly land in the form of *awqāf*. The Party-State's claiming of religious property was part of a wider reorganization of urban space, transforming Linxia from being a spiritual center oriented around its mosques and Sufi tombs to serving as a secular administrative unit, the capital city of Linxia Hui Autonomous Prefecture. Beginning in the 1950s, the state expended tremendous resources to document all aspects of mosques and Sufi organizations, including the number of clerics and students,

---

[34] See Linxia Religious Measures, art. 29, starting in part, "Declaring oneself a missionary and a missionary's conducting of illegal proselytizing and preaching activities are prohibited."

number of followers, and land holdings.[35] Land reform had begun in Linxia in 1951 by confiscating large courtyards from wealthy families and dividing them for multiple poor families. According to official statistics, 1,179.36 *mu*[36] of land owned by the "Three Mas" was expropriated and divided among 1,069 households, a total of 5,860 people (Linxia City Annals Compilation Committee 1995: 566). The remaining large courtyards in Bafang were mostly destroyed in 1954 and 1958. Only a few, such as Eighteen Courtyards, were preserved, although the former residence of Ma Tingxiang would bear the signature of the PLA, "Dispute the lesson," an anticlerical and anti-establishment diktat. In the 1970s the PLA turned the property over to the local land administration, and it was subdivided and rented out to poor families for 3 yuan per month. In 2010 eighteen families, a total of forty-two people, occupied the courtyard.

From 1952 to 1958 the state took the extensive landholdings of tomb complexes and mosques, not by operation of law, but by force. Urban planning has been an agenda for the Representative Meeting of All Nationalities of All Walks of Life since its first meeting in 1949. In the 1950s the government began constructing a new city on what locals refer to as "inner city," the area that had been protected by the imperial walls. The south gate, the last remnant of the wall, was razed in 1958. One goal of the new city plan was to unite the Han and Hui populations, although official city planning has not mapped onto popular consciousness. As noted above, to this day, Hui and Han alike refer to the new city as inner city and Bafang as outer city. These spatial distinctions have their own set of associated norms and behaviors. Hui associate inner city with behaviors and values that much of the global South associates with the North: moral laxity, mindless consumption, illicit sex, and egoism. Bafang Hui refer to such behaviors not as "Western" but as "non-Muslim" (*fei Musilin*)—that is, "Han"—in the local idiom of Linxia's interethnic relations.

In 1958, during the first wave of the anti-rightist movement and the start of the Great Leap Forward, the state implemented the "struggle against the privileges of feudalism and religion" (*fanfengjian fanzongjiao tequan douzheng*) to eradicate all "superstitions" in Linxia. It had devastating effects. From 1958 to 1961 most mosques in Bafang and Sufi

---

[35] For instance, according to an internal report conducted by the Linxia Prefectural Party, as of 1953, for the whole prefecture there were 1,500 mosques and tomb complexes, 2,500 teaching clerics and "heads of teachings" (*jiaozhu*), 3,000 nonteaching clerics, and 10,000 students. There were on average one mosque for every 300 people and one cleric for every 80 people (Linxia Prefectural Party Committee 1953).

[36] One *mu* is equal to one-sixth of an acre.

tombs on the outskirts of the city were destroyed. Only the Grand Tomb Complex was saved. Clerics and Sufi *murshidūn* were arrested and often paraded in the streets with signs around their necks saying that they were enemies of the state. There were armed rebellions in 1958 in the Dongxiang Autonomous County and Guanghe County, although the PLA suppressed any rebellion in Linxia. In 1968 the Red Guard attacked clerics, Sufi masters, and former members of the National People's Army. Following Mao's interpretation of Marxism, the abolition of private property was an important step in the "people's war."

As a consequence of the Party-State's expropriation of sacred space and urbanization, Linxia has been—partially—secularized (see Figures 2.6 and 2.7). One example is the Qadiriyya Grand Tomb Complex, which held more than eight hundred *mu* of land in 1952 (Linxia Prefecture Committee United Front Work Department 1952). A large portion of its land was a cemetery in the northwest of the city that was claimed by the state in the 1950s. The bodies were exhumed in 1966 and moved to North Mountain, and a statue of Mao Zedong was erected on the holy ground. Today, the area is Red Park Public Square, where youth rollerblade and Hui men play *fang* (square), a version of checkers. (The Mao statue has been taken down.) Additionally, next to the square the state developed Red Park, which features a Chinese-style promenade, pond, a zoo of exotic animals, and a decommissioned PLA helicopter. These hyper-secular spaces literally surround the Grand Tomb Complex that Qadiriyya Sufis consider the holiest ground in Linxia or anywhere in China. Secularization is not just temporal, as it obliterates and remakes history (Duara 1995; Jing 1996), but spatial as well. Many younger Hui have no idea of the earlier significance of Red Park Public Square.

After the reforms of the 1980s, the state promised the return of expropriated property to religious institutions, including mosques and Sufi tomb complexes. The return of property is known under the rubric of "the working out of the policies" (*luoshi zhengce*). The first word, *luoshi*, is composed of two characters that, respectively, denote "fall," "drop," or "go down" with "solid," "true," or "real," and the second word, *zhengce*, means "policy." As used by clerics in Bafang, the phrase connects governmental policy, reconstruction (often in a physical or material sense), and the continuance of the divine mission. The phrase has become synonymous with Islamic revival in places such as Linxia, and clerics speak of it almost in the same terms in which they speak of blessings from Allah. My point is not that Hui apotheosize the Party, but that they resolve the antinomies of living a life in accordance with Islam and as a citizen of

Figure 2.6 A view of Linxia (Hezhou) in the 1920s, looking south, as photographed by Carter D. Holton

Courtesy of Harvard–Yenching Library of the Harvard College Library, Harvard University

a socialist state through a higher-order faith in God. Such meme-like phrases reflect the entanglements of local and official discourses and point to the nature of Islamic revival as one that takes physical form, for instance, mosque and madrasa reconstruction. This is not to say that Islamic revival is exclusively infrastructural or bereft of spiritual reawakening. Rather, "the working out of the policies" as a synonym for religious reform is one of the subtler ways in which the Party-State discursively produces Islam.

In Linxia, however, only the land for the government-designated "religious activity areas" was returned and not any other holdings in land. For example, Red Park Public Square and Red Park have not been returned to the Grand Tomb Complex. Several descendants of officers in the National People's Army have been petitioning the government for thirty years for the return of their property, which they claim is occupied by cadres in the local government. Of the surviving Bafang grand courtyards, those, like Eighteen Courtyards, that have been converted into low-income housing have not been returned to their original owners (see Figure 2.8). In its approach to shaping local Islam, including bureaucratizing Hui leaders,

Figure 2.7 A view of Linxia in 2012, looking south. The city wall was pulled down in the 1950s

Source: the author

dismantling the *hanyisi* system, limiting proselytization, and nationalizing religious property and secularizing space, the Party-State has been
much more invasive than imperial rulers in penetrating the Hui social
field. Collectively, these measures have appropriated religion to enhance
the Party-State's own legitimacy in line with secularist projects elsewhere
(Mahmood 2006, 2008; Agrama 2012).

A Muslim civil society?

The Party-State's domination of the public sphere in which religious values
may be deliberated has been one of the main ways in which it has contained
the Hui social field, which might otherwise espouse an alternative source
of law, such as shari'a. As applied to the China case, the notion of civil society has had a rather distinct definition. Some scholars have identified forms
of associational life—professional associations, locality clubs, teahouses, lineages, ancestral halls, chambers of commerce, and even brothels—as premodern institutions that may function as political communities.[37] Other scholars

[37] See Sangren (1984), Pei (1998), and Weller (1999).

Figure 2.8 A view of the south end of the former home of Ma Tingxiang

Source: the author

Located in the center of Bafang, the home is one of the few surviving examples of late Qing "mansions" (*dagongguan*) in Linxia. The courtyard was confiscated by the PLA in the 1950s. The original blue stenciled letters are still visible on the face of the pillars: "Dispute the lesson ... smash the stone-leaning conservatism."

have emphasized that such communities were not necessarily autonomous but existed between social constraints and state regulation.[38] Such forms of civil society are believed to have emerged during the late imperial period (Duara 1995: 150). After an initial florescence in the Republican period followed by a decline and then extinguishment in the early Communist period, such associational forms have returned, alongside new virtual communities.[39] My use of the term "civil society" underscores the idea that voluntary associational life is very much embedded within (albeit not dominated by) state institutions. Civil society thus develops out of *minjian* networks and communities that together with state manipulation of institutional life give form to the Hui social field.[40]

[38] See Chamberlain (1993), Huang (1993), He (1997), and Tan (2003).

[39] On Muslim minority use of cyber-networks, see Peterson (2006), Yang (2009), and Ho (2010).

[40] The topic of a Hui civil society has attracted the interest of many scholars of Islam in China (Gladney [1991] 1996; Gillette 2000; Ma 2006).

The Republican period (1912–1949) witnessed the burgeoning of a Muslim civil society in cosmopolitan centers in Beijing, Nanjing, and even to some extent in the Northwest in the form of publications (Muslim newspapers, gazettes, journals, and magazines) (see generally Mao 2011), private schools (e.g., Shi 1987), charitable organizations, and *minjian* silver-backed banking institutions (Compilation Leading Group 1986). To take one example, the newspaper *Yuehua* (*Moonlight*), founded in Beijing in 1929 by a group of modernist Muslims, had wide circulation among Chinese Muslims throughout the country and discussed a variety of domestic and international political issues, with a focus on the Middle East. I first discovered the newspaper in 2009 when conducting archival research in a *minjian* institution I call the Islamic resource center (IRC).[41]

The IRC is an unregistered nonprofit organization founded in 1993 by a group of Yihewani Hui. It was founded in Lanzhou, but most clerics in Linxia are familiar with it and use it frequently. The fact that the IRC could be established only in the provincial capital and not in Linxia gives credence to the assertion that civil society organizations in Linxia are particularly constrained. The IRC is part library, part Muslim salon, part charity foundation for Muslim women and the disabled, part prayer space, and part matchmaking agency. It has the most complete collection of books on Chinese Islam's history, Hui studies, and Hui literature in the Northwest. It also has copies of the Qur'an in five languages, jurisprudential texts in Arabic and Persian, and books on Chinese Islamic art and architecture. Its holdings include newspapers dating to the early 1990s printed by state-authorized Islamic organizations and associations in China, and *minjian* as well as official Hui periodicals. On a horizontal scroll over the periodical section, the hadith "Seek knowledge even unto China" is written in traditional Chinese script.[42] In a locked cabinet was a *Yuehua* issue that the director allowed me to see (but not photograph), in which an article discussed the "problems in the Northwest." He emphasized that during the Republican period, *Yuehua* was not censored, and therefore, it was perhaps, in fact, the last uncensored Hui periodical.[43]

The juxtaposition of the text of *Yuehua*, a literary product of an effervescent period in Muslim civil society, inside the locked cabinet of the library of an unregistered, nongovernmental organization in contemporary

---

[41] The IRC is a pseudonym to protect the actual organization.

[42] The authenticity of this hadith, heavily cited by Chinese Muslims and in the literature on Islam in China, is disputed.

[43] In 2010 Ningxia People's Publishers edited and bound *Yuehua* as a ten-volume set.

Lanzhou, encapsulates the paradox of religious liberalization in reform-era China. There are other educational and philanthropic organizations like the IRC in China. One was founded in Oxen Street, Beijing's Hui enclave, in 1936 but was closed in the 2000s. There is another in Lanzhou and one in Ningxia, but it is for-profit. Linxia also had a very prominent civil society center called the You Read Books Room (Ni Du Shu Wu), hereinafter, "the Room," named after the first line (*iqra'*, or "recite") of the ninety-sixth sura. The contentious history of the Room epitomizes not only the state's aversion to a Muslim civil society in Linxia, with its connotations of extremism, terrorism, and "splittism," but also to teaching schools as multiple and competing regimes of orthodoxy—a perspective on Linxia I address more fully in Chapter 3.

The Room was established in Bafang on December 6, 1994 (Shan 1995). It was founded by a cleric of a progressive Yihewani mosque and funded by prominent Hui businessmen. The main part of the establishment was a library and reading room, where up to fifteen people could sit. Young Hui men began congregating at the Room, where they could purchase and borrow books. The owner began holding classes there on topics related to Islam, and eventually invited clerics, Chinese Muslim scholars, and even foreign scholars to give lectures. The reputation of the learning center grew, and men came from Shaanxi, Yunnan, Qinghai, and Xinjiang. The center organized courses around the study of the Qur'an, hadith, and the Hanafi text *Sharh al-Wiqaya* (Ch. *Weigaiye*).

As the center expanded its services, its internal organization was formalized, and a board of directors was formed. Delegations of clerics, senior instructors, scholars, teachers at Chinese-Arabic schools, and prominent leaders of mosques from other cities with large Muslim populations visited the Room. In a span of a few years it became well known through Hui intellectual networks spanning most of the country. However, around 2006 the learning center was closed by government fiat, and the cleric was fired. This much is generally agreed upon.

Muslims in Linxia hold a range of opinions as to why the government closed the Room. Many non-Sufis hold the view that it was closed because, they say, Zhang Chengzhi, the famous Maoist revolutionary-turned-Sufi intellectual, gave a talk there in 2005.[44] Sufis, however, relate that the reason for the closing of the Room was not Zhang Chengzhi's talk but rather that it was run by Salafis. They had organized a series of events

---

[44] Zhang never gave a talk in the Room. Rather, his talk was in Linxia's only high-end hotel. For more on Zhang's impact on Hui intellectual life, see Choy (2006).

attracting young converts from Qinghai. "Ten buses for one event!" one Sufi exclaimed. Yet another view, held by Linxia Hui regardless of teaching school, was that the Room was in the midst of forging ties with students in Xinjiang. Others also linked the closing to contemporaneous unrest in Xinjiang, arguing that security forces in the Northwest often tighten around Muslim networks following violence in the far western autonomous region.

The example of the Room illustrates the Party-State's anxiety about allowing underground networks, in this case educational ones, to flourish in Linxia. Such learning centers threaten the state's monopoly on defining Islam and Islamic law. Linxia Hui referred to the Room as a *minjian zuzhi* (popular organization), with the additional undertone that it was unregistered. The secular aspiration of the Party-State is, first, to survey and monitor all Muslim organizations and, second, to depoliticize those that are permitted to open their doors by dictating their promotional or teaching material. This version of secularism does not tolerate unmapped spaces that allow for unscripted discourse about Islamic law and doctrine.

Such Muslim civil society institutions as the IRC or the Room are never completely autonomous from the state, even if, having evaded registration and licensing requirements for nonprofit organizations, they function "off the grid." They are inscribed within the Party-State's surveillance mechanisms, which operate ambiguously toward such grassroots centers of learning. For instance, I had met several cadres and officials who visited the IRC regularly. These representatives of the Party-State were all Muslim and benefited from and participated in the IRC's services. The Room was closed not because it was an unregistered nonprofit organization (these are all too common),[45] but rather because it was organizing Islamic study groups and supporting networks of learning that diverged from state-sanctioned education.

The closure of the Room also shows that the Party-State's anxieties about radical Muslim youths are infectious. The agents of infection are state-controlled media, including Internet commentary. Through the state's monopolization of outlets that elsewhere are mobilized by civil society, the Party propagates not only its own policies but also state-sanctioned relations between the different Muslim minority groups in China. While "ethnic unity" and a "unified Islam" remain official slogans, in

---

[45] Based on my experience providing legal services to nonprofits in the PRC while working at a law firm in Beijing, most such organizations are operating "in the gray," outside of the formal registration system.

postsocialist China, particularly after the 2009 Urumqi riots and the attacks of 2013 and 2014, Uyghurs are equated with anti-state violence. Linxia Muslims, as a response, dissociate themselves from such behaviors. As one Dongxiang mother told me as she, her eight-year-old daughter, and I sat at a noodle shop in Linxia, "We don't like those Uyghurs here. They used to come here and do business. But after the July 5 riots [qi wu shijian], we don't let them enter our mosques anymore." Amid the crossfire of sectarian and ethnic divisions, maintained by mutual accusations, the state purports to maintain a lofty transcendence, a position that it never fully attains.

OPENING AND CLOSURE OF THE HUI SOCIAL FIELD

Muslim communities in Bafang have developed an ordering of norms and laws, some of which derive from shari'a, that structure their communities as a social field. The Hui social field is hardly uniform, however. Teaching schools have varied understandings of law and doctrine. State law and bureaucracy circumscribe and interpenetrate these competing orders of localized Islamic law. Both the *minjian* order and the official sphere generate their own rules. These rules are not exclusive; rather, they impinge on each other.

Eighteen Courtyards provides a touchstone for understanding Bafang as a social field. Eighteen Courtyards reveals the historical formation of the interpenetration of Bafang's layers of norms and rules. As a domestic and administrative place, it has assumed a number of different meanings over the course of Linxia's history. It has been a sign of commercial wealth, a locus for the prestige of lineage, evidence of class oppression, a site of state violence, and in contemporary Linxia, the remnants of the state's social welfare system. As a result, Eighteen Courtyards has been—and continues to be—subject to multiple normative and legal authorities.

As with the Hui social field, Eighteen Courtyards must be "open" to authoritative use and interpretation. At the same time, the Party-State has sought to direct if not foreclose wider connections between Linxia and cross-border Muslim communities. This chapter catalogs the various ways in which state law and policy try to structure and define the internal social field. These include vetting clerics, regulating mosque activities, secularizing sacred spaces and expropriating religious property, arresting the spread of Sufi networks, and stifling civil society institutions. In all cases, the Party-State has discretion as to whether or not it will tolerate the *minjian*, nonstate sources of law and their authorities. The boundary between what is tolerable and what is anathema to the official Islam of the Party-State is ever-changing.

In this chapter I have described the Party as another doctrinal group in Linxia that has tried to impose its definition of official Islam on other groups. The imposition of secular law and bureaucracy over the Hui social field is not an accomplished fact but an ongoing process. Linxia Hui are also producing multiple and competing approaches to integrating Islam and its law into their daily lives, an effort intrinsic to self-understandings of religious authenticity, gender relations, access to justice, control of land and space, and definitions of modernity. Resurgent education networks, for instance, exemplify such efforts. Through trans-local, regional, and international contacts, Muslim youths gain exposure to domestic and foreign scholars, some of whom are viewed as antistate. There are other examples of such illegal networks. For instance, a revived heroin trade from Burma through Yunnan to Linxia Hui Autonomous Prefecture, especially the town of Sanjiaji, has been a controversial source of income for local Muslim communities (Xia Ming 2009: 111–12).

Overall, in the socialist period the Hui social field, including mosque communities and networks based in Bafang that extend throughout the Northwest and potentially beyond, has been subject to a significantly higher degree of state intervention than in the imperial period. Consequently, the capacity of Hui to generate their own rules in accordance with Islamic law, called customary law after the 1950s, has been constrained. Rather than adopt an oppositional strategy toward the Party-State, Hui have sought to abide by the injunctions of Islam through *minjian* means, which are unofficial, nonconfrontational, and even symbolic, by which devotional aspects of law substitute for political ones.

3

RITUAL LAWFARE

Ikhtilāf ummatī rahmatun li-l-nās.
(The difference of opinion in my community is a mercy for the people.)

A widespread (but disputed) hadith

Dangnei liang tiao luxian douzheng jiang changqi cunzai, hai hui chuxian shi ci, ershi ci, sanshi ci ...
(If the struggle between two factions within the Party persists, then there will appear ten times, twenty times, thirty times [more factions] ...)

Zhou Enlai (1973)

TROUBLING INCENSE

In 2000 a standoff occurred between one of the oldest Gedimu mosques in Linxia and the Grand Tomb Complex, the base of the Qadiriyya order in China, over the use of incense. The origins of the debate can be traced back to the previous year, when the cleric of the mosque criticized the Qadiriyya Sufis of the Grand Tomb Complex for their practice of the *sujūd* (prostration by touching forehead to ground) to the Sufi master as a contravention of Islamic law. The young cleric, recently returned to Linxia from his second hajj, had reproached the Qadiriyya Sufis in his sermons, arguing that *sujūd* was reserved for God. Muslims could study Sufi saints for their moral worth but not kowtow to them. Many saw a new way of thinking in the prominent cleric's teaching and said he had been influenced by Salafism abroad.

Later that year, after the cleric went to Cairo for a training course on law at al-Azhar University, the student who replaced him in giving the weekly sermon also began to criticize the Grand Tomb Complex—this time, for its burning of incense during prayer. The practice had been tainted by Buddhist and Daoist religious observances, he reasoned. The Grand Tomb Complex responded by defending its use of incense as consonant with Islamic law. The vitriol intensified upon the cleric's return to Linxia. Members of the mosque marched on the tomb complex and there was a physical confrontation. Fights also broke out between Qadiriyya Sufis and the cleric's supporters in Lanzhou in 2001.

Eventually, Qi Jiequan (d. 2012) of the Bright Heart order, intervened. The eighty-year-old Naqshbandi-Mujaddidi Sufi shaykh met with the young cleric. In an instance of pan-Sufi solidarity against a reformist cleric, the followers of the Bright Heart order compiled a list of ten "words and deeds of [name deleted] who viciously attacked a Sufi order, harming ethnic unity" (*edu gongji gongbei menhuan pohuai minzu tuanjie yan-xing*). Following a long tradition in the resolution of inter–teaching-school doctrinal disputes called "scriptural debate" (*jiangjing*), a version of *munāzara* (debates) common to Muslim communities particularly in South Asia, Qi Jiequan engaged the younger cleric on the issues raised. Qi Jiequan prepared for the debate by collecting Arabic and Persian texts on law, doctrine, and theology to defend the Sufi practice, including the use of incense. He persuaded the younger cleric that the practice was not corrupt, and the confrontation cooled.[1]

This chapter asks, as an initial question, why do things that would otherwise appear commonplace, such as burning incense, matter to Hui and to the Party-State?[2] I argue that, for a number of reasons, ritual matters have become tied to teaching-school identity, and interpretation over what ritual represents is also instrumental to Party rule in Muslim regions. To address the question of ritual's importance in Muslim cities such as Linxia, I note as a general observation that among all fields of Islamic law (criminal, personal status, and so on) it is in ritual matters where the Party-State has granted Hui the most freedom. On one level,

---

[1] The conflict did not end, however. The Sufis claim that eight years later they obtained their revenge. Apparently, the cleric in question had a side business of forging documents for Muslims, especially from Xinjiang, to go on the hajj via Thailand. The authorities discovered the illegal business and suspended the cleric's license. He was on a probationary period in 2008 and could not lead any religious activity, but he did so in violation of his probation. A 2009 letter from the prefectural-level Bureau of Religious Affairs (BRA) once again temporarily suspended his license. In the Sufis' eyes, the punishment was for his insults against them several years earlier, although the letter does not mention the cause of the suspension (most likely it was for the forged visas). Bafang Hui say that because of his behavior, the government removed the cleric from his post, although he obtained a position in a larger mosque outside of Linxia.

[2] This question has been asked before in different guises in the anthropology of ritual. For instance, Evans-Pritchard (1976) investigated the significance of blighted groundnut crops among the Azande; Obeyesekere (1981) studied the consequences of matted hair among Sinhalese Buddhists; and Valeri (2000) queried the meaning of betel nut juice among the Huaulu. In each case—blights, hair, and betel—were found to be foci of collective affect.

such controversies as the use of incense in prayer matter very little to over-worked bureaucracies in local or higher-level governments. Ritual is the banal, esoteric, and emphatically *minjian*. The teaching schools, however, have adopted a traditional Chinese view that rites are the path to ethical cultivation. The result of combining these factors—external constraint on Islamic law practice and internal valorization of ritual—is that Hui invest tremendous psychic energy in matters of correct rites. Orthodoxy takes the form of correct practice and its representation. In the domain of ritual law, Chinese Muslims have a discursive space replete with "repertories of justification" (Bowen 2003: 7) for their authenticity, or the inauthenticity of Muslim others, as seen in the example of the troubling incense. Ritual law is thus largely the terrain upon which Muslim communities fight for their definition of the good life. Conflicts over correct practice lead to violence more quickly than interpretive differences over other areas of Islamic law.

The Party-State would remain aloof from teaching-school disputes but for two reasons. Most immediately, the Party has an incentive to quell any type of violence. In Hui enclaves, violence may arise from such quotidian acts as the burning of incense. Also, the Party, not unlike teaching schools, is invested in appropriating rites to cultivate ethical subjects, not necessarily as individual members of teaching schools, or *jiaomin* (lit. "person[s] of the teaching," or religious adherent[s]), but as *guomin*, citizens of the nation. Historically, the state was itself an exponent of correct practice. Ritual practice was a key category in the imperial state's definition of orthodox spiritual authority.[3] In turn, the state derived popular support by adopting practices of religious or philosophical schools.[4] As a stakeholder in religious belief,[5] the historical Chinese state regarded heterodox sects as rebellious and a cause of political and spiritual instability.[6]

---

[3] On this question, see Ahern (1981) and Feuchtwang ([1992] 2001a, 2001b).

[4] The authorities on the state's definition of orthodoxy are Yang (1961), Wolf (1974), Gates and Weller (1987), Sangren (1987a, 1987b), and Chau (2006, 2011).

[5] Cases in which imperial courts in Gansu decided on matters of Islam mostly touched on issues of "orthropraxy [sic], textual purity, and ritual rectitude" (Lipman 1999: 555)—that is, practice. Chinese Muslims, as Sunnis, share a common belief in the Five Pillars, so at a macro level, practice rather than belief is the fulcrum of debate in such places as Linxia. At a granular level, disagreements over whether, for example, a shaykh can serve as intercessor between a believer and God combine elements of "belief" and "practice." Thus, to some extent, orthopraxy touches on orthodoxy.

[6] See, for instance, de Groot (1903), Naquin (1976), Nancy Chen (2003), and Jansen (2014).

While legally the Party cannot arbitrate sectarian differences within religious populations, it has nevertheless joined the teaching schools in the interpretation of Islam, including ritual aspects of Islamic law. In contemporary Linxia, Hui will not bring ritual law conflicts to state courts. The government does not intervene in inter-teaching-school disputes judicially. Rather, it relies on its own practice of governmentality to shape ritual law through regulation. The Party-State limits, for example, the number of Hui who can perform the hajj, restricts certain dress in public buildings, and discourages state employees from fasting during the month of Ramadan.

While the Party-State endeavors to depoliticize ritual law by confining it to the private sphere, contradictorily, through its regulation, ritual aspects attain greater importance. The politicization of ritual aspects of Islamic law, namely, 'ibādāt (acts of worship) that include ṭahāra (purity) occurs at the intersection of teaching schools' will to follow Islamic law and the Party-State's attempts to mold an official Islam from the minjian. The pivotal role of teaching schools in deciding orthodoxy would seem to leave no room for individuals as interpreters of the law. While teaching schools are not hegemonic, Hui often lodge their arguments with reference to them. The self-perpetuation of teaching schools, the Party-State's attempts to assuage their purchase on Hui, and individual Hui efforts to carve out their own understandings of the law take the form of debates that I call "ritual lawfare."[7]

Since the seventeenth century, a defining feature of Islam in China has been contests over ritual and devotional aspects of the law. Hui past and present have engaged in a number of debates on matters of ritual, including whether to break the fast at the end of Ramadan before prayer or vice versa, who can read the Qur'an during a funeral service, the nature of the fidya (an expiatory act for the dead), the correct interpretation of a ritual book, and the burning of incense. The prevailing explanation of these contests, first espoused by the Chinese Marxist scholars who helped establish the current "orthodox" conception of the teaching schools and subsequently by Western scholars, is that Muslim leaders seek to gain followers and material assets and thus manipulate what has been called "liturgical minutiae" for their own ends. In this view, Hui are pawns of materialist interests and have no freedom.

---

[7] In recent years, scholars of Islam have turned to ritual aspects of law as a domain of argumentation about authenticity, both within Muslim groups and against other Abrahamic faiths (Katz 2002; Mahmood 2003, 2006, 2012; Gauvain 2005; Halevi 2007; Haider 2011).

The materialist explanation fails to account for the symbolic dimensions of law and doctrine as well as the tremendous psychic investment that nonelite Hui place in ritual protocol, or ʿibādāt. I take the view that teaching schools are traditions that interpret Islamic law, and specifically ʿibādāt, in the context of secular China. My view is informed generally by Talal Asad's contributions to the anthropology of Islam. Particularly, following MacIntyre's (2007) work on tradition, Asad has proposed approaching Islam as a "discursive tradition" or, alternatively, an "authorizing discourse" that aims to form moral selves (Asad 1993: 37; [1986] 2009b: 10). Asad has criticized Clifford Geertz's (1973) approach to the study of religion as privileging meaning without considering the relations of power through which meaning is made. While I borrow from Asad's notion of discursive traditions to understand teaching schools, I qualify his approach in finding that teaching schools interpret symbols as part of the reproduction of their tradition. Muslims are continually reinterpreting shariʿa and forming arguments, particularly about ethical and moral matters, with reference to the revealed sources. Meaning is thus appurtenant to power in the process of forging autonomous selves.

In addition to material interest, ritual law matters to Hui because of the minority status of Muslims, as well as the narrowed field of Islamic law in China, the centrality of rites to teaching-school ethics, and the politicization of ritual law, as mentioned. Ritual matters have affective value fundamentally because of Muslims' minority status in Chinese society. In the rhetorical (and sometimes military) campaigns between and within the schools, many of the most hotly contested elements of the ʿibādāt—for instance, modes of worship, ritual cleanliness, and dietary restrictions—have symbolic value when juxtaposed with practices of the Han majority. Incense smoke in the Chinese context, for example, can be interpreted by scripturalist Muslims as metonyms of Daoist or Buddhist cosmologies of purity/impurity or as popular religion in the form of ancestor worship. Alternatively, incense can be an expression of devotion, as in the Sufi experience. Hence, the domain of ritual law is also a semiotic one.[8] Activities, texts, and even gestures are associated with broader meanings through conventions learned through the discursive traditions of schools.

[8] By semiotics, I refer not to Ferdinand de Saussure's model, abstracting signs from social context, but to traditions that foreground the materiality of the sign, as embedded within social interaction (Voloshinov [1929] 1986; Keane 2007).

The remainder of this chapter is divided into six parts. The first two parts assess teaching schools as bodies that interpret Islamic law, specifically ritual law. I begin with the question of teaching schools themselves, which do not readily conform to definitions of "sects" in Islam (whether organized by doctrine or jurisprudence). I view the Party as another type of interpretive body, which has also tried to organize sectarian difference through social-scientific categories. With this orientation of the schools in mind, I turn to their partisan views of Islamic law.

Parts three through six address disputes between and among the schools. I supplement the conventional theory for the cause of sectarian violence among Muslim communities to account for the symbolic elements of disputes. I explain this modified approach with reference to ethnographic data about a long-standing cause of disputes: funerary practices. In the absence of representational politics, teaching schools orient their members to certain understandings of Islamic law through the discursive domain of ritual practice, eclipsing the Party-State's definition of privatized and depoliticized religion. Teaching schools have a monopoly on the interpretation of ritual law, which complicates the assumption that ethics operate through the rise of individualism in contemporary China. Lastly, I draw attention to the ways in which ritual matters underscore tensions between Islamic law and Party policy for Hui cadres.

PARTY VERSUS SECT

In the social life of Bafang Hui, there are few identities as significant as one's teaching-school affiliation. This affiliation determines largely where a Bafang Hui lives, where she eats, whom she marries, where she prays, how she studies the sources of Islam, and whether and how she works. Teaching schools are the "bearer of values," to use Montgomery Watt's term (1953), for Hui in Bafang as well as for Muslim minorities throughout the Northwest. Most notably, the teaching schools are traditions through which China's Muslims realize life in accordance with localized versions of Islamic law and ethics.

Some scholars of China have used the term "sect" to describe the teaching schools (Dillon 1999; Israeli 2002d; Israeli and Gardner-Rush 2007). In Islamic studies, the term has been applied narrowly to the distinction between Sunni and Shiʻi Muslims, and this meaning has become dominant in understandings of Muslim sectarian difference.[9] But there

[9] There is another tradition stemming from the *hadith al-tafriqa* ("tradition concerning division") that appears in four of the six canonical collections of hadith: "The Jews divided into

135

are shortcomings to applying this understanding of "sect" to teaching schools. Among Hui, all teaching schools are Sunni, although historically this was not the case. The head of the Islamic Studies Institute at Lanzhou University, Ding Shiren, has argued that up until the Ming Dynasty at least some Hui were Shi'i.[10] Ding believes this shift from Shi'ism to an orthodox Sunni practice centered on the Hanafi school of law occurred during the sixteenth century. Today, all Hui are Sunni, with the possible exception of traces of Shi'i thought among Jahriyya (Israeli 2002a) and Qadiriyya Sufis (Wang 2014).

If "sect" is a problematic term for describing the teaching schools, then so is *madhhab* (pl. *madhāhib*), or school of jurisprudence. All teaching schools follow the Hanafi school, with the exception of the Salafiyya. (Qadir al-Jilani, the eponymous founder of the Qadiriyya, followed the Hanbali school, but Qadiriyya Sufis in contemporary Linxia follow the Hanafi school.) Non-Salafis will frequently refer to the Salafiyya as followers of the Hanbali school, the strictest of the jurisprudence schools, but the Salafis reject this characterization. During a conversation with a leading Salafi cleric in Lanzhou, he asked me, "Who is best suited to interpret the Qur'an?" In answer to his own question, he responded with "Shengmendizi" and then, in Arabic, "Aṣḥāb al-Nabī," or the Companions of the Prophet. His meaning was that the Salafiyya follow the practice of the Prophet and his Companions before the formation of the schools of jurisprudence. As I explain below, the Salafiyya's relationship to the Hanbali school is complicated and has implications for their theology. *Madhhab* is thus mostly unhelpful in understanding the teaching schools and their antagonisms.

In their explanation of what "teaching school" means to them, Hui frequently make reference to *jiaofa* and *jiaoyi*, "religious law" and "religious doctrine," respectively. If Islamic law and doctrine are the basis of the teaching school, and all teaching schools excepting the Salafiyya are Sunni and follow the Hanafi *madhhab*, then how do differences come in? They

seventy-one sects (*firqa*), the Christians into seventy-two sects, and my community will divide into seventy-three sects" (Mottahedeh 2010: 32). Along with the term *milla* (religious communities), *firqa* has been used to describe sects in medieval Islamic writings, although the criteria by which such sects are differentiated are unclear.

[10] Ding bases his argument on evidence from the *Gang Zhi* (1721), the history of the Hui community of Oxen Street in Beijing, which includes the phrase "*Lianbanzhi wu, qilai jiuyi*" (the successive group [prayer] system is mistaken [even if] they have practiced it a long time). He interprets the "successive group [prayer] system" (*lianbanzhi*) to be a specifically Twelver Shi'a practice, whereby the imam stands not at the front of the group but within the front row of men praying (Ding 2014: 43–44).

appear to be the result of the localization of doctrine in China, affected by factors of genealogy, history, and politics. Some teaching schools are representatives of Islamic communities outside of China, whereas others are emphatically Chinese realizations of Islam. All have linkages—material and imaginary—with centers beyond the Chinese nation-state, and yet all are, at the same time, thoroughly localized. The struggle for correct practice rides these circuits: to interpret the law is to lay claim to an authorizing tradition.

While the teaching schools cannot be labeled sects or *madhāhib* as understood in Islamic studies, their histories and ongoing debates are nonetheless "sectarian" in nature.[11] By sectarian, I refer to the disintegrative and combative effects when actors resort to disputes over correct practice, particularly when religious difference becomes the basis for political action. In Northwest China, rather than formal politics (e.g., political parties or civil society organizations), teaching-school contests become political when they dissolve the secular state's boundaries between privatized religion and the public sphere. Teaching schools as discursive traditions interpret incense, for example, as one sign that is linked to other signs that, in the aggregate, are both reflections of teaching-school doctrine and productive of such interpretations. When conflicting interpretations erupt into open-air accusations and fighting in public streets, doctrinal matters become blueprints for imposing orders alternative to those of other schools.

In the Middle East, sectarianism has been affected by colonialism (Makdisi 2000; Weiss 2010). In Linxia's case, the teaching schools are neither primordial nor purely a construction of the state. Members of schools have inherited long-standing differences between their school and others. At the same time, the formalization of teaching schools in China has been part of the state's production of social-scientific knowledge for purposes of rule. The conflict between the state, through its successive regimes, and sects has defined the place of religion in China (Naquin 1982; Weller 1982). David Palmer (2008) notes that the term *xiejiao* (evil cult) has been used by each regime but with nuanced meaning. *Xiejiao* has been used historically by both the state and teaching schools primarily in relation to Sufi groups. Members of both the Qadiriyya and Jahriyya in Linxia told me that in the past the state and rival schools have labeled them *xiejiao*

---

[11] The Deobandi and Barelvi in India and Pakistan, groups that are both Sunni and follow the Hanafi school but have different interpretations of the law, broadly "Wahhabi" and "Sufi," respectively, present one analogous situation to that of Northwest China's teaching schools (Zaman 1998; Metcalf 2002).

or *wudao* (lit. "without the way").[12] Following ethnic violence in Xinjiang after 2009, Internet commentators have invoked *xiejiao* and such corollaries as *xiejiao fenzi* (cultists) as a synonym for "splittists" (*fenlie fenzi*) and "terrorists" (*kongbu fenzi*).

Palmer (2008) observes a shift in the Party-State's determination of orthodoxy from using *xiejiao* to mean counterrevolutionary to deploying social-scientific knowledge to order religious groups and legitimate policies. His insight has broad applicability to the Party-State's penetration of teaching schools. The teaching schools have a taken-for-granted quality. The history of the schools outlined in Chapter 2 would seem to give credence to their self-evident nature. However, there has been widespread disagreement over how many teaching schools there are in China and how to classify them. As Lipman (1997: 71) points out, there is a cottage industry within Hui "ethnic studies" for the development of systems for schools and orders. One example of a pre-Communist classification system comes from an English translation of an article entitled "Mohammaden Factions in Northwest China," translated from the Chinese and first appearing in the newspaper *Ta Kung Pao* (*Da Gong Bao*) in Tianjin in 1934. The author, Chin Lin, provides the following classification: Old Religious Faction (Laojiao Pai), Pro-China Faction (Neixiang Pai), and New Religious Faction (Xinjiao Pai). The last one is subdivided into Hsuan Hua Kang (Xuanhuagang), Hsi Tao Tang of Lintan (Xidaotang), Hung Men Tao Tang (Hongmen Daotang), Ho Kung Pei (Huo Gongbei), and Hsin Hsing Sect (Xinxingpai) (Chin 1934). Reverend Claude L. Pickens, Jr., who lived in Linxia for a short time during the 1930s, divides Muslims into "old and new schools," which, from the description, refer to Gedimu and Yihewani, respectively (Pickens 1949). Japanese scholarship—for example, Iwamura Shinobu's survey on Islam in Mongolia—provides another schema of three schools: Laojiao (Khufiyya), Xinjiao (Jahriyya), and Xinxingjiao (Yihewani) (Iwamura 1950: ch. 5). Still another view is that Chinese Muslims together constitute one macro teaching school, unlike any other among Muslims elsewhere. These classifications have been largely overridden, however,[13] as scholars' understanding of the schools became calcified around the "three great teaching schools and four great Sufi orders" taxonomy.

---

[12] The way is a concept that is central to Chinese philosophy and has most often been associated with the philosophy-religion of Daoism. It is a concept of guidance, usually with prescriptive or normative meanings.

[13] A recent summary (Wang Xuemei 2012) omits many of these classification schemas.

The architect of this system is a Hui scholar named Ma Tong. Although Ma Tong did not invent the number of schools or orders (see, e.g., Tang (1942) for the typology of the four Sufi orders recognized today), he presented them in a more comprehensive and systematic fashion than had previously been attempted. It is rare in the social sciences for one figure to dominate a field, as Ma Tong has done in the study of Islam in China. A small man with watery eyes behind round-rimmed glasses, he was living in a hospital facility in Lanzhou, where he received treatment when I visited him over the course of my time in Gansu. He was born in 1927 in southern Gansu into a Jahriyya Sufi family, and he first developed an interest in Islam while studying law at Northwest University in Xi'an in 1946. In that year he began working for the Gansu Province Nationalities Affairs Commission in Lanzhou, where he served as secretary to Ma Qingnian, the vice minister of the Gansu Province United Front Work Department (UFWD), the Party organ that interfaces most closely with minorities. Ma Tong described Ma Qingnian as the Party secretary of Linxia City. Ma Tong was in charge of all matters regarding ethnicity and religion. The relationship between the two men would last until 1962 and define both their careers.

Ma Tong first went to Linxia in November 1949, as the people's governments were being installed, and began collecting data on Muslim minorities and their schools. Over the next twenty years he met with many leaders of orders in Linxia and the Xidaotang in Lintan. In 1952 he joined the Party and in that year began working for the Linxia Public Security Bureau. By 1956 Ma Tong had documented the basic situation of the teaching schools and orders, including the Xidaotang. According to his biographer, Ha Baoyu (2009: 160), drafts of his writings were circulated by the prefectural Party committee and the UFWD. As for his methodology, Ma Tong identifies his position vis-à-vis his interlocutors as a "common average cadre" (putong yiban ganbu) and not as a researcher. He explains, "The research was not for my work, it was separate. At that time, there was no such thing as social science." He went to mosques or tomb complexes alone or sometimes accompanied by a Muslim leader, such as Qi Mingde, the founder of the Bright Heart order and father of Qi Jiequan. He denied being part of any political meetings or the public trials in 1958 designed to elicit information from Hui leaders. In that year, during the anti-rightist purges, Ma Tong was attacked from within the Party. In 1968 he was forced to do manual labor.

Although he completed a draft of his field-forming study as early as 1954, only in 1983 was his research published as a book, entitled A Historical Record *of China's Islamic Teaching School and Sufi Order System* (*Zhongguo Yisilan jiaopai yu menhuan zhidu shilüe*) (hereinafter, the *System*). The reason for the postponed publication was the sensitivity of the content. The study addresses, in remarkable detail and breadth, the historical formation, doctrinal particularities, and interrelationships of the "three great teaching schools and four great Sufi orders:" the Gedimu, Yihewani, and Xidaotang schools, and the Qadiriyya, Khufiyya, Jahriyya, and Kubriwaya orders. Ma Tong's study has been foundational for a number of reasons. Foremost, he elaborated an extensive, detailed taxonomy, generating a set of qualifications for a group's status, based on its historical composition and presence through the Northwest, including the number of followers.

Moreover, he recognized the Xidaotang as a teaching school. The Xidaotang have struggled since their founding, sometimes violently, with Gedimu and Sufi groups in Lintan for recognition as an orthodox interpretation of Islam (Min 2007; Xidaotang 1987). Although the Xidaotang obtained governmental recognition in 1919, Ma Tong's authoritative inclusion of them in his study catapulted them from *xiejiao* to one of the "three great teaching schools." As one Xidaotang member remarked half-jokingly, "Mr. Ma Tong is our saint."

In short, the *System* has become the authoritative archive of Chinese Islamic schools, a case of "sectarianization from above" to employ Max Weiss's phrase (2010: 128). A major three-year study conducted by the Chinese Academy of Social Sciences, for example, uses the "four great Sufi order" system, citing Ma Tong's work (Li Weijian 2011: 4), and his students occupy positions of influence in research institutes in Lanzhou and Beijing.[14] Foreign scholars have elevated the *System* to nearly the status of primary source (Dillon 1999: xvii). Indicative of the penetration of academic knowledge into the lanes of Bafang, some Sufis today regard Ma Tong's work as a charter, a public grant of rights to practice as they desire, and they cite the *System* in their own written histories.

Yet the sanctification of the *System* is not unanimous. Yihewani and Salafiyya denounce Ma Tong's work. Their reason for doing so is not based on any evaluative criteria but rather the fact that the *System* recognizes

---

[14] Only in the last few years have Chinese scholars begun to write studies partially critical of the *System*. The first work observed that Ma Tong simplified the complexity of the Famen Sufi order's system of succession (Ma 2007). Lanzhou University's Ding Shiren has offered an alternative classification (Ding 2009). A Taiwanese study on Northwest teaching schools does without his nomenclature altogether, preferring *zongpai*, or "denominations" (Zhao 2010: 6). One of the first uses of *zongpai* was in Yang Zibai's ([1939] 1984) schema, which was developed in 1939 and which had six orders and three schools.

Sufis. Some Sufis likewise criticize his work. Their comments address his methodology and theory, showing that even the *System* can be subject to the process of refutation and contestation that characterizes Linxia's discursive exchange. A member of the Xidaotang concludes, "He was influenced by the political environment of the time." A member of the Qadiriyya goes further, claiming, "He got his data from the police station. He would go to tomb complexes and speak to masters, using his position as a representative of the state, and particularly during a time when there was much fear about the police arm of the state." Several Sufis at different tomb complexes said Ma Tong never actually visited their order and merely accepted some written accounts given to him, or people simply made things up. From these assessments, it is clear that Ma Tong was a technocrat concerned with engineering an analytical system. He was not interested in what Paul Bohannan (1957: 4) named the "folk system" or an emic experience of doctrine. Certainly, Marxism colored his vision of Chinese Sufism, which he described as "a unique feudal Sufi order system" (Ma [1979] 2000: 75). Yet it may be too much to consider the *System* as an analog to the *littérature de surveillance*, or "police report scholarship," such as the French historiography of North African mystical orders or Russian colonial administrators' writings on Central Asian Sufis (Vikør 1995: 11; Knysh 2002: 140).

Nonetheless, Ma Tong's *System* has become one method by which the secular state organizes and manages doctrinal difference among Muslim minorities. Like "customary law" (*xiguanfa*) and "ethnicity" (*minzu*), "teaching school" (*jiaopai*) has become a tool of discursive governance. It makes sense of and imposes order over the messiness of the fractious rival groups within Islam in China. As mentioned in Chapter 1, the purpose of the China Islamic Association (Yi-Xie) is to unite Muslim minorities under the leadership of the Party. Whereas the teaching schools each have a partisan view as to who constitutes the *umma*, the task of the Yi-Xie is to take the *umma*'s diverse and sometimes conflicting imaginings and unite them under a sense of national belonging. To cultivate national unity from Muslim heterogeneity, the state has tried "carefully to count the objects of its own feverish imagining" (Anderson 1983: 169). The state, however, has not recognized the legality of teaching schools. They have no legal status or rights, unlike "ethnic minorities." Consequently, their contests for correct practice occur through informal venues (e.g., scriptural debates in the mosques and lanes of Bafang).

To be clear, scholars such as Ma Tong have ambiguous relationships to the Party-State. Rather than the state directing research, often such "establishment intellectuals" (Mullaney 2011: 11) lead the state. Authoritarianism has many faces. In practice, an authoritarian regime is rarely uniform and must, by necessity, not only integrate but also depend on diverse views to hold the center.

SCHOOLS OF LAW

Teaching schools' interpretation of or orientation toward law is a result of their imaginary,[15] which links them to authenticating origins either inside or outside of China. Piety, particularly in reference to ritual matters, is cultivated with reference to such imaginaries, even as they are constrained and shaped by the Party-State and its preferred imagined unit, the multi-ethnic nation. In providing an overview of how the teaching schools interpret Islamic law, my goal is not to reify the schools according to official taxonomies but to show that each is anchored in its own authorizing discourse of law, which is practiced, performed, and argued. Such discourses are not only mutually defining and interactive (Gladney 1999b: 109–10) but also internally polyphonous.

Gedimu: China's Islamic legal tradition

The Gedimu approach to Islamic law is a result of their imagined descent from the first Central Asian Muslims to enter China, and their view of themselves as the beneficiaries of the "canonical" thought of the Chinese Muslim scholars who composed the books known as the Han Kitab. Historical consciousness and intellectual legacies have combined with nationalism to produce a distinctly Chinese Muslim approach to law. The sentiment underlying this view is conveyed in the statements of the Gedimu Hui policeman Officer Zeng: "Chinese Islam is unique. It is Chinese, and its Chineseness should be encouraged. Chinese Muslims are not Arab Muslims ... In terms of language, race, and culture, Chinese Muslims cannot forget their Chinese origins."

The opinion of the part-Tibetan Officer Zeng reflects some of the complexities of the Gedimu desire to emphatically and distinctly promote

---

[15] By "imaginary," I draw on a line of thought, informed by Benedict Anderson and Arjun Appadurai as much as Louis Althusser and Jacques Lacan, that posits the social world as a registry of images (of the nation, post-nation, *umma*, and the like). These images are perceived by, may possibly be created by, and potentially constitute, what has been called "the subject," a term I address later in this chapter. Olivier Roy (2004) has shown that this process of constructing an imaginary *umma* is heightened following the deterritorialization of Islam among Muslim minorities.

a Chinese form of Islamic practice. This principle undergirds much of their thought about law, with the exception of those learned Gedimu clerics who have studied law abroad. Such clerics bristle at the thought of a "Chinese Islamic law," believing instead, as one former mosque head and graduate of al-Azhar in Cairo told me, "There is only one Islamic law."

Gedimu privilege the revealed sources, the Qur'an and the sunna, as the basis of their law. Like other teaching schools, Gedimu do not produce the nonrevealed sources of law, namely, *qiyās* (analogies) and *ijmā'* (consensus), and they decry their lack of credentials to practice *ijtihād* (independent reasoning). When asked whether Hui used *qiyās*, one cleric explained:

> China has never had *mujtahidūn*, those who can practice *ijtihād*, because we Chinese clerics do not have the credentials.[16] The criteria to be a *mujtahid* are extremely high: he must master Arabic, know five hundred verses from the Qur'an, specialize in the principles of the religious law, study the various branches, memorize some three hundred thousand hadith, and attain six ranks.[17] The credentials are so high because the *mujtahid* represents God.

The young cleric further relates:

> This is a problem, because China—in fact, the whole world—needs *ijtihād* to create law to deal with a changing world and modern challenges. For example, the Qur'an does not mention organ transplants, and this has caused many legal problems not only in the Middle East but here in China. How are we Muslims supposed to abide by the religious law if it is silent on an issue?

When confronted with such an issue, Gedimu may consult compilations of Hanafi cases from abroad that are based on *qiyās* and *ijmā'*. If those sources fail to address the matter at hand, then Gedimu consult reference works by foreign scholars such as Yusuf al-Qaradawi. Yet such intellectual borrowings are diffuse. The interpretive frame for the Gedimu is very much Sinocentric.

---

[16] The cleric equates *qiyās*, a method, with *ijtihād* (Ch. *chuangzhi*), which means literally "to exert oneself" by using the faculty of reason to discern a point of law. Thus, *ijtihād* is going beyond the revealed sources based on individual reason. Classical jurists and contemporary scholars differ on whether *qiyās* can be equated with *ijtihād*, although most would categorize the former as a subtype of the latter (Vikør 2005: 53).

[17] The cleric's list of criteria for becoming a *mujtahid* concurs roughly with that of shari'a scholar Wael Hallaq. Hallaq adds the criteria of training in the theory of abrogation; training in the art of legal reasoning, specifically, how *qiyās* is conducted, and in the principle of causation; and knowledge of all cases sanctioned by consensus (Hallaq 1997: 24; 2005: 146).

Many Gedimu anchor their notion of a Chinese approach to Islamic law in the Han Kitab, of which Liu Zhi's *Tianfang Dianli* (*Laws and Rites of Islam*) (1710) is the primary work. *Tianfang Dianli* explains Islamic law through Neo-Confucian cognates.[18] It includes the two branches of Hanafi jurisprudence, *'ibādāt* and *mu'āmalāt*, which Liu Zhi explains through the Neo-Confucian cognates of "five meritorious deeds" (*wugong*) for the Five Pillars and the "five laws" (*wudian*) corresponding to the five Confucian relationships (Tontini 2011). Liu Zhi, however, grounded his study in the Neo-Confucian term *li* (rites) rather than *fa* (law) (Frankel 2011). The character *fa* has multiple meanings (e.g., transcendent, positive, natural), invoked by scholars according to their various intellectual commitments, whether Neo-Confucian, Legalist, Buddhist, or Huang-Lao, for example. Liu Zhi, who was writing not just for Muslim literati but also for Neo-Confucian readers, was strategic in his translation of Islamic law, using terms that would gain the most acceptance. Thus, it was not just because of the state's monopoly on civil law that Islamic law among Chinese Muslims privileged the ritual aspects over those of social relations.

Contemporary Gedimu claim Liu Zhi as their own. They also take pride in works that have long been used in "scriptural hall education" as pedagogical texts on law. For instance, Gedimu are proud of their knowledge of the *Wiqaya*, a fourteenth-century Central Asian synopsis of a text of legal rulings in the Hanafi school, not despite but because of it being an uncommon text for Muslims outside of China. As one local scholar put it, "They do not use it anymore, even in Central Asia!" Thus, from the Gedimu view, the Hui have preserved a classic text against the various forces of state-led secularization.

As for substantive law, following the long-term preference for ritual law, Gedimu say *'ibādāt*, including *ṭahāra*, is most important to their daily lives. They understand the core of *'ibādāt* as the Five Pillars, and particularly the correct instructions for prayer. In addition, they refer to *gongxiu*, a concept from Confucian ethics that means "self-cultivation" and that suggests standards of pious behavior and thought. Second in importance are family law matters, namely marriage and divorce.

Sufis: the three vehicles

The Sufi orientation toward law is complicated by their path (Ar. *ṭarīqa*), the basis of their imaginary that links them with centers of Sufi learning

---

[18] Sachiko Murata has discussed Liu Zhi's integration of Neo-Confucianism, Daoism, and Islam, including Sufi thought (Murata 2000, 2006; Murata, Chittick, and Tu 2009).

from Central Asia to India. In the official and popular nomenclature, Sufis are identified not as part of teaching schools but as a separate branch of the taxonomy (i.e., *menhuan*). The category "Sufis" itself encompasses a variety of paths, each with its own understanding of Islamic law. Nevertheless, there are commonalities among the Sufi orders, and so I consider them en masse here.

The path is a methodology distinct to the order, involving prayer, meditation, study, and sometimes isolation, asceticism, and other forms of self-discipline. The goal of the path is to increase proximity to God by removing egoistic impulses. Gnosis is known as *ḥaqīqa*, meaning reality, or truth. The practice of shariʿa is integrated into the path, and the path into reality. Because of the primacy of the path, the Sufi imagination is oriented both temporally and geospatially through the *silsila*, the chain of spiritual descent, which usually originates with a master in Central Asia, India, or the Middle East. For Sufis in China, the holy genealogy has taken a specifically Chinese form in the patriline. Furthermore, their practice is, like that of the Xidaotang, influenced by Confucianism, Buddhism, Daoism, and popular ancestor worship.

Sufis understand law as the "three vehicles": shariʿa, the path, and reality—or, respectively, the "vehicle of the teaching" (*jiaocheng*), the "vehicle of the way" (*daocheng*), and the "vehicle of the truth" (*zhencheng*) (Aubin 1990), sometimes collectively called "the three vehicles" (*sancheng*) of religious law.[19] These vehicles represent the stages in a Sufi's self-cultivation and trajectory toward gnosis. The observance of the three vehicles is traced through the *silsila* to an imagined genesis that lies beyond China but is nevertheless realized in the holy city of Linxia, where the tombs of the founders of Chinese orders reside. The path, to which shariʿa is wedded, is the line of legitimacy that connects these realities. The shaykh has attained the highest level of cultivation and thus has immeasurable authority in his order—so much so that one neophyte in a Khufiyya order told me, "He *is* the law." The shaykh, as ethical center of the order, must be followed even if his behavior violates Islamic law. A famous example is that of the Mufti Tomb Complex order in Lintao. According to a story involving the ninth-generation leader Ma Yun (1807–1876), during the anti-Qing rebellion, to evade capture by Han, Ma Yun smoked tobacco

---

[19] There is a fourth vehicle Chinese Sufis refer to as *mai'erleifuti*, or *marefeiti* (Ar. *ma'rifa*): knowledge of God. Sufis usually do not include this fourth vehicle in the "three vehicles" of religious law, because it is nearly unattainable for mortals, although they usually say the founder of their order in fact attained this level.

and thus escaped suspicion that he was a Muslim. As a result, adherents in the tomb complex in Kangle pass around a pipe during communal prayer.

Sufis differ in opinion as to whether the path directly informs a Sufi's observance of shariʿa. A Sufi of a Naqshbandi-Mujaddidi order says emphatically, "No. *Ṭarīqa* is inside knowledge, whereas shariʿa is outside knowledge." This distinction conforms generally to the distinction in Islam, and in Qurʾanic exegesis in particular, between the inner (Ar. *bāṭin*) movements of one's soul and the outer (Ar. *ẓāhir*) commands and prohibitions. A Jahriyya teaching cleric disagrees, arguing:

> The special characteristic of the Jahriyya, which sets them apart from the other three orders, is that we totally integrate shariʿa and the path. Most orders place the path over shariʿa, and the Yihewani place shariʿa over the path, of course. But we see the path as the deeper extension of shariʿa. So while shariʿa means the Five Pillars, the path means stricter [adherence]. So for reading, the path means reading the Qurʾan more and more often with deeper understanding. To see the difference, under shariʿa, a Muslim must work, but under the path, he must work as hard as he can. To give an example from dietary law, under shariʿa, a Muslim cannot eat what is haram. But under the path, he should avoid eating not only that which is haram but also that which is reprehensible [*makrūh*].[20] The path, like shariʿa, touches on interpersonal relations. For instance, while under shariʿa, it is permitted to sit with one's legs crossed casually when talking to another, under the path, this is impolite. Similarly, while one does not have to wear a head covering to pray, under the path, one must wear one. And while one can pray wearing a short-sleeve shirt, under the path, he cannot.

Interpretations of the three vehicles are fundamental to the self-definition of the orders.

As with the Gedimu, Sufis emphasize *ʿibādāt* as the core of their Islamic law, although their perspective is filtered through their path. The path may be based within China or beyond it: for example, the Bright Heart order in Linxia is based in India, and the Dongxiang Beizhuang order is based in Altishar (southern Xinjiang). Practice of Islamic law thus links their worship with the base of their path in a continuous and self-authenticating chain. Often, the chain of succession and the particulars of the path override shariʿa in importance, yet ritual matters of law

---

[20] Islamic law categorizes acts into one of five standards: obligatory, recommended, permitted, reprehensible, and prohibited.

continue to be a defining criterion demarcating Sufis from other schools, as seen in the case of incense.

Xidaotang: legal syncretism in the eastern *umma*

The Xidaotang conception of Islamic law is inseparable from their notion of the *wuma* (Ar. *umma*) as an intellectual project and imagined place. Whereas classically the *umma* refers to the earliest community of believers in Medina, and the term evolved into a concept that describes the global community (see, generally, al-Faruqi 2005), when Ma Qixi founded the Xidaotang, he interpreted the concept to apply to his particular school. The *wuma*, as he conceived it, was to be not only a spiritual and intellectual community but also a social and economic one. The religious heart was West Phoenix Mountain in the old city of Lintan, where the Xidaotang built a mosque, a number of schools, including girls' schools, and eventually tombs for their successive leaders. The Xidaotang sought to integrate Islam into everyday life in their Chinese milieu and rigorously studied the Han Kitab authors; because of their emphasis on classical Chinese learning and the Han Kitab, they are also called the Han Studies School (Hanxuepai). A member of the Linxia Xidaotang mosque told me what it means to be a part of the Xidaotang: "You are a member at birth. But you do not take up responsibilities until after you have graduated from high school. Only then do you have knowledge of Han Chinese language and literature. This is the core of one's cultural quality. We are Chinese first and Muslims second."

The Xidaotang therefore share with Gedimu a close identification with China as a geographic and cultural place, but their identification is localized in Lintan. According to the official history, *The Light of the Crescent Moon* (*Xinyue zhiguang*) by Shaykh Min Shengguang (2007), the *wuma* was a religious commune that united the community not by blood ties but by common faith and the observance of "strict shari'a law" (Min 2007: 2). The memory of a strict shari'a may reflect a utopian vision of the *wuma*. Indeed, many members spoke of the *wuma* with a kind of longing. Such past-referential aspiration suggests a kind of "structure of memory" (Ho 2006: 46) characterized by idealization. Their application of Islamic law within the multiethnic borderland of Lintan was in fact quite creative. Their syncretic approach to spiritual, intellectual, and commercial life drove them to adapt Islamic law, particularly in the fields of marriage, inheritance, and property.

To collectivize the labor and worship of families, the Xidaotang built massive compounds called "grand houses." The only surviving grand house is an artifact of Xidaotang legal syncretism. Located outside Lintan old city, it is named the "Eastern Umma" (Dongfang Wuma). Built in 1943, the Eastern Umma was occupied by two families, who practiced communal marriage and child rearing there until 1966. Under the communal family system, nuclear families were dissolved, radically altering rights and responsibilities between members of the house. A woman who grew up in the Eastern Umma describes a communal wedding:

> Ten or twenty pairs, all members of the Xidaotang, would marry at the same time in the *daotang* [center of instruction] in Lintan. The couples would meet for the first time during the ceremony, their parents and families having done preparation work and inquiries. But the actual couple would not meet until that day, and they would have final say as to whether they thought they were compatible. The bride's costume was provided by the Xidaotang, namely the *baiyin zuode hua* [silver flower], a large circular plate of silver worn around the bride's neck that fell around her waist [see Figure 3.1]. There was no bridal gift [Ar. *mahr*]. After the wedding, the couple would move into the home of the man's family. Both would work, but the Xidaotang would provide for their daily needs by giving money.

Couples who married communally and followed virilocal customs, common to both Han and Hui, maintained a monogamous pairing. Couples who subsequently moved to the Eastern Umma would, however, join the collective family. There is no evidence of polygamy, but the obligations of a member to the collective family trumped duties to one's spouse. The husband would provide neither *mahr* nor maintenance to the wife.[21] Rather, all living costs and material security were provided by the center of instruction, and all property was communal. There was no inheritance system. Family law and domestic life, more generally, were shaped by the needs of the Eastern Umma and so diverged in significant ways from both the practices of the Prophet Muhammad's *umma* in Medina and the classical Hanafi jurisprudence that developed in the tenth and eleventh centuries.

Yihewani: scriptural return

If the Sufi imaginary of law consists of multiple ellipses concentrated around Linxia, then the Yihewani imaginary is predominantly Hijaz-oriented. In theory, their views on law embrace the revealed sources

---

[21] See Chapter 5 for explanations of these terms.

Figure 3.1 A Xidaotang bride wearing a "silver flower." The photograph dates to the mid-1990s

Source: Ding family archive

and the studies of *fiqh* that Ma Wanfu brought back to China from Mecca. They reject as *shirk* (idolatry) the notion that a Sufi master can embody the law. Just as the Muslim Brothers in Egypt and Saudi Arabia reacted against what they viewed as "cultural accretions" in Islamic practices among Muslims in such regions, so too did the Yihewani inveigh against traditionalist Chinese Islam. This component of the Yihewani movement is that of "respecting the scripture, reforming the customs" (*zunjing gesu*).

Ma Wanfu called for a return to the scriptural basis of the law, the mandatory use of Arabic for proclamations of faith and associated prayers, and the abolition of all activities associated with Sufi tomb complexes. Specifically, he advocated a ten-point plan of reform: (1) do not collectively read the Qur'an—only one person can read, the others must listen; (2) do not recite the *dhikr* out loud; (3) do not perform supplication (Ar. *duʿāʾ*) too much; (4) do not worship tomb complexes; (5) do not collectively recite *taobai* (Ar. *tawba*, the atonement of sins); (6) do not commemorate the death date of loved ones; (7) do not use the Qur'an to "turn *fidya*" (i.e., make atonement for the dead); (8) perform zakat and do not

149

perform supererogatory prayers beyond the five daily prayers; (9) advocate the use of *shenghailei* (Ar. *sahl*, easy);[22] and (10) perform *ermaili* (Ar. *'amala*, "to do") oneself and similarly, read the Qur'an oneself (Compilation Committee 2004: 269). Many of the prohibited acts are the foundations of Sufi practice.

For the Yihewani, their opposition to the Gedimu and Sufis might have failed to develop a following had it not been for the patronage of temporal authority. In the Republican period, not only did Ma Wanfu benefit from the patronage of Ma Bufang and Ma Buqing, but young Yihewani scholars, in the 1930s and 1940s, also studied at al-Azhar University, the great center of Islamic law instruction, "reuniting" exilic Chinese Islam with that of the "heartland" (Benite 2008). These returnees would initiate many of the Yihewani modernization campaigns through publishing magazines and journals, translating canonical texts, and establishing civil society organizations (Mao 2011). Their interests were nonetheless congruent with, rather than opposed to, those of the Republican state. Henceforth, the Yihewani program supported political China.

In the Communist period, the Yihewani again anchored their interests with those of the state (Lipman 1997: 208–9). As part of this accommodation, the Yihewani aligned their program for Islamic reform with state-led modernization. Maris Gillette (2000: 76) calls this process "Arabization," meaning "a cluster of ideas about development for Muslims" that serves as an alternative to a state-defined path and yet does not conflict with the Party's program. Within this mutuality of interests, the Yihewani have advocated an interpretation of Islamic law that downplays conflicts with state law. Rather, the two are harmonized under the umbrella of modernity. Yihewani are most likely to argue that the Qur'an contains the basis for scientific and medical knowledge—for example, that dietary rules and prohibitions pertaining to blood prefigured germ theory. Such interpretations of Islamic law are consistent with the secular state's project of admitting a rational form of religion into modernity (Palmer 2007: 300; Nedostup 2009: 3).

The Yihewani in the contemporary Northwest are far from uniform in their doctrinal orientation. On one end of the spectrum are those, such as the cleric of a major mosque in Yinchuan and head of the Ningxia Yi-Xie, who recognize the works of the Han Kitab as their intellectual patrimony. Such moderate Yihewani consult a number of traditional translated texts

---

[22] This injunction appears to refer to an approach toward law that should not be strenuous or exacting but, rather, natural.

to resolve legal problems presented by members of their communities. The cleric showed me, as an example, his well-worn copy of *The Translation and Annotation of the Islamic Compass (Qingzhen zhinan yizhu)*. This work is a condensation of *The Islamic Compass (Qingzhen zhinan)* (1683), a ten-volume doctrinal exegesis by the Yunnan Hui scholar Ma Zhu (b. 1640). Ma Zhu composed the work, I was told by the cleric, to provide instructions on law for wayward Muslims. With *The Islamic Compass* in one hand, the cleric reached for 'Abd al-Rahman al-Jaziri's encyclopedic *Islamic Jurisprudence according to the Four Sunni Schools (al-Fiqh 'ala al-Madhahib al-Arba'a)* with the other hand. Al-Jaziri (1882–1941) was an Egyptian jurist who composed the didactic text to cover the major positions of all four schools during a period of modernization in Egypt. Moderate Yihewani are comfortable applying rules derived from the Ming-era Han Kitab just as much as those from modern works from the Muslim "heartland," and they see no contradiction in such intellectual endeavor.

On the other end of the spectrum are puritanical Yihewani. These Yihewani tend to prefer using *fiqh* texts from Saudi Arabia and Egypt, rather than indigenous Hui works, and emphasize learning from Arabic sources—in translation, if need be—which they consider unadulterated explanations of Islamic law. The differences between moderate and puritanical Yihewani is partly due to the entry of different streams of reformist thought into Linxia.

In Linxia, several so-called Yihewani mosques are heavily influenced by Salafism: Han Family Mosque, West Gate Grand Mosque, New Glory Mosque, Lower Wooded Field Mosque, Village Mosque, and Lower Second Society Mosque. The Salafi imprint on these mosques has reoriented their legal tradition around a perceived closer link to the Middle East, and these mosques all have clerics who have studied abroad in Saudi Arabia or Egypt. Their study of such materials connects them to what they perceive as a purist Islamic law, despite their school's own localization in Northwest China.

Salafiyya: theology and politics

Perhaps more than other teaching schools, the Salafiyya feel disconnected from their idealized version of correct practice (itself based on an imagined Hijaz-based past) because of their political circumstance. As Bernard Haykel (2009: 35) has noted, "The Salafi imagination reconstructs the early Muslims' sartorial, linguistic, cultural and ethical habits and insists on being exactly like them." The Salafiyya surmount the difficulty of this reconstruction by imagining law as transcending both time and space.

151

One of the most recent schools to emerge in China, the Salafiyya valorize the earliest (i.e., revealed) sources, nearly exclusively. Their center of gravity is uncomfortably poised between Mecca and China's Little Mecca.

The Salafiyya promote a return to the first three generations of Islam. They are the only school to explicitly distinguish themselves from the Hanafis, identifying with Islamic law before the schools of jurisprudence evolved. A *minjian* Salafi cleric, defined as one who is not attached to a mosque and may not have a cleric license, described the Salafi view on the hierarchy of legal sources as the following: "The Salafiyya take the Qur'an and hadith as the basis. After this, [we consider] the words and deeds of the disciples found in the legacy [*yixun*] often included in the hadith, as the second part. Lastly are the legal experts."

Other teaching schools describe Salafis as adhering to the Hanbali school of jurisprudence, which prefers a literalist approach to legal reasoning. For instance, on the matter of the correct practice of the *wuḍu'* (Ch. *xiaojing* 小净), the partial ablution required before all prayer, the Qur'an does not specify how the head should be ritually cleansed. The Salafiyya reject the prescriptions of each of the four schools out of hand as violations of the central tenet of *tawḥīd*, the oneness of God, since following a jurist, in their view, means placing him at the level of God (al-Sulayman 2009: 11–13). Nonetheless, as to the actual practice Salafis adopt to perform *wuḍu'*, they most likely follow the Hanbali recommendation, since they perceive it to be minimalist and since it approximates Saudi practice.

The Salafis cultivate a revival of Arab Islam by emulating Saudis. Consequently, they imitate Arab Muslims in their dress (the *thawb* and *shimāgh*), their preference for their Arabic "scriptural name" (*jingming*), and their goatees. The architecture of River's Edge Front Mosque, the largest Salafiyya mosque in China, most resembles that of mosques from the Arabian peninsula, and their reading material includes images of the mosque superimposed onto images of the Sacred Mosque, the two together in photographic synchronicity. All of their literature is Chinese-Arabic bilingual. Their literature also includes documentation of contacts with Saudi organizations, including visits by past and present general secretaries of the Muslim World League, such as Muhammad al-'Abudi in 1985 and 'Abdallah bin 'Abd al-Muhsin al-Turki in 2004 and 2010. Such contacts have helped form links to Saudi-based groups that have provided financial support to budding Salafi networks.

Near the end of 2010, I had the opportunity to observe a ceremony in which the Salafiyya, as well as other schools, welcomed back hajjis from

Mecca (see also Gillette 2003). Such ceremonies underscore the Salafi imaginary of law. Men and students of River's Edge Front Mosque had formed a line from the mosque entrance down the street to welcome the thirteen men from the mosque who had participated in the hajj. The hajjis were dropped off at the end of the line and, one by one, shook the outstretched hands of those gathered, who would also often hug the hajjis, sometimes kissing them on both cheeks. Unlike the Gedimu, Sufis, and Xidaotang, however, after the embrace or the kiss, the men did not "touch face" (molian), a symbolic act of receiving the blessing from hajjis, who had been cleansed of their sins after the hajj. And unlike other schools, once the Salafiyya hajjis arrived at the mosque to pray, they did not burn incense.

I pointed these differences out to a man standing next to me. He responded, "That's not Islam, that's Chinese practice, and we do not do it. Go to Saudi Arabia, you will see that we are one and the same mosque." For the Salafiyya, practice is inextricably tied to their origins in Saudi Arabia, seen as the heartland of Islam, and the perceived continuity of their practice with that of the earliest Muslims there. Yet the Salafiyya's own history belies the imagined connection with Saudi Arabia. It was missionary activity from Central Asia that brought the Salafi teaching to Linxia.[23] The desire among the Salafis to re-create the link with the "pure" Islam of the Saudis, however, mystifies such displacements.

Like the other schools, the Salafiyya are internally diverse. The doctrine of the oneness of God, or tawḥīd, has been a particular point of contention for the Salafiyya, both in their efforts to differentiate themselves from other schools and within the school itself. Historical differences in hermeneutical approaches to tawḥīd created two factions within the early Salafiyya. The debate began over the correct translation of the Qur'an, specifically, the word istawā, which appears in the phrase istawā 'alā al-'arshi, found in seven verses of the Qur'an.[24] One of the founders of the Salafiyya in China, Ma Zhengqing, preferred the Chinese translation "Allah sits rightfully on the throne" (Anla duanzuo zai baozuo shang). Another early convert, Ma Debao, however, advocated the translation "Allah has surpassed the throne" (Anla gaoguo le baozuo). Ma Debao gained a foothold in New Wang Mosque, the earliest Salafiyya mosque in China (est. 1950), whereas Ma Zhengqing was more successful in cultivating students throughout the Northwest and especially in Huangzhong County

[23] On the social construction of Salafiyya ideology, see Lauzière (2010: 373).
[24] See Q. 7:54, 10:3, 13:2, 20:5, 25:59, 32:4, and 57:4.

in Qinghai. In the 1930s and 1940s several Bafang mosques were converted to Salafiyya. Gladney (1999b: 104) has called the two factions the immanentalists and the transcendalists, and noted that the Salafis' debate echoed that of medieval Christians.

Taking up where Gladney left off, I understand the disagreement as an expression of tension between the Salafi view of a divinely ordered world and the practicalities of living in a postsocialist state. Or, in other words, it shows one edge of the Hui social field. In Islamic theology, the ambiguity of the word *istawā*[25] lies at the heart of *tawhīd*, what Hui call *renzhuxue*, or "the science of recognizing the Lord." The doctrine of one truth, independent of all creation, was central to Salafi thought. Salafis discuss *tawhīd* as the opposite of *shirk*, or idolatry, a perpetual concern in Linxia with its fusions of religions and ethnicities, and they invoke the concept as the basis for reform and in their critique of other teaching schools. To do so, they translate works from Arabic and cite them in arguments with other schools and among themselves. While *tawhīd* is central to spiritual matters, their discussions of it also hold meaning as part of their coming to terms with their own limited autonomy, understood broadly as encompassing religious, political, and economic life.

The debates between Linxia Salafis over the nature of God reflect agitation over what Agamben (2011) would call their conception of "economy," or the administration of God's will in this world. Emphasizing a transcendent or immanent divinity are divergent approaches to rationalizing a purist Islamism that continually runs up against the circumscribing authority of the state. More so than the other schools, with the exception perhaps of the Sufis, the Salafiyya have encountered resistance in establishing mosques and madrasas and in developing larger networks. It is telling that the one *minjian* (unregistered) mosque in Bafang is Salafiyya. In other words, the political reality of practicing Islam in Linxia contrasts with their theology.

From teaching schools to jural communities

In assessing the various schools' orientations toward law, I infer the following: First, schools differ in their textual authorities, including their sources, whether Chinese, Arabic, or Persian. Translation, the hallmark

---

[25] The Arabist Hans Wehr includes the following definition of the verb (the eighth form of root *s-w-y*): "to stand upright, erect, straight; to straighten up; to sit down (on), mount (s.th.); to sit firmly" (Cowan 1976: 444).

of Chinese Muslim hermeneutics, and the means of localizing Islamic law in the Chinese context are particularly prone to generating debate.[26] This tendency is particularly so among the Salafis, who have formed transla-tion groups to make *fiqh* more accessible to Hui. Chinese Muslim scholars during the Ming and Qing periods, most famously the authors of the Han Kitab, mined the language of the Confucian classics for terms suitable to convey the divine message. In reform-era China, the issues of authori-tative sources and translation are again fostering innovation and dissen-sion. Clerics across the schools mimic scholars such as Yusuf al-Qaradawi, the "global mufti" (Gräf and Skovgaard-Petersen 2009), in mobilizing new media to spread school interpretations. Several clerics in Xining and Lanzhou, for example, have established websites to address questions Hui have regarding proper dress and decorum.

Second, ritual aspects of law, including prayer, forms of reading, and dress, are the building blocks of an ethical life when observed in accord-ance with school prescriptions. From the elaborate paths of the Sufis to the minimalist methods of the Salafiyya, ritual law is a valorized domain of school epistemology. Perhaps most importantly, correct practice of ritual is the chief means by which one imagines a connection with an author-izing center of Islam. As Maurice Godelier wrote, "The sacred ... always has to do with power insofar as the *sacred is a certain kind of relationship with the origin*" (cited in Shneiderman 2014: 281, emphasis is Godelier's). Linxia's Muslims gain access to a multiplicity of origins—Lintan, Xinjiang, India, Saudi Arabia, Egypt, and so on—through their objectified practice of ritual law. The Party-State has tried to shape these imaginaries, to make them "turn inward." One of its subtler methods is bureaucratizing leading clerics—such as the moderate Yihewani cleric in Yinchuan, the leader of the Ningxia Yi-Xie—who then exercise a kind of "double hermeneutic," interpreting Islamic law through both Islamic and Chinese socialist tenets.

Third and related, because teaching schools are "communities of inter-pretation" (Habermas 2008: 20), they prescribe guidelines for an ethical life in accordance with Islamic law as well as the demands of the postsocial-ist state. Schools differ in their understanding of the restrictions imposed on them, whether political or linguistic. For instance, all teaching schools face the limitation of not using *qiyās* and *ijmā'* to create law specific to the conditions of Muslim minorities in China. Rationales for this omission

---

[26] A conservative position since the Ash'ari school of philosophy in the tenth century has been that the Qur'an cannot be translated. Without translation, however, there would be no Muslims in China.

run the gamut. The Gedimu cleric, for example, agonizes over the lack of scholarly credentials that prohibit clerics from engaging in *ijtihād*. For the Salafiyya, however, minimalist use of these sources is rationalized according to their doctrinal tradition: the *ijmā'* of the Companions is the only one that matters and only *qiyās* from them is valid. Schools wrestle with resolving tensions between the limitations of their lawmaking capacity and their own authorizing discourses. Whereas Muslim minorities in China have not developed specific reasoning methods that would enable *ijtihād*, each school has its own "consensus."

Fourth, even if schools explicitly refer only to religious sources in orienting their followers to a certain engagement with Islam, the interpretations they advocate touch on issues of secular life. Like Indonesian Muslim communities, schools each have their own project of "encompassing pluralism" (Bowen 2003: 254) in its various expressions—normative, legal, religious, customary, and secular. The difference is that Chinese Muslims are bereft of a representative political system or public sphere through which they can communicate and channel their voices, opinions, and perspectives into policy making. Much of the angst of the Salafiyya is a result of their efforts to reconcile their theology, which contemplates God's presence in the world, with the political system of ethnic autonomy, which operates contrary to self-rule.

GRAVEYARD POLITICS

Having suggested that the teaching schools are discursive traditions of Islamic law that address issues that cannot be compartmentalized into a privatized religion, the question remains as to why, when such traditions interpret signs of their social world (especially ritual), divergence of opinion incites violence. The conventional view on teaching-school disputes, as established by Ma Tong's *System*, is that such doctrinal differences are excuses: Ritual difference is manipulated by charismatic leaders to mobilize their followers, attack rivals, and gain more converts and power. Historically, such conflicts also involved potentially vast wealth in the form of pious endowments (*awqāf*) and other assets that were seized in the course of disputing. Ma Tong (1989: 19; [1979] 2000: 86) first advocated this position in the 1950s. The materialist view[27] has gained recognition

---

[27] Ma Tong was not the first to advocate this position, nor was it distinctly Marxist. For example, Reverend Claude L. Pickens, Jr., who lived in Linxia during the 1930s, wrote in 1949 that the differences between the schools are "mainly on the surface" (Pickens 1949).

not just from the Party-State but also from Western scholars.[28] Ma Tong wrote explicitly against the explanation for sectarian violence that uncritically accepted doctrinal difference as the underlying cause for conflict (Ma Tong [1979] 2000: 109). In the materialist-realist explanation, differences are objectified, manipulatable, and superstructural.

This dominant explanation, however, does not explain the symbolic dimensions of law and doctrine, the tremendous psychic investment nonelite Hui place in ʿibādāt. In contrast to Orientalist studies of Islamic law, which emphasized its civil and penal aspects over its ritual ones, scholars of Islam have demonstrated the ways in which rituals produced difference within Muslim communities (see, e.g., Haider 2011). Along these lines, in the study of Islam the pendulum needs to swing back from a vulgar Marxist approach[29] to the center, so as to incorporate both material interests—among Muslims as well as between Muslim minorities and the Party-State—and the symbolic aspects of arguing for authentic versions of Islam.

I do not dispute that power is always present in inter-teaching-school contests. There is a strong element of educational elitism, control of knowledge, and socioeconomic-lineal prestige in the discourse and practices of clerics and Hui leaders. Clerics monopolize knowledge about Islamic law, and through their charisma they elicit obedience from their piously devoted communities of nonelite Hui, who follow them as representatives of Islam. At the same time, average mosque attendees talk about ritual concerns on their way to and from prayer. When a young cleric returns from abroad with a novel understanding of the law, such nonelite Hui respond, often influenced (but not unreflectively) by their own clerics' reactions. For its part, the Party-State's control of debate about Islam in the public sphere has exacerbated rather than suppressed doctrinal disagreement. The case of burial rites is exemplary of these politicized aspects of ritual lawfare.

Differences in funerary practices have been one of the most common causes of interschool friction in Hui communities. To explain the differences, I describe the ritual practice called guizhen (lit. "return to the truth," or dying)[30] as it is carried out and represented by the different teaching

---

[28] Pillsbury (1978) provides a similar analysis between xinjiao (new teaching) and laojiao (old teaching) schools among Taiwanese Muslims.

[29] Marx himself privileged imagination as a constitutive feature of the consciousness of man-as-producer (see Graeber 2001: 58).

[30] The term guizhen derives from the Buddhist lexicon for "to die." Hui, whose name for Allah is Zhenzhu (the true Lord), have adapted the term guizhen to mean "return to Allah."

schools in Linxia. Leor Halevi (2007) has argued that in the early period of Islam death rituals were foundational to an emergent Islamic identity vis-à-vis Christianity, Judaism, and Zoroastrianism.[31] In much the same way, Muslim minorities in the Northwest reproduce teaching-school differences within Islam through everyday burial ritual. Discourse about such distinctions, in the form of accusations, defenses, polemics, and scriptural debates, works both to represent one's school and (mis)represent other schools. Such discourse suggests religious orthopraxy is at stake, and also broader meanings of the relationship between faith, community, and authority, including ideas of economic justice, participation, and equality. Teaching-school practices of burial rites signify these broader meanings and reproduce, at a granular level, their distinct interpretations of law (see Table 3.1).

Historically, the most controversial aspect of the funeral was who was authorized to read the Qur'an during the funeral prayer (Ar. *jināza*). To the north of Linxia, in the Muslim Public Cemetery, amid the headstones and tiered, crumbling loess, teaching schools perform their differences in burial rites, reproducing school distinctions. On any given day, there are two, three, or more funerals conducted at the same time on North Mountain. Funeral attendees include the deceased's friends and business associates from different schools. In my observations of burials, these non-members would often approach me and quietly instruct me in Bafanghua on the differences between their school's practice and the present one.

Hence I often experienced a voice in my ear describing the "correct" practice as I was watching the practice of another school. The chief concern was that I, as an outsider, would be misinformed about proper burials. Among most Salafiyya and puritanical Yihewani, only the cleric will read the Qur'an for the duration of the service. Other Salafis reject the practice of reading the Qur'an altogether, arguing that there is no basis for it in the Qur'an, and elect instead to merely pray for the deceased by performing *du'ā'*. Among Gedimu and Sufis, the students join the cleric in reading the first sura of the Qur'an, "al-Fātiha." Salafiyya and Yihewani make a clear distinction in this regard. A Salafi cleric explains their position: "The main purpose of the funeral rites is to pray for the deceased. The head of the mosque community reads the Qur'anic sura and no one else." A Yihewani man attending the funeral of a Gedimu

---

[31] Similarly, in the context of Chinese religion, James Watson (1988: 3) has argued, "To be Chinese is to understand, and accept the view, that there is a correct way to perform rites associated with the life cycle, the most important being weddings and funerals."

TABLE 3.1 A summary chart of teaching-school interpretations of law

Teaching School	Self-Ascribed Origin	View of Law	Geographic Imaginaries	Links between Law and Imaginary
Gedimu	Descendants of original Arab and Persian migrants to China (7th c.)	Emphasis on ʿibādāt Pragmatic	China	Intellectual: Han Kitab Spiritual: hajj Economic: regional and national networks, limited ties to the Middle East
Sufi	Recipients of the path from missionaries from outside China (17th c.)	Path-based	China Central Asia Iran Yemen India	Intellectual: Han Kitab Spiritual: pilgrimages to tombs within and outside China
Xidaotang	Ma Qixi as founder of this unique community within China (early 20th c.)	Syncretic Communal	Lintan, Gansu	Intellectual: Han Kitab Economic: regional and national networks within China
Yihewani	Ma Wanfu as founder of the Chinese version of the Muslim Brothers in Egypt and Saudi Arabia (early 20th c.)	Emphasis on Qur'an and hadith Limited allowance of fiqh	Saudi Arabia Egypt Pakistan	Intellectual: study abroad in Gulf states, translation of Arabic fiqh Spiritual: hajj Economic: financial support for education from the Middle East, business with Arab Muslims
Salafiyya	Ma Debao and Ma Zhengqing as founders of the Chinese version of Salafi movements in Egypt and Saudi Arabia (early 20th c.)	Emphasis on Qur'an and hadith Allow secondary sources from the Companions	Saudi Arabia	

friend complained to me, "When they [the Gedimu] all read the Qur'an together, it is a cacophony." The Sufi shaykh Qi Jiequan, by contrast, stated:

> For us Ancient School, every person must read the Qur'an. Everyone's diligence is at a different level, so all must read at their own level. The Yihewani have only one person read! Can you imagine? Such a practice violates the spirit of the sacred law. The Salafiyya emphasize the Qur'an and the hadith to the exclusion of Islamic law. There is much in the Qur'an and hadith, but they do not cover the entire field of the holy law that has developed for centuries. They discount the contributions of generations of scholars to developing this law. For instance, the Qur'an does not say precisely how to pray, and so the law of self-cultivation [gongxiu] has been developed to explain this. It is incredulous to discount the works of the four great imams.

The issue of who reads the Qur'an indexes the schools' various approaches to interpreting Islamic law. Qi invokes the *fiqh* of 'ibādāt as a basis for his order's practice, whereas Salafis, consistent with their hermeneutics of Islamic law, base their practice purely on its authorization in the revealed sources. All arguments are based on the assertion "as was done in the time of the Prophet," implicitly referring to the sunna.

Other seemingly incidental differences in burial rites are similarly grounded in debates about the correct reading of the law. For instance, Gedimu, Sufis, and Xidaotang, after performing a *du'ā'* at the conclusion of the funeral prayer, may place incense over the fresh mound of earth and recite a *dhikr* (see Figure 3.2). Salafis and all Yihewani may also perform a *du'ā'*, but never a *dhikr* (see Figure 3.3). Likewise, Gedimu will return to the grave of a family member to pray and burn incense several times a day and sometimes at night during the first forty days, when they consider the soul to still reside in the grave. Slaughtering sheep, inviting the cleric to the home of the bereaved, performing *du'ā'*, and reading the Qur'an may occur during the first seven days after the death, with smaller observances on subsequent multiples of seven days. Neoconservatives inveigh against such postmortem practices as having no basis in scripture and being dangerously akin to ancestor worship.

In the domain of Hui ritual law, the issues of whether the Qur'an is read at graves, as well as other components of the burial liturgy, are symbolic acts that touch upon the school's internal organization, attitude toward leadership, and most prominently, its approach to following religious law. Such proxy arguments among China's Muslim minorities are

Figure 3.2 Sufis reciting the *dhikr* after a funeral. Note that they have embedded incense sticks in the grave

Source: the author

hardly unique and define both disagreements among Muslims and—in more general, comparative contexts—among opposing sides of tradition and modernity in religion. In the highlands of Indonesia, to take one example, traditionalist and modernist Muslims argue over mortuary recitations, with the latter dismissing the former as following pre-Islamic custom (Bowen 1993: 26). For both sides, specific practices are windows onto larger issues of scriptural interpretation. In the context of Christian conversion in Indonesia, Protestants called Sumbanese "fetishists" for conflating agentic subjects and objects (Keane 2007: 77). Muslim reformists and Christian missionaries alike have denigrated Sufi practice as "tomb worship," that is, elevating the tomb itself to an object of veneration, rather than as a place to seek intercession with God.

What distinguishes the China case from Indonesia is that there are no representational bodies that intervene to resolve religious disputes (Bowen 1993: 64–65). The state's predominant role is regulating the social space and its use (in this case, the Muslim Public Cemetery), leaving clerics to address disputes that emerge from activities in that space.

Figure 3.3 A Salafi burial. Note that no student reads from the Qur'an

Source: the author

The Muslim Public Cemetery is operated by the Muslim Public Cemetery Administration Committee, under the Linxia City Yi-Xie, which consists of a group of elder men from various teaching schools. The prefectural government was permitted to issue rules on burial and interment that were an exception to the law that requires all bodies interred to be cremated before interment.[32] The Muslim Public Cemetery Administration Committee charges a fee for a plot of land. However, it does not operate as a body that resolves disputes arising as a result of activities conducted at the cemetery.

Disagreements over everyday practices have led to the formation of teaching schools and orders or led communities to change their allegiance. Schools mythologize such historical events, which serve as evidentiary proofs for their authorizing discourses. The well-known event among Linxia Muslims is the "lightning incident." In 1933 Gedimu and Yihewani held a series of debates that lasted fifty-three days, during which the leaders

[32] See Funeral and Burial Administration Regulations (*Binzang guanli tiaoli*), passed by the State Council, July 21, 1997, arts. 2 and 4.

of the two sides addressed seventy-three questions of law, doctrine, and theology known as the "seventy-three rules [*aḥkām*]."[33] The scriptural debate was meant to resolve an argument over burial rites—specifically, whether Yihewani or Gedimu practices for Qur'anic reading would be used at the burial of a Gedimu woman who lived in a home located within the jurisdiction of a Yihewani mosque (Mingde Mosque of Linxia City 2004: 28–29). The debate resolved the issue (in favor of the Gedimu), but Yihewani backers rejected the outcome and tried to murder the leader of the Gedimu. The would-be attackers were killed by lightning, and followers of the Gedimu cleric interpreted the event as a miracle (Ar. *karāma*) and proof of his blessing from God (Mingde Mosque of Linxia City 2004: 53). This "lightning incident" formed the Bright Heart order, which was transformed into a Sufi order from a Gedimu community.

Following the Islamic renaissance in the reform period, and given the lack of channels to air grievances, disagreements have festered and entrenched school differences. Burial practices test some of the notions Hui commonly hold about the schools. It is often said, for example, that Yihewani are more modern, progressive, or "democratic" and the Gedimu more patriarchal. In fact, burial rites demonstrate that the Gedimu and Sufis are more inclined to have all of the assembled actively participate in the rite by reading "al-Fātiha." Whether they have the Arabic ability to do so is a different matter. In the different interpretations of burial rites, the Yihewani and Salafiyya perceive authority as taking the form of the exclusive right to read, whereas for Gedimu and Sufis it is the right to lead others. Among scripturalists and neoconservatives, young men learn by emulation, whereas the traditionalists learn by doing. Through modeling correct practice and criticizing examples of improper conduct (Cook 2004), the teaching schools are engaged in *ijtihād* in the broad sense of the term: the struggle over interpreting scriptures (Bowen 2003: 148; Feener 2007: 25).

AGENTS OF INTERPRETATION

To describe the teaching schools as the primary agents that shape orthopraxis in China's Northwest is not "groupism," the reification of internally

[33] Such enumerations of doctrine as points of disagreement between rival schools have a long history in Chinese Islam. Japanese scholar Tatsuya Nakanishi has examined a stele from the seventeenth century in Kaifeng, written in Arabic, Persian, and Chinese, that details thirteen doctrines of "law and rites," with twenty-seven textual sources as authorities, that were the subject of dispute between proponents of the "ancient behavior" (*guxing*) and the "new behavior" (*xinxing*). The latter were led by Chang Zhimei (d. 1670) and She Qiling (d. 1710), who advocated the reform of traditional Chinese Islam according to the Qur'an and sunna (Nakanishi 2012).

homogenous entities as the basic units of social life (Brubaker 2004). Teaching schools are internally dissonant, and the boundaries between schools continually blur. For its part, the Party-State has tried to objectify the teaching schools for purposes of governance. As the former leader of the Linxia Prefecture Chinese People's Political Consultative Conference told me, "the Party has long tried to assuage teaching-school differences." Through sermons and publications, the Yi-Xie relays its message of unity under the Party to clerics who proselytize official Islam to Hui.

This view would seem to overlook the role of individual believers. Yet a teaching school or the Party does not practice Islam—individuals do. Whereas schools have corporatized tradition,[34] and the Party has tried to envelop such traditions within a nation united by Chinese socialism, neither is hegemonic. In considering the relationship between the teaching schools and individual believers, the materialist explanation (which normally excludes analysis of the role of the Party) reduces Hui to either egoistic profit maximizers or unreflective automatons. But the relationship between schools and persons invites other notions of power (some complementary, others subversive) than that suggested by the picture of a self-interested elite dominating guileless urban poor and peasants. Hui have affective attachments to charismatic leaders of schools; so too do they seek intimate knowledge of particular traditions.

The question is thus: Can individuals, not just teaching schools or proxies for the Party, interpret the law? One of the chief problems with the materialist explanation is that it eschews any examination of Hui ethical life, what could be described as "the complexity and specificity of ethical reflection, reasoning, dilemma, doubt, conflict, judgement, and decision" (Laidlaw 2014: 23). In the aftermath of poststructuralism, which was partly a response to materialism, it has become de rigueur in social-scientific analysis to write of "subjects" rather than "persons."[35] Centrally, anthropology affirms that people's values, reasoning, and affect are socially produced. Yet social production does not mean eliding

---

[34] I use the term "corporatized" loosely. Unlike traditional Chinese lineage corporations, members of schools do not buy shares in a common estate (Sangren 1984). The Xidaotang are an exception in this sense and did have school-owned stock-holding companies. Most schools consist of an interpretation of Islamic law and doctrine that is "branded" by the school, and members self-identify as such.

[35] Poststructural theory holds the subject to be not the individual but rather a position that is determined by discourse. In a defining debate, critics have mined the possibility of whether the "subject" can have agency outside the discourse within which it is lodged (Butler 1997; Žižek 1989; Moore 2007).

individual assessment of collective morals and ethics, a problem caused by too rigid a materialist explanation or too airy a poststructural one. Islamic traditions—and law is no exception—operate through both revelation and rational deliberation. I retain the term "subject" but use it in reference to subjects of traditions who have a sense of the ethical that is not wholly determined by or congruent with their specific teaching school.

Among Hui, *jiaomin* (persons of the teaching) are the actors of teaching-school discourse. Just as teaching schools are entrenched in scriptural debates with one another, their proponents also engage in arguments to attract and maintain their constituencies. Composing school histories, reiterating hagiographies, and prescribing correct practices of worship and piety are not only activities delineating interschool differences but also methods of ensuring membership. In Linxia it was difficult to find a Hui who did not profess membership in a school and who did not speak as *jiaomin*. In a word, one could not be a *huimin* (Muslim) without being a *jiaomin*.

Being a *jiaomin* could, however, exceed one's commitment to being a *huimin* or Hui. There were a few, such as a Hui cadre I knew who smoked, drank, and consumed American pornography, who claimed to belong to a school but whose practice of Islam was hollowed out of meaning. Such individuals attended Friday prayer and ceremonial events and knew the teaching-school lore, but admitted that they themselves were "unqualified Muslims" (*bu hege de Musilin*).[36] Even Han converts, many of whom are the "have-nots" of China's economic modernization and are attracted to the study of Islam in Linxia, displayed a desire to speak as a *jiaomin* by joining a teaching school and acquiring its tradition.

Schools and followers are not isomorphic, however. Membership is not obligatory, and some Hui change affiliation, particularly after private study. Others change their school by traveling outside the social field of Linxia Muslim communities to study abroad and perform the hajj. Then there are those who appear influenced by reformist schools without formally changing their affiliation, as was the case, allegedly, of the Gedimu cleric at the start of this chapter. Hui may switch allegiance if they find their school fails to address their needs or, worse yet, is morally bankrupt. Followers are always evaluating their clerics and shayhks. If they find them wanting, new traditions may form, such as when at the beginning of the twentieth century members of the Khufiyya dissatisfied with the order's

---

[36] For more on "qualified Muslims," see Chapter 4.

leader left to form Linxia's first Xidaotang mosque. Such behavior suggests that Hui are more than passive followers.

Yet from the poststructural view, these instances are merely the shifting of subject position from *jiaomin*$_{\text{school A}}$ to *jiaomin*$_{\text{school B}}$. It seems impossible to escape the need for an authorizing tradition in the form of teaching schools. The capacity to make meaning of law (i.e., exercise hermeneutics through translation, sermonizing, argumentation, and so forth) is tied to schools. While Hui interpret law through teaching schools, an anthropology of ethics emphasizes that they may also struggle against or within such discursive traditions. For example, when a Sufi from Xining tried to establish his own Sufi tomb complex in 2009 in Linxia without reference to one of the existing orders, he was shunned by almost all Sufis. Yet charismatic leaders such as Qi Jiequan began attending events at the tomb complex founded by the pariah to commemorate the entombed saint. Followers of Qi, who denounced the competitor to me in private, found themselves placing incense at the tomb under Qi's gaze. Such acts, replete with doubt and sometimes loathing, show that piety results from individual conscience as much as it does from teaching-school prescriptions, the two not always being the same. The Xining master's following has grown in recent years, although it remains modest compared with other established Sufi paths.

In fact, there are a number of trends that are eroding the monopoly of teaching schools on interpretations of Islamic law, ritual, or otherwise. Under Saudi influence, some Yihewani and Salafis claim to be "without school" (*wu pai*). Members of the Tablighi Jama'at similarly claim to transcend sectarian identity. While their behavior, including with whom they eat, where they buy goods, and most importantly where they pray, clearly identifies their affiliation, a younger generation of students is being trained in madrasas or prayer halls under such direction. Their level of deference to teaching schools as interpreters of law will most likely differ from that of their parents. Trans-sectarian consciousness is most prominent in the larger cities of Xining, Lanzhou, and Yinchuan. As more Hui youth migrate to cities, the purchase of the teaching schools on their thinking may wane. The Party also mitigates teaching-school association through the work of the Yi-Xie and governmental organs. The Party's goal is less to develop "global" awareness of Muslims and their connections to those outside China than it is to either reinforce Chinese identity or shape consciousness of transnational connections. Still, the "global" individual has not superseded the teaching school at this stage in China's

Islamic renaissance, and especially in places such as Linxia. This does not mean, following Émile Durkheim, that the social nature of moral and ethical authority precludes freedom (Laidlaw 2002: 312). Rather, for Hui in Bafang and elsewhere in the Northwest, to pursue school prescriptions for ortho-praxic behavior via their imagined local, regional, and transnational links produces a freedom of religion that differs from the Party-State's definition.

PARTY VERSUS SECT IN REDUX

The CCP has made ritual obligations a political question. By imposing limits on certain ritual obligations, the CCP signals that they are incongru-ent with Party doctrine and, in so doing, elevates them to the status of the practices of an alternative doctrine. Prayer, fasting, and the hajj each test Hui cadres' ability to toe divergent lines of loyalty between the Party and the teaching schools. Decisions that cadres make reveal some of the ethical questions that arise in their attempts to reconcile their careers with their obligations under Islamic law. Not all difficulties are surmounted, and Hui cadres may feel profound malaise in reconciling conflicting demands.

Hui who have joined the Party and work in a governmental office do not wear a white cap or a headscarf. The injunction is not written into law, and the source of it varies. Hui cite "red-headed documents" (*hongtou wenjian*), internal directives for governmental employees and Party mem-bers, and most commonly, internal work unit (*danwei*) pressure. Similarly, Hui are not permitted to pray at work. Occasionally, senior governmental employees or officials can leave work for the daily prayers. These men and women shuffle back and forth between their government office and their mosque during the course of the day, removing their head coverings as they go. It is not uncommon for junior civil servants to work overtime, making prayer impractical.[37] One elder I met at a Gedimu mosque said he could not pray for forty years while working at the city real estate bureau and called the day he retired "the great relief of my life." Governmental offices are zones of atheism, which prohibit many obligations under *'ibādāt*.[38]

---

[37] One of my younger Hui friends had recently graduated from a top university in Gansu to return to Linxia and work in the government. Even though his parents lived in Bafang and he had a room in their courtyard, he slept in the office most nights because of the intensity of the work.

[38] The traditional rule in the Hanafi school of jurisprudence is that those who do not know of their obligations while living in *dār al-ḥarb* (the Abode of War) do not then have to make them up upon learning of their obligations (Abou el-Fadl 1994: 177–78).

Among Hui civil servants, joining the CCP is a difficult and fraught decision. Most civil servants, regardless of ethnicity, ultimately join the Party ranks. Hui Party members emphasize that prohibitions of external religious dress or prayer at work take the form of not just red-headed documents, which are extralegal, but extra-extralegal social sanctions from more senior Hui Party members. The self-doubt that accompanies the decision to enter the Party was evident during a series of meals I shared with a Salafi friend who worked at a school in Linxia Prefecture. In early 2010 he said, "There is no direct correlation between joining the Party and career advancement, but let me put it to you this way: if they have two candidates for a position and one is a member and the other is not, they will always choose the former." The entire application process takes three to five years. If an application is successful, the relevant-level Party unit will perform a background check, after which the applicant becomes a candidate and eventually a full Party member. Several months later, the teacher had begun taking courses to become a Party member. While chain-smoking over dinner, he explained to me: "I am doing this [joining the Party] for career advancement only. I want to become principal [of my school] one day. I have some great ideas. But to do any of them, I will need to enter the Party. I have put this off for many years. I feel there are definite conflicts between Salafism and Communism. But I will do this for myself and my family." When I asked him what he meant about the conflicts, he just continued to look ahead, his sight transfixed on the mushrooming cloud of smoke that filled the air above our dinner table, signaling the end to the conversation.

The conflicting demands of the Party and the teaching schools give rise to ethical dilemmas and various justifications, some based on necessity or family obligations, as in the case of the Salafi teacher. Dilemmas arise when there is a choice. In the rivalry between the Party and the teaching schools for the affections of Hui, the state may enjoin the performance of an obligation, such as the hajj. The hajj has historically been the primary vehicle for the entry of reformist strains of Islam into the Northwest.[39] As a result, the PRC has tried to limit the number of pilgrims.[40] Based on

[39] The founders of all teaching schools, including Ma Laichi (Khufiyya), Ma Mingxin (Jahriyya), Ma Qixi (Xidaotang), Ma Wanfu (Yihewani), and Ma Debao and Ma Zhengqing (Salafiyya), all acquired novel teachings while either performing the hajj or trying to do so.

[40] Saudi Arabia established a quota system for all countries with Muslim citizens in 1987 (Boissevain 2012: 22). The quota is based on the population of Muslims in that country and is negotiated during an annual meeting between representatives of the foreign country and Saudi

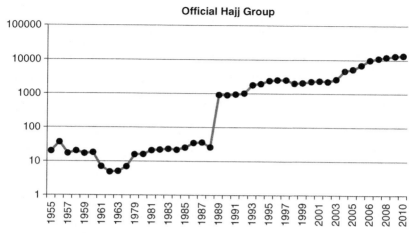

Figure 3.4 Number of Chinese Hajjis (1955–2010)
Source: China Islamic Association (2010)

conversations with the Ministry of Foreign Affairs, which sends a delegation to negotiate the national quota with Saudi counterparts every year, it
appears that it is the PRC government and not the Saudi government that
limits the number of hajjis. Although the reform era has seen an increase
in the number of hajjis (see Figure 3.4), the state sets a tight quota for
those wishing to travel to Mecca. All would-be pilgrims must apply at their
local branch of the BRA, which, together with the relevant-level Yi-Xie,
administers the hajj.[41] In 2009 in Linxia, the quota was 160 pilgrims per
year. A friend registered his mother, who was given number 3,478, which
means she could travel to Mecca in twenty-two years, a difficult trip for a
woman in her late sixties at the time.

The limits imposed on their capacity to uphold their obligation to perform the hajj has elicited a number of responses, including developing
black markets to go on the hajj and even violating the law. Up until recently,
it has been common for individuals to obtain a counterfeit PRC passport
(required to leave the country), after which they would enter Saudi Arabia

Arabia. Most governments, such as those of Turkey, Indonesia, and India, have called for increasing the quota.
[41] See Provisional Measures on Muslims' Signing Up and Queuing in Order to Leave the Country
on the Hajj (*Zhongguo Musilin chuguo chaojin baoming paidui banfa (shixing)*), announced by the State
Council on Religious Affairs Department of Politics and Law, December 20, 2010.

on the quota of another country. After a leading cleric in Linxia was found guilty of a side business of producing fake passports for Uyghurs in 2010 (the same impassioned cleric whose anti-Sufi attack opened this chapter), security forces cracked down on such operations in the Northwest. Some frustrated Hui even approached me, when they knew I was an American, to see if I could devise a way for them to perform the hajj.

The ardor with which Hui speak about the hajj and the opportunity to join Muslims from all over the world is one manifestation of Hui will to follow their law. When their capacity to fulfill the obligation is blocked, Hui feel a disquiet that is rarely articulated but may take the form of law evasion. Hui may not be able to reconcile the "value pluralism" (Laidlaw 2014: 166) between the traditions of the teaching school and those of Chinese socialism or between the global *umma* and the nation-state. Rather, while conflicts may lead to strategic behavior, more often they cause angst or are internalized as part of being Muslim in China.

THE POLITICS OF RITUAL

Ritual lawfare in Linxia and other Muslim enclaves in Northwest China consists of ritual performance and its representation. Muslims of different schools follow their own traditions in proper prayer, worship, and liturgy. They further legitimize their practice through reference to a number of authorizing discourses, including the Qur'an and the sunna as well as their own school histories, which are often grounded in an imagined origin. The Party-State also engages in the sphere of contesting interpretations. For instance, officials visit tombs before observances to ask disciples to limit the number of burning incense sticks, citing fire prevention and public safety. The state invokes the rationale of "public interest" to curtail what it deems to be superstitious practices. Ritual lawfare is not reducible to "liturgical minutiae" but rather entails a variety of disputes—theological, methodological, and hermeneutic. As the state apparatus prohibits any representative or participatory mechanism to allow disagreements to be aired, conflicts become physically charged and violent, such as one internal teaching-school dispute I witnessed in 2010 over the meaning of a smuggled book on Islamic doctrine.[42]

---

[42] The text in question was *The Book of the Beneficial Sciences* (Ar. *Kitab al-'Ulum al-Nafi'a*) by Jasim al-Muhalhal wa-Akhirun. The book had been smuggled into Linxia from Hong Kong in 2000, and for reasons unknown, the cleric who obtained it did not use it for ten years. In 2010 he began

Certainly, one cause for arguments over ritual matters is leaders' efforts to maximize their interests in terms of increasing their followers within the social field of Muslim networks. However, materialist causes provide only a partial explanation. I have made the case that ritual law is a semiotic landscape. Seemingly superficial devotional items, such as incense or books, and ritual protocol, such as graveside Qur'anic reading, are linked to broader notions of school organization, leadership, and understandings of law. Schools are constantly engaged in the work of what Stuart Hall (1980) called decoding the semiotic chain. Yet events, like objects or activities, are not just "exemplifications of an extant symbolic or social order;" rather, they reveal "substantial areas of normative indeterminacy" (Moore 1987: 729). Schools engage in competing claims to make sense of the signs that make the tensions within Hui's bounded social field explicit. Following the increasing visibility of Islam in China's domestic and international politics, schools are not just religious bodies; they also have important social, economic, and political roles. They continue to provide social welfare to members and to organize collective action—for example, in the event a member's home is illegally demolished. Hence, burning an incense stick and reading the Qur'an are instances of "tactics" (Certeau 1984: 37) or "symbolic acts" (Scott 1990: 227), which simultaneously subvert the alternative orthodoxies of other schools while providing the everyday grounds for the discursive position of one's own school. Likewise, oral and written pronouncements about correct practice and refutations of those of other schools can encompass broader tensions attendant to political and economic justice.

School discourses do not directly confront the Party-State's image of society as a totality. Instead, through the production of deeply partisan views, they consciously reflect the gaps between Islamic practice and the Party-State's attempts at its representation. Sufis, for example, may dispute officially sanctioned translations of the Qur'an as produced in Beijing, the center of (Han) national power. Following anthropological studies that have shown how the local ritual of the colonized, indigenous, or ethnic minority can make sense of the politics of the state in ritual terms,[43] ritual lawfare among Muslim minorities in the borderlands of the Qinghai-Tibet plateau can likewise

illegally printing it and distributing it to mosques under the administration of his mosque. This led to a confrontation with an opposing cleric that resulted in a standoff involving several thousand Hui and Dongxiang and several battalions of armed police.

[43] See Kapferer (1997), Keane (1997), Mueggler (2001), Siegel (2006), and Willford (2006).

be seen as disrupting narratives of Islamic unity in a socialist mold. Schools try to transcend their own sectarianism, contingency, and uncertainty, and claim the correct interpretation of Islam in a universalist posture.

4

LEARNING THE LAW

Xiu tian dao, qin wugong;
jin ren dao, dun wu lun.
(Cultivate the heavenly law,
Strive toward the Five Pillars;
Exhaust the man-made law,
Sincerely [guard] the five Confucian relationships).
From *Islamic Three Character Classic*
(*Tianfang Sanzijing*) by Liu Zhi (1660–1739)

Ethnic minority education is a fruitful site for understanding how tradi-tions, including those of the teaching schools and the Party-State, pursue different notions of the ethical life in the Hui social field. Among the aspects of ethnic policy in the PRC are preferential policies, intended to help minorities attend public institutions, and schools that focus specif-ically on minority populations.[1] The former directs minority elite toward the labor market, whereas the latter, which emphasizes instruction in minority languages, is often a second choice for minority students. These graduates are less well prepared to compete with Han and ethnic elite in securing careers. Such "ethnic schools" are commonly, but not neces-sarily, found in ethnic autonomous areas. Most observations of ethnic minority education focus on such schools as socialization for patriotic citi-zens of the nation-state.[2]

In reform-era China, however, there are a number of alternatives to state-run education that make possible other formulations of ethical

---

[1] There are additional "bridging" institutions between the two, such as university preparatory schools (*yuke ban*); see, e.g., Yamada (2012).
[2] Education has been a favored topic for the study of minority policy in China; see Sautman (1998), Hansen (1999), Postiglione (1999, 2000), and Zhou and Hill (2009).

subjects. For over a century Linxia has been known as one of the centers of Islamic learning in China. The primary educational institution is known as "scriptural hall education" (*jingtang jiaoyu*), which offers the equivalent of a madrasa education. In my use, scriptural hall education refers to the institutional form of education, and madrasa denotes a concrete place of instruction and learning. Scriptural hall education is the *minjian* institution par excellence, because the curriculum and teaching were developed by Hui for over a century independent of state intrusion. The narrow aim of scriptural hall education is to produce leaders of the Muslim community who study the Qur'an and sunna and have a working knowledge of Arabic, and possibly Persian. The instruction of Islamic law is central to this goal.

Beyond producing clerics, the broader goal of scriptural hall education is to make what Hui call "qualified Muslims" (*hege de Musilin*). Understandings of what constitutes the qualifications of such Muslims vary according to the teaching schools. A baseline definition would be pious believers who have enough grasp of the revealed sources to practice, articulate, and, as needed, defend their faith. Hui model themselves after the Prophet Muhammad; Hui leaders are more immediate examples of this model and thus they also serve as ethical models. Qualification is a manifestation of having learned the law.

The teaching schools, as authorizing discourses, have sought to incite desire among their followers to pursue their particular version of the ethical self. Generally, desire has an ambivalent relationship to the law. According to the psychoanalyst Jacques Lacan ([1973] 1998), for instance, desire arises out of one's incompleteness. The subject seeks reunification with the mother, but society establishes a taboo or law against such acts, the imposition of which causes the subject to want to both obey the law and surmount it. Along these lines, Raphael Israeli has written of the Hui that "their yearning is not merely to migrate to a land of safety, but to return to Arabia, as the only way for their physical and spiritual redemption" (Israeli 2002b: 47). The Hui, however, neither operate under the Oedipal complex,[3] nor do they seek unification with the Muslim heartland. Rather, the teaching-school imaginaries orient their followers to multiple genealogical and geographic centers

---

[3] Sunni Islam rejects the doctrine of original sin. In a thought-provoking analysis, however, Katharine Ewing (1997) has adapted aspects of Lacanian psychoanalysis to understand the construction of the Sufi subject vis-à-vis postcolonial projects in Pakistan.

of authority, none of which (not even the Salafis) are detached from a grounding in Chinese textual and social forms. The way in which the simultaneous transcendence and rootedness of teaching-school imaginaries influence Hui ethical life is through their constant evaluation of sinful acts against meritorious and expiatory ones. Their immersion in a Han-dominated consumerist society with its temptations (sexual, gastronomic, commercial, polytheistic or atheistic, and so forth) affords the teaching schools no shortage of opportunities for imposing rules of correct behavior. Through the imaginaries of the teaching schools, Hui desire positive ethics.

Positive, or virtue, ethics is a major topic in the anthropology of Islam and can be traced through MacInytre to Aristotle. While anthropologists of Islam may also draw on the writings of Foucault, other scholars such as James Faubion (2001, 2011), James Laidlaw (2002, 2014), and in a different vein Giorgio Agamben (1998), base their analytics of ethics more centrally on Foucault.[4] The Aristotelian approach (Lambek 2010a: 28), the Foucaultian one (Faubion 2001: 84, 90; Laidlaw 2014: 92), or some combination, however, expose rather than foreclose distinctions between desire and norm (or that which is elicited versus that which is obligated). Here, the Hui case is instructive. Given that shari'a is a *minjian* law in China, teaching schools can enforce their ethical regimes as obligatory norms to be followed only to the extent permitted by followers' commitments. Often, norms by themselves are insufficient. Teaching schools thus endeavor to make the norm desirable. They use encouragement and inducement to try to attract students, often invoking powerful imaginaries—for example, by highlighting students' opportunities to study abroad in the Middle East.

The Party-State is also interested in the making of qualified Muslims. It does so by entering the fray of educational institutions in the reform era

---

[4] The difference between Aristotle and Foucault on ethics is more a matter of degree than kind. In his *Nicomachean Ethics*, Aristotle underscores the exercise of ethics rather than their innate nature. But as Faubion (2001: 91) notes, Foucault did not share Aristotle's assumption that there was an embodiment of the ethical good—for example, the Athenian polis—that underwrote ethical cultivation. Contrary to Faubion, Mahmood (2005: 27) emphasizes the continuities between Aristotle's and Foucault's analysis of ethics. Foucault expanded Aristotle's notion of ethics as a set of practices that were specific to a certain way of being in the world. Specifically, Foucault's approach has four elements: (1) the "substance of ethics," or what ethics acts upon, (2) the "mode of subjectivation," or the means by which one acquires ethical knowledge, (3) the "techniques of the self," meaning the training or pedagogy, and (4) the telos, or ultimate aim of ethical cultivation (Faubion 2001: 90; Mahmood 2005: 30).

and creating "ethnic" and "Islamic" public schools to compete with scriptural hall education.[5] The state aims to make "qualified" Muslims secular and nationalistic (i.e., productive members of the nation-state), ethnic (e.g., self-identifying as "Hui"), and depoliticized (e.g., understanding shari'a as "customary law"). But the state's embrace of Muslim minorities as citizens does not go beyond this mold. Following the Uyghur-Han riots in Xinjiang in July 2009, from the vantage of the security state, Muslim students in the Northwest in particular are to be held at a distance as suspect citizens. Post-2009 security interests have given new life to secular law and its capacity not only to bend Muslim minorities to the sovereign state but also to turn them away from autonomous Islam.

Desire for learning is thus malleable and can orient young Hui in different and, indeed, unpredictable directions. Across the landscape of education in Linxia, the respective projects, of the Party-State and of the teaching schools, to cultivate qualified Muslims constantly impinge upon each other. Students migrate across the boundaries of the Hui social field through the various forums for learning, acquiring legal knowledge from authorities—spiritual, secular, local, national, and transnational—that vie for preeminence in the marketplace of learning.

In this chapter I assess the formal education institutions through which Muslims in Linxia, like elsewhere in the Northwest, learn about the law. My focus is on the ways in which Muslim minorities gain, extend, and use their consciousness of Islamic law. While scriptural hall education has been the traditional learning institution, in recent decades private schools, founded by Muslim businessmen with contacts overseas, and state-run Islamic Scriptural Institutes (Yisilanjiao Jingxueyuan) have created competition with scriptural hall education. In addition, public "ethnic schools" (minzu xuexiao), which are not religious schools, teach secular subjects, including "business Arabic." Each of these types of school is equivalent to secondary education, with student ages ranging from sixteen to the mid-twenties, although there are important gendered differences in teaching approaches among the formal institutions. As a whole, the diversification of formal education institutions in Linxia is a result of local Muslim initiative and entrepreneurship, state policy, the expansion and pluralization of education nationwide, regional and transnational market forces, and revivified global networks of Muslims. In the next section I describe the main types of learning centers, their

[5] For the literature on Islamic education in China, see Gladney (1999a), Chérif-Chebbi (2004), Armijo (2008), and Tan and Ding (2014).

impact on shaping legal consciousness, and the Party-State's regulatory framework.

SCRIPTURAL HALL EDUCATION

Following the Qing government's suppression of the Muslim riots in the late nineteenth century in Shaanxi, said to have been the birthplace of scriptural hall education, the center of Islamic education shifted westward to Linxia (Zhe and Guo 1992; Ding 2006). In contemporary Linxia almost all mosques have at least one classroom, and some feature several large halls devoted to daily instruction. Of the thirty-four mosques I visited, only four did not have a school.[6] The madrasas are intergenerational and single-sexed communities within the larger mosque that supports the school. The heart of scriptural hall education is the relationship between teaching clerics (*kaixue ahong*) and students (*manla*). The relationship assumes a variety of forms, from approximations, in Sufi tomb complexes, of the master-disciple pairing with its "ethics of closeness" (Hammoudi 1997) to more joking and fraternal relationships in some mosques. The teacher is the most immediate ethical model for students.

Before 1949 there were three grades for scriptural hall education: the primary level, during which children began their study of Arabic, a secondary level, based on Arabic and Persian texts, and an advanced level, for study in philosophy and Sufism (Dillon 1999: 38; Zhou 2013). Upon the establishment of the PRC, law required that students be at least eighteen years old to begin study in a madrasa,[7] although most students are much younger. Usually, mosques encourage students to attend a state-run primary school to obtain a foundation in standard Mandarin. Consequently, most students enter scriptural hall education at the age of twelve, after which they may stay for four or more years. Some students stay well into their twenties and are absorbed into the mosque administration. The Sufi tomb complexes differ from mosques in their recruitment, taking in boys at the age of six or seven. The Grand Tomb Complex of the Qadiriyya order requires boys to sever all ties to their family and renounce any plans to start their own families.

---

[6] An additional two mosques did not respond to this question on the survey I conducted.
[7] Under PRC law, a person can believe in religion only if they have the legal capacity to do so, which is defined as being eighteen years of age or older. See General Principles of the Civil Law of the PRC (*Zhonghua renmin gongheguo minfa tongze*), promulgated by the National People's Congress, April 12, 1986, art. 11.

In those mosques with schools, the average number of students was 48, the largest with 106 and the smallest with 10. Thus, the approximate number of students in the city is over 2,000.[8] The number of students, like the size of the mosque community, is an indicator of the mosque's relative strength. Among teaching schools, twelve of the fifteen Gedimu mosques had a school (avg. no. students: 40), twelve of the fifteen Yihewani mosques had a school (avg. no. students: 58), and three of the four Salafiyya mosques had a school (avg. no. students: 43). The Xidaotang mosque does not have a school, as Lintan remains their center for education. Sufi tomb complexes also have students, with the Naqshbandi-Mujaddidi Bright Heart Mosque having the largest school, with 80 students. The mosque community provides funding for the students' costs as well as the additional expenses of the school; madrasas receive no state funding.

Historically, madrasas trained clerics as the literary elite who embodied "quality" (*suzhi*), a term with roots in Confucian humanism that the Party has revived in the reform era (Anagnost 2004; Kipnis 2006, 2007). If "quality" is the aim, then this is procured through meritorious self-cultivation, or *gongxiu*. As an Islamic technique of the self, *gongxiu* means different things to the teaching schools. Salafis, for example, refer to the Five Pillars as *gongxiu*, while Sufis have a much more elaborate conception, which includes meditation and exercising the body's *laṭa'if* (Ar. for "centers of energy"). Books, instructional pamphlets, sermons, and individual consultations with clerics and shaykhs elaborate these different conceptions of *gongxiu* to followers.

The purposes of madrasa education have broadened during the reform period. Given the variety of more profitable post-graduate careers for Hui youths, the prestige of becoming a cleric has faded, but it has not disappeared. Despite the growth of mosques, there are far more students graduating than there are clerical positions. Partially because of the oversupply, most students seek to study abroad in the Middle East, Pakistan, or Malaysia, and eventually to conduct business. Hence, teaching schools incite a desire that is ambiguous. On the one hand, they propagate the centrality of acquiring an ethical Islamic education. One Gedimu mosque in Linxia, for instance, posted a flyer to attract students that read, "This year [name deleted] mosque ... hired, in addition to graduates of this mosque, additional superb teachers to handle teaching and continuously improve

---

[8] In terms of historical data, in 1955 the city had 1,533 students, and 1,600 in 1985 (Hai 1993: 98, 105).

the teaching ranks, raise the quality of teaching, and shorten the time required for making something of oneself [chengcai]." On the other hand, the teaching schools' technologies and aims of self-making have changed in China with the emergence of what Yan Yunxiang (2013) calls "the striving individual." Even such dense Muslim enclaves as Bafang are not untouched by these larger material and spiritual shifts. The same Gedimu madrasa flyer indicated that its graduates, in addition to becoming clerics or teachers, choose to become translators or to study abroad. In responding to these trends, madrasas have become more multifaceted in their curricula and have sought to strengthen their networks both within and beyond China.

The daily regime of the madrasa directs students through certain techniques of the self: study, daily prayer, and ritual hygiene (see Table 4.1). The curriculum is central to improving oneself. Among traditionalist madrasas it includes the Thirteen Classics,[9] which cover eight core subjects: Qur'anic exegesis (Ar. tafsīr), hadith sciences, fiqh, Arabic grammar, Arabic morphology, rhetoric, philosophy, and literature. To modernize the curriculum, secular courses such as Mandarin and history were added in the mid-twentieth century. Most recently, madrasa educators have added computing and "thought and morality" to equip students with skills beyond religious instruction.

In addition to the Qur'an, Qur'anic exegesis, and the hadith—all foundational to Islamic law—the standard text on shari'a used in nearly all mosques is the Sharh al-Wiqaya (Ch. Weigaiye). Additionally, many mosques use texts entitled Usul al-Fiqh (Ch. Wusuli feigeihai) for the study of the rules upon which Islamic jurisprudence is based. As reference material, Gedimu and Yihewani teaching clerics alike use al-Sarakhsi's Kitab al-Mabsut (Ch. Mishenkaqi), which is a commentary on another work that summarizes the legal opinion of the Hanafi school. Although not jurisprudence, the preeminent text for Qur'anic exegesis is the Tafsir al-Qur'an (Ch. Gazui or Gazhui) by al-Baydawi. Learning shari'a, or what the Qing Muslim scholar Liu Zhi called "the heavenly law," was thus central to becoming a qualified Muslim.

Traditionalist madrasa education, including that of the Gedimu, Xidaotang, and Sufis, as well as some Yihewani, has been informed by the same principles behind Liu Zhi's thought. Writing in the eighteenth

---

[9] Teaching schools and even mosques within teaching schools vary in which texts they deem to be the "Thirteen Classics." Pang Shiqian (1902–1958) compiled a list of eight Arabic texts and six Persian ones—thus, the "Fourteen Classics" (1937).

TABLE 4.1 Typical daily schedule for a student in scriptural hall education

Time	Activity
5 a.m.	Wake up
5:30 a.m.–6 a.m.	Perform *wuḍū'* (Ch. *xiaojing* 小净)
6 a.m.	Perform *fajr* (morning prayer)
8 a.m.	Eat breakfast
8:40 a.m.	Clean living quarters
9 a.m.–10 a.m.	Class
10 a.m.–11 a.m.	Independent study
11 a.m.–11:30 a.m.	Rest
11:30 a.m.–1:30 p.m.	Rest and lunch
1:30 p.m.	Perform *ẓuhr* (noon prayer)
1:35 p.m.–4 p.m.	Class
4 p.m.–5 p.m.	Perform *'aṣr* (afternoon prayer); independent study
5 p.m.	Perform *maghrib* (sunset prayer)
5:30 p.m.	Dinner
Evening	Perform *'ishā'* (evening prayer); take "high-level" classes, independent study, and practice Qur'anic recitation

century, Liu Zhi united Islamic law with Neo-Confucian ethics. For the founders of scriptural hall education, such as Hu Dengzhou (1522–1597) and the writers of the so-called Han Kitab, the tenets of Islam should be explained through the postulates of Neo-Confucianism. For Liu Zhi, Confucius's five cardinal relationships (ruler and subject, father and son, husband and wife, elder and younger brother, and friends) provided an epistemological framework for a Chinese understanding of Islamic law. The relationships explained the duties and rights that inhere in the law of social relations. But because Abrahamic monotheism was a foreign concept, the *'ibādāt*, with its emphasis on obligations to God, presented a challenge for Confucian ethics (Frankel 2011: 79). In such cases, Liu Zhi made analogies, extending the Confucian relationships to the interpretation of "there is no god but God."[10] For instance, in the *Islamic Three*

[10] As mentioned in Chapter 3, Liu Zhi and contemporaneous Muslim scholars used the neologism "true Lord" (*Zhenzhu*) for Allah (Murata, Chittick, and Tu 2009: 7; Frankel 2011: 160–61).

Character Classic, he wrote, "Esteem the Peerless Master above all, He is the Emperor of the emperors and Sovereign of sovereigns" (*Zhu wu er, nai du zun, di zhi di, jun zhi jun*). The founders of scriptural hall education and the authors of the Han Kitab wedded Islamic law to Neo-Confucian ethics to create a blueprint for the qualified Muslim.

For example, in a 2009 Īd-e-Qurbān[11] sermon entitled "Scrupulously Abide by the Orthodox Teaching, Show Respect to Your Parents" (*Keshou zhengjiao, xiaojing fumu*), a Xidaotang cleric in Linxia weaved Neo-Confucian ethics into Islamic law. He exhorted:

> Worshipping Allah is the basis of the heavenly law, respecting one's parents is the basis of the human law ... The orthodox five constant Confucian virtues include benevolence, the emotional recollection of Allah's nature; justice, an agent for Allah's universality; prayer, which expresses formal gratitude for Allah's mercy; knowledge, the recognition of Allah's uniqueness; and belief, the clear command of Allah. All other relationships between sovereigns and subjects, fathers and sons, husbands and wives, elder and younger brothers, and friends stem from this origin. It is probable that each [relationship] is like this[12] ... In this way, we mix together Islamic belief and the intention of the four cardinal virtues of Chinese traditional culture. Such mixing makes the theory of "the ethical relations of heavenly law" agree with the intrinsic concepts of Chinese Muslims and further develops their glory. Respect the Lord and show filial piety toward one's parents. This makes human law obey the kernel of the heavenly law and emphasizes that besides respecting Allah, filial piety is the most important duty of one's life. "On human matters, you [obey] Allah, and you [obey] your parents."[13] With this, one respects Allah and shows filial piety, this is being loyal to one's country and filial to one's parents; only in this way can belief be complete.

Such exhortations are representative of madrasa instruction about law and ethics. Good family relations are the core of one's *mu'āmalāt* obligations and a reflection of a Muslim's relationship with God *and* country. The cleric's justification cuts across Neo-Confucian and Islamic registers, equating ethics with normative obligations.

---

[11] Hui refer to the commemoration of Ibrahim's near sacrifice of his son Ismail as "Gu'erbangjie," or "festival of the sacrifice." An additional Hui term for the festival is Zaishengjie ("festival of slaughtering the domestic animal"). Hui generally do not use the Arabic expression for the festival: 'Īd al-Aḍḥā. Gu'erbangjie is closer phonetically to the Persian 'Īd-e-Qurbān.

[12] The cleric's reference is to Wang Daiyu's *Answers to the Rare Truth* (*Xizhen Zhengda*) (1658).

[13] The cleric refers here to Wang Daiyu's *True Interpretation of the Orthodoxy* (*Zhengjiao Zhenquan*) (1642).

The Yihewani and Salafiyya have questioned whether the law of relations in the Islamic sense is analogous to the relationships of Neo-Confucianism, and they have looked to scriptural hall education as a base for broad reform of what it means to be a qualified Muslim. For them, reform has become its own telos, a desire that shapes the pursuit of ethical and legal correctness. Their reformist approach to sacred law and the ethical subject began in the early twentieth century, when modernist Yihewani sought to change the language of instruction, texts, study aids, and pedagogy. From the sixteenth century until the Yihewani reforms, students learned to read Arabic texts through a system of phonetic equivalents in Chinese characters. The Chinese sounds would be written above the original Arabic script, and students read the Chinese while associating it with the Arabic words beneath. This transliteration method is called "scriptural hall language" (*jingtangyu*). Muslims in Northwest China use the term to refer to the spoken creole—incorporating Chinese, Arabic, and Persian—that Hui use in mosques across the Northwest.

The Yihewani, under Ma Tianmin (1916–1959) and others, made purifying scriptural hall education a centerpiece of reform. They began by expunging Persian-inspired sounds from scriptural hall language (Ding 2006: 52). These reforms were continued by Ma Tianmin's son Ma Xiqing (1941–2003), who served two years of hard labor in coal mines in northern Gansu at the start of the Cultural Revolution. Ma Xiqing took another traditionalist mode of transliteration called "minor script" (*xiaojing* 小经), which represented Chinese sounds in Arabic script, and replaced it with modern Mandarin. Many of the pro-Arabic and pro-Chinese reforms were directed specifically against writing traditions developed by Gedimu and Sufis that integrated Chinese language and literature into their learning of the languages of Islam. For Yihewani and Salafiyya, mastery of Arabic became mandatory for their approach to education. In Linxia today, puritanical Yihewani and Salafiyya use Arabic texts in their madrasas while some use scriptural hall language in continuing-education classes held for working men. Speaking and reading Arabic is one way that reformist Hui desire can orient students toward Hijaz imaginaries.

Salafis, in particular, look down on those who use scriptural hall language. One Salafi instructor said, "Scriptural hall language cannot keep up with social change. We have an expression at our mosque: *xing-da-ya*. *Xing* means 'the most popular or current language'; *da* means 'changing meaning'; and *ya* is for 'standard, correct, or elegance.' Scriptural hall language is not capable of *xing-da-ya*." The presence of Persian in scriptural hall language along with such vernaculars as Bafanghua has diminished greatly under the Yihewani and Salafiyya linguistic reform, although Sufis continue to use Persian.

Textual reform also provided modernists the opportunity to determine the types of qualifications for the making of Muslims. Ma Xiqing introduced a number of texts, including Muhammad Amin ibn 'Abidin's *Radd al-Muhtar 'ala al-Durr al-Mukhtar*, an eighteenth-century work on Hanafi jurisprudence. He also attempted to standardize instructional texts by writing in Arabic three works that are today better known for their Chinese titles: *Yisilan xinyang* (*Islamic Belief*), *Yisilan gongxiu* (*Islamic Meritorious Cultivation*), and *Yisilan lunli* (*Islamic Ethics*). These works were pragmatic interpretations of Islamic law and ethics for everyday use (Ding 2006: 53). In contemporary Linxia, puritanical Yihewani and Salafiyya may use the Hanbali *fiqh*, the strictest of the four Sunni schools of jurisprudence.

The ways in which students learn, the techniques of the self, have been another facet of modernist reform. Up until the mid-twentieth century the pedagogy of scriptural hall education was uniform across madrasas in Linxia. Teaching clerics read relevant passages of the revealed sources or exegetic aids, and students would record the clerics' commentary, a method many Muslims in Linxia call "Confucian." I participated in such learning at a moderate Yihewani madrasa in Linxia. The cleric lectured on points of the *Wiqaya* as the students around me and I recorded his commentary. The lesson outlined the aural and bodily mechanics of the five daily prayers, with specific reference to those that are pronounced out loud and those that are uttered silently. The cleric also alluded to al-Shafi'i's distinctions. After class, the senior students conducted private Qur'anic study while younger students went out to the courtyard, where they memorized suras. In his study of the education of qadis in Morocco, Eickelman (1985: 57) wrote that students would take "mnemonic possession" of the Qur'an. In Linxia, although teaching aids are not written in rhyme verse as they were in Eickelman's Boujad, modernist Muslims have emphasized "Arab" techniques of memorizing the Qur'an and the hadith.

While studying in madrasas, I asked students how they viewed the importance of Islamic law and ethics in cultivating one's pious self. When I questioned two Yihewani students about the value of the *Wiqaya* in their daily lives, one replied, "It is every Muslim's duty to study the *aḥkām* [rules] of the Five Pillars. Studying the law is *wājib* [obligatory]." The other explained, "It is like the Constitution of the PRC." Students unequivocally equated studying the letter of the law with universal normative injunctions. However, when I asked students to reflect on the study of Islamic law *in a socialist country*, their reflections were mixed. "*Ḥukm* [rule] is the important word. But for most aspects in life, we must follow state law, as China is a large Han nation," one reasoned. "We cannot cut off hands," explained his classmate. "It is a literary product," a student remarked on another occasion. "We study the *Wiqaya* because it improves our language, our mastery of the grammar, and so on."

Conversations suggested that many Hui students understand legal and ethical texts as literary products that could nonetheless conflict with state law. Legal texts have didactic value in cultivating behavior that conforms to an ethical standard. It is not surprising that Hui students do not learn Islamic law as a set of positive rules to apply to disputes in mosque communities (a responsibility they will assume if they graduate to become clerics of mosques). Traditional legal education in the United States, for instance, does not necessarily teach law students the practicum of lawyering (e.g., how to write a purchase and sale agreement) but rather a set of black-letter rules that may be quite detached from actual practice. The equation of literacy with the production of a cultured subject is one legacy of scriptural hall education (Gladney 1999a: 60), itself a manifestation of the underlying aim of the Confucian cultivation of the self (Tu [1978] 1998). Although each of the teaching schools has its own idea of a "qualified Muslim," invariably the educational projects exist to reproduce the schools.

Even if mosque administrators, under the guidance of state officials, render Islamic law into an ethical program, would-be clerics learned to apply rules from shari'a to factual problems, for example, brought by members of their mosque community. They learned to do so not in classrooms but rather in the hallways and offices of teachers. There, informal conversations centered on these problems, as older students sought to rub shoulders with teachers who had recently studied Islamic law abroad in Pakistan or Egypt. It is in these spaces—where the reach of the state is most limited—that the *minjian* attains prominence in knowledge production about the law.

The making of qualified Muslims occurs through a tacking back and forth between teaching-school models and individual Muslims' own assessment of such ethical models. Part of this process is identifying Islamic law and ethics as desirable and conducive to life in contemporary China. Ethics is not apolitical. Teaching schools' educative and interpretive contests to stake out the reach of their law, though bounded by the state ("we cannot cut off hands"), nevertheless disturb the state's monopoly on making subjects. Whereas Chinese Muslim students rarely take up antistate opinions, their learning of the sacred law connects them with authorizing traditions that overleap the Party-State's sovereignty. For instance, while studying Arabic in Amman in 2012, I was astounded to learn that the son and daughter of a Hui cleric friend from Linxia were likewise studying there. Such movements between Linxia and Amman mark a new dimension in the globalization of the Hui social field.

THE DESIRE OF THE PARTY-STATE

Given the traction teaching schools have in serving as models for ethical subjects in the Northwest, the Party-State has also tried to inject into such projects its own desire for making ethical Hui. The Party-State's aim differs from that of the teaching schools, however. In the first decades of the reform period, it endeavored to impose rationality onto popular religious practices (Xie 2006). Since the 2009 riots and subsequent terrorist attacks, rationality has been inflected with the anxieties of national security and counterterrorism. Such anxieties have supplemented the state's sense of nationalist belonging and socialist citizenship. The result is that whereas the Party-State post-2009 has tried not to demonize Uyghurs, state anxieties have nonetheless exacerbated Han Chinese xenophobia toward Uyghurs. The desire of the Party-State is thus unsettled, and it has shaped behaviors on the ground in contradictory ways.

The Party-State employs both hardware (e.g., laws, regulations, registration, and licensing) and software (Foucault's techniques of the self) to steer Hui youths toward a certain orientation of Islamic law and ethics. The hardware and software apply to mosques generally, and to madrasas in particular. To begin with the hardware, the state, as gatekeeper of Islamic knowledge, regulates all aspects of scriptural hall education, including the space itself and the teachers, students, and curriculum. The establishment of a madrasa, like the building of a mosque, requires the mosque leadership, usually the mosque administration committee, to obtain a series of approvals from the government. Before construction begins, the mosque administration committee must, in addition to obtaining the necessary construction permits, register with the relevant county's Bureau of Religious Affairs (BRA). It must also select a "legal representative" (*faren*), who also registers with the BRA and who personally accepts liability for activities at the mosque, including instruction at madrasas.[14] Thus, the *minjian* institution of scriptural hall education is brought under the surveillance of the state.

The BRA controls the hardware used to instill the Party-State's desire into Hui who are based in mosques or madrasas. The BRA is the "responsible unit" for the registered mosque and has complete oversight of its affairs. Subsequently, the mosque is subject to yearly inspection of the status of its internal administration, the nature of its religious activities, finances, and any commercial enterprise or real estate that it manages.[15] Failure to meet such requirements results in administrative action taken against the mosque administration committee and the legal representative.[16] The committee members and the legal representative handle relations with their counterparts in the BRA, as well as in the Bureau of Ethnic Affairs and the United Work Front Department, the Party organ that implements policy in ethnic minority regions, who may also require approvals and make inspections. According to relevant regulations, opening a madrasa requires amending the registration permit for the mosque on file with the relevant BRA. However, most mosque administration committees report that opening a school requires another round of formal applications to multiple governmental and Party organs, including the BRA and the China Islamic Association (Yi-Xie). The ease of obtaining such approvals depends on a number of factors, some of which the teaching school can accommodate, while others are beyond their control—for instance, instability in Xinjiang or Tibet, which sends tremors of (in)security throughout the Northwest, including Hui areas.

Teaching clerics, the most immediate models of correct behavior for students, are tightly regulated. Usually hired by the mosque administration committee for a three-year term, teaching clerics typically come from outside the mosque community, although some schools prefer to hire clerics who previously studied at their madrasa. Other mosques endeavor to hire clerics with outstanding credentials, such as a master's degree in Arabic or Islamic law from a university in Saudi Arabia, Egypt, Pakistan,

---

[14] See Religious Activity Area Administration Regulations (*Zongjiao huodong changsuo guanli tiaoli*), promulgated by the State Council, January 31, 1994, art. 2; Measures for the Examination, Approval, and Registration of the Establishment of Religious Activity Areas (*Zongjiao huodong changsuo sheli shenpi he dengji banfa*), promulgated by the State Administration for Religious Affairs, April 21, 2005, arts. 3 and 6.

[15] Religious Affairs Activity Annual Inspection Measures (*Zongjiao huodong changsuo niandu jiancha banfa*), promulgated by the State Department, July 29, 1996, art. 4.

[16] *Ibid.*, art. 14.

or Malaysia.[17] Teaching clerics cycle through mosques and "spiral up" to more prestigious mosques within their teaching school. Outstanding ones attain positions in the government or even public universities in eastern China, where they teach Arabic.

According to PRC law and religious regulations, to become a teaching cleric (or cleric, generally), an individual must either obtain a cleric certificate (*ahong zhengshu*) or earn a degree from a state-run school, where one receives a patriotic education, the Party-State's equivalent to ethical training. Only a minority pursues the latter route, however. Of Linxia's clerics, only one attended a state-run school; the rest took the route of scriptural hall education. The vast majority—those who attend a mosque-based or private school—must pass an exam administered by the relevant-level Yi-Xie to obtain a cleric certificate.[18] The exam tests the candidate's knowledge of the Qur'an, hadith, *fiqh*, and applicable state law and regulations. Yet separated from most clerics' actual training, the cleric certificate is more a gatekeeping device than a formal recognition of proficiency in a body of legal knowledge. The cleric's mastery of Islamic knowledge, including law and ethics, is mostly determined by the mosque administration committee, who may have a higher standard than that of the Yi-Xie.

Like their teachers, students are subjected both to the regimen of scriptural hall education and to the state's supervision. Specifically, the Party-State is concerned with the mobility of students within the Northwest and across the border. In terms of foreign Muslims studying in China, I encountered a few Pakistani students who had studied in Lanzhou, one of whom surprised me by commenting, "There is more freedom to study Islam here than in my home country." Teachers told me foreign students were not allowed in Linxia, however. Nonetheless, students come from all over China to study in Linxia. In addition to local students from Linxia and other counties in Gansu, there are students from Qinghai, Ningxia, and northern Xinjiang, including Hami and Yining (Gulja). At certain mosques, for example Front River Front Mosque, the largest Salafiyya mosque in China, upward of 90 percent of the students are from outside Linxia.

---

[17] Jackie Armijo (2008: 179) cites the number of 500 to 1,000 Chinese Muslims studying abroad, with 300 alone at al-Azhar University in Cairo. Her number accords with Chinese sources, which place 200 Hui in al-Azhar several years earlier (Liu 2005: 85). Chen Tianshe (2008: 44) places 40,000 overseas Chinese living in Saudi Arabia in 2002, including short-term stays, long-term inhabitants, and those who have obtained Saudi nationality. Chen does not specify what percentage is Muslim.

[18] But see Chapter 7 for changes to this system.

Following the events of July 2009, most Uyghur students were expelled from madrasas throughout southwestern Gansu and elsewhere in the Hui-dominated parts of the Northwest. Public security organs delegated such responsibility to the mosque administration committees. Thus, the state stood behind the authority of Hui elders to enforce state law. A series of measures restricted students' movements. For instance, in April 2010 the Linxia City BRA required all students to register with the bureau. I saw students filling out a form that asked for their scriptural name, Chinese name, hometown, age, and ethnicity. At one Gedimu mosque, the member of the mosque administration committee who was making students complete the form joked, "Now you are eating the Communist Party's food!" (*ni xianzai chi gongchandang de fan*). A cleric told me that these measures were developed to identify local students versus "outsiders," and particularly those from Xinjiang (i.e., Uyghurs).

The Party-State's role in "safeguarding religion" is, elliptically, a way to securitize the state. Population control measures such as randomly checking students' identity cards that specify their ethnicity are not new in China and are remnants of earlier Leninist approaches to population control. Sweeps through Linxia mosques to weed out "nonlocal" (i.e., Uyghur) students are legitimized on the same grounds—that it is the state's right to purify the sacred. Identity cards exemplify the "double-sided" nature of the law (Agamben 1998: 121): they are both the basis of citizen's rights and the means by which authorities can suspect the person of terrorism.

The hardware of law, however, is supplemented by the activities of nonstate actors (Greenhalgh and Winckler 2005: 4–5), "softer" tactics that are directed toward inhabiting Hui ethics. For instance, in the aforementioned 2009 ʿĪd-e-Qurbān sermon the Linxia cleric cited the Yi-Xie's favored Qur'anic verse[19] and warned:

> Islam still considers patriotism and safeguarding social stability to be parts of belief. At this present moment, the building of our country's socialist-modernism is at a critical juncture ... From the high vantage of national and social development, we Muslims recognize and safeguard unity and [seek to] recover stability. We do not cause disputes, but treasure this hard-earned opportunity. Only in this way will families be happy, the nation be prosperous and strong, society stabilize, religion be amiable, and the people live and work in peace and contentment. On the contrary, if we alienate one another, provoke disturbances, and manufacture contradictions, then we will only leave more stumbling blocks in the face

[19] Q. 3:103.

of development, disadvantaging it. Not only [does such behavior] influence the unity and progress of ethnicity and religion, but even worse, it destroys the face of national stability and influences economic development ... Therefore, in all social activity, we want to respect one another, unite all our ethnic brothers, all teaching schools. Especially between teaching schools, we should allow minor differences while seeking a common ground.

The Linxia cleric's sermon echoes official statements by the Yi-Xie and governmental bodies. Indeed, the cleric consults "prize-winning" sermons published by the Yi-Xie. Through the cleric, the Party's message gains a legitimacy it would not otherwise have. Such messages graft the desire for national unity and Muslim patriotism onto belief through the Party-State's techniques of the Muslim self.

PRIVATE SCHOOLS

Enterprising Hui educators have established private schools (minban xuexiao)[20] that teach Islamic law as a way to circumvent the dogma of both mosque-based madrasas and the Party-State. By private schools, I refer to a broad category of schools that neither depend on government funding nor have attachments to a mosque community.[21] Most private schools do have strong ties to a teaching school, however, which may also financially support them. Private schools vary to the degree that they make this affiliation known. In some instances, establishing a private school outside of a mosque community may be a means to produce qualified Muslims outside of the conventional teaching-school matrix. Colloquially called "Chinese-Arabic schools" (Zhong-A xuexiao), private schools provide instruction in subjects beyond language and have emerged in the reform period as vital institutions for cultivating qualified Muslims.

Some of the most innovative experiments with private schools occurred in the mid-twentieth century in Lintan. The Xidaotang established one of these in 1943, the Qixi Private Girls' School (Sili Qixi Nüxiao), named after the founder of the order, Ma Qixi, although the school was taken over by the government in 1949 (Min 2007: 127). Financed principally by the

---

[20] The term begins with the character min for "people," the same as minjian.
[21] Tan and Ding (2014: 61) note that such schools began in the 1920s and are once again growing in the reform era.

Xidaotang's stock-holding companies even after the government takeover, the school had about 150 female students per year by 1949 and 200 in 1958 (Ma Fengyi 2010: 200, 202). The Qixi Private Girls' School was concerned chiefly with educating young women in the Xidaotang tradition of Islam, with its heavy emphasis on Chinese classics and Confucian learning. Contrary to accounts that identify only the Yihewani tradition as compatible with Chinese nationalism, the Xidaotang tradition also oriented women toward active participation in building the young Chinese nation, and the school thus sought to educate women in an ethics of national belonging.

In his portrayal of the school's establishment, for instance, Shaykh Min Shengguan relates that the school participated actively in the founding of "New China" and a society in which everyone, including women, could develop their potential (Min 2007: 9). The emphasis on complementary—if not egalitarian—gender roles was a feature of the Xidaotang discursive tradition. According to Xidaotang official histories, the school was a center of patriotism during the Sino-Japanese War. The students sang a number of patriotic songs:

The waters of the Tao River surge, the morning arrives, Hui children's large battalion,	*Taoshui yong zhaori liu, Huimin ertong de da ben ying,*
We do not speak of narrow nationalism, we do not distinguish between any line of division,	*Women bu jiang xia'ai de minzu, women bu fen renhe jiexian,*
[We] get rid of the boundaries of the past,	*Guoqu de zhenyu wanquan yao ba ta huachu,*
Reading books is our duty, sweeping away the illiteracy of the borderlands,	*Dushu shi tianzhi, saochu bianqu de wenmang,*
Classmates, hold hands and press onward!	*Tongxuemen xie qishou, xiang qianjin!*
Take our blood and our flesh, join together to behead the enemy.	*Na women de xue he rou, qu pindiao diren de tou,*
Classmates, hold hands and press onward!	*Tongxuemen xie qishou, xiang qianjin!*
Contribute to the future nation-state!	*Ba jianglai xian gei guojia minzu!*
Contribute to the nation-state. Hey!	*Xian gei guojia minzu. Hai!*

(Min 2007: 17)

Figure 4.1 Pupils and teacher of Qixi Private Girls' School

Source: Xidaotang archives

The blackboard in the rear identifies the students as the class of 1957, including third and fourth graders. Note the absence of the hijab.

The Xidaotang's interpretation of Islamic law and ethics valorized the collective as the rights-bearing entity within the community, and Qixi Private Girls' School raised its students accordingly, forging modern Xidaotang women through learning, song, and dress (see Figure 4.1). As studies of pluralized ethical projects among Muslims elsewhere have shown (Schielke 2009; Jouili 2011; Simon 2012), the idea that the female students could be Muslim, modern, and nationalist presented no contradiction to the Xidaotang. Importantly, their tribute to the nation-state was not the version that the Communists ordained. Throughout the 1930s and 1940s the Xidaotang supported the Nationalists over the Communists. Their songs are evidence that at that period, the certainty with which the "Party" became wedded to "the State" was far from a foregone conclusion.[22]

---

[22] During the civil war, the Communists and Nationalists were briefly united from 1926 to 1927 and then again against the Japanese from 1936 to 1938.

Likewise, before the Party-State's imposition of ethnic autonomy, the Sino-Tibetan periphery was a wellspring of competing projects to modernize Islam as part of New China. Teaching Hui girls was crucial to such efforts. Historically, female students became the "family instructor" (*jiating jiaolian*) for the children and sometimes for the husband as well. Lanzhou University's Yang Wenjiong has found, based on his study of the sources of Islamic traditional culture among Hui in Yinchuan, Xi'an, and Xining, that "family members' discourse" (*jiarenjiang*) is by far the most common source of Islamic knowledge (Yang 2007: 614). The home has been a privileged domain for learning, and some women move back and forth between home and the mosque, madrasa, or private school, using and dispensing knowledge about the revealed sources and the building blocks of Islamic law.

Following economic reforms and religious policy liberalization in the 1980s, educators have established a number of private schools in Linxia.[23] Two of these, what I will call the "Yihewani private school" and the "Sufi private school," are locked in a turf war over resources, transnational connections, and different conceptions of qualified Muslims. The Yihewani private school is not attached to any one mosque, but it has a strong Yihewani sensibility. In 1977, on the cusp of Deng Xiaoping's economic reforms, Ma Zhixin (d. 2012), an early member of a branch of puritanical Yihewani, established the Yihewani private school and a sister school called the Chinese-Arabic Girls' School. The schools began as small meetings that Ma Zhixin organized in his courtyard home, where he taught Arabic. After raising funds in his mosque community and with some Saudi assistance,[24] he purchased rooms in which to hold the classes.

Private religious schools face difficulties in China in terms of registration, official recognition, funding, and staffing, given that the PRC regulatory regime does not have such a category. Being unaffiliated with mosques carries benefits and burdens. State law regards mosques as "religious activity areas," and they therefore receive a higher level of scrutiny than do schools. Nonetheless, during the late 1970s and 1980s the schools faced difficulty obtaining permits from the state. In 1989 the schools received government approval from the Linxia City Education Bureau to establish the equivalent of a four-year high school or professional school. However, universities did not recognize their diplomas until 2007 when

---

[23] For developments in Yunnan, see Ma Xuefeng (2014).

[24] The 1997 addition of a computer lab and library was funded by Saudi and Gulf money. Ma Zhixin also developed relationships with shaykhs from the Egyptian education institute Dar al-Ifta' al-Misriyya, in addition to other overseas institutes (al-Sudairi 2014: 43).

the Linxia Prefecture Education Bureau approved the schools. However, the boys' school had to change its name from using "Arabic" to describe its focus as "foreign language." One benefit of this approval was that the prefectural government began providing the school with an annual stipend of RMB 80,000 (Ding 2011: 25).

Both schools are managed under the same board of trustees, composed of well-off businessmen, primarily Yihewani, from Linxia. The board of trustees raises all capital for improvements to the school, in addition to tuition, and in 1997 raised RMB 1 million to construct a new building for the girls' school. Some of those funds were derived from business contacts overseas, and the schools have also received some subsidies from the government. In 2010 the Chinese-Arabic Girls' School had forty-five teachers, 20 percent of whom had studied abroad. In that year, between the two schools, there were about 600 male students and 730 female students.

The curriculum for the boys' school reflects many of the initiatives undertaken by Ma Tianmin and Ma Xiqing, with particular emphasis on practical learning, mainstreaming religious instruction, and Arabic-language training. In other words, the Yihewani private school has tried to integrate its Hijaz-oriented imaginary with the demands of the market. Years one and two focus on Arabic language, the Qur'an and sunna, Qur'anic recitation, and the rudiments of Islamic law (*faxue*). Students also have classes in computers, athletics, and "morality," which covers general rules for good comportment and pragmatic instruction in daily living. The third year continues Arabic instruction, adding classical Arabic literature, and also incorporates Islamic history, in addition to increasingly advanced studies in the Qur'an, sunna, and Islamic law. Year four introduces more advanced courses in law, including legal principles (*faxue yuanli*), jurisprudence (*jiaofaxue*), and inheritance law (*yichanfa*). A standard teaching aid used by instructors in law is the *Fiqh al-Sunna*, written by the Egyptian jurist Sayyid Sabiq (d. 2000) and translated by a group of Salafis based in Linxia.

The girls' school curriculum consists of Arabic, Islamic knowledge, history, classical Arabic literature, Mandarin, and computing. Instruction of Islamic law plays a much more marginal role, with teachers making reference to collections of hadith. The school's official literature describes the objectives as follows:

> We strive to study advanced scientific-cultural technology by cultivating Muslim "new type" women and ethnic specialized talent who have culture, morals, quality, ideals, self-respect, self-love, self-confidence, and

self-independence. [We aim] to form the school into an advanced-level women's professional school that is a place for bilingual Chinese-Arabic instruction, full of ethnic characteristics and of vast scope. [Our school] struggles ardently toward the revival of ethnic education, [raising] the quality of ethnicities, developing the local economy, and building social-ism and harmonious society.

As this statement suggests, the private school fills a perceived gap in eth-nic minority education in the Northwest: it provides a learning envir-onment where Muslim women can modernize themselves on Yihewani terms, many of which echo Party propaganda.

As with private Islamic schools elsewhere (Metcalf 2007), private schools in China must not only make pious Muslims but also nurture loyal citizens, a task that has become even more complicated in the post-2009 Northwest. Following the Urumqi riots, the schools' adminis-trations have had to assure officials that the schools do not teach militant fundamentalism. One result of the state's tepid approval of the private schools is the schools' appropriation of official discourse. Their produc-tion of qualified Muslims upholds the Party-State's definition of "good" Muslims, which entails working for the improvement of the local econ-omy and contributing to national development. Along these lines, the principal of the Yihewani private school told me that "to be a *qualified Muslim* is a precondition to being an *excellent citizen*" (his emphasis).

The female leaders of the girls' school all wear the hijab, and as part of the school's project of grooming young women of high quality, the students are likewise required to wear the hijab. Unlike public schools, where Muslim minority women are not allowed to wear headscarves, in the private schools they are outward signs of personal piety. Such expres-sions are showcased by the school administration as a particularly modern mode of female piety that is congruent with the goals of the Party-State. Female Muslims' headwear has emerged as the screen upon which is pro-jected the battle between Islamic religiosity and secularism in the West.[25] Yet headwear is a fluid sign, open to plural meanings even within the same national jurisdiction. Uyghur women in Xinjiang have donned the full veil in increasing numbers in cities like Kashgar for multiple reasons, including to maintain their modesty against the increasing number of tourists (Muslim, Han, and foreigner) into their neighborhoods. In 2015 the Urumqi city government banned burqas, based on the rationale that

---

[25] For scholarly appraisals of this contest, see Scott (1990), Abu-Lughod (2002), Brown (2006), Bowen (2007), and Rohe (2007).

such a prohibition "checks the infiltration of the ideology of religious extremism" (*ezhi zongjiao jiduan sixiang shentou*).[26] What is "oppressive and anti-modern," from the viewpoint of the Party-State in one context (i.e., southern Xinjiang), redeems secular rule in another context, such as Linxia. As one Uyghur woman from Hami told me, "Linxia? Oh, that's where they are extremely strict, like the girls don't have long, uncovered hair like mine and they often don't go outside." The woman's perception shows that some Uyghurs at least see Hui as enjoying greater freedoms to practice piety than they have. Meanwhile, the Yihewani girls' school contributes to writing the public script of state-sanctioned Islam through symbols that can be both Islamic and modern.

The Yihewani private schools' success is mixed. Students said that the attrition rate increases dramatically, such that by year four only about 10 percent of the entering class remains. Likewise, for the Chinese-Arabic Girls' School, in 2009 there were 318 girls in year one but only 72 in year four. The primary reason for dropping out was financial hardship. At the boys' school, of those few who complete the four years, almost all will study abroad in the Middle East, Pakistan, or Malaysia. Following their achievements and particularly their advanced study abroad, these students are imbued with a kind of "charisma ideology" (Bourdieu and Passeron [1964] 1979: 69), which fuels their subsequent careers.

The Yihewani private schools are more oriented than most madrasas toward post-secondary-level education abroad and internationalizing students, although they do not have formal ties with foreign universities, and their diplomas were not recognized by foreign universities until after gaining approval by the prefectural government in 2007. Top students are sent to Beijing for an annual exam that Cairo's al-Azhar University administers. In the past, the boys' school had foreign teachers, but in 2009 the Public Security Bureau (PSB) clamped down on foreigners

---

[26] See Article 1 of the Regulation Prohibiting Wearing Burqas in Public Places in Urumqi City (*Wulumuqi shi gonggong changsuo jinzhi chuandai meng mianzhao pao de guiding*), passed by the Twenty-First Meeting of the Standing Committee of the Fifteenth Session of the Urumqi City People's Congress on December 10, 2014, approved by the Thirteenth Meeting of the Standing Committee of the Twelfth Session of the People's Congress of the Xinjiang Uyghur Autonomous Region on January 10, 2015, effective February 1, 2015. See also the Xinjiang Uyghur Autonomous Region Religious Affairs Regulations (*Xinjiang Weiwu'er Zizhiqu zongjiao shiwu guanli tiaoli*), passed by the Eleventh Meeting of the Thirteenth Session of the Standing Committee of the People's Congress of the Xinjiang Uyghur Autonomous Region on November 28, 2014, effective January 1, 2015, art. 38, prohibiting organizations or persons from compelling others to wear "religious extremist dress or accessorize [with] religious extremist signs or symbols" (*zongjiao jiduan fushi, peidai zongjiao jiduan biaozhi, biaozhi*).

teaching in Linxia. Of the fewer than 100 students who finish three years, about 30 percent become translators in eastern cities such as Shenzhen, Guangzhou, or Yiwu. Most students, about 70 percent, study abroad, continue to study within China, or teach at mosques. At the same time, 20 percent of the graduates of the Chinese-Arabic Girls' School study outside the Northwest—either in Beijing or abroad in Saudi Arabia, Malaysia, Pakistan, Thailand, or Sudan. Ten percent become translators, with Yiwu as the top destination. Fifty percent become teachers at other private schools in China, and 20 percent marry and raise families. None become female clerics.

Although Linxia's private schools are not attached to mosques, their mission to engender qualified Muslims derives from the discursive traditions of teaching schools. For example, several hundred meters from the Yihewani private school is the Sufi private school, which was founded in 1993 by members of a nearby mosque affiliated with the Qadiriyya Ma Wenchuan Sufi order. Whereas the Yihewani private school focused on Arabic language, the Sufi private school identifies Persian as a key language for cultivating Islamic knowledge and is one of the only two private schools in China to specialize in Persian instruction.[27] In contrast to the Yihewani private school's cultivation of ties with business contacts in Saudi Arabia, the Sufi private school builds ties with Iran. The Yihewani and Sufi private schools, anchoring their teaching in opposing authorizing traditions, thus represent in Northwest China the ideological tug-of-war between Saudi Arabia and Iran.

Like its rival, the Sufi private school, which had 170 students, all male, encountered problems in gaining official recognition. In 2007 the Linxia City Department of Education suggested it change its name from using "Arabic" to "foreign language," which it did, like the Yihewani school. However, indicative of the greater scrutiny of Sufi institutions, the Sufi school still did not receive governmental approval. The school offers three concentrations: Persian, Arabic, and Islamic theory. The current principal studied in Iran for eleven years and has changed the curriculum to align with that of schools there. Law instructors teach the *Wiqaya*, al-Sirhindi's *Maktubat*, and *al-Tafsir al-Hussayn* (Ch. *Housaine jingzhu*), but also integrate such Sufi poetry as the *Garden of Roses* (Ch. *Zhenjing huayuan*)

---

[27] The other, according to instructors at the school, is located in faraway Hainan Island, which has a small population of Hui from Linxia.

by Sadi (1184–1263). While the school depends largely on funding from Linxia businessmen, the principal has maintained channels with Iran. In 2009 the school established an arrangement with the Iranian embassy so that every year a representative goes to the school to select students for scholarships to study at top universities in Iran. Five students were chosen in 2010.

Like the Yihewani private school down the street, the Sufi private school is also concerned with the relationship between Islamic law and ethics, on the one hand, and the requirements of PRC citizenship and state laws, on the other. Yet unlike the administration of the Yihewani private school, which has sought to align its interests with nationalist desire and thus willfully overlooks conflicts of law, teachers at the Sufi school exercise a more pragmatic view. One teacher offered the following assessment: "What's most important, for Hui, is neither religious law nor state law, but rather Chinese traditional law. Custom holds that the son should get all and the daughter nothing, so neither an equal portion as under state law nor one half of the male heir's [portion] as under religious law. In applying law, our teachers never say *should*; rather, they state what Islamic law holds, but we know that this is limited by customary traditions." If the Yihewani private school's approach to cultivating ethical awareness in their students emphasizes practicality, then the Sufi approach is doubly so. Consonant with their valorization of the localized forms of Islamic knowledge in China, the Sufis may remind students of their obligations under shari'a as over and above customary behaviors, but in doing so, they acknowledge the prevalence of pre-Islamic customs.

ISLAMIC SCRIPTURAL INSTITUTES

As Robert Hefner (2007: 3–4) has observed, at the global level Muslim education is responsive to the increasing pluralism of contemporary societies. Pious Muslims, however, are not the only ones designing educational institutions to teach Muslims ethics and law. Since the advent of nationalism and the decline of Western imperialism, secular states in the Middle East have turned to religious schools to produce devout and modern citizens. In Egypt, for instance, the Department of Preaching and Guidance was established in 1918 to train and supervise Muslim clerics, and Gamal Abdel Nasser, the second president of Egypt, founded the Ministry of Religious Affairs in 1960 to bring mosques under the direct administration of the state (Hirschkind 2006: 44). Nasser also imposed secular law over the operations of al-Azhar University, long viewed throughout the Middle East and, indeed, globally as an epicenter for Islamic legal instruction. The most far-reaching secularization of traditional Islamic educational institutions occurred in Turkey. Soon after Mustafa Kemal Atatürk founded the Turkish Republic in 1923, he abolished madrasas, and in 1924 the Imam-Hatip schools were formed to train imams (Agai 2007; Ozgur 2012).

In China, the Party-State, in addition to influencing pedagogical material in madrasas and mosques, has founded its own educational institutions to produce a Muslim elite who support state-sponsored Islam. Specifically, the Yi-Xie has established Islamic Scriptural Institutes (Yisilanjiao Jingxueyuan) throughout the country, four of which are located in the Northwest. The Islamic Scriptural Institutes are based on the Hui Institute (Huimin Xueyuan), which was established in Beijing in 1955 and subsequently developed a separate school for women.[28] The Islamic Scriptural Institutes thus grew out of an effort in the early Communist period to cultivate Muslim elite who were equally conversant in the revealed sources of Islam and Chinese socialism. According to Ma Wenlong of the Islamic Scriptural Institute in Lanzhou, the goal was to train clerics in line with Party thought, as "practice proves that a good imam, who is familiar with the Party and government's laws, regulations and policies on freedom of religious belief and who is able to keep close contact with the masses, plays a crucial role locally in safeguarding religious harmony, ethnic unity, and a peaceful and prosperous life for all" (Ma Wenlong 2011: 33).

The institutes include grades equivalent to both secondary and university-level education. Most students enter having completed middle school in a state-run (secular) school and then, within the institute, pursue the lower-level, or professional school (*dazhuanban*), normally for three years. Ages of entering students vary from fifteen to nineteen. Most did not test into high school in a state-run (secular) school, and most come from poorer rural backgrounds. The curriculum is apportioned between 70 percent religious content (e.g., Arabic language and Islamic doctrine, including elementary Islamic law), 20 percent cultural content (e.g.,

---

[28] In addition to the China Islamic Scriptural Institute (the successor to the Hui Institute), there are Islamic Scriptural Institutes in Beijing, Kunming, Lanzhou, Yinchuan, Urumqi, Xining, Zhengzhou, Shenyang, and Shijiazhuang.

Chinese language and Islamic history), and 10 percent political content. In terms of the political content, students I spoke with in the lower level meet once a week for a course on PRC law and policy, which is not limited to regulations affecting religion. In addition, their political courses included content on "thought and morality," a watered-down treatment of socialist thought.

Upon completing the lower level, students can then enter the higher, or university, level (benke), which entails four years of instruction. Higher-level courses are Islamic law, Islamic doctrine, Qur'an, sunna, Arabic, and Chinese. Those who wish to pursue advanced studies can enter the "clerical training class," which includes an additional three years of learning, although most candidates take only one extra year of classes. At this level, political content becomes a greater focus. According to official statements, the political, or patriotic, courses include "Deng Xiaoping Theory" and "Theories on Constructing Socialism with Chinese Characteristics," as well as such electives as "Basic Legal Knowledge," "Policy and Political Situation Analysis," and "Lessons on Muslim Patriotism" (Ma Wenlong 2011: 34).

For the instruction of law, most Islamic Scriptural Institutes use the Wiqaya as a main text. Ding Bingquan, one of the translators for a recent edition, teaches at the Lanzhou Islamic Scriptural Institute. Nonetheless, there is some variation in teaching material across the institutes. The Ningxia Islamic Scriptural Institute in Yinchuan, for instance, also uses the Wiqaya as a traditional Hanafi text, but teachers there called it "outdated," particularly on matters of purity, such as smoking. They developed their own teaching aid, which the institute published in 2002, called A Concise Course in Islamic Law (Yisilanjiao jianming jiaocheng). The book contains sections on belief (imān), etiquette (adab), devotional matters ('ibādāt), the law of social relations (mu'āmalāt), and, for sake of comprehensiveness, punishments ('uqūba).

The emergence within the various Islamic Scriptural Institutes of individual methods of instruction gave rise to curricular reform emphasizing greater standardization. The Yi-Xie convened the Symposium on National and Local Scriptural Study Institutes' Teaching Materials Work in 2001.[29] The following year it established the Office for Coordinating the Editing

---

[29] This is the same year that the Educational Administration Guidance Committee, formed under the Yi-Xie, began the ill-fated project of developing exegetical texts, known as jiejing. See Chapter 1.

TABLE 4.2 Textbooks created by the Yi-Xie for the Islamic Scriptural Institutes

Original Chinese Title	English Translation of Title
Gulanjing jichu jianming jiaocheng	A Concise Course in the Basics of the Qur'an
Shengxun jichu jianming jiaocheng	A Concise Course in the Basics of the Hadith
Gulanjing fenlei jianming jiaocheng	A Concise Course in the Classifications in the Qur'an
Shengxun fenlei jianming jiaocheng	A Concise Course in the Classifications of the Hadith
Yisilanjiaoyi jianming jiaocheng	A Concise Course in Islamic Doctrine
Yisilanjiaofa jianming jiaocheng	A Concise Course in Islamic Law
Shijie Yisilanjiao shi jianming jiaocheng	A Concise Course in Global Islamic History
Zhongguo Yisilanjiao shi jianming jiaocheng	A Concise Course in Chinese Islamic History
Gulanjing songduxue jianming jiaocheng	A Concise Course in Qur'anic Recitation
Alabo wenshufa jianming jiaocheng	A Concise Course in Arabic Calligraphy

of the Yi-Xie Teaching Material. After five years of work reforming the curriculum, the Yi-Xie published a series of textbooks to be used in the Islamic Scriptural Institutes (see Table 4.2).

The textbooks provide the state's view of Islamic law, history, and doctrine and seek to consolidate understandings of Islamic law through established state discourses. The curriculum is uniform across the different institutes and prevents any regional or ethnic disparity. Thus, *A Concise Course in Islamic Law* includes a section on "Islamic Law in China," which uses the trope of "domestication" (*bentuhua*), common in academic writings on Islam in China to describe shari'a not as a transcendent order of law that unites the global *umma*, but as a localized and ethnicized religious belief (China Islamic Association 2008: 103–5).

Although the stated goal of the Islamic Scriptural Institutes is to produce clerics who assume positions of leadership in mosques, based upon my conversations with students and teachers, I concluded that the vast majority of their graduates, like graduates of Turkey's Imam-Hatip schools, enter the civil service. Mainly, they join the BRA or the Yi-Xie.

There appear to be multiple reasons for graduates' career decisions. First, as a technical matter, within the PRC educational system, Islamic Scriptural Institutes are merely "institutes" (*xueyuan*) and not universities (*daxue*). Consequently, the government does not recognize the diplomas students receive from the higher-level school as university degrees, a qualification that is not required to work in the BRA or other governmental bureaus, although increasingly they recruit college graduates and even Ph.D. holders. Similarly, foreign universities do not recognize Islamic Scriptural Institute diplomas and instead require students to take a qualifying exam. Furthermore, the institutes face intense competition from scriptural hall education. Most clerics choose a graduate from their own madrasa to succeed them and look down on graduates from the state-sponsored school. Hence, for Muslim minorities, as for Han Chinese graduates from professional and secondary schools throughout China, entering the bloated civil service provides a viable and stable career.

Islamic Scriptural Institutes are one of the government's key intermediaries between overseas Muslim organizations and domestic Muslims. As the sites for educating China's Muslim elite, the Islamic Scriptural Institutes have received official approval to court Saudi financial support for their development, as opposed to, for example, private schools. For instance, in 1986 the Islamic Development Bank reportedly gave US$4 million to construct institutes in Beijing, Ningxia, and Xinjiang (Allès, Chérif-Chebbi, and Halfon 2003: 17). At the Lanzhou Islamic Scriptural Institute, founded in 1984 and expanded in 2004 with a grant of US$290,000 from the Islamic Development Bank, there were 220 students in 2010, all male. The lower-level grade graduates about 120 students per year. Forty percent plan to study abroad, mostly at al-Azhar or in Saudi Arabia, although some go to Iran, Pakistan, or Malaysia. The latest trend is for students to study abroad directly after middle school or high school at a secular public school. The rest go to the east coast to try their fortunes as translators. Only one out of ten becomes a cleric at a mosque.

It is within the institutes' mandate to provide an array of secular courses alongside religious instruction. In 2009, for instance, English was added to the courses for the lower-level students. With the job market for clerics narrowed by external constraints and competition, it is possible that the institutes will go the way of Imam-Hatip schools, which offer more nonreligious coursework than religious classes (Ozgur 2012: 2).

As embodiments of ethical exemplars that follow both the sunna of the Prophet Muhammad and his successors as well as the Party's ideology (i.e., Mao-Deng-Jiang-Hu-Xi thought), state-trained clerics exhibit their dual inheritance through regular competitions, featuring Qur'anic recitation, sermon competitions, and Arabic oral examinations. Sermons, in particular, reflect the priorities of the Party-State in interpreting Islam through patriotism and the unity of ethnic groups.[30] These oral performances are the Chinese Islamic equivalent of the entertainment industry complex that commoditizes ethnic minorities throughout China.[31] Such performances are self-effacing acts, censoring the performer's own critical or political voice. They align the message of the faith with that of the Party. State-trained clerics become the grassroots supports to Party rule through invoking a transcendent divine sovereignty.

ETHNIC SCHOOLS

In addition to influencing instruction in madrasas and founding its own rival Islamic institutes, the Party-State has established ethnic schools, which steer Muslims away from a religious education altogether, exciting them with the commercial prospects of Arabic-language acquisition. Public education for ethnic minorities that guarantees minority language and culture is a defining feature of PRC ethnic minority policy. Organized under the Ministry of Education, ethnic schools are particularly prominent in autonomous areas, although they are not limited to them. They specialize in providing bilingual education, which consists of instruction in Mandarin, the language of the Han Chinese majority and the official language of the PRC, and the language of the ethnic minority group in question.

There has been widespread criticism of state-run ethnic schools in China. Unlike Xinjiang, where Mandarin has largely superseded Uyghur as the preferred language for entering the labor market,[32] in Linxia the question among Hui is not whether the minority language, in this case Arabic, should receive official support but to what purpose should Arabic be learned. The Linxia vocational technical college was established in 1980 as a three-year professional school offering courses in Arabic, computing,

---

[30] For instance, the cleric who recited the ʿĪd-e-Qurbān sermon studied at the Islamic Scriptural Institute in Yinchuan for three years. However, demonstrating the multiple influences on clerics' education, he also studied in Pakistan for six years in the late 1990s.

[31] For case studies, see, e.g., Schein (1997, 2000), Makley (2002), McKhann (2002), Oakes and Sutton (2010), and Tenzin (2014).

[32] See, for instance, Dwyer (2005), Schluessel (2007), and Ma (2009a, 2009b).

and accounting. The state recognizes a diploma from the college as equivalent to a high school degree. It has six hundred male and female students,
who come from thirteen different provinces. The students are mostly
Muslim minorities, although 30 percent are Han. Of the total student
body, the majority (approximately four hundred) study Arabic.

The Arabic the students learn, however, is divorced from Islam. The state
curriculum has severed the body of knowledge that comprises Islam, specifically, the Qur'an, from its linguistic expression, a relationship Arabist
Irfan Shahid (1999: 68) characterized as "inseparably linked." Reasoning
in Islamic jurisprudence, in particular, was instrumental to developing
Arabic grammar, metaphors, and logic (Carter 1997; Modarressi 1986). At
the vocational technical college, however, neither the course materials nor
instruction touch on matters of religion, let alone Islamic law.

The commercialization of the Arabic language is nothing new.
Universities from Amman to Hong Kong offer "business Arabic" courses.
Yet the classroom as a space that prohibits religious speech, acts, and signs
marks an extreme secularization. For instance, female students cannot
wear headscarves. The faculty uses Arabic textbooks published by foreign language presses in Beijing that exclude any religious content. And
no prayer is allowed during class. On the one hand, while such prohibitions force religion into the private sphere, Hui students and teachers
have accommodated such carve-outs. For instance, they have adapted
their prayers around secular time. As one teacher explained to me, "The
requirements for prayer [salat] are flexible. We pray first in the morning
before class, then during lunch break, and the afternoon prayers we are
also able to perform during breaks. Lastly, we pray in the evening. This
way it does not interfere with school or work. Sometimes we must make
up missed prayers." By flexibly adapting religious obligations, Hui (even
Salafis) uphold their devotional obligations.

Despite extreme secularization's zone of exclusion, religion permeates
the relationships between teachers and students, which can mirror the
ethics of intimacy shared by master and pupil in the more traditionalist
madrasas. I was exposed to the much wider spectrum of topics, including
religion, permitted through conversations outside of class while studying
Arabic with one of the teachers. I met with the teacher every weekend for
several months, until one day when I was no longer permitted to enter the
school.[33] Prior to my expulsion, we held class in his on-campus dorm room,

---

[33] My rejection occurred shortly after the KTV affair (Chapter 7), which occurred in the same
week. As with other towns in the Northwest, after any kind of public disturbance, authorities

which was large enough for one desk and one bed. While I was studying with the teacher, students who also lived on campus regularly interrupted us. Students censored their own speech in class, but in the teacher's private space, as with traditional mosque-based schools, students and teachers discussed matters ranging from points of *'ibādāt* and the determination of innovation (Ar. *bid'a*) in Islamic law to recent Arabic works translated by local scholars and examples of a "Coca-Cola Muslim."[34]

Additionally, many of the teachers were devout Salafis who considered it their moral duty to inform young Muslims in particular of the substance of Islamic law. As one teacher exhorted, "The most meaningful thing is to tell people how to live their lives. People nowadays smoke, drink, and have casual sex with women. They spend their time trying to figure out ways to sleep with women. These people are lost … In the West, people emphasize freedom. 'Oh, if I have freedom, I can do anything!'" The teacher's initiative to impart ethical guidelines to his students, to form moral selves, takes the form of opposition not to the Chinese state or the laxness of non-Muslim Han, but to Western amorality, a favored object of critique within Salafism. The goal, as indicated by the teacher, is not freedom of choice, consumption, or sexuality, but living in accordance with a tradition. Putting the teacher's critique in broader terms, the Western liberal definition of freedom as autonomous action has become synonymous with the march of modernity such that alternative notions of freedom are passed over or, worse, demonized (Keane 2007; Asad 2009a). What is striking about this instance of Salafiyya ethical cultivation is that it operates in *minjian* spaces and discourses within public schooling in a panoptic, postsocialist state.

That state-run schools prefer to hire Salafis may, at first, seem unlikely. But the Salafiyya stress Arabic proficiency, and the majority of Salafi instructors have spent time studying Arabic abroad; from the state's perspective, assessment of the teacher's mastery of the foreign language takes priority over their doctrinal orientation. From the Salafi teacher's view, employment is a double bind. All teachers at state-run ethnic schools are, by definition, civil servants, as they are employed under the Ministry of Education. While such employment confers benefits, such as a pension, it also entails self-loathing. As a teacher, referring to the requirement to register every morning at the school, deplored, "Don't they know? We are

in Linxia temporarily tighten control (including surveillance of any foreigners, Muslims and non-Muslims alike).

[34] *Coca-Cola Muslim* is a term that expresses the vitiating effects of Western culture on one's spirituality.

supervised by Allah, not by man!" The Salafi instructors' insertion of their moral mission into a government-run school and the ministry's use of Salafi Arabic talent for education on the Muslim borderlands typify the kinds of mutual access that characterizes the Hui social field and the Chinese state.

The purpose of the school is to produce students with Arabic proficiency for commercial benefit, rather than to mint experts in Islam or its law. Observers of post-Mao China have described a shift in state-society relations from one whereby the sovereign state rules over subjects to one that elicits desires, from health and sexuality to consumerism and prestige, through multiform governance.[35] These studies stress that the pursuit of personal interest was not antithetical to the interests of the nation, or of the state. As Deng Xiaoping famously quipped, "To get rich is glorious." Maris Gillette (2000), in her ethnography of Hui in Xi'an, provided an important modification to understandings of mainstream Han market behavior by demonstrating how Hui cultivated tastes accented by both Arab- and Han-inspired factors. Hui desire may not just take the form of consuming Western or domestic Chinese fashions but may also be oriented toward Middle Eastern markets.

Such market diversification does not in any way injure the secular state, and it may assist the state's aim of increasing economic ties with energy-rich countries from Kazakhstan to Saudi Arabia. Education in Linxia, specifically through state-run ethnic schools that cultivate the desire for knowledge of the Arabic language, may operate in parallel to consumption patterns that Gillette observed in the late 1990s. The majority of graduates from the Arabic program of the vocational technical college, for instance, become translators in Yiwu, Guangzhou, and Shenzhen, whereas top students apply to study abroad in locations such as Libya. The vocational technical college and other ethnic schools are forerunners in the commercial Arabic market in China. Public schools' encouragement of their graduates to seek work in urbanized southeastern China is not an exception to the Party-State's attempt to isolate and contain Islam in Linxia. Eager youths intent on financial security may leave, but missionaries and educators from abroad cannot enter. The broader point, which I elaborate below, is that the drive to learn commercial Arabic exemplifies a secular ethic, or desacralized "calling," to use Weber's (1930) term, produced by the convergence of the Party-State's interests, the market, and Hui desire.

---

[35] For a partial selection, see Hoffman (2008), Zhang Li (2010), Zhang (2011b), and Osburg (2013).

EXCURSUS: THE SILK ROAD 2.0

In recent years, the regime has endorsed the idea of a "New Silk Road" (Xin Sichou Zhilu), the "Silk Road Economic Belt" (Sichou Zhilu Jingjidai), or "One Belt, One Road" (Yi Dai Yi Lu).[36] The New Silk Road is less a specific policy and more a broad orientation toward economic and security ties with the Middle East and Central Asia—a coalescence of a number of bilateral trade relationships, multilateral institutions, and security pacts.[37] To take one example, relations between the PRC and Central Asian states were formalized in 2001 with the formation of the Shanghai Cooperation Organization (SCO).[38] The member states of the SCO coordinate to prevent cross-border terrorism.[39] The PRC government, in its erecting of a panoptic state, has been increasingly concerned with the movement of Muslim minorities both across international borders and within the territory of the PRC. Such concern is reflected in official reports of the 2014 Central Ethnic Work Meeting. Following the meeting, reports in state-run media emphasized controlling the flow of minorities and the communities they form:

> The meeting noted that following reform and opening, our country has entered a period of the expansion of a great flow of all ethnic groups across the region. This trend has made urban ethnic work more important. Regarding ethnic minorities' floating population, we cannot adopt a "closed door" attitude; we also cannot adopt a laissez-faire attitude. The key is to capture the points of the flow's entrance and egress. We should focus on the community and encourage mutually embedded social structures and social environments. We should pay attention to protecting the legal rights of all ethnic minorities.
>
> (Central Ethnic Work Committee 2014)

---

[36] The name of the effort has changed over time. Xi Jinping first announced the "Silk Road Economic Belt" during a speech on September 7, 2013, at Nazarbayev University in Kazakhstan. Subsequently, China led the creation of the Asian Infrastructure Investment Bank in 2014, worth US$57 billion, to finance a Silk Road Fund. China subsequently pledged US$46 billion to the fund, which will build an infrastructural link between Kashgar and Gwadar Port in southern Pakistan.

[37] Political scientists, economists, and policy makers have spearheaded interest in the "New Silk Road" (Karrar 2009; Simpfendorfer 2009; Krahl 2013).

[38] The SCO was formed pursuant to the Declaration on the Establishment of the Shanghai Cooperation Organization, issued June 15, 2001, by the following member states: Kazakhstan, China, Kyrgyzstan, Russia, Tajikistan, and Uzbekistan. Observer states include Afghanistan, India, Iran, Mongolia, and Pakistan.

[39] See the Shanghai Convention on Combating Terrorism, Separatism, and Extremism, effective May 7, 2009, art. 2(1).

Beyond the Xinjiang theater, this approach of directing the flow of minorities has been taken up by authorities in Linxia, who encourage Hui youths to migrate to the southeastern coast to take up employment as Arabic translators and cultural intermediaries between Han sellers and foreign Muslim buyers. The Party-State has sought in Arabic language instruction a way to marshal a foundational aspect of Hui identity for the development of the nation-state. To do so, the Party-State works mainly through the multiple forms of educational institutions, as one way to keep an eye on the *minjian*. The private schools, which could otherwise be potential sites for antistate interpretations of Islam, have been a focus of such steering. In 2004 a team of experts under the Ministry of Education visited the Yihewani private school in Linxia to "investigate, study, and provide guidance" to the school, and concluded in its report that "the expansion of Arabic language education in the country's Northwest and other concentrated areas of the Hui ethnic group is an important work for the development of the regional economy and the implementation of the Strategy for the Development of the Great Northwest" (cited in Ding 2011: 24).

Enticing young Hui to leave the Northwest for the coastal cities thus benefits the state in many ways. Above all, it channels impressionable Muslim youths who may otherwise be drawn to radical messages in Islam into a market in which linguistic proficiency is more valued than piety. This marketization of Arabic in the Northwest has reoriented Muslim minority desire away from using Arabic to learn sacred law and toward applying it to building the nation-state. The Party-State's association of Arabic with nation building also reflects its attempts to craft China's reemergence in the global *umma*. The market's production of desire, however, does not isomorphically map onto the desire of Chinese Muslim minorities to form connections with Muslim communities abroad.

As mentioned in Chapter 1, such coastal cities as Guangzhou have had a large number of Muslim merchants and traders from as early as the Tang Dynasty (618–907). In the modern period, as economic liberalization has once again attracted large numbers of foreign Muslims to the southeast, one popular destination has been Yiwu, in Zhejiang Province. Yiwu, as previously mentioned, is home to "the world's largest small commodities market."[40] The county government established the small commodities

---

[40] The secondary literature on Yiwu attributes this accolade to a 2005 report jointly issued by the United Nations, World Bank, and Morgan Stanley (see, e.g., Mu 2010: 92, 110); however, I have been unable to verify the existence of this report.

market in 1982, and although it was not initially meant to attract foreign Muslims, as early as 1998 Muslims from the Middle East and North Africa began arriving in Yiwu, almost wholly a Han Chinese city, to buy wholesale goods—from rubber sandals and pens to alarm clocks and stuffed animals—that would be sold to distributors in their home countries.[41] Transient business networks have created more enduring communities as foreign businessmen reside in Yiwu, marry and convert Han Chinese women, and assume permanent status. According to one study, there were 260 Muslims in 2000, most of them foreign (Ma 2012: 23). Ten years later, of a total population of around two million people, there were some 20,000 Muslims living in the city, of whom 65 percent were foreign (Ma 2012: 23). The linchpin of the market are the Hui from Northwest China who work as translators and middlemen between foreign Muslim buyers and Han sellers. As of 2010, there were about 4,000 such translators in Yiwu.[42]

While based in Northwest China, I traveled to Yiwu several times to gain an appreciation of Hui youths' efforts to earn a living from their Arabic training. Yiwu's small commodities market is one of the great successes of the reform period. Its growth has been exponential. In 2011 Sino-Arab trade accounted for US$64 billion, an increase of 1,600 percent from ten years earlier (al-Tamimi 2014: 126), and in 2009 Yiwu's markets alone generated US$49.23 billion in total volume of trade (i.e., not limited to Arab states) (Wu 2010: 297).[43] A young Hui trader from Ningxia who has worked in Yiwu since 1996, Mr. Ma, describes the growth of the market:

> Yiwu developed out of this context: growing cash flows through southeastern China, a hungry market for cheap Chinese goods, particularly among Arab Muslims, and demand from Europe. The reason for Yiwu's success is not the government, but the people. The emphasis here is on building relations and maintaining them. Their work ethic is also

---

[41] There are a number of different markets in Yiwu that are organized by commodity type—for example, eyeglasses, toys, electronics, kitchen supplies, hardware, shoes, and so forth. Most of these are housed in sprawling buildings called International Trade City on the northern side of the city, although markets have popped up throughout Yiwu.

[42] An experienced translator from Ningxia who subsequently founded his own trading company in Yiwu broke down the translators' origin by province as follows: 3,000 Ningxia, 300 Gansu, 300 Xinjiang, 200 Qinghai, 100 Henan, 70 Yunnan, 50 Shaanxi, and 50 Shandong, for a total of 4,070.

[43] Iran, Iraq, India, Afghanistan, and Malaysia were the top export destinations for Yiwu's small commodities in 2010.

formidable. So Yiwu's fortunes are not the work of the government (for example, tax cuts, preferential policies, and favorable laws). In Yiwu, the government depends on the people and not the other way around. Once the government recognized the value of the networks Yiwu businesspeople were developing, they sought to facilitate such business ties. The government became the agent of the people.

The Yiwu business community has procured no small degree of self-regulation in building the small commodities market. Indeed, there is an annual meeting during which representatives from the business community meet with officials from the county-level bureaus of commerce, tourism, and industry to tell them how to design and implement policies on fiscal management. When Mr. Ma and his peers spoke of the relationship between the state, the market, and Muslim entrepreneurs, I understood them to describe the role of private enterprise in global capitalism. In Yiwu, as opposed to Linxia, the state feels far away. The crucial distinction is that Yiwu is not a Muslim city, and although its numbers of foreign Muslims increase annually, their purpose is almost exclusively related to business and self-interest, not Islamic radicalism.

My point is that the secular state's transfiguring of Islamic ethics into Arabic-language acquisition for commercial purposes is only part of the story of Yiwu. In the case of the small commodities market, besides the promotion, through education, of the labor market for Arabic-language translation, the state's role is minimal. Renewed contacts between Chinese and overseas Muslims bespeak the initiative of Muslims themselves. The small commodities market and the revival of the Silk Road show that "life-making," what Ann Anagnost (2013: 2) defines as "investments in the self to ensure one's forward career progression as embodied human capital," is not just a result of the state's stimulation of desires but also of intrareligious communitarian sensibilities.

A closer look at the transactions between Chinese Muslim minorities and foreign Muslims, in their respective roles as translator and buyer, sheds light on the desacralization of the Chinese Muslim desire to master Arabic and the excision of Islamic law from their studies. State education policies and the private market operate through yearnings Hui have as "a diasporic group seeking to find a link to its place of exile" (Benite 2005: 16). When young Hui travel to Yiwu, they try to gain employment in a trade or business company (*maoyi gongsi* or *shangmao gongsi*), where they act as middlemen who assist foreign buyers in purchasing goods in the small commodities market. As of 2010, there were several thousand of these companies in Yiwu, of which 90 percent were owned by foreign Muslims, with the remainder owned and operated by Chinese Muslims. The foreigners who own such companies are men who have decided to take up permanent residence in China and either annually renew their visa by returning briefly to their home country or marry a Chinese woman and obtain permanent residence status.

In the typical transaction the buyer is a foreign Muslim, the seller is a Yiwu Han, and the go-between is a Northwest Hui. Mr. Ma related that when the buyer comes to Yiwu, "he is like a child. He needs constant attention and supervision." The go-between performs due diligence on the products the buyer wants. Once they identify a suitable seller and negotiate the purchase price, during which the go-between (or his employer) serves as interpreter, the buyer and seller will write an invoice (*dinghuodan*). The invoice is boilerplate, and the key portion is the "description of goods," in which the buyer writes (in Arabic) precisely what he wants, which the go-between then translates for the seller. In a minority of transactions the buyer pays the seller in cash at the time of delivery. More commonly, the buyer (who may return to his country soon after the transaction) buys on credit. He gives the money to the go-between, who then has several months to pay the seller upon receipt of goods. One reason for the buyer to provide the go-between with the payment before delivery is that it includes the middleman's fee or commission. The invoice is not a contract under PRC law, but the small commodities market has its own management office that mediates most commercial disputes, sometimes in concert with local courts. Alternatively, disputes can be brought to the economic affairs desk within the PSB, although parties rarely avail themselves of such methods.

The relationship between the buyer and the go-between is based not on contract but rather Islamic ethics. Most people I spoke to—foreign businessmen and Northwest Hui alike—told me that common faith precludes the requirement for a formal writing that would make the parties beholden to either PRC state law or Islamic law. The buyer and the go-between's faith in Islam is, in fact, the glue that holds the Yiwu small commodities market together.[44] In short, inter-Muslim ethics, not state law, guides market transactions at the granular level. Nonetheless, clients and go-betweens cheat each other all the time. Parties accept risk and potential loss as part of their building of business networks. Some of these

---

[44] Muslim ethics provides a basis for trust that, rather than formal law, provides transactional security within *guanxi* (social relationships) that have fueled China's economic growth (Chung and Hamilton 2001; Hamilton 2006; Greif and Tabellini 2010: 5).

losses can be quite high. For instance, one stationery seller was cheated out of RMB 400,000 by an Egyptian buyer. He did not take any steps to rectify the matter. Common rationales given were that formal remedies were costly at best, and sellers' energies and money were better used in identifying reliable buyers in the future.

The motives for Hui to go to Yiwu include both market rationality and broader desires. Financial security and career prospects are one motivation. A twenty-five-year-old man from Ningxia said, "I decided to come to Yiwu because there are not as many jobs at this salary for a person in Ningxia. I never wanted to become a cleric, and there are too few positions, anyway." However, many young would-be translators from the Northwest who planned to travel to Yiwu for work, as well as those who were "fresh" to Yiwu, expressed their excitement to work with foreign Muslims. The opportunity to interact with, converse, and pray with foreign Muslims in Yiwu is a strong incentive, particularly for those who cannot afford to study abroad. While the hajj affords the supreme experience of the *umma*, Northwest Muslims' participation in the small commodities market and the remaking of the Silk Road offers another type of connection with the global community of believers.[45]

For many Hui youths, a foreign Muslim is de facto a qualified Muslim, somehow closer to the origin of the faith. Despite or because of the sectarian nature of the teaching schools in the Northwest, Hui view places such as Yiwu as the *umma* materialized within China. Yiwu is not just a "global city" (Sassen 1992) with Chinese characteristics but also a global market facilitated by the go-between role of Hui. As Lawrence Rosen has pointed out (1984; 1989: 306), the market is where personal networks are formed and versions of reality are "bargained for." Whereas Linxia stands for divisiveness in the Hui imaginary, in Yiwu Chinese Muslim minorities imagine that they can realize Islam's ecumenism. The assembly at Yiwu's mosque of more than seven thousand men—including Sudanese in their bright-colored *jalābiyya*, Algerians, Indonesians, Turks, Saudis dressed in white *thawbs*, Somalis, Tajiks, Iranians, Malays, and Hui wearing their white caps, all standing shoulder to shoulder in prayer—is, for China's Hui, the archetypal vision of Islam's universality (see Figure 4.2).[46] That

---

[45] For studies of imagined diasporic or transnational communities of Muslims, see Ewing (2003), Laffan (2003), Ho (2006), Feener and Sevea (2009), and Tagliacozzo (2013).

[46] The growth of the Yiwu mosque community is one metric for the expansion and internationalization of the small commodities market. Before 2000 there were about 200 people who gathered for prayer. In 2003 there were 1,500. Starting in 2007, the number mushroomed to more than 7,000 (Ma 2012: 5).

Figure 4.2 Muslim men from all over the world gathered for Friday prayer at the Yiwu mosque

Source: the author

this vision is realized in an authoritarian state presents no contradiction to Hui. Members of all races and nations, backgrounds and classes, supplicate to God, as one. The common aspiration of Hui translators from the Northwest was to be part of this community.

However, among the young translators I spoke with both in the Northwest and in Yiwu, there was a common refrain of unmet expectations, if not disappointment, concerning their experience in the small commodities market. Part of the issue is the failure of the educational institutions that are training translators to provide gainful employment. For example, the administration of the vocational technical college in Linxia claims to have an employment center in Yiwu, and the college's publicity material makes similar claims.[47] Their website states:

> High-paying jobs at home and abroad: Following the deepening of the
> Silk Road economic belt construction and the increasing closeness of ties

[47] State media have also trumpeted the success of some eight thousand Hui from Ningxia working as translators in Yiwu (Su 2006; Su and Li 2006; China Ethnic Groups 2009; but see Tang 2012).

between China, the Middle East, Central Asia, and Muslim countries, [those with] advanced Arabic abilities have vast employment prospects. In recent years, a few outstanding graduates of our school, through either study abroad or experience and training in the foreign markets of the southeast, have obtained employment at major multinational companies, making up to RMB 10 to 30 million a year.

Linxia Prefecture Vocational Technical School 2014

However, no such on-site facility exists. In reality, students depend on networks of other students and family friends who have contacts in Yiwu, or they seek employment through the Internet. The deal breaker in Northwest Muslims' participation in the small commodities market, however, is their Arabic-language ability. Foreign Muslim businessmen I spoke with were nearly uniform in assessing the Chinese Muslims' Arabic level as insufficient for purposes of conducting business transactions. One Darfurian buyer told me, "The language level of the Chinese for Arabic or English is very low. Communication inevitably becomes frustrating. These are the transaction costs one must consider in doing business in China."

Thus, in contrast to the grand claims of the ethnic schools' Internet advertising, many translators encounter hardship in making a living. The average income for a translator is about RMB 1,500 per month, slightly below the average household income for Bafang Hui as of 2012.[48] The cost of living in Yiwu and similar cities is, however, much higher than in Northwest China. Because most translators are unable to secure a permanent contract with a trade company and obtain individual clients through personal connections, the amount and quality of work is unpredictable. Many youths experience homesickness and boredom and return to their families in the Northwest.

The situation is doubly complicated for female translators. If foreign businessmen had a negative assessment of Chinese Muslims' Arabic ability, then translators (both male and female) who had been in Yiwu for an extended period of time found that foreign Muslim businessmen failed to meet their expectation of the qualified Muslim, the ethical ideal. Descriptions I heard repeatedly emphasized the term *lustful* (*haose*). As a nineteen-year old Hui woman from Ningxia stated:

When I first came to Yiwu, my mother accompanied me to settle me in and to make sure I was safe. My first impression of the foreign Muslims

[48] The most talented Arabic translators can make up to RMB 500,000 per annum.

was that they are lustful [*haose*]. I found in many respects, whether the food they eat or their prayer habits, or drinking alcohol, or sexual behavior, that they are wanting. Although I myself have never been subject to sexual advances, my friend was groped by her foreign boss. Yiwu changes people, both Chinese Muslim women and foreigner men. Chinese women who wore hijab [*gaitou*] back home will begin to wear less and less because that's how local Yiwu girls dress. Foreign Muslim men who come here will also lower their standards. I have heard Arab clients say [to their female translators], "Don't use Arabic. Just accompanying me is fine."

The line between business relationships and intimate ones is thin, and prostitution has grown at a fever pace. Foreign Muslim businessmen's desire (as libido) frustrates Hui desire to find models of piety by encountering "the real" Muslim, and Hui ethics is subverted.

Nonetheless, the Party-State has aimed to promote the connection between Yiwu and foreign Muslims for purposes of stimulating growth. As part of this, the local government has seized on Linxia's reputation as a center for Islamic instruction and plans to expand secondary-level education in the city with an emphasis on "vocational" (i.e., desacralized) Arabic. As of 2012 it had developed a new and expanded vocational secondary school that would incorporate Linxia's vocational technical college with other faculties. Although in such places as Linxia and Yiwu the desires of Hui and the Party-State are mutually supportive, they are not coterminous. Some Hui benefit from attempts to commercialize Muslim contacts. Others become disenchanted and critical of such versions of Islamic modernity.

ETHICAL OPTIONS

From scriptural hall education (madrasas) and private schools to Islamic Scriptural Institutes and ethnic schools, a variety of education forums undertake their own projects to make qualified Muslims as ethical subjects. Most of these—namely, madrasas, private schools, and Islamic Scriptural Institutes—provide instruction on aspects of Islamic law, each to different effect. Madrasas offer the most rigorous instruction in the law for the purpose of training the next generation of clerics, although much of the practicum of solving disputes in accordance with Islamic law is learned through relationships with mentors and through study abroad. By raising future leaders, madrasas also reproduce teaching-school traditions. Whereas madrasas represent a conventional approach to acquiring Islamic knowledge, private schools are alternative vehicles for instructing

Muslim youths, following the traditions of teaching schools. Private schools have resurged in the reform era and, in the spirit of the commercialization of Chinese society, are more focused than madrasas in preparing students for entry into a global labor force. Public ethnic schools are the state equivalent of private schools, although Arabic-language training has replaced religion as the core of the curriculum. In contrast to such market-responsive schools, state-run Islamic Scriptural Institutes produce mainly civil servants and Muslim cadres. Hui youths confront a menu of educational institutions (see Table 4.3).

Thus far I have mainly assessed the prescriptive projects of educational institutes for training qualified Muslims. To review, the Party-State intervenes in ethical subject making in a number of ways. First, it influences the content of instruction—for example, through state-sanctioned communications such as sermons. Second, it creates institutions, such as the Islamic Scriptural Institutes, that reproduce the sovereignty of the Party-State through state-educated Muslim clerics. The Islamic Scriptural Institutes are not unlike the guilds Durkheim ([1937] 1957) described, professional bodies determined by collective will through secularized sacred law. The goal is to license "religious personnel" who embody state-sanctioned Islam and become the Party-State's local agents within mosques. Third, ethnic schools create qualified Muslims in another instance of secularization. These public schools divorce the language of Arabic from the message of Islam. The commercialization of Arabic reassigns it value that has meaning not in the field of religion but in the labor market. The market then elicits Muslim youths' desires, while the Party-State plays a less active role. Yet the success of the market in increasing the number of Hui translators depends on *umma* imaginaries that do not necessarily valorize the Party-State's preferences (e.g., that Hui should prioritize income in Yiwu over deepening their faith in Linxia). While financial gain is one motive, it does not subsume Hui desire, which is multifaceted and either enhanced or thwarted through encounters with foreign Muslims.

At this point I want to change perspectives to ask: Where is Hui freedom in cultivating ethical selves? While some students pursue a single track for their secondary education, the variety of educational institutes enables students to forum-shop. Depending on their resources and aims, students may attend multiple institutes, acquiring different aspects of the various ethical projects. For instance, one twenty-two-year-old Hui from Ili in Xinjiang arrived in Linxia in 2008 after middle school. His aim was to improve his knowledge of Islam and, in his words, "get closer to

TABLE 4.3 Comparison of secondary-level educational institutions in southwest Gansu

	Scriptural hall education (e.g., Linxia)	Private schools (e.g., Linxia)	Islamic scriptural institutes (e.g., Lanzhou)	Ethnic schools (e.g., Linxia vocational technical college)
Student body	Approx. 2,000; mostly male; separate schools for females; all Muslim	Separate male and female schools; all Muslim	Male only; all Muslim	600 total (400 Arabic majors); co-ed; 70% Muslim, 30% Han
Islamic law course	Yes	Yes	Yes	No
PRC state law course	No	No	Yes	No
Responsible governmental agency	Gansu Province BRA and YiXie	Gansu Province Department of Education	YiXie	Gansu Province Department of Education
Purpose of Arabic instruction (in order of importance)	Religious	Commercial and religious	Administrative, commercial, and religious	Commercial
Teachers	Local clerics trained in scriptural hall education	Most are regional experts; some are Ph.D.s	Most are local teachers; some are published scholars	Most are local teachers

Cost (tuition, room and board, etc.)	Free	Approx. RMB 3,500/yr. (financial aid available)*	Approx. RMB 4,000/yr. (financial aid available)*	Approx. RMB 6,250/ yr. (financial aid available)*
Holidays	All state and Islamic holidays	All state holidays, 3 days during Ramadan, 3 days during 'Id-e-Qurbān	All state holidays, 1 week for Ramadan, 5 days for 'Id-e-Qurbān	All state holidays
Graduates' post-graduate path (in order of frequency)	Clerics, translators, business, advanced study abroad	Translators, advanced study abroad, clerics	Government, translators, business, clerics	Translators, study abroad

Note: Numbers are as of 2011.

* Financial assistance includes a loan of approximately RMB 1,400/yr. and a subsidy from the government (up to RMB 1,000/yr.) if the student's family qualifies as an "economically troubled home."

Allah." Although a Gedimu, he attended a well-known Yihewani madrasa that had a large number of students. After a year, he moved to one of the private schools. He found the religious atmosphere of the school wanting, however. After speaking to many teachers there, he concluded, "After graduation, most of their students study abroad, and then concentrate on business. They live for business and sometimes don't even pray ... I seek to emulate the grand scholars [da xuezhe] and the clerics and felt the school would not prepare me for that path." He considered the ethnic school but only momentarily, as "it is even less interested in teaching or promoting Islamic studies to the extreme of not even mentioning the afterlife [houshi]. They just want to make money." When I last spoke to him, he was frustrated with the options for education in the Northwest and was preparing to go to Yiwu to connect with foreign Muslims.

Unlike the young Ili man, an eighteen-year-old Hui student from Lintan was explicit about *not* wanting to learn Islamic law. "I want to build practical skills," he told me. "And I'll go to whichever school will best prepare me to get a job." This student began at one of the private schools and left because it was "too religious." He planned to practice Arabic and English in Yiwu for a year before studying abroad in the Middle East.

These two students represent how desire pervades the norms of Islamic ethics and the socialist market. Between these options, Hui seek to improve themselves, what James Laidlaw (2002: 322) described as "mak[ing] oneself into a certain kind of person." They exercise reflection between responding to the calling and individual choice. The accounts of the two students show that their sense of freedom does not necessarily accord with Party-State dictates. The Party-State has replaced socialist-era accounts of "liberation" with the myth of the market as the place where minorities realize their potential. The Party-State designs ethnic autonomy and preferential policies to prepare minorities for, and encourage their participation in, the labor market. Like authoritarian definitions of freedom as "positive liberty," which force people to be free (Laidlaw 2014: 145), Muslim minorities must either migrate toward market opportunities outside the Northwest or face obsoleteness in southwestern Gansu. Come East, young men, beckons the market—and they do.

Nonetheless, the experiences of young Hui demonstrate that the making of qualified Muslims may not be the same as the state's use of the market to commodify Arabic. Hui may migrate to Yiwu and the coastal cities but for reasons that differ from state incentives. A minority of Hui may opt out of the market and become clerics. In the contemporary Northwest, successful businessmen have wide visibility in Hui communities, yet no one rivals clerics for their monopoly on interpreting Islamic law. Most students choose a career in entrepreneurship or commercial translation, not necessarily because they know these professions to be financially sound but because they cannot become clerics. Or they may devise alternative routes to markets that leapfrog those of the Chinese nation-state, as in the case of private schools. Students who study abroad may return to China to bring their knowledge to bear on its distinct developmental challenges. They may be equally likely to decide to stay in the Middle East and Africa, where there are growing communities of Chinese (Hui and Han) in major cities. Chinese Muslims' contacts with foreign Muslims—both through state-sanctioned avenues, such as Yiwu's small commodities market, and through means the Party-State tolerates, such as study abroad and transnational business networks—expand the social field of Muslims beyond the milieu of the nation-state. Hui desire to make such connections, a desire aroused in part by state policy, loosens the social field from its moorings in the nation-state.

5

WEDDING LAWS

Do you think for a Hui girl who is married at nineteen and lives for her husband and it is the only happiness she knows – that she will work for her emancipation?

Hui woman from Lanzhou

Mu'āmalāt refers to the *fiqh* of interpersonal exchanges and transactions, including purchases, sales, marriage, and rights of succession, meaning inheritance. In the nineteenth century colonial law in the Middle East and Southeast Asia preserved *mu'āmalāt* by making family law the privileged domain for Islamic law. The designation "family law" is itself a Western legal construct.[1] I use it to refer to what the Hui call *jiatingfa*, the generic Chinese translation for the Western term, or, more specifically, *hunyinfa* ("marriage law"). Family law among Muslims in Muslim-majority countries was an exception to imperial Western, secular law. As a consequence, family law has become integral to debates about female agency in Islam, as it both regulates the most intimate spheres of personal and familial life and provides grounds for women to lay claim to specific rights in initiating, maintaining, and dissolving such relationships.

The anthropologist Saba Mahmood (2003, 2005) has provided the most cogent argument for the idea that Muslim women believe in and actively perform a type of agency that differs from Western feminist preoccupations with resistance to patriarchal norms. In her study of Salafi women's piety movements in Egypt, Mahmood finds that mosque movement participants accept patriarchal norms in conducting *da'wa* by teaching others correct Islamic practice, but in doing so, they are

---

[1] Secondary literature may also refer to this field of law as "personal status laws" (Rosen 1989; Nasir 1990; el-Alami 1992; Layish 2004: 90).

not subjugated to patriarchy. Rather, their work provides grounds for performing agency experienced as suffering and survival, rather than radical individualism (Mahmood 2005: 167). Mahmood's interventions have ignited a sustained critique of secular-liberal definitions of female agency,[2] a project that I endorse, based upon my encounters with Hui women.

Mahmood's analysis is focused primarily on *'ibādāt* as a means for women to embody piety. Whereas *'ibādāt* pertains particularly to techniques of cultivating the ethical self, *mu'āmalāt* is, by definition, social. Mahmood concludes her study by moving beyond personal ethical cultivation to the ways in which the piety these women embody instructs wayward male others, namely husbands (Mahmood 2005: 179, 184–87). I extend this analysis to consider Muslim women's capacity to interpret and "enforce" Islamic law, particularly in circumstances where the impiety of male intimates—fathers or husbands—potentially endangers women's financial, psychological, or bodily well-being through an excess of *minjian*. That is, behaviors that exceed men's rights under Islamic law and that are unregulated by the state are particularly pernicious to the interests of women. I approach this problem through Hui women's experience with family law in China, where the state, unlike in many Muslim countries, has identified family law as a field of reform. Rather than a zone of privacy that exists within but beyond the reach of the state, family law in China has been a primary focus of the Party-State's legal modernization program.

In spite of such efforts, Hui continue to practice family law according to the revealed sources of Islam. Their practice has been heavily influenced by Han Chinese family organization. While Hui practice of Islamic law is generally *minjian*, because of the centrality of the family and also because the family unit has rested on the razor's edge of PRC law reform, family law has become, along with the taboo against eating pork, a kernel of Hui *minjian* law. Illustrating the limits of the state and the reach of the Hui social field, the state has not been able to expunge the prevalence of Islamic norms in family life among Hui. The result is a two-tiered, or dual-track, legal process for marriage and divorce, in which women encounter patriarchy from multiple sources, including Chinese custom, Islamic law, and state law. By patriarchy, I mean, generally, rules

---

[2] For a selection of the expansive literature that has followed upon Mahmood's study, both critical and supportive of Mahmood's project, see Wadud (2006b), Deeb (2011), Bangstad (2011), Abu-Lughod (2013), and Weir (2013).

221

and institutions that reinforce male authority. Whereas the Party-State has made claims to liberate women, marriage law in the reform period has paradoxically exacerbated the marginalization of women. This predicament raises the question: Can Hui law be gendered? Specifically, how do Hui women protect and further their interests in property, custody, and sexual and bodily health in the face of considerable patriarchal pressures that may be immanent in the very sources of law that would be the basis for their protection?

In this chapter I argue that Hui women operate within two incompletely functioning bodies of law, religious and secular, which are deeply patriarchal; at the same time, women may work across legal orders to protect their spiritual, mental, and bodily integrity. Whereas women's movements in the Middle East have at their disposal a repertoire of Islamic discourses and institutions with which to articulate female-centered interpretations of Islamic law,[3] Chinese feminism has been understood as primarily an effect of the state and secondarily as responsive to global intellectual currents (Wesoky 2013). While historically insulated from nascent women's movements in the Middle East, "Hui women's studies" have increased awareness of women's positions in Hui communities and promoted women's advancement, primarily through education (Ma 2008). Female Chinese scholars have argued that Hui women have internalized such Confucian morals as obedience (*shun*) and piety (*xiao*) (Xu and Sun 2008: 29). Ding Hong, a senior female Hui scholar, argued in a seminal article that Hui women "embody" Hui culture, more so than do men, and that as both the creators and bearers of Hui culture, they stand in a complex and continually redefined relation with a patriarchy that they "cannot shake off" (Ding 1998: 72).

Bereft of organizational capacity, civil society, or even grassroots publications, Hui women have few resources to redefine their place in the mosque community and their relationship to men. Merely enacting ethics may not be enough to protect women's legal interests. Thus, an examination of the ways in which the rights of women are imbricated not just with Islamic law but with state law, too, provides a more comprehensive view of the process of becoming a pious Muslim woman (Osanloo 2009: 121). Women reflect on, interpret, and "enforce" Islamic law as they compare Hui male behavior against prescriptions in the revealed sources. If Hui

---

[3] For a partial list of the relevant literature, see Mernissi (1987), Ahmed (1992), Afshar (1996, 1998), Mir-Hosseini (2000, 2006), and Barazangi (2004). For readings beyond the Middle East context, see Wadud ([1992] 1999, 2006a) and Hidayatullah (2014).

women cannot shake off patriarchy—that is, if the Party-State's dream of gender liberation is deferred then they nevertheless exercise their own interpretive authority in making men accountable for their actions. In so doing, as Ding Hong has argued, Hui women may embody dimensions of Islamic family law.

Teaching schools, which dominate religious life, and the Party-State, which claims to control the public sphere, each produce patriarchal versions of their laws. Teaching schools as authorizing discourses reproduce the authority of husbands, fathers, clerics, and shaykhs. Such discourses are a result just as much of the influence of Chinese customs as of understandings of Islamic law. Patriarchy, as expressed through patrilineal descent and kinship, is a defining element of pre-Communist China (Harrell 2002; Sangren 2009: 256). The Party-State, as part of its localization in the Muslim Northwest, has also assumed a male-dominated structure, as it has elsewhere in the country, despite official rhetoric of gender equality. Thus, in both *minjian* and official versions of Islam, the station of women appears secondary. Nonetheless, Hui women cultivate their standing in the home by acting as a wellspring of Islamic legal knowledge, particularly as applied to intrafamilial relations. Such knowledge extends into matchmaking (a role not necessarily inimical to brides' decision-making capacity), instruction beyond the home, Qur'anic interpretation, and even mobilization of state law to enforce Islamic law.

In what follows, I first describe the status of women in Hui enclaves such as Linxia where, despite the Party-State's agenda of gender parity, Hui women are generally more active in the home than in the markets and public spaces. Next, I assess the aspiration of socialist law to emancipate women from patriarchy, and I determine that legal reforms have contradictorily sidelined Hui women's matrimonial rights partly because of state law's nonrecognition of Islamic law. I then discuss the ways in which Hui women in the Northwest protect and promote their interests via limited textual production and nascent women-centered education. The core of this chapter is an analysis of the ways in which Hui women getting married or seeking divorce navigate the tensions between patriarchal authorities and the protection of their interests in Islamic law. On the one hand, state legal reforms have, in certain areas of family law, blocked women's resort to legally cognizable forms of marriage that would support their interests; on the other hand, women mobilize state law to make men accountable for such transgressions of Islamic law as unrestricted polygamy. Women's interpretive interventions have the potential to bridge the

223

gaps between Islamic law and state law in responding to the demands of Chinese Islamic piety and socialist gender reform.

PATRIARCHIES IN THE NORTHWEST

As clerics mediate the legal orders through dispute resolution in the Northwest, the gender of clerics is a helpful starting point in evaluating the magnitude of patriarchy in the region. Men monopolize almost all positions of authority at mosques and Sufi tomb complexes in the Northwest. There are no female clerics in Linxia, for example. A well-respected Yihewani cleric told me, "You cannot use the word cleric [*ahong*] to describe a woman."

However, there are some female clerics in the neighboring autonomous region of Ningxia. In Haiyuan County, for instance, the Qingzhen Grand Mosque includes a women's mosque, which also has a madrasa attached. The women's madrasa has approximately two hundred students and five teachers called, contrary to the Linxia cleric's admonition, "female clerics" (*nü ahong*). These clerics, who live at the madrasa, mediate disputes among women and men in the community; the majority of the cases they handle involve conflicts between mothers- and daughters-in-law, marital discord, and traffic accidents.

Additionally, female clerics are well documented in central China (e.g., Zhongyuan) (Shui and Jaschok 2002). The tradition of female clerics in central China dates back to the late Ming period and is thus a Gedimu innovation, long predating the arrival of the reformist strains of the Yihewani and Salafiyya. The female clerics trace their role not to a specific basis in the revealed law but rather to the role of female religious scholars who came from prominent families of scriptural teachers (Jaschok and Shui 2000: 83). In recent years, the state media have spotlighted female clerics in official accounts of Islam. In the mediatized production of official Islam, female clerics represent China's unique contribution to global Islam: a privileged status for women. It is not just Islamic law, but also gender under Islam that obtains a spectacular quality through such official reproduction.

The Northwest is not central China, however. Of the thirty-four mosques in Linxia, only five have a prayer hall for women, while others may draw a curtain for women around a portion of the prayer hall. There are no women's mosques in Linxia. There is one women's mosque in Lanzhou, which was founded in 1938 by women from Henan, and several more in Ningxia, as mentioned. Of the twenty-three Sufi tomb complexes I visited in Linxia, there is one exception to the rule that Sufi patrilineages are male: Madam Tomb Complex (Taitai Gongbei) is devoted to a female Sufi shaykh. Guo Tomb Complex had two female initiates from Ningxia in 2011. During saints' days, women rarely read liturgical texts and do not receive *nietie* (alms) for such demonstrations of piety. Women and children wait for husbands and fathers to communally eat the meal that concludes the observance. The role of uneducated women is defined as bearing children and maintaining the home. The emphasis on women's wifely role—that is, as a certain relationship to her husband—is consonant with Qur'anic dictates (Spectorsky 2010) and also with traditional Confucian expectations (Barlow 2004: 37–65). Male dominance in positions of leadership is not limited to religion, however. While in my visits to governmental offices I encountered many female workers, I never met a female director of a bureau or department. Despite heavy propaganda advocating gender equality, patriarchal values pervade the secular spaces of governmental offices and meeting rooms.

SOCIALIST LAW AS EMANCIPATION OF WOMEN

The social effects of the PRC's modernization of marriage and family law as a way to combat patriarchy warrant closer examination. China anthropologists have underscored the paramount role of the family in the production of Chinese society.[4] The family was the nexus of blood relations, interpersonal rules, and emotive ties that ordered the household and, through the household's agnatic ties with other households, formed extended kin groups, namely the lineage. The patriline was the ideology that gave the lineage its form and was the basis of ancestor worship, corporate property ownership, and village identity.[5]

Given the material, social, and religious assets of the family, it is little surprise that the Communists made the family and extended kinship a centerpiece of reform through birth control and family planning policy, as well as through legislation. In a quantitative study conducted during the collectivization period, Parish and Whyte (1978: 135–37) found that Communist

---

[4] See Fei (1939), Wolf (1972), Wolf and Huang (1980), and Judd (1989).
[5] See Hsu (1948), Freedman (1958), Pasternak (1972), Ahern (1973), and Chun (1996).

laws and policies had relatively slight impact on family life. The major exceptions were land reform and the 1950 Marriage Law,[6] the first law of New China. The Marriage Law was directed at reforming the family, its organization and reproduction, by replacing "feudal" elements with socialist ones. It prohibited arranged marriage, polygamy, concubinage, marriage of children, interference in the remarriage of widows, and extraction of money as a precondition for marriage. This vast scope effectively made it the legislative centerpiece of the Communists' social engineering of the family.[7]

The Marriage Law was based, in part, on the Communists' first marriage regulation in China, enacted on April 4, 1939: the Marriage Regulations of the Border Area of Shaanxi, Gansu, and Ningxia (hereinafter, "Marriage Regulations") (Meijer 1971: 56). The Marriage Regulations and the space over which they had jurisdiction (though labeled a "border area") were central to the Communists' drafting of the Marriage Law, which inaugurated a "family revolution" (Meijer 1971: 5). Both the Marriage Regulations and the Marriage Law envision a "modern" conjugal family, characterized by equality between husband and wife in resources and rights, including divorce. In other words, socialist gender equality was to root out Chinese patriarchy. To do so, the Party-State sought to redefine marriage as interpersonal relations between equal partners rather than as exchange of women between different kin groups (Croll 1981: 3).

Given this history of the Marriage Law, it is little wonder that one of the specific targets of modern PRC legal reform has been the ethnic minority family, particularly those customs and forms that Communists deemed repugnant to socialist morality.[8] These include non-monogamous arrangements, including polygyny and polyandry, early marriage, arranged marriage, and bride price. The ethnic identification project of the 1950s categorized such ethnic minority marriage practices as "feudal" (Fei 1951: 294; Lin 1940). Reform of the family, however, was balanced with concern about extinguishing anti-CCP agitation among widespread ethnic minority populations located in the strategic border regions. As a result, in the early years of the PRC, ethnic minorities residing in ethnic autonomy regions were exempt from specified requirements

---

[6] Marriage Law of the PRC (*Zhonghua renmin gongheguo hunyinfa*), hereinafter "Marriage Law," passed by the National People's Congress (NPC), promulgated and effective April 13, 1950, amended April 28, 2001.

[7] Marriage Law, art. 3. See also Parish and Whyte (1978: 158), Croll (1981: 2–3), and Diamant (2000: 4).

[8] See, e.g., Goldstein (1987), Levine (1988), Harrell (1995: 10), McKhann (1995), Diamant (2000: ch. 4), Litzinger (2000: 207), Schein (2000: 83–84), and Yao (2002: 80).

of the Marriage Law, along with land reform and certain taxes (Dreyer 1976: 119). Thus, in the 1950s the Party-State allowed autonomous areas to make adjustments to national legislation, such as the Marriage Law.

The Communists' earliest use of ethnic autonomy was broadly congruent with how Western colonialists in Egypt, India, and Indonesia and Russians in Central Asia approached the problem of multiple systems of law—namely, by permitting a domain of private nonstate law regulating marriage. As I show through the case of Hui marriage, divorce, and polygamy, however, the deepening of reform and the building of the state has led to greater standardization of marriage law across ethnic and religious differences. Hui women have adjusted to these changes by situating themselves in multiple discourses that both overlap and diverge, including those of teaching-school traditions and Chinese socialism, to pursue their conception of freedom within Islam.

HUI MARRIAGE

Mama Mu, who works at the *minjian zuzhi* (popular organization) the Islamic resource center (IRC) in Lanzhou,[9] sits at her desk flipping through records of prospective matches. One function of the IRC is to provide a venue through which Hui singles can meet and find a life partner. It is a modern version of a much-venerated (and satirized) institution in Chinese society: the matchmaker. I ask Mama Mu what she believes the requirements are for a valid marriage in Islam. She lists the requirements for marriage as legal capacity (including age requirements and sanity) for those entering into the marriage, the *nikāḥ*, a bridal gift (Ar. *mahr*), and witnesses. The witnesses serve, in part, to publicize the marriage so as to prevent private or secret multiple marriages.

Mama Mu's inclusion of the *nikāḥ* is representative of popular Hui views on marriage. Among Hui, if Islamic marriage can be boiled down to a single concept, it is *nikāḥ*. *Nikāḥ* traditionally means penetration, or sexual intercourse, but its legal meaning in the Qur'an is contracted marriage, specifically, the offer and acceptance. Most Muslim societies have developed elaborate ceremonial rituals attached to the *nikāḥ*, and Chinese Islam is no exception. The ceremony also serves to publicize the marriage. While some jurists argue that the *nikāḥ* as a contract must be in writing, as all contracts under shari'a must be in writing,[10] there is no

---

[9] For more on the IRC, see Chapter 2.
[10] Such arguments usually cite Q. 2:282.

consensus that writing is mandatory. Northwest Hui, like Muslim minorities in many places, rely exclusively on oral statements. When foreign Muslims from North Africa and the Middle East doing business in Yiwu get married to converted Han Chinese women, by contrast, they often go to the mosque to have a simple document "chopped" by the cleric—that is, given a local seal. This document carries more weight in their home countries than the marriage license under PRC law. The ceremony itself, contrary to what many Hui believe, is not required under Islamic law. When Hui speak of *nikāh*, they most often do so in the sense that the "cleric reads *nikāh*,"[11] meaning the Qur'anic verses of prayer that conclude the marriage contract, rather than the actual contract between husband and wife. The subtle semantic shift from the contract between the marrying parties to the act of the cleric suggests the great emphasis Hui place on the authority of the cleric as patriarch of the Muslim community. In this section I examine those elements of marriage law that are most contested in the Hui social field and that have been shaped by both socialist legal reform and Hui women's interpretive practices.

Legal capacity (age)

Legal capacity is the status through which a legal subject assumes the rights and duties of a particular legal system and, in particular, the right to engage in legally enforceable transactions. The Hanafi school provides that a Muslim can marry as soon as she or he reaches puberty, although the marriage can be contracted before that time. Furthermore, unlike in other jurisprudential schools, in the Hanafi school a woman of full legal capacity does not require the permission of a male guardian to marry (Johansen 1999: 203). In the contemporary context outside of China, one view presumes that puberty is reached at the age of fifteen, although the minimum age is twelve years old for males and nine for females (Fyzee 2009: 93–94).[12] PRC state law establishes that people over the age of eighteen (regardless of ethnic or religious affiliation) possess "complete capacity for civil acts."[13] Age has been a sticking point in the Party-State's reform of marriage.

---

[11] There seems to be some slippage in the colloquial use of "*nikāh*," as opposed to the term *khutba*, as understood by Muslims outside of China to refer to the marriage sermon that the cleric or qadi pronounces.

[12] Nasir (1990: 190) has a different age for the Hanafi school's standard for the age of puberty: seventeen for females and eighteen for males.

[13] General Principles of the Civil Law of the PRC (*Zhonghua renmin gongheguo minfa tongze*), promulgated by the NPC, April 12, 1986, art. 11, as noted in Chapter 4. One of Linxia's most successful entrepreneurs, a member of a prominent Yihewani family, drew my attention to the

Marriage in pre-Communist China typically took place at a young age. The primary reason for early marriage, particularly the marrying off of young women, was that the family head perceived the value daughters added to the household's labor capacity as less than that of sons. Their economic value to the household was maximized by marrying them out of the home as soon as they were of age. While class, region, and ethnicity differentiated the age at which people married, Parish and Whyte (1978: 157) have found that before 1949 the average marriage ages were seventeen to nineteen for females and nineteen to twenty-one for males. Village studies have found lower marriage ages. For instance, Fei Xiaotong's dissertation on his natal village in Jiangsu Province found that, in the 1930s, 92 percent of females and 75 percent of males were married before the age of sixteen (Fei 1939: 40, 52).

One of the major goals of the Marriage Law was to raise the marriage age and to educate villagers against the dangers of "early marriage" (zao-hun) (Croll 1981: 60–61). Article 4 of the Marriage Law set the statutory age of marriage at eighteen years for females and twenty for males. The standard was raised in the 1980 revision to twenty and twenty-two, respectively. In so doing, the regime established a statutorily defined minimum age limit for the entire nation. The national standard, violation of which resulted in possible criminal liability, tied the nation-building project of creating national citizen-subjects to the rite of passage of marriage.

In Northwest China, despite state campaigns to "marry late," young adults remain attuned to the cultural prerogative to marry early, well before the age of thirty, the "ceiling" in cities, and even earlier in the countryside (Zang 1993). The Qur'anic preference for marriage[14] compounds the urgency of young Hui to find a partner—belief meets anxiety. Two consequences follow: First, Hui take the state's legal minimum age for getting married as obligatory rather than recommended (the standard in Islamic law) (Yu and Zhang 2007: 140). Second, despite the increase in the legal marriageable age, the socially accepted bar for marriageable age is lowered in the case of Chinese Muslims.

Early marriage is a problem in Linxia. Muslim leaders, parents, teachers, and officials who talked about early marriage acknowledged that

repercussions of the state definition of legal capacity for Chinese Muslims: anyone under the age of eighteen does not have the legal capacity to believe in religion, that is, only at the age of eighteen does one have the right to choose to believe in religion. By that time, the socialization of a young adult into the secular nation, a process that begins with primary school, may displace piety altogether.

[14] Q. 24:32.

Linxia Muslims, and particularly those in the countryside, are likely to marry at ages those in Linxia City consider too young. Residents of Bafang say that both Hui and Han women from the city will marry as early as sixteen and, in the countryside, as early as thirteen. The head of one of Linxia County's judicial bureaus cited a slightly higher average, stating that in the countryside around Linxia City, females, regardless of ethnicity, marry at the age of fifteen or sixteen. Conversations with would-be paramours and their parents at the IRC in Lanzhou yielded roughly consistent statements that rural Hui females marry at the age of sixteen.[15] There is considerable pressure for girls to marry out of their natal home early, and thus the maximum age of marriage is socially significant. If females beyond the age of twenty-five are still single, one mother said, there is a kind of stigma attached to them—they are "too old."

As an organ of ethnic autonomy, the Linxia Prefecture People's Government is empowered by the PRC Constitution and the Law of the PRC on Regional Ethnic Autonomy to pass autonomous regulations that tailor national legislation to the needs of an ethnic minority population.[16] In 1987 adjustments to the minimum marriageable age were made with the promulgation of Linxia Hui Autonomous Prefecture Autonomous Regulations (hereinafter "Linxia Regulations"). The Linxia Regulations adjusted the national standard to accommodate an age of marriage two years lower than the national standard: in Linxia, the minimum age for females was changed to eighteen and for males, twenty.[17]

The regulations justified the change not as an approximation of Islamic law's standard for minimum marriageable age but as an adaptation of prefectural regulations to Linxia Prefecture's "practical situation"—that is, socioeconomic disparity.[18] While the Linxia Regulations may have closed the gap between the national law's standard and that of Islamic law, this change was not to last. In 2011 an amendment to the Linxia Regulations

---

[15] In her study on marriage among rural Hui in Tongxin County, Ningxia, Hui scholar Yang Zhixin found that within the entire county, those Hui aged fifteen and up who were unmarried totaled 39,879 people, or 24.9 percent of their age cohort, whereas those who had partners (although most likely not legally married) totaled 113,862, or 71 percent of their age cohort (Yang 2004: 54). (In Yang's analysis, 4.1 percent of the population is unaccounted for.) Yang's study most likely captures a large number of unmarried men well over the age of fifteen.

[16] Constitution of the PRC, art. 116, and Law of the PRC on Regional Ethnic Autonomy, art. 6.

[17] Gansu Province Linxia Hui Autonomous Prefecture Autonomous Regulations (Gansu Sheng Linxia Huizu Zizhizhou zizhi tiaoli), passed by the First Meeting of the Ninth Session of the Linxia Hui Autonomous County People's Congress, June 30, 1987, and approved by the Twenty-Sixth Meeting of the Sixth Session of the Gansu Province People's Congress Standing Committee, August 29, 1987, art. 51.

[18] Linxia Regulations, art. 6.

abolished the age adjustment, bringing the marriageable age back up to the national standard. Hence, if autonomous regulations are the means for recognizing difference, then such efforts are nullified by legal modernization, led by the central government to "raise" ethnic minorities to the national level of economic development, thereby overriding the discretion of autonomous areas' governments.

To communicate the legal standards, the Linxia government uses techniques found throughout China and some unique to Linxia. The most ubiquitous tactic involves periodic public awareness campaigns consisting of red banners hung across Linxia's main avenues alerting passers-by to the minimum marriageable ages in the Linxia Regulations. These propaganda campaigns also have their online equivalents, and so, for example, the Linxia Government website will occasionally feature special marriage law websites. On the sixtieth anniversary of the promulgation of the Marriage Law (April 28, 2010), newspaper stalls in Linxia were overflowing with newspapers exalting the social significance of the law, replete with photographs of conferences commemorating its passage, and government news organs posted journalistic commentaries on various government websites. The Party-State also mobilizes religious leaders across Muslim minority communities in the Northwest to raise youths' awareness of the dangers of early marriage. When giving sermons, clerics exhort members of their congregation to follow the standards set out in the Linxia Regulations. The head of the Linxia vocational technical college, where business Arabic is taught, works applicable laws into his lessons.

In the course of my fieldwork, I collected information from sixty-six young couples in Linxia who were planning to marry. To render the ethnographic data numerically, the age range was sixteen to twenty-six for females, with twelve females, or 18 percent, under the standard imposed by the Linxia Regulations of eighteen years of age. The age range for males was eighteen to thirty, with four males, or 6 percent, below the legal standard age of twenty. The average age was 20.45 for females and 24.25 for males (see Figure 5.1). Despite violators, the average ages are safely above the Linxia Regulations' limits.

The efforts of the Party-State and its intermediaries have thus met with some success. While social pressure and patriarchal authority influence the age of marriage, women are involved in decision making to varying degrees. The question of *when* to marry is closely related to *how* and *whom* women marry. Among Han and Hui, the traditional instrument for selecting a marriage partner has been arranged marriage (*baoban*

231

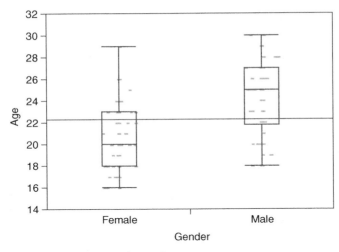

Figure 5.1 Marriage age by gender
Source: the author

hunyin), often with the use of a matchmaker.[19] For Linxia parents, while the socioeconomic compatibility of the two families is a priority, whether their children are a match in terms of ethnicity, religion, and, if Muslim, teaching-school affiliation are all important factors.[20] As opposed to Hui elsewhere in China, in the Northwest the "taboo against marrying women out" (*funü waijia jinji*), both a kinship rule of endogamy and an ethnic prohibition against Hui women marrying Han men specifically, is strongly observed.[21] In the large eastern cities and throughout the southwest, interethnic marriage is quite common among Hui and Han;[22] in

---

[19] See, for instance, Wolf and Huang (1980: 71), Ebrey (1991), and Jaschok and Miers (1994: 2, 56).

[20] Each one of these ascriptive factors may differ between a given family and their son or daughter who is of marriageable age. Thus, a family looking for a spouse for their child cannot simply look to the other family's (i.e., parents') religion, ethnicity, or teaching-school affiliation.

[21] Hui in smaller villages around Linxia show some evidence of cross-cousin marriage, although this practice is not common in the city. It is most strongly pronounced among rural members of conservative Sufi orders, for whom endogamy is the norm. In-marriage has produced a high number of Hui children born with cognitive and physical handicaps, usually the offspring of marriage unions within three generations (Jiang 2007: 106). Thus, the "five-generations rule" has been a focus of Party-State scientific policy addressed at reforming Hui endogamy (Gladney [1991] 1996: 252–53).

[22] In 1996 the rate of interethnic marriage in Beijing's Oxen Street district was 56.7 percent; in one district of Ningxia's capital city of Yinchuan Hui-Han intermarriage was 26 percent; and in a town in Ningxia's Guyuan County it was 6 percent (Li 2004: 26). Another study found city-wide Hui-Han intermarriage in Yinchuan to be as high as 54.01 percent in 1998 (Yang 2007:

Linxia it is broadly condemned. The prohibition also applies, in a muted form, to marriages across teaching schools. Sufis and Salafis, in particular, discourage intermarriage with each other.

For its part, the Party-State has advocated "freedom to marry" (*hunyin ziyou*), meaning that young people have the freedom to choose their partners without parental intervention and can marry whomever they wish.[23] Studies, however, have noted the difficulties in implementing the Marriage Law and effecting true freedom within marriage. According to the first survey on the status of Chinese women, conducted in 1990, 20.1 percent of marriages of urban women were still arranged by the woman's parents, and in rural areas the percentage was 36.5 (Chen 2004: 161). A decade later, these percentages were 6.8 and 16.1, respectively (Chen 2004: 161–62). Thus, while the efficacy of the Marriage Law as catalyst of social change directed at the family is incontrovertible, the particular circumstances under which such change occurred are in dispute.[24]

Hui youths are increasingly empowered to make their own decisions, although parents, other family members, and relatives still exert a strong influence in identifying the pool of potential spouses. Despite the general conservatism of clerics, especially as espoused in opinions against Hui women's marrying men of different teaching schools or Han men,[25] Hui women exercise their piety through either courtship or their parents and a matchmaker. That is, decisions are negotiated, with the bride as an active participant. Many persuade their parents or matchmaker to support their choice. As Ma Yaping, a Hui female scholar based in Lanzhou, writes in her female-centered Qur'anic exegesis:

> Islam requires that the male and female parties both have, in marriage, the "right to self-selection" [*zizequan*], especially the woman. Although women cannot leave the home, they have the right to choose their own husband. "The command of the parents and the speech of the matchmaker"

614). At a national level, according to official statistics, Hui-Han intermarriage had risen marginally from 11.29 percent in 1980 to 11.85 percent in 2000 (Jiang 2006: 101).

[23] See the Marriage Law, art. 3.

[24] Many studies confirm the difference in contemporary marriage practices between cities and the countryside. For instance, Zang Xiaowei has shown that by 1982 four out of five Chinese couples married of their own volition in China's largest eastern cities (Zang 1993: 39–40). Andrew Kipnis's study of rural Shandong in the late 1980s, however, demonstrates the persistence of traditional gender and age hierarchies in institutionalized forms of marriage (Kipnis 1997: 136).

[25] Several clerics in Bafang regarded interethnic marriage as a conflict of law. When they meet a Hui-Han couple, they seek to teach the couple that, according to the Qur'an, a Muslim can marry only another Muslim. One Yihewani cleric claimed a 90-percent conversion rate.

is effective only after obtaining the agreement of both the man and the woman. If the man and woman do not agree, then the marriage is invalid.

(Ma 1992: 182)

Hui female educational entrepreneurs also teach Hui girls their rights under the revealed sources. For instance, a Gedimu woman has opened several girls' schools in the major mosques of Bafang, where there is also a private puritanical Yihewani Chinese-Arabic Girls' School. In teaching Arabic, the Qur'an, the hadith, and female piety, teachers are particularly attuned to matters of marriage.

Alternatively, a few women avail themselves of online dating or the IRC to find a partner. One woman from Linxia, age twenty-one, sought the help of the IRC in finding a partner against the wishes of her upwardly mobile parents, who were recently relocated to Lanzhou. She told me, "They think this place [i.e., the IRC] is too run-down, but I wanted to come here, to see for myself if I could find a Muslim partner." Thus, Hui women avail themselves of both religious sources of knowledge and opportunities afforded by new media and urbanization to decide—often in conversation with clerics and other patriarchal figures—when, how, and whom to marry.

Marriage finance

The transfer of property from the husband to the wife is one of the chief interests of women getting married. Hui women must advocate adherence to Islamic legal requirements in the face of Chinese customary rules and state law, both of which militate against their economic interests. As a threshold matter, the *mahr*, or bridal gift, has been localized by many Hui as an equivalent to the Chinese dowry. Due to the effects of Chinese custom on the bridal gift, there is much confusion in social practice among Chinese Muslims, across the teaching schools, and in the scholarship.[26] In protecting their material interests, Hui women must address the following issues: (1) the amount of money or property the groom owes; (2) to whom the groom owes it; (3) the legal reason for this conveyance; and (4) the timing of this transaction. The confusion surrounding how to resolve these issues highlights a direct conflict between Islamic law and Chinese custom: whereas Islamic law protects the bride's interests, in many cases the

---

[26] Scholarly confusion is not unique to Chinese Muslim practices of marriage finance. Beyond the study of Islam generally, the diversity of social practices entailing property exchange in marriage has frustrated sociological definitions of dowry, dower, bride price, and related terms (Goody 1973).

dictates of the Chinese father overrule the safeguard it provides. A Hui woman, as a result, is bound by two competing obligations—filial piety (subsequently subsumed by matrimonial piety) and personal piety, in which adherence to shari'a requires pursuing her own financial well-being upon marriage.

The position taken within the Hanafi school of Islamic law is that the husband must pay the wife a bridal gift as an effect of the marriage.[27] *Mahr* has been translated as bride price, but according to the Qur'an, it is a bridal gift whose recipient is not the bride's father but the bride herself.[28] The difference is that a bride price is a cash amount or property of equivalent value given by the groom to the bride's family (i.e., the father) in consideration for the marriage contract. The *mahr*, on the other hand, is a result of the marriage contract and is given to the bride as her property, of which only she can dispose (el-Alami 1992: 107–8; Nasir 1990: 83). It is conferred not as currency in a material transaction but as a token of respect. Although some early legal scholars wrote of the *mahr* in terms of legitimizing sexual intercourse and justifying the dominion of the husband, the Hanafi tradition has differentiated marriage from notions of sale, ownership, and slavery (Ali 2010: 49–51).

Chinese custom looms large in marriage finance among Hui. In pre-Communist China, Han grooms gave a "betrothal gift" (*pinli*) to the bride's father. This amount was used as consideration for the bride and to compensate the family for the loss of the daughter. Less commonly, in some areas the father would use part of this gift to invest in a dowry, which is then given to the newlyweds or becomes the property of the groom (Ebrey 1991: 97; Parish and Whyte 1978: 156). The modern legal regime has prohibited bride price as a mercenary and feudal practice that led to the dehumanization and commodification of women as well as the deepening of class stratification.[29] The Linxia Prefecture People's Government has not used autonomous regulations to make adjustments to state law. Bride price remains illegal, even though the practice is nearly ubiquitous among Muslims in the region. Moreover, in contravention of Islamic law, Hui widely regard bride price as a basic requirement of marriage, and not an effect of the contract.

This double violation of Islamic and state law might be better understood as an integration of elements of both Chinese customary and

---

[27] Q. 4:24. I follow the translation in the *Encyclopaedia of Islam*, "bridal gift" (Spies 2014).

[28] Q. 4:4; see also 5:5.

[29] See Marriage Law, art. 3.

Islamic practices. Some Linxia Hui superficially divide the money or property conferred by the groom into *pinli*, gifted during the engagement period, and *mahr*, given either during the wedding ceremony or afterward. In social practice, however, these categories may collapse. Other Hui in Linxia confer one lump sum of money along with material goods. In both cases, there are two major complications in the understanding of *mahr*. First, to confuse matters, the postengagement amount is sometimes referred to as *pinli* or, less frequently, as *caili*, betrothal payment (Cohen 2005: 97–98). Very few Hui, outside of clerics, are familiar with the Arabic word *mahr* or its legal definition. In everyday discourse and social practice, the Hui *pinli* shows closer approximation to the Han Chinese *pinli* than to the Islamic *mahr*. Specifically, Hui practice is for the groom to give the (first) *pinli/caili* to the bride's family as part of the premarriage engagement—that is, as a bridal gift, but one that goes to the bride's guardian, usually the father, and sometimes to the mother or elder brother. This amount is then used to pay for the wedding or to purchase items for the newlyweds' home; in this way it resembles a classical dowry system. The second complication is that the second or postengagement *pinli*, which, depending on the teaching school and religiosity of the couple, may be less important than the first *pinli*, will go to the bride, either directly or indirectly through the father.

Neither of these conveyances accords with Islamic law. The first violates Islamic law because it is given in consideration of the marriage, and both transactions violate Qur'anic rules because they position the bride's guardian as ultimate property holder. According to Imam Abu Hanifa, the eponymous founder of the Hanafi school, and as noted by Hui female scholar Ma Yaping (1992: 180), the *mahr* is the property of the wife and continues to be her property in the event of divorce, if the marriage was consummated and the divorce was not her fault. Hence, the pull of Chinese custom, and specifically of the institution of gifting, is particularly strong in marriage finance.

As to the amount of *mahr*, different Muslim communities and schools of jurisprudence hold different standards for the minimum acceptable sum. The Hanafi school decided on the sum of ten dirhams. In Linxia there is no consensus as to the socially acceptable minimum amount. A Gedimu cleric based the minimum amount on twenty silver dollars, citing the Qur'an.[30] Since one silver dollar is equal to 300 yuan, at current

---

[30] The Qur'an is silent as to the amount. There is a consensus among the schools, usually with reference to Q. 4:4 and Q. 4:24, that the *mahr* is mandatory.

monetary value he understood the minimum amount to be 6,000 yuan. Other Gedimu clerics claim that before 1980 the accepted amount was, on average, 500 yuan and a *caili* of eight sets of clothes, plus a certain weight of tea leaves, beef, and mutton. These clerics state that the amount, as of 2010, is based upon a lump sum of money, such as 500,000 yuan. Yihewani and Salafi clerics, by contrast, refer to the practice in Muslim states whereby the general rule is that the couple is permitted to set any amount they agree upon in their marriage contract.

While there is a socially imposed floor, there is no ceiling. Anything above the minimum is subject to negotiation. Hui and Dongxiang suitors cited a number of factors affecting the value, including (in the order of frequency of response) the girl's overall appearance and figure, whether she is officially employed by the state (i.e., as a civil servant), family background, and moral character. Additionally, value seems to be inversely proportional to age. In general, based on living costs and the relative higher social class of many urban Hui, the price in Linxia is half that in Lanzhou. A young Gedimu man whom I call Brother Tang paid 20,000 yuan plus thirty pieces of jewelry, consisting of rings and earrings. This property was in addition to the clothes Tang gifted in the courtship period before the wedding day was set. In the rare instance when a Hui bride marries a Han groom, the bride can request that the man use his conversion as the *pinli*.

In both Linxia and Lanzhou the *pinli* comes from the groom's parents, as most men in their early twenties do not have adequate personal savings. Most pointedly, the recipient is not the bride, as is required for the *mahr*, but the bride's father. According to one Salafi teacher in Linxia, the father will apportion some of it to buy furniture and household goods for the young couple, give some of it directly to his daughter, who keeps this money as her own, and keep the remainder for himself. When I asked the teacher how this differed from Han practice, he blurted out, "Han fathers keep more for themselves!"

In addition to the *mahr*, the right to receive maintenance (Ar. *nafaqa*, Ch. *shenghuofei*) is an important element of marriage finance. The general rule in Muslim societies is that during the course of a valid marriage, a wife is entitled to maintenance, which consists of food, clothing, and shelter. This practice is based on the Qur'an as well as several hadith (Doi 1984: 207–8; Verma 1988: 328).[31] While maintenance is a major component of Islamic marriage law, Linxia Hui place less emphasis on it than on

---

[31] Q. 4:34.

the *mahr*. Clerics speak of the wife's right to receive maintenance, but they rarely single out the husband's failure to provide it as grounds for divorce.

In marrying, the bride's competing obligations to her father and husband mark her transition from "child" daughter to "adult" wife. The person of the father often casts a shadow over this transition. As a consequence, a woman may respond by expressing devotion to her father. At the same time, the woman seeks to cultivate her own piety by adhering to the rules of marriage finance. Her desire may lead her to demand that others, including her father or groom, also obey the law. A woman resorts to suasion to protect her interests through her intimate relationships with her parents or the matchmaker, often a relative or friend of the family.

Nikāḥ versus registration

The existence of both Islamic law and state law in the field of marriage law in the Hui social field gives rise to a dual track for marriage. Theoretically, a couple fulfills the obligations under both systems, and thus the two are cognizable as "husband and wife" under both regimes. Yet more often than not, the husband takes advantage of the legal dualism, and the couple pursues the requirements of only one system, usually obtaining a *nikāḥ* from a cleric but not officially registering the marriage at the local bureau of civil affairs and thereby obtaining a marriage license. This problem, when a marriage is recognized under Islamic law but not state law, is known as "limping marriage" and is common among Muslim populations from the former Soviet republics to the United Kingdom (Ahmed 2008; Brusina 2008; Bowen 2011). Limping marriages can disadvantage women in terms of the security of both their economic interests and custodial rights over any children born from the marriage. In the Northwest, Hui use the expression "no registration, no administration" (*lingbugao guanbujiu*), meaning that there are a large number of Muslim couples that are *minjian*: their marriage is not under any management by the state, nor are they protected by PRC law.[32] Hui women avoid the bind of limping marriages by cultivating legal consciousness in both Islamic law and state law among themselves and their intimates.

In Hui communities the *nikāḥ* is understood as a ceremony, the solemn rite during which the groom and bride exchange offer and acceptance. As such, it is the formalization of consent. Jaschok and Shui (2000: 141)

---

[32] Based on my conversations with clerics, PRC law and regulations do not place an affirmative duty on clerics to verify that a couple who come to them for a *nikāḥ* have already obtained a marriage license. Some clerics make inquiries, but that is the extent of their enforcement power.

argue that before the Communist period, brides did not act autonomously in giving their offer or acceptance, that they were themselves objectified within the rite, and that only in the 1950s and after, when the bride was allowed to meet the groom before the ceremony, was she truly giving her consent. In other words, their view is that the modern marriage regime, beginning in the early Communist period, combined with the revival of Islamic law in the reform era, liberated Hui women from the hegemonic hold of traditional Chinese patriarchy, and this emancipation took place through the reformation of the Islamic ceremony, the nikāḥ. While there seems to be evidence for a broad gender liberalization, patriarchy acts on the nikāḥ in ways that may diversify or complicate general trends.

"We get the nikāḥ because we want to have sex," Brother Tang tells me, his face inches away from mine as we sit in a crowded noodle shop in Linxia. "We cannot have sex before the nikāḥ or we violate religious law. The marriage license ... can wait." His voice trails off as he returns to slurping his noodles. He continues: "We get nikāḥ read first because this is important for our religion. The marriage license is the ceremony of the Communists." When I push him on why he does not get a marriage license, he dismisses it as "too much trouble."

Such positions suggest distrust of formal law and its institutions. Avoidance of law is a problem endemic to reform-era China. Evasion of state law strengthens the husband's capacity to maximize his interests in the marriage. If there is no marriage license, then in the event of divorce there is no court that will enforce the legal rights of the wife. Property and children remain with the husband, and the wife is left with the heavy stigma of being a divorcée. It seems that Linxia Hui men have no shortage of legal consciousness when it comes to state law; they know state marriage law seeks to protect the rights of women. Some couples will go without a marriage license for many years and will get one only upon the birth of their first child. The motive is the "household registration" (hukou) for the child, for which the marriage license is a prerequisite.

Secular education improves the likelihood that women will require registration of the marriage at the Bureau of Civil Affairs. Among the couples I interviewed, no woman had a level of education higher than that of her husband. In all cases either their level of formal education was equal or the man's was higher. In the event that both attended university, it is less likely that the husband dominates the decision making. A married Dongxiang woman who was university educated and a civil servant in a Linxia City judicial organ stated, "In some cases in Linxia, the husband will put pressure on the wife not to get a marriage license. I would never allow my husband to do that." Most women in Linxia do not have a university-level education, however, and so generally husbands can pressure their wives to forgo full legal protection.

The response of most of these men is akin to that of Brother Tang—not wanting to acknowledge that their actions are derelictions of state law. Instead, they avoid the issue, resort to indirection and noodle slurping, not unlike the behaviors anthropologist Hans Steinmüller (2010) observes as formative of what he names "communities of complicity." In his study of rural Hubei, Steinmüller studied the gap between official discourse, which denigrated popular religion, and local sociality, which valorized it. His informants resorted to a variety of verbal means to address such ambiguity. He writes, "Covertness, embarrassment, cynicism, and irony are communicative strategies that make it possible for them to acknowledge both sides of the contradiction, to avoid confrontation, and to maintain communication" (Steinmüller 2010: 540). The relation of Hui to state law is the obverse: the Party-State glorifies law, and residents outwardly feign compliance while secretly mocking the law. Such responses demonstrate that ethical reflection on value pluralism can lead just as much to negative adjustments as to positive ones: unabashed opportunism as the flipside of pious devotion.

The process of marriage thus presents a number of dilemmas, including arranged marriage or free choice, bridal gift or absence thereof, and nikāḥ or marriage registration.[33] Hui women largely rely on their level of education and Islamic legal knowledge as well as their abilities of moral suasion to induce parties involved to safeguard their matrimonial and especially their economic rights. For instance, if a husband is having an illicit affair, female clerics in Haiyuan County, Ningxia, "do work" (zuo gongzuo) in persuading a husband and his lover to end their relationship in order to maintain the family unit, including the husband's moral and financial commitments to his wife. Embodiment of female virtue may not, however, be enough to persuade entrenched patriarchies to protect a wife's interests. Divorce and the problem of polygamy show that even though state law does not recognize Islamic law, Hui women mobilize socialist law to protect their rights under Islamic law.

---

[33] A couple could decide to obtain both a nikāḥ and a marriage license.

DIVORCE

Chinese feminists have heralded divorce as a power equalizer between the sexes. However, state law has actually made it more difficult for Hui women, particularly those in limping marriages, to gain a divorce. Such restrictions are exacerbated by male clerics' propensity to mediate marriage disputes toward an outcome of reconciliation rather than divorce, divesting women of the right to divorce. Despite these considerable patriarchal hurdles, women mobilize state law to further their own piety, including women's adherence to Islamic law.

A centerpiece of marriage law reform since the 1950s has been to empower women with the right to divorce. Citing a threefold increase in the number of divorces from 1950 to the first half of 1952, 75 percent of which were initiated by women, Kazuko Ono (1989: 179) concludes that the Marriage Law "became an influential weapon for the emancipation of such women from traditional marriages". At a macroscopic level, the Marriage Law has given women a basis on which to exercise the freedom to divorce—and they have. The divorce rate increased from 4.7 percent in 1979, to 8.9 percent in 1992, to 19 percent in 2000 (Yu 2004: 173). The conventional position is that women have generally enjoyed greater social mobility in the reform period.[34] According to statistics released by the Ministry of Civil Affairs (MCA) in 2009, 2,468,000 couples filed for divorce, compared with 285,000 divorced couples in 1978 (Wang 2011: 34).

Marriage law reform has undoubtedly made it easier for women to initiate divorce. Likewise, marriage law reform has increasingly responded to the reasons women may want divorce. In 1980 the Marriage Law was amended to include a clause providing a basis for divorce if one party believes "mutual affection no longer exists."[35] Procedurally, divorce became easier as courts automatically granted divorce if mediation failed (under the 1950 Marriage Law a divorce may be granted in the event of failed mediation) (Croll 1983: 83). Legal reform, in turn, combined with several other factors—including the breakdown of Cultural Revolution marriages, changing gender statuses, a rise in extramarital affairs, and failed material expectations—to increase the number of divorces (Honig and Hershatter 1988: 210–23).

---

[34] See, for instance, *White Paper: Gender Equality in China* (State Council Information Office 2005).
[35] Marriage Law, art. 25.

Moving from the macro level to a regional one, divorce rates show differences across regions. The divorce rates of provinces in the Muslim Northwest, with the exception of Xinjiang,[36] are the lowest in the country (see Table 5.1).

Gansu and Qinghai are near the bottom, and Ningxia occupies the middle of the list. Whereas Honig and Hershatter (1988) conducted their research in the wealthier eastern region of China, the standard of living in the Muslim Northwest is much lower. To cite just one indicator of economic disparity, the per capita annual income of western China is 13,917.01 yuan, whereas that in eastern China is 20,965.49 yuan (National Bureau of Statistics 2009: 322). Honig and Hershatter hypothesize that material wealth led to more divorces (i.e., women's status has been affected by their ability to accumulate savings and to consume commodities, and more wealth among men correlates with more opportunities to engage in extramarital affairs). But while poverty helps to account for marriage stability in the Northwest, it is not a full explanation. Social, cultural, and religious factors also contribute to divorce and its (in)frequency in Muslim areas.

Disagreeing about divorce

In Linxia, divorce among Muslim couples is rare. It is uncommon primarily because of the domination of the husband and the patriarchal authority of the cleric, who enforces Islamic law's negative view of divorce. Although Islamic law permits divorce, it discourages it. One hadith states, "Of all things permitted by law, divorce is the most hateful in the sight of God."

Under one common view of Islamic law, the form of the dissolution of the marriage contract is *ṭalāq*, or unilateral repudiation, which is the exclusive right of the husband. As with formation of the marriage contract, there are requirements for a legal *ṭalāq*: majority age, sanity, and, according to some scholars, voluntariness. *Ṭalāq* may take the form of a verbal utterance, a written statement, or a gesture (Nasir 1990: 107, 109). There are three types of dissolution. The first and preferred type, called the "best divorce" (Ar. *ṭalāq aḥsan*), takes the form of a single utterance said when the wife is not menstruating, which is followed by abstinence from sexual intercourse during a specified waiting period (Ar. *ʿidda*,

---

[36] The exceptionally high rate of divorce in Xinjiang is best understood in the context of anomie felt by Uyghurs in the region. Along with drug and alcohol abuse as well as other health issues, divorce has increased among Uyghurs in the reform era (Dautcher 2004). For a comprehensive study of divorce among Uyghurs in Xinjiang, see Nijim (2009).

TABLE 5.1 Ranking of divorce rates per administrative unit

No.	Administrative Unit	Divorce Rate*
1	Xinjiang	4.12
2	Chongqing	3.56
3	Heilongjiang	3.30
4	Jilin	3.27
5	Liaoning	3.05
6	Shanghai	2.53
7	Sichuan	2.45
8	Beijing	2.40
9	Tianjin	2.29
10	Inner Mongolia	2.15
11	Zhejiang	2.07
12	Hunan	2.06
13	Ningxia	2.05
14	Hubei	1.91
15	Jiangsu	1.87
16	Hebei	1.81
17	Fujian	1.61
18	Shandong	1.60
19	Guizhou	1.53
20	Anhui	1.52
21	Shaanxi	1.47
22	Jiangxi	1.39
23	Qinghai	1.37
24	Guangxi	1.36
25	Yunnan	1.34
26	Henan	1.31
27	Hainan	1.28
28	Guangdong	1.24
29	Shanxi	1.14
30	Gansu	0.94
31	Tibet	0.60

* This figure is based on a comparison between the number of divorces filed in that administrative unit and the population's annual mean.
Source: Ministry of Civil Affairs (2010: A12).

Ch. *daihunqi*). This type of divorce is the most meritorious, because it is revocable. The second type, called "better divorce" (Ar. *talāq ḥasan*), is the less preferred way. In this type, the husband makes three pronouncements over the course of three consecutive periods of menstrual purity. No sex can take place during the course of the three utterances. This type is final and irrevocable upon the third pronouncement. In the third type, called the "divorce of innovation" (Ar. *talāq al-bid'a*), the husband pronounces three divorces at the same time during a period in which his wife is not menstruating, whereupon she enters the waiting period. This type, commonly referred to as the "triple *talāq*," is also irrevocable (Tucker 2008: 86–87).

As with arranged marriages and the effects of *pinli* on Hui understandings of *mahr*, the traditional Chinese method of divorce, *xiuqi* (lit. "discard wife"), has also shaped Hui practices of *talāq*. Divorce among Han was primarily the right of the husband or, mirroring the pivotal role of parents in arranging marriages, his parents (Wolf 1975: 89; Stacey 1983: 34); women had only a restricted right to divorce under a specified set of conditions (Bernhardt and Huang 1994: 189). But because Chinese custom, like Islamic law, does not favor divorce, it occurred only infrequently (Freedman 1966: 60; Wolf and Huang 1980: 179). Furthermore, historically divorce has rarely been a means of addressing marital problems. The point is that both forms of divorce—Islamic and Chinese—have favored the prerogative of the husband and discouraged divorce, which can severely constrain women's freedom.

In Linxia on average, 1,300 marriages are registered per year and 130 divorces are obtained per year.[37] When Linxia Muslims do divorce, they use *talāq*. Just as Linxia Muslims show a preference for *nikāḥ* over lawful marriage registration, so too do they prefer *talāq* over pursuing a divorce through the formal state procedure. While aversion to formal law is one reason, another is their preference to be married and divorced in the sight of God through *nikāḥ* and *talāq*. As one Yihewani cleric said, for Hui "religious law trumps state law" in matters of marriage and divorce. But Hui Muslims, whether clerics or laypeople, do not share a single understanding of the minimum requirement for *talāq* under Islamic law. While opinions differ somewhat according to teaching-school lines, reflections are clouded by the lack of an indigenous *fiqh* or authoritative 'ulama'.

---

[37] Statistics from the Linxia City Bureau of Civil Affairs (BCA), covering the period January 1, 2010, to December 20, 2010.

In particular, Chinese Muslims, like Muslims elsewhere, vary in their usage of *ṭalāq aḥsan*, *ṭalāq ḥasan*, and *ṭalāq al-bidʿa*. A Gedimu man, age twenty-five, said *ṭalāq* means to say " 'I divorce you' [*wo xiu ni* or *wo bu yao ni*] three times." However, when asked whether all three pronouncements can be uttered at the same time or must there be a grace period between them (i.e., whether he is referring to *ṭalāq ḥasan* or *ṭalāq al-bidʿa*), he was uncertain.[38] Other Gedimu men confirmed that it takes three utterances made over a period of time that they referred to as *san xiu*, the term in the local dialect for *ṭalāq ḥasan*. Men of other teaching schools say that divorce entails a single pronouncement of "I divorce you," but they differ as to whether the pronouncement must be uttered during the wife's period of menstrual purity, which determines if it is the *ṭalāq aḥsan* or the *ṭalāq al-bidʿa*. A Yihewani cleric explained to me that in divorce "what the husband says goes," but he must provide his ex-wife three months of maintenance and compensation based on their time together and situation, and he must ensure her access to their children. This Yihewani cleric detailed two ways to divorce: In the first (*ṭalāq aḥsan*), the husband says "I divorce you" one or two times, but if he says "I take you back," then the husband and wife must remarry. However, if he says "I divorce you" a third time, then the husband and wife are divorced. The second procedure conflates *ṭalāq ḥasan* and *ṭalāq al-bidʿa*: the husband says in a single utterance, "I firmly do not want you" or "I do not want you three times," which brings about divorce.

In the course of my ethnographic study of Bafang's mosques, clerics nearly unanimously identified marriage and divorce, subsumed under "marital relations" (*fuqi guanxi*) or "family conflicts" (*jiating maodun*), as the most prevalent source of conflict among families in their community and the issue they most frequently mediate. In handling divorce cases, clerics in Linxia show a strong preference for maintaining marriages, although their rationales for doing so differ across teaching schools.

For example, a cleric at a Gedimu mosque explained how he handled a case where a man had two wives, and the first wife sought divorce, arguing that the second marriage violated Islamic law:

> *There is a preference in Islam to maintain marriages*, and so I will try to persuade the two [i.e., the husband and the first wife] to remain married if the second marriage is legal. In this case, it was not legal under Islamic

---

[38] In certain Muslim societies outside of China, such uncertainty may result from the differences of opinion that jurists hold on the matter. In China, diverse views are entering Hui communities and form a nascent legal consciousness.

law, for a ceremony was never held. Thus, I pronounced the husband in dereliction of his duties and said there was ground for divorce [of the first marriage]. However, China is a country of "rule by law," not "rule by religion," and so my power stops there. I told them the rest is up to them to decide [emphasis added].

The cleric provides a blanket rationalization, grossly consistent with predominant views of Hanafi doctrine, for the durability of marriage under Islamic law. By contrast, a former cleric of one of Linxia's most active Yihewani mosques veers from prevailing opinions of Hanafi law in his interpretation of Islamic law's barriers to divorce. When a cleric receives a case, he explains:

> he will determine whether (a) the intention or will to divorce was said in a moment of anger or (b) it was a thought-out, rational statement. If it was the former, then it does not count, and the cleric will ask the two to go back and live together for a period of three months, after which they must reassess. If it is the latter, then they will again be requested to go back and live together (separate bedrooms is okay). The difference is the pronouncement counts as one of three required "divorce statements." After the three months, the cleric will see if they are reconciled. If not, then it is the second time, and they are requested to go back to live together again for a minimum of three months (sometimes six months or one year). And if they are still dissatisfied, then that is the third time and it's a legal divorce.

The Yihewani cleric makes a distinction between a pronouncement said in anger and one that is rational. Despite the Qur'an's strong disapproval of *ṭalāq*,[39] Hanafi jurists have broadly interpreted the husband's power to make the declaration, although there is disagreement within the school as to whether *ṭalāq* uttered in a moment of anger is valid.[40] This seemingly technical point of law sheds light on the differences between the teaching schools in their interpretations and applications of Islamic law. Some Middle Eastern jurists cite the Qur'an directly as evidence that any anger invalidates a *ṭalāq*.[41] Others follow authoritative Hanafi texts, such as the *Radd al-Muhtar 'ala al-Durr al-Mukhtar*, which classifies anger into three levels, arguing that only extreme anger, near insanity, nullifies a

---

[39] Q. 2:229.
[40] Modern legislation in Muslim states has put limits on the *ṭalāq* pronounced in anger. See, for instance, the Republic of Iraq's Unified Code of Personal Status (1959) (Mallat and Connors 1990: 182).
[41] Q. 2:228.

pronouncement.[42] In almost all instances the authority doing the inter-preting is male.

The substantive law of Islam through state procedural law

Given that the primary venue for spousal conflicts is overseen by male clerics who, more often than not, try to reconcile the couples, women have looked to state law as a means to protect their interests. According to interviews with officials in the Linxia City Bureau of Religious Affairs (BRA), Hui women seeking a divorce in the people's courts frequently invoke their rights under the nikāḥ, the basis for a minjian marriage. Generally, court mediators may be more flexible in considering such argu-ments than judges in the event of divorce proceedings through litigation. Thus, although modern legal institutions in the form of people's courts may provide a venue for women to assert their rights, in a curious inver-sion of the logic of legal modernization, women often base their argu-ments on shari'a.[43]

The consequences of divorce, whether legal, material, or emotional, affect women's long-term rights. In Islamic law, if a husband initiates divorce after consummating the marriage, then the wife has a right to the full mahr and maintenance. If the ṭalāq is uttered prior to consumma-tion, then the wife may not have the right to the mahr (Nasir 1990: 135). Ṭalāq also terminates all mutual rights of inheritance. As for custody of offspring from the marriage, a common view is that the mother is entitled to custody of any son below the age of seven years old and any daughter who has not reached puberty (Verma 1988: 272), although opinions differ as to the relevant ages of children, and the best interests of the child may also be taken into consideration.

In Linxia and surrounding areas, the general rule is that any property held by either the bride or the groom, including the bride's dowry (i.e., the property she brought with her, often given by her father), is jointly owned. A Yihewani cleric in Linxia's sheep hide district comments that, in theory, any property the wife brings into the marriage is hers in the event of divorce and that, according to religious law, no one can use the mahr, although her family members often use it to pay for the wedding (see Figure 5.2).

[42] The text was written by the scholar-jurist Muhammad Amin ibn 'Abidin (1783–1836).
[43] Muslim minority women are not alone in advocating nonstate norms in state courts. Impoverished Hindu women, for instance, have argued for customary divorce in state courts in India (Holden 2004).

Figure 5.2 A bride's family moves her assets to the home of the groom's father
Source: the author

   As explained by a Hui civil servant who frequently mediates divorce among Muslim couples in Linxia, a key criterion is the length of the marriage. Usually, if the marriage lasted several years and it is the husband who seeks to dissolve the marriage, then the wife keeps the *mahr*. However, if the marriage was short and she initiates divorce proceedings, then she must return the *mahr*, if she has not already spent it.[44] The rationale behind the law aims to discourage women from marrying for material gain. Although property is held in common by husband and wife, there is no doctrine of equitable distribution in the event of divorce. Hence, the wife may not receive any portion of the marriage assets to which she contributed, either directly or indirectly.

   In the event that judicial mediation is unsuccessful and the couple litigates in a people's court, state law limits the legal bases upon which a woman can make her arguments. When a Chinese Muslim woman with only a *nikāḥ* and not a marriage license seeks to dissolve her marriage in a people's

[44] The Qur'an (2:229) varies from this statement: the husband has the right to ask for the *mahr* back but is encouraged not to do so; the wife is not required to give it back if the husband does not ask for it.

248

court, she has no legal recourse, as the court does not recognize *nikāḥ*, and thus there is no lawful union for the court to dissolve. Historically, the state responded to this problem through the de facto "common law" marriage or "marriage-in-fact" (*shishi hunyin*).[45] In the event that one or both parties wanted to end the union, a PRC judge had the right to recognize a marriage-in-fact even in the absence of a lawfully registered marriage. This allowance benefited a woman seeking to divorce her husband, as she could still protect her interests in property and her custody of any offspring from the union. The marriage-in-fact serves as a gap filler between the Islamic *nikāḥ* and state divorce law. The policy was based on the recognition that, particularly in the countryside, many citizens, whether Han or belonging to an ethnic minority, did not register their marriages.

Then in 1994 the MCA issued the Marriage Registration Administrative Regulations (hereinafter, "1994 Regulations"), which expressly prohibited any legal recognition of cohabitation between a man and a wife that is not based on a registered marriage.[46] Most legal and judicial officials in Linxia and elsewhere in the Muslim Northwest view the 1994 Regulations as closing the door on marriage-in-fact. The jurisprudence on marriage-in-fact is not settled, however, and this indeterminacy is reflected in the varying views of officials on the ground.[47] While

---

[45] The earliest legal basis for the marriage-in-fact in New China is a document issued by the Supreme People's Court of the East China Branch Institute, dated July 29, 1953. In it, the court permitted marriage-in-fact while limiting its application and stressing continued education. On February 2, 1979, the Supreme People's Court issued the Opinion on Implementing and Executing Regulations and Laws Pertaining to Civil Affairs (*Guanyu guanche zhixing minshi zhengce falü de yijian*), which defined marriage-in-fact as a situation in which a "man and woman have not properly obtained a marriage registration, but cohabit as husband and wife, and the people regard them as husband and wife" (art. 4).

[46] Marriage Registration Administrative Regulations (*Hunyin dengji guanli tiaoli*), promulgated by the MCA on February 1, 1994, art. 24. See also the Supreme People's Court's Notice Regarding the Applicable New Regulations on the Management of Marriage Registration (*Zuigao renmin fayuan guanyu shiyong xin de hunyin dengji guanli tiaoli*), issued April 4, 1994, stating unequivocally, "As of February 1, 1994, men and women without a spouse who have not properly registered their marriage, even if they outwardly have a life of cohabitation, should be handled as illegally cohabiting."

[47] The amended Marriage Law, promulgated April 28, 2001, states, "Those who have not registered their marriage should acquire a supplementary registration" (art. 8). Supplementary registration was addressed in the Supreme People's Court Explanation Regarding Certain Questions under the Applicable PRC Marriage Law (*Zuigao renmin fayuan guanyu shiyong Zhonghua renmin gongheguo hunyinfa ruogan wenti de jieshi*), issued December 27, 2001, which differentiated between those cohabitations before and after 1994, permitting those before 1994 to be recognized as marriage-in-fact while requiring those established after 1994 to acquire a supplementary registration before any divorce action. Those couples who failed to do so would be regarded as illegally cohabiting (arts. 4 and 5).

officials, lawyers, and judges in Linxia County and Linxia City as well as Haiyuan County in Ningxia all say that marriage-in-fact no longer exists under law,[48] officials in Yinchuan, Ningxia, say marriage-in-fact still has legal force.

The practice of divorce in Linxia and surrounding areas in the Northwest shows, to borrow from Margery Wolf (1985), a "revolution postponed." Despite the patriarchy of both Hui clerics and the Party-State, as demonstrated in laws that close off the few bases of argumentation available to women in failing marriages, Hui women navigate such difficulties and, as the following section shows, may cite state law in defense of their rights under Islam. The persistence of polygamy, in particular, sheds light on the difficulties accompanying such legal mobilization.

THE PROBLEM OF POLYGAMY

Polygamy, as a violation of women's security and dignity, presents Hui women with a unique problem for which they turn to state law—despite its limitations—to protect their own rights. While monogamy remains the most widespread form of marriage in the Muslim Northwest, polygamy also exists in the region. In Linxia, the topic is not openly discussed, given the broad condemnation of multiple-party marriages in state law and socialist morality more generally. Nevertheless, nearly every person I spoke with about the topic knew someone who was involved in such a relationship. The common denominator across teaching schools and ethnicity is class. Men who have multiple wives are in their late forties or older and have accumulated the wealth necessary to afford multiple households and the consumption habits of women who often compete for the husband's attention by out-consuming rivals. A common profile

---

[48] The common response is that all marriages not registered go under "illegal cohabitation" (feifa tongju). Thus, a divorce case brought to the court or judicial bureau is filed under "conflict of property division and child support." In other words, property division/child support provides the cause of action. The law acts on that which it recognizes—property and children—even if the relationship in which these legal objects are contextualized is unrecognizable. If the (nikāḥ) marriage was short in duration (i.e., little property accrual and no children), then the court will not touch it. If the marriage was long, then it will be considered under the above cause of action. A Hui lawyer in the Linxia County judiciary said that, in the course of a divorce proceeding, judges will take a three-statement ṭalāq as evidence of the husband's desire to divorce, but not as a de jure basis for divorce. He argued that state law is a corrective to this acknowledgment, as either party, a husband or a wife, can initiate divorce proceedings.

of a polygamist is an elder businessman with households in several locations throughout southwestern Gansu and even the Tibet Autonomous Region.

The economic reforms beginning in the 1980s have, contrary to state law's praise for gender equality, increased the gap between men and women. Leta Hong Fincher (2014), in her study of "leftover women" (women stigmatized for being unmarried in their late twenties), finds a correlation between women's lack of property rights and gender inequality. Conversely, the accumulation of property by Hui businessmen who have benefited from economic policies and resurgent commercial networks has enabled these men to afford multiple wives. As living standards have increased, a wider range of professionals, including teachers, school principals, and other civil servants, have also begun to acquire second, and sometimes third wives. It is rare for a man to have the material assets to afford four wives. Many accounts I collected have the common element that the second or third wife is a Tibetan woman whom the man met in Lhasa or Gannan when conducting business. The Tibetan woman will convert to Islam, and the two often (but not always) have a cleric read the nikāḥ. Several Hui women I talked with in Linxia shifted the problem of polygamy onto Tibetan women, saying, "Tibetan women are loose about having sex." If official marriage licenses are not the rule among Linxia Muslims in monogamous pairs, then they are nonexistent in polygamous arrangements. The first wife may have a marriage license, but the second does not. The record of the first marriage would prevent a second registration. The woman's ability to protect her property, inheritance, and custodial rights are compounded when her husband has multiple wives.

Women are usually caught in polygamous marriages because of their limited material resources that, in turn, inhibit their ability to protect their rights. A thirty-four-year-old unmarried Linxia Hui woman relates:

> Islam gives freedom to women. For example, if I want to go outside, all I have to do is get my father's permission. Polygamy [yifuduoqi] is another aspect of Islam that has to be understood in this context. There is polygamy in my family. My senior male cousin, age fifty-seven, had first married a woman, now sixty years old, the "senior wife" [da laopo], who resides in Linxia with their two children. He then married a thirty-year-old woman, "junior wife" [xiao laopo], who lives in Lanzhou. He spends most of his time with junior wife, which goes against religious law. He had the nikāḥ read at both weddings but has a marriage license only for the first marriage. Senior wife hates junior wife but cannot divorce her husband, even

though she has this right under religious law and state law. She is dependent on him financially, as are her children.

From the perspective of Hui women, polygamy may be more of a response to the influence on Hui men by Han custom than a distortion of Islamic law. When I ask what percentage of Chinese Muslim men have a second wife, she replies, "Thirty percent of Hui men have a second wife, although very few have more than two. This is more than Han men. Han men call their second wife 'little third' [*xiao san*]."

Whereas 30 percent is a very high estimate, and a cleric of the largest Yihewani mosque in Xunhua County, Qinghai, estimated that only one out of every ten Salar men had more than one wife, the woman's use of the term "little third" displaces blame for Hui polygamy from Islam to Hui adoption of Han custom. The Linxia woman's equation of "little third," a colloquial term for mistress, with the Hui practice of polygamy suggests that, in her eyes, Hui men's taking multiple wives may be less an emulation of the Prophet under the Islamic law and more a manifestation of Chinese custom.[49] While matrimonial infidelity among Chinese men, Han and minority, is a problem in the reform era, that this woman understands polygamy in the context of freedom in Islam is telling of the extent to which Hui women have internalized patriarchy in their defense of Islam.

As polygamy can have disastrous effects on women's material security as well as their emotional and physical well-being, women have turned to state law to seek redress for injustices. In the following case, Teacher Ding, a woman whose husband had a second wife, sought remedy through both more traditional nonstate means (e.g., family members) and state law. Her family members' role in mediating the problem demonstrates that the family, like the cleric, is an institution that reproduces patriarchy. While the Party-State's invalidation of common-law marriage has closed off avenues of argumentation available to women, Teacher Ding's case shows that skillful mobilization of law can provide redress.

Teacher Ding is a small-framed, soft-spoken woman who wears a traditional black hijab. She comes from a rural background, and thus most Linxia Hui would consider her socioeconomic level to be average among

---

[49] Most Han I spoke with in Linxia and surrounding areas made a clear distinction between Hui polygamous practices and the historical male Han practice of having multiple wives. In this respect, the Han majority identifies state law (i.e., the 1950 Marriage Law) as a marker of progress over "feudal" pasts. It should be noted that polygamy gained recognition as a Chinese customary law among Chinese outside mainland China under colonial rule—that is, in Singapore and Malaysia in the 1960s, and 1971 in the case of Hong Kong (Hooker 1975: 168).

her peers or slightly below average. I spent an afternoon with her and her lawyer, Lawyer Wang, a Hui man who works for the prefectural judiciary and takes on many cases of polygamy. Teacher Ding's experience is representative of the situation of Hui women in polygamous relationships. Given its representativeness and, at the same time, the absence of such data in the ethnographic record, I include her testimony in its entirety.

> I'm twenty-eight years old, a Muslim. My family is from Hezheng [County]. I met my husband, who is thirty-one, in 1998, when we were studying at Linxia Teachers' School. We dated for three years and then got married soon after graduation. My husband was not active in any one mosque and rarely went to the mosque on Friday. We had a relative, my mother's brother, read *nikāḥ*. We lived in Linxia and commuted to Hezheng. He was originally teaching at another school in Hezheng. In December 2003 our daughter was born. Only when I was pregnant did we get a marriage license.

> In late 2006 I discovered that my husband was cheating on me. One day, while at school, I received a text message on my phone asking, "Has [name deleted] had lunch?" I sent a text back, "I don't know who you are." I thought, at the time, the texter was a colleague, a fellow teacher, who was playing a joke. However, after this exchange and subsequent text exchanges, my husband found out and told me about the "third party" [*disanzhe*]. At the time, my child was two years and ten months old. From 2006 to 2008 my husband lived part time with the third party in Linxia. In April 2007 the third party called me, asking if my husband was there, saying "Let me see him" and "I want him to leave you and to support me financially." At that time, a female friend working in the Linxia hospital took me to the third party to confront her. The third party was a Han woman, thirty-two years old (four years older than I and one year older than my husband), who was married at the time as well, with children. She worked at her father's medical clinic.

> In March 2007 I filed for divorce at Linxia City People's Court. During the hearings, the court sought to mediate the dispute. I had moved out. I was sleeping at the school's dormitory, where other teachers stayed. I stayed there for three to four months. Also, the third party had moved out from her family, as her affair with my husband was now openly known, and she was separated from her own husband. Further, family members and clerics were involved in trying to reconcile me and my husband. At that time, he promised to leave the third party and return to me.

> I decided to move back in with my husband to try to make the marriage work, mainly thinking of our child. In 2008 my husband got promoted.

He left the larger school where he had taught and became the principal of the primary school where I taught, so we saw each other every day.

But he did not keep his promise. It was his custom each Ramadan to go to the mosque. In 2008 he told me he was doing so, but I thought he was acting strange. I followed him and saw that in fact he was going back to the residence of the third party. Further, I found out that in that year he had gotten married to the third party. A different cleric, not knowing of my husband's previous marriage, had married them. The Han woman first converted to Islam.

I left my husband again, but I soon returned when my father-in-law was ill in Lanzhou. I went to the hospital with my husband and our daughter, and there he begged me to come back, and I forgave him. I did not want to expend my heart caring for him, but for my daughter, I returned to him.

Family members were involved trying to reconcile my husband and me. During one family meeting, my brother-in-law strongly advocated that we get a divorce, mainly because if the husband left the third party, then she would return to being a Han. Islam prohibits apostasy. The family also argued for divorce, because both I and my husband, as workers in a state-run school, were bound by laws and regulations. It would be more convenient for me to initiate divorce and for my husband to start over with a new wife than to try to patch up a marriage that was causing so many problems. Basically, they were afraid my husband would lose his job.

In 2008 the three of us [Teacher Ding, her husband, and his lover] met. A physical struggle ensued. My husband, who is 170 cm [5 ft., 6 in.], intervened and struck me. During a subsequent meeting, I sought to get him to sign an agreement saying that Monday, Wednesday, and Friday he would stay with me and Tuesday, Thursday, Saturday, and Sunday he would stay with the third party. My true aim in doing this was to get a written statement in which he admitted to having an affair.

However, I discovered that my husband and the third party had had a child, also a girl, before he married the third party. My husband sold our house in Linxia, and I moved back to living at the school. The child was grounds for divorce, and so I undertook—a second time—to file for divorce in Linxia City People's Court.

Typical of many Hui women, Teacher Ding was limited in her options of obtaining redress. Her parents were in Lanzhou and did not know what was happening. She was not close to any cleric, and talked only to a few close friends late in the process. It was her brother-in-law who introduced her to Lawyer Wang. In terms of the divorce action, the specific ground for divorce was the crime of bigamy, for which the maximum sentence is two years in prison. Also, the plaintiff can be awarded up to half of the couple's total earnings. In 2011 the Linxia City People's Court mediated the dispute. During the proceedings, Teacher Ding discovered that her former husband had an affair with yet another lover—a university student in her early twenties. The court found the husband at fault and awarded Teacher Ding RMB 180,000 but did not impose criminal liability. As for severing the limping marriage (i.e., the union was still potentially valid under Islamic law), in this case, because a family member and not a cleric had read the *nikāḥ*, Teacher Ding did not exercise her right under Hanafi law to seek a divorce from a cleric. She considered the Islamic marriage void, pursuant to the finding of the judicial mediators.

Lawyer Wang comments that in his fourteen years of lawyering, he has handled some two hundred civil cases, fifty to sixty of which were what he called "lovers' relationships" (*qingren guanxi*). Twenty percent of these were a situation in which the man had obtained multiple *nikāḥ*, and the others involved a man who had a *nikāḥ* with his wife but then one or more lovers. Only those situations in which a Muslim man has a *nikāḥ* with more than one woman are considered cases of bigamy. His interpretation suggests that criminal law judges (almost half of whom are Muslim in Linxia Prefecture) take into consideration multiple *nikāḥ* as determinative evidence of bigamy. This is an example of state law implicitly recognizing Islamic law.[50]

As for the profile of women who find themselves in polygamous relationships, Lawyer Wang states that generally they are poor, many are illiterate, and they have only a rudimentary understanding of their legal

---

[50] The definition of bigamy under PRC law has changed over time. The PRC Criminal Law (*Zhonghua renmin gongheguo xingfa*), adopted by the National People's Congress, July 1, 1979, revised March 14, 1997, art. 258, defines a bigamist as "a person already having a spouse who marries another person or [a person who] marries another, knowing that that person has already married." Under the pre-1994 regime of marriage laws and regulations, when state law gave limited recognition to marriage-in-fact, any relationship that satisfied the definition of marriage-in-fact could, when the circumstances showed that the marriage-in-fact was in addition to a registered marriage, be the basis for the crime of bigamy. After the 1994 Regulations, which did not recognize marriage-in-fact, went into effect, the criminal law that gave recognition to marriage-in-fact was out of date. The Supreme People's Court addressed this conflict in the same year. In The Supreme People's Court's Official Reply on Whether After the Implementation of the Marriage Registration Administrative Regulations, a Bigamy Case Involving a Nominal Husband and Wife Who are Discovered in Illegal Cohabitation Should be Guilty and Punished According to the Crime of Bigamy (*Guanyu hunyin dengji guanli tiaoli shixing hou fasheng de yi fuqi mingyi feifa tongju de chonghun anjian shifou yi chonghun zui dingzui chufa de pifu*), issued December 14, 1994, the court declared that "a person already with a spouse who, with another, assumes a relationship of nominal husband and wife in cohabitation life-style or [a person who] knowing that the other person has a spouse, forms with that person a nominal husband and wife cohabitation life-style, should, as before, be guilty and penalized as a bigamist." Thus, there remains a kind of soft recognition of marriage-in-fact in criminal law but not in administrative law or marriage law.

rights. Teacher Ding adds that during the lawsuit she read books and newspaper articles about marriage law and watched law-themed television shows—common forms of state law popularization. Most Linxia Hui women learn of their rights during the litigation process[51] in conjunction with working with a lawyer, who charges a set fee of 5,000 yuan per case, prohibitive to many rural Chinese women. Many women in polygamous arrangements are economically dependent on the husband and allow him to take a second or third wife. Conversely, those women who are proactive in defending their rights are economically independent, as Teacher Ding's case shows. For instance, on her teacher's salary she can afford a life for both herself and her daughter.

Lawyer Wang says that while the number of polygamous marriages is very low, he sees polygamy increasing in Linxia and surrounding areas. The main cause is higher living standards, which enable more men to afford multiple wives or lovers. Polygamy may be one practice that is bolstered by both religious revival and secular commercialism, in spite of law and gender modernization campaigns. The case of Teacher Ding demonstrates, however, that Hui women do use state law to escape a polygamous marriage.

Muslim women acquire knowledge of Islamic and state laws through grassroots or local-level networks centered on local women who have taught themselves law or even studied it abroad. One Gedimu woman who has started several women's schools attached to mosques in Bafang stated, "Our goal is to educate the illiterate women of Bafang, to teach them Islamic culture so that they can be a qualified Muslim." Of the approximately three hundred women who study at the Gedimu schools (not all of whom are Gedimu), the vast majority are homemakers. In studying the Qur'an, hadith, and Arabic, women attain consciousness of their basic rights under Islamic law.[52] Additionally, women may communicate knowledge about using state law through such networks. Beyond the grassroots level, scholars such as Ma Yaping, based in the provincial capital of Lanzhou, apply a female-centered hermeneutic to interpret the Qur'an. She writes, for example, about the Qur'an's conditions for

---

[51] See, for instance, Diamant, Lubman, and O'Brien (2005), Gallagher (2006), and Erie (2012).

[52] Contrary to Élisabeth Allès (2004), who considers scripturalist (what she terms "fundamentalist") women's schools conforming to male authority and limiting female agency, I do not see evidence of such male domination in grassroots Gedimu schools, although the administration of the Yihewani Chinese-Arabic Girls' School in Linxia is predominantly male.

polygamy.[53] In Beijing, Ding Hong and other senior Hui scholars advocate "Hui women's studies."

Unfortunately, while there are a number of "horizontal" networks of Muslim women—at the local, regional, and national levels—there are few institutionalized "vertical" linkages between these networks. Knowledge about the law (religious and secular) regarding women circulates through a patchwork of horizontal networks but does not travel as readily "up" and "down." As a result, Hui women have little organizational support to effect broader women-based reform. The All-China Women's Federation, the Party's official women's rights organization, for instance, is far removed from most legal and ethical dilemmas Hui women face in places such as Linxia. One of the pressing questions for the study of Islamic law in China as the PRC enters its fourth decade of reform is the extent to which Muslim minority women will be able to bridge different levels of networks and, further, marshal emergent transnational connections to reform gender relations on the ground.

THE LIMITS OF MODESTY

Hui women embody filial piety as obedience to the father's will, but they also may bend such will. Women's capacity to do so depends on a variety of factors, including teaching-school affiliation, level of education, and geography (rural or urban). Within scripturalist teaching schools, especially those in cities such as Lanzhou or Yinchuan, women exercise a greater capacity to embody the demands of both Islamic law and Chinese tradition in the transition from daughter to wife. In enclaves such as Linxia the codependence of the local Party-State and clerics tends to reproduce patriarchal values in both mosque mediation and people's courts. The effects of the reform of marriage laws have proven limited. Hui still arrange marriages, perform the *nikāḥ*, give *mahr*, and divorce according to the *ṭalāq*. Even polygamy, by which Islamic law most clearly breaks with socialist norms of gender equality, has not only survived but is resurgent in postsocialist China. Furthermore, many reforms at the national level, such as abrogating common-law marriage, have militated against women's capacity to ensure their own autonomy.

At the same time, state law's nonrecognition of Islamic law, specifically the *nikāḥ*, divests Hui women of the protection Islamic law affords

---

[53] Citing the Qur'an (4:3), Ma Yaping (1992: 182) draws attention to the conditions of equal treatment of wives and reciprocal love, pleasing, and concord within the marriage.

to women. Consequently, although state law and socialist gender policy is predicated on a notion of gender equality, the effects of state law in Muslim communities prevent Hui women from articulating arguments based on religious law that would provide greater guarantees for gender justice. Proponents of "depoliticizing" ethnicity by dissolving legal recognition of ethnic and religious difference would seek to further standardize substantive and procedural law. Such reforms, however, would decrease rather than increase Hui women's ability to protect their interests under Islamic law and thereby limit their access to justice.

Women's interiorization of patriarchal norms may have limited their ability to make others accountable to the law. Violations of religious or state law and, further, deprivations of basic human rights, such as security and well-being, can lead some women to differentiate the law from male domination. Specifically, women draw attention to men's behavior when they exceed their legal entitlements. As couples and families are inherently relational, impiety of one member affects the piety of others (cf. Mahmood 2005: 185). In spite of or because of the reinforced and overlapping patriarchies originating in Chinese custom, Islamic law, and state socialist law, women adopt a number of postures—discursive, textual, and juridical—vis-à-vis marriage inequities. Women acquire knowledge about their rights from *minjian* organizations, private Arabic schools, female clerics and scholars, and various other sites and sources at the margins of male dominion in localized Islamic law. A few women, such as Teacher Ding, step outside communal expectations to seek redress based on their own understanding of marital relations and gender justice. Such initiatives assert a female-centered view of gender relations in marriage that itself may cross the Party-State's line between privatized religion and public citizenship. Women access state law to obtain justice even if state law fails to recognize the religious basis of their claims. In short, their piety is not only internalized but transforms social relations partly through state law.

For many Hui women growing up in rural Gansu, Qinghai, or Ningxia, being a wife and mother are primary aspirations. Only a small percentage of those who attend religious schools—for example, the Chinese-Arabic Girls' School—assume positions in the government or work for companies domestically or abroad. Thus, for most women freedom resides in the ability to assume established roles within the family and mosque community. Most have no longing for separation or individualism unless their rights as wives, sisters, mothers, and daughters are infringed upon. Such infringement precipitates ethical reflection, through which they recast their relationship to others in light of legal prescriptions. Learning the law or using the law within patriarchal relationships does not mean that women tolerate abuse. Through growing legal consciousness, women seek to conform their relationships to the expectations of Islamic law. In doing so, women go beyond embodying normative models of female piety and assert themselves as orthopraxic models for familiars.

6

MORAL ECONOMIES

Allah will deprive usury of all blessing, but will give increase for deeds of charity.

Qur'an 2:276

PINCHING THE PRICE

On a frigid day in December 2011, I stood at one of Linxia's major inter-sections, which is also a node of the city's sheep hide market. The burly Hui towering over me, wearing a Tibetan ox hide overcoat and donning an ushanka over his white cap, who was engaged in such haggling, smiled a toothless grin in answer to my question as to whether Hui used Islamic law in their commercial transactions. He slapped the Chinese translation of a work on Islamic commercial law that I had been toting, knocking it onto the ground, and pulled my hand into the cavernous sleeve of his overcoat. With his grin changing into an expression of soft concentration, he began pinching my fingers together in sequences that corresponded to numerals to represent cash amounts. "Six-seven-eight-nine," he instructed in Bafanghua, the local dialect. He then took my hand and drove it into a warm, steaming pile of sheep intestines that lay by the side of the road, next to the hides of sheep that had been recently slaughtered in nearby mosques. "*Yah!*" he exclaimed, grinning wildly. My face blanched, and I managed a weak smile as the dozen Hui and Dongxiang men around us laughed at my initiation into the sheep hide market.

The sheep hide market links the economics of mosques, built mainly around members' charity, with one of the chief commercial activities of Hui in the Northwest, "flipping" sheep hides for profit. About half of the hides come from animals raised and slaughtered in Qinghai and Tibet. These hides are trucked directly to processing centers located on the south side of the Da Xia River. The hides come from Hui who have donated animals to mosques, particularly during such festivals as Ramadan and ʿĪd-e-Qurbān when alms are said to count seventy more times than those given at other times of the year (Benthall and Bellion-Jourdan 2009b: 9). Mosque representatives subsequently sell these local hides "upstream" through the city via a sequence of middlemen who collect ever larger numbers of hides and, through flipping, drive up their price. After being flipped three or four times, the hides reach the market, where the final buyer and seller negotiate a sale. In the Linxia market, the second largest in the Gansu-Ningxia-Qinghai area, the hides are collected, assessed for quality, and loaded on trucks that transport them to tanneries, leather factories, and finally buyers and consumers in Henan and other eastern provinces. By the mid-2000s Linxia's sheep hide market was processing over five million hides per year and employing approximately five thousand people (Editorial Group 2008: 160).

From the vantage of mosques, taking animals donated by members as an expression of piety and turning them into a commodity is an essential practice and significant source of funding. Mosques depend on charity from members almost exclusively, since generally they do not receive support from the government. At the same time, the transformation of charity into a commodity raises important questions about how religious influences give rise to particular forms of secular, and especially economic, activity. Whereas political theologians (Kantorowicz 1997; Agamben 1998, 2011; Schmitt [1922] 2005) trace the roots of state power and sovereignty to the divine, their approach does not adequately provide a basis to understand how, among Hui, commercial exchange and profit derive from religious values. Like the echoes of the Protestant calling in worldly morality (Weber 1930), ethics of giving shape barter and exchange in the Hui social field. Specifically, sheep hide transactions occur through the mechanics of what Linxia Hui call "price pinching" (niejia),[1] which depend on the ethics of Muslim solidarity.

Being a Muslim is a necessary but ultimately insufficient condition for a successful exchange.[2] Skill in price pinching supplements piety, the

---

[1] An older term for this haggling technique is "handle the price inside the sleeve" (xiutong gaojia) and is found throughout the Northwest, although among Muslim minorities, including the Kazakhs in Altay, there are city-specific variations in its techniques. Niejia is a Northwest Chinese version of haggling (jiangjia), a method of negotiation found throughout Chinese society.

[2] There are a few Tibetan and Han truckers who bring hides directly from Qinghai and Tibet, but these men rarely engage in price pinching. Also, the processing centers often staff Dongxiang women, but price pinching seems primarily a male pastime.

two meeting in Hui attitudes toward business practices, especially toward cheating (*pianren*). Trust comes from familiarity, common faith and ethnicity, and sometimes even teaching-school membership. It also comes from the skill of the negotiator. A negotiation begins when a buyer assesses the price of a sheepskin based on its size, thickness and quality of the down under the hair, cut, and color. After this evaluation, the buyer raucously disparages the quality of the hide, to begin negotiating at the lowest price possible. As he does this, he takes the hand of the seller under his coat. The two men face each other as the buyer proceeds to pinch the seller's fingers. The purpose is to prevent other buyers from knowing the offered price. Only after the parties agree upon the price will the buyer cry out "*Uht!*" and then hold up a single yuan bill, which he must place into the hand of the seller. This part becomes physical as rivals attempt bodily to block the buyer. Up until the reform period, which saw a turn against the interpersonal violence of the Cultural Revolution, such movements commonly devolved into brawls. When the buyer succeeds in getting the note into the seller's hand, he cries "*Uht!*" and when the seller also yells "*Uht!*" the oral contract is formed. The buyer takes possession of the hides, and ownership is passed upon the seller's receipt of payment, which may come immediately thereafter or some time later. Buyers or their partners become sellers in the next transaction. Despite rising prices, their profit margin decreases as hides travel "upstream."[3]

The transaction becomes both dependent on and productive of piety: both buyer and seller ground the exchange in their mutual identity as Muslims. As one hide flipper said, "Between Muslims, we have the same belief [*xinyang*]. Our oral contract is written on our hearts. If one side transgresses the terms, Allah will punish him."[4] Trust as the basis for exchange is not limited to Linxia Hui but also characterizes transactions between Hui translators and Middle Eastern Muslims in such places as Yiwu. As one Hui businesswoman, a former female cleric from Inner Mongolia, told me, "[In Yiwu] we rely on oral agreements. These are not enforceable in PRC courts. If you write a contract, you need formalities. This is trouble." The informalization of procedures is partly a

[3] For instance, a sheep donated by a member of a mosque initially may be sold, hypothetically, for 50 yuan for a 50 yuan profit. At the next transaction, it may be sold for 75 yuan for a 25 yuan profit. Then 95 yuan for a 20 yuan profit, and so on until it reaches the processing centers, which make as little as 1 yuan per sheep hide and 5 to 10 yuan per ox hide. The market price creates a ceiling, and each "upstream" flipper makes profit on volume.

[4] Because distributors are mainly Han, Hui write contracts with them in the processing centers.

rejection of state law. Faith makes parties more accountable, because it is internally guaranteed; at the same time, it exposes parties to cheating, without recourse for those cheated to be "made whole" by the cheater. Price pinching also rejects formal Islamic contracts in favor of the ethics of solidarity.[5] Similarly, though it introduces risks, they are not as great as in the case of Yiwu's commodities market, where deals are for much larger sums and, oftentimes, one is negotiating with a stranger, not a next-door neighbor. In either case, however, pious ethics enables transactions and, in so doing, produces social relations, whether locally, as in the case of Hui-Hui negotiations in Linxia, or more globally, through Yiwu's commodities market.

The descriptive argument of this chapter is that Hui charitable giving reproduces their moral economy as a dimension of the Hui social field that lies largely outside of the state's purview. E. P. Thompson (1971) and James Scott (1977) developed the concept of moral economy to explain interactions between elite and peasants in the provision of basic goods. The core idea is that elite violation of commonly held norms legitimates peasants' rioting or other forms of resistance. Hui also have a sense of a moral economy, yet this diverges from the Thompson-Scott concept in the following ways: Hui moral economy concerns expectations about proper behavior involving giving and the ends to which one gives. It applies not just to subsistence but also to social welfare and property (its provision, transfer, or enjoyment) more generally. Unlike Thompson's "paternalist model" (1971: 95), the Hui conviction is that it is God, not the state, who provides through the *umma* (however defined by the teaching schools). Hui view the tie of paternalism as weaker than the eighteenth-century Englishmen in Thompson's study did, and the ethical center resides in the local Hui community, not in an authoritarian state. Moreover, while the teaching schools in Linxia present views as a consensus, that does not mean, as critiques of the concept of moral economy (e.g., Popkin 1979) have pointed out, that shared values and assumptions necessarily form a totalizing imperative. Rather, the moral economy is subject to individual reflection and manipulation (Laidlaw 2014).

The Hui moral economy comprises a certain set of ideas about how economic behavior constitutes "the good."[6] These ethical ideas are realized

---

[5] The Qur'an (2:282) encourages written contracts.

[6] Moral economy has been used by Communist scholars (An 2014) and in studies of reform-era China (Polachek 1983; Little 1989; Steinmüller 2013; Zhang 2011a).

through practice, internal consideration, and social interaction. As with other matters of religious belief, they are expressed publicly. As such, inner motivations are subject to public assessment, praise, debate, and scorn as well as private commentary, including disparagement or affirmation. The Hui moral economy enables their sociality; without it, Hui would not be able to raise their mosques, staff "scriptural hall education," or spread learning about the revealed sources. The Hui moral economy illustrates the pressures, internal and external, that define the boundary between the Hui social field and the Party-State.

My normative argument is that the Hui moral economy consists of dispositions and exchanges of property that are shaped by, but not wholly reducible to, "Islamic," "socialist," or "capitalist" models of economic behavior. The Hui moral economy is not necessarily more just than Islamic economics and is certainly not maximizing social welfare, as socialist and capitalist models purport to do; however, its value lies in its attempt to close the gap between such aspirations. "Islamic economics" emerged in the 1970s in the Middle East as an economic system that provided an alternative to Western, or postcolonial, capitalism as well as Soviet-led versions of socialism. Islamic economics comprises different fiscal behaviors, including charity, namely zakat and *awqāf*, as well as Islamic finance—that is, shariʿa-compliant financial instruments organized around the prohibition against interest (Ar. *ribā*). Following the 2007 global economic meltdown, economists from the Middle East and Southeast Asia have touted Islamic finance as an answer to the lack of ethics in investment and money management in Western capitalism.[7]

At the same time, Chinese scholars have trumpeted the "China model" of economic development for its stability and good governance as opposed to the volatility and weak regulatory oversight that has come to characterize democratic capitalism.[8] The China model is a statist approach to economic reform. The state opens markets to foreign direct investment while retaining ownership and control of key industries and requiring the banking industry to support state-owned companies. Crucially, the China model diverges from Western "law and development" orthodoxy by privileging such measures without political liberalization; this approach is the crux of the "socialist market economy."[9] Hui are at the forefront of linking Islamic economics and China's hybrid socialist-capitalist economy. They

---

[7] See, for instance, Çizakça (2011), Cattelan (2013), and Iqbal and Mirakhor (2013).

[8] For leading voices, see, e.g., Zhu et al. (2009).

[9] The "socialist market economy" was initially announced during the First Plenary Session of the Fourteenth Central Committee of the CCP, October 19, 1992.

do so through their moral economy and primarily through charity, based on extensive regional, national, and, increasingly, transnational business networks—a kind of "shadow finance" (Tsai 2002; Bolton, Santos, and Scheinkman 2012) that enables the growth of Hui communities.

This system is mostly *minjian*. The sheep hide market, for instance, which developed in the late Ming or Qing period, typifies Linxia as a node on the historic Silk Road and the deep localization of Islam in Hui commercial life. Its relationship to the state economy is complex. It operates in parallel with state-run industries (whether agriculture, forestry, or real estate), but its revenues are also bound up in secular markets. At the "supply" side of the sheep hide market, mosques, given their designation under PRC law as "religious activity areas," cannot run businesses. Islamic law, too, discourages profit earning within the space of a mosque.[10] Mosques depend on donations, because their legal status under applicable rules for both systems, secular and Islamic, limits the sources of their revenue. Likewise, at the consumption side of the sheep hide market, the sheep intestines are combined with pork and made into sausages for the consumption of Han in eastern China. The sheep hide market, born of gestures of Hui piety, is thus linked to other markets in Han cities. To summarize, the Hui moral economy is produced at the intersection of the religious and the commercial, *minjian* and national, and Hui and Han.

Economists from Karl Polanyi ([1944] 1957a) to Amartya Sen (1993) have emphasized that the deprivation of the material capabilities of people is a constraint on their ability to govern themselves.[11] The rest of this chapter explains how the gift upholds the moral economy of Hui as the wellspring of their ability to develop private markets. Hui build communities through voluntary donations as a *minjian* form of economy, which is, nonetheless, never completely delinked from the state economy. I turn to Linxia to evaluate the moral economy of giving that operates through conflicting ethical demands. Although Linxia has long served as an important market for Hui transactions, it is in practices of charity rather than the market that Islamic law and ethics matter most to Hui.

---

[10] The Chinese translation of the Egyptian jurist Sayyid Sabiq's writings on transactional law, entitled *Yisilan shangyefa* (*Islamic Commercial Law*), by the Salafi Muslim Youth Translators Group describes, in the Hanafi school, economic exchange within mosques as permitted, but because bringing goods into the mosque may contaminate its hygiene, it is reprehensible (*makrūh*) (Sabiq 2002: 21).

[11] Although their prescriptions for privatizing property rights differ, liberals and libertarians have also equated self-governance with ownership of property (Epstein 1997; cf. Kennedy 2006: 152–56; Ryan 1994). Hui *minjian* property differs from liberal views in that it is not necessarily based on rights guaranteed by the state but, rather, rights grounded in Islamic law and ethics.

Contrary to the argument of Marcel Mauss ([1950] 1990), whose theory of the gift has had an enduring influence over economic anthropology, the "freedom" of the gift[12] may reside less in its reciprocity than in the performance of legal and ethical obligations that undergird such gifting.

Next, I examine the nascent Islamic finance industry based in Ningxia Hui Autonomous Region, hereinafter, "Ningxia." Ningxia, about 580 kilometers from Linxia, is an important rival of Linxia in terms of the Islamic revival, and it has enjoyed opportunities unknown to the Linxia Hui. In Ningxia, Islamic banking shows the consequences of the Party-State's integration of a community-based initiative for development into the official banking system. In including both charitable giving and commercial transactions within the Hui moral economy, I follow the insights of the "substantive" economic anthropologists, who observed that such economic behaviors (whether disposition or exchange) are part of larger social systems.[13] Extending this line of thought, a number of major theorists of economic anthropology have sought to bring gift exchange into the same analytical purview as more conventional "economic" transactions.[14] In this case, the mosque community, organized according to the teaching schools, is the larger social organization that incorporates the resources of Hui families. I conclude by addressing how the Hui moral economy offers an alternative understanding of money from capitalist ideas of interest maximization, as expressed either in the West or in postsocialist China.

A MARKET TOWN WITHOUT A MARKET

The renaissance of Islam in China requires considerable material resources. Hui are building mosques at a remarkable rate across the "Qur'an belt" between Lanzhou and Linxia in southwest Gansu, and there are similar zones of development in Qinghai and Ningxia as well.

---

[12] The basic notion of the "free gift" is that it is a gift that does not require a counter-gift and thereby violates the principle of exchange at the heart of Mauss's definition of economy. For literature on the free gift, see Douglas (1990), Laidlaw (2000), and Hann (2006).

[13] The substantivists responded to the formalists in a debate that defined anthropology in the 1960s. Briefly, the formalists believed that the model of the market, developed mainly in Western industrial states, could be applied to non-Western societies (e.g., Firth 1938). Substantivists critiqued the idea of a self-regulating market. Instead, they analyzed the processes through which societies provisioned themselves, including not just market-based transactions but also reciprocity and redistribution, as well as parts of wider systems (Bohannan 1959; Polanyi 1957b; Dalton 1961, 1965). David Graeber (2001) has argued that theoretical debates in the discipline from the 1980s onward reframed issues broached but ultimately left unresolved by the substantivists and formalists.

[14] See Bourdieu (1977), Appadurai (1988), and Mauss ([1950] 1990).

Once constructed, mosques require maintenance. There are additional costs for the living expenses of clerics and students, madrasas, educational supplies, and goods for religious holidays. Generally, Muslims have a number of ways to finance their religious communities, including business, internal donations, civil society and foundations, state funding, and international aid. Hui have developed such resources, in spite of the fact that the state has placed legal restrictions on civil society organizations and does not normally provide subsidies to mosques or other religious institutions, and the fact that, as mentioned, under both PRC and Islamic law, mosques face restrictions against engaging in business activities. As a result of such limitations, mosque finances derive primarily from donations from members who own proprietorships or family businesses that may entail regional, national, or even transnational commercial networks. One of the most remarkable aspects of China's Islamic revival is that Hui are able to finance religious practice and institutions despite constraints imposed by the Party-State. How they accumulate and manage property to develop such mosque communities reveals the interpenetration of localized Islamic law and formal law in the Hui social field.

Generally, Hui in the Northwest regions have looked to Hui business networks and charity as the primary means of building their communities, and charitable giving has become one of the main activities through which they express their piety. At the same time, Han Chinese notions of gifting have shaped Hui charitable practices. The state also intervenes in beneficence when its regulations touch upon land issues. Hui moral economy in the economic sphere thus takes the form of a struggle to piously support their communities while navigating between the influence of the Han gift economy and state-imposed limitations. In what follows, I examine how Linxia Hui are developing "China's Little Mecca" despite the state's imposition in the Northwest of considerable controls on transnational Islam.

By the measure of per capita net income for rural households, Gansu is the poorest province in China (National Bureau of Statistics 2012: 366). Gansu is also one of the provinces targeted for the "Great Western Development Policy" (GWDP), started in 2000. Sometimes referred to in the literature as "Opening the West," the GWDP has aimed to decrease the regional inequality between eastern and western China through governmental investment, fiscal transfers, tax incentives, credit support, and initiatives to attract foreign direct investment. As part of the GWDP, the state has invested in infrastructural projects and urbanization to stimulate migration to the cities, with the aim of growing a consumer class, including in such places as Linxia.

According to the policy rationales of the GWDP, foreign direct investment would supplement state subsidies, but to date the region has attracted little foreign investment. Interethnic tension and instability create an environment unattractive to investors, but many people I spoke with also suggest that rather than incentivizing international investment in Gansu, Qinghai, and most parts of Xinjiang, the central government discourages foreign investment. The popular conception among foreign observers is that Xinjiang is tightly controlled, and "inner China" is more loosely governed; in reality, however, there is a gradation. While Xinjiang remains much more strictly controlled than elsewhere in Northwest China, affairs in Gansu and Qinghai, including economic matters, are also subject to considerable oversight by the government.

The Hui moral economy, through which teaching schools cultivate overlapping ideas of what constitutes ethical management of finances, is, as a result of the Party-State's control, primarily a local matter. The state-imposed closure of Hui and Tibetan areas of Gansu as well as portions of eastern Qinghai makes mosques dependent on local funding sources. The entrenched role of the teaching schools, as arbiters of orthopraxy, has further sharpened conflicts attendant to the ethics of money. As in other conflicts about Islamic law, the critical focus is the presence of pre- or non-Islamic customs in Hui practices.

To assess Hui business as the primary source of charity, I consider two common types of charitable giving: voluntary donations (*nietie*) and pious endowments (*awqāf*). The former shows Hui trying to follow Islamic law shaped by Chinese customs, whereas the latter demonstrates how state socialist law constrains Muslim altruism. Taken together, the examples underscore the ethical dilemmas of the so-called "free gift" in the Hui context. Hui ethicized reflections concerning these conflicting demands present windows into reconsidering the "freedom" of such gifts. Rather than equating the "free," or "pure," gift with non-reciprocity, the Hui case suggests that following Islamic law and ethics, and specifically voluntary giving, is itself a form of freedom.

"In the East, there is Wenzhou. In the West, there is Hezhou" (*Dong you Wenzhou, xi you Hezhou*). People in Linxia (formerly Hezhou) often repeat this phrase, attributed to the anthropologist Fei Xiaotong during one of his visits there in the 1980s (Fei 1987). The expression means that Linxia is the Northwest equivalent of the prosperous commercial city of Wenzhou on the coast. Specifically, the phrase extols the role of private enterprise and trade networks in building local and regional economies. When China scholar A. Doak Barnett visited Linxia in 1988, officials who received him reiterated the phrase. Indeed, Barnett lauded Linxia as a "remarkable enclave of modernity," making particular reference to its benefiting from economic reforms in the 1980s (Barnett 1993: 246–53). More than twenty years later, official propaganda outlets and local newspapers such as the Ethnic Daily (Minzu ribao) regularly repeat Fei's comparison.

Yet when contemporary Bafang Hui mouth the expression, their tone is mocking. Hui and Han alike bemoan Linxia's economic condition. A common way to pass the time in Linxia is to sip fine green tea in a Bafang courtyard, tend the coal-burning furnace, and gripe about the city. If economic prosperity is the national desire, then Hui in Linxia feel left behind. Many Bafang Hui complain of the poor condition of their households and blame the local government, which they see as favoring the Han. Other Hui I spoke with blame Linxia's proximity to Tibet, a "non-development zone" (bu kaifa qu).

Linxia Han hold a different view. A farmer whose land in a peri-urban collection of Han farms on Linxia's eastern outskirts has been requisitioned for development deplores the Hui favoritism of the local government. "It's a systematic problem, a vicious circle. The Hui benefit from the policies without any true merit or hard work. Once they become leaders, they have no work ability, nor do they have the cultural level to handle problems." "If I have money, I can buy you an official. They all want your money," his neighbor, also Han, complains. A young Dongxiang Sufi cadre in the Linxia City government vents:

> Linxia has not received the investment it needs to develop. Places like Yiwu are totally different, as all the central government's money goes there. For Linxia to be a trade center, it would need a highway,[15] a railroad,[16] an airport,[17] modern infrastructure[18] ... these are just basics ... but

---

[15] Linxia historically was the hub of a network of roads linking southern Gansu and Tibet to Lanzhou. Because of the steep loess mountains that divide Linxia from Lanzhou, the state has been unable to cut highway access through to Linxia. The route taken by most buses and transport trucks is a second-class highway, built in the 1990s, which follows a route through the Qur'an belt of Guanghe County. A second route, opened in 2009, cuts an artery through the mountains of Dongxiang Autonomous County but is far too steep for most trucks or buses. In 2011 a third route, the Kanglin highway, was completed, which may meet some of the transportation demand. There is one second-class highway, completed in 2005, that links Linxia to Hezuo and southern Gansu.

[16] There are no trains that pass through Linxia, although there has been talk for years of putting a line through the plain beyond North Mountain.

[17] The nearest airport to Linxia is over two hundred kilometers away.

[18] Where residents of Linxia do see capital investment facilitating traffic and trade, it does not benefit them and may even further marginalize them. A proprietor in Bafang complained

269

most importantly, it needs resources, human talent, and a necessary production base. It lacks all of these things. Historically, yes, Linxia played an important role via the tea-horse trade and Silk Road, but that was in the context of the empire. Things are totally different now. Planes, e-commerce, and so on have all replaced the need for a middle-point in China.

While there is no shortage of blame circulated and rationales for the plateauing of Linxia's economy vary, one explanation struck me as particularly salient. A Hui woman born and raised in Bafang, and married to a Hui government official, articulated this view, which was held by others with whom I spoke: "Linxia never changes. It hasn't changed in thirty years. You look at cities out east and how modern they are. Our government is controlled by the Han. They don't want Linxia to develop. They are afraid of so-called China's Little Mecca attracting terrorists." Such perceptions, which are common in Linxia, give evidence to the view that after 2009 the category "Muslim" warrants strict scrutiny by the government, even beyond ethnic distinctions.

Security trumps economics in Linxia, which is inconveniently located between two security zones. The most glaring example of the priority of social stability over economic well-being in the Northwest was the government's shutting down of the Internet in Xinjiang the day after the riots of July 5, 2009. Because the riots were allegedly incited by members of the Uyghur diaspora through social media, the authorities imposed an Internet blackout. Internet restrictions continued for another six months. Similarly, travel was restricted across the Xinjiang border during this period. As a result of the security restrictions, some experts estimate that Xinjiang lost RMB 20 billion in tourism revenue alone (Du and Haimiti 2011: 17). Similarly, following the Tibetan riots on March 14, 2008, travel was restricted in Gannan Tibetan Autonomous Prefecture (hereinafter "Gannan"), which shares Linxia Prefecture's southern border. As several of the demonstrations carried out by Tibetan monks occurred in Gannan, authorities closed the area to foreign tourists for the following two years. Even though tourism is one of the major industries of Gannan, closing the prefecture to such a revenue source was not given second thought.

Such examples from the Northwest show that "coercive closure" of Chinese communities can occur not only as a result of dynastic cycles,

that the Qinghai-Tibet railroad, completed in 2006 to much international fanfare, has broken Linxia's hold as the gateway to Tibet.

as Skinner (1971) hypothesized at the macro level, but also as a result of responses to ongoing interethnic violence. The closure of Linxia, however, is different from that of Xinjiang or Gannan. The causes of its closure are not proximate and "hot" but enduring and potential. From the view of the Party-State, the negative externalities of Islamic extremism and the risk of antistate activity taking root in Linxia outweigh the loss of economic viability through regional and international integration. Linxia gives evidence of China's "trapped transition," by which market and political developments under authoritarian rule lose their momentum (Pei 2006).

Linxia no longer holds the same strategic importance as a gate into Tibet and Xinjiang that it once did before the reform period. That is, while Linxia remains a regional crossroads between the Qinghai-Tibet plateau and the Han-dominated lowlands to the east, the nature of the market has changed in the course of China's economic modernization. The GWDP—under which the central government has invested in infrastructural projects, including highways, railways, irrigation canals, and dams—has altered the regional economy, with disparate effects on local populations. As Skinner (1965) presciently observed, technology obviates many market towns as goods, services, money, and credit "leapfrog" smaller markets for larger ones based in provincial capitals, coastal cities, or markets outside of China.

The agricultural, meat-processing, and forestry industries that sustained the local economy during the 1980s have not grown in pace with national development. Barnett (1993: 263) reported that while revenues of the Linxia Prefecture government had increased 124-fold in 1987 compared with 1950, its expenditures had grown 189-fold, so that the government suffered a deficit of RMB 96.55 million, which was offset by subsidies from the provincial government. According to official statistics, the deficit in Linxia in 1986 was RMB 394,000. By 1995 expenditures had grossly outstripped revenue, so that the deficit mushroomed to RMB 19.3 million (Linxia City Chronicles Committee 2011: 261), making the municipal government dependent on higher-level government grants.

Private and collective industries, such as construction, chemical manufacturing, leather and carpet production, and food service, continue to have a strong hand in Linxia's commercial economy. By 2005 privately owned enterprises employed some 28,000 people and accounted for 78 percent of the city's total economic output (Linxia City Chronicles Committee 2011: 220). Yet private enterprise has proven mostly inadequate in ensuring that Linxia keeps up with Hui regional rivals, such as Ningxia.

Hui in Linxia have encountered difficulty translating China's Little Mecca into a money-making enterprise. For example, Linxia Hui entrepreneurs have established halal food factories, and there are about a half dozen such factories in and around Linxia City. Most are family-owned operations that manufacture halal meats, dairy products, cookies, and candies. Yet only one enterprise has been able to acquire the necessary licenses to produce halal foodstuffs for export abroad. Such bureaucratic impediments handicap Linxia.

Some Hui businessmen complain that there are few incentives to build enterprises in Linxia. Indeed, the local government's financial policies have worked to stifle entrepreneurship. In 1994 the central government enacted a tax reform that shifted a significant share of fiscal revenues from local governments to the central government but did not proportionally reassign expenditure responsibilities to the central government; local governments thus ended up with less than half their prior revenues even as they were responsible for 77 percent of public expenditures (Man and Hong 2010).[19] In response, local governments have increased taxation on primary and secondary industries. In Linxia, these industries, including agriculture, forestry, and husbandry, do not generate significant revenue in the form of value-added tax. At the same time, increased taxes have strangled entrepreneurship in these industries. Following revisions to the land value-added tax in 2007, local governments became increasingly dependent on land sales to finance their debt. One of the main sources of land-sale revenue is expropriating collectively owned land that is then sold to developers for massive profits. During the ten-year period from 1995 to 2005, revenue from land tax increased by 79 percent (Linxia City Chronicles Committee 2011: 280).

The government's solution to Linxia's blighted economy has been to build. In 2009 the government began an urbanization project to expand Linxia eastward, effectively quadrupling the area of the city. The urbanization plan is part of a nationwide effort to relocate rural populations to the cities in order to expedite national development. In official documents, the project is known as "build a new district in the east, build a

---

[19] The GWDP has offered preferential tax policies to governments in western China. These include a reduced income tax rate for those enterprises (domestic and foreign) that conduct business in categories that are encouraged by the central government, and up to two years of tax exemptions for domestic enterprises working in those categories (Lu and Deng 2011: 4). During my time in Linxia, however, I did not come across evidence of a single foreign-invested enterprise, and Hui entrepreneurs did not mention GWDP-related tax reductions or exemptions.

park in the west." The initial design called for urban expansion to the west of Bafang, but Hui mass gathering and protest halted the proposed plan. The portion of the valley east of Linxia, while more rural than the western district, is dotted with mosques,[20] and one Sufi village there has blocked demolition, even though thugs hired by the local government have kidnapped and beaten up village leaders. The plans for the urbanization of the eastern district continue apace, however, with the idea that Hui from the countryside around Linxia will move to the city and become urban consumers. The city government has invested RMB 1.18 billion in the urbanization project (Linxia Prefecture Government 2012).

Bafang itself, which remained relatively untouched during the reform era, is also slated for urbanization, or as it is known among Bafang Hui, "moving from a single-story to a multistory building." The first high-rise was built in the Old Glory Mosque community in 1995 (see Figure 6.1). Two additional high-rise complexes were constructed in the south end of Bafang in 2010. Upon returning to Bafang in 2012, I discovered high-rises on all four sides of the old Muslim quarter. Bafang Hui are highly ambivalent about the reconstruction of Linxia. Some Bafang families aspire to move to a high-rise where they will have a brand-new apartment with central heating and, they hope, a view of Bafang neighborhoods below. Like Han Chinese, they equate a modern apartment with material success. One study, based on a survey of cadres, found that 70 percent of respondents consider urbanized life "good" (Gao 2005: 64).[21]

On the other hand, urbanization has resulted in the demolition of courtyard homes held in families for generations, resulting in protest.[22] In October 2009 residents of Small South Lane, a neighborhood of sixty families, organized a "rights defense" (weiquan) campaign when developers sought to illegally enter into direct negotiations with the residents to intimidate them, rather than go through relevant government bureaus. By employing the official rhetoric of state law and citing local regulations, residents gained attention from the government and were successful in raising the amount of their "property switch" compensation from a ratio of 1:1.5 to

[20] According to one official, originally four mosques were to be razed for the urbanization plan. As of 2015, the mosques were still in negotiation with the developers about their relocation and the amount of compensation, although one mosque had managed to change the course of a street to preserve its location.
[21] As of 2010, graduate students have been conducting their own surveys, not exclusively based on government officials.
[22] Several studies have been conducted on the impact of "demolition and relocation" (chaiqian) and resettlement on urban Hui (Bai 2005; Liang 2006; Yang 2007).

Figure 6.1 An aerial view of Bafang, looking southeast, taken from Bafang's first high-rise

Source: the author

1:1.7.[23] Unlike conflicts in Han neighborhoods, this collective action was based on the preexisting residential-based collectivity of the mosque community.

One consequence of urbanization is the rearrangement of mosque communities based on teaching-school divisions. For example, residents of Bafang's first high-rise[24] are not the residents of the previous court-yard homes.[25] Instead, many are wealthier Hui families, with an average monthly income of 4,077 yuan (i.e., twice that of the average Bafang resident) and a civil servant as the family head (36.2 percent). They are not

---

[23] This means that the residents are given space in the new high-rise that is 1.7 times greater than the surface area of their original home. However, residents must then pay the developer for the difference in property value between their original home and the high-rise apartment. Furthermore, residents must pay for utilities, which are a luxury to most Bafang residents.

[24] The complex that obtained full occupancy of 238 families in 2006 consists of four towers of four-teen floors. In 2006 the price for an apartment was 1,760 yuan per square meter. In 2010 it had risen to 3,400 yuan per square meter.

[25] I collected data from 58 of the 238 families in the complex, or 24.4 percent of the total number of residents.

all Gedimu, the teaching school of the closest mosque, but rather a mixture of three different teaching-school communities. While the mixing of teaching-school communities may not necessarily decrease the importance of teaching-school identity, and indeed cohabitation may intensify such distinctions, initial conversations suggest that many residents, after moving, attend the closest mosque, whether or not it belongs to their teaching school. The purchase of an apartment, an aspiration shared by Chinese throughout the country, thus may facilitate homogenization of Islamic doctrine. From the vantage of the Party-State, growing a Hui urban middle class may not only provide a stronger base for domestic consumption but may also mollify inter-teaching-school frictions.

In 2012 the newly appointed Party head of Linxia Prefecture gave a speech announcing plans to make Bafang into an "ethnic tourist attraction." Thus, urban development proceeds apace in Linxia, but cautiously, and under the close direction of the local government, so as to avoid making Linxia attractive to Uyghurs. As one Bafang resident stated, "Linxia is developing, yes, there are more apartment high-rises, but this isn't necessarily good for our religion." The long-term impact of urbanization is difficult to predict but may lead to the dissolution of the tight networks within neighborhoods, and the uncanny combination of ghettoization and sterilization of Bafang, not unlike the ethnic urban dystopias of Lhasa and Kashgar.

THE FREEDOM OF THE GIFT

Due to state controls that limit the capacity of Hui to connect with Muslims overseas, in most of the Northwest the Hui moral economy is understood in local terms. In charity, Hui find a means to unite their desire to follow Islamic law and ethics with the practical needs of their mosque. Mosque members' voluntary donations (*nietie*) are the primary source of funding for mosques and madrasas and a chief expression of piety among Hui. Donations are made not just at mosque services, but also at weddings, funerals, Sufi saint memorial dates, and other life-cycle events. Charity is broadly consonant with Chinese socialism, and philanthropists have been in the limelight in recent years in the wealthier cities in eastern China.

Unlike secular philanthropy, however, Hui charity originates in divine injunctions. It also has been influenced by Han Chinese practices of giving. Hui beneficence raises questions about the "free" gift—that is, unilateral disbursements, often given as a result of religious obligations.

Whereas *nietie* is a "total system of gift" (Douglas 1990: ix), the "freedom" of the gift has conventionally been construed as non-reciprocity. But Hui charity demonstrates that its freedom resides in its conveyance in accordance with Islamic ethics. At the same time, competitiveness and egoism, which are universal human qualities, have entered into *nietie*, through practices that look very similar to the Han gift economy. As a result, Hui confront quandaries, including whether to pursue altruism or rivalry. A young Hui official frames the dilemma in the following way: "Certainly, someone can lose face in regards to *nietie*. This happens all the time. If two men are of the same relative socioeconomic position and one gives more than the other, then the one who does not give as much will lose face and must make up for it. The fact that all the *nietie* numbers are publicly displayed in the mosque courtyard makes it hard for someone not to lose face in this circumstance." As the official explains, donation may become self-interested, violating Islamic law. Self-interest has been a puzzle in understanding the "free" gift, which would otherwise appear to preclude selfish motives (Bourdieu 1977: 171; Laidlaw 2000: 627). In giving "free" gifts, Hui adopt different strategies to reconcile the conflicting demands of Islamic rules governing voluntary donation and Chinese customs of gifting.

The ethics of gifting

Although state law has prohibited Hui from establishing charitable organizations that could potentially accept funds from Muslims nationally and internationally, it does permit Hui to donate to mosques as "religious activity areas." Members of a mosque community give charitably in one of three ways: *nietie* (voluntary donations), the obligatory zakat (an annual contribution of a specified percentage of an individual's income), and *awqāf* (pious endowments). I concentrate on the first and third as examples of localized Islamic law and the cornerstones of Hui moral economy.

Without income generated through *nietie*, mosques could not function in China. Nearly every mosque in the Northwest has a placard in the central courtyard upon which is written the amounts donated by individual members or families of the mosque (see Figure 6.2). Such signs are also commonly found in Daoist temples, although most Hui do not entertain the comparison, for to do so would be to acknowledge syncretism in their practice of Islam. Men, in coming or going, will pass by this sign and give it a quick once-over or linger before it, making a mental note of donors.

Nietie is the principal source of funds for the upkeep of all of a mosque's physical property, books for the library and madrasas, teachers'

Figure 6.2 Xidaotang collecting *nietie* on the birthday of the Prophet Muhammad in 2012

Source: the author

salaries, the clerics' maintenance, utilities, all costs for students, and food and edibles for holidays and special observances. A mosque's inflow of funds from *nietie*, in turn, is determined by the number of men who regularly attend the Friday service. Large mosques have an accountant who records donations. *Nietie* is seen at all major life-cycle events, including births, weddings, and funerals, where family members and friends will donate money to parents, the newlyweds and their cleric, or relatives of the deceased, respectively. *Nietie* is also one of the ways in which Hui link their traditional practices to the building of the Chinese nation-state (Gillette 2000: 177).[26] After disasters such as the 2008 Wenchuan earthquake in Sichuan Province and the 2010 Yushu earthquake in Qinghai Province, for example, Hui communities collected *nietie* for government-sponsored disaster relief. Through such public acts of charity, Hui reconcile their ethical obligations as Muslims and their duties as Chinese citizens.

Nietie, which could be called the linchpin of Hui financial and spiritual life, is based upon conceptual slippage, evidencing the localization of Islam. The Arabic referent for *nietie* is *niyya*, which means "intent" or "intention" (Schacht 1964: 116; Bourdieu 1977: 173). As anthropologist Lawrence Rosen explains, while Muslims declare *niyya* at the start of each prayer as a specifically religious sign of an act arising from the heart, *niyya* has also been a central concept in law, both in criminal contexts, where it is part of determining the seriousness of an offense, and in civil affairs, where it is required to determine the validity of a bequest or contract (Rosen 1984: 49–52; 1989: 51–52). In the original Arabic, the term applies exclusively to the motivation or volition behind the gifting, rather than the thing itself.

The legal basis for what the Hui call *nietie* is *ṣadaqa*. In some hadith, *ṣadaqa* is understood as an expression of one's love for God and an act that absolves sin. As a Yihewani cleric stated, "Giving alms leads to rewards from Allah in the afterlife." The Arabic word *ṣadaqa* is cognate with the Hebrew term for "justice" (Singer 2008: 4). It is this meaning that Mauss ([1950] 1990: 18) cites as root for the Arabic, and the term *ṣadaqa* has retained echoes of this definition along with its more commonly understood meaning of gift or alms. Among Hui, to give *ṣadaqa* is to recognize divine right in this world.

Hui linguistic terms for giving reflect the ambiguity caused by the influence of Han gifting practices. In mosques and tomb complexes, *nietie* is often spoken of alongside such terms as "donate money" (*juankuan*), "donate property" (*juanzi*), "give alms" (*shishe*), and "collect donations" (*mujuan*). Often, the Chinese verb-object construction does not distinguish between the thing given and the act of giving. Hui linguistic vernacularization—for example, *wo gei/song/juan nietie* ("I give/gift/donate nietie")—suggests that Hui think of *nietie* as the material object given, the thing itself, in accordance with the ethics of the Chinese gift economy (Yang 1994; Yan 1996; Kipnis 1997).

---

[26] Muslim charity work is standard content on Muslim websites (see, e.g., China Muslim Youth Net 2010).

Nietie blurs the distinction in the anthropology of gifts between Mauss's reciprocated gift and the "free" gift. Mauss rebuked Malinowski's notion of the pure, or "free," gift, arguing that all gifts, even those of the Trobrianders, are reciprocated (Mauss [1950] 1990: 73), and indeed Malinowski later revised his analysis to emphasize reciprocity. Reappraisals of Mauss, particularly through the example of *dana* in Hinduism (Parry 1986) and Jainism (Laidlaw 2000), suggest Mauss's criticism of Malinowski may have been overreaching. In its sense as *ṣadaqa*, *nietie* is similar to *thaan* (also from the Sanskrit *dana*) in Theravada Buddhism (Bowie 1998). Nonetheless, even within the logic of such gifts, the donation is not "free" but rather an exchange: veneration of a deity or its representative that, in return, absolves the donor's sin or accrues her merit, and thus confers cosmic or future returns.

As the currency of Muslim communities' moral economy and a localized practice of Islamic law, *nietie* also entails aspects of Mauss's (i.e., social or inter-personal) gift. Specifically, *nietie* exhibits the sociality of the Chinese gift economy, which is based on the ethics of social connections (*guanxi*) and the conferral of respect to superiors or "face" (*mianzi*). In Daoist practices, donors follow these ethics in giving privately, whereas public giving is strictly tributary, or "free" (Yang 2005: 132). Hui donating may also be done in private or public. Similarly, donating may be motivated by a number of compulsions, including self-interest.

Hui thus conceive of *nietie* as a reified *thing* that embodies Islamic and Chinese rules of giving. Egoistic behavior violates the Islamic rule that donation may benefit the donor by expiating sin but should not be given to further the donor's interests in this world.[27] In giving alms, Hui are aware of other mosque members' donations. *Nietie* combines an awareness of social relationships with an act of piety. It is at this level that Chinese notions of "face" enter the social observance of *nietie*, as remarked upon by the young official. As Mauss ([1950] 1990: 15–16, 65) noted, charity is not free of antagonism. So while Chinese Muslims are hardly unique in their self-consciousness about giving, their customization of *ṣadaqa* reflects a particularly Chinese way of maintaining social status. Unlike conceptions of *ṣadaqa* among Arab Muslims,[28] Chinese custom has put a "face" on intention and, in the process, made it material, thing-like.

---

[27] See Q. 76:8–9.

[28] This is not to say that Arab Muslims, or Berbers for that matter, shy away from potlatch-like contests of giving (see, e.g., Jamous 1981).

Given such ethical confusion, different doctrinal schools among Hui make sense of the tensions in *nietie* in a variety of ways. Opinions over Sufi *nietie* practices highlight the differences between Gedimu, Sufis, and Xidaotang, on the one hand, and Yihewani and Salafis, on the other. Yihewani and Salafis seek greater adherence to "pure" shari'a and promote stricter rules about giving. For example, donations are to be given to the mosque's accountant. Scripturalists such as the Yihewani, who are predisposed to finding evidence of modernity in the Qur'an, conceive of *nietie* as an Islamic income distribution system. So while giving alms absolves the sins of the donor, it ultimately "ensures social equality." Thus, the social and secular aims of *nietie* are harmonized with its religious importance in the Yihewani interpretation.

Sufis regard *nietie* as particularly vital to the operation of their tomb complexes, sites of pilgrimage for tens of thousands of followers on the anniversary of the death of the order's founding saint. Donations cover all costs of the tomb complex (e.g., maintenance and repairs, costs of students, the living expenses of the shaykh, the tomb manager's living expenses, food for celebrations, and so on). A teaching cleric from the Grand Tomb Complex in Linxia, the center of the Qadiriyya Sufi order in China, observes, "The zakat is more important from the vantage of Islamic law, but the *nietie* is the real money maker." For instance, the Glory Mosque Tomb Complex, resting place of Ma Laichi, founder of the Khufiyya path in China, grossed some RMB 700,000 by the sixth day of the celebration in 2010.

The Sufi practice of *nietie* is to give copiously to the shaykh, as Sufis believe the shaykh can intercede on their behalf and transmit God's blessing to them. The Sufi shaykh will go to homes of followers to conduct a prayer of invocation (Ar. *du'ā'*), often on behalf of a sick family member, and receive donations in return. The shaykh is supposed to then use the offerings for the benefit of the order. However, charges of corruption are common. The shaykh of the Grand Tomb Complex has been attacked by non-Sufis (and Sufis, too) for selling cows donated during Ramadan for his personal profit. The relationship between the shaykh and his followers bears similarity to that of Daoist shamans and their clients (Yang 2005: 132), as governed by the ethics of Chinese gift exchange.

The marketization of Chinese society, even in such relatively poor western cities as Linxia, has exacerbated gaps between the wealthy and the disadvantaged, as can be seen in their different capacities to give. One young Sufi blushed in remarking, "A follower gave [the shaykh] a brand new Toyota SUV, which is worth RMB 700,000. He uses this for his personal transportation!" While hypocrisy is a common problem among self-proclaimed holy men (see, e.g., Gilsenan 1982: 9; Ewing 1997: 63), envy among Hui comes at a particularly critical juncture in China's economic modernization and the Party-State's call for unity among Muslims. Some Hui have also benefited from the material conditions afforded by the "get rich is glorious" maxim of Deng Xiaoping, and conspicuous consumption and display of material assets demonstrate how the market economy has become wedded to the gift economy.[29] Yet material excess may militate against Islamic piety, and further exacerbate teaching-school tensions. Scripturalists and the government alike strongly oppose such practices as institutionalized gift giving as exploitative, and both inveigh against the problem of commodities taking the form of gifts (see generally Venkatesan 2011), though on different grounds. Yihewani, for instance, base their disapproval on their reading of the revealed texts, whereas the Party-State labels such practices as "feudal," a violation of the tenets of Marxism-Leninism.

Altruism and competition thus may exist side by side in Hui charitable giving practices, complicating assumptions of the uniformity of intent. The conflicts that Hui must navigate when making voluntary donations are also apparent in the giving of real property. As voluntary charity, *awqāf* are a subset of *ṣadaqa*. Whereas *nietie* illustrate tensions between Islamic ethics and Chinese custom, *awqāf* point to the Hui capacity to follow Islamic law in spite of state law's constraints.

Pious endowments through socialist property rights
Despite state law preventing the transfer of property to establish pious endowments, Northwest Hui are founding different versions of *awqāf* (sing. *waqf*) as another aspect of the Hui moral economy. According to Islamic law, the *waqf* is a complex institution that lies at the intersection of property, administrative, and inheritance law.[30] *Awqāf* assume two main forms, including "public *awqāf*," which are donated by the founder for the benefit of the poor or public utilities, much like a trust under Anglo-American common law, and "family *awqāf*," which, as the name indicates, are granted for the benefit of heirs and agnates. The former

---

[29] For a partial list of sources on this topic, see Smart (1993), Smart and Hsu (2013), Yang (2002), and Osburg (2013).

[30] Regarding literature on the "classical" *waqf*, see Leeuwen (1999) for the Ottoman Empire; McChesney (1991) for Central Asia; and Powers (1999) for the Maghrib. For studies that examine the survival and revival of *awqāf* in colonial, postcolonial, or secular regimes, see, e.g., Reiter (1996), Husain (1939), and Kozlowski (2008).

is more prominent among Hui, and so I limit my discussion to "public" forms of *awqāf*, although the descriptor "public" is misleading in the China case, as most property transfers are *minjian*.[31] As a Salafi *minjian ahong* (unofficial cleric) expressed:

> We see the clearest conflict between state law and shari'a in the area of inheritance law ... The shops [*puzi*] one sees outside Chinese mosques are not true *awqāf*. At one time, they were. But we don't have a recording. We have lost the name of the donor. A true *waqf* is a donation from a mosque member to the *waqf* for public benefit. Historically, there have been many of these in Linxia. [Now] nearly every mosque has its *awqāf*, but these are not public [*bu gongkai*, a euphemism for "illegal"].

While *awqāf* are important as a material representation of the capacity of Hui to circumvent the limits that secular law imposes on Islamic legal practice, at the same time they underscore some of the contradictions of Hui charity.

According to Islamic law, to qualify as a *waqf*, the founder must (1) own rights in the property and (2) convey them for the public good in perpetuity (Powers 1999: 1171–73). The founder gives up all property rights in the object. Once the conveyance is concluded, the object is considered to be the property of God.[32] Unlike *niyya*, the term *waqf* refers both to the act of transferring property for some charitable purpose and to the property itself (McChesney 1991: 6). However, neither (1) nor (2), the elements of the *waqf*, are legal under PRC property law.

Before the Communist period, Chinese Muslims used *awqāf* for a variety of purposes (Li 2000: 51). Additionally, there were welfare foundations that served pilgrims on the hajj and Sufis traveling to holy sites in South Asia (Bakhtyar 2000: 40). In Linxia, many mosques and Sufi tomb complexes were initially built through a *waqf* donation. The Old Glory Mosque (est. 1368), the Naqshbandi-Mujaddidi Sufi Bright Heart Mosque (est. 1978), and the New Glory Mosque (est. 1946) are just some of the Linxia mosques built on land donated in the form of *awqāf*. Similarly, many Sufi tomb complexes were constructed on land gifted to the order as *awqāf*.

---

[31] The institution of the *waqf* spread through Central Asia, Afghanistan, and into China after the formation of the Hanafi *fiqh* on *awqāf* in the eighth and ninth centuries (Hennigan 2004). As a result, *awqāf* have a long history in Hui communities throughout China. There are mosque steles dating from at least the Ming era memorializing land grants to mosques (Yu and Lei 2001).

[32] The *Sharh al-Wiqaya*, the Hanafi commentary that is used in nearly all mosques in Linxia and throughout the Northwest, contains a chapter on donations, including the *waqf*.

The classical Islamic idea of a *waqf* and its Chinese instantiation diverged in the mid-twentieth century as a result of the creation of the modern state. Nationalization of land was a priority of the Communists in the 1950s. The large tracts of land held by Sufi tombs and mosques as *awqāf*, in their view, buttressed the landlord class and were requisitioned under the land reform. Before 1949 Sufi tombs had been particularly dependent on *awqāf* as sources of income. Under the socialist property regime, ownership rights in land are held by the state (Erie 2007). While individuals may obtain land use rights for thirty years in the countryside and seventy years in the city, they can only sell and transfer the latter.[33] The current property regime thereby militates against pious endowments established in perpetuity. Many Sufis report that due to extra restrictions on tomb complex finances, they are no longer legally allowed to hold pious endowments and so are doubly dependent on "internal funding"— that is, *nietie*.

The status of land use rights in the Northwest is tied to the historical relationship between property and religion. In the early Communist period, mosque lands were guaranteed legal protection. The land reform began in 1952 in Linxia but was mired by violence when cadres redistributed Sufi lands without observing legal protection of *awqāf* (Khan 1963: 68). Furthermore, the 1958 "struggle against the privileges of feudalism and religion" campaign and the 1966 Cultural Revolution entailed the destruction and burning of most mosques and Sufi tombs. At the start of the reform period in the 1980s, administrative regulations issued at the national level sought to return all requisitioned lands to Islamic organizations, mosques, and tomb complexes.[34] But as a cadre in the Gansu Province Ethnic Religious Committee told me, the people's

---

[33] Article 149 of the 2007 Property Law provides that upon the expiration period for residential areas (a seventy-year term), the right to use land is automatically renewed; however, it is not clear that this rule applies to rural land.

[34] In 1980 the State Council, Bureau of Religious Affairs (BRA), State Construction Bureau, and related organs issued reports, such as the *Report Regarding Problems in the Implementation of Policies on Religious Groups' Real Estate Property* (*Guanyu luoshi zongjiao tuanti fangchan zhengce deng wenti de baogao*), reproduced in *Anthology of New-Period Religious Work Documents* (*Xin shiqi zongjiao gongzuo wengong xuanbian*), that sought to return property expropriated during the Cultural Revolution to religious organizations. Section 3, article 1 of the report reads: "Return all property rights of real property in its entirety to religious groups, and that property which cannot be returned, must be returned in the equivalent monetary amount" (Policy and Law Department of the BRA 1995: 25). Such documents note the economic duress of mosques while underscoring the need to keep religious organizations independent of foreign influence.

government of Gansu Province issued no regulations about the return of property.[35] Instead, when issues arose, experts were sent out to consult with local Muslim leaders, and they decided on the amount of property to be returned on an ad hoc basis. As to whether all lands, including *awqāf*, were returned, her response was, "consider reality" (*zhaogu xianshi*). PRC land policies have strangled the income flow of Sufi tomb complexes, in particular.

The *waqf* survives, however, in abbreviated form, illustrating Hui desire to abide by Islamic law. *Awqāf* are resurging in Northwest China in a number of forms: educational facilities for boys, girls, or adults; libraries and reading rooms; and even commercial enterprises that generate revenue for the mosque. There are a variety of ways, with varying degrees of legality, that Hui can found a *waqf*. Starting with the most official type, the majority of mosques in cities have "storefront *awqāf*" (*puzi wagefu*) (see Figure 6.3). These *awqāf* are legal, as they reside within the perimeter of the land allocated by the state to the mosque. Most mosques in Linxia have shops facing the street at the periphery of their property. These shops sell a wide variety of halal goods. Shopkeepers lease space from the mosque, and the income generated from the lease goes to support the daily operations of the mosque. In some cases, it exceeds the *nietie* as the greatest source of cash flow for the mosque. For example, West Gate Grand Mosque in Lanzhou, one of the largest and wealthiest mosques in Gansu, may generate RMB 3 million per year, of which approximately two-thirds derives from storefront *awqāf*, with the remainder from *nietie*. The owners of the lease are usually members of the mosque community, but not always. For instance, a mosque in Linxia rents out its street-front property and the mosque's basement to a Han-owned pharmaceutical company. That some Yihewani and Salafis point out that it is unlawful (Ar. *haram*) for a mosque to permit business on its grounds does not gain much traction in Linxia, where all teaching schools have little choice but to combine prayer space with the generation of revenue.

A second type of *waqf* occurs when a mosque collects *nietie* from members and purchases property outside of the mosque's state-allocated property in order to build a school, daycare center, or commercial space leased

---

[35] Based on my conversations with leaders of teaching schools, mosques and tombs received the equivalent of "allocated land use rights" (*huabo tudi shiyong quan*), as opposed to "granted land use rights" (*tudi shiyong quan churang*). The difference is that the former allows land use without payment to the government for a theoretically unlimited period, although the state can requisition the land at any time.

Figure 6.3 Storefront *awqāf* along one of the main streets in Bafang
Source: the author

out to members. This type is semilegal and draws attention to the distinc-tion between use rights in land and ownership of fixtures above land. Under PRC law, developers obtain both the use rights in land and the rights to develop real estate above ground. The legal definition of a real estate developer appears to exclude religious entities, however.[36] Under the Regulations on Religious Affairs, religious entities may not engage in the transfer, mortgaging, or development of property.[37] A Hui lawyer in the Linxia County Judicial Department explained that a mosque may purchase the real estate certificate for fixtures above the land, but the use rights in the land on which the fixtures rest remain in the name of the original grantee. Thus, the acquisition results in a bifurcation of prop-erty rights: the grantee owns the land use rights, and the mosque owns the rights in fixtures. This splitting of property rights, while not a direct

[36] The legal definition is set out in the Urban Real Estate Administration Law of the PRC (*Zhonghua renmin gongheguo chengshi fangdichan guanlifa*), passed by the NPC, August 30, 2007, art. 30.
[37] See Regulations on Religious Affairs (*Zongjiao shiwu tiaoli*), issued by the State Council, July 7, 2004, effective March 1, 2005, art. 32.

contravention of state property law, runs afoul of the Islamic legal requirement that the founder of a *waqf* fully relinquish her rights in the property.
The work-around nonetheless allows mosque communities to follow the
spirit of Islamic law in using land for religious purposes.

A third type of *waqf* in China occurs when individual members transfer
or will[38] their land use rights to the mosque. Hui describe these transfers
as *minjian*. This instance of *minjian* is not just unofficial but illegal. The
Hui moral economy takes form around the various blockages imposed by
state law. These hindrances fail to meet the requirements under Islamic
law, specifically that of perpetuity. When Hui convey their land use rights
without having their land use certificate notarized and without registering the conveyance at the relevant land bureau, they directly contravene
state land law.[39] One mosque in Linxia is particularly known to accrue
property through this means. The cleric vouched that the mosque had the
land transfer registered by the land bureau and had the "chopped" land
use transfer certificates to prove it, but that he would not show them to
me suggests that there was no legal basis for the transfer.

Minjian awqāf as "free" gifts initiate a chain of gifting that further blurs
the boundaries between legal and illegal. There are tax consequences to
such illegal transfers as well, but mosque leaders and real estate officials
trade in favors and thereby address problems. For example, in return for
not registering a transfer of property, Hui officials consult the mosque
cleric for religious guidance regarding personal or family matters. And
while the initial donor of land may not receive direct benefits in the form
of return gifts, donors undoubtedly gain reputational recognition in giving, as word of mouth spreads within and beyond the mosque community
of the donors' acts despite their unlawfulness. Economic capital is thus
converted to social capital (Bourdieu 1986) as a result of the Hui moral
economy.

Nonetheless, unlike the *nietie*, which receives immediate acclaim
through the up-to-date boards in the center of mosques, conveyances of
minjian awqāf are not publicly displayed. Unlike the "free" gift in Hindu
India, which conveys the sin of the giver and so requires the recipient to
give it to another or invite misfortune (Parry 1986), the *waqf* initiates a
sequence of gifts, "licit" and "illicit," under different registers that travel

---

[38] Wills are extremely rare among the Hui (as they are for rural Han), although the heads of some of
the elite families that have accumulated considerable wealth following three decades of reforms
do manage the disposition of their estates through writing wills.

[39] See the PRC Land Administration Law (*Zhonghua renmin gongheguo tudi guanlifa*), adopted by the
NPC, June 25, 1986, amended August 28, 2004, arts. 2, 73, and 81.

various circuits. What is pious under one legal regime (i.e., Islamic) may be "contrary to public interest" in another (i.e., socialist). In the case of *minjian awqāf*, the discrepancy is reconciled by concealment—that is, by burying any conflict that would come to the surface, as for example in the case of the alleged use rights transfer certificates that were *bu gongkai* (not public/illegal).

Hui adaptation of the *waqf* to a socialist property rights regime has, however, resulted in ethical questioning about the *waqf*'s beneficiary. According to Hanafi *fiqh*, a founder can establish a *waqf* for public utilities or for the poor. Since the state provides public works projects, in Hui practice the default recipient is the mosque. But it is unclear whether the mosque is the beneficiary or a trustee for the poor. Among most teaching schools, *awqāf* are for the mosque's use, and proceeds from them are managed by the mosque administration committee. Individual Hui and the poor may indirectly benefit from donations to the mosque. "Anything given to the mosque," one Yihewani mosque administrative committee member says, "are considered *awqāf*: donated books, a chair, or a blackboard. These are given to the mosque for the use of its members." Hui funnel their material resources to the mosque, which may, in turn, redistribute them—for example, during holidays such as Ramadan and particularly the Night of Power (Ar. Laylat al-Qadr), when the mosque provides meals for members and the poor. As the center of Hui communities, mosques illustrate what Polanyi ([1944] 1957a: 49) called "centricity," a principle for collecting and redistributing goods and services.[40] As Polanyi, following Malinowski, observed, redistribution can be a form of economics.

Voluntary beneficence, whether as movable property (e.g., sheep or ox) or real estate in the form of *awqāf*, is an economic activity and inflow of material resources to mosques, as well as an occasion for Hui to practice—and exhibit—their piety. Donations, mainly structured through the mosques and unrecorded by the state (e.g., through tax deductions), are a mainstay of the Hui moral economy, even as they link the Hui in the Northwest with larger Han consumer markets in the east, as

---

[40] The mosque does not necessarily use revenue from the *waqf* for the benefit of the poor. For instance, regarding *awqāf* from pooled *nietie*, mosques and Sufi tombs increasingly engage in contests to expand the structure's size. Hui understand the physical proportions of the mosque and the size of the prayer hall to indicate the number of followers, and thereby the relative strength of the teaching school. Hence, donations may contribute to the capacity of the teaching school to perpetuate its standing in the community and region.

in the case of the sheep market. In the following section, I shift from private beneficence to Islamic finance. Banks in Ningxia have recently begun offering shariʿa-compliant products. Unlike donation in Linxia or other Hui enclaves in the Northwest, Islamic finance in Ningxia is a Hui community-based initiative officially recognized by the Party-State; as such, it raises the question of when and why the Party-State sanctions *minjian* practices as opposed to simply tolerating them.

ISLAMIC FINANCE IN NINGXIA

Islamic finance is the one area of Islamic law that the Party-State recognizes, albeit not in the form of legislation but through policy. It is unsurprising that the exception to the state's nonrecognition of Islamic law would be in the field of finance. After the 2007 global meltdown, Islamic finance increasingly evokes images of a shimmery Gulf metropolis. Such images resonate with the Party-State's desire to broadcast itself as offering alternatives to the problems of Wall Street: loose monetary policies, ego-driven risk, inadequate supervision, and the creation of global imbalances in capital flows (Ho 2009). As a result, Ningxia, in recent years, has experimented with a budding Islamic finance industry.

Yet Islamic finance raises the possibility of a flood of Middle Eastern money that could fuel antistate activity. Hence, the central banking system has tightly controlled Islamic finance. The banking regulators were quick to incorporate Islamic finance into the official banking system in order to prevent a cross-border source of income for Hui communities. Whereas charity, in the Hui moral economy, looks ceremonial but is not, Islamic finance looks like a hyper-modern development in China's economy but remains mostly ceremonial, a result of official Islam subsuming and transforming the *minjian*.

The status of Islamic finance in mainland China illustrates the tensions between China's emergence in the global *umma* and its security and secular priorities. A closer integration between Asian economies and Islamic finance has been identified by the governments of Greater China (i.e., the PRC, Hong Kong, Taiwan, and Macau) as a means to increase their competitive advantage over the West. Since the global economic crisis, both Hong Kong and Taiwan have experimented with Islamic finance. Taiwan established a Taiwan Shariʿa Index in 2008, which has been used for shariʿa-compliant investment products that focus on shariʿa-compliant companies listed on the Taiwan Stock Exchange. Likewise, in 2007 the financial secretary of Hong Kong, John Tsang Chun-wah, expressed interest in making Hong Kong a center of the Islamic bond (*sukūk*) market in Asia (Ho Wai-Yip 2013: 123). After amending profit tax and property tax laws, which the legislative council is empowered to do, given the relatively high degree of political autonomy[41] that Hong Kong's "one country, two systems" approach offers, in September 2014 Hong Kong issued its first set of *sukūk* worth US$1 billion.[42]

In Northwest China, security concerns have complicated provincial and autonomous region governments' capacity to develop Islamic finance. Since the early 2000s, the PRC government has hailed the "New Silk Road" as serving both economic and security interests. There have been multiple platforms for trade and investment. As explored in Chapter 4, one portal of renewed integration between China and Muslim countries is the "maritime Silk Road" along China's southeastern coast, where capital and labor are mobile and largely unfettered by state regulation. Another portal for revitalized commercial ties is Kashgar, Xinjiang's far western city, which the government nominated as China's first inland special economic zone (SEZ) in 2010. Although the broader religious and political effects of the Kashgar SEZ remain to be seen, the radical transformation of the city and increasing surveillance suggest that security interests rather than economic ones dominate in the far west.

Ningxia represents a midpoint between an opened east coast maritime Silk Road and a closed and monitored overland Silk Road. Whereas Xinjiang opens China to investment and trade with Central Asia (a region the PRC perceives to be grooming Islamic terrorists) and thus has received governmental support in the form of highly directed investment, the Party-State has heralded Ningxia as China's portal to the Middle East. The Northwest region is, as a whole, poorer than the rest of China by the metric of per capita net income. Ningxia is generally wealthier than Gansu and Qinghai but not as wealthy as Xinjiang, given Xinjiang's oil and natural gas reserves (see Table 6.1).

Of Ningxia's 6.3 million people, 2.2 million (35 percent) are Hui, nearly twice the amount of Gansu's approximately 1.26 million Hui. In Ningxia,

---

[41] This power is provided for in the Basic Law of the Hong Kong Special Administrative Region (*Zhonghua renmin gongheguo Xianggang tebie xingzhengqu jibenfa*), adopted by the NPC, April 4, 1990, effective July 1, 1997, arts. 66–79.

[42] The *sukūk* oversubscribed 3.7 times with US$4.7 billion in orders received, including institutional investors from the Middle East, Asia, Europe, and the United States (Hong Kong Monetary Authority 2014; Yiu 2014).

TABLE 6.1 Per capita income of rural households by area

| Area | Per Capita Net Income of Rural Households (unit = RMB) | |
	1990	2011
National average	686.31	6,977.29
Xinjiang	683.47	5,442.15
Ningxia	578.13	5,409.95
Qinghai	559.78	4,608.46
Gansu	430.98	3,909.37

Source: 2012 China Statistical Yearbook (National Bureau of Statistics 2012: 366).

the densest pockets of Hui communities are in the rural west and south, which are also the poorest. In Haiyuan County, for instance, the average income for the county's approximately 315,000 Hui is RMB 2,640 per month,[43] slightly higher than that of Hui in Bafang. In 2010 Ningxia had a total budgetary revenue of RMB 28.7 billion and expenses of RMB 55.5 billion. In that year, it received RMB 16.03 billion in subsidies from the central government (Yang Jing 2011: 407), as opposed to Gansu, which, indicative of its status as one of China's poorest provinces, received RMB 103.2 billion in subsidies in the same year (Gansu Provincial People's Government 2011: 138). For Ningxia or Gansu, Islamic finance could theoretically provide a flow of investment to supplement state subsidies.

It would be Ningxia where Islamic finance would gain purchase in China. Ningxia Hui have enjoyed closer relationships with the Party since before the Communists assumed power in 1949. In the 1930s the Red Army required Hui support in Ningxia during the civil war with the Nationalists. On October 20, 1936 the Red Army established the Yuhai County Hui Autonomous Government of the Shaanxi-Gansu-Ningxia Provinces. Its foundation marks the first time that the Communists used the conception of "autonomous government" in administering ethnic minorities, eleven years before the Inner Mongolia Autonomous Region was created. Although the Yuhai County Hui Autonomous Government lasted only about one month,[44] a commemorative sign still hangs over Tongxin Grand Mosque, where the government was founded. This early

[43] The average expenses for Haiyuan Hui is RMB 2,283 per month, allowing for minimal, if any, savings. These statistics are for the year 2009 (Zhang Jinhai 2011: 96).

[44] The Nationalist Army dismantled the government in late November 1936.

concession of the Communists to Hui ethnic autonomy appears sincere, according to its foundational documents (Qiu 2009), and has set the tone for CCP-Hui relations in Ningxia.

As a consequence of this history, Ningxia Hui have academic institutions and publication houses that promote Islam and closer ties with Arab nations through cultural exchange, trade, and investment. In Northwest China, where autonomy appears in shades, Ningxia enjoys "ethnic autonomy" at the level of an autonomous region, theoretically the same administrative level as a province. However, as noted in Chapter 1, administrative hierarchies are complicated by the central government's reluctance to approve autonomous regulations issued by autonomous region governments.

Part of the relative freedom enjoyed by Ningxia Hui is fiscal innovation. In 2010 I visited the Bank of Ningxia (BON) in Yinchuan, the capital of the autonomous region, a year after Ningxia launched the mainland's pilot project for Islamic finance.[45] The project began at the insistence of the Hui business community, which sought shari'a-compliant instruments through which to invest savings. As in Malaysia,[46] which has sought to displace the Gulf as the world's Islamic finance hub, the earliest demands for Islamic banking in China came from local Muslim communities rather than from governmental agencies at the local or national level. In fact, Malaysia was one of the inspirations for the project. The BON sent a delegation of representatives to Malaysia to study its Islamic finance system. Although Muslims in Malaysia primarily follow the Shafi'i rather than the Hanafi school of jurisprudence, Malaysian Islamic finance is known for its flexible structures and was thus perceived as a suitable model.[47]

In a rare instance of grassroots lobbying through official channels, an effort more likely to be successful in Ningxia than elsewhere in the Northwest, a small but powerful clique of Hui businessmen consulted with the clerics at their mosques. The goal of the businessmen was to create financial services that were in accordance with Islamic law and notions of justice, and were responsible to local communities.

---

[45] There were precedents for Islamic banks in China, but they were either short-lived, Islamic in name only, or both. Some Hui say there were Islamic banks in Linxia and Qinghai in the 1980s. In 1986 an attempt was made to establish an Islamic bank in Yinchuan through a joint venture between the Ningxia Islamic International Trust and Investment Company and the Faisal Islamic Bank of Egypt (Harris 1993: 199).

[46] The community basis of the effort is not unlike the practice of Islamic finance in Malaysia (Balala 2011; Rudnyckyj 2014).

[47] Malaysian bankers conducted follow-up visits to Yinchuan, such as the one in 2012, during which Malay and Hui discussed common problems in designing shari'a-compliant products.

The clerics approached the Ningxia Islamic Association (hereinafter "Ningxia Yi-Xie"), of which some of the clerics were members. It is not clear from my conversations whether the businessmen wanted to make the Islamic bank official or not, but ultimately the Ningxia Yi-Xie took over the project. Its senior members discussed the possibility of the BON starting Islamic banking services, with the Ningxia Yi-Xie clerics, including Yihewani and Khufiyya Sufis, playing a pivotal role in communicating their constituencies' interests to bank officials. In so doing, the idea of Islamic finance transformed from a community-based initiative to one that could be integrated into the state's official banking system.

The case demonstrates that there are multiple interests in such collaborations. The Ningxia Yi-Xie clerics seemed to believe that the Hui could realize their aims through the official system better than they could through *minjian* banks. The Ningxia Yi-Xie, as the liaison between the Hui business community and the Party-State, is more inclined than is the Hui community to work with the government to protect weak property rights in China's transitional economy.[48] In so doing, however, the Ningxia Yi-Xie aligns Hui interests with state interests, making them official. Furthermore, this casting of the elite (both the clerics and officials) as the caretakers of Hui social welfare further reinforces the "paternalistic tradition of the authorities" (Thompson 1971: 79). Yet, instead of Hui businessmen and nonelite holding such authorities to their promises with passion and riots, the elite's failures are met with cynicism, circumvention, or noninterest.

Once the Ningxia Yi-Xie had taken over advocating the position of the Hui business community, it worked with the BON to gain approval from the governmental regulators. The BON is the Ningxia bank organized under the People's Bank of China, which historically has served as the BON's supervisory organ. In 2003 the China Banking Regulatory Commission (CBRC) took over this role from the People's Bank of China. The CBRC must approve all changes and innovations to the services offered by banks under its supervision, including Islamic finance. Upon completion of the study tour in 2009, the BON applied to the CBRC to begin the pilot project to introduce Islamic finance to Ningxia. On December 24, 2009, the BON began offering shari'a-compliant financial services at five of its branches.

---

[48] On property rights see, e.g., Ho (2003, 2005).

To summarize, there are three distinguishing features of the Islamic finance project: one, it grew out of a grassroots demand, which was, two, taken over by the Ningxia Yi-Xie as mediator between the Hui community and the government, and three, its legal basis was not exercised via Ningxia's power of ethnic autonomy but rather through the regulatory regime of the banking sector.

Making Islamic finance work in a socialist banking system

Since the macroeconomic reform of the 1990s, the Party-State has both centralized and diversified the banking industry. The incorporation of Islamic finance into the PRC banking system represents the adaptability of Islamic finance (Maurer 2006) as well as the high degree of elasticity if not inventiveness of state institutions concerning commercial matters. Under Islamic law, debt transactions are charitable transactions, under which the creditor should not earn profit. Any return to an investor should be based on profits derived from commercial risk, through contracted provisions, and not uncertainty (Ar. *gharar*). Further, shari'a encourages investors to act not as creditors but as partners sharing profits and risk. Under partnerships, profit should not be assured, nor should fixed returns on investments be guaranteed. Investments should be halal, meaning that industries such as alcohol, drugs, gambling, and pork production are unlawful.[49]

In accordance with these principles, the BON offered a range of services. The no-interest savings accounts (*wuxi cunkuan zhanghu* or *baoguan zhanghu*) are based on a contract signed between the BON and the customer. The BON safeguards the customer's savings and allows withdrawals. The customer does not earn interest, but the BON can provide "gifts" (*lipin*). In an investment account (*caifu zhangfu*) the BON and customer form a contract under which the BON raises funds from individuals or institutions. Investment projects accord with the rules of Islamic law. Rather than pay dividends based on the investment's performance, the BON distributes the income to its customers pursuant to the terms of the contract, which specify a proportion of the dividends to be paid to investors. In a third financial instrument, called a *murābaha* (Ch. *jiajia maoyi*), the BON and the customer enter into a contract of sale, and the BON purchases goods on behalf of the customer and then resells the goods to the customer at the price of cost plus profit. Subsequently, the customer pays a deferred payment plus profit to the BON.

---

[49] For a helpful overview of Islamic finance law, see Vogel and Hayes (1998).

As with Islamic banks in the Middle East and Southeast Asia, clerics provided "expert advice" on matters of Islamic commercial law. Upon the commencement of the BON project, clerics affiliated with major mosques in Yinchuan and with the Ningxia Yi-Xie formed the Islamic Finance Consulting Committee, which works with the bank managers to decide whether the enterprises that apply for financing as *murābaha* are halal. Clerics reported that they specifically verify whether the entrepreneurs are Hui (although a few Han businesses have been permitted) and whether their business is lawful according to Islamic law. Following clerical approval, the BON gives interest-free loans up to RMB 300,000.

There were roadblocks from the beginning of the proposed project, however. According to my conversations with BON managers, the BON applied for an initial investment of RMB 200 million, but finance ministries initially approved a mere fraction of that amount for the entire project.[50] In addition, the government imposed caps on the size of loans and deposits. Loans were graded on a scale of RMB 50,000 to RMB 300,000, and the size of the deposit was limited to RMB 10 million. Only about a thousand customers had used the savings account as of mid-2012, for a total balance of RMB 53 million. Many Hui customers have been able to use the account for costs associated with the hajj, on average RMB 3,000 per person. This use of the account was a result of the BON negotiations with the autonomous-region-level BRA.

There were additional problems with the types of investments the BON could make and the legal expertise of the Islamic Finance Consulting Committee. The BON could not invest in trust companies, for instance. BON managers privately complained about the committee, saying that the clerics did not really have financial expertise or knowledge of Islamic law. Managers admitted that they searched the Internet for Islamic finance instruments that they could then include in their promotional material circulated to mosques.

Like microfinance, the *murābaha* was meant to stimulate small local proprietorships and businesses, such as clothing shops and restaurants. It met with limited success, attracting some four hundred clients for a total of 222 *murābaha* projects by mid-2012. Approval for more sophisticated instruments—such as the *muḍāraba*, a noninterest "profit sharing" account, and the *mushāraka*, a joint venture under which the customer would provide expertise and the BON would provide startup funding for

---

[50] One manager told me the actual amount approved was only RMB 4,000, although this is such a meager amount that I must have misheard.

a business—was still pending as of 2012. By that time, the total amount of money generated by the Islamic finance project was RMB 1.34 billion. However, managers claimed that total savings would be significantly higher with more advanced instruments, such as the *muḍāraba*.

Although fifteen months had passed since the Urumqi riots when I visited the BON, it was intimated to me that the reason for the difficulty in getting the project off the ground was the Party-State's fear that Islamic finance would permit funds from overseas Muslims to enter China, benefiting secessionist movements in Xinjiang. A BON manager said, "The government is afraid Uyghurs will use the bank in Yinchuan. This is the reason why such a bank will not open in Urumqi—for fear that it will increase financial ties between Muslims in Xinjiang and Central Asia." Indeed, Uyghurs in Xinjiang had called for Islamic financial services before the 2009 riots, but their requests went unheard. The sub-optimality of the project, however, was not just a result of state-imposed limits. Hui had also not used the shariʿa-compliant services to the extent the BON had hoped. Bank managers looked embarrassed when they admitted that even after three years, the project was still in the testing phase. Although the bank's Yinchuan branch had installed teller windows specifically for shariʿa services, during several site visits I failed to see any customers use such windows. As a result of this lack of demand, the Islamic finance service department of the BON had shrunk from six employees in 2010 to only four in 2012.

Ceremony, specter, and money

The empty windows of the BON Islamic finance services may suggest that Hui do not wish to follow Islamic law in commercial affairs—that here, there is no desire to live in accordance with the Islamic law of finance. Another explanation is that Ningxia's Hui, who may have initially called for Islamic banking, have not been satisfied with the official banking system's offering of shariʿa-compliant products. The Xinjiang specter has cast its shadow over the genesis of Islamic finance in Ningxia, and the would-be customers have realized that the services were constrained in scope and monitored by the Party-State.

One manager of the BON told me, "We propagated the financial services by going to many mosques and handing out flyers and gifts to encourage the Hui to become customers ... but the numbers [of clients] have been disappointing." While the standard criticism of Islamic finance is that it is, to use a Chinese expression, "old wine in new bottles," or conventional banking with an Islamic gloss, in the BON project the state banking system has additionally limited the scope of the services. While the BON's Islamic finance services are mainly ceremonial in their current form, that does not mean that they are necessarily empty of significance. As with the medieval European doctrine of the king's two bodies,[51] the ceremonial display of Islamic finance appropriates any economic justice afforded by Islamic banking for the Party-State's own perpetuation.[52] Yet, because of the unpredictable nature of the Islamic resurgence in Ningxia, the Party-State is not the sole arbiter of the form its institutions take. Moral economy is generated from below, requiring adaptations by the Party-State. As the community sets the rules for ethical business and giving, Hui look to the community, not to the Party-State, for economic justice.

Putting the Islamic finance project in the context of the geopolitics of Sino-Middle Eastern relations, the provision of Islamic banking in Ningxia is congruent with the state's sanctioning of Ningxia as the focal point of China's engagement with the Muslim world. Hui share the view that Ningxia has a key diplomatic role to play. Beginning in the 1980s, Ningxia Hui engaged in *minjian waijiao* (popular diplomacy) with Muslim states (Ai and Xia 2008); in 1984 they invited representatives from the Muslim World League to Yinchuan and, in that same year, convened the International Islamic Economic Technology Consultation Conference, which inaugurated a series of exchange visits between Ningxia Hui and experts from Saudi Arabia, Iran, Egypt, and Tunisia (Ai and Xia 2008).

Nearly two decades later, such nongovernmental ties have borne fruit. Walking down the central business district in Yinchuan in 2012, I saw a number of real estate development projects that are financed by overseas companies based in the United Arab Emirates. Media organs have painted Ningxia as a geostrategic location of moderate Islam and a successor to the historic Silk Road. For example, in 2005 I attended the "International Symposium on Cultural Exchange between China and the West under Zheng He" on the six-hundredth anniversary of the maritime travels of the Chinese Muslim admiral.[53] Hosted by the Ningxia Academy of Social Sciences, the symposium featured scholars and intellectuals from Iran,

[51] The doctrine of the king's two bodies refers to the practice in medieval England and France of replacing the natural body of a deceased king with an effigy that could be worshipped as a representation of the immortal "body politic" (Kantorowicz 1997).

[52] E. P. Thompson (1971: 88) described how state prosecutions of thieves in England were designed for "symbolic effect, as demonstrations to the poor that the authorities were actively vigilant in their interests."

[53] In a series of voyages from 1405 to 1433, Zheng He (1371–1433), a native of Yunnan, traveled to Ormuz, Mecca, Aden, Mogadishu, and Mombasa to extend China's trade and its tributary reach.

Bulgaria, and Japan. Such Silk Road revivals, which are part of Ningxia's imagined modernity, are the product of a consortium of actors—including clerics, academics, businessmen and women, and officials—who have similar though not identical interests and motivations.

Ningxia has benefited from central-government support to establish several other pilot projects to develop halal enterprises for export to the Middle East. In 2006 Ningxia established the annual "Halal Food Muslim Everyday Product Festival" to introduce Ningxia products to foreign markets. By 2008 Ningxia halal food and Muslim product manufacturers had garnered US$6.2 million in foreign contracts. By the following year, the industry had some ten thousand halal production and processing enterprises and twenty thousand halal proprietors, generating a production value of RMB 200 billion.[54]

Ningxia has enjoyed more opportunities for exchange—economic, intellectual, educational, and cultural—with Muslim-majority countries than has anywhere else in the Northwest.[55] One of the focal points of renewed engagement with the Middle East is the China-Arab States Economic and Trade Forum (hereinafter, the "Forum"). The groundwork for the Forum was laid during former CCP General Secretary and PRC President Hu Jintao's 2004 visit to Cairo to meet with representatives of the Arab League (Yao 2006). Since 2010, the Forum, hosted by leaders in the central and autonomous region governments,[56] has been a spectacle of official Islam, a cornucopia of diplomatic and commercial delights. As of the 2013 Forum,[57] 18 heads of state had attended as well as 195 high-ranking delegates from a total of 76 countries.[58] The Forum has featured 5,000 Chinese enterprises specializing mainly in halal food, Muslim products, energy and chemical commodities, electronics, and agricultural products (An 2014).

---

[54] These statistics are from the Ningxia Academy of Social Science, on file with the author.

[55] Generally, teaching schools and Sufi orders have all benefited from these opportunities, although Salafis remain small in number in Ningxia. There are only 10,000 Salafis, compared with 540,000 Gedimu, 480,000 Jahriyya, 450,000 Yihewani, 370,000 Khufiyya, and 100,000 Qadiriyya (Zhang Jinhai 2011: 154).

[56] The 2011 Forum, for example, was attended by members of the Politburo Standing Committee, the Chinese People's Political Consultative Conference National Committee chairman, the NPC Standing Committee, and the NPC Nationalities Affairs Commission, as well as the president of the China–Arab Friendship Association, the director of the State Ethnic Affairs Commission, and the director of the Overseas Chinese Affairs Office, to name a few.

[57] The 2013 meeting was renamed the China–Arab States Expo (Zhong–A Bolanhui).

[58] In the past, foreign delegates and officials came from Bahrain, Egypt, Ethiopia, Kuwait, Tunisia, and the United Arab Emirates, among other countries. In addition, there have been representatives from Turkey and Indonesia, a deputy of the Hungarian parliament, the former deputy prime minister of Thailand, and the president of the Islamic Republic of Mauritania.

Official media have spotlighted the Forum as a keystone in China's New Silk Road. The economic incentives of renewed exchange with Arab states are unmistakable. As one of the fastest-growing economies in the world, China consumes 9.9 million barrels of oil per day, making it the world's second-largest consumer of oil after the United States (US Energy Information Administration 2014). While China has extensive oil reserves, it became a net importer of oil in 1993, and oil consumption has increased 8 percent annually since 2002 (Kemp 2012: 68). The PRC has become increasingly dependent on the Middle East—Saudi Arabia and Iran, in particular—as its source of oil (Kemp 2012: 68–69).[59] Trade between China and the Middle East grew from US$36.7 billion in 2004 to US$194.9 billion for the first ten months of 2013, an increase of 531 percent.[60] According to its official website, the 2013 Forum grossed US$42.3 billion, or 21.7 percent of that year's total trade to date, making the Forum a substantial source of burgeoning trade between the regions (see also Ma Haiyun 2014).

The Forum would seem to present an ideal opportunity to link the BON's Islamic finance initiatives with foreign investors. However, the Party and its media outlets have been ambivalent about Islamic finance; consequently, the project has been betwixt and between censor and celebration. It seems that bank managers were dissuaded from making Islamic finance a focus of the earlier Forums. During the 2012 Forum, attendees made some mention of the issue. Reem Badran, vice chairman of the Amman Chamber of Commerce in Jordan, discussed the prospects of *sukūk*, and during the "Issue Ceremony of China-Arab Finance Development Strategy Framework Initiative" panelists mentioned the potential of Islamic finance in Ningxia. The press embraced these disclosures and glowed about the prospects for Yinchuan becoming an "internationalized Islamic finance center" within five to ten years and the possibility that Arab Muslims would invest in Yinchuan and that the BON would partner with the Arab Development Bank. But to date no foreign Muslim has been able to invest in the BON's project, despite the Forum's handing out BON China-Arab State Trade Forum co-branded debit cards for cross-border transactions. Moreover,

---

[59] For more on China's Middle East oil dependence and energy security, see Simpfendorfer (2009: ch. 2) and Olimat (2012: ch. 2).

[60] These figures are derived from a comparison of Yao (2006: 223) and official statistics from the Ministry of Commerce (2013).

in 2014, against the backdrop of unrest in Xinjiang and terrorist attacks in Beijing in October 2013 and Kunming in March 2014, the Forum was canceled.[61]

The example of the BON shows that the state is constantly wary of *minjian* institutional capacity, particularly those that are economic in nature and that cross borders. The Party-State maintains a watchful eye over such developments and will seek to control them by sanctioning them in the event that they have potential to support its needs. So while the *minjian* is frequently surveilled, it can also be transformed, or even shut down, as the case of the BON shows.

Closure of some *minjian* practices may, however, open new opportunities for Hui to pursue other ones. Whereas the BON officially represents Islamic finance and commerce, *minjian* organizations are also emerging as important drivers of Ningxia's connections with the Middle East. Following a rise in international Islamic humanitarian organizations, often based in the Middle East but directed to such places as Afghanistan, Bosnia, and China, Islamic philanthropy is reconfiguring global trajectories of aid dollars, previously dominated by Western aid organizations.[62] Hui "business promotion associations,"[63] aware of these trends, have worked to connect Middle Eastern businessmen eager to pursue philanthropic opportunities abroad with "charitable causes" (*cishan shiye*) in Ningxia, ranging from mosque education to poverty relief.

One association based in Yinchuan has channeled Kuwaiti dollars into Ningxia-based charities. In truth, the funneling association is nominally a "promotional association" (*cujinhui*) but is really a "chamber of commerce" (*shanghui*), a legal entity for which it is easier to gain approval under the Ningxia Bureau of Civil Affairs and which does not require administrative oversight, at least under the arrangement arrived at by entrepreneurial Hui. There are some forty charities that pay a membership fee to belong to the association. A board member says:

---

[61] The Central Office for the Leading Group on Foreign Affairs issued the decision in its Notice Regarding Holding the China-Arab States International Fair and Related Matters (*Guanyu juban Zhongguo-Alabo guojia bolanhui youguan shixiang de tongzhi*), April 16, 2014.

[62] See, e.g., Burr and Collins (2006), Alterman and von Hippel (2007), and Benthall and Bellion-Jourdan (2009a).

[63] These associations blur the distinction under PRC law between a charitable organization and a business entity. Many charitable organizations and especially "social enterprises" may try to register as for-profit companies but have a charitable purpose for their business scope, in order to circumvent the restrictive registration regime for such associations in China.

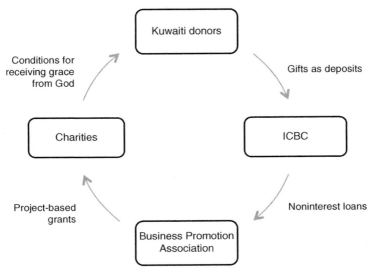

Figure 6.4 *Minjian* gift circulation
Source: the author

> The government does not provide adequate funds to Hui communities. Banks like the BON do not have branches in the Middle East and so cannot attract foreign customers. We have solved this problem. We work with the Industrial and Commercial Bank of China (ICBC).[64] The ICBC has branches in Kuwait. Kuwaitis deposit their money in interest-free savings accounts. This is important, as it complies with Islamic law. The ICBC then issues noninterest-bearing loans to charitable organizations that we identify here in Ningxia. No one assumes risk: not the Kuwaiti who is complying with Islamic law, the bank that is not charging interest, or the charity that is receiving money from an official bank.

The Kuwaitis deposit money as an act of charity; it is considered a gift (Ar. *hadiyya* or, generally, *sadaqa*). Foreign donors feel safe interfacing directly with an official bank, according to the board member. The ICBC then distributes the money to the association, based in Yinchuan, often packaged in the form of interest-free mortgage loans. The association subsequently grants the money to the charity (see Figure 6.4).

An example of one transaction benefiting Hui in Ningxia involves a nonprofit educational organization that needed money to assist rural

---

[64] The ICBC is one of China's four major state-owned banks.

students who wanted to attend university. The charity asked the business promotion association for RMB 250,000. The association, as middleman, raised the required amount abroad, charging a fee of approximately 0.25 percent for its services, and provided the charity its funding. One such program provided RMB 3,000 a year to several students in rural Ningxia. The students do not pay back the funds they receive. The Kuwaitis, in return, receive the "grace" (*huici*) of God. In this way, the "gift" of charity migrates across various distinctions (official and *minjian*, secular and religious, domestic and transnational) to promote "faith, community, [and] jurisdiction" (Maurer 2005: 7), which does not necessarily accord with the Party-State's vision. As Emily Yeh (2013) has argued in the context of Tibet, the "gift" of Chinese development (i.e., infrastructural projects and housing) demands the counter-gift of ethnic citizens' fidelity to the nation-state. Hui have generated their own transnational gifting system, which accords with Islamic law and which makes use of state institutions without requiring loyalty to the state, although it does not militate against national belonging, either. Such arrangements are part of the global extension of Islamic charity, which challenges secular jurisdictions and monetary controls, particularly charity from the Middle East to Muslim populations at the margins of the *umma*. The Islamic Development Bank,[65] for example, has disbursed some US$284.5 million between 1978 and 2011 to Muslim communities in nonmember states, improving access to health services, providing microfinance, and securing scholarships (Islamic Development Bank 2013: 9). The bank has made inroads into financing mosques in the Northwest, including the Yihewani West Gate Grand Mosque in Lanzhou, to which it gave RMB 2 million in 2003.

While linkages between Hui charities and Middle Eastern dollars permit Hui to exercise their moral economy through material ties, such initiatives may raise ethical questions. For instance, members of the business promotion association in Yinchuan claimed that the majority of charities in the association were Muslim (including Hui, Dongxiang, Bonan, and Salar of different teaching schools but no Uyghur ones). I subsequently discovered, however, that only eight of the forty charities were Muslim; the rest were Han. In such multiethnic communities as Ningxia, Hui may overstate their success in achieving transnational Muslim solidarity.

---

[65] The Islamic Development Bank, founded in 1975, promotes economic development and social welfare in both its fifty-six member countries (chiefly in the Middle East, North Africa, Central Asia, and Southeast Asia) and nonmember states.

While the Yinchuan association claimed to have attracted an astonishing RMB 500 million in funds from Kuwait in a three-month period, not all the money went toward the needs of Muslim minority social welfare; Han, too, benefited. Whereas the Hui community may set the agenda for matters of both charity and commerce, it nonetheless encounters economic constraints and may depend on the Han majority. In a word, imaginaries may exceed material connections. The gift circulates, but the Hui moral economy may not acknowledge its beginnings and ends.

HUI SHADOW ECONOMIES

In the past four decades and especially after the 2007 world financial crisis, Muslim scholars have proffered Islamic economics as an alternative to both Communism and global capitalism.[66] Although Islamic foundations and development institutions have, since 9/11, been an object of government suspicion,[67] their provision of international aid continues apace. In addition, Islamic finance has emerged as an alternative source of wealth to capitalist banking. The rationale for adopting this alternative model of economics is expressed in terms of Qur'anic notions of economic justice that privilege egalitarianism and individual flourishing based on divinely sanctioned exchange and redistribution. By banning interest, Islamic economics intends to obviate the problem of inequality and exploitation common in capitalist societies while retaining the primacy of God's will, unlike the socialist privileging of the state as representative of the people.

Hui have their own version of Islamic economics, which is a response to both the transitional Chinese economy and Chinese society's traditions of money management. Due to political pressures, Hui cannot establish sophisticated Islamic finance and banking instruments, and yet Ningxia's Hui work as bricoleurs, assembling official and *minjian* legal instruments and entities, to channel money to Hui communities. Hui in Gansu, Qinghai, and eastern Xinjiang do not have these capabilities, as provincial and central governments prohibit charitable associations.[68] However,

---

[66] See, for instance, Sirageldin (1995), Siddiqui (1996), Ahmed (2010), Venardos (2010), and Askari, Iqbal, and Mirakhor (2011).

[67] For a sample of this emergent literature, see Crimm (2008), Benthall (2014) and Lacey and Benthall (2014).

[68] I came across one exception, a charity called The Overwhelming Compassion of the Hezhou Public Granary (Hezhou Canyi Aixin Yongdong), formed in 2000 and organized by a network of Yihewani mosques in Linxia and Lanzhou. It collects clothes and foodstuffs such as cooking

Hui in these areas are developing business networks with the Middle East, Pakistan, and other locations, and these networks may prove to be one way funds from Muslim-majority countries enter Hui communities. As international links are nascent, Hui depend mostly on local community finances, some official and others not. Their *minjian* transactions provide a window into thinking about shadow economies at the intersection of Islamic, socialist, and capitalist property systems.

The *awqāf*, as sources of wealth for mosque communities, are central to informal or *minjian* Hui property rights. In addition to *wagefu*, the phonetic transliteration for *waqf*, Hui colloquially refer to *awqāf* as *sichan*, a homophonous Chinese word that means both "mosque property" and "private property." The designation underlines the mosque's importance to collective life (including the redistribution of property), at the same time as it distinguishes the *waqf* from "public property" owned by the state. In the Hui conception, the mosque has its own legal personality, independent of the official state designations of "religious activity area" or "religious property," suggesting a system of property transactions beyond the realm of the state. Despite the Party-State's fixation on property as a lever of social revolution and reform, China has developed a "spontaneous order" of property rights.[69] The economist Timur Kuran (2001, 2004, 2005) has called Islamic property devices such as the *waqf* a brake on economic development. Beyond the Islam question, Party-State orthodoxy in the reform of the "extralegal law" of property is to officially recognize it, incorporate it into the formal legal system, and further, privatize such rights (cf. Soto 1989). The Hui approach diverges from those of both Kuran and the Party-State in at least two regards. First, Hui exercise piety in transferring, disbursing, and redistributing property in a way that supports communities economically, and second, they do so without full recognition from the state.

Taking these aspects of the Hui approach to property in turn, Hui aspire to use disposable income that is just by the standards of the revealed sources. Self-interest and egoism, patriarchal authority, and other sources

---

oil for the extremely poor (Muslim and non-Muslim) in Linxia County and surrounding areas. It is funded purely by *nietie* and zakat. During Ramadan in 2010 it partnered with the Linxia City Compassion Relief Committee (Linxia Shi Aixin Qiuzhu Hui) for a major charity in Jishishan County.

[69] Friedrich A. Hayek (1973) first proposed the concept of spontaneous order, meaning generally one obtained by individuals following rules but pursuing their own interests, independent of state intervention. Recently, legal scholars have used Hayek's concept to describe property rights in China (P. Ho 2013; Qiao and Upham 2015).

of hierarchy insert themselves into egalitarian ethics. Hui never resolve these tensions, but they objectify them through comparative assessments of both individuals and teaching schools. They evaluate their own and others' behavior according to teaching-school affiliation in the continual interpretation of what constitutes correct practice.

Next, it is unlikely that official recognition of unofficially founded *awqāf* would increase the security of property rights in Northwest China. Prescriptions to do so are predicated mostly on liberal private property rights. In China, official registration means that property becomes subject to state control and disposition, as in the example of Islamic finance. In integrating *minjian* practices into the official property system, Hui may lose the capacity to achieve their aims. The relationship between the Hui moral economy and the state economy is not one of resistance; however, it resides below or beyond regulators until it touches upon the interests of the Party-State, in which case it becomes regulated and thereby official.

7

PROCEDURAL JUSTICE

The gods would die if their cult were not rendered.

Émile Durkheim (1912)

DISPUTING HARMONY

Linxia's social landscape is a minefield of disputes. Hui confront Han for playing music too loud in their stores, Han complain of the *adhān*, Salafi clerics condemn Sufi shaykhs, Yihewani students vilify Salafis, pupils vie to succeed their master, wives pursue errant husbands to get them to fulfill their financial duties, farmers protest illegal takings, residents boycott gas stations expanding into their neighborhoods, Bafang Hui denounce high-rise developers, and third-generation homeowners petition the government for adequate compensation for the demolition of their homes. Some of these controversies—for example, property disputes—can be found anywhere in China. Others, such as the inter-teaching-school contests, are unique to Linxia and the surrounding region. The doctrinal, religious, and ethnic complexity of Linxia, coupled with its pained experience of modernity, means that even seemingly innocuous disagreements can carry a tinge of ferocity and possibility for violence. One Hui, a Salafi who worked in the city government, put it this way: "Linxia people are different. They are closed-minded to the point where they will not tolerate the views of others."

In response to the volatility of disputes in Linxia and their potential to snowball into mass conflicts, the Party-State has installed the kinds of legal and extralegal apparatuses that characterize grassroots dispute resolution throughout China. These include local people's courts, the main judicial venues, and mediation across the lowest-level administrative units, including neighborhood committees. While scholars have refuted the notion that East

Asians are averse to litigation,[1] an erroneous idea based on an essentialization of Neo-Confucianism, the fourth and fifth generations of CCP leadership have resuscitated such anachronisms by touting "harmonious society" (*hexie shehui*) as an aspiration for Chinese.

Official discourse on harmony, which overlaps with the Party line on Islam in China, reflects what Laura Nader has called a "harmony ideology," which is defined as "an emphasis on conciliation, recognition that resolution of conflict is inherently good and that its reverse—continued conflict or controversy—is bad or dysfunctional" (Nader 1991: 2). Linxia Hui do not balk at defending their rights and interests or at disagreeing with others. Hui are not averse to disputing, yet they rarely seek redress in people's courts. They cite the same reasons as Han: high transaction costs and reputational harm from disrupting close-knit relationships. Instead, the preferred venue for disputes is often mediation[2] in the mosque.[3] Hui preference for mediation, while not divorced from Neo-Confucian ethics (cultural, historical, or the Party-State's reinvention of the foregoing), is often rationalized on the basis that mosque mediation is most suited to the problems of Muslims.

Clerics are the pivot between Islamic law and socialist state law in Northwest China.[4] Charismatic clerics attract followers for a number of reasons, one of which is their knowledge of Islamic law (or the public perception of their knowledge). Because of his centrality to the mosque community, the cleric is also the targeted recipient of Party-State propaganda

[1] See, e.g., Haley (1978), Ramseyer (1988), Upham (1987), and Feldman (2000).

[2] Shapiro (1981: 3, 10) offers a generic definition of mediation. The mediator operates only with the consent of the parties and may not impose solutions. While mediation is not binding, the mediator works through suasion to align not just the interests of the parties but also the dispute with social norms. Mediation does not necessarily exclude law, but rather it is often based on either previously announced judicial rules or is conducted in the shadow of courts.

[3] The Chinese (Han or Hui) preference for mediation should not be overstated. Johanna Meskill's (1979: 87) historical study of the Lin family in Qing-era Taiwan, to provide just one data point, clearly demonstrates a strong countercurrent of a "culture of violence [that] accounted for the near-permanent feuding that overtook the island" in the 1840s and 1850s. Linxia's own history from the late nineteenth century to the beginning of the Communist period is further evidence that local society was as quick to militarize as it was to mediate.

[4] The significance of the clerics' role is parallel to that of the local or "grassroots" judge, whom Zhu Suli (2000: 5–6) views as irreplaceable in filling in the gaps of law and making concrete decisions from otherwise unclear law, and whom historian Philip C. C. Huang (2001: 7) has conceived as the mediator between custom and code. Outside of the China context, among the Hadrami diaspora of Yemen living in Southeast Asia in locales such as Singapore, a parallel role was played by the "family solicitor," who was a specialist in translating Islamic law into English law (Gilsenan 2012: 184).

efforts that aim to wed the consciousness of the cleric to the will of the Party, even if the cleric himself does not formally join the Party. More broadly, the Party-State tries to mobilize *minjian* authority in the figure of the cleric.

This chapter argues that the relationship between clerics and cadres demonstrates a common ground of the secular and the religious in the Northwest. The relationship between, on the one hand, clerics as well as Sufi shaykhs, mosque elders, and madrasa teachers and, on the other hand, cadres and officials in judicial, religious, ethnic, and security bureaus raises the question of the role of the *minjian* in power relations in Hui communities. The Party-State rarely resorts to coercion to steer clerics to uphold the state-sanctioned understanding of official Islam. While clerics are involved in the "manufacture of consent" (Gramsci 1971: 263), consent only partially explains the production, distribution, and multiplication of power in the triangular relationship between the local Party-State, clerics, and their teaching-school followers.

Agamben (2011) has proposed "glory" as an alternative to power (as either coercion or consent). Drawing on Foucault's concept of governmentality, Agamben further disarticulates the state from law, asserting that glory operates not through courts but through police, not via sovereignty but via government, and by reference not to God but to his angels. Agamben's interventions into the Christian roots of the concept of sovereignty in Western liberalism prompts the present query: How does praise for God underwrite the glory of the socialist Party-State? In this chapter I address this question through a study of the procedural aspects of *jiaofa* or Hui religious law in Northwest China. Clerics, as interstitial nodes of authority between the Party and the Hui masses, glorify God and the Party. They do so through a variety of means, including sermons and, to a lesser extent, textual production—and also through dispute resolution. It is in addressing disputes that clerics and other mosque elders choose, apply, and proselytize law—both secular and Islamic. Clerics operate in an environment of constraint and conflict, however, as they reproduce both the traditions of teaching schools and those of the Party-State.

Personalistic relationships between Hui leaders and governmental officials in legal and judicial bureaus as well as Party organs cross over distinctions PRC law makes between "law" and "non-law." They are also what allow the blood to flow through the arteries of governmental bureaucracies. The interests of Hui leaders and representatives of the Party-State may be aligned when it comes to solving disputes, but that does not mean their interests are one and the same. The informality of cleric-cadre relationships, which are often glossed as *guanxi* (connections based on reciprocity) in Chinese, opens the door to the use of Islamic law. Whereas popular perceptions have viewed *guanxi* as a hindrance to "rule of law" (Shen 2000: 23) and as inviting corruption (Li Ling 2011), it also shapes legal practice.[5] While *guanxi* may increase transaction costs, it is equally plausible that it may lower them by circumventing institutional and bureaucratic hurdles. In Hui communities, thick ties between cadres and clerics complicate the state law's nonrecognition of Islamic law.

Despite the work personalistic relationships perform, collaborations between clerics and cadres are fraught with anxiety. In the remainder of this chapter I examine the ways in which Hui negotiate this anxiety in the practice of Islamic law, a *minjian* law. I do so through two extended case studies that reveal the matrix of interests and sources of law in Hui disputes. I call the first type, which deals with the benign collaboration between cadres and clerics in communicating policy to nonelite Hui, the "formalization of mediation" and the second type, which diffuses conflicts that may otherwise snowball into broader communal strife, the "informalization of adjudication." These types differ according to community in the Northwest, and so I situate them in their geographical and historical setting. Whereas the formalization of mediation operates to reproduce Party-State authority and socialist law at the local level through Hui leaders, the informalization of adjudication shows skilled clerics carving out the Hui social field at the points of contact with state judges and officials. I begin with a closer examination of clerics, who are the linchpin of procedural justice in the Northwest.

MAKING HUI CLERICS

Only after a student has made it through the four or more years of training in scriptural hall education and passed the examination to become a cleric[6] does he fully realize the commitments of serving multiple masters. When I entered a mosque in Northwest China, men would direct me to speak with the cleric. However, clerics were not easy to find. A cleric is often outside the mosque, attending to the matters of community members—whether childbirth, the naming of a child, illness, weddings,

---

[5] See, e.g., Potter (2002), Lo and Otis (2003), Osburg (2013), and Smart and Hsu (2013).

[6] The typical cleric is a married Hui man in his forties. (Only a handful of clerics I met in Ningxia were female, so I will use the masculine pronoun when referring to a cleric.)

funerals, or family disputes. Yet he is just as likely to be attending the meetings of the local government and Party organs.

The cleric is the chief dignitary of the mosque community and plays a central role in its well-being. He assumes the tasks of the imam (the one who leads prayer) and the *khaṭīb* (the one who gives the Friday sermon). Additionally, though he does not formally adjudicate, the cleric is a proxy who takes on the traditional role of the qadi, addressing the panoply of the community's legal concerns and performing many of the qadi's duties—for instance, in pronouncing divorces. Therefore, the cleric is a community leader, problem solver, public relations expert, storehouse of Islamic knowledge, and judge. Like the qadi, he is the touchstone of communitarian values (Geertz 1971: 50-51; Rosen 1984: 4, 11).

The cleric embodies Islamic traditions and, as such, exhibits tremendous charisma in his community. A number of factors define charisma locally, including: performance of the hajj; study abroad in Islamic countries such as Saudi Arabia, Egypt, and Pakistan; mastery of Arabic; knowledge of the Qur'an; lineage and kinship ties; and reputation among mosque communities. Many of the requirements for charismatic leadership are a result of the vast majority of Muslims' inability to travel abroad and interact with coreligionists. Hui, particularly but not exclusively Sufis, recognize certain leaders as embodying grace from God.[7] As a kind of realization of both the Confucian and the Islamic scholar, the cleric possesses charisma that potentially transcends his specific community. The founders of teaching schools demonstrated such charisma, but so have such contemporary leaders as the Yihewani cleric Nasim, first introduced at the beginning of this book and whom I will discuss later in this chapter, whose mosque has witnessed a growth in students and followers. Individual charisma can also be threatening to teaching schools. Thus, over time, teaching schools have "routinized" charisma—that is, transformed it from a quality embodied by a revolutionary figure to a permanent position within "offices" (Weber [1922] 1978a: 245), some of which are hereditary, as in the Sufi tradition. The charismatic authority of clerics is, in Weber's language, charisma routinized by tradition (Weber [1922] 1978a: 245-48; [1922] 1978b: 1121-22).

Clerics' knowledge of shari'a is one source of their reputational charisma. In many instances, due to their high level of education and Arabic literacy, clerics have a monopoly on interpreting and applying the law.

---

[7] The Arabic term *baraka*, loosely translated as "blessing," describes the local currency for charisma.

They reference the revealed sources of Islamic law in mediating disputes, extracting rules directly from the Qur'an and the sunna, and applying them to cases. Generally, they adopt the view that shari'a is a living and breathing law that can be understood by common sense, although Salafis and some Yihewani may apply an originalist conception to legal analysis. They examine the Qur'an through the sunna, with particular reference to the explications of the first three generations after the Prophet Muhammad. Inevitably, in identifying and applying rules to disputes, clerics apply their own reasoning, sometimes with reference to Hanafi *fiqh* manuals. They do not write down their reasoning or ruling, however, for fear that state authorities would find it subversive. Chinese *fiqh* thus remains primarily oral, unconsolidated, and driven by problem solving.

According to my study of Linxia's thirty-four mosques, each mosque cleric, with one exception, mediated civil disputes. The one particularly nervous cleric who flatly denied settling any kind of dispute among his community told me that "religious law cannot exceed state law" (*jiaofa chaobuguo guofa*), and so he deferred to the police. Clerics mediate a broad spectrum of civil disputes: in order of frequency, these disputes concern family matters, including: marital relations, father-son relations, and inheritance; neighbor problems; accidental death, or what would be called tort in common law systems or "delict" (*qinquan*) in continental law systems such as the PRC's; and, lastly, property concerns and dietary rules. Due to the dense ties Hui have to fellow teaching-school members in their mosque communities, such disputes have the potential to mushroom into larger conflicts beyond the immediate parties.

Members of the mosque community tend to follow the instructions of their cleric, whose authority could be unchallenged in the absence of checks by the mosque administration committee. One senior member of a Linxia mosque implied that the cleric's authority is unquestioned, stating, "Here, we have a problem. The faithful do what the cleric says." Although the speaker was describing Linxia, his statement, which renders explicit Hui behaviors and attitudes toward their clerics, has broad applicability to Hui communities. It is precisely such loyalty that troubles the Party-State.

Hence, the Party-State, like the teaching schools, also tries to routinize the charisma of clerics. It attempts to do so by incorporating them into the lowest tiers of its legal-juridical apparatus. Max Weber viewed bureaucracies as a requirement for the rationalization and systematization of justice. The bureau, as the form of modern organized action by officials, was one category of "rational legal authority" (Weber [1922]

1978a: 219). Bureaucracy and law proceeded in lockstep in the modernization of procedural justice. In contemporary Northwest China, the relationships between the Party-State and local Muslim societies are shaped by bureaucracy and law. While both have traction in the everyday lives of Hui leaders, they are made meaningful only through personalistic relationships between the Muslim elite and officials and cadres.[8] There are numerous religious and ethnic bureaus under the government that enfold Muslim minority leaders into the Party-State, including the State Administration of Religious Affairs (SARA), the State Administration of Ethnic Affairs (SAEA), and the State Ethnic Affairs Commission (SEAC). Bureaucracies also include organs of the CCP, such as the United Front Work Department (UFWD) (see Table 7.1). Collectively, these bureaus, like their counterparts in Muslim-majority societies such as Egypt, are engaged in "the fashioning of religion as an object of continual management" (Agrama 2012: 24). They do so by accessing the Hui social field through those charged with maintaining it—the clerics.

Whereas many senior members of mosque communities in a variety of teaching schools had joined the Party, no cleric I talked to had joined. They cited a conflict between Islam and socialism, although Salafis and Yihewani were generally more adamant than were Gedimu, Sufis, or the Xidaotang that Party membership would violate their responsibility to their community. Nonmembership did not, however, prevent clerics from attending regular meetings and, in some cases, serving as advisers to governmental bodies and Party organs. Most clerics have formal membership in the organizations constituted under the Party-State, such as the China Islamic Association (Yi-Xie), which function as a bridge between the Party and Muslim citizens.

The bureaucratization of clerics begins with their licensing, which historically has been the responsibility of the Yi-Xie. The Yi-Xie's mandate has evolved over recent years, affecting its work at both the national and local levels. For instance, the exam clerics must pass for state certification[9] was historically administered by the local Yi-Xie, but in 2010 the

---

[8] Frank Upham (1987: 17-27) observed a similar characteristic of what he called "bureaucratic informalism" in Japan.

[9] The basis for the requirement that all clerics (Muslim or otherwise) obtain certification is found in local regulations—for instance, pursuant to article 33 of the Temporary Administrative Measures of the Linxia Hui Autonomous Prefecture Religious Affairs (*Linxia Huizu zizhizhou zongjiao shiwu guanli zanxing banfa*), hereinafter "Linxia Religious Measures," passed by the Linxia Hui Autonomous Prefecture People's Government, December 31, 2001, implemented January 7, 2006.

TABLE 7.1 Bureaucracies in the Muslim Northwest

	Government			CCP		Government-Constituted Organizations
National-level entity	*State Administration of Religious Affairs (SARA)*	*State Administration of Ethnic Affairs (SAEA)*	*State Ethnic Affairs Commission (SEAC)*	*United Front Work Department (UFWD)*	*Chinese People's Political Consultative Conference (CPPCC)*	*Yi-Xie's Educational Administration Guidance Committee (EAGC)*
Supervening entity	State Council			Central Committee of the CCP		SARA
Entity at relevant administrative level*	BRA	BEA	Ethnic Affairs Commission	UFWD	CPPCC	Yi-Xie
Jurisdiction and function	All matters pertaining to the officially recognized 5 religions	All matters relating to the officially recognized 56 ethnicities	Implement policy in ethnic minority areas	Coordinate relations between CCP and non-Party elite	Represent CCP and non-Party leaders, including religious leaders	Implement policies on Islam
Local management of Hui clerics	Approve appointment of clerics, approve election of mosque committee, establish mosque curricula, conduct training sessions		Train Hui cadres, supervise mosque activities and mosque space	Train Hui cadres, consult Hui leaders on local problems		Publish model sermons, hold sermon competitions, establish mosque curricula, produce research for Hui consumption

* Each bureau exists at every administrative level (e.g., autonomous region or province, prefecture, county, and city) except for the Education Administration Guidance Committee (EAGC), which exists only at the national level and convenes in Beijing.

rule changed in Gansu so that now only the Yi-Xie in Beijing has the authority to administer the test. Several clerics said this restriction made obtaining certification, which is a state requirement, much more difficult. As mentioned in Chapter 4, because most clerics prefer to be educated in mosque-based madrasas rather than the state-run Islamic Scriptural Institute, which grants certification automatically upon graduation, most must take the examination administered by the Yi-Xie. Upon passing the examination and obtaining certification, clerics undergo training at the local Bureau of Religious Affairs (BRA) as part of the requirement that they "ceaselessly increase [their] religious knowledge, policy proficiency, and legal consciousness."[10] Upon completion of the training, clerics are placed on the local bureau's payroll. The pay scale appears to vary depending on location within the Northwest. For instance, clerics are nominally paid by the Linxia City BRA,[11] but in Ningxia, clerics can supplement their income by mediating disputes under the guidance of the judicial bureau.

Influential clerics who have high appointments in the Yi-Xie usually have a corresponding position in the Chinese People's Political Consultative Conference (CPPCC). The CPPCC, formalized during the First Plenary Session of the CPPCC on September 21, 1949, is an organization of the CCP and non-Party groups, often religious in nature and recruited by the Party, that serve an advisory function in developing policy for Muslim minorities, among other groups. I met several high-ranking figures in mosques, including Salafis, who were vocal and active members of the CPPCC. Such representatives would lead public meetings during which officials sought to communicate policy initiatives or changes to Hui attendees. Muslims in Gansu call dual appointments in both the Yi-Xie and CPPCC "one set, two brands" (yitaoliangpai).

There is the perception that Yihewani dominate as "model clerics" through their participation in such organizations as the Yi-Xie. But while neither quasi-governmental organizations nor governmental bureaus release data on the teaching-school affiliation of their constituents, based on interviews in both Beijing and the Northwest, the Party-State appears to be ecumenical in bureaucratizing clerics. The local Yi-Xie and CPPCC organs have selected charismatic clerics from all teaching schools for membership. As to the Yi-Xie based in Beijing, and particularly within its research institute, many of the most productive individuals identify

---

[10] See, e.g., Linxia Religious Measures, art. 31.
[11] The local government constantly changes such policies.

as Gedimu or Xidaotang, although there are few Salafis. Whereas the past presidents of the Ningxia Yi-Xie and the Gansu Province Yi-Xie were Yihewani,[12] Sufis have made inroads in both organizations at the sub-autonomous region and sub-provincial levels. For example, Ma Guoyu, a member of the Jahriyya, was appointed the president of the Gansu Province Yi-Xie in 2010, and one of the most active vice presidents of the Gansu Province Yi-Xie has been Ma Bailing, also of the Jahriyya. The president of the Lanzhou City Yi-Xie, Su Guanglin, is another politically active Sufi who regularly speaks at commemorations of the anniversaries of death dates of Sufi saints, giving an official imprimatur to such occasions. Sufis generally talk more about their leaders' positions than do Yihewani and Salafis.[13] My sense of the reason for this is that Sufis feel that the state has historically discriminated against them more than against other groups, and thus to receive any official status is an indication that their version of Islam is closer to state-supported official Islam.

These relationships illustrate the interdependence of the secular state and Islam in China. Through licensing, formal appointments, informal consultations, meetings, training, continued education, propaganda sessions, conferences, committee formations (each with its own reporting requirements), and payrolls, the charisma of clerics is contained and channeled by the bureaucracies. Clerics are trained in Party policy affecting

[12] In Ningxia, the lead cleric of Central Mosque in Yinchuan holds the following positions: member of the National Committee of the CPPCC, standing member of the Yi-Xie, president of the Ningxia Yi-Xie, vice chairman of the Yinchuan Committee of the CPPCC, and president of the Yinchuan Yi-Xie. In Gansu, Yang Sen (1922–2008), former cleric of the Yihewani West Gate Great Mosque in Lanzhou and one of the most well-known clerics of his generation, was concurrently the vice chairman of the Lanzhou City CPPCC, vice president of the Lanzhou City Yi-Xie, and president of the Gansu Province Yi-Xie. In 1993 the Yi-Xie dispatched him to Egypt, where he was given a gold medal by then-president Husni Mubarak. The following year he went to Malaysia, where he founded several exchange programs. Clerics such as Yang Sen have served vital roles in (re)establishing Chinese Muslims' ties to foreign Muslims.

[13] For instance, in Ningxia, Khufiyya Sufis are proud of such members as Wang Zhiwei, who assumed the position of Party secretary of the autonomous region, and Li Rei, who is vice chairman of Haiyuan County. In Linxia, the current shaykh of the Grand Tomb Complex is the vice chair of the CPPCC of Gansu Province and a member of the provincial Yi-Xie. Ma Jincheng (d. 2009), the sixth shaykh of the Beizhuang Sufi order in Dongxiang Autonomous County, was a revered Sufi leader. His ties to quasi-governmental organizations were extensive: he was a member of the Standing Committee of the Gansu Province CPPCC, vice president of the Yi-Xie at both the national level and the Gansu provincial level, vice chairman of the Linxia Prefecture CPPCC, and president of the Linxia Prefecture Yi-Xie. He further had regular contacts with the UFWD at the national and provincial levels. His funeral was attended by 130,000 Muslims as well as a host of dignitaries, including the Gansu Province Party secretary and director of the Gansu People's Congress Standing Committee, the head of the UFWD, and the vice director of the Gansu People's Congress, to name a few.

every aspect of "religious work," from the types of textbooks used in mosque classrooms and the content of sermons to mosque financial management. Beyond socialization into a state-defined Islam, the bureaucracy includes clerics as decision makers, informants, and even recipients of orders from various bureaus. By assuming diverse types of delegated powers of mediation, clerics become partners with cadres in maintaining social stability in Muslim communities.

While it is clear that the BRA and the Bureau of Ethnic Affairs (BEA) benefit from bureaucratizing clerics and other Hui leaders, such relationships can also benefit the bureaucratized Hui elite. To give one example, the ninth shaykh of the Grand Tomb Complex of the Qadiriyya order, Yang Shijun (1903–1997), was an eminent Sufi leader and religious head in Linxia.[14] In 1984 he successfully brokered a deal between the tomb complex and the Linxia City government when the latter sought to build a "sky bridge," or pedestrian walkway, over the front entrance of the tomb complex so that people could enter the neighboring Red Square Public Park from the front street access, particularly on the New Year Lantern Festival, a secularized holiday. The Qadiriyya considered such a construction an insult to Qi Jingyi, their founder buried at the site, for the sky bridge would be taller than his tomb. Over a period of several days, tens of thousands of angry Sufis gathered at the entrance of the tomb complex to protest the proposed construction, and when the city police could not maintain control, armed police were brought in from Lanzhou. The head of the Nationalities Affairs Commission, the main governmental representative body for ethnic minorities, which implements recommendations from the UFWD, came from Beijing and told those gathered to leave peacefully or the armed police would forcefully remove them. The protesters remained.

Through negotiations, Yang Shijun and the Linxia City Yi-Xie persuaded the city government to build an underground entrance to the park. Many Qadiriyya Sufis claim that one of the reasons Yang Shijun was successful in his negotiations was that he was vice chair of the Gansu Province CPPCC and a member of the Yi-Xie at the provincial level. They argue that these positions conferred upon him a measure of "symbolic capital" and leverage vis-à-vis the city officials; furthermore, he had existing social ties within the city government's BRA and BEA. He was able to mobilize these resources in defense of the tomb complex. Indeed, the

[14] Yang Shijun is remembered by Qadiriyya Sufis for leading the restoration of the order in the 1980s after the order was particularly singled out for destruction in the 1960s and 1970s.

teaching clerics at the Grand Tomb Complex say that attaining such a position is a criterion of becoming a shaykh—that is, recognition of leadership within the order depends on recognition by the government.

Others, including Qadiriyya Sufis, disagree, saying such titles are "empty cups" (*kong beizi*) that are used only to appease Muslim leaders, and that the titles suggest that the Party-State has positive relations with Muslims when the reality may be murkier. Naysayers argue the reason for Yang Shijun's success was not his stature in the eyes of the government, but rather his charisma among his followers and the support of "popular sentiment" (*minxin*).[15] The most cynical view espoused by Linxia Hui is that such titling does not confer entitlement but, instead, constructs fetters around influential Muslims. The bureaucratization of clerics and other Hui leaders is the subject of intense reflection and debate among followers.

Bureaucratizing nonstate authorities is a form of governance that predated Communist rule.[16] One of the defining debates in the anthropology of Chinese religion is whether popular religions' description of celestial bureaucracies reflected bureaucratic forms of government or vice versa.[17] This question gains immediacy in contemporary partnerships between the local Party-State and minority elites, whether Tibetan (Yeh 2003; Pirie 2013b), Yi (Diamant 2001; Yan 2012), Mongol (Bulag 2010), or Hui. The Party-State endeavors to co-opt the charisma of religious elites (Feuchtwang 2010), resulting in a condition of "mutual dependence" (Chau 2006: 14) between religious leaders and the local state. Beyond instrumentalist aims—that is, "using the Hui to rule the Hui" (*yi Hui zhi Hui*), as the Qing policy was known—the mirroring of

---

[15] The word *minxin* is closely related to *minjian*, as it shares the character *min*, meaning "people" or "of the people." The second character, *xin*, is usually translated as "feeling," "heart," or "center."

[16] Ma Zhan'ao, for instance, was one of the Ma family warlords whom the Qing won over by offering entitlements and military posts.

[17] Adapting a structural-functionalist approach, Arthur Wolf (1974) argued that social categories determine cosmological order. Steven Sangren (1987a, 1987b) has argued that relations between officials provide "structures of value" that are reproduced through social practice and that provide a model for thinking about analogous social relations. Stephan Feuchtwang ([1992] 2001a: vi) has drawn upon Wolf's writing to argue that popular religion is not determined by imperial rule but is a "supplementary universe" to state orthodoxy. Robert Weller (1987: 23–24), like Sangren, emphasizes "pragmatic flexibility of interpretation" in practitioners' use of universal sets of relationships, such as between gods, ghosts, and ancestors. The central tenet of Islam, the oneness, or indivisibility, of God (*tawḥīd*), distinguishes Islam in China from such popular religions as ancestor-based worship. At the same time, Chinese Muslims are culturally Chinese. Although there is no bureaucracy in the Islamic vision of heaven, there are sub-bureaucratic mediators among Chinese Muslims.

what Agamben (2011: 144) calls "angelology and bureaucracy" is not just a form of power delegation but rather one of making piety an expression of civility.

Islamic law and charismatic Muslim authorities present a potential threat to the Party-State, particularly given the history of the Ma family warlords, most of whom were anti-Communist,[18] but also given the transnational ties emerging between clerics in the Northwest and scholars and ideologues outside the PRC. For example, several clerics from Qinghai and Gansu who had studied in Saudi Arabia and Egypt have established websites on which they answer questions from Hui about everyday matters ranging from dress to intermarriage with Han.[19] These online clerics emulate muftis in the Middle East who mobilize social media to reach audiences broader than their mosque communities. Many of these websites have been shut down, because the government censors consider them to threaten social stability. Clerics, in turn, establish multiple online venues in a cat-and-mouse game with the Internet police, in addition to using other media, including pamphlets and DVDs. The Party-State perceives them as glorifying an alternative legal order, not officially sanctioned by governmental bureaus.

THE FORMALIZATION OF MEDIATION

Hui leaders play an important role in some of the extrajudicial forms of dispute resolution that the PRC has actively promoted. China has a history of mediation that long antedates the popularity of "alternative dispute resolution" in Anglo-American common law (Shapiro 1981: 160–61). The model was the family head, who would mediate tensions within the family, but the authority to mediate disputes could also be seen in the heads of lineages, and even in the local magistrate, who favored extrajudicial adjustments and referred cases to nongovernmental mediators.[20] As historian Philip C. C. Huang (2006: 286) has shown, the Communists' use of mediation was a result of their dependence on local communities in Northwest China before 1949. With the establishment of the PRC, Mao

---

[18] Most of the Ma warlords fled China to Taiwan or Saudi Arabia before 1949, with the exception of a minority, such as Ma Hongbin, who joined the Communists.

[19] Unlike 'ulama' in Pakistan, where Muhammad Qasim Zaman (2002) found a distinction between public Muslim intellectuals, who use new media, and Deobandi 'ulama', who choose not to reproduce their authority through such means, the most educated Chinese clerics try to incorporate the Internet as one of several mechanisms for spreading Islamic legal consciousness.

[20] See, for instance, Freedman (1958: 36), Ch'u (1965: 20–21), and Cohen (1966: 1209).

Zedong abolished the legal system but retained mediation as a means to control conflict in the population (Lubman 1967).

A basic tripartite structure, first established in Northwest China, remains the template for mediation throughout the country: *minjian tiaojie* (popular mediation), which is led by community leaders; "administrative mediation" (*xingzheng tiaojie*), which is organized under government officials; and "judicial mediation" (*sifa tiaojie*), which is integrated into the courts. Although the Party-State prioritized legal development over mediation in the 1990s, beginning in 2002 there has been a revitalization of mediation (Halegua 2005)[21] as part of a governmental response to populist pressures as well as to arguments from government officials that the court system is overburdened (Liebman 2011). In all cases, state law is the applicable law.

Critics of the return of mediation argue that it is a response to an uptick in socially destabilizing petitioning and protests and that legal reform according to Western standards erodes the autonomy of the CCP (Fu and Cullen 2011; Fu 2014). They view mediation and informalization as a retreat from commitments to the "rule of law" (Minzner 2011; Pissler 2012). Such critics echo the sentiments expressed in Nader's "harmony ideology." They argue, as did critics of previous forms of mediation in China, that mediation depoliticizes conflict (Lubman 1999: 13; Katz 2009: 8).

In this context, state-appointed Hui leaders play a significant role. Although the Party-State does not recognize Islamic law, it co-opts religious figures into the larger apparatus of dispute resolution by involving them in "people's mediation committees" (*renmin tiaojie weiyuanhui*), hereinafter PMCs. Although Mao Zedong created PMCs, it was not until 2011 that they were given a basis in law.[22] Their purpose has shifted over time. In the 1950s they were instruments of political ideology, but by the 1990s their function was dispute resolution. Beginning in 2002, they have served

---

[21] See article 1 of Several Provisions of the Supreme People's Court on Hearing Civil Cases Involving Mediation Agreements (*Guanyu shenli sheji renmin tiaojie xieyi de minshi anjian de ruogan guiding*), hereinafter "Several Provisions," promulgated by the Supreme People's Court, September 5, 2002. Several Provisions made mediation agreements enforceable as contracts in people's courts.

[22] Article 7 of the People's Mediation Law of the PRC (*Zhonghua renmin gongheguo renmin tiaojiefa*), issued August 28, 2010, by the Standing Committee of the National People's Congress, and effective as of January 1, 2011, defines people's mediation committees as comprising three to seven members, with one person serving as director and, optionally, one or more people serving as deputy director(s). The law specifies that in ethnic minority regions PMCs should have ethnic minority members.

several functions,[23] and today they are used in a wide variety of settings, including villagers' committees in the countryside and residents' committees in the cities (Read and Michelson 2008: 739). The use of PMCs has grown exponentially in the reform era: in 1981 PMCs mediated 673,936 cases, and in 2009 they mediated 5,800,144 cases (Zhu 2011: 303–4), an increase of 761 percent. In the Northwest, PMCs have taken a particular form in mosques, both addressing individual Hui disputes pursuant to state law and communicating broader state policies toward Islam to parties beyond the dispute.

One subset of PMCs is what I call "Islamic PMCs." The Party-State uses Islamic PMCs to address conflicts and prevent them from devolving into interethnic or antistate confrontations. Among Hui communities, Islamic PMCs are most prominently found in Ningxia.[24] As of 2012, there were 3,423 PMCs in Ningxia for Hui and other ethnic groups, employing 21,888 mediators.[25] There are 30 Islamic PMCs attached to mosques in Ningxia, and a total of 7,800 Hui mediators (some of whom are not based in mosques), comprising 36 percent of the AR's total number of mediators. Among these, some 2,000 are "religious personnel" (*zongjiao renshi*) and members of the mosque administration committee.

Cadres in legal and judicial bureaus run training sessions and create educational propaganda to prepare Hui clerics and elder members of the mosque community to serve as mediators. These bureaus then employ trained clerics, shaykhs, and Hui elders to mediate disputes in their communities through Islamic PMCs. In rural Haiyuan County, which has a population of 450,000, of whom 75 percent are Hui, the judicial bureau hired ten clerics in 2010, and the number was set to increase in the following fiscal year. The basic-level people's courts, the lowest level of the judiciary, and grassroots mediation bodies also hire clerics. The funding does not come from the local government, however, but from the Ministry of Finance. In 2010 in Haiyuan County, one of the poorest counties in Ningxia, clerics were paid 50 yuan per case and 100 yuan for particularly challenging cases. Dockets include mainly marital disputes but also

[23] These transitions are reflected in the documents that have formalized PMCs under law, including the General Rule on the Organization of the Temporary People's Mediation Committees (*Renmin tiaojie weiyuanhui zanxing zuzhi tongze*), promulgated by the Administration Council, March 22, 1954; the Regulations on the Organization of People's Mediation Committees (*Renmin tiaojie weiyuanhui zuzhi tiaoli*), promulgated by the State Council, May 5, 1989; and the Several Provisions.

[24] Fernanda Pirie (2013b: 81), however, has observed Tibetan PMCs in Qinghai.

[25] In 2010 mediators in Ningxia handled 57,410 cases; 2011 saw a drop to 29,300 cases plus an additional 5,268 "difficult cases" (*yinan fuza maodun*) (Wang Yingmei 2012: 51).

inheritance and property cases as well as torts, such as those arising from traffic accidents.

Mediation work in Ningxia exhibits what I call the formalization of mediation. Much like what Galanter (1989) revealed in his study of the *Panchayat* in India, the Chinese state has gradually incorporated into the juridical apparatus potentially alternative nonstate authority, in the form of Hui leaders. The function of the formalization of mediation is not just to curb disturbances but also to communicate broader policy to nonelite Hui through a face most familiar to them: a cleric or an elder. Simon Roberts (1993: 462) noted that in-court mediation (called "judicial mediation" in the PRC) can be coercive, because the face of the third-party mediator is the authoritative judge. In Islamic PMCs, however, the face of authority is not the judge as representative of the state but rather a local charismatic community Hui elder.

A man I call Old Dong exemplifies the formalization of mediation. One of the most prolific and publicly praised mediators in the area surrounding Ningxia's capital, Yinchuan, Old Dong is a seventy-year-old Sufi Hui who is the director of his mosque's administrative committee and the head of the mosque's PMC. The mosque is located in a hamlet of approximately ten thousand people, all Hui. The town has several mosques, of which most are Khufiyya Sufi with a smaller number of Jahriyya Sufi and Yihewani. This demographic and doctrinal pattern is replicated throughout most of Ningxia.

The mediation room, located off the mosque's courtyard opposite the prayer hall, looks like a classroom for PRC legal propaganda. There is a small chalkboard in the front of the room and a group of desks with small stools in the middle. Each wall is decorated with large posters, such as "Traffic Safety Propaganda Enters the Mosque," which shows photos of members of the mosque's PMC arm in arm with police conducting propaganda sessions in the mosque, attending meetings on traffic safety in Yinchuan, and participating in class sessions in the mediation room itself. In one corner are a series of placards reading "Civil Dispute Mediation Work Room" and "Site of Legal System Propaganda Education." One image is particularly striking: a photograph of Old Dong holding a Qur'an as if in deep study. Old Dong, however, can read neither Arabic nor Chinese. He tells me:

> I never went to school. I worked mainly in the fields, doing manual labor for most of my life. I can't read Chinese or Arabic. But I speak Chinese, some Arabic, some Turkic, some Persian, and a little Mongolian … I have

been a judicial mediator for seven years. I have been hired by thirteen work units [*danwei*], including the court, judicial bureau, bank, traffic police, police station, and the people's congress.

Old Dong's illiteracy calls into question his capacity to apply any kind of text-based law to a dispute. (In his defense, he mentions that the Prophet Muhammad himself was illiterate.) It highlights his discretion in handling cases rather than his capacity for legal reasoning. Despite his illiteracy, he has considerable status in his community, not only because he embodies local norms of rectitude but also because of the official mediator titles that thirteen governmental bodies have conferred on him.[26] It is the combination of his lack of formal legal education and his grassroots charisma that is attractive to the Party-State and that makes him a model state-sanctioned Hui leader. Old Dong describes how he began as a mediator, a process of envelopment by bureaucracy: "I began doing this voluntarily—that is to say, without a mandate from the local government. But soon local officials came and began to notice the value of my work. They said, 'Even though you have never studied law, you handle these problems.'" In 2003 his town's traffic police nominated him as a people's mediator, and since then he has been recognized as a mediator by over a dozen governmental departments and Party organs. Old Dong says he has not joined the CCP and has never been paid for his work. "I have never made money from it. But recently, I was given a reward of thirty thousand yuan!" he exclaims.

The procedure for people's mediation may take different forms, including forms modeled on adjudication. The two parties sit at tables opposite each other, one identified by the sign "petitioner" and the other by "respondent." Six members of the PMC sit at a large table before the parties, each with his or her own sign identifying the member's position in the committee. Five of the PMC members are part of the mosque administration; the sixth is the assistant director, who is a police officer. Old Dong sits in the middle, with the policeman to his left and another committee member to his right. Because all individuals in the room are Hui, men wear a skullcap and women a black scarf. As Hui mediators are not technically civil servants and the mosque is not a governmental unit, their religious markers are not only permitted but also encouraged.

---

[26] Adam Yuet Chau (2005) wrote in his study of local elites and popular religion that the local state, as part of what he calls "legitimation politics," would often confer titles on such figures as temple officers.

The one exception is the police officer. Although he too is Hui, he wears his full police uniform and hat. Thus, despite the venue being a forum for people's mediation, the police officer is a constant reminder of the state's presence. He is both a symbolic fixture of state power and one of its "intimate collaborators" (Garces 2010: 463) with religious authority. As a representative of the socialist state, he delegates powers to Hui clerics, but at the same time, Old Dong informed me, he ensures that state law, not Islamic law, is the governing law. He does not need to directly address the parties in dispute, nor does he himself need to vocalize state law. Old Dong speaks for the state. Just by being there, the police officer guarantees state interests. During a visit in 2015, I learned that Old Dong increasingly handles disputes without a police officer, and that much mosque-based mediation is conducted without a state representative. The absence of police in popular mediation has not necessarily allowed a greater role for Islamic law, however. Hui leaders like Old Dong have adopted the position of enforcing state law, marking a greater internalization of secular legal consciousness.

In seven years of mediating, Old Dong had personally handled 107 cases (for an average caseload of fifteen cases per year). Of the sixteen cases he mediated in 2010,[27] nine (56 percent) were traffic accidents. Of these, three were "major accident disputes" that resulted in the death of one or more people. The remaining seven cases concerned housing loans (3), contracted land (2), an economic dispute (1), and "other" (1).

What he lacks in caseload, Old Dong makes up in success rate (defined as those cases that were not appealed). He claims 100 percent of the cases he mediated were met with satisfaction by both sides and were not appealed. Old Dong's assertion was not completely accurate. Several archived case reports I reviewed entailed judicial mediation—that is, disputants dissatisfied with Old Dong's mediation "appealed" to a people's court, which in turn tried to mediate the dispute before adjudication. Just as judicial mediation is rarely appealed in China (Fu and Cullen 2011: 34), so too is appeal from people's mediation infrequent. It is likely that disputants, who might not all be satisfied by Old Dong's mediation work, lump their claims.

Because of his success, Old Dong has been heralded by official institutions. The archive of cases Old Dong handled is full of praise by judicial and security organs. For instance, in October 2010 Old Dong mediated

---

[27] My visit to the judicial bureau that archives Old Dong's cases occurred in November 2010; thus the total number of cases mediated by Old Dong in 2010 would be slightly higher.

a contentious dispute arising out of a traffic accident. A man driving a bus hit another man riding a motorcycle, resulting in the death of the latter. Both men were Hui. The offender then drove directly to the driving school office where he worked. The family members of the deceased took the body and carried it to the driving school office to confront the offender. A conflict ensued that quickly became violent. The family members, enraged, took the daughter of the head of the school, who owned the offender's vehicle, and forced her to kneel down before the dead body. The wife of the school head gathered ten men to defend the school. Soon, over a hundred people were fighting, and guns were drawn. The police finally arrived, including ten policemen in riot gear, who disrupted the brawl. Public security officials contacted Old Dong. He worked for three days and three nights to mediate the dispute among the three parties: the family of the deceased, the family of the offender, and the family of the owner of the driving school. The aggrieved family wanted 280,000 yuan in compensation, and the school owner suggested 120,000 yuan, whereas the offender's family said it could afford only 20,000 yuan. After mediation, the settled amount was 180,000 yuan: 150,000 yuan from the school head and 30,000 yuan from the offender's family. This amount included compensation for the loss of the life of the family head and life subsidies for his wife and two children. The official case report highlights the role of Old Dong: "Through [Old Dong's] ceaseless effort and energetic mediation of the drivers' dispute, they [finally] signed a People's Mediation Agreement Book." Beyond the official record, Old Dong has been heralded as a kind of local Muslim Lei Feng by judicial and security organs and the Yi-Xie in the local media.[28]

Islamic PMCs are not a true alternative to official law. State law has thus colonized informal justice (Merry and Milner 1993: 5). Colonization takes the form of integrating alternative venues of dispute resolution into the official apparatus through supervision, archiving, and formalizing their procedures. Significantly, Old Dong, who is not trained in PRC or Islamic law, is a model people's mediator. He has been commended by the official propaganda organs more than any other Hui leader I encountered. Such commendation is part of the spectacle of the law: the display of the signifiers of justice exceeds procedural justice. In the context of socialist law, which is anathema to Islamic law, Islamic PMCs exemplify the seeming paradox of

---

[28] Lei Feng (1940–1962) was a model soldier eulogized by the CCP for his selfless devotion to Communism. See Minzner (2011) for a similar example of a "model judge" from Jiangsu who was likewise extolled for handling 3,100 cases in fourteen years without a single complaint or appeal.

Islamic law in China. Whereas some Western states have established Islamic arbitration, Islamic PMCs maintain the appearance of "Islamicness" while applying state law, not Islamic law.

The formalization of mediation acts on those members of Muslim communities who are both charismatic and nonthreatening to the regime. Its highest function is to communicate the benign collaboration between the local government and individuals respected by the community. There are precedents for such arrangements in Western imperialism, namely, the relationship between the British judge and the maulvies (Anderson 1990) or pundits in the Punjab (Bhattacharya 1996), as well as French employment of qadis, chieftains, and charismatic notables as instruments of local rule in Morocco (Eickelman 1985). As Hannah Arendt noted, colonial bureaucratization entailed exploitation. Arendt traces the "philosophy of the [imperial] bureaucrat" to Lord Cromer, British consul general in Egypt from 1883 to 1907, who sought a "hybrid form of government" (Arendt [1966] 1976: 213). The legacies of such hybrid governments can be found in the contemporary Middle East, in the state's use of tribal dispute resolution (see, e.g., Antoun 2000). Similarly, such relationships in China co-opt clerics as agents of Party-State policy on religion and ethnicity.

Beyond exercising power through local ethnic delegates, however, the formalization of mediation draws on the Hui experience of Islam, and Islam's legitimacy in the eyes of nonelite, to administer Hui issues on behalf of the Party-State. State-supported Hui leaders are analogous to those whom Agamben would call "angels," who through hymn and liturgy acclaim the sovereign. The acclamation, or "an exclamation of praise, of triumph," links the law and liturgy (Agamben 2011: 169–70). As the counterpart to official law and policy, the acclamations of angel Hui resonate with the Muslim masses. When Old Dong engages in mediating a dispute, he first "calm[s] and propagandize[s]" the parties (*gei tamen zhenjing xuanchuan*) through both state law and religious knowledge. He does so by explaining patriotism and unity through Chinese Islamic myth: "The Prophet gave the three legendary Sufi saints Gaisi, Gasa, and Wan Gasa instructions to ... love their country. Today, we call this love nation, love religion [*aiguo aijiao*]."[29] The efficacy of the acclamation derives from the authorizing discourse of Islam. In other words, the angels' praise is a form of administration in this world.

[29] Old Dong, like many Chinese Sufis, refers to Gaisi, Gasa, and Wan Gasa as (proto-)Sufis, although they purportedly arrived in China as missionaries during the Tang Dynasty, well before the emergence of recognizable Sufi orders.

Since 2009, Chinese sovereignty over Muslim minority populations has become increasingly dependent on such celestial glorification.
Typically, after a violent episode between Uyghurs and Han Chinese, a
Hui or Uyghur leader of the Yi-Xie will denounce the act as "not representative of Islam," which is a "peaceful religion." The underlying causes
of the dispute are glossed over in the Party-State's appropriation of the
meta-discourse of apolitical Islam. It was Hui clerics at the helm of the
Yi-Xie who most vocally called for the enactment of an antiterrorism
statute days after a terrorist attack in Kunming in March 2014. It is not
only through sermons and news statements but also through resolving
disputes that Hui leaders articulate versions of official Islam, ideological
counter-radicalization. Through the formalization of mediation and its
representation through local media, Hui clerics, in conjunction with
police and public security officers, communicate law and policy to Hui
communities beyond the dispute. In sum, the form of dispute resolution
routinizes the charisma of Hui elite, severs Muslim authority from Islamic
law, and reproduces the Party-State's version of Islamic orthodoxy.

THE INFORMALIZATION OF ADJUDICATION

Whereas sociolegal studies have theorized the state's integration of nonstate law and alternative dispute resolution, they have given less attention to the effects of such integration on the formal legal system itself.[30]
The Party-State's use of Islamic law through *minjian* channels provides
an inroad to addressing this question. In addition to the formalization of
mediation, another type of collaboration between Hui leaders and their
counterparts in the local Party-State is what I call the informalization of
adjudication. This type of collaboration, most prominent in Linxia but
apparent also in other areas of Gansu and Qinghai, is in some regards the
opposite of the formalization of mediation. It acts not to glorify the Party's
beneficial religious and ethnic policies through nonexpert Hui, but rather
to appropriate educated clerics' knowledge of Islamic law. If, during adjudication, a Hui litigant makes an oral argument based on Islamic law that
is integral to the matter under dispute or uses Islamic law as a basis of
evidence (e.g., a wife arguing that because she and her husband had an
Islamic marriage contract, they were validly married under Islamic law), a
state judge may turn the case over to a cleric. Social networks channel the
dispute away from the court and toward informal venues such as mosque

---

[30] See Henry (1985), Harrington (1992), and Norrie (1999).

chambers. There, the cleric may apply general principles from shariʿa to a dispute through mediation. This process operates in the gray area of PRC procedural law, where the official hands over authority to the *minjian*.

In Hui communities, when disputes arise between family members or neighbors, they often seek mediation by a cleric, who applies Islamic law, but sometimes they go to the neighborhood office, the smallest unit of the municipal government, which has state-appointed mediators who apply state law. Only rarely does an unresolved dispute involve litigation in a basic-level people's court. If the judge is Hui and a disputant invokes Islamic law during the proceedings, the judge, who cannot opine on a matter of religious law, may call what could be described as a "cleric hotline" to request that a cleric come and mediate the dispute. This cleric may not necessarily be one of the clerics officially sanctioned by the state to mediate disputes. Once the cleric takes over, Islamic law becomes the relevant law. The procedural law of judicial mediation is ambiguous concerning the legality of remanding a case to a nonstate authority. Given that the trial's "record of speech" (*tanhua bilu*) strikes any reference to Islamic law and that case records omit any use of clerics, court procedure suggests that the use of religious law contravenes civil procedure law.

Nasim receives many of these cases. The process by which he became a delegate of the judiciary illustrates the informalization of adjudication. Upon returning to Linxia from studying Islamic law and jurisprudence in Saudi Arabia in the 1990s, he began teaching his mosque community, through both sermons and dispute mediation, the importance of following Islamic law. Over the years he gained a reputation as an expert in Islamic law, and the local government took notice of his standing in the community. A bureau hired him as a "supervisor." Officially, his expertise is limited to advising the bureau on vehicular accidents, but representatives from a variety of bureaus come to the mosque to consult him on matters touching on Islamic law that they encounter in their work. In return, Nasim, who is never paid for his services, has acquired a reputation as a resource for the Party-State's bureaucrats, and this reputation confers benefits, such as having his mosque selected for a visit by high-ranking Party leaders. Judges also consult him on cases that touch upon Islamic law.

Sometimes he is invited to court to mediate, and sometimes the judge asks the disputants to seek Nasim at his mosque. Or they meet in a neutral environment, such as a restaurant or a hotel. Bafang Hui call this procedure "the custom of popular mediation" (*minjian tiaojie xiguan*). It is a process by which a dispute that initially takes the form of a lawsuit in a people's court is taken out of the state venue and into a *minjian* one. Usually, the referring judge is Hui and knows Nasim personally. Of the ninety-two cadres in the Linxia City People's Court, forty are Muslim. Social ties among coreligionists transcend the Party-State's attempt to demarcate secular and religious domains. When these cadres call on their cleric, they do so both as representatives of the Party-State and as members of the mosque community. Nasim relates:

> I may come across issues relating to inheritance, marriage, or divorce. The procedure of referring a case back down to the local religious authority is, in fact, illegal. The case should not be taken out of the state venue. Once the complaint is lodged there, it should be decided by that authority. This has been going on for many years. Not only will official PRC court decisions exclude any mention of religious law, but there will be no instances of even remnants of Islamic law in decisions, or references of any kind, however vague.

Here there is a direct conflict between Islamic law and state law. Nasim told me he encounters cases in which the Qur'anic shares for inheritance directly clash with the PRC Law of Succession. For instance, a daughter argues state law (for an equal portion of the inheritance) and a male relative cites shari'a, claiming women receive only one-half of what men receive.[31] To understand how to apply rules from the primary sources of shari'a, Nasim consults a small library of Hanafi *fiqh* compendia in his office as guidance. As to whether Islamic or state law is controlling, he assesses the relative position of the parties concerned, and the fairness of outcomes under the different regimes. (Usually, in inheritance disputes, he applies state law.) Procedurally, Nasim characterizes as unlawful the use of a cleric as temporary judicial mediator, but the cleric is used despite the law's prohibition. Article 95 of the 2012 amended PRC Civil Procedure Law allows a court to "invite" (*yaoqing*) a governmental unit or individual to "assist" (*xiezhu*) with mediation. Though it is unclear whether a cleric can be considered an "individual," the statute indicates that the court is still in charge of the mediation.[32]

---

[31] Article 9 of the PRC Law of Succession (*Zhonghua renmin gongheguo jichengfa*), promulgated by the NPC on April 10, 1985, effective October 1, 1985, provides for an equal right to inheritance, in the absence of a legally enforceable will. For the Qur'anic inheritance scheme, see 4:11.

[32] The 2010 Mediation Law did not clarify the issue. Article 18 states: "The basic-level people's courts [and] public security organs, in order to find a suitable way to resolve a dispute through mediation, may, before accepting a case, inform the parties to apply for mediation by a PMC."

Furthermore, according to article 33 of the 2010 Mediation Law, the relevant people's court may review the agreement that results from a PMC's mediation. Judicial oversight does not occur in the informalization of adjudication, however. Rather, the cleric takes over the case. Nor do clerics draft a mediation agreement; the entire process is done orally and circumvents any recording. Complicating the notions of the authorities' "legalization" of interpersonal and wider social conflicts (Diamant, Lubman, and O'Brien 2005: 3), the referral of cases to religious specialists demonstrates law's dramaturgical purpose. Law provides a veneer for the thick, personalistic ties that otherwise blur the divide between official and *minjian* legal venues.

This covering function of law is literally displayed in mosque administrative offices. Upon walking into the office of any mosque or Sufi institution in Northwest China, a visitor is confronted with the entire corpus of laws, rules, and administrative regulations governing Islam—on the walls. Laws are displayed in full text, with regulations issued by numerous governmental bodies at the relevant administrative level printed in small font on sheets of paper a meter square, so that the laws, in their entirety, can be viewed at a glance. From Lintan in southern Gansu to Haiyuan County in Ningxia to Hami in northeastern Xinjiang, the administrative offices of mosques and Sufi shrines are wallpapered in legal texts, literally wrapped in the letter of the law (see Figure 7.1). Although public display of PRC religious rules does not itself appear to be a formal requirement of the law, clerics and senior members of mosques display them to demonstrate their compliance with the law to Party cadres, who frequently visit the mosques.[33]

Clerics do not have the right to mediate under national law, nor does local regulation provide them with such a basis.[34] Of note, applicable rules do not give clerics any express grant of authority to mediate disputes,[35] and they omit any mention of the Qur'an and hadith or other sources of

---

[33] This observation is my inference. While clerics are required to uphold state law, they are not necessarily required to popularize it. Based on my experience visiting mosque offices, when cadres stopped in, usually unannounced, the cleric had to have his house in order.

[34] Provisional Measures for the Administration of Gansu Province Islamic Clerics (*Gansu sheng Yisilanjiao ahong guanli shixing banfa*), hereinafter "Clerics Measures," promulgated by the Gansu Province Bureau of Religious Affairs, December 12, 2000.

[35] In contrast, the mosque administration committee is required by state law to assist the government in mediating disputes within its community. See, e.g., the Linxia Religious Measures, art. 15, requiring the mosque committee to assist the government in dealing with conflicts and disputes of a religious nature. The policy rationale seems to be that clerics may accrue too much authority by becoming state-appointed mediators, whereas the conservative mosque elders who comprise the mosque administration committee do not represent such a threat.

Figure 7.1 A cleric's chambers
Source: the author

Islamic law.[36] Rather, the informalization of adjudication is characterized by relationships between the Hui elite and government officials.

These relationships are marked by discretion rather than transparency, and there are no traces of them in the official record. The work of mediating disputes is done "backstage," to use Erving Goffman's apt phrase (Goffman [1959] 1969). The "back room," not the courts, is often the site for brokering power between stakeholders (Martin 2013: 628). As Li Ling has written, "More seems to take place behind courtrooms than in them in litigation in China" (Li 2012: 853). Meanwhile, the courtroom is the venue for the public performance of the law (Trevaskas 2004). In this sense, the formal legal institutions of secular "rule of law" are dependent on the informal authority of Hui leaders and their capacity to mediate in accordance with Islamic law. Whereas the formalization of mediation operates through state propaganda, the informalization of adjudication rests on discretion and concealment.

Although the informalization of adjudication cannot be officially recognized, it is an open secret. Within this arrangement, Nasim seeks to educate his mosque community and others about Islamic law. Linxia Muslims of all teaching schools come to his quarters to ask him to mediate problems. As secular law and its institutions depend on Islamic

[36] One exception to official omission of Islamic law is the Clerics Measures, which do mention the Qur'an, hadith, and *fiqh*.

authority, Hui elite use the social capital conferred through such delegations to spread Islamic legal consciousness.

Nasim's visibility to both Muslim followers and officials (overlapping pools of clients) brings with it no small degree of danger. He whispers: "The CCP cannot know that I am explaining Qur'anic law to members of my mosque. And it's not even enforcing Qur'anic law, but merely explaining it. Much of Qur'anic law is at odds with state law. If they knew I was doing this, they would say I was interfering with the judiciary." From the view of the Party-State, Nasim can work only to put disputants back on a course where they can negotiate their own problem. In this, his work parallels that of a qadi (Rosen 1989: 61), the crucial difference being that clerics cannot enforce the law. Consequently, Islamic law operates here not through implementing institutions but through continual education, instruction, sermon, and prayer.

As many commentators have observed, weak courts remain the Achilles' heel of legal reform in the PRC.[37] Most critics point to the CCP's oversight of people's courts as invalidating their independence. Courts, meanwhile, rely on local authority figures to mediate claims. As a normative point, although such relationships deviate from Western "rule of law" prescriptions, it is arguable whether such reliance is a weakness or a strength. Indeed, scholars have analyzed connections between the CCP, lawyers, and judges as "political embeddedness" (Michelson 2007b, Liu and Halliday 2011). Such social connections have generally been viewed as a net good, as a resource and means of protection for lawyers. So, too, do Hui elite accrue benefits from collaborating with local officials.

However, clerics must be wary of being perceived as "too close" with cadres. Because of such relationships, they may lose credibility in the eyes of nonelite Hui. In serving two masters, they must toe a line that is continually shifting, as demonstrated during a riot in Linxia. The incident, which I will call the "KTV affair," illustrates the potential for violence in attempts to enforce Islamic law and morality in the Northwest, and the point at which the Party-State pushes back against an assertive Hui social field. The KTV affair began in late 2010. Whereas Linxia has been holy for Hui since at least the seventeenth century, urbanization in the reform period has brought social ills, including alcohol, drugs, gambling, and prostitution. When a local Hui man opened the KTV (karaoke bar) as a brothel near the heart of the Muslim quarter, the residents were enraged.

---

[37] See, for example, Lin (2003), Clarke (2008), and Peerenboom (2009).

Whereas the neighborhood police station initially rebuffed neighbors' attempts to close the establishment, as officials had received kickbacks from its owner, the neighborhood mosque clerics listened to the complaints of their constituents. "I told the members of my community," one cleric said, "the things that go on in that KTV—gambling, alcohol, drugs, whoring—these are haram [unlawful] and against religious law [zongjiaofa]. We must oppose such behavior."

Clerics exhorted their followers to take action in their Friday sermons. A half-dozen mosques organized a group to meet with the KTV owner. The mosques were all Salafi-influenced Yihewani communities, suggesting that inter-mosque networks organized by teaching schools can effectively set in motion collective action and that the "administrative mosque" (hanyisi) system, a target of state reform, is not yet defunct. One cleric involved in urging followers to protest remarked:

> The organizers came and talked to me. I then talked to my congregation and told them, "On such and such a day, we are going to the KTV to talk to them—talk only." But of course, as we know, on that day, things went otherwise than according to plan. There were several thousand people there, not several hundred as the police later reported. There were many youths, and they began getting excited. The police were already there, but they didn't do anything. Even when the youths began picking up rocks and bricks and threw them at the KTV, smashing its windows, the police didn't do anything. But when they broke down the door by kicking it in and stormed in—the owner wasn't there—the police began to get worried. They talked to me and [name deleted]. We talked to the protesters and told them to disperse, which they did.

Bafang Hui were outraged at the KTV and its sale of sex, which offended their conscience. The Hui were particularly upset that the direction and scope of Linxia's development was occurring without public opinion. Instead, they reasoned, profiteers who trafficked in prostitution were more important to the local government than the residents. None of the statements of reproach, however, admitted that some of the patrons of the KTV were Hui.

When the police were unable to quell the rioters, they called the clerics. These clerics were the same ones who had initially called upon their followers to take action, and they intervened, demanding an end to the violence. The crowds melted away. In the aftermath of the KTV affair, the UFWD under the Linxia City government began an investigation. They interviewed clerics in the affected area. The Public Security Bureau posted notices. The announcement posted around Bafang read in part:

On the evening of September 21, a large crowd of several hundred people gathered at Northern Front River Street's middle section, and some members of the crowd engaged in smashing One Million Lotuses K Song bar, which was in the process of starting to do business. These people caused significant property damage and created a vile social impression. This is altogether a typical case of an illegal act of smashing and ruining property. In order to severely punish illegal criminal activities and in order to maintain social stability and order, the public security organs are sparing no effort to investigate this case.

In the aftermath of the KTV affair, two clerics were arrested and detained in a town outside Linxia. They were detained in another town, because it is not uncommon for hundreds of followers to march on the municipal police station if their cleric or leader has been arrested. The two clerics were charged with the crimes of destruction of property and "gathering the masses," with a maximum penalty of three years in jail. The more senior cleric's sentence was commuted to one year and ten months, although he returned home ill, and his health has suffered since.

The KTV affair shows the arbitrariness of the line between the official and the *minjian*. Even though state socialist law does not recognize Islamic law or morality as a basis of urban order, the police relied on clerics to resolve the conflict. The clerics, for their part, framed their opposition in terms of "religious law." While shari'a prohibits gambling as well as the sale and drinking of alcohol, for example,[38] the clerics' understanding of "religious law" is heavily moral in its tones. The moralization of law is largely an effect of the coding of morality as ethnic (i.e., Han as corrupt). Collective action organized, in part, by this moralized law was intolerable to the state. The clerics had crossed the indiscernible line between permissible and unlawful conduct. This uncertainty (i.e., today an ally, tomorrow a detainee) injects anxiety into cadre-cleric collaborations. While relying on each other, they are also surveilling each other. While sharing, they also guard information close to the chest.

The potential for violence percolates beneath collaborations, creating suspicion for both Hui leaders and their official counterparts. The ability of clerics to straddle the demands of the Party-State and those of their communities is even more precarious among Uyghurs. There is a much higher degree of distrust among nonelite Uyghurs for imams than there is among Hui. For this reason, Islamic PMCs are rare in Xinjiang. Moreover, distrust may boil over into antipathy for those clerics who are

[38] Q. 2:219.

most vocal about supporting the Party-State. For instance, on July 30, 2014, Juma Tahir, the imam of the largest mosque in Xinjiang and head of the Kashgar Yi-Xie, was stabbed to death allegedly by radicalized Uyghur teenagers who believed the imam owed loyalty more to Beijing than to his own people. Juma Tahir's predecessor had also been stabbed in 1996 but survived, and there have been numerous other incidents of attacks on state-supported imams in southern Xinjiang. In the polarized environment there, clerics' attempts to praise the Party through sermons, publications, and dispute resolution are more likely to fall on deaf ears than in Hui communities in the Northwest.

THE DISPUTING CONSTELLATION AMONG MUSLIMS IN NORTHWEST CHINA

The formalization of mediation and the informalization of adjudication, prevalent in different parts of the Northwest, represent parts of a larger continuum of dispute resolution in the region. In this section I locate these two processes within the larger picture, and I discuss the implications for dispute resolution as glorification. In *The Legal Process: Basic Problems in the Making and Application of Law* (1958), Henry Hart et al. proposed the "great pyramid of legal order" as a model for understanding the disputing process: from a grievance, once recognized as such, to a legally cognizable claim, and finally to a judicable dispute—the number of disputes decreasing the longer the life of the conflict, such that few become judicable disputes. The pyramid model became foundational to the "law and society" literature in the 1970s and 1980s[39] and more recently has been adapted to study Chinese disputes (see, e.g., Michelson 2007a: 460). Crucial to the pyramid model was the inclusion of a wide array of dispute institutions, not all of which are "legal" per se. Along these lines, many Chinese who are engaged in conflicts choose to avoid formal channels, whether legal or administrative (Zhu 1996; Xin 2005). Rather, they look to informal or *minjian* means. Disputing in China entails a mélange of venues and methods of solving conflicts, ranging from formal adjudication to the extralegal.[40] Some disputes "move up" (O'Brien and Li 2006),

---

[39] See, for instance, Nader and Todd (1978), Felstiner, Abel, and Sarat (1980), Miller and Sarat (1981), and Galanter (1983).

[40] These venues and methods include mediation via "premodern" corporate groups and associational life in rural society that were revitalized in the reform era (e.g., lineage corporations, clan organizations, surname associations, deity cults, temple communities, women's networks, and trade associations) (Sangren 1984; Liang 1999; Weller 1999; Feuchtwang 2001b); leftover Soviet

and others "move down" (Michelson 2008b). The diversity of forums and the multidirectionality of disputes is a consequence of China's legal diversity.

There is a constellation of nodal points, each representing an authority and means of dispute resolution that may or may not have a relationship (synchronic or diachronic, hierarchical or ahierarchical) to other nodes. At a general level, these nodes can be placed in two overlapping spheres: *minjian* and state venues of dispute resolution (see Figure 7.2). These nodes exist along a spectrum from *minjian* to state forms. The *minjian* sphere comprises such *minjian* authorities as family heads and Sufi shaykhs. The status of the *minjian* cleric lies on the far end of the spectrum. These clerics opt out of the kinds of relationships that such clerics as Nasim find themselves in. *Minjian* clerics also mediate disputes either within the community of their own mosque or others. Many clerics and officials believe *minjian* clerics have more capacity to address conflicts than do registered clerics. A Hui city civil servant in Linxia stated, "*Minjian* clerics have more room to maneuver; the registered clerics are tightly regulated."

Next are the teaching clerics, who are registered but not empowered to mediate. Moving farther toward the "state venue" end of the spectrum are such clerics as Nasim, who have been chosen to serve as supervisors (*jianduyuan*) to a formal governmental or Party body. Figures such as Old Dong, nominated to be members of an Islamic PMC, whether or not they possess knowledge of the law, are located within the state sphere. Beyond the Islamic PMC are officials of a number of public organs and institutions who mediate disputes, including the neighborhood office and police.

Disputes involving Muslims in Northwest China may proceed from *minjian* venues to state ones, crossing over the Hui social field. A civil dispute will begin with the family head and then may move to a cleric or the village head, PMC, village committee, or an official organ such as the judicial bureau, and finally to the people's court.

However, disputes may just as frequently zigzag across the *minjian/* state distinction. The formalization of mediation takes a dispute out

and Maoist organizations (Huang 2005); "letters and visits" (*xinfang*) (Thireau and Linshan 2005; Minzner 2006; Fang 2009); petitioning higher bureaucratic levels (*shangfang*) (Diamant, Lubman, and O'Brien 2005); lawsuits (Zhu and Wang 2008); and arbitration (Gallagher 2005)— as well as protest, demonstration, civil disobedience (Frazier 2005; van Rooij 2010; Perry and Selden 2001), and their online equivalents (MacKinnon 2008; Yang 2009).

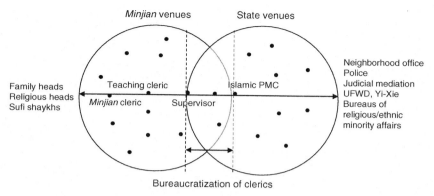

Figure 7.2 The disputing constellation in Northwest China
Source: the author

of *minjian* venues and, while preserving the appearance of nonstate authority (through the physical setting of the mosque and the role of the Islamic PMC), brings it within the realm of state law. The informalization of adjudication, on the other hand, begins in a formal venue but ends up in a *minjian* one. Sometimes disputes explode outward and at other times contract, or they exist in multiple forums simultaneously.[41] For instance, the KTV affair did not end with the arrest of the clerics who organized the protest. Incensed at the treatment of the clerics, family members of the clerics filed a lawsuit in the Linxia Prefecture Intermediate Court, naming the KTV owner as defendant. Their goals were not only to permanently close the KTV but also to force the local government to recognize the Bafang Hui's right to want the KTV closed. With the financial assistance of their mosque communities and under the guidance of clerics who were not arrested, the families hired eight Han lawyers from Qinghai. As to why they did not hire local Hui lawyers, one cleric stated, "Criticism is more likely to be heard by those who belong to the same group as the rulers than from those who are ruled."

Initially, the KTV owner refused the summons. The government tried to persuade the parties to settle out of court. Ultimately, the KTV owner appeared in court—to file a counterclaim against the neighbors. The basis

[41] Similarly, Paul Katz (2009), examining ideologies of justice and legal practice, finds a "judicial continuum" that links official settings and popular rituals, such as chicken beheadings and oath swearing.

of his claim was property damage. He sued for 940,000 yuan, the cost of the damage. The judge's verdict in the suit was conveyed in heavy moral tones. It stated, in part, that while the Muslim citizens were right to reject the presence of the KTV, their method of violence was wholly unlawful. Rather, they should have relied on the proper authorities. Ultimately, the plaintiffs did not have to pay any of the damages the KTV owner sought in his countersuit. The consequences of the verdict were complicated. Six leaders of government bureaus were fired as a result of their corruption (i.e., collusion with the KTV owner), which the families interpreted as a victory. One cleric involved in the suit argued:

> Although the suit named the KTV owner as defendant, it was really a case against the government [and their misfeasance]. We sued the state.[42] It was the first case of its kind in China. We won. We did not have to pay a single yuan. The case made the government lose face. It gave us a platform from which to speak. I don't see them building any KTVs in that area in the future.

The KTV affair was a dispute that devolved into violent protest—the form of disputing most intolerable to "harmonious society"—but upon the state's use of law to punish those responsible for the protest, the dispute transformed into a lawsuit against the state. Hui communities' attempt to live in accordance with moralized religious law may take the form of protecting such rights through socialist law.

Given the plurality of venues, forum shopping is common. Venue selection depends on a number of factors, including the nature of the dispute, the identity of the disputants (e.g., ethnicity, age, religion, education, teaching-school membership if Muslim, general socioeconomic background and resources) and whether these categories of identity are shared between the parties, and the quality and number of such venues available to the disputants. The choice of venue is usually a result of negotiation between the parties, and involvement from a Muslim authority or representatives of the state. Members of the same teaching school will seek a cleric of their school. If the disputants belong to different schools, they may consult a neutral third-party cleric from a different teaching school or resort to a grassroots state authority, such as neighborhood committees.

The most striking instance of forum shopping in Linxia occurs when one party is Han and the other is Hui. As the population of Linxia City is

---

[42] The cleric, like others in Bafang, understood the suit to be between the mosques involved and the local government. As a technical matter, mosques as "social organizations" (*shehui tuanti*) do not have legal status to sue in their own name.

nearly evenly split between Han and Hui, intercourse between the ethnic groups is regular. The common site in Linxia for interethnic interaction is roadways. Vehicular accidents have increased steadily in Linxia since the 1980s. In an accident in which the defendant is a Han who accidentally injures or kills a Hui pedestrian or bicyclist, the Han defendant will often-times agree to use a cleric, as he sets a standard for compensation that is lower than that of the official system.

Within the continuum, where *minjian* authority potentially challenges state authority, the Party-State tries to transform it into official authority. Through laws and regulations, appointments, and personal relationships, local bureaucrats appropriate *minjian* resources and channel them into support for official Islam as harmonious, peaceful, and united. *Minjian* clerics are a constant source of worry among religious officials, particu-larly as many of them are puritanical Yihewani and Salafis. In 2009, after the Urumqi riots, the BRA in Linxia City began transitioning to a sys-tem under which registered clerics would receive a salary of 1,500 yuan per month. However, two years later no cleric I spoke with who had reg-istered had received any money. Many clerics thought the measure was introduced to encourage *minjian* clerics to register so as to identify and remove them.

At the same time, public security may depend on *minjian* forms of Muslim authority. For instance, at the premediation stage of a dispute, police may undertake what Hui refer to as a *minjian diaocha* (popular inves-tigation), working alongside clerics to gather evidence about the cause of a conflict. As with informalized adjudication, there is no legal basis for *minjian* investigations, except for the legal right of the mosque committee to settle disputes and, in the course of which, to conduct an investigation and collect evidence. Nor are *minjian* investigations institutionally bureau-cratized. However, not only are *minjian* investigations common, but public security organs may also actually seek the assistance of mosque members to lead a *minjian* investigation. The cleric and the board of trustees of one of Linxia's oldest and most prominent Gedimu mosques have led *min-jian* investigations on several occasions. In a 2009 case, a hit-and-run that resulted in the death of a Hui by a Han, the cleric and the board of trustees led an investigation that helped the police find the man responsible. The cleric said, "We organized mosque members to interview people who saw the incident, took photographs, and so on. The board of trustees worked with police during this period. Ultimately, together [with the police] we found the offender. The police later thanked the mosque." What distin-guishes the process of *minjian* investigation from the figure of a *minjian* cleric is that the police can appropriate the knowledge, resources, and connections of the former for its own purposes.

The disputing constellation shows one of the defining features of Chinese legal culture: the presence of multiple sources of law and authorities that coexist with or compete with state law. The Party-State tolerates such nonstate normative orders to the extent that they maintain "harmonious society" in line with state prescriptions—for example, *minjian* investigations. However, if enforcing a nonstate norm, such as injunctions against haram behavior, conflicts with state law, exposes its inadequacies, or threatens social stability, then the state's public security forces will crack down on such behavior and its proponents. The KTV affair marks one such forceful transgression (and equally forceful reassertion) of an unwritten boundary in the plural legal landscape of Chinese Muslim communities in Northwest China.

By examining clerics and Muslim leaders who operate within the informal sphere of dispute resolution more closely, it becomes apparent that arrangements between clerics and the Party-State take numerous forms. The most widespread use of mediation by teaching clerics in Northwest China occurs without government consent. As with the relationship between the judiciary and popular institutions for dispute resolution among ethnic minorities throughout China,[43] local legal and judicial bureaus have sought to the fullest extent possible to diminish this nonregulated mediation, which potentially challenges state authority. Contrary to what Foucault and his successors, such as Agamben, have argued, law is not divorced from governmentality or glory. To except law from such forms of rule (including self-rule) is to reproduce the fallacy of the state's monopoly on law. Rather, for Hui, living in accordance with Islamic law is an expression of God's glory in this world—and therein lies the test to CCP rule. The Party-State assimilates those who praise God's glory (the clerics), so that their acclamations—for example, those of Old Dong—reproduce state order. Further complicating Agamben's approach, glory in the Muslim Northwest works both ways: local government bureaus praise Old Dong, just as he touts the prerogatives of patriotism and national belonging.

The test, ultimately, of collaborations between Hui leaders and the local government is whether the Hui masses internalize the celestial publicity of co-opted elite. Generally, Hui view state law with arm's-length suspicion. During the annual Legal Popularization Day, for example,

---

[43] See, for instance, Bai (2008) and Wang Qiliang (2009, 2010).

government officials sat at tables in Linxia's main square with stacks of colorful flyers with legal texts. Hui ambled by the tables. There was little interaction or discussion, however, with the government representatives. Later, I saw an older Hui man on a bicycle, its basket stuffed with colorful handouts like an origami whirlwind. I asked him what he was going to do with them and whether he needed them for his business. He replied, "No, they have nothing to do with my work, but I will read them. Otherwise, I'll never know if I'm doing something illegal!" Apprehensive attitudes toward state law are typical among minorities in the Northwest.

When confronted with questions of conflict between religious and state law, Hui often resort to a conceptual schema that the revealed sources provide but that nevertheless includes state law. The most common Qur'anic reference for this schema is "O ye who believe! Obey Allah, and obey the Messenger, and those charged with authority among you."[44] Hui interpret "those charged with authority among you" as the Party-State. Hui resist interpreting the sources of law in a hierarchical fashion that would privilege one source over the other. Similarly, a female elder in the Naqshbandi Sufi order told me, quoting a part of a hadith, "Patriotism is like the bird that cherishes the nest [xiang niao aihu wochao shide aihu zuguo]. You must obey both Allah and the Party, which is like the ruler." A Ningxia Jahriyya Sufi echoed this sentiment: "Seventy percent of state laws and regulations are in accordance with religious law ... Both Islam and the state promote peace, and the laws of both systems are designed with this goal in mind." The Hui think of conflicts as reconcilable primarily because their clerics, in sermons and through mediation, tell them so. "Patriotism is part of belief [imān]" (aiguo shi yimani de yi bufen), a saying attributed to the Prophet, is espoused by clerics and generally permeates Hui discourse.

Islamic legal consciousness does not necessarily "trickle down" from authoritative sources. Those Hui who consult such experts as Nasim, and particularly more senior students, acquire skills to reflect on conflicts of law, either on their own or through consultation with clerics who have studied Islamic law abroad. Despite the Party-State's efforts to co-opt minjian Muslim authority, Hui do have a choice of law and multiple venues for resolving disputes. Although alternatives to state law reside at the margins of the official legal order, they nonetheless have considerable traction in everyday life. In choosing state venues or Islamic PMCs, the Hui may contribute to the glorification of the Party-State. Just as likely, they may opt for nonstate venues such as mediation by mosque-based clerics or minjian

---

[44] Q. 4:59.

clerics as an expression of glory not commissioned by the local government. This glory does not stand in a relation of opposition or resistance to the glory of the socialist state but rather dwells both within and beyond it. Glorification is a practice that occurs in extralegal spaces, including hotel rooms and even car garages, and that transpires through emergent networks of learning outside the Chinese nation-state.

CONCLUSION

LAW, MINJIAN, *AND THE ENDS OF ANTHROPOLOGY*

> *It is because law matters that we have bothered with this story at all.*
>
> E. P. Thompson (2013: 209)[1]

HYSTERIA AND SILENCE

The post-9/11 period has heightened irrational fears about "shariʿa creep" in many Western societies. The Law Society of the United Kingdom, for example, issued guidelines for solicitors to draw up wills in accordance with Islamic law in 2014. Eight months later, in the face of intense pressure, the Law Society retracted the guidelines and, in an unprecedented move, issued a formal apology. Also in 2014, Alabama became the seventh US state[2] to ban shariʿa through constitutional amendment. France and Belgium have recently undergone yet another wave of calls to ban the burqa.[3] As these examples illustrate, secular states often find in such items as clothing threats to constitutional orders. Concerned publics cite national security, public safety, and counter-radicalization as rationales for prohibiting shariʿa and its physical markers from public spaces. In France, the November 13, 2015 attacks in Paris allegedly committed by predominantly French nationals trained in Syria by the so-called Islamic State in Iraq and Syria[4] has led to yet another wave of Islamophobia and anti-immigrant and anti-refugee sentiment across Europe and North America. Free-speech fundamentalists have drawn the ire of Muslims across the world, resulting in attacks on Christians—for example, in

---

[1] Permission to republish obtained from copyright-holder.
[2] The others are North Carolina, Arizona, Kansas, Louisiana, South Dakota, and Tennessee. In 2013 a federal judge struck down a shariʿa ban in Oklahoma as unconstitutional. See *Awad v. Ziriax*, 966 F. Supp. 2d 1198 (W.D. Ok. 2013).
[3] See, e.g., *S.A.S. v. France* (No. 43835/11) Eur. Ct. H.R. (2014).
[4] Approximately 130 people were killed in the attacks that targeted multiple venues across Paris.

Nigeria. Following such events, actors on the ground conflate a number of categories (e.g., Muslims with terrorists or Christians with neoconservatives), conflations that impede meaningful dialogue. Through ballots and public laws, non-Muslim majorities redraw a line in the sand between private religion and public life. As US Supreme Court Justice David Souter wrote, it is the "constant tension between security and liberty" that may be the "defining character of American constitutional government."[5] Although Western states have different approaches to secularism, multiculturalism, and religious difference, a common denominator in recent debates has been anxieties about the separation of church and state in a world at war with terror.[6]

Unlike the hysterical debates in Western liberal democracies about shari'a creep, in China one rarely hears about Islamic law. This silence is striking, given China's large Muslim population, their importance to modern Chinese history, and the dynamic and evolving relationship between the PRC and Muslim states in Central Asia, the Middle East, and Southeast Asia. But the absence of public discussions about Islamic law does not mean it is a nonissue to Muslim minorities or to the state. The Party-State's domination of public discourse and the absence of freedom of speech mute such discussions. More so, as with anxieties of shari'a creep in Western states, the crucial factor is the fear of the institutional recognition of some aspect of Islamic law. The PRC, as a socialist state, accords no formal recognition to Islamic law, and hence, Chinese citizens have not rallied against so-called shari'a creep.

Recent voices on Hui social media platforms such as Internet blogs and discussions on Weixin, a popular instant messaging service in China, suggest that popular commentaries are drawing more attention to the relationship between Islamic law (*jiaofa*) and state law (*guofa*) (see, e.g., Ding 2015; Zhong Mu Qing Wang 2015). While describing the relationship as mutually supportive and avoiding empirical observations, online opinions are nonetheless calling, for the first time in postsocialist China, for greater recognition of the importance of Islamic law in the lives of China's growing Muslim population. Whether or not such *minjian* discussions can affect policy at the local or national levels remains to be seen.

---

[5] See Rascoff (2012: 131), citing *Hamdi* v. *Rumsfeld*, 542 US 507, 545 (2004).
[6] For a sample of a growing literature, see Juergensmeyer (2008), Fadel (2013), Ghachem (2013), Huq (2013), and Turner (2013: 24–25).

It is the absence of institutional recognition that distinguishes China on the matter of Muslim minorities and their law. China lacks formal institutional bridges or civil society organizations that could communicate Hui public opinions to the state. There are no representational politics,[7] Muslim NGOs, shari'a councils, official forums for private mediation in accordance with religious law, 'ulama', or professional associations for Muslim lawyers. The Party-State has monopolized any form of Muslim institutional life in the China Islamic Association (Yi-Xie), Islamic people's mediation committees are empty of Islamic law, and even the Bank of Ningxia's Islamic finance project is countenanced as "Islamic doctrine" (not law).

Rather, Hui practice of Islamic law is *minjian*. In this conclusion, I explain why it is that Hui can practice their own form of Islamic law in certain fields of law as opposed to others. I then draw out some of the implications for studying the *minjian* in order to understand both broader issues of Islamic law in modern secular states and law, generally, in contemporary China. Focusing on the *minjian* and its relationship to formal law may mean changing assumptions that inform the study of Islamic law and Chinese law, as well as the methodologies for empirical research in such areas. Anthropology is one disciplinary lens, among others, that can contribute new approaches to these systems of law that are of critical importance to states beyond China.

FROM STATE LAW TO *MINJIAN* AND BACK AGAIN

As illustrated in the case of Hui, the *minjian* is a middle ground where the Party-State and Hui meet to solve problems, articulate needs, and most importantly work toward their respective views of "the good." The centrality of the *minjian* in mediating relationships between political authority in the state and religious authority in Hui mosques differs from familiar concepts in either Western liberal states or transitional Middle Eastern ones. Because the regime does not permit a public sphere, in Jürgen Habermas's ([1962] 1989) sense of a place, for critical public discussion, analytical

---

[7] Articles 113 and 114 of the PRC Constitution require that the chairman and vice chairman of the standing committee of the people's congress of an autonomous area as well as the head of the autonomous area belong to the ethnic group that exercises regional ethnic autonomy in the area concerned. See also the PRC Law on Regional Ethnic Autonomy, arts. 16–18. Unfortunately, Hui in Gansu, Qinghai, and Xinjiang complain that such titular roles do not translate into meaningful representation. Ningxia may be a partial exception in this regard.

terms such as "public space" and "public reason," so crucial to liberal thought, particularly as applied to the question of Muslims in multicultural states (Fadel 2008; March 2009), are problematic in Northwest China. Nor do Hui enjoy an "Islamic public sphere"[8] or a "counterpublic" (Hirschkind 2006), concepts that originated in Muslim-majority countries such as Morocco, Egypt, and Indonesia. Rather, Hui in the Northwest exercise the *minjian*, reproduced not in the town square but in mosque sermons and madrasa lessons, on saints' days at tomb complexes, and through gossip at halal restaurants. The *minjian* generates its own forms of speech/rules, even as it borrows from state discourse/laws—for example, "evil cult" (*xiejiao*) and "ethnic unity" (*minzu tuanjie*). Yet while the *minjian* is a middle ground for borrowing, sharing, and negotiation, it is also marked by discord.

One of the key questions, then, is when does the Party-State seek to appropriate the *minjian* by formal recognition of law, when does it suppress the *minjian* by institutional blockages, when does it transform it by, for example, discursive methods, and when does it tolerate it, even if the *minjian* is illegal or semilegal? Outcomes depend on whether the *minjian* practices in question bring together different views of a just and ordered society or draw attention to their divergences. For Hui, much of their everyday is centered around living in accordance with their version of Islamic law as a way to realize distinct interpretations of Islam. Most of these interpretations are based outside of China, and so the work of the teaching schools is to accommodate their various approaches toward Islamic law and ethics in Chinese society. Their work of localization requires a certain space, the Hui social field, through which they can move back and forth between Linxia and their respective "centers," through pilgrimage, textual production and translation, education, and even replication through modes of dress and prayer.

The Party-State, on the other hand, is concerned chiefly with maintaining the political status quo by ensuring social stability. Economic performance has become the litmus test of the regime during the reform era. Developmental goals and interethnic relations converge on the borders, where China is expanding relationships with Central Asia and the Middle East through the so-called "New Silk Road." Counterterrorism has become a priority, following increased activity across the borders of

---

[8] See Eickelman and Salvatore (2004), Salvatore (2007), Eickelman (2008), Dahlgren (2010), and McLarney (2011).

the Northwest region. The Party-State achieves its aims of political stability and interethnic coordination through ongoing nation-building programs and promarket policies to alleviate poverty and increase household wealth. To do so, the Party-State relies not only on official tactics (e.g., state-run media, public schooling, and five-year economic plans) but also on the *minjian*.

The Party-State has developed different approaches to the various fields of Islamic law as practiced by Hui in China. As a general observation, the *minjian* in many ways leads the state, not the other way around, as seen most clearly in the example of economic initiatives, whether in Linxia's small-scale sheep hide market or Ningxia's Islamic finance industry. The Party-State expends considerable resources in tracking the *minjian*. They include monitoring, surveillance, and information gathering. In addition to security concerns, tracking enables the state to tap the creativity of the *minjian*. Much of the dynamism of Chinese economic life originates with the *minjian*, as illustrated in the "New Silk Road," which was a result of transnational contacts between Muslims in China and coreligionists abroad before it became a slogan of the Party.

Beyond tracking the *minjian*, the Party-State's allowance for Hui practice of Islamic law depends on a variety of factors, mainly whether the practice and its social effects accord with the Party-State's view of a unified, multiethnic state. On one end of the spectrum, the Party-State has monopolized criminal law. It does so to preserve its control over organized coercive violence within its jurisdiction (Weber [1922] 1978a: 314). The Party-State does not just exclude formal recognition of Islamic penal law; it further aligns that law with antimodern barbarity, as exemplified in the display of the whips at the *qadihana* in Xinjiang. The state's monopoly on force is thus not a foregone conclusion but requires continual reaffirmation.

At the other end of the spectrum, the administrative state has granted considerable powers of local enforcement to Hui communities in the area of public safety. In some areas, Hui can even apply Islamic norms, such as food production and food quality inspection. There, the Yi-Xie and the Bureau of Religious Affairs license vendors and factories as *qingzhen* (halal). In the area of traffic safety, the government allows Hui to apply broad principles of Islamic law to questions of compensation and redress, but generally PRC laws and regulations, especially criminal liability, are controlling. Such partnerships, as between police and mosque personnel who conduct *minjian* inspections, are valuable to the Party-State for both limiting its resource expenditures and also signaling to Hui communities that the Party collaborates with Hui leaders in meaningful ways. Pragmatics mix with other concerns in such arrangements, and cadres will defer to clerics and shaykhs not just to appropriate their authority over the community but because the cadres too may belong to the Hui leader's teaching school or even attend his mosque.

Between these two ends of the spectrum are a number of legal fields that are less certain. These include the fields of family law, namely, marriage and divorce, as well as property, such as real property, private markets, and to lesser extent, questions of inheritance. These fields of law are characterized by a high degree of normative indeterminacy and procedural complexity. The reason for the grayness of these fields is that they are areas where vested state interests intersect with jurisdictions of Islamic law over Muslim minorities in China and elsewhere. The state has sought to control both family organization and property relations, as these are aspects of Chinese society that have been the fulcrum of change and continuity.[9] Yet the family and property are also enduring subjects under Islamic law, even as practiced by Muslim minorities, including Hui. In China, these areas of law have been shaped by the historical state's successive legal modernization programs and are also gaining new life among Hui as they increase their interaction with foreign Muslims, both outside of China and in such "New Silk Road" cities as Yiwu or Kashgar. The result is that as the two incomplete legal systems interact with each other through the *minjian*, the Hui social field accommodates conflicts of law, though not always seamlessly. Generally, the Party-State tolerates Hui practice of family or property law, even if it contravenes state law, as long as it does not directly jeopardize state interests. For regulating the family, these interests include preserving the conjugal unit, managing family reproduction, and controlling population growth. For property regulation, the state is interested in transferring land to those who use it for its highest use value (i.e., real estate developers). Hui dual-track marriages, by which a couple marries by obtaining a *nikāḥ* or divorces by *ṭalāq*, or *minjian* transfers of *waqf* property may, in the aggregate, present challenges to state control of its population and assets.

The controlling law is a result of compromise and negotiation between state actors and Hui. Cadres and officials may allow Hui to apply their

---

[9] On relationships between the family and larger kin groups and the historic Chinese state, see Freedman (1966, 1970), Ebrey (2003), and Esherick (2011); for property relations, see Schurmann (1956), Macauley (2001), and Zelin, Ocko, and Gardella (2004). On property and the family, see Ocko (1991), Bernhardt (1999), and Brandstädter (2003).

rules if such allowance keeps small claims out of overworked courts and enables the local state to appear to give some autonomy to Hui. The state may also intervene, sometimes by Hui initiative, as in the case where Hui husbands have surpassed their rights under Islamic law. The common ground in the areas of family and property does not take the form of an equilibrium; rather, it is uneven, and violence percolates around points where Hui and Party-State versions of the just and ordered society are irreconcilable. The KTV affair in Linxia is one example where urban development was out of touch with Hui notions of morality, and violence ensued with remarkable speed and ferocity.

The area of ritual law also lies within the gray area of the spectrum in terms of fields of law prohibited or permitted by the state. Historically, in China, the (self)-regulation of the body through the performance of rites was a valorized dimension of social production as part of larger projects to reproduce ethical wholes (Zito and Barlow 1994). The historical state was invested in maintaining such sociocosmic order, and thus heterodox practices were to be uprooted. Hui have also practiced ritual modes of worship in their own traditions, the teaching schools. Generally, such practices to mold "qualified Muslims" are consonant with the Party-State's efforts to groom citizens of high "quality." In the past, certain Sufi protocols, such as asceticism, have drawn the ire of local governments. In the post-2009 period, the ambit of suspicious Muslim activity has expanded such that even learning Arabic in a madrasa or carrying a certain type of book on ritual can be suspicious, depending on the student's birthplace or ethnicity. In an environment, not just in China but in postindustrial democratic states as well, where a headscarf attains symbolic value as extremism, ritual has again become politicized. As a result, control over how to dress or even move one's body present flashpoints for teaching schools and the Party-State alike.

ISLAMIC LAW AND TOLERATION

What does *minjian* Islamic law in China teach about Islamic law more generally? Whereas in the West, where the misperception of shari'a creep is based on the supposed opposition of Islamic law to Western Enlightenment versions of law, China's experience with Islamic law derives from a different set of oppositions (Chapter 1). The Chinese adaptation of Soviet law and policy toward religious minorities assumes that any law other than that of the Party-State is "customary law," something other than "true" law. Contemporary China's experience with Islamic law has been complicated by its own experience of irrationality, which is part and parcel of the global discourses on terrorism.

Meanwhile, Hui are growing their communities partly based on precepts from the revealed law. The key point is that this process occurs not necessarily through formal institutions but through Hui's own relationship building, translating, and bridgework among their local communities, the Party, the state, and foreign Muslims. Such formal institutions as ethnic autonomy may frustrate rather than enable Hui desire to implement their own ideas about community organization and development, particularly when doing so incorporates aspects of Islamic law. The Hui experience under socialist rule is unique, but their capacity to navigate systemic blockages, institutional and ideological, may represent dilemmas and opportunities shared by ethnic and religious minorities elsewhere.

Whereas Hui sometimes hear from Uyghurs and other Muslim minority groups in China as well as from Western observers that they are "not real Muslims," Hui view their relationship to Chinese society, including political rule, differently. Hui constantly engage in managing relationships understood broadly, from those between literary canons to financial interests. Their intellectual patrimony, the Han Kitab, is one expression of an intellectual accommodation between currents of Islamic thought and Neo-Confucianism. Similarly, in contemporary China, through commercial transactions and mediation, Hui manage their relationships not just with members of their own ethnicity or religion but also with the majority Han. Much of this work relies upon line drawing and boundary maintenance—for example, upon labeling products "*qingzhen*" (halal), upon wearing ethnic markers such as the headscarf or skullcap, and upon habitually performing practices such as daily prayer. Law and ethics are the basis for these boundaries. Yet, and similar to Muslims everywhere, such boundaries overlap in important ways with non-Muslim constituencies, as seen in Linxia's sheep hide market, which produces goods for Han consumption, or in the "world's largest small commodities market" in Yiwu, where Hui translate for foreign Muslim businessmen who make purchases from Han sellers. Thus, just as Islamic law may mark boundaries of communities, it also provides internalized instruction for Muslims to engage ethically with non-Muslims.

Hui practice of Islamic law has two edges, one sharp and the other dull: while teaching-school projects compete with those of others, fomenting intrareligious intolerance, generally Hui adopt a flexible and tolerant form of Islamic law in regard to interactions with the Han majority. From their daily prayer obligations to disposing of real property and marrying in accordance with scripture, Hui work through and around both the rules of the Party and those of the state. Such adaptability has enabled them to integrate into China's markets and state bureaucracies. While Hui impose clear lines on "illicit" as opposed to "licit" behavior, and teaching schools disagree internally and among themselves as to where to draw these lines, the flexibility of Hui law towards state law and the Han majority is one hallmark of its legal culture, one that has the potential to contribute to contemporary debates about the place of shariʿa in plural societies.

STUDYING THE *MINJIAN*

What does the study of religious law among minorities teach about Chinese law and institutional life? The *minjian* is not preformed although the state dominates certain fields of law (e.g., criminal law); rather, it is an outcome of the on-going practices between and among Hui groups, the Han majority, and the state. Without the *minjian*, Hui could not practice their form of religious law, and, arguably, it would be more difficult for the Party-State to maintain the kind of rule it does over Muslim minorities. Hui follow, produce, and enforce the rules of Islamic law through the *minjian* that may reside in places where state law is silent. Islamic law, in China, is, as a result, not wholly illegal, nor is it inherently opposed to state law and socialist morality. The thick interpenetration of different sources of law—including religious and secular, state and nonstate, or *minjian* and official—is perhaps what most distinguishes the Hui social field. As the *minjian* takes the form of unregistered mosques, unlicensed clerics, unrecorded property transfers, and parallel-track marriages, however, it is potentially a threat to the Party-State's monopoly on law. The Party-State attempts to render threats into resources. It does so by constantly accessing and mobilizing the *minjian*.

The historian Prasenjit Duara has called a similar inversion that occurred in China's transition from empire to nation the "cultural nexus of power" (Duara 1988). For Duara, the cultural nexus comprised those informal institutions (e.g., the market, kin ties, religion, and so on) and their norms (i.e., "popular culture") that gave legitimacy to local society. The imperial state also became dependent on this cultural nexus. To put it another way, *minjian* dimensions of society became integral to the early Chinese notion of sovereignty. Contrary to the governance approach of the late Qing Dynasty, however, the Party is trapped in its own ideological straitjacket. It cannot publicize its dependence on Hui authorities and Islamic law. Even the Yi-Xie's project to develop a *fiqh* of the revealed sources crossed the Party's line between private belief and public life.

The study of the *minjian* and its vexed relationship to power is not a fringe question about minorities in one corner of China; it resonates with the study of Chinese law and society more generally. Much of the "rule of law" industry in China, including Chinese lawyers, academics, policy experts, and activists and their American and European counterparts, focuses predominantly on state law as an object of reform. Legal institutions, specifically the judiciary, have been the object of scholarly fixation. The *minjian* requires analysis not just of "unofficial law," as it has been traditionally understood as interactions between formal and informal sources of law—for example, by legal pluralists (Chiba 1989; Menski 2006)—but also of the legitimating normative roots of formal law and its institutions.[10]

Max Weber's theory of the rationalization of law—namely, the systematization of substantive law and procedure for the aim of achieving juridical precision and predictability of legal consequences—is often construed in teleological terms, and indeed, this may have been how Weber understood his categories of legal thought. For the first thirty years of the PRC's legal modernization campaign, the Party-State's goal has been, broadly, Weberian. It has tried to build an efficient and predictable environment for commercial transactions that excludes "irrational" sources of law, whether religious or customary, and that purges internal "spiritual pollution," even as it exempted itself from the law. Yet Weber himself gives a more nuanced view of legal modernization in *The Protestant Ethic and the Spirit of Capitalism* (1930), which underscores that rationalization is fueled by religious belief. For Weber, it was not engineers and technocrats who laid the cornerstones for the capitalist system, but God-fearing Puritans.

After three decades of capitalistic reforms, the legitimating ideology of Maoism has become increasingly effaced (Lin 2006: 65), and Party leaders have turned to the language of belief to substantiate the law. The 2014 Fourth Plenary Session of the Eighteenth Central Committee of the CCP identified "rule of law" as a source not just of transactional guarantees but

[10] The glaring example is Anglo-American common law, which has roots in Christian "natural law" theory. A distinction should be made between revealed law and natural law. Whereas revealed law refers to the scriptural basis of religious law as understood by believers, natural law refers to comprehending God's revelation through applying reason to the natural world (Zuckert 1997; Miller 2012).

also of political and national legitimacy. The fifth part of the Decision of the Fourth Plenary Session states:

> The authority of law originates in the endorsement and belief of the inner being of the people. The rights and interests of the people will depend on legal guarantees, and legal authority depends on its being upheld by the people. [We] must carry forward the spirit of the socialist rule of law, build a socialist rule of law culture, strengthen all of society's enthusiasm and initiative in enforcing rule of law, and allow the glory of honoring the law and an atmosphere of disgrace for those who violate the law to take shape. [We] must make the whole body of the people into the faithful venerators, conscious observers, and staunch defenders of the socialist rule of law.
>
> (Fourth Plenum of the Eighteenth Congress of the Central Committee of the CCP 2014)

Whereas CCP leaders in the past have made references to Confucian morality and ethics in support of Party rule, the Fourth Plenary Session marks the Party's most overt attempt to found its own political theology through law, although such statements tend to be more rhetorical than substantive.[11] The role of law in Chinese society enters a new phase as "faith in the rule of law" (Merry 2000: 259). It is no longer the "command of the sovereign" that matters but rather the acclamation of those governed. Law is not imposed from above; instead, it resides within the hearts of those who would be its defenders.[12] Belief, spirit, initiative, honor, faith, and consciousness—these are reflections of the divine, appropriated by the Party-State and made the inspiration for citizen-acolytes.[13] In one sense, the Party-State's proselytizing of belief in the "rule of law" substantiates the Weberian view that secular belief displaces religion.[14] It is perhaps more compelling, however, to regard China's movement, to use Talcott

---

[11] The Fourth Plenary Session is not the first time the Party has committed itself to "rule of law." The commitment can be traced back to the Fifteenth National Congress in 1997. However, it is the first time the Party has introduced language that equates the "rule of law" so unequivocally with faith.

[12] Liang Zhiping, one of the foremost proponents for the social-scientific study of law in China, has written of the fifth part of the Decision, "Belief, these two characters [i.e., *xin yang*], set a very high goal. You can demand a member of the CCP to believe in Communism, but whether or not you can make her do it is another thing. Similarly, you can demand a religious believer to be faithful, but to make the people believe in law—what is the basis? How do you do it? ... These are very high goals, and in order to achieve them, the rulers must first make such demands or even higher demands of themselves" (Liang 2014).

[13] This is a tall order for a country that experienced "legal nihilism" under Mao only forty years ago (Lo 1992: 649; Miyazawa, Chan, and Lee 2008: 333–34; Sapio 2010: 33).

[14] This view is the conventional interpretation of the secularization thesis (Habermas 2008; Casanova 2011).

Parsons's translation of Weber (1930: 123), not from the saint's cloak to the iron cage and back to the saint's cloak again, but rather to the current depiction of the saint's cloak wrapped around the iron bars. One insulates rather than replaces the other, and the Party-State gains legitimacy through such layering.

At the same time, criticism of the Party-State's "rule of law" discourse as "mere rhetoric" goes too far; rather, commitments to the spirit of the law should be taken seriously. Like Islamic law for Hui, state law may attain an aspirational quality for officials, lawyers, and the lay, yet their efforts to live in accordance with law matter. Law in China, whether revealed or secular, invites thinking about law beyond rules (ethical, religious, customary, and so on). Rules can be bent or even ignored. Nonetheless, the plethora of projects to make selves, citizens, communities, and nations out of law, projects that may be glorified just as well as concealed, by, for instance, Salafis or cadres (or Salafi cadres), are changing China and beyond.

The Party-State's concern over nonstate law suggests anxieties about its own ethics. Judgments on subjects often reflect agitations the ruler has over his own ethical standards as prerequisite to govern, a theme with a very long history in China. The Party's current anticorruption campaigns[15] are designed to raise such standards among officials, low and high. What qualifies as "corruption" in China overlaps with the *minjian*: person-to-person relationships, family or kinship ties, transnational business networks, under-the-table informalities, legal evasion, and so on. Yet, as the category of "the official" expands and increases its panoptic sight, so too does the *minjian*. Anticorruption may appease critics and bolster legitimacy, but the *minjian* endures. The *minjian* is not to be romanticized, however. An excess of *minjian*, defined by the abuse of informal rights that deprive others of theirs, requires state intervention as a corrective. Hui open KTV parlors as brothels and practice polygamy across the Qinghai-Tibet plateau. Hui women engage Islamic and formal legal sources to protect their rights against such violations. As seen from the Hui social field, the *minjian* and state law are in many respects inseparable.

More broadly, including the *minjian* in the analysis of Chinese law and governance sheds light on the experience of those living under normative

---

[15] In 2012, when he assumed power, Xi Jinping, general secretary and president of the CCP, commenced an aggressive anticorruption campaign that has reformed cadre behavior at all levels. It has led to the sacking of several Party leaders, including Bo Xilai, former member of the Politburo, and Zhou Yongkang, former member of the Politburo Standing Committee, the most powerful organ in the PRC.

pluralism in China. The great challenge of studying Chinese law—and, I would add, its reward—is grasping the relationship between law and the *minjian*, that which happens off the court transcript and beyond the four corners of the legal document. Formal law is almost always bound up in processes located beyond formal institutions and legal texts, yet "out of court" relationships and backroom conversations can also invoke *minjian* sources of law, which may have significant impact on the rights and duties of those in question. Ethnography, as situated learning, is one methodology among others that is suited to this task. While the Chinese legal system continues to develop and lawyers are increasingly professionalized, such development is uneven, in terms of geography and ethnicity and class, not to mention public interest as opposed to private commercial law. Researching only formal law may omit half the picture.

Studying the *minjian* also illuminates the evolving nature of the Party. The general view is that Party leadership is aware that in order for it to rule the diverse populations, particularly in its border regions, it must reform its own internal rules and more piously adhere to the letter of its own law. From the perspective of the Hui, a question is whether the Party can stand in as legislator of the *qingzhen* (lit. "pure and true," or halal). Hui are constantly reminding one another that belief is "written on their hearts." Commitments to law—and their deviations from it—by the sovereign as well as by the citizen should be taken together. This is particularly so in a world of constraints. Hui are reminded every day of the disconnect between the "ought" and the "is." Learned clerics, for instance, bemoan such government appointees as Old Dong. Frustrations have real-life consequences. One cleric lost his clerical position after a dispute with the local government. Following standard procedure, the public security organs made the mosque administration committee reprimand the cleric, after which he left the mosque. In such results, one sees the legacies of "custom"-making imperial projects, modern panopticons, ethnic heteronomy, the opacity of the state's law, and hollow glorification and fallen angelology. Hui would be the first to profess that they are neither a perfect model of following one's law nor a model for the integration of Islamic law into state legal systems. Indeed, it is their imperfections that warrant study for efforts to close the gap between faith, conscience, and aspiration, on the one hand, and the everyday exigencies of living in diverse societies, on the other hand.

GLOSSARY

The study of Islam in China presents numerous linguistic and terminological difficulties given the presence of multiple languages and the creolization of terms through Chinese and its local dialects. Although there exist several excellent glossaries for the study of Islam in China,[1] there is no glossary that addresses the question of Islamic law in China. Thus, I have compiled a list of related terms. Doubtless this list is both under-inclusive in the sense that there are other terms important to the Hui practice of Islamic law and over-inclusive by enumerating some terms not directly related to law, but which are nevertheless important to religion and politics in Northwest China. I have attempted to weigh importance, predominance, and frequency of terms used among Hui throughout the Northwest with a focus on Linxia. The glossary includes the Chinese term as used by the Hui, the original in Arabic, Persian, Tibetan, or Uyghur, and the English meaning. In certain cases, the text of the book includes both the Chinese and the original term. In other instances, the text mentions only the original (e.g., Arabic) and not the Chinese translation. In these cases (noted by an asterisk, *), I have listed, for the purpose of uniformity, both the original and the Chinese, according to the alphabetical order of the Chinese term. For orthographic rules, I use IJMES Style for Arabic and Persian words, Wylie for Tibetan, and the pre-1950 "Modern Uyghur" system for Uyghur.

---

[1] See Gladney ([1991] 1996); Allès (2000); J. Wang (2001); Zhao (2010); and P. Wang (2012).

Chinese Term	Non-Chinese Equivalent	English Meaning of Chinese Term
Phonetic Equivalent (PE) and Semantic Equivalent (SE). All terms are included in Bafanghua, although Bafanghua may have divergent pronunciation, as indicated by (B).	Unless otherwise indicated as Persian (P), Tibetan (T), or Uyghur (U), all terms are Arabic.	Where the Chinese term and that of the original language diverge in meaning, I note herein.
ahong 阿訇 (PE)	*ākhūnd* آخوند (P)	Imam, cleric, or one who leads the prayer in a mosque.
Anla 安拉; *Anlahu* 安拉乎 (PE)*	Allah الله	God. See *Zhenzhu*.
baigong 拜功 (SE)*	salat صلاة	Worship, one of the five pillars. See *libai*.
bai maozi 白帽子 (SE); *bei homo* (B)	qubba'a قبّعة	White cap worn by Hui.
Buharla Shengxun 布哈利圣训 (PE)*	*Sahih al-Bukhari* صحيح البخاري	One of the six canonical collections of the sayings and deeds of the Prophet.
buli 晡礼 (SE)*	'aṣr عصر	Afternoon prayer.
canyu gufen zhi 参与股份制 (SE)*	*mushāraka* مشاركة	A joint venture through which a bank usually provides capital and the investor the management expertise. The parties share profits based on a percentage and share losses.
chaogong 朝功; *chaojin* 朝觐 (SE)*	hajj حجّ	Pilgrimage, one of the five pillars.
chenli 晨礼 (SE)*	*fajr* فجر	Morning prayer.
chuangzhi 创制 (SE)	*ijtihād* اجتهاد	Independent reasoning in rule creation.

Chinese Term	Non-Chinese Equivalent	English Meaning of Chinese Term
daihunqi 待婚期 (SE)*	ʿidda عدّة	Mandatory waiting period after pronouncement of *ṭalāq* during which husband and wife cannot have sex. See *jiejingqi*.
dangran 当然 (SE)*	wājib واجب	Obligatory [duty or act] (one of the five categories of evaluating behavior under Islamic law). See *fuzhuming*, *tianming yiwu, wazhibu*.
daocheng 道乘 (SE)	ṭarīqa طريقة, pl. ṭuruq طرق	Lit. "vehicle of the way," or path, the second of the three Sufi vehicles. See *tuoleigeti*.
dazhong 大众		Lit. "the masses," means Han.
du'a 都阿 (PE)*	duʿāʾ دعاء, pl. adʿiya أدعية	Supplication.
ermaili 尔麦里 (PE)	ʿamala عمل;	Lit. "to do; to act," used for anniversary of death date of a Sufi saint. Also used by Yihewani to mean, more generically, study and prayer.
falixue 法理学 (SE)*	fiqh فقه	Jurisprudence. See *feigehai*.
faren 法人		Legal representative of a mosque or Sufi tomb complex.
fatewa 法特瓦; *feitewu* 菲特伍 (PE)*	fatwa فتوى	Juristic ruling on a specific issue.

356

Chinese Term	Non-Chinese Equivalent	English Meaning of Chinese Term
faxue 法学 (SE); *faxue yuanli* 法学原理 (SE); *faxue dagang* 法学大纲 (SE)	*uṣūl al-fiqh* أصول الفقه	Lit. "the roots of the law," refers to the study of the sources of Islamic law and the methodologies for deriving rules from the sources.
faxuejia 法学家 (SE)*	*'ulama'* علماء	Legal scholars, jurists.
faxuepai 法学派 (SE)*	*madhhab* مذهب, pl. *madhāhib* مذاهب	School of jurisprudence.
feidiye 费底耶; *feijiye* 非吉也; *feitulu* 费突鲁 (PE)*	*fidya* فدية	Lit. "ransom," used to describe a preburial practice of atoning for sins of the deceased. Also used to describe the practice of giving 10 percent of one's income to charity (distinguished from zakat).
feifa 非法 (SE)*	haram حرام	Prohibited (one of the five categories of evaluating behavior under Islamic law). See *hailamu, halamu.*
feigehai 费格海 (PE)*	*fiqh* فقه	Jurisprudence. See *falixue.*
fei Musilin 非穆斯林 (SE)	*kafir* كافر	Generally, non-Muslim, disbeliever. It is debated by theologians and jurists in the Middle East as to whether this term applies to Christians and Jews.
fengsu xiguan 风俗习惯		Social customs and habits.

Chinese Term	Non-Chinese Equivalent	English Meaning of Chinese Term
fuzhuming 副主命 (SE)	*wājib* واجب	Obligatory [duty or act] (one of the five categories of evaluating behavior under Islamic law). See *dangran, tianming yiwu, wazhibu*.
gaitou 盖头 (SE)	hijab حجاب	Headdress commonly worn by Hui women.
Gajirenye 嘎吉忍耶; *Gadelinye* 嘎德林耶 (SE)*	al-Qadiriyya القادرّية	One of the four Sufi orders of China.
gazhui 嘎锥; *gazui* 噶最 (PE)	qadi قاضي	See *kadi*.
Gedimu 格底木 (PE)	*qadīm* قديم	Lit. "old" or "ancient," meaning one of the teaching schools believed to be descendants of the original Arab and Persian traders in China.
geyasi 格亚斯 (PE)*	*qiyās* قياس	Analogical reasoning, one of the two man-made sources of shari'a. See *leibi*.
gongbei 拱北 (PE)	*qubba* قبّة; *dgon pa* དགོན་པ (T)	Sufi tomb complex. This word may have origins in the Arabic term for "dome" and/ or Tibetan word for "monastery."
gongxiu 功修 (SE)	*awrād* pl. أوراد	"Meritorious work" or "regular spiritual works," referring to *dhikr, du'ā'*, recitation of the Qur'an and meditation as part of a Sufi's adherence to the *ṭarīqa*.

Chinese Term	Non-Chinese Equivalent	English Meaning of Chinese Term
gongyi 公议 (SE)*	*ijmā'* إجماع	Consensus of the scholars, one of the two man-made sources of shari'a.
Gu'erbangjie 古尔邦节 (PE)*	'Īd-e-Qurbān عيد قربان (P)	Festival of sacrifice. See Zaishengjie.
guizhen 归真 (SE)	*māta* مات	Lit. "return to the truth" or "return to the true Lord." Or, to die.
Gulanjing 古兰经 (PE, SE)	Qur'an القرآن	Lit. "ancient classic of moral excellence," for "recitation," one of the two sacred sources of shari'a.
guofa 国法		State law.
guomin 国民		Citizen(s) or national(s).
hadisi 哈迪斯 (PE)*	hadith حديث	Sayings of the Prophet Muhammad, one of two sacred sources of shari'a.
hageishanti 哈给盖体 (PE)*	*ḥaqīqa* حقيقة	Truth, the third of the three Sufi vehicles. See *zhencheng*.
haijiye 海吉也 (PE)*	*hadiyya* هديّة	Gift.
hailamu 海拉母; *halamu* 哈拉目 (PE)*	haram حرام	Prohibited (one of the five categories of evaluating behavior under Islamic law). See *feifa*.
hailiali 海俩里 (PE)*	halal حلال	Lawful, permissible. See *hefa*.
haituibu 海推布 (PE)	*khaṭīb* خطيب (imam إمام)	One who gives the Friday sermon.
Hanaifei 哈乃斐 (PE)*	Hanafi حنفي (adj.)	One of the four schools of Sunni jurisprudence and the school of jurisprudence to which most Chinese Muslims belong.

Chinese Term	Non-Chinese Equivalent	English Meaning of Chinese Term
Hanbaili 罕百里 (PE)*	Hanbali حنبلى (adj.)	One of the four schools of Sunni jurisprudence and the school that most non-Salafis associate with the Salafiyya.
hanyi dasi 罕乙大寺; *hanyisi* 罕乙寺 (PE)	*hay'at al-masjid* هيئة المسجد	"Administrative mosque" or "authoritative mosque," referring to a large mosque that administers smaller mosques.
hefa 合法 (SE)*	halal حلال	Legal, lawful, used for halal. See *hailiali*.
houshi 后世 (SE)	*al-ākhira* الآخرة	Afterlife.
Hufeiya 虎非耶 (PE)*	al-Khufiyya الخفيّة	Naqshbandi Sufi *ṭarīqa*.
Hui 回, Huihui 回回, *huimin* 回民, Huizu 回族		One of the fifty-five officially recognized ethnic minorities and the largest group of Muslim minorities in China.
Huihui hadesi 回回哈的司		Bureau of the Qadis. An institution, begun by the Yuan Dynasty, that integrated Muslim clerics into the official bureaucracy.
Huizu xiguanfa 回族习惯法		Hui customary law.
hukun 呼昆 (PE)	*ḥukm* حكم, pl. *aḥkām* أحكام	Islamic commandment, rule, or judgment made by God, judge, or jurist.
hunli 昏礼 (SE)*	*maghrib* مغرب	Sunset prayer.

Chinese Term	Non-Chinese Equivalent	English Meaning of Chinese Term
jiajia maoyi 加价贸易 (SE)	*murābaḥa* مرابحة	Islamic finance instrument by which a buyer signs a contract of sale with a bank that purchases a good from a seller at a prearranged price and then resells it to the buyer with an increased cost.
jiangjing 讲经 (SE)	*munāẓara* مناظرة	Debate (regarding the scriptures).
jiaocheng 教乘 (SE)	*shariʿa* شريعة	Lit. "vehicle of the teaching" and the first of the three Sufi vehicles. See *jiaofa*, *sheruo'ati*, *sheli'erti*, *zongjiaofa*.
jiaofa 教法 (SE)	*shariʿa* شريعة	Lit. "law of the teaching." See *jiaocheng*, *sheruo'ati*, *sheli'erti*, *zongjiaofa*.
jiaofang 教坊 (SE)	*jamāʿa* جماعة	Community. See *zhemati*.
jiaogui 教规 (SE)*	*fiqh* فقه	Lit. "teaching rules."
jiaolü 教律 (SE)*	*ʿibādāt* جهاد	Ordinances of divine worship. See *yibadade*.
jiaomin 教民		Lit. "person(s) of the teaching" or religious adherent.
jiaopai 教派		Lit. "teaching school."
jiehade 杰哈德 (PE)*	*jihad* عيادات	Generally, "struggle."
jiejing 解经 (SE)	*tafsīr* تفسير	Qur'anic exegesis.
jiejingqi 洁净期 (SE)*	*ʿidda* عدّة	Mandatory waiting period after pronouncement of *ṭalāq* during which husband and wife cannot have sex. See *daihunqi*.

Chinese Term	Non-Chinese Equivalent	English Meaning of Chinese Term
jingtang jiaoyu 经堂教育		Lit. "scriptural hall education."
juban 举伴 (SE)*	*shirk* شرك	Idolatry.
kadi 卡迪 (PE)*	*qadi* قاضي	Judge. See *gazui*.
kaixue ahong 开学阿訇		Teaching *ahong*.
karemeti 卡热么提 (PE)*	*karāma* كرامة	Wonder, miracle.
kegong 课功 (SE)*	*zakat* زكاة	Obligatory alms, one of the five pillars. See *tianke, zakate*.
kouhuan 扣环 (SE)	*ijāza* إجازة	Permission.
laorenjia 老人家 (SE)	*murshid* مرشد, pl. *murshidūn* مرشدون	Lit. "respected parent," meaning "spiritual guide" or Sufi master. See *shehe*.
leibi 类比 (SE)*	*qiyās* قياس	Analogical reasoning, one of the two man-made sources of shari'a. See *geyasi*.
libai 礼拜 (SE)*	*salat* صلاة	Prayer, one of the five pillars. See *baigong*.
manla 满拉 (PE)	*mawlā* مولى (charge); mulla ملا (teacher); *murīd* مريد (pupil), pl. *murīdūn* مريدون	Student (Arabic equivalent uncertain).
menhuan 门宦		Sufi organization.
minjian 民间		Lit. "between people." Used to mean popular, unofficial, folk, nongovernmental, nonstate, and grassroots.
minjian ahong 民间阿訇		Unofficial cleric or imam.
minjian diaocha 民间调查		Popular or unofficial investigation.
minjianfa 民间法		Popular or unofficial law.
minjian tiaojie 民间调解		Popular mediation.

Chinese Term	Non-Chinese Equivalent	English Meaning of Chinese Term
minjian waijiao 民间外交		Popular or unofficial diplomacy.
minjian xinyang 民间信仰		Popular faith.
minjian zuzhi 民间组织		Unofficial or unregistered organization.
minshi falü guiding 民事法律规定 (SE)*	*muʿāmalāt* معاملات	Shariʿa of social relations. See *muamailiangte*.
minshi xingwei nengli 民事行为能力 (SE)*	*taklīf* تكليف (state)	Having legal capacity for civil conduct.
minzu 民族		Nationality, ethnicity.
minzufa 民族法		Ethnic law.
mu'amailiangte 穆阿麦俩特 (PE)*	*muʿāmalāt* معاملات	Law of social relations. See *minshi falü guiding*.
mu'anjin 穆安津 (PE)	*muezzin* مؤذّن	Person who calls Muslims to prayer.
mudalaba 穆达拉巴 (PE)*	*muḍāraba* مضاربة	A contractual relationship in accordance with Islamic finance law whereby one party contributes money and the other management. Risk is born by the former alone.
mufuti 穆夫提 (PE)*	*mufti* مفتي	Legal counsel who interprets shariʿa.
Muhammode 穆罕默德 (PE)*	*Muhammad* محمّد	The Prophet.
Musilin 穆斯林 (PE)	*Muslim* مسلم	Muslim.
muzhitaixide 穆智台希德 (PE)	*mujtahid* مجتهد pl. *mujtahidūn* مجتهدون	One capable of performing *ijtihād* (independent thinking in creating legal decisions).

Chinese Term	Non-Chinese Equivalent	English Meaning of Chinese Term
Nageshenbandiye 纳格什班迪耶 (PE)	al-Naqshbandiyya النقشبندية	The Sufi *tarīqa* from which the Khufiyya and Jahriyya *turuq* diverged.
nietie 乜贴 (PE)	*niyya* نيّة	Object donated. Used for "intent or "intention."
nikaha 尼卡哈 (PE)*	*nikāḥ* نكاح	Marriage contract.
pinli 聘礼; *pingjin* 聘金* (SE); *pingji* (B)*	*mahr* مهر	Bridal gift.
qingzhen 清真 (SE)	halal حلال	Lit. "pure and true," also lawful, clean, whole.
qingzhenyan 清真言 (SE)*	*shahāda* شهادة	Islamic creed, one of the five pillars.
renmin tiaojie weiyuanhui 人民调解委员会		People's mediation committee.
Sailaifeiye 塞莱非耶 (PE)	al-Salafiyya السلفية	Neoconservative Islamist ideology.
sajida 萨吉达 (PE)*	*sujūd* سجود	Prostration to God by touching forehead to ground.
sancheng 三乘		Lit. "Three vehicles" of Sufism. See *jiaocheng, daocheng,* and *zhencheng.*
Shafeiyi 沙斐仪 (PE)*	Shafi'i شافعي (adj.)	One of the four schools of Sunni jurisprudence.
shangli 晌礼 (SE)*	*zuhr* ظهر	Noon prayer.
shehe 舍赫 (PE); 筛赫;* *shahe* 沙赫;* *shaihai* 筛海*	shaykh شيخ	Elder, master, or leader.
shenghuo guilü 生活规律		Regularizing pattern of life, the way that elite Hui describe shari'a.

Chinese Term	Non-Chinese Equivalent	English Meaning of Chinese Term
shengxun 圣训 (SE)	hadith حديث	Lit. "instructions of the sage," meaning sayings and deeds of the Prophet Muhammad, one of two revealed sources of shariʿa. See *hadisi*.
sheruo'ati 舍若阿提; *sheli'erti* 舍里尔提 (PE)*	shariʿa شريعة	Shariʿa. See *jiaocheng*, *jiaofa*, *zongjiaofa*.
shou qianze de xingwei 受谴责的行为 (SE)*	*makrūh* مكروه	Reprehensible but permitted behavior (one of the five categories of evaluating behavior under Islamic law).
su'er 苏尔 (PE)*	sura سورة	Chapter of the Qur'an.
suodege 索德格 (PE)*	*ṣadaqa* صدقة	Voluntary charity.
suoma 索麻 (PE)	*ṣawmaʿa* صومعة	Cloister, monastery.
talage 塔拉格 (PE)*	*ṭalāq* طلاق	Divorce.
taikebi'er 太克比尔 (PE)*	*takbīr* تكبير	*Allahu akbar* (God is great), a phrase used in formal and informal prayer. See *zanci*.
taobai 讨白 (PE, SE)	*tawba* توبة	Repentance, from the ninth sura of the Qur'an. Considered, among Sufis, to be fuel for spiritual ascent.
tianke 天课; *tianminggongke* 天明功课 (SE)*	zakat زكاة	Obligatory alms, one of the five pillars. See *kegong*, *zakate*.
tianming 天明 (SE)	*ḥukm* حكم, pl. *aḥkām* أحكام	Lit. "mandate of heaven," used for Islamic commandment.

Chinese Term	Non-Chinese Equivalent	English Meaning of Chinese Term
tianming yiwu 天明义务 (SE)*	*wājib* واجب	Obligatory duty (one of the five categories of evaluating behavior under Islamic law). See *dangran, fuzhuming, wazhibu.*
tianshan 天仙 (SE)	*malā'ika* ملائكة	Angels, belief in which is one of the six articles of faith.
tuoleigeti 妥勒格体;* *tuoleishanti* 妥勒善提 (PE)*	*ṭarīqa* طريقة, pl. *ṭuruq* طرق	The way or path and second of the three vehicles of Sufism.
wagefu 瓦格夫 (PE)	*waqf* وقف, pl. *awqāf* اوقاف	Pious endowment.
Wahabiye 瓦哈比耶 (SE)*	Wahhabism الوهّابيّة	Islamist reform movement that believes in strict interpretation of the Qur'an.
wazhibu 瓦直卜 (PE)	*wājib* واجب	Obligatory [duty or act] (one of the five categories of evaluating behavior under Islamic law). See *dangran, fuzhuming, tianming yiwu.*
Weidaojing 卫道经 (SE)*	*Sharh al-Wiqaya* شرح الوقاية	*Explanation of the Protection,* a Hanafi text. See *Weigaye.*
Weigaye 伟尕耶 (PE)*	*Sharh al-Wiqaya* شرح الوقاية	*Explanation of the Protection,* a Hanafi text. See *Weidaojing.*
wo'erzi 卧而子 (PE)	*wa'ẓ* وعظ.	Admonishment. Hui may use as substitute for *khuṭbah* (Friday sermon).
wugong 五功 (SE)	*arkān al-Islām* أركان الإسلام	Five pillars of Islam.
wuma 乌玛 (PE)	*umma* امّة	The Muslim community.

Chinese Term	Non-Chinese Equivalent	English Meaning of Chinese Term
xiaojing 孝敬 (SE)	*birr al-wālidīn* برّ الوالدين	Filial piety.
xiaojing 小净 (SE)	*wuḍūʾ* وضوء	Partial ablution.
xiaoli 宵礼 (SE)*	*ʿishāʾ* عشاء	Evening prayer.
Xidaotang 西道堂		A religious, social, and commercial community based in Lintan, Gansu.
xiejiao 邪教		Heterodoxy or cult.
xiguan 习惯 (SE)	*ʿurf* عرف	Custom.
xiguanfa 习惯法		Customary law.
xijila 希吉拉 (PE)	hijra هجرة	Emigration; the historical migration of Prophet Muhammad from Mecca to Medina in 622 CE.
xijing 洗净 (SE)*	*ṭahāra* طهارة	Ritual purity.
xilixila 西里西拉 (PE)*	*silsila* سلسلة	Chain of spiritual descent between initiate and past masters.
xinzhuduyi 信主独一 (SE)*	*tawḥīd* توحيد	Oneness of God.
xiudaoyuan 修道院 (SE)*	*ṣawmaʿa* صومعة	Cloister, monastery. See *suoma*.
xuanjiao 宣教 (SE)*	*daʿwa* دعوة	Piety, preaching Islam.
xuanli 宣礼 (SE)*	*adhān* أذان	Call to prayer.
xunnai 逊奈 (PE)*	sunna سنّة	Practices of the Prophet Muhammad.
yibadade 伊巴达德 (PE)*	*ʿibādāt* عبادات	Ordinances of divine worship. See *jiaolü*.
yichanfa 遗产法 (SE)	*ʿilm al-farāʾid.* علم الفرائض	Inheritance law.
yiduan 异端 (SE)*	bidʿa بدعة	Innovation.
yifuduoqi 一夫多妻 (SE)	*taʿaddud al-zawjāt* تعدّد الزوجات	Polygamy.

367

Chinese Term	Non-Chinese Equivalent	English Meaning of Chinese Term
Yihewani 伊合瓦尼 (PE)	al-Ikhwan al-Muslimun الإخوان المسلمون	Muslim Brotherhood.
yimamu 伊玛目 (PE)*	imam إمام	One who leads the prayer.
yimani 伊玛尼 (PE)	īmān إيمان	Belief. See zongjiao xinyang.
Yisilanfa 伊斯兰法 (PE)		Islamic law.
Yisilanjiaofa 伊斯兰教法 (PE)		Islamic (religious) law.
yizhitihade 伊智提哈德 (PE)*	ijtihād اجتهاد	Independent reasoning in rule creation.
youhui zhengce 优惠政策		Preferential policies.
Zaishengjie 宰牲节 (SE)	ʿĪd-e-Qurbān عيد قربان; (P)	Festival of sacrifice. See Gu'erbangjie.
zakate 则卡特 (PE)*	zakat زكاة	Obligatory alms, one of the five pillars. See kegong, tianke.
zanci 赞词 (SE)*	takbīr تكبير	Praising God through the expression Allahu akbar (God is great).
zanshi hunyin 暂时婚姻 (SE)*	mutʿa متعة	Temporary marriage.
zeke'er 则克尔 (PE)*	dhikr ذكر	Remembrance of God.
Zhehelinye 哲赫林耶 (PE)	al-Jahriyya الجهريّة	Naqshbandi Sufi ṭarīqa.
zhemati 折麻体 (SE)	jamāʿa جماعة	Mosque community. See jiaofang.
zhenaze 者那则 (PE)*	janāza جنازة	Funerary procession.
zhencheng 真乘 (SE)	ḥaqīqa حقيقة	Lit. "vehicle of truth" or "the vehicle of Allah," the third of the three Sufi vehicles.
Zhenzhu 真主 (SE)	Allah الله	Lit. "true lord." See Anla, Anlahu.
zizhi 自治		Self-rule, legal autonomy.

Chinese Term	Non-Chinese Equivalent	English Meaning of Chinese Term
zongjiaofa 宗教法 (SE)	shariʿa شريعة	Religious law. See *jiaocheng, jiaofa, sheruoʾati, sheliʾerti*.
zongjiao fating 宗教法庭 (SE)*	*qadihana* قاضيخانه (U)	Site where the qadi holds courts (which may or may not be a physical court). Used by Uyghur and not Hui.
zongjiao huodong changsuo 宗教活动场所		"Religious activity area," the PRC legal term for mosque.
zongjiao shehui tuanti 宗教社会团体		"Religious social group," the PRC legal term for teaching school or its mosque community.
zongjiao xinyang 宗教信仰 (SE)	*īmān* إيمان	Faith, belief. See *yimani*.
zongjiao xuexiao 宗教学校 (SE)*	madrasa مدرسة	Islamic school.

Glossaries on Islam in China

Allès, Élisabeth. 2000. *Musulmans de Chine: Une Anthropologie des Hui du Henan*. Paris: Éditions de l' École des Hautes Études en Sciences Sociales.

Gladney, Dru C. [1991] 1996. *Muslim Chinese: Ethnic Nationalism in the People's Republic*. 2nd edn. Cambridge, MA: Council on East Asian Studies, Harvard University.

Wang, Jianping. 2001. *A Glossary of Chinese Islamic Terms*. Richmond, UK: Curzon.

Wang, Ping [王平]. 2012. *Linxia Bafang: Yige chuantong yu xiandai Huizu shequ de jiangou* [*Linxia Bafang: A Traditional and Modern Hui Community Construct*]. Beijing: Minzu daxue chubanshe [Minzu University Publisher].

Zhao, Qiudi [赵秋蒂]. 2010. "Zhongguo xibei musilin zongjiao paibie duoyuanhua yanjiu – yi Linxia wei lunshu zhongxin [Research on the Pluralization of China's Northwest Muslims' Religious Denominations: Taking Linxia as the Center for Discussion]." Ph.D. diss., Minzu xuexi (Ethnic Studies Dept.), National Chengchi University.

REFERENCES

For ease of use, I have categorized the references into two lists according to their language (i.e., Western languages and Chinese). In most cases, it is evident in which list a source can be located. However, some works by Chinese scholars are in English and can be found in the "Western Language Sources" list. Likewise, a handful of non-Chinese authors have published in Chinese—in which case such sources are found in the "Chinese Language Sources" list. Links to online sources are active as of 2015; I have kept online material on file.

WESTERN LANGUAGE SOURCES

Abbas, Tahir. 2011. *Islamic Radicalism and Multicultural Politics: The British Experience*. Abingdon, UK: Routledge.

Abdo, Geneive. 2006. *Mecca and Main Street: Muslim Life in America after 9/11*. Oxford University Press.

Abel, Richard L., ed. 1982. *The Politics of Informal Injustice*. Vol. 2, *Comparative Studies*. New York: Academic Press.

Abou el-Fadl, Khaled. 1994. "Islamic Law and Muslim Minorities: The Juristic Discourse on Muslim Minorities from the Second/Eighth to the Eleventh/Seventeenth Centuries." *Islamic Law and Society* 1(2): 141–87.

Abrahamian, Ervand. 2003. "The US Media, Huntington and September 11." *Third World Quarterly* 24(3): 529–44.

Abu-Lughod, Lila. 2002. "Do Muslim Women Really Need Saving? Anthropological Reflections on Cultural Relativism and Its Others." *American Anthropologist* 104(3): 783–90.

2013. *Do Muslim Women Need Saving?* Cambridge, MA: Harvard University Press.

Afshar, Haleh. 1996. "Islam and Feminism: An Analysis of Political Strategies." In *Feminism and Islam: Legal and Literary Perspectives*, edited by Mai Yamani, 197–216. New York University Press.

1998. *Islam and Feminisms: An Iranian Case-Study*. Basingstoke, UK: Macmillan.

Agai, Bekim. 2007. "Islam and Education in Secular Turkey: State Policies and the Emergence of the Fethullah Gülen Group." In *Schooling Islam: The Culture and Politics of Modern Muslim Education*, edited by Robert W. Hefner and Muhammad Qasim Zaman, 149–71. Princeton University Press.

Agamben, Giorgio. 1998. *Homo Sacer: Sovereign Power and Bare Life*, translated by Daniel Heller-Roazen. Stanford University Press.

1999. "The Messiah and the Sovereign: The Problem of Law in Walter Benjamin." In *Potentialities: Collected Essays in Philosophy*, edited by Daniel Heller-Roazen, 160–76. Stanford University Press.

2005. *State of Exception*, translated by Kevin Attell. University of Chicago Press.

2011. *The Kingdom and the Glory: For a Theological Genealogy of Economy and Government*, translated by Lorenzo Chiesa and Matteo Mandarini. Stanford University Press.

Agrama, Hussein Ali. 2010. "Ethics, Tradition, Authority: Toward an Anthropology of the Fatwa." *American Ethnologist* 37(1): 2–18.

2012. *Questioning Secularism: Islam, Sovereignty, and the Rule of Law in Modern Egypt*. University of Chicago Press.

Ahern, Emily Martin. 1973. *The Cult of the Dead in a Chinese Village*. Stanford University Press.

1981. *Chinese Ritual and Politics*. Cambridge University Press.

Ahmed, Adel. 2010. "Global Financial Crisis: An Islamic Finance Perspective." *International Journal of Islamic and Middle Eastern Finance and Management* 3(4): 306–20.

Ahmed, Leila. 1992. *Women and Gender in Islam: Historical Roots of a Modern Debate*. New Haven, CT: Yale University Press.

Ahmed, Sameer. 2008. "Pluralism in British Islamic Reasoning: The Problem with Recognizing Islamic Law in the United Kingdom." *Yale Journal of International Law* 33: 491–511.

el-Alami, Dawoud S. 1992. *The Marriage Contract in Islamic Law: In the Shari'ah and Personal Status Laws of Egypt and Morocco*. London: Graham & Trotman.

Alford, William P. 2000. "Law, Law, What Law?" In *The Limits of the Rule of Law in China*, edited by Karen G. Turner, James V. Feinerman, and R. Kent Guy, 45–64. Seattle: University of Washington.

Ali, Abdullah Yusuf. 1938. *An English Interpretation of the Holy Qur-ān: With Full Arabic Text*. 3rd edn. Lahore, Pakistan: Shaykh Muhammad Ashraf.

Ali, Kecia. 2010. *Marriage and Slavery in Early Islam*. Cambridge, MA: Harvard University Press.

Allès, Élisabeth. 2004. "Chinese Muslim Women: From Autonomy to Dependence." In *Devout Societies vs. Impious States? Transmitting Islamic Learning in Russia, Central Asia and China, through the Twentieth Century*, edited by Stéphane Dudoignon, 91–103. Berlin: Klaus Schwarz Verlag.

Allès, Élisabeth, Leïla Chérif-Chebbi, and Constance-Hélène Halfon. 2003. "Chinese Islam: Unity and Fragmentation." *Religion, State & Society* 31(1): 7–35.

Alterman, Jon B., and Karin von Hippel, eds. 2007. *Understanding Islamic Charities*. Washington DC: CSIS Press.

Anagnost, Ann. 2004. "The Corporeal Politics of Quality (*Suzhi*)." *Public Culture* 16(2): 189–208.

　　2013. "Introduction: Life-Making in Neoliberal Times." In *Global Futures in East Asia: Youth, Nation, and the New Economy in Uncertain Times*, edited by Ann Anagnost, Andrea Arai, and Hai Ren, 1–28. Stanford University Press.

Anderson, Benedict. 1983. *Imagined Communities: Reflections on the Origin and Spread of Nationalism*. London and New York: Verso.

Anderson, Michael. 1990. "Islamic Law and the Colonial Encounter in British India." In *Islamic Family Law*, edited by Chibli Mallat and Jane Connors, 205–24. Norwell, MA: Kluwer Academic Publishers Group.

An-Na'im, Abdullahi Ahmed. 2005. "The Interdependence of Religion, Secularism, and Human Rights." *Common Knowledge* 11(1): 65–80.

　　2008a. *Islam and the Secular State: Negotiating the Future of Shari'a*. Cambridge, MA: Harvard University Press.

　　2008b. "Shari'a in the Secular State: A Paradox of Separation and Conflation." In *The Law Applied: Contextualizing the Islamic Shari'a*, edited by Peri J. Bearman, Wolfhart Heinrichs, and Bernard G. Weiss, 321–41. London: I. B. Tauris.

Antoun, Richard T. 2000. "Civil Society, Tribal Process, and Change in Jordan: An Anthropological View." *International Journal of Middle East Studies* 32: 441–63.

Appadurai, Arjun. 1988. *The Social Life of Things: Commodities in Cultural Perspective*. Cambridge University Press.

Arendt, Hannah. [1966] 1976. *The Origins of Totalitarianism*. San Diego, CA: Harcourt, Inc.

al-Arian, Abdullah. 2014. *Answering the Call: Popular Islamic Activism*. Oxford University Press.

Armijo, Jackie. 2008. "Muslim Education in China: Chinese Madrasas and Linkages to Islamic Schools Abroad." In *The Madrasa in Asia: Political Activism and Transnational Linkages*, edited by Farish A. Noor, Yoginder Sikand, and Martin van Bruinessen, 169–90. Amsterdam University Press.

Armijo-Hussein, Jacqueline M. 1997. "Sayyid 'Ajjal Shams al-Din: A Muslim from Central Asia, Serving the Mongols in China and Bringing 'Civilization' to Yunnan." Ph.D. diss., Inner Asian and Altaic Studies, Harvard University.

Asad, Talal. 1993. *Genealogies of Religion: Discipline and Reasons of Power in Christianity and Islam*. Baltimore, MA: Johns Hopkins University Press.

　　2003. *Formations of the Secular: Christianity, Islam, and Modernity*. Palo Alto, CA: Stanford University Press.

2009a. "Free Speech, Blasphemy, and Secular Criticism." In *Is Critique Secular? Blasphemy, Injury, and Free Speech*, edited by Talal Asad, Wendy Brown, Judith Butler, and Saba Mahmood, 24–25. Berkeley: University of California Press.

[1986] 2009b. "The Idea of an Anthropology of Islam." *Qui Parle* 17(2): 1–30.

Askari, Hossein, Zamir Iqbal, and Abbas Mirakhor, eds. 2011. *Globalization and Islamic Finance: Convergence, Prospects and Challenges*. Singapore: John Wiley & Sons.

Atkinson, Rowland, and John Flint. 2003. "Snowball Sampling." In *The SAGE Encyclopedia of Social Science Research Methods*, edited by Michael S. Lewis-Beck, Alan Bryman, and Tim Futing Liao, 1043–44. Thousand Oaks, CA: Sage Publications.

Atwill, David G. 2005a. *The Chinese Sultanate: Islam, Ethnicity, and the Panthay Rebellion in Southwest China, 1856–1873*. Stanford University Press.

2005b. "The Dhikr Controversy in Eighteenth-Century Northwest China: Was There a Religious Basis?" Accessed December 15, 2009, www-personal.umich.edu/~yousufh/dhikr.html (copy on file with author).

Aubin, Françoise. 1990. "En Islam chinois: Quel Naqshbandis?" [In Chinese Islam: which Naqshbandis?]. In *Naqshbandis: Cheminements et situation actuelle d'un ordre mystique musulman* [*Historical developments and present situation of a Muslim mystical order*], edited by M. Gaborieu, A. Popovic, and T. Zarcone, 491–572. Istanbul and Paris: Éditions Isis.

Bakhtyar, Mozafar. 2000. "The 'Sufi' Orders in China." *Journal of the Pakistan Historical Society* 48(3): 37–44.

Balala, Maha-Hanaan. 2011. *Islamic Finance and Law: Theory and Practice in a Globalized World*. London: I. B. Tauris.

Ballard, Roger. 2006. "Ethnic Diversity and the Delivery of Justice: The Challenge of Plurality." In *Migration, Diasporas and Legal Systems in Europe*, edited by Prakash Shah and Werner F. Menski, 29–56. London: Routledge-Cavendish.

Bangstad, Sindre. 2011. "Saba Mahmood and Anthropological Feminism after Virtue." *Theory, Culture & Society* 28(3): 28–54.

Barazangi, Nimat Hafez. 2004. *Women's Identity and the Qur'an: A New Reading*. Gainesville: University Press of Florida.

Barlow, Tani E. 2004. *The Question of Women in Chinese Feminism*. Durham, NC: Duke University Press.

Barnett, A. Doak. 1993. *China's Far West: Four Decades of Change*. Boulder, CO: Westview Press.

Barth, Fredrik. 1969. *Ethnic Groups and Boundaries*. Oslo: Universitetsforlaget.

Becquelin, Nicolas. 2000. "Xinjiang in the Nineties." *The China Journal* 44: 65–92.

Beidelman, Thomas O. 1961. "Kaguru Justice and the Concept of Legal Fictions." *Journal of African Law* 5(1): 5–20.

Bellér-Hann, Ildikó. 2004. "Law and Custom among the Uyghur in Xinjiang." In *Central Asian Law: An Historical Overview, A Festschrift for the Ninetieth Birthday of Herbert Franke*, edited by Wallace Johnson and Irina F. Popova, 173–94. Topeka: Society for Asian Legal History, University of Kansas.

    2008. *Community Matters in Xinjiang, 1880–1949: Towards a Historical Anthropology of the Uyghur*. Leiden: Brill.

Bellér-Hann, Ildikó, Rachel A. Harris, M. Cristina Cesaro, and Joanne Smith Finley, eds. 2007. *Situating the Uyghurs between China and Central Asia*. Aldershot, UK: Ashgate Publishing.

Benda-Beckmann, Franz von, and Keebet von Benda-Beckmann. 2013. *Political and Legal Transformations of an Indonesian Polity: The Nagari from Colonisation to Decentralisation*. Cambridge University Press.

Benite, Zvi Ben-Dor. 2005. *The Dao of Muhammad: A Cultural History of Muslims in Late Imperial China*. Cambridge, MA: Harvard University Asia Center.

    2008. "'Nine Years in Egypt': The Chinese at Al-Azhar University." *HAGAR: Studies in Culture, Polity & Identities* 8(1): 105–28.

Benjamin, Walter. [1921] 2000. "Critique of Violence." In *Walter Benjamin: Selected Writings Volume 1 1913–1926*, edited by Marcus Bullock and Michael W. Jennings, 236-52. Cambridge, MA: Harvard University Press.

Benthall, Jeremy. 2014. "Charity." In *The Oxford Encyclopedia of Islam and Politics*, edited by Emad el-Din Shahin, Peri J. Bearman, Sohail H. Hashmi, Khaled Keshk, and Joseph A. Kechichian. *Oxford Islamic Studies Online*. Accessed May 22, 2015, www.oxfordislamicstudies.com/article/opr/t342/e0015.

Benthall, Jonathan, and Jérôme Bellion-Jourdan, eds. 2009a. *The Charitable Crescent: Politics of Aid in the Muslim World*. London: I. B. Tauris.

    2009b. "Financial Worship." In *The Charitable Crescent: Politics of Aid in the Muslim World*, edited by Jonathan Benthall and Jérôme Bellion-Jourdan, 7–28. London: I. B. Tauris.

Benton, Lauren. 2002. *Law and Colonial Cultures: Legal Regimes in World History, 1400–1900*. Cambridge University Press.

    2012. "Historical Perspectives on Legal Pluralism." In *Legal Pluralism and Development: Scholars and Practitioners in Dialogue*, edited by Brian Z. Tamanaha, Caroline Sage, and Michael Woolcock, 21–33. Cambridge University Press.

Benton, Lauren, and Richard J. Ross, eds. 2013. *Legal Pluralism and Empires, 1500–1850*. New York University Press.

Bernard, Harvey Russell. 2006. "Chain Referral, or Network Sampling: The Snowball and RDS Methods." In *Research Methods in Anthropology: Qualitative and Quantitative Approaches*, edited by Harvey Russell Bernard, 192–94. Lanham, MD: AltaMira Press.

Bernhardt, Kathryn. 1999. *Women and Property in China, 960–1949*. Stanford University Press.

Bernhardt, Kathryn, and Philip C. C. Huang, eds. 1994. *Civil Law in Qing and Republican China*. Stanford University Press.

Bhattacharya, Neeladri. 1996. "Remaking Custom: The Discourse and Practice of Colonial Codification." In *Tradition, Dissent and Ideology: Essays in Honour of Romila Thapar*, edited by R. Champakalakshmi and S. Gopal, 20–54. Oxford University Press.

Biersteker, Thomas J., and Cynthia Weber. 1996. "The Social Construction of State Sovereignty." In *State Sovereignty as Social Construct*, edited by Thomas J. Biersteker and Cynthia Weber, 1–21. Cambridge University Press.

Bobrovnikov, V. O. 2001. "Sharia Courts and Legal Pluralism in Soviet Daghestan." *Ètnografičeskoe obozrenie* 3: 77–91.

Bodde, Derk, and Clarence Morris. 1967. *Law in Imperial China: Exemplified by 190 Ch'ing Dynasty Codes (Translated from the "Hsing-An Hui-lan")*, *with Historical, Social, and Juridical Commentaries*. Cambridge, MA: Harvard University Press.

Bohannan, Paul. 1957. *Justice and Judgment among the Tiv*. Prospect Heights, IL: Waveland Press, Inc.

  1959. "The Impact of Money on an African Subsistence Economy." *The Journal of Economic History* 19(4): 491–503.

Boissevain, Katia. 2012. "Preparing for the Hajj in Contemporary Tunisia: Between Religious and Administrative Ritual." In *Ethnographies of Islam: Ritual Performance and Everyday Practices*, edited by Baudouin Dupret, Thomas Pierret, Paulo G. Pinto, and Kathryn Spellman-Poots, 21–30. Oxford University Press.

Bolton, Patrick, Tano Santos, and Jose A. Scheinkman. 2012. "Shadow Finance." In *Rethinking the Financial Crisis*, edited by Alan S. Blinder, Andrew W. Lo, and Robert M. Solow, 247–66. New York: Russell Sage Foundation and The Century Foundation.

Borneman, John, and Abdellah Hammoudi, eds. 2009. *Being There: The Fieldwork Encounter and the Making of Truth*. Berkeley: University of California Press.

Bostom, Andrew G. 2012. *Sharia versus Freedom: The Legacy of Islamic Totalitarianism*. Amherst, MA: Prometheus Books.

Bourdieu, Pierre. 1977. *Outline of a Theory of Practice*. Cambridge University Press.

1986. "The Forms of Capital." In *Handbook of Theory and Research for the Sociology of Education*, edited by J. Richardson, 241–58. New York: Greenwood.

1987. "The Force of Law: Toward a Sociology of the Juridical Field." *Hastings Law Journal* 38: 805–55.

[1991] 2002. *Language & Symbolic Power*, edited by John B. Thompson, translated by Gino Raymond and Matthew Adamson. Cambridge, UK: Polity Press.

Bourdieu, Pierre, and Jean-Claude Passeron. [1964] 1979. *The Inheritors: French Students and Their Relation to Culture*, translated by Richard Nice. University of Chicago Press.

Bourgon, Jérôme. 1999. "La coutume et le droit en Chine à la fin de l'empire." *Annales: histoire, sciences sociales* 54: 1073–107.

2002. "Uncivil Dialogue: Law and Custom Did Not Merge into Civil Law under the Qing." *Late Imperial China* 23(1): 50–90.

2005. "Rights, Freedoms, and Customs in the Making of Chinese Civil Law, 1900–1936." In *Realms of Freedom in Modern China*, edited by William C. Kirby, 84–112. Stanford University Press.

Bovingdon, Gardner. 2002. "Strangers in Their Own Land: The Politics of Uyghur Identity in Chinese Central Asia." Ph.D. diss., Government, Cornell University.

2010. *Uyghurs: Strangers in Their Own Land.* New York: Columbia University Press.

2013. "Hu Wants Something New: Discourse and the Deep Structure of Minzu Policies in China." In *Social Difference and Constitutionalism in Pan-Asia*, edited by Susan H. Williams, 165–94. Cambridge University Press.

Bowen, John R. 1988. "The Transformation of an Indonesian Property System: Adat, Islam, and Social Change in the Gayo Highlands." *American Ethnologist* 15: 274–93.

1993. *Muslims through Discourse: Religion and Ritual in Gayo Society.* Princeton University Press.

2003. *Islam, Law and Equality in Indonesia: An Anthropology of Public Reasoning.* Cambridge University Press.

2005. "Normative Pluralism in Indonesia: Regions, Religions, and Ethnicities." In *Multiculturalism in Asia: Theoretical Perspectives*, edited by Will Kymlicka and Baogang He, 152–69. Oxford University Press.

2007. *Why the French Don't Like Headscarves: Islam, the State, and Public Space.* Princeton University Press.

2011. "How Could English Courts Recognize Shariah?" *St. Thomas Law Review* 7(3): 411–35.

Bowie, Katherine A. 1998. "The Alchemy of Charity: Of Class and Buddhism in Northern Thailand." *American Anthropologist* 100(2): 469–81.

Brandstädter, Susanne. 2003. "The Moral Economy of Kinship and Property in Southern China." In *The Postsocialist Agrarian Question*, edited by Chris Hann, 419–40. Münster, Germany: LIT.

Brown, Wendy. 2006. *Regulating Aversion: Tolerance in the Age of Identity and Empire*. Princeton University Press.

Brubaker, Rogers. 2004. *Ethnicity without Groups*. Cambridge, MA: Harvard University Press.

Brusina, Olga I. 2006. "The Russian Experience of Reforming Nomadic Courts according to *Adat* in Turkestan, 1850–1900." *Journal of Legal Pluralism and Unofficial Law* 52: 31–40.

2008. "Sharia and Civil Law in Marital Relations of the Muslim Population in Central Asia." *Anthropology & Archaeology of Eurasia* 47(2): 53–68.

Bubandt, Nils, and Martijn van Beek, eds. 2012. *Varieties of Secularism in Asia: Anthropological Explorations of Religion, Politics and the Spiritual*. New York: Routledge.

Bulag, Uradyn E. 2002. *The Mongols at China's Edge*. Lanham, MD: Rowman and Littlefield Publishers.

2010. *Collaborative Nationalism: The Politics of Friendship on China's Mongolian Frontier*. Lanham, MD: Rowman and Littlefield Publishers.

Burak, Guy. 2013. "The Second Formation of Islamic Law: The Post-Mongol Context of the Ottoman Adoption of a School of Law." *Comparative Studies in Society and History* 55(3): 579–602.

2015. *The Second Formation of Islamic Law: The Hanafi School in the Early Modern Ottoman Empire*. Cambridge University Press.

Burbank, Jane, and Frederick Cooper. 2010. *Empires in World History*. Princeton University Press.

Burman, Sandra B., and Barbara E. Harrell-Bond, eds. 1979. *The Imposition of Law*. New York: Academic Press.

Burr, J. Millard, and Robert O. Collins. 2006. *Alms for Jihad: Charity and Terrorism in the Islamic World*. Cambridge University Press.

Butler, Judith. 1997. *The Psychic Life of Power: Theories in Subjection*. Stanford University Press.

Cao, Nanlai. 2010. *Constructing China's Jerusalem: Christians, Power, and Place in Contemporary Wenzhou*. Stanford University Press.

Carter, M. G. 1997. "Analogical and Syllogistic Reasoning in Grammar and Law." In *Islam: Essays on Scripture, Thought, and Society: A Festschrift in Honour of Anthony H. Johns*, edited by Peter G. Riddell and Tony Street. Leiden: Brill.

Casanova, José. 2011. "The Secular, Secularizations, Secularism." In *Rethinking Secularism*, edited by Craig Calhoun, Mark Juergensmeyer, and Jonathan VanAntwerpen, 54–73. Oxford University Press.

Cattelan, Valentino, ed. 2013. *Islamic Finance in Europe: Towards a Plural Financial System*. Cheltenham, UK: Edward Elgar.

Certeau, Michel de. 1984. *The Practice of Everyday Life*, translated by Steven F. Rendall. Berkeley: University of California Press.

Chaffee, John. 2006. "Diasporic Identities in the Historical Development of the Maritime Muslim Communities of Song-Yuan China." *Journal of the Economic and Social History of the Orient* 49(4): 395–420.

Chai, Winberg, ed. 1972. *Essential Works of Chinese Communism*. New York: Bantam Books.

Chamberlain, Heath B. 1993. "On the Search for Civil Society in China." *Modern China* 19(2): 199–215.

Chau, Adam Yuet. 2005. "The Politics of Legitimation and the Revival of Popular Religion in Shaanbei, North-Central China." *Modern China* 31(2): 236–78.

2006. *Miraculous Response: Doing Popular Religion in Contemporary China*. Palo Alto, CA: Stanford University Press.

ed. 2011. *Religion in Contemporary China: Revitalization and Innovation*. New York: Routledge.

Chen, Mingxia. 2004. "The Marriage Law and the Rights of Chinese Women in Marriage and the Family." In *Holding Up Half the Sky: Chinese Women Past, Present and Future*, edited by Tao Jie, Zheng Bijun, and Shirley L. Mow, 159–71. New York: Feminist Press at the City University of New York.

Chen, Nancy N. 2003. "Healing Sects and Anti-Cult Campaigns." *China Quarterly* 174: 505–20.

Chérif-Chebbi, Leïla. 2004. "Brothers and Comrades: Muslim Fundamentalists and Communists Allied for the Transmission of Islamic Knowledge in China." In *Devout Societies vs. Impious States? Transmitting Islamic Learning in Russia, Central Asia and China, through the Twentieth Century*, edited by Stéphane Dudoignon, 61–90. Berlin: Klaus Schwarz Verlag.

Chiba, Masaji. 1989. *Legal Pluralism: Toward a General Theory through Japanese Legal Culture*. Tokyo: Tokai University Press.

Chin, Lin. 1934. "Mohammedan Factions in Northwest China," translated by T. M. Chu. *Friends of Moslems* 8: 46–48.

China and the Principle. 2010. "China and the Principle of Self-Determination of Peoples." *St. Antony's International Review* 6(1): 79–102.

China Ethnic Groups. 2009. "Hui People Dominate Arabic Interpretation in Yiwu." Accessed March 15, 2015, www.ningxiaexpo.com/english/Selection/200908/t20090810_611216.htm (on file with author).

Choy, Howard Y. F. 2006. "'To Construct an Unknown China': Ethnoreligious Historiography in Zhang Chengzhi's Islamic Fiction." *Positions* 14(3): 687–715.

Christoffersen, Lisbet. 2010. "Is Shari'a Law, Religion or a Combination? European Legal Discourses on Shari'a." In *Shari'a as Discourse: Legal*

Traditions and the Encounter with Europe, edited by Jørgen S. Nielsen and Lisbet Christoffersen, 57–76. Burlington, VT: Ashgate.

Ch'u, T'ung-tsu. 1965. *Law and Society in Traditional China*. Paris: Mouton & Co.

Chun, Allen. 1996. "The Lineage-Village Complex in Southeastern China: A Long Footnote in the Anthropology of Kinship." *Current Anthropology* 37(3): 429–50.

Chung, Wai-Keung, and Gary Hamilton. 2001. "Social Logic as Business Logic: Guanxi, Trustworthiness, and the Embeddedness of Chinese Business Practices." In *Rules and Networks: The Legal Culture of Global Business Transactions*, edited by Richard Appelbaum, William F. Felstiner, and Volkmar Gessner, 325–46. Portland, OR: Hart Publishing.

Çizakça, Murat. 2011. *Islamic Capitalism and Finance: Origins, Evolution and the Future*. Cheltenham, UK: Edward Elgar.

Clarke, Donald C., ed. 2008. *China's Legal System: New Developments, New Challenges*. Cambridge University Press.

Clarke, Morgan. 2012. "The Judge as Tragic Hero: Judicial Ethics in Lebanon's Shari'a Courts." *American Ethnologist* 39(1): 106–21.

Cohen, Jerome Alan. 1966. "Chinese Mediation on the Eve of Modernization." *California Law Review* 54: 1201–26.

　　1970. "Chinese Attitudes toward International Law." In *Contemporary Chinese Law: Research Problems and Perspectives*, edited by Jerome A. Cohen, 282–93. Cambridge, MA: Harvard University Press.

Cohen, Myron L. 2005. *Kinship, Contract, Community, and State: Anthropological Perspectives on China*. Stanford University Press.

Cohn, Bernard S. 1987. "The Census, Social Structure and Objectification in South Asia." In *An Anthropologist among Historians and Other Essays*, edited by Bernard S. Cohn, 224–55. Delhi: Oxford University Press.

Comaroff, John L. 2001. "Colonialism, Culture, and the Law: A Foreword." *Law and Social Inquiry* 26(2): 305–14.

Comaroff, John L., and Jean Comaroff. 2009. *Ethnicity, Inc.* University of Chicago Press.

Comaroff, John L., and Simon Roberts. 1981. *Rules and Processes: The Cultural Logic of Dispute in an African Context*. University of Chicago Press.

Conley, John M., and William O'Barr. 1990. *Rules Versus Relationships: The Ethnography of Legal Discourse*. University of Chicago Press.

Cook, Joanna, James Laidlaw, and Jonathan Mair. 2012. "What If There Is No Elephant? Towards a Conception of an Un-sited Field." In *Multi-Sited Ethnography: Theory, Praxis and Locality in Contemporary Research*, edited by Mark-Anthony Falzon, 47–72. Burlington, VT: Ashgate.

Cook, Michael. 2004. *Commanding Right and Forbidding Wrong in Islamic Thought*. Cambridge University Press.

Coulson, Noel James. 1959. "Muslim Custom and Case-Law." *Die Welt des Islams* 6(1–2): 13–24.

Cowan, J. M., ed. 1976. *Arabic-English Dictionary: The Hans Wehr Dictionary of Modern Written Arabic*. Ithaca, NY: Munster.

Crews, Robert D. 2006. *For Prophet and Tsar: Islam and Empire in Russia and Central Asia*. Cambridge, MA: Harvard University Press.

Crimm, Nina J. 2008. "The Moral Hazard of Anti-Terrorism Financing Measures: A Potential to Compromise Civil Societies and National Interests." *Wake Forest Law Review* 43: 578–626.

Croll, Elisabeth. 1981. *The Politics of Marriage in Contemporary China*. Cambridge University Press.

1983. *Chinese Women since Mao*. London: Zed Books.

Crossley, Pamela Kyle. 1990a. *Orphan Warriors: Three Manchu Generations and the End of the Qing World*. Princeton University Press.

1990b. "Thinking about Ethnicity in Early Modern China." *Late Imperial China* 11(1): 1–30.

Crouch, Melissa. Forthcoming. "Islamic Law and Society in Southeast Asia." In *Oxford Handbook on Islamic Law*, edited by Anver Emon, Kristen Stilt, and Rumee Ahmed. Oxford University Press.

Dahlgren, Susanne. 2010. *Contesting Realities: The Public Sphere and Morality in Southern Yemen*. Syracuse University Press.

2012. "Making Shari'a Alive: Court Practices under an Ethnographic Lens." In *Ethnographies of Islam: Ritual Performance and Everyday Practices*, edited by Badouin Dupret, Thomas Pierret, Paulo G. Pinto, and Kathryn Spellman-Poots, 153–61. Edinburgh University Press.

Dalton, George. 1961. "Economic Theory and Primitive Society." *American Anthropologist* 62(1): 483–90.

1965. "Primitive Money." *American Anthropologist* 67(1): 44–65.

Dautcher, Jay. 2004. "Public Health and Social Pathologies in Xinjiang." In *Xinjiang: China's Muslim Borderland*, edited by S. Frederick Starr, 276–95. Armonk, NY: M. E. Sharpe.

da Col, Giovanni, and David Graeber. 2011. "Foreword: The Return of Ethnographic Theory." *HAU: Journal of Ethnographic Theory* 1(1): vi–xxxi.

Deeb, Lara. 2011. *An Enchanted Modern: Gender and Public Piety in Shi'i Lebanon*. Princeton University Press.

de Groot, Jan Jakob Maria. 1903. *Sectarianism and Religious Persecution in China*. Amsterdam: Johannes Müller.

de Soto, Hernando. 1989. *The Other Path: The Economic Answer to Terrorism*. New York: Basic Books.

Derrida, Jacques. 1990. "Force of Law: The 'Mystical Foundation of Authority'." *Cardozo Law Review* 11: 921–1045.

Diamant, Neil Jeffrey. 2000. *Revolutionizing the Family: Politics, Love, and Divorce in Urban and Rural China, 1949–1968*. Berkeley: University of California Press.

2001. "Pursuing Rights and Getting Justice on China's Ethnic Frontier, 1949–1966." *Law & Society Review* 35(4): 799–840.

Diamant, Neil Jeffrey, Stanley B. Lubman, and Kevin J. O'Brien, eds. 2005. *Engaging the Law in China*. Stanford University Press.

Diamond, Stanley. 1974. "The Rule of Law versus the Order of Custom." In *In Search of the Primitive: A Critique of Civilization*, edited by Stanley Diamond, 255–80. New Brunswick, NJ: Transaction Publishers.

Dicks, Anthony. 1990. "New Lamps for Old: The Evolving Legal Position of Islam in China, with Special Reference to Family Law." In *Islamic Family Law*, edited by Chibli Mallat and Jane Frances Connors, 347–88. London: Graham & Trotman.

Dikötter, Frank. 1992. *Discourse of Race in Modern China*. Stanford University Press.

2002. *Crime, Punishment and the Prison in Modern China*. New York: Columbia University Press.

Dillon, Michael. 1999. *China's Muslim Hui Community: Migration, Settlement and Sects*. Richmond, UK: Curzon.

Ding, Jun. 2011. "Civilian-Operated Arabic Language Schools and the Development of Muslim Society: A Historical and Contemporary Review." In *Muslims in a Harmonious Society: Selected Papers from a Three-Conference Series on Muslim Minorities in Northwest China (Gansu Province, 2008, Shaanxi Province, 2009, Xinjiang Autonomous Region, 2009)*, translated by Christine Sun. Arlington, VA: Development Research Center of China's State Council and the Institute for Global Engagement.

Dirks, Nicholas B. 2011. *Castes of Mind: Colonialism and the Making of Modern India*. Princeton University Press.

Doi, Abdur Rahman. 1984. *Sharī'ah: The Islamic Law*. London: Ta Ha Publishers.

Douglas, Mary. 1990. Foreword to *The Gift: The Form and Reason for Exchange in Archaic Societies*, by Marcel Mauss, vii–xviii. London: Routledge.

Dresch, Paul. 2012a. "Legal, Anthropology, and History: A View from Part of Anthropology." In *Legalism: Anthropology and History*, edited by Paul Dresch and Hannah Skoda, 1–38. Oxford University Press.

2012b. "Aspects of Non-State Law: Early Yemen and Perpetual Peace." In *Legalism: Anthropology and History*, edited by Paul Dresch and Hannah Skoda, 145–72. Oxford University Press.

Dreyer, June Teufel. 1976. *China's Forty Millions: Minority Nationalities and National Integration in the People's Republic of China*. Cambridge, MA: Harvard University Press.

Duara, Prasenjit. 1988. *Culture, Power, and the State: Rural North China, 1900–1942*. Stanford University Press.

    1995. *Rescuing History from the Nation: Questioning Narratives of Modern China*. University of Chicago Press.

    2009. "The Limits of Legal Sovereignty: China and India in Recent History." *The Journal of Asian Studies* 68(1): 122–27.

Dumont, Louis. 1980. *Homo Hierarchicus: The Caste System and Its Implications*. University of Chicago Press.

Dupret, Badouin, Maurits Berger, and Laila al-Zwaini, eds. 1999. *Legal Pluralism in the Arab World*. The Hague: Kluwer Law International.

Durkheim, Émile. 1912. *Les formes élémentaires de la vie religieuse [The Elementary Forms of Religious Life]*. Paris: Librairie Félix Alcan.

    [1937] 1957. *Professional Ethics and Civil Morals*. Glencoe, IL: The Free Press.

Dwyer, Arienne M. 2005. *The Xinjiang Conflict: Uyghur Identity, Language Policy, and Political Discourse*. Policy Studies 15. Washington DC: East-West Center.

Ebrey, Patricia Buckley. 1991. "Shifts in Marriage Finance from the Sixth to the Thirteenth Century." In *Marriage and Inequality in Chinese Society*, edited by Rubie Sharon Watson and Patricia Buckley Ebrey, 97–132. Berkeley: University of California Press.

    2003. *Women and the Family in Chinese History*. Abingdon, UK: Routledge.

Eickelman, Dale F. 1985. *Knowledge and Power in Morocco: The Education of a Twentieth-Century Notable*. Princeton University.

    2008. *The Public and Private Spheres in Muslim Societies*. Tokyo University of Foreign Studies.

Eickelman, Dale F., and Armando Salvatore. 2004. "Muslim Publics." In *Public Islam and the Common Good*, edited by Dale F. Eickelman and Armando Salvatore, 1–27. Leiden: Brill.

Ekvall, David P. 1908. "A New Station at Ho-Chow, Western China." *The Christian and Missionary Alliance*, March 6.

Ekvall, Robert B. 1938. *Gateway to Tibet*. Harrisburg, PA: Christian Publications.

Elliott, Mark C. 2001. *The Manchu Way: The Eight Banners and Ethnic Identity in Late Imperial China*. Stanford University Press.

    2015. "The Case of the Missing Indigene: Debate over a 'Second-Generation' Ethnic Policy." *The China Journal* 73: 186–213.

Emon, Anver M. 2006. "Islamic Law and the Canadian Mosaic: Politics, Jurisprudence, and Multicultural Accommodation." *La Revue du Barreau canadien* 87: 391–425.

    2007. "Enhancing Democracy, Respecting Religion: A Dialogue on Islamic Values and Freedom of Speech." In *Faith and Law: How Religious Traditions from Calvinism to Islam View American Law*, edited by Robert F. Cochran, 273–90. New York University Press.

Epstein, Richard A. 1997. *Simple Rules for a Complex World*. Cambridge, MA: Harvard University Press.

Erie, Matthew S. 2007. "China's (Post-)Socialist Property Rights Regime: Assessing the Impact of the Property Law on Illegal Land Takings." *Hong Kong Law Journal* 37(3): 919–49.

2012. "Property Rights, Legal Consciousness, and the New Media in China: The Hard Case of the 'Toughest Nail-House in History.'" *China Information* 26(1): 34–58.

Esherick, Joseph W. 2011. *Ancestral Leaves: A Family Journey through Chinese History*. Berkeley: University of California Press.

Esposito, John L. 2001. *Women in Muslim Family Law*. Syracuse University Press.

Esposito, John L., and Ibrahim Kalin. 2011. *Islamophobia: The Challenge of Pluralism in the 21st Century*. Oxford University Press.

Evans-Pritchard, E. E. 1951. *Kinship and Marriage among the Nuer*. Oxford University Press.

1976. *Witchcraft, Oracles, and Magic among the Azande*. Oxford University Press.

Ewing, Katherine Pratt. 1997. *Arguing Sainthood: Modernity, Psychoanalysis, and Islam*. Durham, NC: Duke University Press.

2003. "Living Islam in the Diaspora: Between Turkey and Germany." *The South Atlantic Quarterly* 102(2–3): 405–31.

Fadel, Muhammad H. 2008. "The True, the Good and the Reasonable: The Theological and Ethical Roots of Public Reason in Islamic Law." *Canadian Journal of Law and Jurisprudence* 21(1): 1–69.

2009. "Islamic Politics and Secular Politics: Can They Co-Exist?" *Journal of Law and Society* 25(1): 101–18.

2013. "Seeking an Islamic Equilibrium: A Resonse to Abdullahi A. An–Na'im's Complementary, Not Competing, Claims of Law and Religion: An Islamic Perspective." *Pepperdine Law Review* 39(5), (Symposium: The Competing Claims of Law and Religion): 1257–72.

Fairbank, John King, ed. 1968. *The Chinese World Order: Traditional China's Foreign Relations*. Cambridge, MA: Harvard University Press.

Fang, Qiang. 2009. "A Hot Potato: The Chinese Complaint Systems from Early Times to the Present." *The Journal of Asian Studies* 68(4): 1105–35.

al-Faruqi, Maysam J. 2005. "Umma: The Orientalists and the Qur'ānic Concept of Identity." *Journal of Islamic Studies* 16(1): 1–34.

Fassin, Didier. 2012. *A Companion to Moral Anthropology*. Malden, MA: Wiley-Blackwell.

Faubion, James D. 2001. "Toward an Anthropology of Ethics: Foucault and the Pedagogies of Autopoiesis." *Representations* 74(1): 83–104.

2011. *An Anthropology of Ethics*. Cambridge University Press.

Fay, Mary Ann. 2012. *Unveiling the Harem: Elite Women and the Paradox of Seclusion in Eighteenth-Century Cairo*. Syracuse University Press.

Feener, R. Michael. 2007. *Muslim Legal Thought in Modern Indonesia*. Cambridge University Press.

2013. *Shari'a and Social Engineering: The Implementation of Islamic Law in Contemporary Aceh, Indonesia*. Oxford University Press.

Feener, R. Michael, and Mark E. Cammack, eds. 2007. *Islamic Law in Contemporary Indonesia: Ideas and Institutions*. Cambridge, MA: Harvard University Press.

Feener, R. Michael, and Terenjit Sevea, eds. 2009. *Islamic Connections: Muslim Societies in South and Southeast Asia*. Singapore: ISAS.

Fei, Xiaotong [费孝通]. 1939. *Peasant Life in China: A Field Study of Country Life in the Yangtze Valley*. New York: E. P. Dutton & Company.

1951. "The Minority People of Kweichow." *China Monthly Review* 121: 289–94.

[1947] 1992. *From the Soil: The Foundations of Chinese Society*, translated by Gary G. Hamilton and Wang Zheng. Berkeley: University of California Press.

Feldman, Eric A. 2000. *The Ritual of Rights in Japan: Law, Society, and Health Policy*. Cambridge University Press.

Felstiner, William L. F., Richard Abel, and Austin Sarat. 1980. "The Emergence and Transformation of Disputes: Naming, Blaming, Claiming …" *Law & Society Review* 15(3–4): 631–54.

Feuchtwang, Stephan. [1992] 2001a. *The Imperial Metaphor: Popular Religion in China*. Richmond, UK: Curzon Press.

2001b. "Religion as Resistance." In *Chinese Society: Change, Conflict and Resistance*, edited by Elizabeth J. Perry and Mark Selden, 161–77. New York: Routledge.

2010. *Anthropology of Religion, Charisma and Ghosts: Chinese Lessons for Adequate Theory*. Berlin: Walter de Gruyter.

Fincher, Leta Hong. 2014. *Leftover Women: The Resurgence of Gender Inequality in China*. New York: Zed Books.

Firth, Raymond. 1938. "Work and Wealth of Primitive Communities." In *Human Types*, edited by Raymond Firth, 71–97. London: Thomas Nelson and Sons.

Fiskesjö, Magnus. 1999. "On the 'Raw' and the 'Cooked' Barbarians of Imperial China." *Inner Asia* 1(2): 139–68.

2006. "Rescuing the Empire: Chinese Nation-Building in the Twentieth Century." *European Journal of East Asian Studies* 5(2): 15–44.

2012. "The Animal Other: China's Barbarians and Their Renaming in the Twentieth Century." *Social Text* 29(4): 57–79.

Fitzgerald, John. 1995. "The Stars on China's Flag: Appropriating the Universe for the Nation." In *The State in Transition: Reimagining Political Space*, edited by Joseph A. Camilleri, Anthony P. Jarvis, and Albert J. Paolini, 91–104. Boulder, CO, and London: Lynne Rienner.

Fletcher, Joseph. 1975. "Central Asian Sufism and Ma Ming-hsin's New Teaching." In *Proceedings of the Fourth East Asian Altaistic Conference*, 75–96. Cambridge, MA: Harvard University. Unpublished.

1977. "The Naqshbandiyya and the Dhikr–l Arra." *Journal of Turkish Studies* 2: 113–19.

1995. "The Naqshbandiyya in Northwest China," edited posthumously by Jonathan N. Lipman. In *Studies on Chinese and Islamic Inner Asia*, edited by Beatrice Forbes Manz, 1–46. Aldershot, UK: Variorum.

Fortes, Meyer. 1949. *The Web of Kinship among the Tallensi*. Oxford University Press.

Foucault, Michel. 1991. "Governmentality." In *The Foucault Effect: Studies in Governmentality*, edited by Graham Burchell, Colin Gorden, and Peter Miller, 87–104. London: Harvester Wheatsheaf.

2008. *The Birth of Biopolitics: Lectures at the Collège de France 1978–1979*, edited by Michel Sennelart, translated by Graham Burchell. New York: Palgrave Macmillan.

Fox, Jonathan. 2012. "Separation of Religion and State in Stable Christian Democracies: Fact or Myth?" *Journal of Law, Religion and State* 1(1): 60–94.

Franke, Herbert. 1994. *China under Mongol Rule*. Aldershot, UK: Variorum.

Frankel, James D. 2011. *Rectifying God's Name: Liu Zhi's Confucian Translation of Monotheism and Islamic Law*. Honolulu: University of Hawai'i Press.

Frazier, Mark W. 2005. "What's in a Law? China's Pension Reform and Its Discontents." In *Engaging the Law in China: State, Society, and Possibilities for Justice*, edited by Neil J. Diamant, Stanley B. Lubman, and Kevin J. O'Brien, 108–30. Stanford University Press.

Freedman, Maurice. 1958. *Lineage Organization in Southeastern China*. London: The Athlone Press.

1966. *Chinese Lineage and Society: Fukien and Kwantung*. New York: The Athlone Press.

ed. 1970. *Family and Kinship in Chinese Society*. Stanford University Press.

Fu, Hualing. 2014. "Mediation and the Rule of Law: The Chinese Landscape." In *Dispute Resolution: Alternatives to Formalization*, edited by Joachim Zekoll, Moritz Bälz, and Iwo Amelung, ch. 4. Leiden: Brill.

Fu, Hualing, and Richard Cullen. 2011. "From Mediatory to Adjudicatory Justice: The Limits of Civil Justice Reform in China." In *Chinese Justice: Civil Dispute Resolution in Contemporary China*, edited by Margaret Y. K. Woo and Mary E. Gallagher, 25–57. New York: Cambridge University Press.

Fyzee, Asaf A. A. 2009. *Outlines of Muhammadan Law*, edited by Tahir Mahmood. 5th edn. London: Oxford University Press.

Galanter, Marc S. 1983. "Reading the Landscape of Disputes: What We Know and Don't Know (and Think We Know) about Our Allegedly Contentious and Litigious Society." *UCLA Law Review* 31: 4–71.

1989. *Law and Society in Modern India*, edited by Rajeev Dhavan. Delhi: Oxford University Press.

Gallagher, Mary E. 2005. "'Use the Law as Your Weapon!' Institutional Change and Legal Mobilization in China." In *Engaging the Law in China: State, Society, and Possibilities for Justice*, edited by Neil J. Diamant, Stanley B. Lubman, and Kevin J. O'Brien, 54–83. Stanford University Press.

2006. "Mobilizing the Law in China: 'Informed Disenchantment' and the Development of Legal Consciousness." *Law & Society Review* 40(4): 783–816.

2007. "'Hope for Protection and Hopeless Choices': Labor Legal Aid in the PRC." In *Grassroots Political Reform in Contemporary China*, edited by Elizabeth J. Perry and Merle Goldman, 196–227. Cambridge, MA: Harvard University Press.

Garces, Chris. 2010. "The Cross Politics of Ecuador's Penal State." *Cultural Anthropology* 25(3): 459–96.

Gates, Hill, and Robert P. Weller. 1987. "Hegemony and Chinese Folk Ideologies: An Introduction." *Modern China* 13(1): 3–16.

Gauvain, Richard. 2005. "Ritual Rewards: A Consideration of Three Recent Approaches to Sunni Purity Law." *Islamic Law and Society* 12: 333–93.

Geertz, Clifford. 1971. *Islam Observed: Religious Development in Morocco and Indonesia*. University of Chicago Press.

1973. "Religion as a Cultural System." In *The Interpretation of Cultures*, edited by Clifford Geertz, 87–125. New York: Basic Books.

1983. "Local Knowledge: Facts and Law in Comparative Perspective." In *Local Knowledge: Further Essays in Interpretive Anthropology*, edited by Glifford Geertz, 167–234. New York: Basic Books.

Ghachem, Malick W. 2013. "Religious Liberty and the Financial War on Terror." *First Amendment Law Review* 12: 139–236.

Ghai, Yash. 2000. "Autonomy Regimes in China: Coping with Ethnic and Economic Diversity." In *Autonomy and Ethnicity: Negotiating Competing Claims in Multi-ethnic States*, edited by Yash Ghai, 77–98. Cambridge University Press.

Ghai, Yash, and Sophia Woodman. 2009. "Unused Powers: Contestation over Autonomy Legislation in the PRC." *Pacific Affairs* 82(1): 29–46.

Gillette, Maris Boyd. 2000. *Between Mecca and Beijing: Modernization and Consumption among Urban Chinese Muslims*. Stanford University Press.

2003. "The 'Glorious Return' of Chinese Pilgrims to Mecca." In *Living with Separation in China: Anthropological Accounts*, edited by Charles Stafford, 130–57. New York: RoutledgeCurzon.

Gilmartin, David. 1988. "Customary Law and Shari'at in British Punjab." In *Shari'at and Ambiguity in South Asian Islam*, edited by Katherine P. Ewing, 43–62. Berkeley: University of California Press.

Gilsenan, Michael. 1982. *Recognizing Islam: An Anthropologist's Introduction*. Abingdon, UK: Taylor & Francis.

2012. "Possessed of Documents: Hybrid Laws and Translated Texts in the Hadhrami Diaspora." In *Ethnographies of Islam: Ritual Performances and Everyday Practices*, edited by Badouin Dupret, Thomas Pierret, Paulo G Pinto, and Kathryn Spellman-Poots, 181–92. Edinburgh University Press.

Ginsburg, Tom. 2008. "Administrative Law and the Judicial Control of Agents in Authoritarian Regimes." In *Rule by Law: The Politics of Courts in Authoritarian Regimes*, edited by Tom Ginsburg and Tamir Moustafa, 58–72. Cambridge University Press.

Giunchi, Elise. 2014. *Muslim Family Law in Western Courts*. London: Routledge.

Gladney, Dru C. 1987a. "Muslim Tombs and Ethnic Folklore: Charters for Hui Identity." *The Journal of Asian Studies* 46(3): 495–532.

1987b. "Qingzhen: A Study of Ethnogreligious Identity among Hui Muslim Communities in China." Ph.D. diss., Anthropology, University of Washington.

[1991] 1996. *Muslim Chinese: Ethnic Nationalism in the People's Republic*. 2nd edn. Cambridge, MA: Council on East Asian Studies, Harvard University.

1998. "Clashed Civilizations? Muslim and Chinese Identities in the PRC." In *Making Majorities: Constituting the Nation in Japan, Korea, China, Malaysia, Fiji, Turkey, and the United States*, edited by Dru C. Gladney, 106–31. Stanford University Press.

1999a. "Making Muslims in China: Education, Islamization, and Representation." In *China's National Minority Education: Culture, Schooling, and Development*, edited by Gerard A. Postiglione, 55–94. New York: Garland Press.

1999b. "The Salafiyya Movement in Northwest China: Islamic Fundamentalism among the Muslim Chinese?" In *Muslim Diversity: Local Islam in Global Contexts*, edited by Leif Manger, 102–49. Richmond, UK: Curzon Press.

2004a. "The Chinese Program of Development and Control, 1978–2001." In *Xinjiang: China's Muslim Borderland*, edited by S. Frederick Starr, 101–19. Armonk, NY: M. E. Sharpe.

2004b. *Dislocating China: Reflections on Muslims, Minorities, and Other Subaltern Subjects*. University of Chicago Press.

2008. "Islam and Modernity in China: Secularization or Separatism?" In *Chinese Religiosities: Afflictions of Modernity and State Formation*, edited by Mayfair Mei-Hui Yang, 179–208. Berkeley: University of California Press.

2009. "Islam in China: State Policing and Identity Politics." In *Making Religion, Making the State: The Politics of Religion in Modern China*, edited by Yoshiko Ashiwa and David L. Wank. Stanford University Press.

Gluckman, Max. 1955. *The Judicial Process Among the Barotse of Northern Rhodesia*. University of Manchester.

Goerzig, Carolin, and Khaled al-Hashimi. 2015. *Radicalization in Western Europe: Integration, Public Discourse, and Loss of Identity among Muslim Communities*. Abingdon, UK: Routledge.

Goffman, Erving. [1959] 1969. *The Presentation of Self in Everyday Life*. London: Penguin Press.

Goldstein, Melvyn. 1987. "When Brothers Share a Wife." *Natural History* 3: 39–48.

Goody, Jack. 1973. "Bridewealth and Dowry in Africa and Eurasia." In *Bridewealth and Dowry*, edited by Jack Goody and S. J. Tambiah, 1–58. Cambridge University Press.

Goossaert, Vincent, and David A. Palmer. 2011. *The Religious Question in Modern China*. University of Chicago Press.

Graeber, David. 2001. *Toward an Anthropological Theory of Value: The False Coin of Our Own Dreams*. New York: Palgrave.

Gräf, Bettina, and Jakob Skovgaard-Petersen. 2009. *Global Mufti: The Phenomenon of Yūsuf al-Qaraḍāwī*. New York: Columbia University Press.

Gramsci, Antonio. 1971. *Selections from the Prison Noteboks of Antonio Gramsci*. New York: International Publishers.

Granet, Marcel. 1934. *La pensée chinoise* [Chinese thought]. Paris: La Renaissance du livre.

Greenhalgh, Susan, and Edwin A. Winckler. 2005. *Governing China's Population: From Leninist to Neoliberal Biopolitics*. Stanford University Press.

Greenhouse, Carol. 1986. *Praying for Justice: Faith, Order, and Community in an American Town*. Ithaca, NY: Cornell University Press.

Greif, Avner, and Guido Tabellini. 2010. "Cultural and Institutional Bifurcation: China and Europe Compared." *American Economic Review* 100(2): 1–10.

Griffith-Jones, Robin, ed. 2013. *Islam and English Law: Rights, Responsibilities, and the Place of Shari'a*. Cambridge University Press.

Grillo, Ralph. 2015. *Muslim Families, Politics and the Law: A Legal Industry in Multicultural Britain*. Farnham, UK: Ashgate.

Habermas, Jürgen. [1962] 1989. *The Structural Transformation of the Public Sphere: An Inquiry into a Category of Bourgeois Society*, translated by Thomas Burger and Frederick Lawrence. Cambridge, MA: MIT Press.

2008. "Notes on Post-Secular Society." *New Perspectives Quarterly* 25(4): 17–29.

Haider, Najam. 2011. *The Origins of the Shi'a: Identity, Ritual, and Sacred Space in Eighth-Century Kufa*. Cambridge University Press.

Halegua, Aaron. 2005. "Reforming the People's Mediation System in Urban China." *Hong Kong Law Journal* 35: 715–50.

Halevi, Leor. 2007. *Muhammad's Grave: Death Rites and the Making of Islamic Society*. New York: Columbia University Press.

2013. "A House of Islam or of War: On Republican China's Legal Status in Ma Ruitu's Arabic Correspondence with Rashīd Ridā." Paper presented at the Association of Asian Studies, San Diego, CA, March 21–24, 2013.

Haley, John O. 1978. "The Myth of the Reluctant Litigant." *Journal of Japanese Studies* 4(2): 359–90.

Hall, Stuart. 1980. " 'Encoding/Decoding.' " In *Culture, Media, Language: Working Papers in Cultural Studies, 1972–79*, edited by S. Hall, D. Hobson, A. Lowe, and P. Willis, 128–38. London: Hutchinson.

Hallaq, Wael B. 1997. *A History of Islamic Legal Theories: An Introduction to Sunni Usul al-Fiqh*. Cambridge University Press.

2005. *The Origins and Evolution of Islamic Law: Themes in Islamic Law*. Cambridge University Press.

2009a. *Sharī'a: Theory, Practice, Transformations*. Cambridge University Press.

2009b. *An Introduction to Islamic Law*. Cambridge University Press.

Hamilton, Gary G. 2006. *Commerce and Capitalism in Chinese Societies*. New York: Routledge.

Hammoudi, Abdellah. 1997. *Master and Disciple: The Cultural Foundations of Moroccan Authoritarianism*. University of Chicago Press.

Han, Enze. 2013. *Contestation and Adaptation: The Politics of National Identity in China*. New York: Oxford University Press.

Hann, Chris. 2006. "The Gift and Reciprocity: Perspectives from Economic Anthropology." In *Handbook of the Economics of Giving, Altruism and Reciprocity*, edited by Serge-Christophe Kolm and Jean Mercier Ythier, 208–23. Amsterdam: Elsevier.

Hannerz, Ulf. 2003. "Being There ... and There ... and There! Reflections on Multi-Site Ethnography." *Ethnography* 4: 201–16.

Hansen, Mette Halskov. 1999. *Lessons in Being Chinese: Minority Education and Ethnic Identity in Southwest China*. Seattle: University of Washington Press.

Hansen, Valerie. 2012. *The Silk Road: A New History*. Oxford University Press.

Harrell, Stevan. 1995. Introduction: *Civilizing Projects and the Reaction to Them. Cultural Encounters on China's Ethnic Frontiers*, edited by Stevan Harrell, 1–36. Seattle: University of Washington Press.

2001. *Ways of Being Ethnic in Southwest China*. Seattle and London: University of Washington Press.

2002. "Patriliny, Patriarchy, Patrimony: Surface Features and Deep Structures in the Chinese Family System," accessed November 23, 2015 http://faculty .washington.edu/stevehar/PPP.html.

Harrington, Christine B. 1985. *Shadow Justice: The Ideology and Institutionalization of Alternatives to Court*, Contributions in Political Science. Westport, CT: Greenwood Press.

1992. "Popular Justice, Populist Politics: Law in Community Organizing." *Social & Legal Studies* 1: 177–98.

Harris, Lillian Craig. 1993. *China Considers the Middle East*. London: I. B. Tauris.

Harrison, Henrietta. 2001. *Inventing the Nation: China*. New York: Oxford University Press.

Hart, Henry M., Jr., Albert M. Sacks, William Eskridge, Jr., and Philip Frickey, eds. 1958. *The Legal Process: Basic Problems in the Making and Application of Law*. St. Paul, MN: Foundation Press.

Hayek, Friedrich A. 1973. *Law, Legislation, and Liberty*. Vol. 1. University of Chicago Press.

Haykel, Bernard. 2009. "On the Nature of Salafi Thought and Action." In *Global Salafism: Islam's New Religious Movement*, edited by Roel Meijer, 33–57. New York: Columbia University Press.

He, Baogang. 1997. *The Democratic Implications of Civil Society in China*. London: Palgrave Macmillan.

He, Xin. 2014. "The Party's Leadership as a Living Constitution." In *Constitutions in Authoritarian Regimes*, edited by Tom Ginsburg and Alberto Simpser, 245–64. Cambridge University Press.

Hefner, Robert W. 2007. "Introduction: The Culture, Politics, and Future of Muslim Education." In *Schooling Islam: The Culture and Politics of Modern Muslim Education*, edited by Robert W. Hefner and Muhammad Qasim Zaman, 1–39. Princeton University Press.

ed. 2011. *Shari'a in Politics: Islamic Law and Society in the Modern World*. Bloomington: University of Indiana Press.

Hennigan, Peter Charles. 2004. *The Birth of a Legal Institution: The Formation of the Waqf in the Third Century AH Ḥanafī Legal Discourse*. Leiden: Brill.

Henry, Stuart. 1985. "Community Justice, Capitalist Society, and Human Agency: The Dialectics of Collective Law in the Cooperative." *Law & Society Review* 19(2): 303–27.

Hermes, Nizar F. 2013. "The Orient's Medieval 'Orient(alism)': The Riḥla of Sulaymān al-Tājir." In *Orientalism Revisited: Art, Land, and Voyage*, edited by Ian Richard Netton, 207–22. London and New York: Routledge.

Hevia, James Louis. 1995. *Cherishing Men from Afar: Qing Guest Ritual and the Macartney Embassy of 1793*. Durham, NC: Duke University Press.

Hidayatullah, Aysha. 2014. *Feminist Edges of the Qur'an*. Oxford University Press.

Hillman, Ben. 2014. *Patronage and Power: Local State Networks and Party-State Resilience in Rural China*. Palo Alto, CA: Stanford University Press.

Hinsley, F. H. 1986. *Sovereignty*. Cambridge University Press.

Hirsch, Susan F. 1998. *Pronouncing & Preserving: Gender and the Discourses of Disputing in an African Islamic Court*. University of Chicago Press.

Hirschhausen, Ulrike von. 2008. "Imperial Legacies: The Afterlife of Multi-Ethnic Empires in the Twentieth Century." Workshop conducted at the German Historical Institute, London, September 14–16.

Hirschkind, Charles. 2006. *The Ethical Soundscape: Cassette Sermons and Islamic Counterpublics*. New York: Columbia University Press.

Ho, Engseng. 2006. *The Graves of Tarim: Genealogy and Mobility across the Indian Ocean*. Berkeley: University of California Press.

Ho, Karen. 2009. *Liquidated: An Ethnography of Wall Street*. Durham, NC: Duke University Press.

Ho, Peter. 2003. "Ningxia: Environmental Degradation, Rural Poverty and Ethnicity." In *Das große China-Lexikon*, edited by Brunhild Staiger, Stefan Friedrich, and Hans-Wilm Schütte, 542–43. Darmstadt, Germany: Primus Verlag.

2005. *Institutions in Transition: Land Ownership, Property Rights, and Social Conflict in China*. Oxford University Press.

2013. "In Defense of Endogenous, Spontaneously Ordered Development: The Institutional Structure of China's Rural Urban Property Rights." *Journal of Peasant Studies* 40(6): 1–32.

Ho, Ping-Ti. 1998. "In Defense of Sinicization: A Rebuttal of Evelyn Rawski's 'Reenvisioning the Qing.'" *The Journal of Asian Studies* 57(1): 123–55.

Ho, Wai-Yip. 2010. "Islam, China and the Internet: Negotiating Residual Cyberspace between Hegemonic Patriotism and Connectivity to the Ummah." *Journal of Muslim Minority Affairs* 30(1): 63–79.

2013. *Islam and China's Hong Kong: Ethnic Identity, Muslim Networks and the New Silk Road*. London and New York: Routledge.

Hoffman, Lisa M. 2008. "Post-Mao Professionalism: Self-Enterprise and Patriotism." In *Privatizing China: Socialism from Afar*, edited by Li Zhang and Aihwa Ong, 168–81. Ithaca, NY: Cornell University Press.

Hofrichter, Richard. 1987. *Neighborhood Justice in Capitalist Society*. Westport, CT: Greenwood Press.

Holden, Livia. 2004. "Official Policies for (Un)Official Customs: The Hegemonic Treatment of Hindu Divorce Customs by Dominant Legal Discourses." *Journal of Legal Pluralism and Unofficial Law* 49: 47–74.

Hong Kong Monetary Authority. 2014. "HKSAR Government's Inaugural Sukuk Offering," accessed November 23, 2015, www.hkma.gov.hk/eng/key-information/press-releases/2014/20140911-3.shtml?_ga=1.150803710.977559890.1412166547.

Honig, Emily, and Gail Hershatter. 1988. *Personal Voices: Chinese Women in the 1980s*. Stanford University Press.

Hooker, M. B. 1975. *Legal Pluralism: An Introduction to Colonial and Neo-colonial Laws.* Oxford, UK: Clarendon Press.

1978. *Adat Law in Modern Indonesia.* Oxford University Press.

Horowitz, David. 2004. *Unholy Alliance: Radical Islam and the American Left.* Washington DC: Regnery.

Hsu, Francis L. K. 1948. *Under the Ancestors' Shadow: Chinese Culture and Personality.* New York: Columbia University Press.

Huang, Philip C. C. 1993. " 'Public Sphere'/'Civil Society' in China? The Third Realm between State and Society." *Modern China* 19(2): 216–40.

2001. *Code, Custom, and Legal Practice in China: The Qing and the Republic Compared.* Stanford University Press.

2005. "Divorce Law Practices and the Origins, Myths, and Realities of Judicial 'Mediation' in China." *Modern China* 31(2): 151–203.

2006. "Court Mediation in China, Past and Present." *Modern China* 32(3): 275–314.

Huntington, Samuel P. 1993. "The Clash of Civilizations?" *Foreign Affairs* 72(3): 22–49.

1996. *The Clash of Civilizations and the Remaking of World Order.* New York: Simon & Schuster.

Huq, Aziz Z. 2013. "The Social Production of National Security." *Cornell Law Review* 98(3): 638–709.

Husain, Fida. 1939. *The Musalman Law of Wakf.* Nagpur, India: Self-published.

Iqbal, Zamir and Abbas Mirakhor, eds. 2013. *Economic Development and Islamic Finance.* Washington DC: The World Bank.

Islamic Development Bank. 2013. *39 Years in the Service of Development.* Jeddah: Economic Research and Policy Department.

Israeli, Raphael. 2002a. "Is There Shiʻa in Chinese Islam?" In *Islam in China: Religion, Ethnicity, Culture, and Politics*, edited by Raphael Israeli, 147–68. Lanham, MD: Lexington Books.

2002b. "Muslim Minorities under Non-Islamic Rule." In *Islam in China: Religion, Ethnicity, Culture, and Politics*, edited by Raphael Israeli, 43–56. Lanham, MD: Lexington Books.

2002c. "Muslims in China: The Incompatibility between Islam and the Chinese Order." In *Islam in China: Religion, Ethnicity, Culture, and Politics*, edited by Raphael Israeli, 7–30. Lanham, MD: Lexington Books.

2002d. "The Naqshbandiyya and Factionalism in Chinese Islam." In *Islam in China: Religion, Ethnicity, Culture, and Politics*, edited by Raphael Israeli, 133–46. Lanham, MD: Lexington Books.

Israeli, Raphael, and Adam Gardner-Rush. 2007. "Sectarian Islam and Sino-Muslim Identity in China." *Muslim World* 90(3–4): 439–58.

Jamous, Raymond. 1981. *Honneur et Baraka: Les structures sociales traditionnelles dans le Rif.* Paris: Atelier d'Anthropologie Sociale, Maison des Sciences de l'Homme.

Jansen, Thomas. 2014. "Sectarian Religions and Globalization in Nineteenth Century Beijing: The Wanbao Baojuan 萬寶寶卷 (1858) and Other Examples." In *Globalization and the Making of Religious Modernity in China: Transnational Religions, Local Agents, and the Study of Religion, 1800–Present*, edited by Thomas Jansen, Thoralf Klein, and Christian Meyer, 115–35. Leiden: Brill.

Jansen, Thomas, Thoralf Klein, and Christian Meyer, eds. 2014. *Globalization and the Making of Religious Modernity in China: Transnational Religions, Local Agents, and the Study of Religion, 1800–Present*. Leiden: Brill.

Jaschok, Maria, and Suzanne Miers, eds. 1994. *Women and Chinese Patriarchy: Submission, Servitude, and Escape*. Hong Kong University Press.

Jaschok, Maria, and Jingjun Shui. 2000. *The History of Women's Mosques in Chinese Islam: A Mosque of Their Own*. Richmond, UK: Curzon Press.

Jing, Jun. 1996. *The Temple of Memories*. Stanford University Press.

Johansen, Baber. 1999. *Contingency in a Sacred Law: Legal and Ethical Norms in the Muslim Fiqh*. Studies in Islamic Law and Society, 7. Leiden: Brill.

Jouili, Jeanette S. 2011. "Beyond Emancipation: Subjectivities and Ethics among Women in Europe's Islamic Revival Communities." *Feminist Review* 98: 47–64.

Judd, Ellen. 1989. "Niangjia: Chinese Women and Their Natal Families." *The Journal of Asian Studies* 48(3): 525–44.

Juergensmeyer, Mark. 2008. *Global Religion: Religious Challenges to the Secular State, from Christian Militias to al Qaeda*. Berkeley: University of California Press.

Jun, Sugawara. 2010. "Tradition and Adoption: Elements and Composition of Land-Related Contractual Documents in Provincial Xinjiang (1884–1955)." In *Studies on Xinjiang Historical Sources in 17–20th Centuries*, edited by James A. Millward, Shinmen Yasushi, and Sugawara Jun, 120–39. Tokyo: Toyo Bunko Research Library.

Kamali, Mohammad Hashim. [1991] 2003. *Principles of Islamic Jurisprudence*. 3rd rev. and enl. edn. Cambridge, UK: Islamic Texts Society.

Kantorowicz, Ernst Hatwig. 1997. *The King's Two Bodies: A Study of Mediaeval Political Theology*. Princeton University Press.

Kapferer, Bruce. 1997. *The Feast of the Sorcerer: Practice of Consciousness and Power*. University of Chicago Press.

Karrar, Hasan Haider. 2009. *New Silk Road Diplomacy: China's Central Asian Foreign Policy since the Cold War*. Vancouver: UBC Press.

Katz, Marion Holmes. 2002. *Body of Text: The Emergence of the Sunni Law of Ritual Purity*: SUNY Series in Medieval Middle East History. Albany: State University of New York Press.

Katz, Paul R. 2009. *Divine Justice: Religion and the Development of Chinese Legal Culture*. New York: Taylor and Francis.

2014. *Religion in China and Its Modern Fate*. Boston, MA: Brandeis University Press.

Kaup, Katherine Palmer. 2000. *Creating the Zhuang: Ethnic Politics in China*. Boulder, CO: Lynne Rienner.

2003. "Regionalism versus Ethnicnationalism in the People's Republic of China." *China Quarterly* 172: 863–84.

Keane, Webb. 1997. *Signs of Recognition: Powers and Hazards of Representation in an Indonesian Society*. Berkeley: University of California Press.

2007. *Christian Moderns: Freedom & Fetish in the Mission Encounter*. Berkeley: University of California Press.

Keeton, G. W. 1969. *The Development of Extraterritoriality in China*. Vol. 1. New York: Howard Fertig.

Kemp, Geoffrey. 2012. *The East Moves West: India, China, and Asia's Growing Presence in the Middle East*. Washington DC: Brookings Institution Press.

Kennedy, Duncan. 2006. *Rise and Fall of Classical Legal Thought*. Washington DC: Beard Books.

Khan, M. Rafiq. 1963. *Islam in China*. Delhi: National Academy.

Kidder, Robert L. 1979. "Toward an Integrated Theory of Imposed Law." In *The Imposition of Law*, edited by Sandra B. Burman and Barbara E. Harrell-Bond, 289–306. New York: Academic Press.

Kim, Ho-dong. 2004. *Holy War in China: The Muslim Rebellion and State in Chinese Central Asia, 1864–1877*. Stanford University Press.

Kim, Marie Seong-Hak. 2008. "Ume Kenjirō and the Making of Korean Civil Law, 1906–1910." *Journal of Japanese Studies* 34(1): 1–31.

Kipnis, Andrew B. 1997. *Producing Guanxi: Sentiment, Self, and Subculture in a North China Village*. Durham, NC: Duke University Press.

2006. "Suzhi: A Keyword Approach." *China Quarterly* 186: 295–313.

2007. "Neoliberalism Reified: Suzhi Discourse and Tropes of Neoliberalism in the People's Republic of China." *Journal of the Royal Anthropological Institute* 13(2): 383–96.

Knysh, Alexander. 2002. "Sufism as Explanatory Paradigm: The Issue of the Motivations of Sufi Resistance Movements in Western and Russian Scholarship." *Die Welt des Islams* 42(2): 139–73.

Kozlowski, Gregory C. 2008. *Muslim Endowments and Society in British India*. Cambridge University Press.

Krahl, Daniel. 2013. "Springtime on the New Silk Road? China and the Arab World after the Revolutions." In *China's South-South Relations*, edited by Bettina Gransow, 50–62. Zurich: LIT.

Kuran, Timur. 2001. "The Provision of Public Goods under Islamic Law: Origins, Contributions, and Limitations of the Waqf System." *Law & Society Review* 35(4): 841–97.

2004. "The Economic Ascent of the Middle East's Religious Minorities: The Role of Islamic Legal Pluralism." *Journal of Legal Studies* 33: 475–515.

2005. *Islam and Mammon: The Economic Predicaments of Islamism.* Princeton University Press.

Kuru, Ahmet T. 2009. *Secularism and State Policies toward Religion: The United States, France, and Turkey.* Cambridge University Press.

2012. "Assertive and Passive Secularism: State Neutrality, Religious Demography, and the Muslim Minority in the United States." In *The Future of Religious Freedom: Global Challenges,* edited by Allen Hertzke, 235–55. Oxford University Press.

Lacan, Jacques. [1973] 1998. *The Four Fundamental Concepts of Psychoanalysis: The Seminar of Jacques Lacan.* Book 11, edited by Jacques-Alain Miller, translated by Alan Sheridan. New York: W. W. Norton & Co.

Lacey, Robert, and Jonathan Benthall, eds. 2014. *Gulf Charities and Islamic Philanthropy.* Berlin: Gerlach Press.

Laffan, Michael Francis. 2003. *Islamic Nationhood and Colonial Indonesia: The Umma below the Winds.* New York: Routledge Press.

Lagerwey, John. 2010. *China: A Religious State.* Hong Kong University Press.

Laidlaw, James. 2000. "A Free Gift Makes No Friends." *Journal of the Royal Anthropological Institute* 6(4): 617–34.

2002. "For an Anthropology of Ethics and Freedom." *Journal of the Royal Anthropological Institute* 8(2): 311–32.

2014. *The Subject of Virtue: An Anthropology of Ethics and Freedom.* Cambridge University Press.

Lambek, Michael. 2010a. Introduction to *Ordinary Ethics: Anthropology, Language, and Action,* edited by Michael Lambek, 1–38. New York: Fordham University Press.

ed. 2010b. *Ordinary Ethics: Anthropology, Language, and Action.* New York: Fordham University Press.

Lauzière, Henri. 2010. "The Construction of Salafiyya: Reconsidering Salafism from the Perspective of Conceptual History." *International Journal of Middle East Studies* 42: 369–89.

Layish, Aharon. 2004. "The Transformation of the Shari'a from Jurists' Law to Statutory Law in the Contemporary Muslim World." *Die Welt des Islams* 44(1): 85–113.

Lee, Ching Kwan. 2007. *Against the Law: Labor Protests in China's Rustbelt and Sunbelt.* Berkeley: University of California Press.

Lee, Ching Kwan, and Yonghong Zhang. 2013. "The Power of Instability: Unraveling the Microfoundations of Bargained Authoritarianism in China." *American Journal of Sociology* 118(6): 1475–508.

Leeuwen, Richard van. 1999. *Waqfs and Urban Structures: The Case of Ottoman Damascus.* Studies in Islamic Law and Society. Leiden: Brill.

Leibold, James. 2013. *Ethnic Policy in China: Is Reform Inevitable?* Policy Studies 58. Honolulu: East-West Center.

Lev, Daniel S. 1972. *Islamic Courts in Indonesia: A Study of the Political Bases of Legal Institutions.* Berkeley: University of California Press.

Lévi-Strauss, Claude. [1967] 1969. *The Elementary Structures of Kinship,* edited by Rodney Needham, translated by James Harle Bell and John Richard von Sturmer. Boston, MA: Beacon Press.

——— 1976. *Structural Anthropology,* translated by Monique Layton. Vol. 2. New York: Basic Books.

Levine, N. E. 1988. *The Dynamics of Polyandry: Kinship, Domesticity, and Population on the Tibetan Border.* University of Chicago Press.

Lewis, Bernard. 1990. "The Roots of Muslim Rage." *The Atlantic,* September 13.

Li, Cheng, ed. 2008. *China's Changing Political Landscape.* Washington DC: Brookings Institute.

Li, Ling. 2011. "Performing Bribery in China—Guanxi-Practice, Corruption with a Human Face." *Journal of Contemporary China* 20(68): 1–20.

——— 2012. "The 'Production' of Corruption in China's Courts: Judicial Politics and Decision Making in a One-Party State." *Law and Social Inquiry* 37(4): 848–78.

Liang, Zhiping [梁治平]. 1999. "Tradition and Change: Law and Order in a Pluralist Landscape." *Cultural Dynamics* 11(2): 215–36.

Lieberman, Joseph. 2008. "Violent Islamist Extremism, the Internet, and the Homegrown Terrorist Threat." United States Senate Committee on Homeland Security and Governmental Affairs. Washington DC.

Lieberthal, Kenneth. 1992. "The Fragmented Authoritarianism Model and its Limitations." In *Bureaucracy, Politics, and Decision Making in Post-Mao China,* edited by K. Lieberthal and David M. Lampton, 1–30. Berkeley: University of California Press.

Liebman, Benjamin L. 2005. "Watchdog or Demagogue? The Media in the Chinese Legal System." *Columbia Law Review* 105(1): 1–157.

——— 2011. "A Return to Populist Legality? Historical Legacies and Legal Reform." In *Mao's Invisible Hand,* edited by Sebastian Heilman and Elizabeth J. Perry, 165–200. Cambridge, MA: Harvard University Press.

Lin, Chris X. 2003. "A Quiet Revolution: An Overview of China's Judicial Reform." *Asian-Pacific Law & Policy Journal* 4(2): 255–319.

Lin, Chun. 2006. *The Transformation of Chinese Socialism.* Durham, NC: Duke University Press.

Lin, Yaohua. 1940. "The Miao-Man Peoples of Kweichow." *Harvard Journal of Asiatic Studies* 5: 261–325.

Lindsey, Tim, and Kerstin Steiner. 2012. *Islam, Law and the State in Southeast Asia.* New York: I. B. Taurus.

Lipman, Jonathan N. 1984. "Ethnicity and Politics in Republican China: The Ma Family Warlords of Gansu." *Modern China* 10(3): 285–316.

1996. "Hyphenated Chinese: Sino-Muslim Identity in Modern China." In *Remapping China: Fissures in Historical Terrain*, edited by Gail Hershatter, Emily Honig, Jonathan N. Lipman, and Randall Stross, 97–113. Stanford University Press.

1997. *Familiar Strangers: A History of Muslims in Northwest China*. Seattle and London: University of Washington Press.

1999. "Sufism in the Chinese Courts: Islam and Qing Law in the Eighteenth and Nineteenth Centuries." In *Islamic Mysticism Contested: Thirteen Centuries of Controversies and Polemics*, edited by Frederick de Jong and Bernd Radtke, 553–74. Leiden: Brill.

2005. "'A Fierce and Brutal People': On Islam and Muslims in Qing Law." In *Empire at the Margins: Culture, Ethnicity, and Frontier in Early Modern China*, edited by Pamela Crossley, 83–112. Berkeley: University of California Press.

Little, Daniel. 1989. *Understanding Peasant China*. New Haven, CT: Yale University Press.

Litzinger, Ralph A. 2000. *Other Chinas: The Yao and Poetics of National Belonging*. Durham, NC: Duke University Press.

Liu, Dajun. 1931. *Le recensement de Chine en 1912* [*The 1912 census of China*]. Shanghai: International Statistical Institute.

Liu, Lydia H. 2009. *The Clash of Empires: The Invention of China in Modern World Making*. Cambridge, MA: Harvard University Press.

Liu, Sida, and Terence C. Halliday. 2011. "Political Liberalism and Political Embeddedness: Understanding Politics in the Work of Chinese Criminal Defense Lawyers." *Law & Society Review* 45(4): 831–65.

Lo, Carlos W. H. 1992. "Deng Xiaoping's Ideas on Law: China on the Threshold of a Legal Order." *Asian Survey* 32(7): 649–65.

Lo, Ming-Cheng M., and Eileen M. Otis. 2003. "Guanxi Civility: Processes, Potentials, and Contingencies." *Politics & Society* 31(1): 131–62.

Lombardi, Clark B. 2006. *State Law as Islamic Law in Modern Egypt: The Incorporation of the Sharīʿa into Egyptian Constitutional Law*. Leiden: Brill.

2013. "Constitutional Provisions Making Sharia 'A' or 'The' Chief Source of Legislation: Where Did They Come From? What Do They Mean? Do They Matter?" *American University International Law Review* 28: 733–74.

Lu, Zheng, and Xiang Deng. 2011. *China's Western Development Strategy: Policies, Effects and Prospects*. Munich Personal RePEc Archive.

Lubman, Stanley B. 1967. "Mao and Mediation: Politics and Dispute Resolution in Communist China." *California Law Review* 55(5): 1284–360.

1999. *Bird in a Cage: Legal Reform in China after Mao*. Stanford University Press.

Ma, Haiyun. 2014. "'Muslims We Can Do Business With': China Welcomes Arab Trade in Its Hui Muslim Heartland," accessed November 4, 2014, http://islamicommentary.org/2014/03/muslims-we-can-do-business-with-china-welcomes-arab-trade-in-its-hui-muslim-heartland/.

Ma, Rong [马戎]. 2009a. "The Development of Minority Education and the Practice of Bilingual Education in Xinjiang Uyghur Autonomous Region." *Frontiers of Education in China* 4(2): 188–251.

2009b. "Issues of Minority Education in Xinjiang, China." In *Affirmative Action in China and the U.S.*, edited by Mingliang Zhou and Ann Maxwell Hill, 179–98. New York: Palgrave Macmillan.

[For Ma Rong. 2009c and other dates, see Chinese language sources.]

Ma, Tong. 1989. "China's Islamic Saintly Lineages and the Muslims of the Northwest." In *The Legacy of Islam in China: An International Symposium in Memory of Joseph F. Fletcher*, edited by D. C. Gladney, 266–306. Conference volume. Cambridge, MA: Harvard University Press.

Ma, Wenlong. 2011. "Religious Institutes and the Construction of a Harmonious Society in a New Era." In *Muslims in a Harmonious Society: Selected Papers from a Three-Conference Series on Muslim Minorities in Northwest China (Gansu Province, 2008, Shaanxi Province, 2009, Xinjiang Autonomous Region, 2009)*, translated by Christine Sun, 31–40. Arlington, VA: Development Research Center of China's State Council and the Institute for Global Engagement.

Ma, Xuefeng. 2014. "From *Jingtang* Education to Arabic School: Muslim Education in Yunnan." In *Muslim Education in the 21st Century: Asian Perspectives*, edited by Sa'eda Buang and Phyllis Ghim-Lian Chew, 70–89. New York: Routledge.

Macauley, Melissa. 2001. "A World Made Simple: Law and Property in the Ottoman and Qing Empires." *Journal of Early Modern History* 5(4): 331–53.

McCarthy, Andrew C. 2012. *The Grand Jihad: How Islam and the Left Sabotage America*. New York: Encounter Books.

McCarthy, Susan K. 2009. *Communist Multiculturalism: Ethnic Revival in Southwest China*. Seattle: University of Washington Press.

McChesney, R. D. 1991. *Waqf in Central Asia: Four Hundred Years in the History of a Muslim Shrine, 1480–1889*. Princeton University Press.

MacInnis, Donald E. 1989. *Religion in China Today: Policy and Practice*. New York: Orbis Books.

MacIntyre, Alasdair. 2007. *After Virtue: A Study in Moral Theory*. University of Notre Dame Press.

Mackerras, Colin. 2003. *China's Ethnic Minorities and Globalisation*. London and New York: RoutledgeCurzon.

McKhann, Charles F. 1995. "The Naxi and the Nationalities Question." In *Cultural Encounters on China's Ethnic Frontier*, edited by Stevan Harrell, 39–62. Seattle: University of Washington Press.

2002. "The Good, the Bad, and the Ugly: Observations and Reflections on Tourism Development in Lijiang, China." In *Tourism, Anthropology, and China*, edited by Tang Chee Beng, Sidney Cheung, and Yang Hui, 147–66. Bangkok: White Lotus Press.

MacKinnon, Rebecca. 2008. "Cyber Zone: How China's Online Pioneers Are Pushing the Boundaries of Free Speech." *Index on Censorship* 37(2): 82–89.

McLarney, Ellen. 2011. "The Islamic Public Sphere and the Discipline of Adab." *International Journal of Middle East Studies* 43: 429–49.

Madsen, Richard. 2011. "Secular State and Religious Society in Mainland China and Taiwan." In *Social Scientific Studies of Religion in China*, edited by Fenggang Yang and Graeme Lang, 273–96. Leiden: Brill.

Mahmood, Saba. 2003. "Ethical Formation and Politics of Individual Autonomy in Contemporary Egypt." *Social Research* 70(3): 1501–30.

2005. *Politics of Piety: The Islamic Revival and the Feminist Subject*. Princeton University Press.

2006. "Secularism, Hermeneutics, and Empire: The Politics of Islamic Reformation." *Public Culture* 18(2): 323–47.

2008. "Is Critique Secular? A Symposium at UC Berkeley." *Public Culture* 20(3): 447–52.

2012. "Sectarian Conflict and Family Law in Contemporary Egypt." *American Ethnologist* 29(1): 54–62.

Makdisi, Ussama. 2000. *The Culture of Sectarianism: Community, History, and Violence in Nineteenth-Century Ottoman Lebanon*. Berkeley: University of California Press.

Makley, Charlene E. 2002. "On the Edge of Respectability: Sexual Politics on the Sino-Tibetan Frontier." *Positions: East Asia Cultures Critiques* 10(3): 575–630.

Malinowski, Bronislaw. 1926. *Crime and Custom in Savage Society*. New York: Harcourt, Brace and Co.

Mallat, Chibli, and Jane Connors. 1990. *Islamic Family Law*. London: Graham & Trotman.

Mamdani, Mahmood. 2002. "Good Muslim, Bad Muslim: A Political Perspective on Culture and Terrorism." *American Anthropologist* 104(3): 766–75.

Man, Joyce Yanyun, and Yu-Hung Hong, eds. 2010. *China's Local Public Finance in Transition*. Cambridge, MA: Lincoln Institute of Land Policy.

Mao, Yufeng. 2011. "A Muslim Vision for the Chinese Nation: Chinese Pilgrimage Missions to Mecca during World War II." *The Journal of Asian Studies* 70(2): 373–95.

March, Andrew F. 2009. *Islam and Liberal Citizenship: The Search for an Overlapping Consensus*. Oxford University Press.

Marcus, George E. 1995. "Ethnography in/of the World System: The Emergence of Multi-Sited Ethnography." *Annual Review of Anthropology* 24: 95–117.

Martin, Jeffrey T. 2013. "Legitimate Force in a Particularistic Democracy: Street Police and Outlaw Legislators in the Republic of China on Taiwan." *Law and Social Inquiry* 38(3): 615–42.

Massell, Gregory. 1968. "Law as an Instrument of Revolutionary Change in a Traditional Milieu: The Case of Soviet Central Asia." *Law & Society Review* 2(2): 179–228.

Maurer, Bill. 2005. *Mutual Life, Limited: Islamic Banking, Alternative Currencies, Lateral Reason.* Princeton University Press.

  2006. *Pious Property: Islamic Mortgages in the United States.* New York: Russell Sage Foundation.

Mauss, Marcel. [1950] 1990. *The Gift: The Form and Reason for Exchange in Archaic Societies,* translated by W. D. Halls. New York: W. W. Norton.

Meijer, Marinus Johan. 1971. *Marriage Law and Policy in the Chinese People's Republic.* Hong Kong University Press.

Meijer, Roel. 2009. Introduction to *Global Salafism: Islam's New Religious Movement,* edited by Roel Meijer, 1–32. New York: Columbia University Press.

Menski, Werner F. 2006. *Comparative Law in a Global Context: The Legal Systems of Asia and Africa.* Cambridge University Press.

Mernissi, Fatima. 1987. *Beyond the Veil: Male-Female Dynamics in Modern Muslim Society.* 2nd edn. Bloomington and Indianapolis: Indiana University Press.

Merry, Sally Engle. 1990. *Getting Justice and Getting Even: Legal Consciousness among Working-Class Americans.* The University of Chicago Press.

  2000. *Colonizing Hawai'i: The Cultural Power of Law.* Princeton University Press.

Merry, Sally Engle, and Neal Milner. 1993. Introduction to *The Possibility of Popular Justice: A Case Study of Community Mediation in the United States,* edited by Sally Engle Merry and Neal Milner, 3–30. Ann Arbor: The University of Michigan Press.

Mertha, Andrew. 2008. *China's Water Warriors: Citizen Action and Policy Change.* Ithaca, NY: Cornell University Press.

Meskill, Johanna Menzel. 1979. *A Chinese Pioneer Family: The Lins of Wu-feng, Taiwan 1729–1895.* Princeton University Press.

Messick, Brinkley. 1993. *The Calligraphic State: Textual Domination and History in a Muslim Society.* Berkeley: University of California Press.

  2008. "Shari'a Ethnography." In *The Law Applied: Contextualizing the Islamic Shari'a,* edited by Peri J. Bearman, Wolfhart Heinrichs and Bernard G. Weiss, 173–93. London: I. B. Tauris.

Metcalf, Barbara D. 1998. "Women and Men in a Contemporary Pietist Movement: The Case of the Tablighi Jama'at." In *Appropriating Gender: Women's Activism and Politicized Religion in South Asia*, edited by Amrita Basu and Patricia Jeffrey, 107–21. New York: Routledge.

——— 2000. "Tablighi Jama'at and Women." In *Travellers in Faith: Studies of the Tablighi Jama'at as a Transnational Islamic Movement for Faith Renewal*, edited by Muhammad Khalid Masud, 44–58. Leiden: Brill.

——— 2002. "'Traditionalist' Islamic Activism: Deoband, Tablighis, and Talibs." *ISIM Papers*: 1–17.

——— 2003. "Travelers' Tales in the Tablighi Jama'at." *Annals of the American Academy of Political and Social Science* 588: 136–48.

——— 2007. "Madrasas and Minorities in Secular India." In *Schooling Islam: The Culture and Politics of Modern Muslim Education*, edited by Robert W. Hefner and Muhammad Qasim Zaman, 87–106. Princeton University Press.

Michelson, Ethan. 2006. "The Practice of Law as an Obstacle to Justice." *Law & Society Review* 40(1): 1–38.

——— 2007a. "Climbing the Dispute Pagoda: Grievances and Appeals to the Official Justice System in Rural China." *American Sociological Review* 72(3): 459–85.

——— 2007b. "Lawyers, Political Embeddedness, and Institutional Continuity in China's Transition from Socialism." *American Journal of Sociology* 113(2): 352–414.

——— 2008a. "Dear Lawyer Bao: Everyday Problems, Legal Advice, and State Power in China." *Social Problems* 55(1): 43–71.

——— 2008b. "Justice from Above or Below? Popular Strategies for Resolving Grievances in Rural China." *China Quarterly* 193: 43–64.

Miller, Nicholas P. 2012. *The Religious Roots of the First Amendment: Dissenting Protestants and the Separation of Church and State*. Oxford University Press.

Miller, Richard E., and Austin Sarat. 1981. "Grievances, Claims, and Disputes: Assessing the Adversary Culture." *Law & Society Review* 15: 525–66.

Millward, James A. 1989. "The Chinese Border Wool Trade of 1880–1937." In *The Legacy of Islam in China: An International Symposium in Memory of Joseph F Fletcher*, edited by Dru C. Gladney. Cambridge, MA: Harvard University Press.

——— 1998. *Beyond the Pass: Economy, Ethnicity, and Empire in Qing Central Asia, 1759–1864*. Stanford University Press.

——— 2007. *Eurasian Crossroads: A History of Xinjiang*. New York: Columbia University Press.

Minzner, Carl F. 2006. "Xinfang: An Alternative to Formal Chinese Legal Institutions." *Stanford Journal of International Law* 42: 103–80.

2011. "China's Turn against Law." *American Journal of Comparative Law* 59: 935–84.

Mir-Hosseini, Ziba. 2000. *Marriage on Trial: Islamic Family Law in Iran and Morocco*. Rev. edn. New York: I. B. Tauris.

2006. "Muslim Women's Quest for Equality: Between Islamic Law and Feminism." *Critical Inquiry* 32(4): 629–45.

Miyazawa, Setsuo, Kay-Wah Chan, and Ilhyung Lee. 2008. "The Reform of Legal Education in East Asia." *Annual Review of Law and Social Science* 14: 333–60.

Modarressi, Hossein. 1986. "Some Recent Analyses of the Concept of *Majāz* in Islamic Jurisprudence." *Journal of the American Oriental Society* 106: 787–91.

Moore, Henrietta L. 2007. *The Subject of Anthropology: Gender, Symbolism and Psychoanalysis*. Malden, MA: Polity Press.

Moore, Kathleen. 2002. "A Part of U.S. or Apart from U.S.? Post-September 11 Attitudes toward Muslims and Civil Liberties." *Middle East Report* 224: 32–35.

Moore, Sally Falk. 1973. "Law and Social Change: The Semi-Autonomous Social Field as an Appropriate Subject of Study." *Law & Society Review* 7(4): 719–46.

1978. *Law as Process: An Anthropological Approach*. Oxford: James Currey Publishers.

1987. "Explaining the Present: Theoretical Dilemmas in Processual Ethnography." *American Ethnologist* 14(4): 727–36.

ed. 2005. *Law and Anthropology: A Reader*. Malden, MA: Blackwell Publishing.

Morgan, David. 2007. *The Mongols*. 2nd edn. London: John Wiley & Sons.

Morrison, Alexander. 2008. "Review of Robert D. Crews 'For Prophet and Tsar. Islam and Empire in Russia and Central Asia.'" *The Slavonic & East European Review* 86(3): 553–57.

Mosca, Matthew. 2013. *From Frontier Policy to Foreign Policy: The Question of India and the Transformation of Geopolitics in Qing China*. Stanford University Press.

Mottahedeh, Roy P. 1996. "The Clash of Civilizations: An Islamicist's Critique." *Harvard Middle Eastern and Islamic Review* 2(2): 1–26.

2010. "Pluralism and Islamic Traditions of Sectarian Divisions." In *Diversity and Pluralism in Islam: Historical and Contemporary Discourses amongst Muslims*, edited by Zulfikar Hirji, 31–42. London: I. B. Tauris.

Moustafa, Tamir. 2014. "Judging in God's Name: State Power, Secularism, and the Politics of Islamic Law in Malaysia." *Oxford Journal of Law and Religion* 3(1): 152–67.

Mu, Guo. 2010. "The Yiwu Model of China's Exhibition Economy." *Provincial China* 2(1): 91–115.

Mueggler, Erik. 2001. *The Age of Wild Ghosts: Memory, Violence, and Place in Southwest China*. Berkeley and Los Angeles: University of California Press.

Mullaney, Thomas S. 2004. "Ethnic Classification Writ Large: The 1954 Yunnan Province Ethnic Classification Project and Its Foundation in Republican-Era Taxonomic Thought." *China Information* 18(2): 207–41.

2011. *Coming to Terms with the Nation: Ethnic Classification in Modern China*. Berkeley: University of California Press.

Mundy, Martha, ed. 2002. *Law and Anthropology*. Aldershot, UK: Ashgate Press.

2004. "Ownership or Office? A Debate in Islamic Hanafite Jurisprudence over the Nature of the Military 'Fief', from the Mamluks to the Ottomans." In *Law, Anthropology, and the Constitution of the Social: Making Persons and Things*, edited by Alain Pottage and Martha Mundy, 142–65. Cambridge University Press.

Mundy, Martha, and Richard Saumarez Smith. 2007. *Governing Property, Making the Modern State: Law, Administration and Production in Ottoman Syria*. London: I. B. Tauris.

Murata, Sachiko. 1987. *Temporary Marriage (Mut'a) in Islamic Law*. London: Muhammadi Trust.

2000. *Chinese Gleams of Sufi Light: Wang Tai-yu's Great Learning of the Pure and Real and Liu Chih's Displaying the Concealment of the Real Realm*. Albany: State University of New York Press.

2006. "The Creative Transformation in Liu Chih's 'Philosophy of Islam.'" In *Islamic Philosophy and Occidental Phenomenology on the Perennial Issue of Microcosm and Macrocosm*, edited by Anna-Teresa Tymieniecka, 141–48. Dordrecht: Springer.

Murata, Sachiko, William C. Chittick, and Weiming Tu. 2009. *The Sage Learning of Liu Zhi: Islamic Thought in Confucian Terms*. Cambridge, MA: Harvard University Center for the Harvard-Yenching Institute.

Nader, Laura. 1991. *Harmony Ideology: Justice and Control in a Zapotec Mountain Village*. Stanford University Press.

Nader, Laura, and Harry Todd. 1978. "Introduction: The Disputing Process." In *The Disputing Process: Law in Ten Societies*, edited by Laura Nader and Harry Todd, 1–40. New York: Columbia University.

Naquin, Susan. 1976. *Millenarian Rebellion in China: The Eight Trigrams Uprising in 1813*. New Haven, CT: Yale University Press.

1982. "Connections between Rebellions: Sect Family Networks in Qing China." *Modern China* 8(3): 337–60.

Nasir, Jamal J. 1990. *The Islamic Law of Personal Status*. London: Graham & Trotman.

Nedostup, Rebecca. 2009. *Superstitious Regimes: Religion and the Politics of Chinese Modernity*. Cambridge, MA, and London: Harvard University Asia Center.

Nielsen, Jørgen S. 2010. "Shari'a between Renewal and Tradition." In *Shari'a as Discourse: Legal Traditions and the Encounter with Europe*, edited by Jørgen S. Nielsen and Lisbet Christoffersen, 1–14. Farnham, UK, and Burlington, VT: Ashgate.

Norrie, Alan. 1999. "From Law to Popular Justice: Beyond Antinomialism." In *Laws of the Postcolonial*, edited by Eve Darian-Smith and Peter Fitzpatrick, 249–76. Ann Arbor: University of Michigan Press.

Oakes, Tim, and Donald S. Sutton, eds. 2010. *Faiths on Display: Religion, Tourism, and the Chinese State*. Lanham, MD: Rowman and Littlefield Publishers.

Oba, Abdulmumini A. 2002. "Islamic Law as Customary Law: The Changing Perspective in Nigeria." *International and Comparative Law Quarterly* 51(4): 817–50.

Obeyesekere, Gananath. 1981. *Medusa's Hair: An Essay on Personal Symbols and Religious Experience*. University of Chicago Press.

[1992] 1997. *The Apotheosis of Captain Cook: European Mythmaking in the Pacific*. Princeton University Press.

O'Brien, Kevin J., and Lianjiang Li. 2006. *Rightful Resistance in Rural China*, Cambridge Studies in Contentious Politics. New York: Cambridge University Press.

Ocko, Jonathan K. 1991. "Women, Property, and Law in the People's Republic of China." In *Marriage and Inequality in Chinese Society*, edited by Rubie Sharon Watson and Patricia Buckley Ebrey, 313–47. Berkeley: University of California Press.

Ocko, Jonathan K., and David Gilmartin. 2009. "State, Sovereignty, and the People: A Comparison of the 'Rule of Law' in China and India." *The Journal of Asian Studies* 68(1): 55–100.

Ogden, Suzanne. 1974a. "Chinese Concepts of the Nation, State, and Sovereignty." Ph.D. diss., Political Science, Brown University.

1974b. "Sovereignty and International Law: The Perspective of the People's Republic of China." *New York University Journal of International Law and Politics* 7(1): 1–32.

Olimat, Muhammad. 2012. *China and the Middle East: From Silk Road to Arab Spring*. Abingdon, UK: Routledge.

Ono, Kazuko. 1989. *Chinese Women in a Century of Revolution, 1850–1950*. Stanford University Press.

Osanloo, Arzoo. 2009. *The Politics of Women's Rights in Iran*. Princeton University Press.

Osburg, John. 2013. *Anxious Wealth: Money and Morality among China's New Rich*. Palo Alto, CA: Stanford University Press.

Ozgur, Iren. 2012. *Islamic Schools in Modern Turkey: Faith, Politics, and Education*. Cambridge University Press.

Palmer, David A. 2007. *Qigong Fever: Body, Science, and Utopia in China*. New York: Columbia University Press.

2008. "Heretical Doctrines, Reactionary Secret Societies, Evil Cults: Labelling Heterodoxy in 20th Century China." In *Chinese Religiosities: Afflictions of Modernity and State Formation*, edited by Mayfair Yang, 113–34. Berkeley: University of California Press.

Papas, Alexandre. 2011. "So Close to Samarkand, Lhasa: Sufi Hagiographies, Founder Myths and Sacred Space in Himalayan Islam." In *Islam and Tibet: Interactions along the Musk Routes*, edited by Anna Akasoy, Charles S. F. Burnett, and Ronit Yoeli-Tlalim, 261–80. Farnham, UK: Ashgate.

Parashar, Archana. 2013. "Religious Personal Laws as Non-State Laws: Implications for Gender Justice." *Journal of Legal Pluralism and Unofficial Law* 45(1–3): 5–23.

Parish, William L., and Martin King Whyte. 1978. *Village and Family in Contemporary China*. University of Chicago Press.

Parry, Jonathan. 1986. "The Gift, the Indian Gift, and the 'Indian Gift.'" *Man* 21(3): 453–73.

Pasternak, Burton. 1972. *Village and Family Life in Contemporary China*. Chicago University Press.

Peerenboom, Randall. 1993. *Law and Morality in Ancient China: The Silk Manuscripts of Huang-Lao*. Albany: State University of New York Press.

2002. "Law and Religion in Early China." In *Religion, Law and Tradition*, edited by Andrew Huxley, 84–107. New York: RoutledgeCurzon.

ed. 2009. *Judicial Independence in China: Lessons for Global Rule of Law Promotion*. Cambridge University Press.

Pei, Minxin. 1998. "Chinese Civic Associations: An Empirical Analysis." *Modern China* 24(3): 285–318.

2006. *China's Trapped Transition: The Limits of Developmental Autocracy*. Cambridge, MA: Harvard University Press.

Peletz, Michael G. 2002. *Islamic Modern: Religious Courts and Cultural Politics in Malaysia*. Princeton University Press.

2015. "A Tale of Two Courts: Judicial Transformation and the Rise of a Corporate Islamic Governmentality in Malaysia." *American Ethnologist* 42(1): 144–60.

Pendlebury, Michael. 2004. "Individual Autonomy and Global Democracy." *Theoria* 103: 43–58.

Perry, Elizabeth J., and Mark Selden. 2001. "Introduction: Reform and Resistance in Contemporary China." In *Chinese Society: Change, Conflict and Resistance*, edited by Elizabeth J. Perry and Mark Selden, 1–19. London and New York: Routeledge.

Peterson, Kristian. 2006. "Usurping the Nation: Cyber-Leadership in the Uighur Nationalist Movement." *Journal of Muslim Minority Affairs* 26(1): 63–73.

Pickens, Jr., Claude L. 1949. "The Old and New Sects, Some Differences." *Friends of Moslems* 23(3): 48.

Pillsbury, Barbara L. K. 1974. "No Pigs for the Ancestors: Pigs, Mothers and Filial Piety among the Taiwanese Muslims." Symposium on Chinese Folk Religions, University of California, Riverside, April 24.

    1978. "Factionalism Observed: Behind the 'Face' of Harmony in a Chinese Community." *China Quarterly* 74: 241–72.

Pils, Eva. 2014. *China's Human Rights Lawyers: Advocacy and Resistance.* New York: Routledge.

Pirie, Fernanda. 2005. "Segmentation within the State: The Reconfiguration of Tibetan Tribes in China's Reform Period." *Nomadic Peoples* 9(1–2): 83–102.

    2006. "Legal Complexity on the Tibetan Plateau." *Journal of Legal Pluralism* 53/54: 77–100.

    2013a. *The Anthropology of Law.* Oxford University Press.

    2013b. "The Limits of the State: Coercion and Consent in Chinese Tibet." *The Journal of Asian Studies* 72(1): 69–89.

Pissler, Knut B. 2012. "Mediation in China: Threat to the Rule of Law?" In *Mediation: Principles and Regulation in Comparative Perspective*, edited by Klaus J. Hopt and Felix Steffek, 959–1010. Oxford University Press.

Polachek, James. 1983. "The Moral Economy of the Kiangsi Soviet (1928–34)." *The Journal of Asian Studies* 42(4): 805–30.

Polanyi, Karl. [1944] 1957a. *The Great Transformation.* Boston, MA: Beacon Press.

    1957b. "The Economy as Instituted Process." In *Trade and Market in the Early Empires: Economies in History and Theory*, edited by Karl Polanyi, Conrad Maynadier Arensberg, and Harry W. Pearson, 243–270. New York: The Free Press.

Popkin, Samuel L. 1979. *The Rational Peasant: The Political Economy of Rural Society in Vietnam.* Berkeley: University of California Press.

Postiglione, Gerard A., ed. 1999. *China's National Minority Education: Culture, Schooling, and Development.* New York: Garland Press.

    2000. "National Minority Regions: Studying School Discontinuation." In *The Ethnographic Eye: Interpretive Studies of Education in China*, edited by Judith Liu, Heidi A. Ross, and Donald P. Kelly, 51–71. New York and London: Falmer Press.

Potter, Pitman B. 2002. "Guanxi and the PRC Legal System: From Contradiction to Complementarity." In *Social Connections in China: Institutions, Culture, and the Changing Nature of Guanxi*, edited by Thomas Gold, Doug Guthrie, and David Wank, 179–96. Cambridge University Press.

    2003. "Belief in Control: Regulation of Religion in China." *China Quarterly* 174: 317–37.

Povinelli, Elizabeth A. 2002. *The Cunning of Recognition: Indigenous Alterities and the Making of Australian Multiculturalism*. Durham, NC: Duke University Press.

Powers, David S. 1999. "The Islamic Family Endowment (Waqf)." *Vanderbilt Journal of Transnational Law* 32(4): 1167–90.

Qiao, Shitong, and Frank Upham. 2015. "The Evolution of Relational Property Rights: A Case of Chinese Rural Land Reform." *Iowa Law Review* 100(6): 101–128.

Rabb, Intisar. 2008. "'We the Jurists': Islamic Constitutionalism in Iraq." *University of Pennsylvania Journal of Constitutional Law* 10(3): 527–79.

    2014. *Doubt in Islamic Law: A History of Legal Maxims, Interpretation, and Islamic Criminal Law*. Cambridge University Press.

Radcliffe-Brown, A. R. 1950. Introduction to *African Systems of Kinship and Marriage*, edited by A. R. Radcliffe-Brown and D. Forde, 1–85. London: Oxford University Press.

Rahman, Noor Aisha Abdul. 2006. *Colonial Image of Malay Adat Laws: A Critical Appraisal of Studies on Adat Laws in the Malay Peninsula during the Colonial Era and Some Continuities*. London: Brill.

Ramseyer, Mark. 1988. "Reluctant Litigant Revisted: Rationality and Disputes in Japan." *Journal of Japanese Studies* 14(1): 111–23.

Rascoff, Samuel J. 2012. "Establishing Official Islam? The Law and Strategy of Counter-Radicalization." *Stanford Law Review* 64(1): 125–90.

Rashid, Salim, ed. 1998. *The Clash of Civilizations?: Asian Responses*. Oxford University Press.

Read, Benjamin L., and Ethan Michelson. 2008. "Mediating the Mediation Debate: Conflict Resolution and the Local State in China." *Journal of Conflict Resolution* 52(5): 737–64.

Reinhart, A. Kevin. 1983. "Islamic Law as Islamic Ethics." *Journal of Religious Ethics* 11(2): 186–203.

Reiter, Yitzak. 1996. *Islamic Endowments in Jerusalem under British Mandate*. London: Frank Cass & Co.

Renaudot, Eusèbe. 1733. *Ancient Accounts of India and China by Two Mohammedan Travelers Who Went to Those Parts in the 9th Century*. London: Sam Harding.

Reynolds, Douglas R. 1993. *China, 1898–1912. The Xinzheng Revolution and Japan*. Cambridge, MA: Harvard University.

Riles, Annelise. 2004. "Law as Object." In *Law and Empire in the Pacific*, edited by Sally Engle Merry and Donald Brenneis, 187–212. Santa Fe, NM: School of American Research Press.

Roberts, Simon. 1993. "Alternative Dispute Resolution and Civil Justice: An Unresolved Relationship." *Modern Law Review* 56: 452–70.

Rohe, Mathias. 2006. "The Migration and Settlement of Muslims: The Challenges for European Legal Systems." In *Migration, Diasporas and Legal*

Systems in Europe, edited by Prakash Shah and Werner F. Menski, 57–72. London: Routledge-Cavendish.

2007. *Muslim Minorities and the Law in Europe: Chances and Challenges*. New Delhi: Global Media Publications.

Rosen, Lawrence. 1984. *Bargaining for Reality: The Construction of Social Relations in a Muslim Community*. University of Chicago Press.

1989. *The Anthropology of Justice: Law as Culture in Islamic Society*. The Lewis Henry Morgan Lectures. Cambridge University Press.

Rossabi, Morris. 1981. "The Muslims in the Early Yuan Dynasty." In *China Under Mongol Rule*, edited by John D. Langlois, Jr., 257–95. Princeton University Press.

Roy, Olivier. 2004. *Globalized Islam: The Search for a New Ummah*. New York: Columbia University Press.

Rudelson, Justin Jon. 1997. *Oasis Identities: Uyghur Nationalism along the Silk Road*. New York: Columbia University Press.

Rudelson, Justin Jon, and William Jankowiak. 2004. "Acculturation and Resistance: Xinjiang Identities in Flux." In *Xinjiang: China's Muslim Borderland*, edited by S. Frederick Starr, 299–319. Armonk, NY: M. E. Sharpe.

Rudnyckyj, Daromir. 2014. "Islamic Finance and the Afterlives of Development in Malaysia." *PoLAR: Political and Legal Anthropology Review* 37(1): 69–88.

Ruskola, Teemu. 2013. *Legal Orientalism: China, the United States, and Modern Law*. Cambridge, MA: Harvard University Press.

Ryan, Alan. 1994. "Self-Ownership, Autonomy, and Property Rights." *Social Philosophy and Policy* 11(2): 241–58.

Sahlins, Marshall. 1995. *How "Natives" Think, about Captain Cook, for Example*. University of Chicago Press.

Saich, Anthony. 2008. *Providing Public Goods in Transitional China*. New York: Palgrave Macmillan.

Salvatore, Armando. 2007. *The Public Sphere: Liberal Modernity, Catholicism, Islam*. New York: Palgrave Macmillan.

Sangren, P. Steven. 1984. "Traditional Chinese Corporations: Beyond Kinship." *The Journal of Asian Studies* 43(3): 391–415.

1987a. *History and Magical Power in a Chinese Community*. Stanford University Press.

1987b. "Orthodoxy, Heterodoxy, and the Structure of Value in Chinese Rituals." *Modern China* 13(1): 63–89.

2009. "'Masculine Domination': Desire and Chinese Patriliny." *Critique of Anthropology* 29(3): 255–78.

Santos, Boaventura de Sousa. 1980. "Law and Community: The Changing Nature of State Power in Late Capitalism." *International Journal of the Sociology of Law* 8: 379–97.

Sapio, Flora. 2010. *Sovereign Power and the Law in China*. Leiden: Brill.

Sassen, Saskia. 1992. *The Global City: New York, London, Tokyo*. Princeton University Press.

Sautman, Barry. 1998. "Affirmative Action, China's Ethnic Minorities and China's Universities." *Pacific Rim Law & Policy Journal* 77(7): 77–114.

———. 2010. "Scaling Back Minority Rights? The Debate about China's Ethnic Policies." *Stanford Journal of International Law* 46(1): 51–120.

———. 2012. "Ethnicity." In *Handbook of Contemporary China*, edited by William S. Tay and Alvin Y. So 137–172. Singapore: World Scientific.

———. 2014. "A US/India Model for China's Ethnic Policies: Is the Cure Worse Than the Disease?" *East Asia Law Review* 9(3): 89–159.

Sauvaget, Jean. 1948. *Aḥbār aṣ–Ṣīn wa l–Hind relation de la Chine et de l'Inde, rédigée en 851/texte établi, traduit et commenté*. Paris: Belles Lettres.

Schacht, Joseph. 1964. *An Introduction to Islamic Law*. Oxford: Clarendon Press.

Schein, Louisa. 1997. "Gender and Internal Orientalism in China." *Modern China* 23(1): 69–98.

———. 2000. *Minority Rules: The Miao and the Feminine in China's Cultural Politics*. Durham, NC: Duke University Press.

Schielke, Samuli. 2009. "Ambivalent Commitments: Troubles of Morality, Religiosity and Aspiration among Young Egyptians." *Journal of Religion in Africa* 39: 158–85.

Schluessel, Eric T. 2007. "'Bilingual' Education and Discontent in Xinjiang." *Central Asian Survey* 26(2): 251–77.

Schmitt, Carl. [1922] 2005. *Political Theology: Four Chapters on the Concept of Sovereignty*, translated by George Schwab. University of Chicago Press.

Schurmann, H. F. 1956. "Traditional Property Concepts in China." *Far Eastern Quarterly* 15(4): 507–16.

Scott, David, and Charles Hirschkind, eds. 2006. *Powers of the Secular Modern: Talal Asad and His Interlocutors*. Stanford University Press.

Scott, James C. 1977. *The Moral Economy of the Peasant: Rebellion and Subsistence in Southeast Asia*. New Haven, CT: Yale University Press.

———. 1990. *Domination and the Arts of Resistance: Hidden Transcripts*. New Haven, CT: Yale University Press.

Sen, Amartya. 1993. "Capability and Well-Being." In *The Quality of Life*, edited by Martha Nussbaum and Amartya Sen, 30–54. Oxford, UK: Clarendon Press.

Shah, Prakash. 1994. "Legal Pluralism: British Law and Possibilities with Muslim Ethnic Minorities." *Retfaerd* 66/67(17): 18–33.

———. 2010. "Between God and the Sultana? Legal Pluralism in the British Muslim Diaspora." In *Shari'a as Discourse: Legal Traditions and the Encounter with Europe*, edited by Jørgen S. Nielsen and Lisbet Christoffersen, 117–40. Aldershot, UK: Ashgate Publishing.

Shahid, Irfan. 1999. "Medieval Islam: The Literary-Cultural Dimension." In *Religion and Culture in Medieval Islam*, edited by Richard G. Hovannisian and Georges Sabagh, 66–78. Cambridge University Press.

Shapiro, Martin. 1981. *Courts: A Comparative and Political Analysis*. University of Chicago Press.

Shen, Yuanyuan. 2000. "Conceptions and Receptions of Legality: Understanding the Complexity of Law Reform in Modern China." In *The Limits of the Rule of Law in China*, edited by Karen G. Turner, James V. Feinerman, and R. Kent Guy, 20–44. Seattle: University of Washington Press.

Shneiderman, Sara. 2014. "Reframing Ethnicity: American Tropes, Recognition beyond Politics, and Ritualized Action between Nepal and India." *American Anthropologist* 116(2): 279–95.

Shryock, Andrew. 2010. *Islamophobia/Islamophilia: Beyond the Politics of Enemy and Friend*. Bloomington: Indiana University Press.

Siddiqui, Mona. 1996. "Law and the Desire for Social Control: An Insight into the Hanafi Concept of Kafa'a with Reference to the Fatawa 'Alamgiri (1664–1672)." In *Feminism and Islam: Legal and Literary Perspectives*, edited by Mai Yamani, 49–68. New York University Press.

Siegel, James T. 2006. *Naming the Witch*. Stanford University Press.

Simon, Gregory M. 2012. "Conviction without Being Convinced: Maintaining Islamic Certainty in Minangkabau, Indonesia." *Ethos* 40(3): 237–57.

Simpfendorfer, Ben. 2009. *The New Silk Road: How a Rising Arab World Is Turning Away from the West and Rediscovering China*. New York: Palgrave Macmillan.

Singer, Amy. 2008. *Charity in Islamic Societies*. Cambridge University Press.

Sirageldin, Ismail. 1995. "Islam, Society, and Economic Policy." *Pakistan Development Review* 34(4): 457–80.

Skinner, G. William. 1965. "Marketing and Social Structure in Rural China: Part III." *The Journal of Asian Studies* 24(3): 363–99.

——— 1971. "Chinese Peasants and the Closed Community: An Open and Shut Case." *Comparative Studies in Society and History* 13(3): 270–81.

——— 1980. "Marketing Systems and Regional Economies: Their Structure and Development." Symposium on Social and Economic History in China from the Song Dynasty to 1900, Chinese Academy of Social Sciences, Beijing, October 26–November 1.

Skovgaard-Petersen, Jakob. 1997. *Defining Islam for the Egyptian State: Muftis and Fatwas of the Dār al-Iftā*. Leiden: Brill.

Smart, Alan. 1993. "Bribes, Gifts, and Guanxi: A Reconsideration of Bourdieu's Capital." *Cultural Anthropology* 8(3): 388–408.

Smart, Alan, and Carolyn L. Hsu. 2013. "Corruption or Social Capital? Tact and the Performance of Guanxi in Market Socialist China." In *Corruption and the Secret of Law: A Legal Anthropological Perspective*, edited by Monique Nuijten and Gerhard Anders, 167–90. Burlington, VT: Ashgate.

Spannaus, Nathan. 2013. "The Decline of the Ākhūnd and the Transformation of Islamic Law under the Russian Empire." *Islamic Law and Society* 20(3): 202–41.

Spectorsky, Susan A. 2010. *Women in Classical Islamic Law*. Leiden: Brill.

Spencer, Robert. 2008. *Stealth Jihad: How Radical Islam Is Subverting America without Guns or Bombs*. Washington DC: Regnery Publishers, Inc.

Spies, O. 2014. "Mahr." In *Encyclopaedia of Islam, First Edition (1913–1936)*, edited by M. Th. Houtsma, T. W. Arnold, R. Basset, and R. Hartmann. Brill Online.

Stacey, Judith. 1983. *Patriarchy and Socialist Revolution in China*. Berkeley: University of California Press.

Stafford, Charles, ed. 2013. *Ordinary Ethics in China*. London: LSE Monographs on Social Anthropology.

Starr, S. Frederick, ed. 2004. *Xinjiang: China's Muslim Borderland*. Armonk, NY: M. E. Sharpe.

State Council Information Office. 2005. *White Paper: Gender Equality in China*. State Council, accessed February 7, 2015, www.chinadaily.com.cn/english/doc/2005-08/24/content_471841.htm.

Steinmüller, Hans. 2010. "Communities of Complicity: Notes on State Formation and Local Sociality in Rural China." *American Ethnologist* 37(3): 539–49.

2013. *Communities of Complicity: Everyday Ethics in Rural China*. London: Berghahn Books.

Stepan, Alfred. 2011. "The Multiple Secularisms of Modern Democratic and Non-Democratic Regimes." In *Rethinking Secularism*, edited by Craig Calhoun, Mark Juergensmeyer, and Jonathan VanAntwerpen, 114–44. Oxford, UK: Oxford University Press.

Stern, Rachel L. 2013. *Environmental Litigation in China: A Study in Political Ambivalence*. Cambridge: Cambridge University Press.

Stewart, Frank H. 2006. "Customary Law among the Bedouin of the Middle East and North Africa." In *Nomadic Societies in the Middle East and North Africa*, edited by Dawn Chatty, 239–79. Leiden: Brill.

Stiles, Erin E. 2009. *An Islamic Court in Context: An Ethnographic Study of Judicial Reasoning*. New York: Macmillan.

Stoler, Ann, ed. 2006. *Haunted by Empire: Geographies of Intimacy in North American History*. Durham, NC: Duke University Press.

Strathern, Marilyn. 1990. *The Gender of the Gift: Problems with Women and Problems with Society in Melanesia*. Berkeley: University of California Press.

Svarverud, Rune. 2007. *International Law as a World Order in Late Imperial China: Translation, Reception and Discourse, 1847–1911*. Leiden: Brill.

Tagliacozzo, Eric. 2013. *The Longest Journey: Southeast Asians and the Pilgrimage to Mecca*. Oxford University Press.

al-Tamimi, Naser M. 2014. *China-Saudi Arabia Relations, 1990–2012*. Abingdon, UK: Routledge.

Tan, Charlene, and Kejia Ding. 2014. "The Role, Developments and Challenges of Islamic Education in China." In *Muslim Education in the 21st Century: Asian Perspectives*, edited by Saʿeda Buang and Phyllis Ghim-Lian Chew, 55–69. New York: Routledge.

Tan, Sor-hoon. 2003. "Can There Be a Confucian Civil Society?" In *The Moral Circle and the Self: Chinese and Western Approaches*, edited by Kim-chong Chong, Sor-hoon Tan, and C. L. Ten, 193–218. Chicago: Open Court.

Tang, Zhenyu [唐震宇]. 1942. "History of the Four Men-Huan." *Friends of Moslems* 16: 5–7.

Tenzin, Jinba. 2014. *In the Land of the Eastern Queendom: The Politics of Gender and Ethnicity on the Sino-Tibetan Border*. Seattle: University of Washington Press.

Thireau, Isabelle, and Hua Linshan. 2005. "One Law, Two Interpretations: Mobilizing the Labor Law in Arbitration Committees and in Letters and Visits Offices." In *Engaging the Law in China: State, Society, and Possibilities for Justice*, edited by Neil J. Diamant, Stanley Lubman, and Kevin O'Brien, 84–107. Stanford University Press.

Thompson, E. P. 1971. "The Moral Economy of the English Crowd in the Eighteenth Century." *Past and Present* 50(1): 76–136.

———. 2013. *Whigs and Hunters: The Origin of the Black Act*. London: Breviary Stuff Publications, 2013.

Thum, Rian. 2014. *The Sacred Routes of Uyghur History*. Cambridge, MA: Harvard University Press.

Tian, Huan. 2012. "Governing Imperial Borders: Insights from the Study of the Implementation of Law in Qing Xinjiang." Ph.D. diss., History, Columbia University.

Tontini, Roberta. 2011. "Tianfang Dianli: A Chinese Perspective on Islamic Law and Its Legal Reasoning." In *Asia Orientale: Ming Qing Studies*, edited by Paolo Santangelo, 487–528. Rome: Raffaele Garofalo.

Trevaskas, Susan. 2004. "Propaganda Work in Chinese Courts: Public Trials and Sentencing Rallies as Sites of Expressive Punishment and Public Education in the People's Republic of China." *Punishment and Society* 6(1): 5–21.

Tsai, Kellee S. 2002. *Back-Alley Banking: Private Entrepreneurs in China*. Ithaca, NY: Cornell University Press.

Tsai, Lily L. 2007. *Accountability without Democracy: Solidary Groups and Public Goods Provision in Rural China*. Cambridge University Press.

Tu, Weiming. [1978] 1998. *Humanity and Self-Cultivation: Essays in Confucian Thought*. Boston, MA: Cheng & Tsui.

Tucker, Judith E. 2008. *Women, Family, and Gender in Islamic Law*. Cambridge University Press.

Turner, Bryan S. 2013. *The Religious and the Political: A Comparative Sociology of Religion*. Cambridge University Press.

Twining, William. 2012. "Legal Pluralism 101." In *Legal Pluralism and Development: Scholars and Practitioners in Dialogue*, edited by Brian Z. Tamanaha, Caroline Sage, and Michael Woolcock, 112–28. Cambridge University Press.

Upham, Frank K. 1987. *Law and Social Change in Postwar Japan*. Cambridge, MA: Harvard University Press.

US Energy Information Administration. 2014. *China*. Washington DC: US Energy Information Administration.

Valeri, Valerio. 2000. *The Forest of Taboos: Morality, Hunting and Identity among the Huaulu of the Moluccas*. Madison: University of Wisconsin Press.

van der Veer, Peter. 2014. *The Modern Spirit of Asia: The Spiritual and the Secular in China and India*. Princeton University Press.

van Rooij, Benjamin. 2010. "The People v. Pollution: Understanding Citizen Action against Pollution in China." *Journal of Contemporary China* 19(63): 55–77.

Venardos, Angelo M., ed. 2010. *Current Issues in Islamic Banking and Finance: Resilience and Stability in the Present System*. Hackensack, NJ: World Scientific Publishing Co.

Venkatesan, Soumhya. 2011. "The Social Life of a 'Free' Gift." *American Ethnologist* 38(1): 47–57.

Verma, B. R. 1988. *Muslim Marriage, Dissolution and Maintenance*. Allahabad, India: The Law Book Co.

Vikør, Knut S. 1995. *Sufi and Scholar on the Desert Edge: Muḥammad b. ʿAlī al-Sanūsī and His Brotherhood*. Evanston, IL: Northwestern University.

2005. *Between God and the Sultan: A History of Islamic Law*. Oxford University Press.

Vogel, Frank E., and Samuel L. Hayes. 1998. *Islamic Law and Finance: Religion, Risk, and Return*. The Hague: Kluwer Law International.

Volokh, Eugene. 2014. "Religious Law (Especially Islamic Law) in American Courts." *Oklahoma Law Review* 66(3): 431–58.

Voloshinov, V. N. [1929] 1986. *Marxism and the Philosophy of Language*. Cambridge, MA: Harvard University Press.

Wadud, Amina. [1992] 1999. *Qur'an and Women: Rereading the Sacred Text from a Woman's Perspective*. Oxford University Press.

2006a. *Inside the Gender Jihad: Women's Reform in Islam*. Oxford, UK: Oneworld Publications.

2006b. "Politics of Piety: The Islamic Revival and the Feminist Subject (Review)." *Journal of the American Academy of Religion* 74(3): 815–18.

Wang, Chenguang. 1997. "Introduction: An Emerging Legal System." In *Introduction to Chinese Law*, edited by Wang Chenguang and Zhang Xianchu, 1–29. Hong Kong: Sweet & Maxwell Asia.

Wang, Jianping [王建平]. 2014. "The Opposition of a Leading Akhund to Shi'a and Sufi Shaykhs in Mid-Nineteenth-Century China." *Cross-Currents: East Asian History & Culture Review* 12 (e-journal): 68–87.

Wang, Qiliang. 2009. "Religion, Legal Pluralism and Order in a Multiethnic Society: A Legal-Anthropological Study in Contemporary China." *Journal of Legal Pluralism* 59: 1–27.

Watson, James L. 1988. "The Structure of Chinese Funerary Rites: Elementary Forms, Ritual Sequence, and the Primacy of Performance." In *Death Ritual in Late Imperial and Modern China*, edited by James L. Watson and Evelyn Sakakida Rawski, 3–19. Berkeley: University of California Press.

Watt, Montgomery William. 1953. *Muhammad at Mecca*. Oxford, UK: Clarendon Press.

Weber, Max. 1930. *The Protestant Ethic and the Spirit of Capitalism*, translated by Talcott Parsons. London: Routledge Press.

   1951. *The Religion of China: Confucianism and Taoism*, translated by Hans H. Gerth. New York: The Free Press.

   [1922] 1967. *On Law in Economy and Society*, translated by Edward Shils and Max Rheinsten. New York: Clarion.

   [1922] 1978a. *Economy and Society*. Edited by Guenther Roth and Claus Wittich. Vol. 1. Berkeley: University of California Press.

   [1922] 1978b. *Economy and Society*. Edited by Guenther Roth and Claus Wittich. Vol. 2. Berkeley: University of California Press.

Weiner, Benno Ryan. 2012. "The Chinese Revolution on the Tibetan Frontier: State Building, National Integration and Socialist Transformation, Zeku (Tsekhok) County, 1953–1958." Ph.D. diss., History, Columbia University.

Weir, Allison. 2013. *Identities and Freedom: Feminist Theory between Power and Connection*. Oxford University Press.

Weiss, Bernard G. 1998. *The Spirit of Islamic Law*. Athens: University of Georgia Press.

Weiss, Max. 2010. *In the Shadow of Sectarianism: Law, Shi'ism, and the Making of Modern Lebanon*. Cambridge, MA: Harvard University Press.

Wellens, Koen. 2010. *Religious Revival in the Tibetan Borderlands: The Premi of Southwest China*. Seattle: University of Washington Press.

Weller, Robert P. 1982. "Sectarian Religion and Political Action in China." *Modern China* 8: 463–83.

   1987. *Unities and Diversities in Chinese Religion*. Seattle: University of Washington Press.

   1999. *Alternate Civilities: Democracy and Culture in China and Taiwan*. Boulder, CO: Westview Press.

Wesoky, Sharon. 2013. *Chinese Feminism Faces Globalization*. New York: Routledge.

Wickham, Carrie Rosefsky. 2013. *The Muslim Brotherhood: Evolution of an Islamist Movement*. Princeton University Press.

Willford, Andrew C. 2006. *Cage of Freedom: Tamil Identity and the Ethnic Fetish in Malaysia*. Ann Arbor: University of Michigan Press.

Wolf, Arthur P. 1974. "Gods, Ghosts, and Ancestors." In *Religion and Ritual in Chinese Society*, edited by A. P. Wolf, 131–82. Stanford University Press.

    1975. "The Women of Hai-shan: A Demographic Portrait." In *Women in Chinese Society*, edited by Margery Wolf and Roxane Witke, 89–110. Stanford University Press.

Wolf, Arthur P., and Chieh-shan Huang. 1980. *Marriage and Adoption in China, 1845–1945*. Stanford University Press.

Wolf, Margery. 1972. *Women and Family in Rural Taiwan*. Stanford University Press.

    1985. *Revolution Postponed: Women in Contemporary China*. Stanford University Press.

Woo, Margaret Y. K. and Mary E. Gallagher. 2011. *Chinese Justice*. Cambridge University Press.

Xia, Chunli. 2009. "Autonomous Legislative Power in Regional Ethnic Autonomy of the People's Republic of China: The Law and the Reality." In *One Country, Two Systems, Three Legal Orders: Perspectives of Evolution: Essays on Macau's Autonomy after the Resumption of Sovereignty by China*, edited by Jorge Oliveira and Paulo Cardinal, 541–64. Macau: Springer.

Xia, Ming. 2009. "The Chinese Underclass and Organized Crime as Stepladder of Social Ascent." In *Marginalization in China: Recasting Minority Politics*, edited by Siu-Keung Cheung, Joseph Tse-Hei Lee, and Lida V. Nedilsky, 95–122. New York: Macmillan.

Xie, Zhibin. 2006. *Religious Diversity and Public Religion in China*. Aldershot, UK: Ashgate.

Xin, He. 2005. "Why Do They Not Comply with the Law? Illegality and Semi-Legality among Rural-Urban Migrant Enterpreneurs in Beijing." *Law & Society Review* 39(3): 527–62.

Yamada, Naomi C. F. 2012. "Education as Tautology: Disparties, Preferential Policy Measures and Preparatory Programs in Northwest China." Ph.D. diss., Anthropology, University of Hawai'i.

Yan, Yunxiang. 1996. *The Flow of Gifts: Reciprocity and Social Networks in a Chinese Village*. Palo Alto, CA: Stanford University Press.

    2009. *The Individuation of Chinese Society*. London School of Economics.

    2013. "The Drive for Success and the Ethics of the Striving Individual." In *Ordinary Ethics in China*, edited by Charles Stafford, 263–92. London: Bloomsbury.

Yang, C. K. 1961. *Religion in Chinese Society*. Berkeley: University of California Press.

Yang, Der-Ruey. 2005. "The Changing Economy of Temple Daoism in Shanghai." In *State, Market, and Religions in Chinese Societies*, edited by Fenggang Yang and Joseph B. Tamney, 113–48. Leiden and Boston, MA: Brill.

Yang, Fenggang. 2011. *Religion in China: Survival & Revival under Communist Rule.* Oxford University Press.

Yang, Guobin. 2009. *The Power of the Internet in China.* New York: Columbia University Press.

Yang, Mayfair Mei-hui. 1994. *Gifts, Favors, and Banquets: The Art of Social Relationships in China.* Ithaca, NY: Cornell University Press.

———. 2002. "The Resilience of Guanxi and Its New Deployments: A Critique of Some New Guanxi Scholarship." *China Quarterly* 170: 459–76.

———. 2008. Introduction to *Chinese Religiosities: Afflictions of Modernity and State Formation*, edited by Mayfair Mei-hui Yang, 1–42. Berkeley: University of California Press.

Yeh, Emily T. 2003. "Tibetan Range Wars: Spatial Politics and Authority on the Grasslands of Amdo." *Development and Change* 34(3): 499–523.

———. 2013. *Taming Tibet: Landscape Transformation and the Gift of Chinese Development.* Ithaca, NY: Cornell University Press.

Yilmaz, Ihsan. 2005. *Muslim Laws, Politics and Society in Modern Nation States: Dynamic Legal Pluralisms in England, Turkey and Pakistan.* Aldershot, UK: Ashgate Publishing.

Yiu, Enoch. 2014. "City Sukuk Opens Door to More Islamic Finance in Hong Kong." *South China Morning Post*, accessed November 1, 2014, www.scmp.com/business/money/markets-investing/article/1592514/city-sukuk-opens-door-more-islamic-finance-hong.

Yu, Dan Smyer. 2011. *The Spread of Tibetan Buddhism in China: Charisma, Money, Enlightenment.* New York: Routledge.

Yu, Xiong. 2004. "The Status of Chinese Women in Marriage and the Family." In *Holding Up Half the Sky: Chinese Women Past, Present, and Future*, edited by Tao Jie, Zheng Bijun, and Shirley L. Mow, 172–78. New York: The Feminist Press.

Yu, Yingshi. 1967. *Trade and Expansion in Han China: A Study in the Structure of Sino-Barbarian Economic Relations.* Berkeley: University of California Press.

Zaman, Muhammad Qasim. 1998. "Sectarianism in Pakistan: The Radicalization of Shi'i and Sunni Identities." *Modern Asian Studies* 32(3): 689–716.

———. 2002. *The Ulama in Contemporary Islam: Custodians of Change.* Princeton University Press.

Zang, Xiaowei. 1993. "Household Structure and Marriage in Urban China: 1900–1982." *Journal of Comparative Family Studies* 24(1): 35–44.

Zarrow, Peter. 2006. "Constitutionalism and the Imagination of the State: Official Views of Political Reform in the Late Qing." In *Creating*

Chinese Modernity: Knowledge and Everyday Life, 1900–1940, edited by Peter Gue Zarrow, 51–82. New York: Peter Lang.

Zelin, Madeleine, Jonathan K. Ocko, and Robert Gardella, eds. 2004. *Contract and Property in Early Modern China.* Stanford University Press.

Zhang, Everett Yuehong. 2011a. "China's Sexual Revolution." In *Deep China: The Moral Life of the Person,* edited by Arthur Kleinman, Yunxiang Yan, Jing Jun, Sing Lee, Everett Zhang, Pan Tianshu, Wu Fei, and Guo Jinhua, 106–51. Berkeley: University of California Press.

——— 2011b. "Introduction: Governmentality in China." In *Governance of Life in Chinese Moral Experience: The Quest for an Adequate Life,* edited by Everett Zhang, Arthur Kleinman, and Tu Weiming, 1–30. London and New York: Routledge.

Zhang, Li. 2010. *In Search of Paradise: Middle Class Living in a Chinese Metropolis.* Ithaca, NY: Cornell University Press.

Zhang, Xiaohui, and Qiliang Wang. 2003. "The Change and Function of Folk Law of Ethnic Minorities in Modern Society: An Analysis of Folk Law in Twenty-Five Ethnic Minority Villages in Yunnan." *Chinese Sociology and Anthropology* 35(4): 33–81.

Zhou, Chuanbin. 2013. "The Paradigm of 'Ulum al–Din in China: Its Institution and Transition." Conference on The Everyday Life of Islam: Focus on Islam in China, Cornell University, April 27–28.

Zhou, Minglang, and Ann Maxwell Hill, eds. 2009. *Affirmative Action in China and the U.S.: A Dialogue on Inequality and Minority Education.* New York: MacMillan.

Zhu, Jiangang, and Chao Wang. 2008. "Seniors Defending Their Rights: Strategies and Culture in Collective Action." *Chinese Sociology and Anthropology* 40(2): 5–34.

Zhu, Suli [朱苏力]. 1996. "The Function of Legal Evasion in China's Economic Reform—From a Socio-Legal Perspective." In *Legal Development in China,* 294–302. Hong Kong: Sweet & Maxwell.

Zito, Angela, and Tani Barlow, eds. 1994. *Body, Subject, and Power in China.* University of Chicago Press.

Žižek, Slavoj. 1989. *The Sublime Object of Ideology.* London and New York: Verso.

Zuckert, Michael P. 1997. *The Natural Rights Republic: Studies in the Foundation of the American Political Tradition.* University of Notre Dame Press.

CHINESE LANGUAGE SOURCES

Ai, Fumei [艾福梅], and Xia Chen [夏晨]. 2008. "'Minjian waijiao' lajin 'Zhongguo Musilin sheng' yu Musilin guojia de juli" ["Unofficial diplomacy" draws China's "Muslim province" closer to Muslim states]. *Renmin ribao [People's Daily]*, May 10.

An, Xiaoxia [安小霞]. 2014. "Zhong–A Bolanhui you meinian yijie gaiwei liangnian yijie" [The annual China-Arab International Fair is changed to a biennial fair]. *Ningxia News*, accessed November 1, 2014, www.nxnews .net/sz/system/2014/04/17/011011114.shtml.

Bai, Rongjing [拜荣静]. 2008. "Shaoshu minzu minjian jiufen jiejue jizhi de xianshi kunjing jiqi pojie" [On the predicament of dispute settlement mechanisms among minority groups and its countermeasures]. *Xibei Minzu Yanjiu [Northwest Minorities Research]* 57(2): 193–99.

Bai, Shouyi [白寿彝]. 1944. *Zhongguo Huijiao xiaoshi [A brief history of Chinese Islam]*. Vol. 3. Chongqing: Shangwu yinshuguan [Commercial Printers].

  [1957] 1992a. "Huihui minzu de xingcheng he chubu fazhan" [The formation and early stages of the Huihui ethnicity]. In *Bai Shouyi minzu zongjiao lunji [Bai Shouyi's theoretical collection on ethnicity and religion]*, 155–68. Beijing Shifan Daxue Chubanshe [Beijing Normal University Publishers].

  1992b. *Huimin qiyi [The Hui rebellion]*. Vol. 3. Beijing: Minzu Chubanshe [Nationalities Publishing House].

  1995. *Zhongguo tongshi [A general history of China]*. Vol. 6. Shanghai Renmin Chubanshe [Shanghai People's Publishers].

Bai, Youtao [白友涛]. 2005. *Pangencao: Chengshi xiandaihau beijing xia de Huizu shequ [Pangencao: a Hui community against the backdrop of urban modernization]*. Yinchuan: Ningxia Renmin Chubanshe [Ningxia People's Publishers].

Bureau for the Revision of the Laws (Xiuding falüguan). 1909. "Diaocha minshi xiguan zhangcheng shitiao" [The regulations on the civil customs survey, in ten articles]. In *Diaocha minshi xiguan wenti [Civil customs survey questions]* 1–3. Beijing: Xiuding Falüguan Shuayin [Printed by the Office of the Revision of Laws].

Central Ethnic Work Committee (Zhongyang minzu gongzuo huiyi). 2014. "Jiaqiang wenhua rentong fandui da Hanzu zhuyi" [Strengthen cultural recognition, oppose great Han chauvinism], accessed October 7, 2014, http://news.sina.com.cn/c/2014-09-29/192930934609 .shtml?bsh_bid=501762237.

Chang, Chung-fu [张中复]. 2001. *Qingdai Xibei Huimin shibian: shehui wenhua shiying yu minzu rentong de xingsi [The Hui incident in the Qing Northwest: sociocultural adaptation and reflection on ethnic identity]*. Taipei: Lianjing Book Publishers.

Chen, Guangyuan [陈广元], ed. 2003. *Xinbian wo'erzi yanjiang ji (shixing ben)* *[A collection of W'az speeches: new edition (trial copy)]*. Edited by "Xinbian wo'erzi yanjianb ji" bianshen weiyuanhui [the editorial and screening committee for "a collection of W'az speeches: new edition"]. Beijing: Zongjiao Wenhua Chubanshe [Religion and Culture Publishers].

2011. "Tuidong jiejing gongzuo chanyang Yisilanjiao zhen jingshen" [Advocating the expounding of the classic work, propagating Islam's true spirit]. *Zhongguo zongjiao [China Religion]* Issue 5: 12–16.

Chen, Jinzhao [陈金钊], and Xie Hui [谢晖], eds. 2002. *Minjianfa [Popular law]*. Jinan: Shandong Renmin Chubanshe [Shandong People's Publisher].

Chen, Long [陈龙], ed. 2002. *Linxia renwu zhi [A record of Linxia personnages]*. Lanzhou: Gansu Renmin Chubanshe [Gansu People's Publishers].

Chen, Tianshe [陈天社]. 2008. "Alabo guojia de Zhongguo liuxuesheng jiqi yingxiang" [Chinese foreign students in Arab nations and their influence]. *Shijie minzu [World Ethnicity]* Issue 2: 44–49.

China Islamic Association (Zhongguo Yisilanjiao Xiehui), ed. 2008. *Yisilanjiao jiaofa jianming jiaocheng [A concise course in Islamic law]*. Beijing: Zongjiao Wenhua Chubanshe [Religion Culture Publishers].

2010. *Zhongguo Musilin linian chaojin qingkuang – lanbiao [A chart of the Chinese Muslims hajj situation over the years]*. Beijing: China Islamic Association.

China Muslim Youth Net (Zhongguo Musilin Qingnian Wang). 2010. "Musilin zongjiao yu cishan shiye" [Muslim religion and charity work], accessed January 21, 2013, www.muslem.net.cn/bbs/article-2718-1.html.

Chinese Academy of Social Sciences Nationalities Research Institute (Zhongguo Kexueyuan Minzu Yanjiusuo). 1958. *Heilongjiang huizu shehui lishi diaocha baogao [The Heilongjiang Hui social-historical survey report]*. Beijing: Zhongguo Kexueyuan Minzu Yanjiusuo [Chinese Academy of Social Science Nationalities Research Institute].

1964a. *Gansu huizu diaocha ziliao huiji [The compilation of the Gansu Hui survey materials]*. Beijing: Zhongguo Kexueyuan Minzu Yanjiusuo Gansu shaoshu minzu shehui lishi diaocha [Chinese Academy of Social Sciences Nationalities Research Institute Gansu Ethnic Minority Sociohistorical Survey].

ed. 1964b. *Gansu Huizu diaocha ziliao huiji [Gansu Hui survey material compilation]*. Lanzhou: Gansu Renmin Chubanshe [Gansu People's Publishers].

Compilation Committee (Bianzuan Weiyuanhui), ed. 2004. *Xining Dongguan Qingzhen Dasi Zhi [Annals of the Xining East Gate Grand Mosque]*. Lanzhou: Gansu Wenhua Chubanshe [Gansu Culture Publishers].

Compilation Leading Group (Bianzu Lingdao Xiaozu), ed. 1986. *Linxia Zhou jinrong zhi [A record of Linxia Prefecture's finance]*. Linxia: Zhongguo renmin zhengzhi xieshang huiyi Linxia huizu zizhizhou weiyuanhui wenshi ziliao weiyuanhui bian [Editorial Committee of the China People's Political Consultative Conference Linxia Hui Autonomous Prefecture Committee Literature and History Materials].

Ding, Hong. 1998 [丁宏]. "Huizu funü yu huizu wennua" [Hui women and Hui culture]. *Zhongyang Minzu Daxue xuebao (zhexue shehui kexueban) [Journal of Central Nationalities University (Humane and Social Science Edition)]* Issue 2: 70–76.

Ding, Shiren [丁士仁]. 2006. "Ershi shiji Hezhou jingtang jiaoyu de liangci zhongda tupo" [The two great breakthroughs in twentieth-century mosque education in Hezhou]. *Huizu Yanjiu [Journal of Hui Muslim Minority Study]* 64(4): 51–55.

———. 2009. "Zhongguo Yisilanjiao menpai huafen de xin jiaodu" [New perspectives to classify China's Muslim sects], accessed July 14, 2014, www.yslzc.com/xsh/Class137/Class139/200911/32073_2.html (on file with author).

———. 2014. "Yisilanjiao Hanaifei jiaofa xuepai jiqi zai Zhongguo de chuanbo" [Hanafi law of Islam and its spread into China]. *Xibei Minzu Xueyuan xuebao (Zhexue Shehui kexuban) [Journal of Northwest Minorities University (Social Sciences)]* 1(1): 38–45.

———. 2015. "Jiaofa da haishi guofa da: xuezhe ru shuo" [Is Religious Law the Law of the Land or State Law? A Scholar Gives His Opinion], accessed July 27, 2015, www.muslem.net.cn/bbs/article-14396-1.html.

Ding, Yangmei [丁杨梅]. 2008. "Huizu xingcheng shi de kaocha" [An investigation into the history of the Hui's formation]. *Shidai renwu [Times Figure]* Issue 6: 246–47.

Dou, Yi [窦仪]. 1984. *Song Xing Tong [Song penal code]*. Vol. 8. Beijing: Zhonghua shuju [China Publishing House].

Du, Yan [杜艳], and Yimiti Haimiti [海米提•依米提]. 2011. "Lüyou weiji shijian yanjiu: yi Xinjiang '7.5' shijian weili" [Research on tourism crisis events: taking the Xinjiang "July fifth" event as an example]. *Hebei Lüyou Zhiye Xueyuan xuebao [Journal of Hebei Tourism Vocational College]* 16(1): 13–19.

Editorial Group (Bianxiezu), ed. 2008. *Linxia Huizu Zizhizhou gaikuang [The situation of Linxia Hui Autonomous Prefecture]*. *Zhongguo shaoshu minzu zizhi difang gaikuang congshu [China ethnic minorities local autonomy collection]*. Lanzhou: Gansu Renmin Chubanshe [Gansu People's Publishers].

Editorial Group for the General Situation of the Changji Huizu Autonomous Prefecture (Changji Huizu Zizhizhou gaikuang bian xie zu). 1985. *Changji Huizu Zizhizhou gaikuang [The general condition of the Changji Hui Autonomous Prefecture]*. Urumqi: Xinjiang Renmin Chubanshe [Xinjiang People's Publisher].

Fan, Changjiang [范长江]. [1937] 1991. *Zhongguo de xibei jiao [China's Northwest corner]*. Part 3, vol. 70. *Minguo congshu* [Republic of China book collection]. Shanghai Shudian (Shanghai Bookstore).

Fei, Xiaotong [费孝通]. 1980. "Guanyu woguo minzu de shibie wenti" [On China's ethnic classification project]. *Zhongguo shehui kexue [China Social Science]* Issue 1: 147–62.

———. 1987. "Linxia hang" [Linxia business]. *Liao Wang Zhoukan [The Weekly Watch]* Issue 23: 30–33.

Feng, Jianshen [冯健身], and Shi Jun [石军], eds. 2012. *Gansu sheng 2010nian renkou pucha ziliao [2010 Gansu Province population survey materials]*. Beijing: Zhongguo Tongji Chubanshe [China Statistics Publishers].

Fourth Plenum of the Eighteenth Congress of the Central Committee of the CCP (Zhongguo Gongchandang Di Shiba Jie Zhongyang Weiyuanhui Di Si Ci Quanti Huiyi). 2014. "Zhonggong zhongyang guanyu quanmian tuijian yifa zhiguo ruogan zhongda wenti de jueding" [CCP Central Committee decision regarding some major questions in comprehensively promoting the governing of the country according to law]. *Renmin ribao [People's Daily]*, accessed December 31, 2014, http://politics.people.com .cn/n/2014/1029/c1001-25926893.html.

Gansu Provincial People's Government (Gansu Sheng Renmin Zhengfu), ed. 2011. *Gansu Nianjian 2011 [Gansu yearbook 2011]*. Lanzhou: Gansu Wenhua Chubanshe [Gansu Culture Publishers].

Gao, Hongjun [高鸿钧]. 2004. *Yisilanfa: Chuantong yu xiandaihua [Islamic law: tradition and modernization]*. Revised ed. Beijing: Qinghua Daxue Chubanshe [Qinghua University Publishers].

Gao, Qicai [高其才]. 2003. *Zhongguo shaoshuminzu xiguanfa yanjiu [Research on the customary law of China's ethnic minorities]*. Beijing: Qinghua Daxue Chubanshe [Qinghua University Publishers].

———. 2013. "Dangdai Zhongguo guojia lifa yu xiguanfa" [Modern Chinese state law and customary law]. Third East Asia Law and Society Association Meeting, Shanghai Jiaotong University Koguan Law School, March 22–23.

Gao, Yongjiu [高永久]. 2005. *Xibei shaoshu minzu diqu chengshihua ji shequ yanjiu [Urbanization in Northwest ethnic minority areas and community research]*. Beijing: Minzu Chubanshe [Nationalities Publishing House].

Government of the Shaanxi, Gansu, Ningxia Border Areas (Shaan-Gan-Ning Bianqu Zhengfu). 1944. *Shaan-Gan-Ning bianqu zhengce tiaoli huiji [Collection of policies and regulations of the Shaanxi, Gansu, Ningxia border areas]*. Yenan: Shaan-Gan-Ning Bianqu Zhengfu [Government of the Shaanxi, Gansu, Ningxia border areas].

Ha, Baoyu [哈宝玉]. 2007. "Zhongguo Yisilanjiaofa de xueshu yuanjiu jiqi tedian" [The characteristics of academic research on Chinese Islamic law]. *Huizu Yanjiu [Journal of Hui Muslim Minority Study]* 68(4): 113–20.

2009. "Jiji xueshe diyun tanjiu suefei zhendi—ji woguo zhuming Yisilanjiao, huizu yanjiu zhuanjia Ma Tong xiansheng" [Collecting the academic reality beneath the surface in exploring the true meaning of Sufism—remembering my country's famous expert on Islam and Hui research studies, Mr. Ma Tong]. *Huizu Yanjiu [Journal of Hui Muslim Minority Studies]* 2(74): 159–65.

Hai, Xuewang [海学旺]. 1993. *Linxia Shi minzu zongjiao zhuanji [Special Collection on Linxia City Ethnicity and Religion]*. Lanzhou: Gansu Minzu Chubanshe [Gansu Nationalities Publishing House].

Hanunai, Anyoubu [哈奴乃 俺由卜]. 1986. "Linxia Yisilanjiao Salaifengye de youlai" [The origin of Linxia Islam's Salafiyya]. In *Linxia shi wenshi [Linxia City literary and historical materials]*, 126–29. Linxia City: Zhongguo Renmin Zhengzhi Xieshang Huiyi Linxia Huizu Zizhizhou Weiyuanhui wenshi ziliao weiyuanhui bian [Editorial committee of the China People's Political Consultative Conference Linxia Hui Autonomous Prefecture Committee literature and history materials].

Hao, Shiyuan [郝时远]. 2011a. "Jianchi minzu quyu zizhi zhidu bixu wanshan minzu zhengce" [In preserving ethnic regional autonomy, the system must complete ethnic policy]. *Chuancheng [Inheritance and Innovation]* Issue 5: 64–66.

2011b. "Zhonghua minzu de weida fuxing—Zhongguo Gongchandang minzu lilun yu minzu zhengce de lilunxing yu shijianxing" [The great rejuvination of the Chinese nation—the Chinese Communist Party ethnic theory and theoreticality and practicality of the ethnic policy]. *Yunnan Minzu Daxue xuebao (zhexue shehui kexueban) [Journal of Yunnan Nationalities University (Social Science)]* 28(6): 5–21.

2012a. "Meiguo shi Zhongguo jiejue minzu wenti de bangyang ma?" [Is America helping in resolving China's ethnic problem?]. *Shijie minzu [World Ethnicity]* Issue 2: 1–15.

2012b. "Ping 'di erdai minzu zhengce' shuo de lilun yu shijian wuqu" [Commentary on theoretical and practical misunderstanding of the "second-generation nationality policy"]. *Xinjiang shehui kexue [Social Sciences in Xinjiang]* Issue 2: 44–62.

Hao, Shiyuan [郝时远], Zhang Haiyang [张海洋], and Ma Rong [马戎]. 2013. "Hao Shiyan, Zhang Haiyang, Ma Rong: Goujian xinxing minzu guanxi" [Hao Shiyan, Zhang Haiyang, and Ma Rong: building a new model of ethnic relations]. *Lingdao Zhe [Leaders]* Issue 53 (September): 79–100.

Hou, Ai'mei [侯爱梅]. 2007. "'Shilin hunshu wenjuan' chutan [An initial exploration of the "documents relating to the lost forest marriage contract case"] *Ningxia Shehui Kexue [Social Sciences in Ningxia]* 2(141): 106–10.

Hu, Angang [胡鞍钢], and Hu Lianhe [胡联合]. 2011. "Di er dai minzu zhengce: zoujin minzu jiaorong yiti he fanrong yiti" [The second generation of ethnic policies: toward integrated ethnic blending and flourishing]. *Xinjiang Shifan Daxue xuebao (zhexue shehui kexueban) [Journal of Xinjiang Normal University: Philosophy and Social Science Edition]* 32(5): 1–12.

Hu, Xusheng [胡旭晟]. 2000. "20 shiji qianqi Zhongguo zhi minshangshi xiguan baogaolu ji qi yiyi (daixu)" [An article in lieu of a preface: the abstracts of the report on civil and commercial customs of the early part of the twentieth century and its significance]. In *Minshi xiguan diaocha baogao lu* [Abstracts of the report on civil affairs customs], edited by Hu Xusheng [胡旭晟], Xia Xinhua [夏新华] and Li Jiaofa [李交发], 1–17. Beijing: Zhongguo Zhengfa Daxue Chubanshe [China University of Political Science and Law Publishers].

[胡旭晟], Xia Xinhua [夏新华], and Li Jiaofa [李交发], eds. 2000. *Minshi xiguan diaochao baogaolu [Abstracts of the report on civil affairs customs]*. Vol. 2. Beijing: Zhongguo Zhengfa Daxue Chubanshe [China University of Political Science and Law Publishers].

Hu, Yunyu [胡韫玉]. 1914. "Zhongguo xiguanfa lun" [Discussing China's customary law]. *Xiaxing [Summer Star]* 1(2): 1–8.

Huang, Kexuan [黄克绚]. 1936. "Meiguo de xiguanfa" [America's customary law]. *Zhongguo faxue zazhi yuekan [Chinese Legal Studies Monthly Magazine]* 1(4):107–19.

Huang, Tinghui [黄庭辉]. 2009. "Huizu de hunyin jiating" [Hui marriage and family]. In *Huizu shehui lishi diaocha ziliao [Materials from the Hui sociohistorical survey]*, edited by Yunnan sheng bianji zu [Yunnan Provincial Editorial Group], 186–93. Beijing: Minzu Chubanshe [Nationalities Publishing House].

Iwamura, Shinobu [岩村忍]. 1950. *Zhongguo Huijiao shehui de gouzao [The structure of Chinese Islamic society]*, translated by Chai Yaxin. Vol. (2). Tokyo: Riben Pinglun She [Japanese Discussion Group].

Jiang, Xin [姜歆]. 2007. "Lun Huizu xiguanfa de xianshi yiyi yu guojia zhidingfa de guanxi" [A discussion of the actual significance and relationship to state statutory law of Huizu customary law]. *Ningxia Shifan Xueyuan xuebao (shehui kexue) [Journal of Ningxia Teachers University (Social Science)]* 28(4): 103–8.

Jiang, Zhenhui [蒋贞慧]. 2006. "Shilun HuiHan tonghun de yuanyin jiqi tedian" [On reasons and features of marriage between Hui and Han]. *Shangluo Shifan Zhuanke Xuexiao bao [Journal of Shangluo Teachers University]* Issue 3: 101–103.

Jun, Sugawara. 2009. "Shengdi Wupa'er: Yiju Maze wenshu de lishi tantao" [Sacred Wupa'er: a historical inquiry into the Mazar documents]. *Xicheng Yanjiu [Research on Western Regions]* Issue 2: 83–92.

Li, Guilian [李贵连]. 2005. *Shen Jiaben pingchuan [Commentary on Shen Jiaben's legacy].* Nanjing Daxue Chubanshe [Nanjing University Publishers].

Li, Weijian [李维建]. 2011. *Gansu Linxia menhuan diaocha [Survey of the Sufi orders in Linxia, Gansu].* Beijing: Zhongguo Shehui Kexue Chubanshe [China Social Science Academy].

Li, Xiaoxia [李晓霞]. 2004. "Shilun Zhongguo zuji tonghunquan de goucheng" [Examining the composition of the circle of Chinese interethnic marriage]. *Guangxi Minzu Yanjiu [Guangxi Ethnicity Research]* 77(3): 20–27.

Li, Xinghua [李兴华]. 2000. "Qingdai Huizu qingzhensi de sichan wenti" [The problem of mosque property during the Qing Dynasty]. *Shijie zongjiao yanjiu [Studies in World Religions]* Issue 2: 46–54.

2006. "Hezhou Yisilanjiao yanjiu" [Research on Hezhou Islam]. *Huizu Yanjiu [Journal of Hui Muslim Minority Study]* 61(1): 109–27.

Liang, Jingning [良警宁]. 2006. *Niujie: Yige chengshi Huizu shequ de bianqian [Oxen Street: changes to an urban Hui community].* Beijing: Zhongyang Minzu Daxue Chubanshe [Central Nationalities University Publishers].

Liang, Zhiping [梁治平]. 1996. *Qingdai xiguanfa: shehui yu guojia [Qing customary law: society and state].* Beijing: Zhongguo Zhengfa Daxue Chubanshe [China University of Political Science and Law Publishers].

2014 "2014ban fazhi diqu tanjing (quanwen)" [A path to find one's way through the 2014 edition of the rule-of-law map]. *Gongzhiwang [Common Understanding Net],* accessed December 31, 2014, www.21ccom.net/articles/china/ggzl/20141210117338_all.html.

Linxia City Annals Compilation Committee (Linxia Shi Difang Zhi Bianzuan Weiyuanhui). 1995. *Linxia shi zhi [Linxia City Record].* Lanzhou: Gansu Renmin Chubanshe [Gansu People's Publishers].

Linxia City Chronicles Committee (Linxia shi difangzhi bianzuan weiyuanhui). 2011. *Linxia Shi Zhi (1986–2005) [Linxia City Record, 1986–2005].* Lanzhou: Gansu Wenhua Chubanshe [Gansu Culture Publications].

Linxia Prefectural Party Committee (Zhongguo Gongchandang Linxia Huizu Zizhizhou Weiyuanhui). 1953. "Guanyu zongjiao jiaopai menhuan jian ruogan wenti jiancha baogao ji jinhou gongzuo yijian" [Report on the inspection with regards to certain problems between religious teaching schools and Sufi orders and opinion for work hereafter]. Gansu Provincial Archives. Catalogue no. 006. Serial no. 0002. Record no. 0129. Entry no. 95. August 21.

Linxia Prefecture Committee United Front Work Department (Zhonggong Linxia Zhouwei Tongzhanbu). 1952. "Jiejue Linxia shi qingzhensi gongbei tudi wenti baogao" [Report on solving Linxia City's mosque and Sufi complex land problem]. Gansu Provincial Archives. Linxia. Catalogue no. 006. Archive no. 0079. Serial no. 0013. Batch no. 95.

Linxia Prefecture Government (Linxia Huizu Zizhizhou Renmin Zhengfu). 2012. "Linxia shi dongqu guihua jianshe qingkuang" [Linxia City eastern section construction plan), accessed July 9, 2014, www.linfang.cc/archive .php?aid=2574.

Linxia Prefecture Vocational Technical School (Gansu Sheng Linxia Zhou Zhiye Jixu Xuexiao). 2014. "Gansu Sheng Linxia Zhou Zhiye Jixu Xuexiao (Alaboyyu zhuanye): 2014nian zhaosheng jianzheng" [Gansu Province Linxia Prefecture Vocational Technical School (Arabic specialized field): 2014 general regulations for student recruitment], accessed August 26, 2014, www.lxzmzxx.com/shownews.asp?newsid=591.

Liu, Baojun [刘宝军]. 2005. "Huizu liuxuesheng zai haiwai de fazhan bianqian shi" [A history of changes in the historical development of Hui overseas study abroad]. *Ningxia Shehui Kexue [Social Sciences in Ningxia]* 129(2): 83–86.

Liu, Junning [刘军宁]. 2014. "Cong kunming shijian fansi minzu quyu zizhi zhengce" [Reconsidering ethnic regional autonomy policy after the Kunming incident], accessed September 8, 2014, http://wenku.baidu.com/link?url=_BF7Ouc6-v2uJ3vifkgmAPqiIVE55bcySe-jXtnrNyBQcAB_ztbdEQ1eCbB-cPCC5L0yPSCZki0T1dfgUWGwmQ2QZpcomLlAQnMgGR51UIq.

Liu, Junwen [刘俊文]. 1999a. *Tang Lü Shu Yi [Commentary and discussion of the Tang Code].* Vol. 8. Beijing: Falü Chubanshe [Law Publishers].

1999b. *Tang Lü Shu Yi [Commentary and discussion of the Tang Code].* Vol. 6. Beijing: Falü Chubanshe [Law Publishers].

Liu, Kangle [刘康乐], and Wang Duo [旺多]. 2011. "Yuanda de zongjiao guanli tizhi ji qi xiandai qishi" [The religious administration system of the Yuan Dynasty and its modern enlightenment]. *Xizang Daxue xuebao (shehui kexueban) [Journal of Tibet University (Social Science Edition)]* 26(2): 111–16.

Lu, Weidong [路伟东]. 2010. "Zhangjiao, xiangyue yu baojiace—Qingdai hukou guanli tixi zhong de Shan-Gan Huimin renkou" [Imam, local rules and regulations, and the book of the baojia [system]—the Muslim population of Shanxi-Gansu region in the Qing Dynasty household registration system]. *Huizu Yanjiu [Journal of Hui Muslim Minority Study]* 78(2): 38–46.

Lu, Zhonghui [鲁忠慧]. 2001. "Shixi Tangsong shiqi Huihui xianmin de guoji hunyin: fanhantonghun" [Foreigner-Han intermarriage: a trial examination of Tang-Song period Huihui ancestors' international marriage]. *Ningxia Shehui Kexue [Social Sciences in Ningxia]* 5(108): 50–53.

Ma, Dongping [马东平]. 2010. *Chuantong yu Shanbian: Hezhou bafang huizuren de shenghuo shijie [Tradition and permutation: the life world of Hezhou Bafang Hui people].* Lanzhou: Gansu Minzu Chubanshe [Gansu Nationalities Publishing House].

Ma, Fengyi [马凤仪]. 2010. "Zhanlüe Lintan musilin nüzi jiaoyu" [Outline of Lintan Muslim girls' education]. In *Zhongguo Yisilanjiao Xidaotang yanjiu wenji* [*Collected research works on the Chinese Islamic Xidaotang*], edited by Min Shengguang [敏生光], 200–202. Lanzhou: Gansu Minzu Chubanshe [Gansu Nationalities Publishing House].

Ma, Jianchun [马建春]. 2005. "Yuandai Dashiman yu Huihui ha de si de shezhi" [The installation of the Dashiman and Hui qasi]. *Zongjiaoxue yangjiu* [*Religious Studies*] Issue 1: 116–17.

Ma, Junhua [马俊华]. 2004. *Jindai hezhou fengyun* [*The wind and clouds of modern Hezhou*]. Linxa Zhou Minzu Shiwu Weiyuanhui Minzu Zongjiao Yanjiusuo [Ethnic-Religious Research Institute of the Linxia Prefectural Ethnic Affairs Committee].

Ma, Kelin [马克林]. 2006. *Huizu chuantongfa wenhua yanjiu* [*Research on Hui traditional legal culture*]. Beijing: Zhongguo Shehui Kexue Chubanshe [China Social Science Publisher].

Ma, Mingxian [马明贤]. 2011. *Yisilanfa: Chuantong yu yanxin* [*Islamic laws, tradition, and renovation*]. Beijing: Shangwu Yin Shuguan Chubanshe [Commerical Press].

Ma, Ping. 1998. "Huizu hunyin ze'ou zhong de 'funü waijia jinji'" ["Taboo against women marrying out" in Hui marriage spouse selection]. *Xibei Minzu Yanjiu* [*Northwest Minorities Research*] 2(23): 180–86.

Ma, Rong [马戎]. 2004. "Lijie minzu guanxi de xin silü—shaoshu zuqun wenti de 'quzhengzhihua'" [New perspective to understand ethnic relations—depoliticization of ethnicity]. *Beijing Daxue xuebao: zhexue shehui kexueban* [*Journal of Peking University: Humanities and Social Sciences*] 41(6): 123–33.

[For Ma Rong. 2009a and 2009b, see Western language sources.]

2009c. "Jingji fazhanzhong de pinfu chaju wenti—quyu chaiyi, zhiye chaiyi he zuqun chaiyi" [Income gaps in economic development—differences among regions, occupational groups, and ethnic groups]. *Beijing Daxue xuebao: zhexue shehui kexueban* [*Journal of Peking University: Philosophy and Social Sciences*] 46(1): 116–27.

2010. "Zhongguo shehui de lingwai yilei 'eryuan jiegou'" [Another kind of "dual structure" in Chinese society]. *Beijing Daxue xuebao: zhexue shehui kexueban* [*Journal of Peking University: Humanities and Social Sciences*] 47(3): 93–103.

Ma, Tong [马通]. [1979] 2000. *Zhongguo Yisilan Jiaopai yu menhuan zhidu shilüe* [*A historical record of China's Islamic teaching school and Sufi order system*]. 3rd edn. Yinchuan: Ningxia Renmin Chubanshe [Ningxia People's Publishers].

Ma, Wen [马雯]. 2014. "Shendu xian shidai minzu wenti baozhang minzu diqu zizhi quanli" [A review of the current era's protection of the rights of ethnic area autonomy]. *Guangxi Minzu Shifan Xueyuan xuebao* [*Journal of Guangxi Normal University for Nationalities*] Issue 1: 97–99.

Ma, Xiaopei [马效佩]. 2007. "Lun Famen menhuan liangfen Alabowen Sufei chuanjiao pingzheng de wenxian jiazhi ji xinxi" [Discussing the value of and information on the Famen Sufi order's two Arabic documents that are proofs to proselytize Sufism]. *Shijie zongjiao yanjiu [Studies in World Religions]* Issue 2: 115–23.

Ma, Xiaorong [马效融], ed. 1994. *Linxia wenshi ziliao xuanji: Hezhou shihua [Selections of literary and historical materials on Linxia: historical narrative of Hezhou]*. Vol. 8. Lanzhou: Zhongguo Renmin Zhengzhi Xieshang Huiyi Linxia Huizu Zizhizhou Weiyuanhui wenshi ziliao weiyuanhui bian [Editorial Committee of the China People's Political Consultative Conference Linxia Hui Autonomous Prefecture Committee literature and history materials].

Ma, Yan [马艳]. 2008. "20shiji 80niandai yilai de huizu nüxing yanjiu shuping" [A review of Islamic women's studies since the 1980s]. *Funü yanjiu luncong [Collection of Women's Studies]* 85(2): 82–94.

Ma, Tong. 2012. *Yige xinyang qunti de yimin shijian—Yiwu Musilin shehui shenghuo de minzu zhi [The migrated practice of a faith community: an ethnography of Yiwu Muslims' social life]*. Beijing: Zhongyang Minzu Daxue Chubanshe [Central Nationalities University Publishers].

Ma, Yaping [马亚萍]. 1992. "Jianshu 'Gulanjing' funü guanzhi jiji yinsu" [A simple explanation of the Qur'an on the positive factors of women's perspectives]. *Xibei Minzu Yanjiu [Northwest Minorities Research]* 11(2): 179–83.

Mao, Zedong [毛泽东]. [1937] 1970. *Mao Zhuxi de wu pian zhuexue zhuzuo [Five philosophical writings by Chairman Mao]*. Beijing: Renmin Chubanshe [People's Publisher].

Mian, Weilin [勉维霖]. 1988. "Zhongguo Huizu Yisilanjiao de zhangjiao zhidu" [China Hui Islamic imam system]. *Ningxia Shehui Kexue [Social Sciences in Ningxia]* Issue 6: 51–56.

Min, Shengguang [敏生光]. 2007. *Xinyue zhiguang [The light of the crescent moon]*. Lanzhou: Gansu Minzu Chubanshe [Gansu Nationalities Publishing House].

Mingde Mosque of Linxia City, Gansu Province (Gansu Sheng Linxia Shi Mingde Qingzhensi). 2004. *Long ahong [Deaf cleric]*. 2nd edn. Vol. 1. Linxia.

Ministry of Civil Affairs (Minzheng bu). 2010. "Sida zhixiashi lihunlü 'minglie qianmao'" [List of names for the "top candidates" for divorce rate among the four large cities under the central government]. *Fazhi wanbao [Legal System Evening Paper]*, October 3.

Ministry of Commerce (Shangwu bu). 2013. "2013nian shangwu gongzuo nianzhong shuping zhi shiyi: Zhong-A jingmao hezuo wenbu fazhan" [A year-end review of 2013's commercial work in November: the steady development of China–Arab trade cooperation], accessed November 4, 2014, www.mofcom.gov.cn/article/ae/ai/201312/20131200433287.shtml.

Nakanishi, Tatsuya. 2012. "17, 18 shiji zhijiao de Zhongguo guxingpai de Yisilanjiao—jiyu Kaifeng yu Zhuxianzhen de Alabowen beiji de fenxi" [The seventeenth to eighteenth turn-of-the-century Islamic ancient behavior faction—an analysis of an Arabic stele based in Kaifeng and Zhuxianzhen]. *Dongyang Wenhua Yanjiusuo jiyao [The Memoirs of the Institute for Advanced Studies on Asia]* 162.

National Bureau of Statistics (Guojia tongji ju). 2009. *China tongji nianjian 2009 [China statistical yearbook 2009]*. Beijing: Zhongguo Tongji Chubanshe [China Statistics Publishers].

⸻ 2012. *China tongji nianjian 2012 [China statistical yearbook 2012]*. Beijing: Zhongguo Tongji Chubanshe [China Statistics Publishers].

Nationality Problem Research Committee (Minzu Wenti Yanjiuhui Bian). [1941] 1980. *Huihui minzu wenti [The Huihui nationality problem]*. Beijing: Renmin Chubanshe [People's Publisher].

Nijim, Anwar 2009. *Xinjiang weiwuerzu renkou lihun wenti yanjiu [Research on Xinjiang Uyghurs' population divorce problems]*. Beijing: Zhongyang Minzu Daxue Chubanshe [Central Nationalities University Publisher].

Ou, Jianfei [欧剑菲]. 2006. "Shaoshu minzu diqu de cungui minyue" [Village rules in ethnic minority places]. In *Shaoshu minzu diqu xisu yu falü de tiaoshi: yi Yunnan Sheng Jinping Miaozu Yaozu Daizu Zizhixian wei zhongxin de anli yanjiu [Adaptability of ethnic minority areas' customs and law: a case study from Yunnan Province Jinping Miaozu, Yaozu, and Daizu Autonomous County]*, edited by Fang Hui, 135–212. Beijing: Zhongguo Shehui Kexue Chubanshe [China Social Science Publisher].

Pang, Shiqian [庞士谦]. 1937. "Zhongguo Huijiao siyuan jiaoyu zhi yange ji keben" [The course of change and development and textbooks of China's Hui mosque education]. *Yu Gong [Tribute of Yu]* 7(4), np.

Policy and Law Department of the Bureau of Religious Affairs (Zongjiao Shiwuju Zhengce Faguisi), ed. 1995. *Xin shiqi zongjiao gongzuo wengong xuanbian [Anthology of new-period religious work documents]*. Beijing: Zongjiao Wenhua Chubanshe [Religion Culture Publishers].

Population Census Office (Renkou Pucha Bangongshi), ed. 1985. *Zhongguo 1982nian renkou pucha ziliao [1982 population census of China]*. Beijing: Zhongguo Tongji Chubanshe [China Statistics Publishers].

⸻ ed. 2012. *Zhongguo 2010nian renkou pucha ziliao [2010 population census of China]*. Beijing: Zhongguo Tongji Chubanshe [China Statistics Publishers].

Qiu, Shusen [邱树森]. 2001a. "Cong Heicheng chu tuwen shu kan Yuan 'Huihui ha de si'" [Looking at the Yuan [Dynasty] Bureau of Qadis in the documents excavated in Heicheng]. *Nanjing Daxue xuebao [Journal of Nanjing University]* 39(3): 152–60.

2001b. "Tangsong 'fanfang' yu 'zhiwaifaquan'" [Tang-Song "foreigner lanes" and extraterritoriality]. *Ningxia shehui kexue [Social Sciences in Ningxia]* 5(108): 31–37.

Qiu, Wangjun [仇王军]. 2009. *Yuhai Xian Huimin Zizhi Zhengfu chengli shimo [The founding of the Yuhai County Hui Autonomous Government].* Yinchuan: Ningxia Renmin Chubanshe [Ningxia People's Publishers].

Que, Chengping [阙成平]. 2013. "Minzu quyu zizhi zhidu yanjiu xianzhuang ji sixiang" [The status of and thoughts on research regarding the ethnic regional autonomy system]. *Xizang Minzu Xueyuan xuebao (zhexue shehuikexueban) [Journal of Tibet Nationalities Institute (Philosophy and Social Sciences)]* 34(4): 85–91.

Sabiq, Sayyid [散伊德•萨比格]. 2002. *Yisilan shangyefa [Islamic commercial law]*, translated by Muslim Youth Translators Group. Neibu ziliao [internal material].

Shan, Zhirong [陕志荣]. 1995. "Linxia chuangban 'Ni Du Shu Wu'" [Linxia creates "You Read Books Room"]. *Zhongguo Musilin [China Muslim]* Issue 3: 40.

Shi, Mingshan [石明珊]. 1987. "Huiyi jiefang qian de sili Xinghua Xiaoxue" [Remembering the preliberation private school Xinghua Elementary]. In *Linxia shi wenshi ziliao xuan [Selections of literary and historical materials on Linxia]*, edited by Zhongguo renmin zhengzhi xieshang huiyi Linxia shi weiyuanhui [China People's Political Consultative Conference], 110–14. Linxia City: Zhongguo renmin zhengzhi xieshang huiyi Linxia huizu zizhizhou weiyuanhui wenshi ziliao weiyuanhui bian [Editorial Committee of the China People's Political Consultative Conference Linxia Hui Autonomous Prefecture Committee literature and history materials].

Shui, Jingjun [水镜君], and Maria Jaschok. 2002. *Zhongguo qingzhen nüsi shi [A history of Chinese female mosques].* Beijing: Sanlian Bookstore.

State Ethnic Affairs Commission (Guojia minzu shiwu weiyuanhui). 2011. "Difang falü fagui" [Local laws and regulations], accessed October 31, 2014, www.seac.gov.cn/col/col63/index.html.

Su, Kelong [苏克龙]. 2006. "Wuzhong Ayu fanyi Zejjiang yanyi duocai rensheng" [Wuzhong Arabic translators in Zhejiang deduce a colorful life], accessed August 25, 2014, www.nx.xinhuanet.com/place/2006-12/27/content_8939926.htm.

[苏克龙], and Li Fuyou [李富有]. 2006. "Ayu fanyi Huizu chuyi: Wuzhong tese pinpan quanguo kaihua" [Arabic translators with culinary skill: Wuzhong speciality brands bloom throughout the nation], accessed August 25, 2014, http://nx.cnr.cn/xwzx/tewh/201012/t20101228_507521778.html.

al-Sudairi, Mohammed Turki. 2014. "Shate dui Zhongguo Sailaifeiya fazhan de yingxiang" [Saudi influences on the development of Chinese Salafism]. MA thesis, Institute of International Relations, Peking University.

Sui, Hongming [眭紅明]. 2004. "Qingmo minchu minshangshi xiguan diao-cha zhi yanjiu" [Research on the late Qing and early Republican civil and commercial affairs survey]. Ph.D. diss., Law (Legal Theory), Nanjing Normal University.

al-Sulayman, Aibu Axiya, [艾卜 阿西亚]. 2009. "Zhengtongpai xinyang gang-yao: cong Gulanjing he Shengxun zhong lijie dao de" [Outline of the ortho-dox sect's beliefs: as understood from the Qur'an and the hadiths], edited by Baishu Xiang Qingzhensi [Cypress Lane Mosque]. Lanzhou: Baishu Xiang Qingzhensi [Cypress Lane Mosque].

Sun, Yi [孙懿]. 2009. "Zhongguo minzu quyu zizhi de lishi guocheng" [The his-torical proces of China's ethnic regional autonomy]. *Heilongjiang minzu congkan [Heilongjiang Ethnic Collection]* 108(1): 8–15.

Tang, Zixin [唐字昕]. 2012. "Ayu fanyi zai Yiwu shi haikuo tiankong hai-shi huaicai buyu" [Arabic translators in Yiwu: are they as bound-less as the sea and the sky or unrecognized talent?]. *Zhezhong xinbao [Zhejiang News]*, accessed May 23, 2015, http://news.cnyw.net/view .php?newsid=12432.

Team of the Guangdong Social-Historical Survey (Guangdong Shehui Lishi Diaochazu). 1963. *Guangdong huizu shehui lishi qingkuang [The Guangdong Hui social-historical situation]*. Guangzhou: Guangdong Shehui Lishi Diaochazu [Team of the Guangdong Social-Historical Survey].

Tian, Chengyou [田成有]. 2005. *Xiangtu shehuizhong de minjianfa [The folk law of native soil society]*. Beijing: Falü Chubanshe (Law Publishers).

United Front Work Department of the Wudou Prefectural CCP (Zhonggong Wudou Diwei Tongzhanbu). 1956. "Guanyu Shengwei Tongzhanbu dui qingzhensi gongbei tudi wenti ji minzu zongjiao renshi anpai wenti huiyi jingshen de zhuanda baogao" [Report communicated in the spirit of the meeting by the Provincial Party Committee United Front Work Department on the mosque and tomb-complex land problem and ethnic-religious personnel placement problem]. Zhonggong Wudou Diwei Tongzhanbu [United Front Work Department of the Wudou Prefectural Chinese Communist Party]. Catalogue no. 001. Archive no. 0394. Serial no. 0006. Batch no. 95.

Wang, Dongping [王东平]. 2002. "Yuandai Huihui ren de zongjiao zhidu yu Yisilanjiaofa" [Study on the religious system and shari'a of the Hui Muslim society in the Yuan Dynasty]. *Huizu Yanjiu [Journal of Hui Muslim Minority Study]* 48(4): 44–50.

Wang, Jian [王鉴]. 2010. "Lun woguo minzu jiaoyu de teshuxing jiqi zhengce zhichi" [The particularity of China's ethnic education and the relevant support in policy]. *Xueshu tansuo [Academic Exploration]* Issue 5: 126–31.

Wang, Min [王敏]. 2011. "Zhongguo gao lihunlü beihou de hunyin kunjing" [The marriage difficulty behind China's high rate of divorce]. *Shehui guan-cha [Social Outlook]*, 34–35.

Wang, Mingke [王明珂]. 2008. *Qiang zai Han-Zang zhijian: Chuanxi Zangzu de lishi renleixue yanjiu [The Qiang between the Han and the Tibetans: historical anthropological research on Sichuan's western Qiangzu]*. Taipei: Zhonghua Shuju [China Publishing House].

Wang, Mingming [王铭铭], and Wang Sifu [王斯福] (Stephan Feutchwang), eds. 1997. *Xiangtu shehui de zhixu, gongzheng yu quanwei [The order, justice, and authority of local society]*. Beijing: Zhongguo Zhengfa Daxue Chubanshe [China University of Political Science and Law].

Wang, Qiliang [王启梁]. 2010. "Zongjiao zuowei shehui kongzhi yu cunluo zhixu ji falü yunzuo de guanlian" [Religion as social control and village order, and the relevance of the functioning of law]. In *Maixiang shenqian zai shehui yu wenhua zhong de falü [Toward the Law Deeply Embedded in Its Social and Cultural Context]*, edited by Wang Qiliang, 175–181. Beijing, Zhongguo fazhi chubanshe [China Legal System Publishers].

Wang, Quanchen [王全臣], ed. 2009. *[Kangxi] Hezhou zhi [Hezhou Annals in the Period of the Kangxi Emperor]*. Beijing: Xueyuan Chubanshe [Academic Institute Publishers].

Wang, Xuemei [王雪梅]. 2012. "Zhongguo Yisilanjiao jiaopai menhuan yanjiu zongshu" [Summary of research on China's Islamic sects and Sufi orders]. *Huizu Yanjiu [Journal of Hui Muslim Minority Study]* 86(2): 117–21.

Wang, Yingmei [王银梅]. 2012. "Kuayueshi fazhan beijing xia minzu diqu shehui maodun jiufen de huajie zhidao—Yi Ningxia de zuofa wei pingxi duixiang" [The path of mediating social disputes in ethnic areas against the backdrop of breakthrough development—assessing the objective through Ningxia's approach]. *Xinan Minzu Daxue xuebao: Renwen shehui kexueban [Journal of Southwest Nationalities University: Humanities and Social Sciences]* Issue 1: 50–54.

Wu, Huhai [吴湖海], ed. 2010. *2009 Yiwu Nianjian [2009 Yiwu yearbook]*. Shanghai Renmin Chubanshe [Shanghai People's Publisher].

Wu, Jianwei [吴建伟] ed. 1995. *Zhongguo qingzhensi zonglan [A general survey of China's mosques]*. Yinchuan: Ningxia Renmin Chubanshe [Ningxia People's Publisher].

Wu, Mu [武沐], and Chen Yunfeng [陈云峰]. 2006. "Qingdai Hezhou musilin xiangyue zhidu kaoshu" [Textual research on the local regulation system of Hezhou Muslims in the Qing Dynasty]. *Xibei Shida xuebao (shehui kexueban) [Journal of Northwest Normal University (Social Science)]* 43(5): 115–21.

Xidaotang [西道堂], ed. 1987. *Xidaotang Shiliaoji [Xidaotang historical material edited]*. Xining: Qinghai Minzu Xueyuan [Qinghai Nationality Institute].

Xie, Hui [谢晖]. 2012. "Lun minjianfa yanjiu de liangzhong xueshu shiye jiqi qubie" [A discussion of the fields of and differences between the two academic approaches to the study of popular law]. *Ha'erbin Gongye Daxue xuebao (shehui kexueban) [Journal of Ha'erbin Institute of Technology (Social Sciences Edition)]* 14(2): 30–40.

2014. "*Lun minjianfa zuowei xianzheng de gonghe jichu*" [*A discussion of popular law as the basis of the constitutional government's republic*]. Beijing Gongli Daxue [Beijing Institute of Technology].

Xiong, Wenzhao [熊文钊], ed. 2010. *Zhongguo minzu fazhi 60nian* [*Sixty years of China's ethnic legal system*]. Beijing: Zhongyang Minzu Daxue Chubanshe [Central Nationalities University Publishers].

Xu, Juan [许娟]. 2014. "*Zhan zai pokou zhi zhong: Zhongguo minjianfa yanjiu xianzhuang jiqi yanjiu quxiang de fansi*" [*Standing on the middle of the tear: thoughts on the direction of research on Chinese popular law and related topics*]. Wuhan: Zhongnan minzu daxue [South-Central University for Nationalities].

Xu, Lili [徐黎丽], and Sun Jinju [孙金菊]. 2008. "Xibei huizu nüxingguan bianqian huanman zhi chengyin—yi Gansu Linxia Huizu Zizhizhou huizu funü wei li" [Reasons for the slow change of Hui female view in the Northwest—taking Linxia Huizu Autonomous Region as an example]. *Hunan Renwen Keji Xueyuan xuebao* [*Journal of Hunan Institute of Humanities, Science and Technology*] 104(5): 28–31.

Yan, Mengchun [严梦春]. 2007. *Hezhou Huizu jiaohu wenhua* [*Hezhou Hui household-on-foot culture*]. Yinchuan: Ningxia Renmin Chubanshe [Ningxia People's Publishers].

Yan, Wenqiang [严文强]. 2012. "'Zhenshi' yu 'jiangou' de eryuanduili: lun guojiafa yu Yizu xiguanfa de duanlie" [Binary opposition of "true" and "construction:" on the breaking and cooperation of state law and Yi's customary law]. *Minzu Xuekan* [*Journal of Ethnology*] 4(12): 45–49.

Yang, Jing [杨晶], ed. 2011. *Zhongguo minzu nianjian* [*China ethnic yearbook*]. Beijing: Minzu Chubanshe [Nationalities Publishing House].

Yang, Shuli [杨淑丽]. 1998. "Ahong peixun gongzuo chutan" [An initial investigation into cleric training]. *Zhongguo Musilin* [*China Muslim*] Issue 4: 19–24.

2010. "Xin quishi xia zhongqingnian ahong peixun gongzuo de diandi xiangfa he jianyi" [A few thoughts and pieces of advice on the new trends in young cleric training work]. The Nineteenth Hui Studies Research Symposium, Beijing, August 5.

Yang, Wenjiong [杨文炯]. 2006. "Huizu xingcheng de lishi renleixue jiedu" [The formation of the Hui nationality: an interpretation of historical anthropology]. *Minzu Yanjiu* [*Ethnic Research*] Issue 4: 30–39.

2007. *Hudong tiaoshi yu chonggou: Xibei chengshi Huizu shehuiqu jiqi wenhua bianqian yanjiu* [*Interaction, adaptation, and reconstruction: a study of the Northwest urban Hui Muslim community and its cultural transition*]. Beijing: Minzu Chubanshe [Nationalities Publishers].

Yang, Zhixin [杨志新]. 2004. "Ningxia nanbushanqu huizu funü zaohun xisu diaocha yu fenxi—yi tongxin xian yuwang xiang zhangjiashu cun wei ge an" [The custom investigation and analysis on the women's early marriage of the Hui in the southern mountainous region of Ningxia]. *Qinghai minzu yanjiu [Nationalities Research in Qinghai]* 15(1): 53–56.

Yang, Zibai [杨子伯]. [1939] 1984. "Zhongguo Huijiao de zongpai." [The Denominations of Chinese Islam] In *Xibei minzu zongjiao shiliao wenzhai: Gansu shouce [Abstracts of historical data on Northwest ethnicity and religion]*, 437–44. Lanzhou: Gansu Sheng Tushuguan [Gansu Province Library].

Yao, Jide [姚继德]. 2002. "Yunnan Tonghai Naguzhen Huizu de hunyin yu jiating" [Marriage and family of Hui from Yunnan Tonghai Nagu town]. *Yunnan Minzu Xueyuan xuebao [Journal of Yunnan University of the Nationalities]* 19(4): 79–83.

Yao, Kuangyi [姚匡乙]. 2006. "Zhongguo-Alabo hezuo luntan" [China-Arab agreement forum]. In *Sichou xinyun: Xin Zhongguo he Alabo guojia 50nian waijiao licheng [New silk music: a record of fifty years of new China-Arab nation relations]*, edited by An Huihou et al., 218–28. Beijing: Shijie Zhishi Chubanshe [World Knowledge Publishers].

Yu, Buren [俞布仁], and Zhang Xulu [张晓露]. 2007. "Shilun Huizu hunyin zhidu de bianhua yiji shehui fazhan dui qi suo chansheng de yingxiang" [A discussion of the changes and influence of social development on the production of the Hui marriage system]. *Xibei Minzu Yanjiu [Northwest Minorities Research]* 5(5): 138–43.

Yu, Zhengui [余振贵], and Lei Xiaojing [雷晓静], eds. 2001. *Zhongguo Huizu Jinshilu [Records of ancient inscriptions of Chinese Hui]*. Yinchuan: Ningxia Renmin Chubanshe [Ningxia People's Publishers].

Yuan, Ziyong [袁自永], and Gao Ting'ai [高庭爱]. 2001. "Qingdai Huijiang de falü shiyong" [The use of law in Huijiang in the Qing Dynasty]. *Kashi Shifan Xueyuan Xuebao (Shehui Kexueban) [Journal of Kashgar Teachers College (Social Sciences)]* 22(3): 38–41.

Yunnan Provincial Editors Group (Yunnan Sheng Bianji Zu). 1985. *Yunnan Huizu shehui lishi diaocha [The Yunnan Hui social-historical survey]*. Vol. 1. Kunming: Yunnan Remin Chubanshe [Yunnan People's Publisher].

Zhang, Haiyang [张海洋]. 2014. "Zhang Haiyang Jiaoshou tan xinxing minzu guanxi" [Professor Zhang Haiyang discusses the new model of ethnic relations], accessed October 27, 2014, www.2muslim.com/forum.php?mod=viewthread&tid=614180&page=1.

Zhang, Jinhai [张进海], ed. 2011. *Ningxia shehui lanpishu 2012 [Blue book of Ningxia society 2012]*. Yinchuan: Ningxia Renmin Chubanshe [Ningxia People's Publishers].

Zhang, Rui [张锐]. 2010. "Shaoshu minzu youhui zhengce tanxi" [An exploratory analysis of the preferential policies of ethnic groups]. *Wenshan Xueyuan xuebao [Journal of Wenshan University]* 23(13): 69–71.

Zhang, Shen [章深]. 2002. "Songdai waishang chengshi juzhuquan tansuo" [Urban residential right for foreign merchants in the Song Dynasty]. *Kaifang Shidai [Blooming Times]* Issue 6: 62–68.

Zhao, Qiudi [赵秋蒂]. 2010. "Zhongguo Xibei Musilin zongjiao paibie duoyuanhua yanjiu—yi Linxia wei lunshu zhongxin" [Research on the pluralization of China's Northwest Muslims' religious denominations—taking Linxia as the center for discussion]. Ph.D. diss., Minzu xuexi [Ethnic Studies], National Chengchi University.

Zhao, Shude [赵树德], ed. 1990. *Linxia jiefang [The liberation of Linxia]*. Linxia: Zhonggong Linxia Zhou Weidang Shi Ziliao Zhengji Bangongshi [Office of the Chinese Communist Party Linxia Prefecture Committee Party Historical Materials Collection].

Zhao, Xudong [赵旭东]. 2003. *Quanli yu gongzheng [Rights and justice]*. Tianjin: Ancient Books Publishers.

Zhe, Malu [哲麻鲁], and Guo Guang [郭广]. 1992. "Linxia zaoqi de Yisilianjiao jingtang jiaoyu" [The early period of scriptural hall education in Hezhou]. In *Linxia wenshi xiliao xuanji [Selections of literary and historical materials on Linxia]*, 94–101. Linxia: Zhongguo Renmin Zhengzhi Xieshang Huiyi Linxia Huizu Zizhizhou Weiyuanhui wenshi ziliao weiyuanhui bian [Editorial Committee of the China People's Political Consultative Conference Linxia Hui Autonomous Prefecture Committee literature and history materials].

Zheng, Xianwen [郑显文]. 2003. "Tangdai shewai minshi falü chutan" [A preliminary study of the civil law concerning foreign affairs during the Tang Dynasty]. *Beijing Keji Daxue xuebao (shehui kexueban) [Journal of University of Science and Technology Beijing]* 19(3): 24–29.

Zhongguo renmin daxue zhexueyuan [中国人民大学哲学院], and Zhongguo renmin daxue Zhongguo diaocha yu shuju zhongxin [中国人民大学中国调查与数据中心], eds. 2015. *Zhongguo zongjiao diaocha baogao [Report on Chinese Religions Survey]*. Beijing: Zhongguo Renmin Daxue Chubanshe [China People's University Publishers].

Zhong Mu Qing Wang [中穆青网]. 2015. "Jiaofa yu falü: Zhongguo Yisilan jiaofa shijian" [Religious Law and (State) Law: The Practice of China's Islamic Law], accessed August 25, 2015, www.muslem.net.cn/bbs/article-14500-1.html.

Zhou, Enlai [周恩来]. 1973. "Zhongguo Gongchandang Di Shi Ci Quanguo Daibiaohui shang de baogao" [Report at the Tenth National Congress of the Chinese Communist Party]. Beijing. August 24.

Zhu, Jingwen [朱景文], ed. 2011. *Zhongguo Renmin Daxue Zhongguo falü fazhan baogao 2011 zouxiang duoyuanhua de falü shishe [China People's University's China law development report 2011: toward a diversifed law enforcement]*. Beijing: Zhongguo Renmin Daxue Chubanshe [China People's University Publishers].

Zhu, Suli [朱苏力]. 1993. "Falü guibi he falü duoyuan" [Legal avoidance and plural law] *Zhongwai faxue [Sino-Foreign Legal Studies]* 30(6): 14–20.

——— 2000. *Songfa xiaxiang: Zhongguo jiceng sifa zhidu yanjiu [Sending the law down to the countryside: research on China's grassroots judicial system]*.

Beijing: Zhongguo Zhengfa Daxue Chubanshe [China University of Political Science and Law Publishers].

[1996] 2004. *Fazhi jiqi bentu ziyuan [Rule of law and native resources]*. Beijing: Zhongguo Zhengfa Daxue Chubanshe [China University of Political Science and Law Publishers].

Zhu, Xiaoyang [朱晓阳], and Hou Meng [侯猛], eds. 2008. *Falü yu ren-leixue: Zhongguo duben [Law and anthropology: a China reader]*. Beijing Daxue Chubanshe [Peking University Publishers].

Zhu, Yunhan [朱云汉], Wen Tiejun [温铁军], Zhang Jing [张静], and Pan Wei [潘维]. 2009. "Gongheguo liushinian yu Zhongguo moshi" [People's Republic at sixty years and the China model]. *Dushu [Read]* Issue 9: 16–28.

INDEX

Books in the Series

China and Islam: The Prophet, the Party, and Law
Matthew S. Erie

Diversity in Practice: Race, Gender, and Class in Legal and Professional Careers
Edited by Spencer Headworth and Robert Nelson

Diseases of the Will
Mariana Valverde

The Politics of Truth and Reconciliation in South Africa: Legitimizing the Post-Apartheid State
Richard A. Wilson

Modernism and the Grounds of Law
Peter Fitzpatrick

Unemployment and Government: Genealogies of the Social
William Walters

Autonomy and Ethnicity: Negotiating Competing Claims in Multi-Ethnic States
Yash Ghai

Constituting Democracy: Law, Globalism and South Africa's Political Reconstruction
Heinz Klug

The Ritual of Rights in Japan: Law, Society, and Health Policy
Eric A. Feldman

The Invention of the Passport: Surveillance, Citizenship and the State
John Torpey

Governing Morals: A Social History of Moral Regulation
Alan Hunt

The Colonies of Law: Colonialism, Zionism and Law in Early Mandate Palestine
Ronen Shamir

Law and Nature
David Delaney

Social Citizenship and Workfare in the United States and Western Europe: The Paradox of Inclusion
Joel F. Handler

Law, Anthropology and the Constitution of the Social: Making Persons and Things
Edited by Alain Pottage and Martha Mundy

Judicial Review and Bureaucratic Impact: International and Interdisciplinary Perspectives
Edited by Marc Hertogh and Simon Halliday

Immigrants at the Margins: Law, Race, and Exclusion in Southern Europe
Kitty Calavita

The Clinic and the Court: Law, Medicine and Anthropology
Edited by Tobias Kelly, Ian Harper and Akshay Khanna

A World of Indicators: The Making of Government Knowledge Through Quantification
Edited by Richard Rottenburg, Sally E. Merry, Sung-Joon Park and Johanna Mugler

Contesting Immigration Policy in Court: Legal Activism and its Radiating Effects in the United States and France
Leila Kawar

The Quiet Power of Indicators: Measuring Governance, Corruption, and Rule of Law
Edited by Sally Engle Merry, Kevin Davis, and Benedict Kingsbury

Investing in Authoritarian Rule: Punishment and Patronage in Rwanda's Gacaca Courts for Genocide Crimes
Anuradha Chakravarty

Iraq and the Crimes of Aggressive War: The Legal Cynicism of Criminal Militarism
John Hagan, Joshua Kaiser, and Anna Hanson

Printed in Great Britain
by Amazon